A Way with WORDS 5

Note to Teachers

A Way with Words is a series of activity books designed to foster the development of oral language, reading and writing from Junior Infants to Sixth Class.

A Way with Words 5 contains:

- a wide and varied menu of comprehension passages;
- comprehensive grammar exercises;
- vocabulary expansion work;
- spelling activities;
- a variety of writing exercises, including cloze procedures and functional and creative writing activities;
- poetry appreciation pages;
- editing exercises;
- opportunities to promote classroom discussion.

Acknowledgements

For permission to use copyright material, the publishers make grateful acknowledgement to the following: Carcanet Press Ltd for *Hide and Seek* from *Complete Poems in One Volume* by Robert Graves.

In the case of some copyright pieces, the publishers have been unable to contact the copyright holders but will be glad to make the usual arrangement with them should they contact the publishers.

Published by
CJ FALLON
Ground Floor - Block B Liffey Valley Office Campus Dublin 22 Ireland

First edition March 2007
This reprint May 2014

Printed by
Turner Print Group
Earl Street Longford

Contents

A Dog's Tale

There are many different breeds of dog, and some dogs are mixtures of many different breeds! The history of each breed is often in its name. Here are some examples.

St Bernard dog

These gentle giants were bred in Switzerland as mountain-rescue dogs by the monks of St Bernard. In winter, when the snow lay deep in the Alps, these big, furry dogs were sent out to rescue travellers caught in drifts. They are often shown in pictures with small casks of brandy around their necks, but this is a myth – they never carried casks around their necks. The most famous St Bernard dog was Barry, who reportedly saved more than 40 lives. There is a monument to Barry in the dog cemetery in Berne.

Poodle

Although the origin of the poodle has long been questioned, France is now officially recognised as the poodle's country of origin. However, the name 'poodle' comes from the German word *pudel*, which means *to splash about in water*. Poodles were often used to collect hunted birds from lakes and ponds because they are very good swimmers. Today, poodles are generally kept as pets.

Irish wolfhound

The Irish wolfhound is the tallest breed of dog in the world. In ancient Ireland, they were called 'Cú', and they could only be kept by kings and noblemen. They were used not only to hunt wolves but also elk and deer, and they were of such importance that battles were fought over them. However, after the last wolf in Ireland was killed in 1786 by a Mr. Watson in Carlow, Irish wolfhounds went into decline, and they are quite a rare pet nowadays.

Pekingese dog

This breed is named after the city of Peking in China. For centuries, these dogs were so precious that they could only be kept by members of the Chinese Royal Family. When British troops attacked the Imperial Palace in 1860, the royal family killed their Pekingese dogs rather than let their enemies take them. However, the British found five of the dogs behind a curtain in the palace. They brought the dogs back to England and presented one to Queen Victoria. She loved her Pekingese, and the breed became very popular.

Question Time

A

1. What information can the name of a breed of dog give about the breed?
2. Where were St Bernard dogs bred?
3. Who are St Bernard dogs named after?
4. In which mountains were the St Bernard dogs used as rescue dogs?
5. What was the name of the most famous St Bernard dog?
6. From what German word does the name poodle come? What does this word mean?
7. What is the biggest breed of dog in the world?
8. (a) Who killed the last wolf in Ireland?
   (b) When did he kill it?
   (c) Where did he kill it?
9. What city in China are Pekingese dogs named after?
10. Which British queen fell in love with Pekingese dogs?

B

1. What is meant by 'breed' of dog?
2. What do we call a dog that is a mixture of many breeds?
3. What myth do many people believe about St Bernard dogs?
4. Look up the word 'retriever' in the dictionary and then name some retriever dogs.
5. Why are Irish wolfhounds no longer used for hunting?
6. Why are Irish wolfhounds rarely kept as pets today?
7. Why are Irish wolfhounds so called?
8. What were poodles used for and why is their name appropriate?
9. Why, do you think, were the Pekingese dogs behind the curtain not killed?
10. Write these words in sentences to show their meaning.

imperial   monument   elk   myth

Think and Talk

1. Imagine you live in an apartment on the fourth floor and your pet is an Irish wolfhound. Write about your pet.
2. Find out how Cúchulainn got his name.
3. Imagine you are a traveller in the Alps in winter. You get caught in a snowstorm. Write about how you are rescued by a St Bernard dog.

Capital Letters

You must always use a capital letter…

- at the start of a sentence.
- when using 'I', meaning '**myself**'.
- for **proper names** and **place names**, e.g. **Mary**, **Galway**.
- for days, months and festivals.
- for the titles of plays, books, songs, films and poems, e.g. Black Beauty.
- for people's titles, e.g. **Mrs**, **Dr**, **Mr**.

A. Correct this passage by putting in capital letters.

Twenty capital letters are missing.

last saturday, my family went shopping in dublin. the city was packed with people, and mum told us to stay close together. i wanted to go to a music shop because auntie mary had given me a gift token. we strolled around a few department stores, and then dad and i went to a record shop. he bought himself beethoven's fifth symphony, and i got *electric shovels*, the new album by dave smith.

B. Now try this passage.

Fifteen capital letters are missing.

my favourite time of the year is the easter holidays in april. there's something special about easter. my friend conor says that it's like a dress rehearsal for the holidays in the summer. for me, easter gives me a feeling of hope. the days are growing longer and becoming warmer. plants are growing again. animals are having their young. nature seems to be waking up from its winter sleep. everyone seems more cheerful. even homework doesn't seem so bad!

C. Correct this passage. Watch out for place names.

Fifteen capital letters are missing.

as soon as i set foot in the airport terminal building, i could feel the sense of excitement there. people were busy. the place was bustling. holidaymakers were boarding planes for majorca and tenerife. a flight had just arrived back from bermuda. the passengers looked pretty cold now. dark-suited business people walked by. maybe i'll fly to australia next year.

Full Stops

You should use a full stop...

- to end a sentence.
- to show an **abbreviation**, e.g. Dr. for doctor, St. for street.

  Example: Dr. Doolittle thought that he could talk to animals.

  (You will learn more about abbreviations in the next unit.)

A. This passage is written without full stops. Rewrite it and put in the eight missing full stops.

I walked slowly into the house It seemed to be deserted The doors were locked, and the windows were covered over with shutters Creepers rambled over the walls, and dead leaves had gathered on the doorstep The curtain in the porch window was dirty and torn Weeds and brambles grew all over the garden Paint flaked from the window frames and doors This was a house that had not been a home for a long time

B. Rewrite this passage and put in the fifteen missing full stops.

Dr Smith lived in Holly St in a quiet part of town That day, she left the house at about 8 pm and strolled down Oak Rd until she reached St Anne's Church The church was being restored, and Rev Simpson had invited Fr Flynn to hold services at St Mary's until the work was completed Dr Smith admired the work of the builders and continued on past Willow St until she turned into Walnut Ave and arrived at St Paul's Hospital where she worked

C. Rewrite this passage and put in the eight missing full stops and the ten missing capital letters.

the fox is one of our best-known wild animals it belongs to the dog family foxes are common in all parts of ireland apparently, foxes are very clever and are able to play tricks on people and on other animals many of aesop's fables are about the fox and his tricks

an adult fox measures about 1·3m from the point of its nose to the tip of its tail the vixen is usually smaller than the dog fox foxes have coats of reddish fur

Digging up the Past

The earth was dark brown in colour. Fortunately, the weather had been kind in recent weeks, and the soil was reasonably dry. It crumbled away easily with each stroke of Tara's brush.

Tara loved this part of the job. Digging down into the earth was like travelling in a time machine. The deeper you went down, the further back in time you travelled. You never knew what was waiting in the ground to be discovered after hundreds, sometimes thousands, of years.

The work required a gentle touch and sensitive fingers. Some of the things Tara had unearthed in previous digs had been so fragile that they were ready to turn into dust in her hands. Without gentle handling, such things could be lost forever, along with whatever could be learned from them.

That's why Tara used a soft brush. It could push away crumbs of clay and dust without damaging any delicate 'finds'. It was slow and difficult work, but Tara loved it because she never knew what she would find or when she would find it.

She and her companions had been working on this dig for a fortnight now, and the early discoveries were quite promising. There were many traces of Roman activity in this region. The site that they had chosen for their dig had once been the villa of a powerful Roman official. They could learn so much about the past here.

Tara's sensitive fingers felt a tiny vibration running through the handle of her brush. She had found something in the dark-brown soil. Perhaps it was only a pebble, but maybe it would turn out to be some great treasure dating back to the time of the Roman Empire. She brushed more of the soil away very carefully.

There was something! It was small, round, dirty, hard ... a coin. She could just make out the word *Caesar* ... it was Roman! As she prised it gently from its earthen tomb, Tara wondered what had happened to this tiny coin. What was its story?

Question Time

A

1. What was Tara doing?
2. What tool was she using?
3. Describe the soil.
4. Did she and her friends have any success at the site?
5. Was her work easy to do?
6. How had the weather been of help?
7. How long had Tara and her friends been working on the site?
8. Who were the ancient people that Tara was trying to find out about?
9. What did Tara find?
10. What led her to believe she had found something important?

B

1. Why was it good to have dry soil on the site?
2. What skills were required for Tara's work?
3. How do we know that she had sensitive hands?
4. Why was this useful to her?
5. Why did she use a brush instead of a shovel or a spade?
6. In what way was the soil like a time machine?
7. Why did Tara love her slow, difficult work?
8. Why had this site been chosen?
9. What do you think the work would be like in wet weather?
10. When Tara used the word 'treasure', do you think she meant gold and other riches? Why?

Think and Talk

1. Why are archaeological digs so important in helping us to understand the past?
2. The Romans came to Ireland, but they never stayed in great numbers, and Ireland never became a part of the Roman Empire. Could you think of some reasons why?

Commas (1)

You must use a comma to separate **adjectives** in **lists**.

Example: It was a cold, bleak, miserable day.

Note the last adjective **does not** need a comma.

You must also use a comma to separate **nouns** in **lists**.

Example: I enjoy rugby, wrestling, boxing and ballet.

However, the noun before the 'and' **does not** need a comma.

A. Put commas into each of the lists of adjectives and nouns in these sentences.

1. Eric was a cold cruel bitter heartless man.
2. The gleaming glittering sparkling drops cascaded from the mouth of the fountain.
3. I took my compass binoculars water-bottle and rucksack with me, and I set off into the hot sandy desert.
4. The aircraft dropped food medicine water and blankets to the desperate starving refugees.
5. The huge majestic volcano spewed lava ash and smoke over the land in a violent terrifying display of power.
6. The yard was a frantic mad crazy chaotic place at playtime.
7. I could make out the parks streets avenues and alleyways of the entire city from the top of the tall majestic skyscraper.
8. The twirling swirling mesmerising snowflakes fell silently to the ground as the cold cruel biting wind blew across the land.
9. Countless tiny unseen hands had worked all through the night to secure Gulliver's hair arms and body to the ground.
10. Joan ate chicken potatoes and cabbage for lunch.

B. Rewrite these sentences and put in capital letters, commas, full stops and question marks where necessary.

1. i met joan in galway yesterday
2. my mother asked me to go to nolan's shop for eggs apples peas and potatoes
3. what happened to your shoes
4. my sister went to london last sunday on the long comfortable train
5. i will be ten years old in june
6. tommy and danny play hurling every saturday
7. we go to school every monday tuesday wednesday thursday and friday
8. did you see what she did to paul's book
9. i would like to get a bike a CD a book and a game for Christmas
10. did you see my sister in london

Titles and Abbreviations

When you abbreviate a word, you **shorten** it... and make it easier to spell!

- **Mrs.** is the abbreviation of **Missus**.
- **Abbreviated** words usually start with a **capital letter** and end with a **full stop**.

A. Write the full title beside these abbreviated words.

Mr.	________	Mrs.	________
Dr.	________	Prof.	________
Fr.	________	Rev.	________

**B. Abbreviated words are often used when writing addresses.
Put the correct abbreviation beside each word.**

Rd.	St.	Gr.	Pk.	Dr.	Tce.	Sq.	Upr.
Lr.	Apts.	Co.	Cres.	Wd.	Ct.	Ave.	Gdns.

Park	________	Square	________
County	________	Terrace	________
Avenue	________	Lower	________
Drive	________	Wood	________
Road	________	Apartments	________
Street	________	Upper	________
Grove	________	Court	________
Gardens	________	Crescent	________

- You can shorten a name by using the first letter of that name.
  Example: **P.** Sayers for **Pat** Sayers.

C. Abbreviate these names and titles.

Father John McCarthy ________

Professor Paula Kelly ________

Mister Frederick Flintstone ________

Missus Patricia Podd ________

Doctor Bernadette Lister ________

Reverend Michael Walsh ________

D. Abbreviate these names of days and months. Use a calendar if you need help.

Monday	________	January	________	Tuesday	________
February	________	Wednesday	________	September	________
Thursday	________	August	________	Friday	________
December	________	Saturday	________	November	________
Sunday	________	April	________	March	________

Write Away!

Walking in the Dark

Read this passage carefully. Many of the words are missing.
Rewrite the passage using the words in the wordbox to fill in the blanks.
Some words can be used more than once.

cut	street	heard	cold	miserable	saw	stopped	walking	house	looked
nervous	walk	louder	tripped	noise	shaking	hands	beside	see	making
		dark	deserted	racing	run	panicked	fell		

It was a ________, ________ night. I was ________ down the ________ towards my ________. The street was ________ and ________. Suddenly, I ________ a noise. I ________ and ________ around but ________ nobody. I kept on ________.

Then I ________ the noise again. It was ________ this time. I ________ around but still ________ nobody. Now I began to feel a bit ________.

I started to ________ a bit more quickly. My heart was ________ and my hands were ________. There! I heard the ________ again! I ________ and began to ________. I couldn't ________ very well and I ________ and ________ over.

I ________ my knee and my ________. Whatever or whoever had been ________ the sound was now right ________ me. I ________ up and saw a ……

Finish the story.
Does this story have to be scary? Could you give it a funny ending?

Writing a Poem

A Close One

Of all the scary creatures
That I've met in my time,
The really, truly worst
Was a tiger in his prime.
I was walking through the jungle
On a nice, hot, sunny day,
When this stripy monstrous brute,
Jumped out and blocked my way.
He looked me up and down.
This made me really quiver.
And said in a quiet voice,
"I think I'll start with your liver."
I fell upon my knees and begged.
"Please give me a break.
I've a wife and twenty kids,
Have a heart for goodness sake!"
The noble beast frowned and said,
"Twenty orphans and one widow,
Oh, all right, I'm feeling kind
So, go on then, scram now, kiddo."
So I turned and galloped off.
I didn't need telling twice.
But it just goes to show,
That even tigers can be nice.

Jim Halligan

A. Discuss and Write

- How did the writer feel when he realised he was going to be the tiger's lunch?
- Was the tiger really all that bad?
- Do you think the writer was telling the truth to the tiger?
- How do you think the writer felt about the tiger after he was let go?
- Do you think all this really happened? Why?

B. Tell the story of this poem from the tiger's point of view. Start like this...

There I was in the jungle one day when this stupid human came blundering along the path. I was feeling a bit peckish so I jumped out in front of the guy. You should have seen his face when I landed in front of him...

C. Write a story or a poem about a close escape that you had. Maybe it was only a small scare... or maybe something a bit more serious... or maybe something that you could make up.

Viva Mayo!

September was All-Ireland month, and the whole county was in a state of feverish excitement. What a week for Señor Filipo Mayo, his wife Señora Lucretia Mayo and their three children, Julio, Martha and little Juanito, to arrive in the town of Westport to start their new lives. Filipo Mayo wasted no time in writing to his brother in Lisbon to tell him all about his family's first few exciting days in Ireland.

Dear Sergio,
I have so much good news to tell you! Ireland is a wonderful country. To think how I and Lucretia worried ourselves sick before leaving our beloved Portugal. It was so hard to leave all our friends and family. To think how Julio and Martha cried their eyes out. Their tears soon turned to smiles when we arrived at Knock Airport. I tell you, Sergio, the place was festooned with Portuguese flags – all to welcome us! Many of the flags even had our family name, Mayo, printed on them!

I can tell you, Sergio, that we need not have worried! The Irish are the friendliest people in the whole wide world. To make us feel welcome, they have hung Portuguese flags everywhere – our lovely red and green flags flutter from every house and shop, across the streets and even from the windows of their cars! When cars drive past and little Juanito waves the flag you gave him in the airport, they shout, "MAYO! MAYO!", and smile and wave at us. The Irish are treating our family like celebrities! "It's crazy," says Lucretio, "but I love it!" Everybody knows our name! "Come on, Mayo!" they call to me in the street.

Sergio, everybody tells me that a man called Sam Maguire is coming to meet us soon. They all love this Sam Maguire. He is a very important person, and to think he wants to greet our little family! Can you believe that?

I will write again very soon and tell you all about Señor Samuel Maguire. Give my love to all the family, and tell them to book their plane tickets immediately and come and live in this crazy, wonderful country!

My best wishes,
Filipo

Question Time

A

1. What month is All-Ireland month?
2. What were the first names of the members of the Mayo family?
3. Who was the youngest child?
4. What was the name of Filipo's brother?
5. Where did his brother live?
6. At what airport in Ireland did the family arrive?
7. What do people shout when Juanito waves his little flag?
8. Who is supposed to be coming to meet them soon?
9. What does Filipo urge his brother to do?
10. What does Filipo say he will discuss in his next letter?

B

1. From what country have the Mayos come?
2. What are the colours of that country's flag?
3. What are the colours of the Mayo flag?
4. Why, do you think, are there Mayo flags everywhere?
5. Name one county that played in the All-Ireland Final that year.
6. In what county is Knock Airport?
7. Who (or what) is Sam Maguire?
8. Explain in your own words how the misunderstanding has arisen.
9. Put these words in sentences to show their meanings.

flutter festooned celebrities beloved

10. Do you think that the Mayo family can speak English? Give a reason for your answer.

Think and Talk

1. Where is the All-Ireland Final usually played?
2. Choose to write about (a) or (b).
   - (a) Mayo wins the All-Ireland and receives the Sam Maguire Cup. Write the letter that Filipo sends to his brother Sergio.
   - (b) Mayo loses the final. Write the letter that Filipo sends to his brother.
3. You are mistaken for a celebrity that you happen to look like. Write a short account of your '15 minutes of fame'.

Commas (2)

A comma must be used with **when, as, if, though, although, unless, after** and **since** to connect sentences.

Example: I woke up. I got dressed.
When I woke up, I got dressed.

A. Write these sentences correctly by putting a comma in each.

1. When the sun rose the landscape was breathtaking.
2. As the blow struck the door the hinges began to give way.
3. Though I like ice cream I prefer chocolate.
4. If you think I'm going to climb that steep mountain you've got another thing coming.
5. Unless I'm seriously mistaken I've just been bitten by a tarantula.
6. Although I'm nearly twelve I still enjoy having a story read to me at bedtime.
7. When I arrived at the airport I discovered that I had left my passport at home.
8. If you look directly at the sun you will seriously damage your eyes.

Commas (3)

You must use commas to separate words in lists. Listing actions (verbs) can make your writing more interesting.

Examples: The kitten hissed, spat, scratched and bit until the dog decided to leave it alone.
Ken peeled, chopped, diced and sliced every vegetable in that kitchen.

Note: The verb before the 'and' does not need a comma.

A. Write these sentences correctly by inserting commas.

1. I woke up showered dressed and had my breakfast.
2. The swallow dived swooped dipped and swerved as it chased insects over the meadow.
3. White water gushed gurgled foamed and splashed over the rocks as it cascaded down the mountainside.
4. The bulldozer scraped pushed gouged and dug its way through the rubble of the collapsed building.
5. The ravenous lions ripped tore hacked and chewed at the body of the antelope.
6. Flames crackled sparks flew smoke billowed and waves of heat rose from the burning house.
7. The stranger stopped turned and smiled at me.
8. The clouds thickened darkened and shut out the light of the sun.
9. The aeroplane landed turned and headed towards the terminal.

Addresses

Addresses are lists of information. Each piece of information goes on a separate line. Each line, except the last line, ends with a **comma**. The last line in an address always ends with a **full stop**.

Look at this address. Notice how it starts with a person's name, followed by her house, followed by where the house is... and so on...

Elanna Dunne,	person
'Villa France',	name of house
16 Ballymore Grove,	number of house and estate
Bray,	town
Co. Wicklow.	county

If an address uses a postcode, this will be on the last line of the address, e.g. Dublin 12.

A. 1. **Write your own name and address in your copybook.**
2. **Write the name and address of your school in your copybook.**

B. Write the names and addresses of the following people.
Remember that the details of an address get more and more general with each new line.

1. John O'Grady lives in house number 16 in Barnaby Street, which is in Drogheda, a town in County Louth.
2. Jeff Murtagh lives in a house called 'Villa Nova' on the Dublin Road in Naas, which is in County Kildare.
3. Helena Troy lives in Apartment 4B in a house called Shamrock Mansion on the Lower Brighton Road, which is in Raheny, a district in Dublin. The postcode for Raheny is Dublin 5.
4. Emma Gillespie lives in 'Brook Cottage' in a townland called Ballymore near Enniscorthy, a town in County Wexford.
5. Adolfo Savonarola lives at 'Mea Culpa', a house on Bonfire Avenue, which is in Florence, a town in Italy.

C. Unscramble these addresses by putting the information in the correct order.

1. Co. Cavan.
Mary O'Sullivan,
Rose Cottage,
Cootehill,

2. Athlone,
Co. Westmeath.
Mary O'Reilly,
15 Mill Road,

3. Apartment 3,
Ciaran Dunne,
Dublin 8.
Inchicore,
Cross Guns House,
Main Street,

4. Hilton Hotel,
Mr. Alec Dwyer,
Room 16,
Dublin 6.
Mulberry Road,
Ranelagh,

5. Castle Lodge,
Philip Shaw,
Leixlip,
Co. Kildare.

6. Co. Meath.
Holly Cottage,
Carlanstown,
Daniel Reilly,

Accident Black Spot

I'll never forget the sound of the accident – the sharp screeching, followed by the loud thunderous boom, followed in turn by the brittle tinkling, then the silence. The silence was probably the most frightening part.

The village is a small place, and that summer evening, I saw most of my neighbours dashing out of their houses. We all ran towards the bridge. That was where the sound had come from. All the locals knew that the bend in the road just before the bridge was a deathtrap.

My heart was pounding as I approached the old, stone humpback bridge. I caught up with Eileen and John who lived next door to me. Their faces were white. John glanced at me as we ran. "Another one," he stated grimly.

As soon as we reached the rise in the bridge, all our worst fears were confirmed. There was a large, white van at the corner. The rear end of the van stuck out across the road. The front of the van was buried in the ditch. A trail of black skid marks led back along the road like two snakes. None of us recognised the van, so we presumed it was just another stranger travelling too fast on a dangerous road. The driver had tried very hard to stop.

I heard others coming behind us as we reached the cab of the van. John and I pulled back branches as Eileen peered inside. "They're alive," she said. Two men, the driver and passenger, were strapped into their seats. They moaned in pain. Neither of them was fully conscious. The two of them were in a bad way. I heard people behind me making urgent calls on their mobile phones.

I reached in and turned off the ignition, to prevent a fire. John was about to pull the driver from his seat when Eileen stopped him. "We won't move them unless we have to," she said, pulling a strip of cloth from her apron. "This lad has a bad cut on his arm." As she tried to slow the flow of blood from the driver's arm, we heard the distant wailing of sirens.

Question Time

A

1. How many sounds did the accident make?
2. Describe the sounds.
3. Where did the accident take place?
4. How did the storyteller feel while running to the accident?
5. Who else did the storyteller meet along the way?
6. What had crashed?
7. What did John want to do to help the driver?
8. What did Eileen do to stop the blood flowing from the driver's injury?
9. What saved the driver and his passenger from being killed instantly?
10. Who called for help?
11. At what time of the day did the accident take place?
12. Describe the van that crashed.

B

1. Describe how you think the accident happened.
2. How did the people of the village react?
3. How do you know that something like this had happened before?
4. (a) Were the people in the van locals?
   (b) Could this be a reason for the accident?
5. What do you think was so dangerous about the road?
6. Why did Eileen stop John from pulling the driver out of the van?
7. Why did the storyteller turn off the van's ignition?
8. How do you know that help was on its way?
9. Why, do you think, was the storyteller's heart pounding?
10. What showed that the driver had tried hard to stop?
11. Who do you think was the most helpful in the emergency? Why?
12. What do you think happened next?

Think and Talk

1. What do you understand by the term 'accident black spot'?
2. How do you think the local people felt about the bend near the bridge?
3. If you were a villager that had just witnessed this crash, how would you feel?
4. What do you think should be done about the dangerous bend?
5. Pretend you are one of the villagers. Write a letter to the county council demanding that something be done about the dangerous bend in the road.

Paragraphs

A **paragraph** is made up of a number of sentences that deal with the **same idea**.
A paragraph starts on a new line. All paragraphs start a little way in from the margin.

Example: → My grandma was old and needed a walking stick to get about.
Her face was as wrinkled as a dried plum. Her wispy hair was completely white.
She always moved slowly.
→ Her sister, by contrast, was a youthful 81-year-old. Her step was sprightly and her smile wide and frequent.

A. Rewrite the following passage in two paragraphs.

Tom pressed his nose against the windowpane and sighed. Rain dribbled down the glass. The young willow tree in the garden flung its branches about in the wind like a crazed dancer. The chimney moaned eerily. It had been different last Christmas. Last Christmas, it had snowed and a cheerful fire had burned in the grate. Last Christmas, the house had been full of people, full of laughter.

B. Rewrite the following passage in three paragraphs.

Laura was fed up. This was supposed to be the first concert of her new band, the Warblers, and it was all going wrong. Anne's throat had been sore all week, and she should have worn a scarf. Now her voice was croaky and hoarse. Singing was out of the question. That wasn't the only problem. Carl had been picked to play in some match or other, and, typically disloyal, he had announced that he would be unavailable. Laura hoped he lost 10-nil!

C. Donna has a pet parrot. Write about it in three paragraphs using the following guidelines.

1st paragraph: its name, age, colour, markings, etc.
2nd paragraph: its strange and wonderful personality.
3rd paragraph: what it did last Sunday!

D. Here are several muddled sentences. Organise them into two paragraphs.

(Hint: Use the seasons.)

- May is mild and full of promises.
- September is rich and full of fruit.
- June days are long and easy.
- October is red and golden with fallen leaves and bright with crisp, blue skies.
- August brings the first rustling winds and shortening days of autumn.
- By July, summer is rich and slow and glorious.

Writing Letters

Here is a model letter:

4 Chestnut Drive,
Bailieborough,
Co. Cavan.

9th August 2007

Dear Aunty Flo,

How are you? I'm fine. I'm in fifth class now. Mam said that I should write to thank you for the lovely jumper you sent me for my birthday.

What a lovely jumper! Pink and fluffy with a purple rabbit on the front… just what I wanted. Mam told me I should say that. It must have taken you ages to knit. All that itchy, scratchy wool must have been very hard to knit with.

Anyway, Mam said she would be sure to get me to wear it the next time you come to visit us. I really hope I don't grow out of it. I'm growing really fast these days. You're not going to visit soon, are you?

Thanks,
Jack.

Common endings for letters include:

Yours truly *or* Yours sincerely *or* Yours faithfully *or* Your friend.

Always sign your name on the last line.

Writing assignment – choose one of these:

1. Write a letter to thank someone for a birthday present you received.
2. Write a letter to an embassy asking for information about that country – great for projects! Addresses of all embassies can be found in the 01 Dublin Area telephone book.
3. Write a letter inviting a famous celebrity to come and give a talk to your class.

Write Away!

Emergency 999 – Emergency 112

You hope it will never happen to you, but you may have to dial 999 or 112 to get help from the emergency services someday. The emergency operator will direct your phone call to the service that you need, such as the ambulance service, the gardaí, the fire brigade or the lifeboat service.
The service operator will request details from you about the emergency and will decide what needs to be done. What you have to do is to remain as calm as you can.

Imagine that you have an emergency on your hands.
Rewrite this passage and include your part of the conversation with the emergency and service operators.

Emergency Operator: This is the emergency operator. Which service do you need?

You: ____

Emergency Operator: I'll transfer you now…

Service Operator: This is the ______________________.
Tell me your name and where you are.

You: ____

____

Service Operator: Now tell me clearly what has happened.

You: ____

____

____

Service Operator: Can you say how many people are involved and if any of them are hurt?

You: ____

____

Service Operator: Tell me exactly where this happened.

You: ____

____

Service Operator: There's a unit on its way to you now. Stay there and remain calm.

Write Away!

Speed

A. Make a list of words that describe speed.
Use a dictionary or thesaurus to help you.
dashing, rushing, hurtling, zipping, ______________________

____

____

B. Think of the sights, sounds and smells of

1. riding on a roller coaster in a fairground.
2. a motorbike zooming past you.
3. a train thundering by in a station.
4. a cheetah chasing an antelope.
5. a jet roaring down a runway.

C. You are on your bike and you are freewheeling down the best (or worst!) hill in your neighbourhood. Write a paragraph to describe what it is like. Talk about how the speed feels as you whizz along and about what you see as you shoot down the hill.
Use the words in the wordbox to help you.

the rumble of the tyres	wind rushing past	eyes wide in fright	thrilling	terrifying
zooming along	things seen in a blur of speed	gripping handlebars tightly		
glad to have a helmet	the whirr of the wheels	the squeal of brakes	relief and triumph	

D. Write two more paragraphs to finish this story.
My Air Corps helicopter bucked and rocked in the strong wind. This was not good flying weather, but I didn't have a choice. We had just winched a seriously injured motorist aboard, and the hospital was waiting for us to deliver him safely… and quickly. That's what Air Corps pilots are trained to do.
In this weather, I couldn't fly over the mountains. I would have to fly through them using the narrow valleys and passes. I gritted my teeth and nudged the joystick forward. The ground seemed to zoom up towards us as we dived. This was not going to be easy…

That Winning Feeling!

As soon as Mum left the house, Sarah wheeled herself into the kitchen and took the letter down from the worktop. She had been itching to read it again, but she had felt embarrassed. "You're not reading it again, are you, love?" Mum had joked when Sarah had last looked at it. "Are you learning it off by heart?" she had continued with a laugh. "Don't go getting a big head!"

However, Sarah was in no mood to be teased just now, even though she knew that, behind it all, her mother was as pleased as Punch. Sarah just wanted a moment all to herself with her letter, to read every word slowly and to savour the excitement brimming up inside her. "… more than 10,000 entries for our essay competition," she read.

Then, closing her eyes and letting the words wash over her, she repeated it out loud, "more than 10,000 entries and mine was the best!" She clenched her small fist and punched the air. "I won it!" she shouted, and a huge smile broke across her face.

Dropping the letter in her lap, Sarah applied the brake on one wheel and pushed the other for all she was worth. The heavy wheelchair began to turn around and around, squeaking on the tiles. Faster and faster, Sarah turned the chair until tiny beads of perspiration appeared on her forehead.

As the chair spun and the kitchen flew past her in a dizzy swirl, she called out, "I won it! I won it! I won it!" Her mother, who had returned unnoticed, stood in the doorway and watched the sparks flashing in her daughter's eyes.

As her spinning slowed and then stopped, it seemed to Sarah as if her body had uncoiled like a spring, leaving her calm and deeply content. She looked up to see her mother beaming at her, and, wheeling her chair over to her, she wrapped her arms around her mother's waist and hugged her as tightly as she could.

Question Time

A

1. Where was the letter?
2. Why was the letter important to Sarah?
3. Why was Sarah embarrassed to reread the letter in front of her Mum?
4. What kind of competition did Sarah win?
5. How many entries were there in the competition?
6. How did Sarah make the wheelchair spin in a circle?
7. How did Sarah show her excitement?
8. What did Sarah call out?
9. Who did Sarah see when she looked up?
10. What did Sarah do when she saw her mother?

B

1. Explain what is meant by "pleased as Punch".
2. How do we know that spinning the wheelchair was hard work?
3. (a) How does the writer describe Sarah's eyes?
   (b) Explain what the writer means by this.
4. Describe how Sarah's mother felt as she watched her daughter from the doorway.
5. Put these words in sentences to show their meanings.

   savour clenched applied uncoiled

6. "Her body had uncoiled like a spring." Explain what this means.
7. Compare how Sarah felt
   (a) before spinning her wheelchair;
   (b) afterwards.
8. How do you react when you are overjoyed or excited by something?

Think and Talk

1. Imagine you have just won an essay competition that had 10,000 entries.
   Describe how you would react to the news.
2. Imagine your best friend has won a sporting competition that you had really wanted to win. Describe your feelings.
3. Suggest ways of staying calm before an important event, such as an exam, a parachute jump, a final, Christmas, etc.

Direct Speech (1)

A. In the speech bubbles, write the actual words that Tom and Jim say to each other in this snippet of conversation.

"Telltale! Telltale!" chanted Tom at his friend.
"I am not," retorted Jim crossly.
"Call me that again and I'll tell on you!"

- The words in the bubbles are the **actual words** that the two boys have said.

B. Write out these snippets of conversation and underline the actual words spoken.

1. "But I was certain that I'd pressed the brake pedal," the young lady told Eddie, her driving instructor, after they had shot out in front of a large truck. "No, Miss Dobbs," Eddie explained quietly, as he waited for his heart to start beating again. "The brake pedal is the one in the middle. I may have mentioned that before." "Oops! Silly me!" Miss Dobbs giggled.

2. "During those voyages, many ships visited the island of Mauritius in the Indian Ocean," the professor explained. "It was a popular place for sailors to take on fresh water and food," added his wife. "It was also the home of the dodo birds," continued the professor. "They were easy to catch and kill for meat." "And that is exactly what the sailors did," finished his wife sadly, "and they didn't stop until every dodo was dead!"

C. Look at the cartoon and write the conversation in the gaps below.

"______________________________" the boy exclaimed, holding his hands wide apart.
"______________________________" replied his mother, shaking her head.

Apostrophes (1)

We put 's at the end of a noun when it owns something.

Examples: the girl's hands = the hands belonging to the girl
the cat's tail = the tail belonging to the cat

A. Change these sentences by using apostrophes and rewrite the sentences in your copybook.

1. The car belonging to Roger is a jalopy.
2. The bill of a pelican is ideal for scooping up fish.
3. The propeller of the ship churned the water into a foaming, white froth.
4. The siren of the police car shattered the silence.
5. The gravity of Earth is six times greater than the gravity of the Moon.
6. The blackbird broke the shell of the snail on the stone.

B. Write these sentences in your copybook and insert the missing apostrophes.

1. Seáns sailing boat is a Laser One.
2. Angelas flowers formed a dazzling display of bright colours.
3. Childrens rights must be respected by everyone.
4. An elephants trunk can lift a tree.
5. The mans face was scarlet with anger.
6. A hares ears are longer than a rabbits ears.
7. Emmas quick reflexes saved her life.

C. Write this passage in your copybook and insert the missing apostrophes.

One summers day, soon after her birthday, Niamhs younger sister, Emma, borrowed her sisters bike without permission to go down to Murphys shop. The bicycles wheels glittered as the suns rays caught the spokes, and the girls hands skilfully steered it down the road.

Just then, Mrs. Smiths young boy ran straight out in front of Emma. She swerved out of the childs way but found herself facing an oncoming van. The vans brakes screeched as the driver tried to stop. Emma leapt from the doomed bike, and the next thing she could remember was the drivers anxious face as he helped her up from the soft grass of the ditch. An ambulances siren wailed in the distance.

Niamhs face fell when she saw what the vans wheels had done to her bike. Still, she would rather have her bold little sister than a bicycle.

An Angry Email

To: complaints@e-buy.com
Re: Order No: 4799-5634-4791
Date: 5th July 2009

Dear Sir / Madam,
Last week (29th of June), I ordered a Chopmaster 5000 High Power Chainsaw, in metallic purple with extra spotlight fitting, from your www.e-buy.com website. I paid €589·95 using my credit card. Today, six days later, I was delighted when I received a package from you. However, I was not delighted when I opened the parcel. Instead of my state-of-the-art chainsaw, the box contained two stone garden gnomes, a lady's pink tracksuit (size 12) and a small, yellow rubber duck. How am I supposed to chop down trees with that lot?????

Somebody has made a serious blunder. I really need that chainsaw for my farm. There's a creaky, old oak tree that is about to fall on to my hen-house, and they are valuable chickens! If anything happens to one of those hens, I'll have your company to blame.

I demand, and expect, that you get to the bottom of this stupid mistake as quickly as possible. If I do not receive my chainsaw within the week, you will be hearing from my solicitors.

You have been warned!!!

Myles Doherty.

P.S. I have posted the other rubbish back to you.

Question Time

A

1. Who is writing this email?
2. To whom is he writing it?
3. What did he order from E-Buy?
4. When did he order it?
5. What arrived at his house?
6. How does he feel about that?
7. How much did his order cost?
8. What use does he have for the tool he ordered?
9. What has he threatened to do if he does not get his order sorted out within the week?
10. What did he do with the items that arrived by mistake?

B

1. What work do you think Myles does?
2. Why is he worried about the chickens?
3. What do you think happened to his order?
4. Do you think that it would be easy to mix up the order number? Why?
5. On what date did the parcel arrive?
6. Why, do you think, did Myles want a chainsaw with a spotlight on it?
7. What do you think will happen if the mistake is not sorted out in time?
8. Why did he call the items in the parcel "rubbish"?
9. What sort of person do you think Myles is?
10. Do you think he is right to be angry? Why?

Think and Talk

1. Doris Delaney ordered a pink tracksuit that she wanted to wear to her grandson's birthday. She also ordered a rubber duck for her little darling and two garden gnomes to go beside her pond. Instead, she received what looks like a do-it-yourself World War Three murder machine… in purple with a silly light on the end!!!!
   Write her letter of complaint to E-Buy.
2. Poor you. You work in the E-Buy complaints department, and it's your job to write a nice letter to Mr. Doherty promising to sort out the mistake as quickly as possible.
3. You want to sell your bottle-top collection on the Internet. Design a catchy ad that will attract many bottle-top collectors and get you a good price.

Direct Speech (2)

- When you write down the **actual** words that are said by people, you must put the words inside **inverted commas** (“.........”).

  Example: “Amy has new shoes,” said Lucy.

  Note that an ordinary comma is also used after the last word that is spoken.

A. Write the following sentences in your copybook and put in the missing inverted commas.
Don’t forget the ordinary comma!

1. Your room is like a pigsty said mum crossly.
2. Your television will work better if you plug it in explained the TV repairman.
3. Teacher is wearing odd socks giggled Justine.
4. I have lost my mobile phone announced Dylan.
5. You do not understand where to put inverted commas said the teacher.
6. Fasten your seat belts dad told the children in the back of the car.
7. Don’t worry, this won’t hurt a bit reassured the dentist.
8. My football jersey has turned pink in the wash shouted Frank in horror.
9. I’ll meet you at half past three Anne suggested.
10. A stitch in time saves nine Mam said.

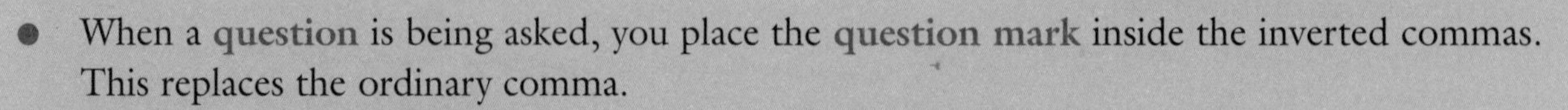

- When a **question** is being asked, you place the **question mark** inside the inverted commas. This replaces the ordinary comma.

  Example: “Were you born in a barn?” asked Mum crossly.

B. Write these sentences in your copybook and put in the missing inverted commas and question marks.

1. When did you last clean your ears asked Aidan.
2. Would you like some mustard on that spaghetti enquired the waiter.
3. How much more time are you going to spend working on that computer Dad demanded to know.
4. What daft excuse for not doing your homework are you going to come up with this time wondered the teacher.
5. What cathedral in London has a Whispering Gallery the quizmaster asked.
6. How big is the spider in the bath Dad asked Mona.
7. At what speed do you think you were driving enquired the garda.
8. Did you put in all the inverted commas and question marks asked the teacher.
9. Have you seen my pet hamster cried Oisín.
10. Where did I put my glasses enquired Dad.
11. Will you please make your bed Mum asked Seán.
12. Can I have some money to buy a CD pleaded Philip.

Apostrophes (2)

- Remember: 's shows that a noun **owns** something, e.g. Ciara's pencil.
- Remember: **Ordinary plurals** do **not** use an apostrophe with the s.

  Example: With their **eyes** shut tight, the boys dived off the **cliff's** edge into the sea below.

A. Rewrite these sentences by putting in the missing apostrophes.

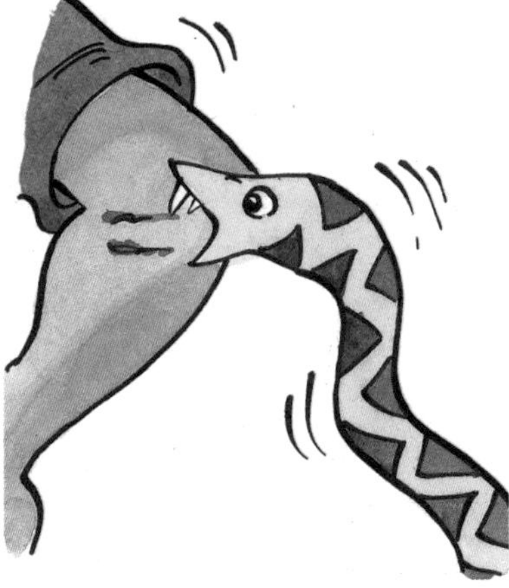
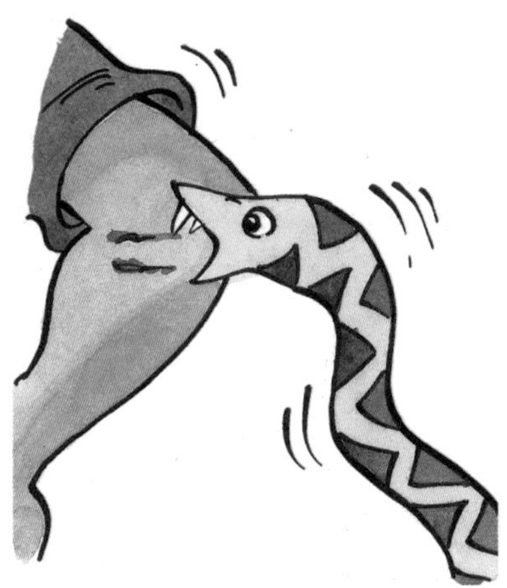

1. Two worms munched through the apples soft flesh.
2. The scientists hands trembled as he picked up the test tubes.
3. Of all the seas, the Red Sea is the worlds warmest.
4. The beaver is Canadas national animal.
5. Slowly, the potters strong hands turned the clay into a beautiful vase.
6. The snakes fangs sliced through the flesh on his arm.
7. Apples, oranges, pears and kiwis were all on display on the shops shelves.
8. The lorrys front wheels were both punctured.

Apostrophes (3)

- When plurals ending in s own something, put an apostrophe **after** the s.

  Example: The two stags' antlers locked in combat.

B. Rewrite these sentences by putting in the missing apostrophes.

1. The soldiers faces were covered in green camouflage paint.
2. Both boys faces were covered in jam.
3. Polar bears bodies are kept warm by thick layers of fur and fat.
4. The police cars sirens wailed in the distance.
5. The Normans military skills helped them to capture large parts of Ireland long ago.
6. Throughout the city, the earthquake had destabilised the buildings foundations.
7. The vultures sharp beaks tore at the carcass of the wildebeest.
8. The deep-sea divers oxygen tanks were running dangerously low, so they decided to abandon the search.
9. The teachers staffroom was out of bounds for all pupils.
10. Tadpoles tails grow shorter as they gradually turn into frogs.

Write Away!

Writing from Notes

Concorde

Use these notes to write your own report on Concorde, the world's first supersonic airliner.

Supersonic passenger jet .... travel at twice the speed of sound (Mach 2) .... designed by British and French engineers in the 1960s .... First flight in 1969 .... 4 powerful Rolls Royce Olympus engines .... very expensive to design and build .... Only 16 Concorde aircraft ever made .... carry about 100 passengers .... cut flight time from London to New York from 7 hours to about 3 hours .... very popular with wealthy business people and famous stars .... Tickets very expensive at up to €10,000 per trip .... high level of luxury .... beautiful plane .... disaster strikes July 25th 2000 .... first and only crash happens after take-off in Paris .... 113 people killed .... September 11th attack on WTC Twin Towers .... people afraid to fly .... wealthy did not want to travel .... Concorde loses most of its customers .... British Airways and Air France decide to retire their Concorde fleets .... 27 years of service over .... Stored in museums for people to visit.

Essay Writing

- When you write an essay, you should try to present all sides of the subject and not just say what you like about an idea (or what you don't like).
- A useful approach to writing an essay:
  1. **P:** Write down the **positive** (good) things about the idea.
  2. **N:** Write down the **negative** (not so good) things about the idea.
  3. **C:** Write down your **conclusions** (what you actually think) about the idea.

A. Using these notes, write an essay in three paragraphs on the following topic:

"TV should not start until 6pm"

Positives:

1. Children would play more.
2. No distraction from homework.
3. It would save electricity.

Negatives:

1. There would be fewer children's programmes.
2. Wet days might be long and boring.
3. Sick children would have no distraction.

Conclusions:

1. ______________________________
2. ______________________________
3. ______________________________

B. Write an essay called "Are School Holidays Too Long?" in three paragraphs following the guidelines above. The first sentence of each paragraph is given to you. Add a few sentences to each paragraph to finish them.

"Are School Holidays Too Long?"

(Paragraph 1): School holidays are wonderful!
(Paragraph 2): However, some children think that school holidays are just too long.
(Paragraph 3): Having considered both the positive and negative sides of school holidays, I personally think that…

- A good essay should be planned beforehand. Taking notes before you write helps you to organise your thoughts and will improve your essay.

The Amazon

The Amazon River is a truly great river!
Here are just some of the facts about the Amazon River to give you some idea of its size:

1. The mouth of the Amazon is 330km wide – that's as wide as Ireland!
2. The flow of fresh water that surges out of the Amazon River is so powerful that it actually pushes back the salt water of the Atlantic Ocean for 150km.
3. There are at least 1,100 tributaries flowing into the Amazon.
4. It is so deep and wide that ocean-going ships can navigate 3,700km up the Amazon.
5. The Amazon Basin, the land drained by the Amazon and its tributaries, is almost as large as Australia (over 6,400,000 sq km).

The Amazon Basin is covered by the world's largest rainforest. The rainforest is home to a rich diversity of plant and animal life. The thick canopy of the forest traps the heat, and the entire area is like a vast greenhouse. It is also very wet, so plants grow rapidly and densely. This lush forest gives off so much oxygen that it actually supplies the world with up to 20% of its oxygen needs.

Sadly, the great Amazon Rainforest is being destroyed. Every year, an area about the size of Belgium is cut down and burnt. Who is causing this destruction? Wealthy countries, including Ireland, want the beautiful hardwood, such as teak and mahogany, that grows in the rainforest to make furniture. However, for every hardwood tree that is cut down to supply our demands, the tangle of smaller trees and shrubs that block access to the hardwood trees are also hacked down and burnt. Thus, whole areas can be devastated in the search for hardwood.

Rich landowners also clear the forest in order to breed cattle. Even the poor people who live there destroy great tracts of the rainforest. They are desperate for land on which to grow food, so they 'slash and burn' large areas of the jungle. However, the rainforest soil is very poor, so after farming it for a few years, the people move on and 'slash and burn' a new farm from the rainforest.

If the destruction continues, it is feared that by the year 2050 the vast Amazon Rainforest will be no more. The world's most important oxygen supply, the beautiful hardwood trees and the habitats of thousands of rare species of plant and animal will be gone forever.

Question Time

A

1. How wide is the mouth of the Amazon River?
2. Approximately how many tributaries feed into the Amazon?
3. How far up the Amazon can large ocean-going ships sail?
4. How far back is the salt water pushed by the fresh water of the Amazon?
5. What grows in the Amazon Basin?
6. What percentage of the world's oxygen does the rainforest supply?
7. How large is the area of rainforest that is destroyed each year?
8. Name two hardwoods that come from the Amazon Rainforest.
9. What type of soil can be found in the Amazon Basin?

B

1. Into what ocean does the Amazon flow?
2. What is a tributary?
3. What is the thick, leafy covering of the rainforest called?
4. Why do rich landowners destroy the forest?
5. In what way do the poor farmers also destroy the rainforest?
6. What are the weather conditions in the rainforest that aid such rapid growth?
7. For what do the wealthy landowners breed cattle?
8. For how many more years will the rainforest survive if its destruction is not halted?
9. The Nile may be the world's longest river, but the Amazon is considered by many to be the world's greatest river. In what ways is this true?

Think and Talk

1. Why, do you think, is hardwood so popular? Could people in Ireland use Irish timber instead? Name some native Irish hardwoods.
2. Why is the Amazon Rainforest so important for our survival? List some of the possible effects for the planet if the rainforest is completely destroyed.
3. You have been given the job of saving the Amazon Rainforest. Describe what actions you would take.

Direct Speech (3)

- When you write speech, put the spoken words on a new line, and place the first **inverted commas** a little way in from the margin.

  Example: The snake curled itself around Charlie's ankles.
  He could feel the hairs on the back of his neck tingling.
  "Do something, please," he whispered desperately.
  "Stay cool, Charlie, I'll think of something," replied Jack reassuringly.

A. Write out the following paragraphs and begin each piece of speech on a new line.

1. "So what did you get for your birthday?" asked the girl's uncle. "A pet rattlesnake, a rugby ball and a bunch of celery sticks," replied his niece.
2. The principal folded his arms and glared at the boy. "Why are you late this time?" he asked crossly. "Well, Mr. Hardline, it's a long story," Roger began. "I have all day," replied Mr. Hardline, leaning back in his chair.
3. The child looked longingly at the biscuit tin on the table. "Please, Mammy, may I have a biscuit?" he asked hopefully. "No, dear, you have already had four," replied his mother, as she took away the tin.

B. Write this passage in your copybook and put in inverted commas where necessary. Put the spoken words on a new line each time.

Robbing a bank is an art form, Nance explained to Ron in her slow, drawling voice. Nance Travers was a small, wiry woman in her early sixties. Her pipe jiggled up and down in her mouth as she spoke. It's not just a matter of pulling a stocking over your head, kicking in a door and waving a sawn-off shotgun at a bunch of screaming customers. Isn't it? wondered Ron, pulling his chair forward to catch her every word. Ron was short and stocky. He looked like a block. No, robbing banks has been given a bad name by brainless yahoos and trigger-happy hoodlums, Nance continued. Has it? butted in Ron, his eyes big and round. I like to do it right. When I rob a bank, it stays robbed, explained Nance. Does it? interrupted Ron – not a man for long sentences, our Ron.

Prefixes

- A **prefix** goes in front of a word to make a new word.
- **Prefixes** (such as **un-**, **anti-**, **dis-**, etc.) often change the meaning of a word to its opposite.
  Examples: able – **un**able, obey – **dis**obey, freeze – **anti**freeze

A. Turn these words into new words by putting a prefix in front of them.
Use the prefixes in the box to help you.

un-	im-	inter-	pre-	anti-	in-	dis-

clockwise	polite	occupied	secure
covered	theft	patient	safe
freeze	pure	edible	complete
prison	kind	septic	capable
embarked	view	historic	grateful

B. Complete these sentences by putting in words that you made in A above.

1. The house next door has been ____________ for some time.
2. Most modern cars are fitted with an ____________ device.
3. Captain Cook ____________ Australia.
4. That disgusting meal is ____________!
5. He is too ____________ to be a good fisherman.
6. In winter, the cliff walk is ____________.
7. Not saying "please" or "thank you" is ____________.
8. In Ireland, we drive ____________ around roundabouts, but they do the opposite in most other countries.
9. The teacher was not pleased when she saw the girl's ____________ homework.
10. In winter, many people put ____________ in their cars to stop the engine from freezing up.
11. The young child was ____________ of tying his shoelaces.
12. The passengers ____________ from the ship.
13. Dinosaurs were ____________ creatures that once roamed the Earth.
14. When Anne grazed her knee on a rusty nail, she made sure to apply ____________ cream to the wound.

C. Write down two words for each of the following prefixes, and then put each word into a sentence to show its meaning. Use a dictionary if necessary.

un-	in-	non-
re-	dis-	trans-
im-	tele-	under-

The Fearless One

The Fearless One was so intent on tracking down a bear that he did not notice how dark it was getting nor how the twists and turns of the forest path had led him deeper and deeper into the dense wood.

A bird bursting out of the undergrowth startled him. He looked up to see a great tree looming above him, its black branches reaching down to envelop him. A shiver ran down his back, and the Fearless One stepped backwards, dropping his spear. A bramble caught hold of his ankle and tripped him so that he fell awkwardly among the briars. Overhead, thick, black clouds raced across the face of the moon.

"Run, run, run!" a voice in his head shouted. He scrambled to his feet and raced back down the path. The trees stretched out their twigs to slap his face and pushed out their roots to trip him. The Fearless One crashed through the trees, tearing his clothes on the brambles and yelling for his father.

The path was going the wrong way surely, leading him not back to the safety of his tent but deeper and deeper into the woods! It was a trick. He turned off the path, fighting through the sharp twigs of the pine trees, which were moving closer and closer together to block his way.

He changed direction again. He didn't know where he was. Something black swooped down over his head, almost brushing his hair. He screamed. Then he saw the light, a thin beam cutting through the trees, and heard his father's voice calling, "Michael, Michael, is that you?"

Question Time

A

1. What was the Fearless One tracking down?
2. What startled him?
3. What was "looming" over him?
4. Why did he fall among the briars?
5. What did the voice in his head shout?
6. What did the trees seem to do to him as he ran along the path?
7. Who was the Fearless One yelling for?
8. Where was the light coming from?
9. What was the Fearless One's real name?
10. In what was the Fearless One living at the time?

B

1. Who do you think gave the boy the nickname the "Fearless One"?
2. Why did the Fearless One not notice how dark it was getting?
3. Is the danger to the boy real or imaginary?
   Give a reason for your answer.
4. The great tree seems to be a living, moving creature.
   What is it about the tree that makes the boy think this?
5. What else in the passage is brought to life
   by the boy's imagination?
6. What do you think swooped over his head?
7. In what way did he think he was being tricked?
   What was the consequence of this thought?
8. Put these words into sentences to show their meanings.

   intent   looming   undergrowth   startled

9. About what age was the boy do you think? Give a reason for your answer.
10. Look up the meaning of **irony** in your dictionary and then explain why the "Fearless One" is an **ironic** name for the boy.

Think and Talk

1. Talk about situations that make you fearful.
2. How does your body react to fear? Describe it.
3. Suggest ways of overcoming imaginary fears.
4. Write a short passage where the main character fantasises that he/she is an imaginary hero (e.g. The Special One, SuperSam, The Brainless One, etc.).

Looking Back (1) – Capital Letters, Full Stops and Commas

A. Can you remember the rules for capital letters? Test yourself by filling in the gaps.

A capital letter is used...

to _______________ sentences.

for _______________ names and ____________ names, e.g. Anne, Dublin.

when using the letter ____, meaning myself.

for ___________ of books, plays, films, music, etc.

for _______________, _______________ and _____________,

e.g. Monday, June, Christmas.

for people's _____________, e.g. Dr, Ms, Sr.

B. Now write out this passage and put in capital letters, full stops and commas.

leonardo da vinci's painting the *mona lisa* hangs in the louvre museum in paris it is perhaps the best known painting in the world leonardo himself was so fond of the painting that he kept it for himself and it is said took it with him wherever he went he certainly took it with him when he moved from italy to france after his death the mona lisa was bought by king francis I of france but it was napoleon who put it in the louvre museum where to this day it attracts thousands of visitors each year

C. Rewrite this passage and break it into paragraphs.

Martha's father is a couch potato. There is nothing more he prefers doing after work than relaxing in his big, comfortable armchair in front of the television, with the remote in his hand. If there is nothing on the television, he will still sit there and read the newspaper or just take a nap. By contrast, Martha's mother is a keep-fit fanatic. She is up at six every morning for her 10km jog and then she power-walks to work. On Monday, Wednesday and Friday evenings, she goes to yoga classes. On the remaining weekdays, she does kick-boxing after work. As well as this, she works as a fitness instructor in a gymnasium. Martha herself is neither a couch potato nor a mad sportswoman. She is somewhere in the middle. She likes playing hockey and dancing, and she loves skateboarding with her friends, but she also likes to relax and watch a little, but not too much, TV. Every night, she reads herself to sleep. In fact, as Martha would say herself, she is just perfect!

Looking Back (2) – Letters and Abbreviations

A. Write these names and addresses properly in your copybook.

1. Seamus Joyce lives in house no. 58 on Riversdale Road, which is in Dublin 22.
2. Aine O'Shea lives in Apartment 11b on Putland Road, which is in Bray in Co. Wicklow.
3. Tents and Caravans Ltd. is in Weston Retail Park on the Nangor Road in Dublin 12.
4. Walter Bee lives in a house called Down Sport on Marsoopeeal Avenue, which is in Sydney in Australia.

B. Write the abbreviation for these titles, addresses, days and months.

Examples: Mister – Mr, Square – Sq, etc.

Professor ________	Doctor ________	Father ________
Avenue ________	Court ________	Park ________
February ________	Saturday ________	April ________

C. Use the information below to write this short letter in the proper layout in your copybook.

Name of writer of letter: Mary Fonda

Address: The Hollows, 24 Ship Street, Liverpool, England.

Person to whom the letter is written: Peter Prendergast

The date: April 1, 2007

The contents of the letter: I hope you are keeping well, Peter. Thank you kindly for offering my son, Seán, a ticket to the Liverpool versus Manchester United match. He is over the moon about it! He is booked on the overnight ferry from Dublin to Liverpool on Friday night, and I hope it's not too inconvenient for you to meet him at the boat at 6.30am. I have booked him on the return sailing at 9 o'clock that evening. He will be exhausted when he gets home, but the thrill of seeing his favourite team in action will make it all worthwhile! Let's just hope they win! Once again, thank you very much, and we look forward to seeing you at Easter when you come to visit us.

D. Rewrite these sentences by putting in inverted commas, ordinary commas and question marks.

1. Citrus fruits are rich in vitamin C explained the doctor.
2. Do you like ketchup on cornflakes asked the young girl.
3. David was raging with his teacher. She gave me detention and I wasn't the one who threw the bell out the window he fumed.
4. The zookeeper got the children's full attention when he said stay clear of the snake's fangs.

Creative Writing (1)

The Fear Factor

A. **Think of as many words as you can that describe fear.**
(Example: terrified…)

B. **List some things that can frighten people.**
(Example: the dark, heights…)

C. **Find the meaning of each of these words and put the words in sentences to show their meaning.**

traumatised	consternation	foreboding	anxiety
agitation	dismay	uneasiness	apprehension

D. **Our bodies react when we are frightened.**
Write sentences describing how the following parts of your body react to fear:

Your hands
Your skin
Your heart
Your hair
Your stomach
Your legs

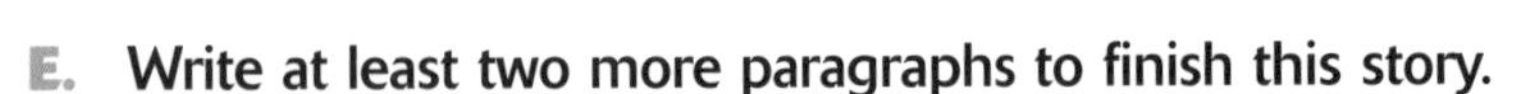

E. **Write at least two more paragraphs to finish this story.**
We stood, hidden in the shadows, hardly daring to breathe. My heart pounded in my chest, and the palms of my hands were sticky with sweat. I knew the others must be feeling the same. We could hear him coming. His unhurried steps drew gradually nearer. He sounded so confident, so fearless. The steps stopped once or twice, as though he was checking between the rows. He knew we were here! A cold pang of sheer terror spread through the small of my back. What would we do?

F. **Young children have many fears. Remember a fear that you once had and write a paragraph or two about it. Try to get into the mindset of a young child.**

Write Away!

Writing a Poem

Hide and Seek

The trees are tall, but the moon small,
My legs feel rather weak,
For Avis, Mavis, and Tom Clarke
Are hiding somewhere in the dark
And it's my turn to seek.

Suppose they lay a trap and play
A trick to frighten me?
Suppose they plan to disappear
And leave me here, half-dead with fear,
Groping from tree to tree?

Alone, alone, all on my own
And then perhaps to find
Not Avis, Mavis, and young Tom
But monsters to run shrieking from,
Mad monsters of no kind?

By Robert Graves

Discuss and Write

A. This poem is written from the point of view of a young child.
Discuss:

- What makes the game frightening for the child?
- How old do you think the child is in comparison to the other children?
- Are the child's fears real or imaginary?
- What does the child think her friends might do?
- Who is the child talking to in the poem?

B. Now write a short account *or* a poem of a frightening experience from the point of view of a young child. You can choose from this list *or* choose any other experience that you remember being frightened of as a child yourself.

(a) First day at school
(b) Lost in a Shop
(c) Visit to Doctor or Dentist
(d) New Teacher
(e) The Dark
(f) Watching a Horror Movie
(g) Uncle's False Teeth

Preflight Check

Rachel Dowling examined her instrument panel once more. The rows of indicator lights all glowed a reassuring green. She glanced over at Sam Kealy and Mike Duffin, who were strapped securely in their seats. "All right, gentlemen, it's time to go through the final checklist," she said, her calm voice gently filling the cramped capsule.

"Fuel tanks?" "Tanks full, external fuel valves closed," replied Kealy, her co-pilot. "On-board computers?" "All three systems are online and running well," drawled Duffin, the electronics specialist. He sounded bored, as usual.

"Communications?" "All radio channels open and operational." "Flight programme?" "Flight plan locked into the main computer," confirmed Duffin as he scanned his beloved computer monitors. "Docking arms?" she enquired. "All docking arms are withdrawing now," answered Kealy. Slowly, the robot arms of the launch tower released their hold on the spaceship and swung out of its way.

"Life-support?" "Life-support systems are fully operational," assured Kealy. On and on it went, with every aspect of the ship's health being checked and double-checked. Rachel placed her hand over a switch on her console. Sam Kealy did the same with an identical switch on his console. Mike Duffin kept a well-trained eye on the computer monitors, watching for any sign of a failure in the ship's complex structure.

"Begin launch countdown on my mark," ordered Dowling. "Three, two, one, mark!" Both engine ignition switches were pressed simultaneously. The launch sequence had begun. Duffin's voice marked off each second. "Internal fuel valves open, ten, nine, eight, engines sparking, six, five, we have ignition, three, two, one…" The engines roared into life. Dowling, Kealy and Duffin lay back in their seats and braced themselves for the launch.

Question Time

A

1. How many astronauts were aboard the spaceship?
2. Who was in command?
3. Who was the co-pilot?
4. What was Mike Duffin's job?
5. What did the crew do to prepare for the launch?
6. List the items mentioned on the checklist.
7. Who gave the order for the launch countdown?
8. Write out the first sentence that Rachel Dowling speaks.
9. What is the last sentence that Sam Kealy speaks?
10. How many questions does Rachel ask?
11. How do you know when someone else begins to speak in the story?
12. What marks are used on the page to show spoken sentences?
13. How many computers were on board?
14. How many ignition switches were used on board?

B

1. What words in the story show that Rachel was not a nervous person?
2. Are there any signs that Mike was a very relaxed person? What are these signs?
3. Why did the astronauts settle back into their seats before take-off?
4. Why were the astronauts so careful in their preflight check?
5. What do you think they would have done if something on the checklist had failed?
6. Think of some words to describe the astronauts.
7. Why, do you think, were they blasting off into space?
8. Why, do you think, did the spacecraft have three computer systems rather than just one?
9. Why, do you think, did they use two ignition switches instead of one?
10. Do you think the three people were suited to their jobs? Why?
11. What do you think the docking arms were used for?
12. What do you think the life-support systems were used for?

Think and Talk

1. Why, do you think, do people who travel to space need so much training?
2. Why do all pilots carry out careful preflight checks before they take to the air?
3. Space travel is extremely expensive. Do you think it's worth it?
   Give a reason.
4. What qualities do you think a person needs to become an astronaut?
5. Write a newspaper report on the launch of the spacecraft.
   Give as many details about the crew as you can.

Nouns

Nouns are names.
A noun can be the name of a person, a place, a thing, an animal, a period of time or an idea.

A. Underline the nouns in the following sentences:

1. Pandas eat the leaves of the bamboo.
2. People are about a centimetre shorter in the evening than in the morning.
3. The Olympic Games were first held in Greece on Mount Olympus.
4. The first people to settle in Australia were the Aborigines.
5. Animals that have pouches are called marsupials.
6. The feather-winged beetle is so small it can sit on a pinhead.
7. Trees are the largest plants of all, and they also live longer than any other plant.
8. The Venus Flytrap is a plant that eats insects.
9. Lemons, oranges, grapefruit and other citrus fruit are rich in vitamin C.
10. Sad plays are called tragedies whereas funny plays are called comedies.
11. Many animals are born during spring.
12. Edmund Hillary was the first person to reach the summit of Mount Everest.

B. Write the following passage in your copybook and replace each space with a noun from the box. (Some nouns are used more than once.)

tooth puller	pain	teeth	gas	noise
dentists	show	patient	crowd	toothache
tooth	stall	ordeal	drummer	people
	market days		anaesthetics	

Nowadays, when __________ pull __________, they use __________ or ____________ to numb the patient's pain. In the past, however, it must have been a terrible __________. __________ probably put up with the __________ of a ______________ for as long as they could bear it rather than face the dreaded __________ __________! He usually set up his __________ on __________ __________, and he was often accompanied by a __________. The drummer's job was to make as much __________ as possible in order to drown out the screams of the __________. Meanwhile, the tooth puller pulled, poked and yanked out the offending __________. It was quite an __________, and a large __________ was sure to cheer on the __________ __________, all except the next __________ in line!

Suffixes

- You can make a new word by adding a **suffix** to the end of the original word.

  Examples: care + less = careless
  king + dom = kingdom

A. Complete each sentence by adding a suitable suffix from the following list.

-hood	-less	-ment	-ness	-ful	-ous	-ish	-wise	-ways

1. The danger________ driver overtook the bus on a narrow bridge.
2. Wine bottles ought to be stored side______ to keep the corks moist.
3. The fool_______ boy thought that the moon had fallen into the lake.
4. It's good to have help______ people living in your neighbour_______.
5. The heart_____ landlord evicted the old couple from their little flat.
6. The move_____ of the ship made me feel quite sick.
7. He is in hospital suffering from a rare ill_____.
8. She did not play as well as usual; other_______, he would not have won.
9. It is help_______ if you understand what a suffix is when doing these exercises.
10. He spent much of his boy_______ playing football.

B. Put a word before each of these suffixes.
Then put each of the new words you have made into a sentence to show its meaning.

Examples: **-ation** imagine – imagin**ation**
-ism tour – tour**ism**

-less	-wise	-ful	-dom	-ation	-hood
-ism	-ess	-fold	-er	-ant	-able

C. List the suffixes and the prefixes used in the following words:

unhelpful	disagreement	unfolding
indefinitely	replaying	implantation

D. Rewrite this passage and replace the underlined words with words from the wordbox.

unable	disagreement	replaying	misunderstanding	unhelpful	indefinitely

Going over and over the same old argument forever is not helpful! You are either deliberately not understanding my point of view or simply not able to admit when you are in the wrong!

____

____

____

____

A Letter to Mam

14 Eaton Manor,
Abbeyvale,
Dublin 37.

Hi Mam,

I know you've only been away for a few days but I thought I'd write to let you know that we are all getting along just fine. I hope the weather in Australia is good. It has to be better than the weather here. It rained all last night, and we forgot to close the attic skylight. Still, we have mopped up most of the water, so no worries there.

Dad cooked us a super tea the day you left on your holiday. We had chips and pizza and a big fry-up. He said it was every bit as good for us as the healthy stuff you cook. Dad will have the scorch marks on the kitchen ceiling painted over by the time you get back, so you'll hardly notice where the chip pan went on fire. We had lots of Coke too. He said he knew we were allergic to it, but he thought it might cheer us up a bit because you were gone. I was only sick twice, but Alan was up most of the night. You should have seen his bed!

Anyway, since then, Dad has bought us a Chinese takeaway, an Indian takeaway and a Southern Fried Chicken takeaway, and he said he might take us to a burger joint tonight. That might depend on when the man comes to fix the washing machine though. Dad thought it was the dishwasher. He said it was a very easy mistake to make, and we were all a bit tired after staying up to watch the late-night horror movie.

Dad was very good at getting the washing sorted out without the washing machine. We had great fun putting all the laundry in the bath and swirling it around with the handle of the sweeping brush. It was a bit strange when all the white clothes changed colour, but Dad says that pinky-grey underwear is all the fashion.

Anyway, never mind all that boring stuff about us! How are you? I bet you're out relaxing in the sun without a worry in the world! Give my love to Aunt Laura and Uncle Ken. I bet their new house is lovely.

I'll have to go now because I promised Dad I'd help him fix that broken vase – the one Granny gave you.

Enjoy the next five weeks. You lucky thing!

Lots of love and kisses,

Emma XXXXXXXXXXXXXXX

Question Time

A

1. Who is writing the letter?
2. To whom is she writing it?
3. Why is she writing it?
4. Where is her mother?
5. How long has her mother been away?
6. Who is in charge of the house while she is away?
7. What did the father cook for the children?
8. What happened to the washing machine?
9. What accident happened in the kitchen with the chip pan?
10. How did the father wash all the clothes?
11. What happened to the clothes when they were washed?
12. For how long is the children's mother going to be away?
13. Make a list of the things you think the father might have done wrong.
14. Name the different countries mentioned in the letter.

B

1. Why did the family have to mop up lots of water?
2. Why did the father let the children have cola to drink?
3. What do you think is the father's opinion of healthy food?
4. Do you think the children's mother would agree with him?
5. List the different types of food mentioned in the story.
6. Why is the mother in Australia?
7. Do you think the children's father knows the contents of Emma's letter? Why?
8. How do you think the mother is going to react when she reads the letter?
9. Do you think the mother will enjoy her stay in Australia? Say why.
10. Do you think the father was doing a good job? Say why.
11. What do you think is the worst thing the father has done?
12. Emma is writing a cheerful letter with lots of news.
    Do you think this will cheer her mother up? Say why.
13. Do you think Emma's letter will cause trouble for her father?
14. What do you think Emma's father might say to her if he knew what she was writing?

Think and Talk

1. Talk about what a healthy lunch should contain.
2. Talk about the effects of eating junk food.
3. Do you think it is easy to take care of a household? Say why.
4. Write the reply the mother might now send to Emma.

Pronouns

- A word that takes the place of a **noun** is called a **pronoun**.

  Example: Anne likes to eat ice cream.

  She likes to eat **it**.

  She replaces Anne while **it** replaces ice cream.

A. Replace each of the underlined nouns in the following passage with a suitable pronoun from the box.

he	her	him	them	she

When Brendan was younger, Uncle Jack would slip Brendan a bar of chocolate, lift Brendan onto his knees and tell him amazing stories of the adventures that Jack himself had had in Africa. Mum would laugh when Brendan recounted the stories to Mum afterwards.
"Tall tales, Brendan," Mum would say, ruffling his hair. "Don't believe everything that brother of mine tells you. Jack always had a lively imagination!"

B. Underline the pronouns in the following sentences:

1. Scavengers are carnivores, but they do not always kill the food that they eat.
2. You can identify a flower by the smell of it.
3. Coughing helps you to clear dust from your lungs.
4. The Indians had animal furs to keep them warm during the long, winter months.
5. Jack always takes a book with him.
6. The footballer caught the ball, and he kicked it over the bar.
7. Mary was late, and the teacher scolded her.
8. Mum helped him with the maths problem.
9. We told him not to tell her about it.
10. She gave them sandwiches, and they thanked her for them.
11. It was a cold day, so they all wore gloves.
12. We have just been talking to them.
13. He asked for money, but I didn't give him any.
14. It's very late now, so you should call her out.
15. My feet are so cold that I have no feeling in them.
16. They like to eat fruit for lunch.
17. I can't understand him when he speaks quickly.
18. He stole the credit card and used it to buy a television.
19. Luckily, the gardaí caught him.

Similes

Comparisons that use the words **like** or **as** are called **similes** (**simil-ays**).
Similes help us to explain or describe things more clearly.
Examples: He ran as fast **as** a speeding bullet.
She looked **like** a million dollars.

A. Complete these similes.

1. The giant was as tall as ____________________.
2. The house with its broken shutters and peeling paintwork looked like ___________.
3. The sprinters left the starting blocks like ____________________.
4. The jet trailed its smoke across the sky like ____________________.
5. The feeling you get before the parachute opens is like _______________.
6. Lying alone in the dark house, knowing that there was an intruder downstairs, Michael felt fear and anger rising in him like _______________.
7. Not quite asleep, not quite awake, stray thoughts and disconnected dreams flitted about her head like ____________________.
8. Paul leaned on the low wall and watched the gulls being blown about like ____________________.
9. Her fingers were so cold they felt like ____________________.
10. The water splashing over his face was as ____________________.

B. Write a sentence to fit these similes.

1. ______________________________ like a kangaroo.
2. ______________________________ as ice.
3. ________________ as a sack of stones.
4. ____________________ like he had been pulled backwards through a ditch.
5. __________________________ like cold mashed potatoes.

C. Some similes are used very often. Complete these common similes.

1. As white as _____________
2. As happy as _____________
3. As pale as _____________
4. As black as _____________
5. As busy as _____________
6. As heavy as _____________
7. As dead as _____________
8. As hard as _____________

D. Common similes are often overused and boring.
Make up your own similes for the list above.
Put these in sentences to make them interesting.

Write Away!

Functional Writing – Taking Notes

- When we read a passage and want to remember the information in it, taking notes is very helpful.
- When taking notes, it is a good idea to spot the **key word** in each sentence.

  Example: Some **French** people eat **snails**.

  Key Words: **French** / **snails**

A. Read this passage and underline the key words in each sentence.

Lions live in packs called prides. A pride of lions can have up to twenty members. Surprisingly, there may be three or four male lions in a pride. It is the male lion that has the majestic mane of hair. The rest of the pride is made up of lionesses and their cubs. A lioness usually has a litter of cubs every two years or so. A litter typically consists of one to four cubs.

Cubs are blind and quite helpless when they are born. Their mothers guard them jealously, teaching them to hunt and stalk prey. It is actually the female lionesses who do most of the hunting for the pride. The male lions protect the territory of the pride.

B. Using these key words as an aid, write a short passage about Italy.

Key Words:

- Capital – Rome
- Foods – pasta / spaghetti
- Language – Italian
- Cities – Florence / Venice / Naples / Milan
- Artists – Michelangelo / Leonardo da Vinci / Raphael
- Vatican City / Pope / Rome
- Sistine Chapel – Michelangelo
- Ancient Rome – Colosseum / Forum / Circus Maximus / Pantheon
- Islands – Sicily / Sardinia / Capri / Pantelleria
- Leaning Tower of Pisa

C. Using these key words, write about *The First Voyage Around The World*.

Key Words:

- Ferdinand Magellan – first voyage, died en route.
- Magellan – a Portuguese explorer.
- Charles I of Spain gave him five ships.
- Three years later, one ship (Vittoria) returned to Spain.
- Magellan found a passage from Atlantic to Pacific Oceans.
- Passage known as the Strait of Magellan.
- Magellan killed in local war on the island of Cebu in Pacific.

Write Away!

An Interview

Thor McGillicuddy – world-famous explorer

It's every journalist's dream! You have bumped into none other than the world's greatest living explorer, Thor McGillicuddy, who is looking for his car in a busy airport car park. Using your notes, you have to write a report about the great man. Good luck!

Where were you born?	*Here in Ireland in Cashel, County… eh… Waterford … no, Tipperary, that's the one! Tipperary.*
Your earliest childhood memory?	*I think it was when I got lost in the woods behind my house… I was always wandering off and getting lost… My mother was furious. Bright red.*
Your mother was bright red?	*No, no, no… my car is bright red… easy to see… I always use bright red tents when I'm exploring. It makes them easier to find when you get lost in the jungle… should work with cars in car parks too, shouldn't it?*
Happiest childhood memory?	*When my parents got me a dog… a bloodhound that could find me when I got lost… Rover…*
Your dog was called Rover?	*No. He was called Sam. Great dog. Could find me anywhere… the car is a Rover… a Land Rover. Did I tell you it was bright red?*
Did you enjoy school when you were young?	*Loved it! Though I was always rotten at geography… useless with maps!*
Is that not a problem for an explorer?	*Suppose… never thought of it that way… after all, if you don't get to where you are going, then you'll probably end up somewhere else, right?*
Your greatest achievement as an explorer?	*Finding the ruins of the lost city of Barak Tu in the African rainforest.*
And your scariest moment?	*Bumping into the rather large and angry gorillas that lived in the ruins of the Lost City of Barak Tu… had to run like mad or it could have got nasty.*
What do you think makes a good explorer?	*Being able to run fast is a big advantage… mostly though, I think you have to like to go wandering around, and you have to be as nosey and as curious as a cat.*
Any big ambitions or plans for the future?	*Finding my car would be nice… ah, there it is… well, goodbye… you don't know the way out of here, do you?*

Now, in your copybook, use your notes to write your newspaper article about Thor McGillicuddy.

For Sale!

When people want to buy or sell things, they often place advertisements in newspapers or on the Internet.

ARTICLES FOR SALE

Bicycle – excellent cond.
New tyres.
€85 ono.
Ph: (01) 453897

Computer – Laptop with broadband connection. IBM PCS model. As new. €745. No offers. P.O. Box 3465

Fridge-Freezer
Unwanted prize. Still in box. Twirlpool. €650 only. Ph: Noreen (0404) 56219154 Evenings only.

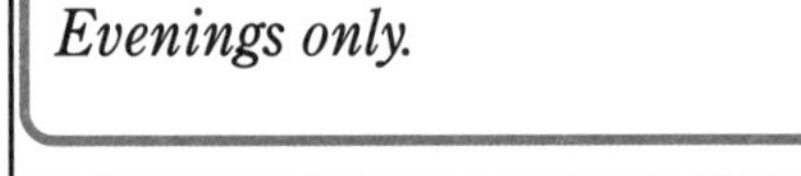

PUPPIES
5-week-old spaniel puppies
€75
each to a good home
www.k-ninesales.ie

Skateboard

Ex. Condition
Genuine reason for sale (broken ankle)
€34 ono
Ph (056) 56432376

Table – Oak, seats 6.
Slightly damaged.
Genuine offers only.
Ph: (01) 453897

Medals

Collector seeks old medals pre-dating World War 1.
Fair prices paid.
Ph: (088) 9876054

PETS

Good home given to puppy.
Small breed of dog preferred.
€60 – €80 paid for healthy dog.
P.O. Box 2210

ARTICLES WANTED

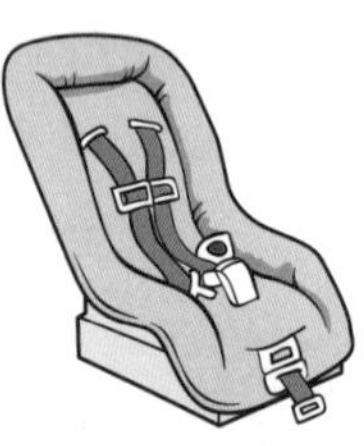

Car Seat – suitable for 2-yr-old. Must be in good condition. Ph: (01) 673290

COMPUTER GAMES – good prices paid for any PC computer games. Ph: 083 6578906

Fridge-Freezer
Young family needs fridge-freezer in good working order.
Price must be reasonable.
Ph: (0404) 43527629

PIANO
Upright piano required for school use.
Must be sturdy.
Will collect. Good price paid.
PO. Box 23189

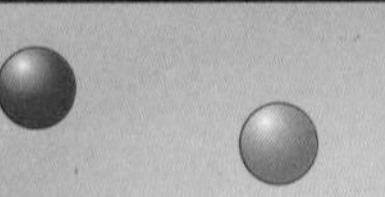

Snooker Table – old table needed for Scouts. We will collect from anywhere in the city. Can you help us out?
Ph: (01) 987657

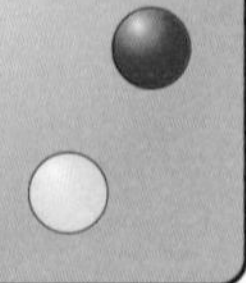

ono = or nearest offer / cond. = condition

Question Time

A

1. What kind of puppies are for sale?
2. Describe the table that is for sale.
3. Why is the fridge-freezer for sale?
4. Which of the items for sale are in good condition?
5. A driver is looking for something. What is it?
6. A young family is looking for something. What is it?
7. What are the scouts looking for?
8. What is the P.O. Box number that is used by the school?
9. How much is the person prepared to pay for a puppy?
10. Who is prepared to collect their purchase?
11. What is the website used by the puppy seller?
12. What is the difference between an upright piano and a grand piano?

B

1. Somebody is trying to sell two items. What are they? Give a reason for your answer.
2. It is generally considered a good idea to be at, or near, the top of the list. Do you agree? Give a reason for your answer.
3. Why, do you think, is the oak table for sale?
4. Would the collector be interested in medals from the 1940s? Give a reason for your answer.
5. Do you think the scouts have a lot of money to spare? Give a reason for your answer.
6. Do you think any of the "For Sale" items might match up with any of the "Wanted" items? Which ones? Why?
7. Which of the articles for sale would interest you most? Why?
8. Which advertisers are prepared to sell for less than the asking price?
9. Do you think that the person selling the puppies cares about animals? Give a reason for your answer.
10. Advertisements do not read like ordinary sentences. Give a reason for this.
11. What abbreviations are used in the advertisements instead of (a) excellent, (b) or nearest offer, (c) condition?
12. Write the full words for each of these: Ph. / P.O. / P.C.

Think and Talk

You have €20 to spend on an advertisement.
You are trying to sell your bicycle.
Each word costs €1.
Write your advertisement for the local newspaper.

Adjectives (1)

Adjectives tell us something about nouns (e.g. people, places, things).
They make language more interesting.

Example: The cat sat on the mat.
The **sleek, graceful** cat sat on the **beautiful, blue** mat.

A. Underline the adjectives in the following sentences:

1. The long, difficult climb up the icy rock-face was the most dangerous I had ever undertaken.
2. Neil Armstrong and Buzz Aldrin were the first people ever to set foot on the barren, desolate surface of the moon.
3. The gigantic Airbus 380 is the world's largest passenger aircraft.
4. Tiny bumblebee bats are the world's smallest mammals.
5. The lovely Arabian princess wore gorgeous, green robes of the finest silk.

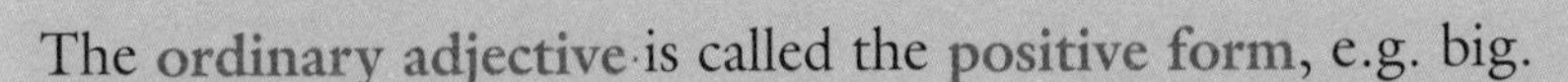

The **ordinary adjective** is called the **positive form**, e.g. big.
The **comparative form** is when we compare two objects, e.g. bigger.
The **superlative form** is when we compare more than two objects, e.g. biggest.

B. Finish this table.

positive	comparative	superlative
fat	fatter	fattest
lucky	luckier	luckiest
late	later	latest
warm	warmer	warmest
tall	________	________
high	________	________
greasy	________	________
funny	________	________
safe	________	________
big	________	________
hot	________	________
dark	________	________
light	________	________
sunny	________	________
cute	________	________

C. Complete each of these.

good	better	________
bad	________	worst
little	less	________
many	________	most

Metaphors – Pushing your Imagination

This passage uses a **metaphor**, a person playing a nasty trick, to describe shoppers in a busy street being caught in a sudden shower of rain. The rain is described as if it is a person. When we use a **metaphor** to describe something, we do not use the words **as** or **like**.

Example: The lonely mountain hunched its back against the wind and the rain of the storm.
(The mountain is compared to a lonely person turning his or her back to the storm.)

A. To what are the underlined words in these sentences compared?

1. The little stream leaped, laughing over the stones, and ran cheerfully down the hillside.
2. The dark windows of the house frowned forbiddingly as I approached.
3. The shepherd's rough, craggy face crinkled into a smile.
4. The witch leaped about and screeched, her black arms flapping, her long fingernails clawing the air.
5. The damaged plane shuddered and swerved as it struggled to limp back to the runway.

B. Complete these sentences.

1. He was a pig the way he ate ______________________.
2. The leaves danced and twirled ______________________.
3. A cruel smile was frozen on her lips and her eyes were ________________.
4. The drops of rain danced merrily on the ______________________.
5. The old oak tree towered above ______________________.
6. The thunder in Jack's face told us that he ______________________.

C. Use metaphors to write sentences describing each of the following.
Remember, you may not use the words *as* or *like*.

1. Waves breaking on the shore.
2. A storm.
3. Somebody losing his/her temper.

High Anxiety

The VIP lounge was filled with specially invited guests. These lucky people chatted and laughed as the final preparations were made. They posed for eager photographers. Some of the guests stood by the window and gazed at the group of pilots marching in protest outside the airport building. They were carrying placards and banners that had statements such as "Unfair!" and "Our Jobs Are At Risk" written on them. Some of the guests laughed.

A special announcement was heard over the airport loudspeakers. "Will all the guests for the first flight of Automated Airways please go to the VIP gate." They shuffled out of the VIP room, trailing fur coats, diamond jewellery and expensive clothes. Everyone was eager for a glimpse of the aircraft itself.

When they did catch sight of it through the passenger gate, everyone remarked on how ordinary it looked. In fact, all the extraordinary aspects of the plane were hidden inside. The only clue to be seen was the absence of windows in the front, where the cockpit was supposed to be. A large band was playing on the tarmac beside the jet.

Each person was escorted to his or her seat on board. As they settled back, a strange, metallic voice came over the intercom. "Ladies and gentlemen, welcome to this, the first official flight of a fully automated jetliner." They applauded. The voice continued. "Today, you will be carried safely across the Atlantic Ocean to New York in 1 hour, 25 minutes and 17 seconds. There is no pilot or co-pilot. This flight will be free of human error." More applause.

The doors closed automatically. The engines powered up automatically. The huge aircraft taxied automatically from the airport terminal to the runway. It automatically built up speed, and then it took off automatically. Within minutes, it was streaking across the sky to America.

The metallic voice began once more: "Ladies and gentlemen, we have reached cruising altitude and are travelling at a speed of 4,375km per hour. You may unfasten your seat belts, and just to reassure you that nothing can go wrong… click… go wrong… click… go wrong… click…"

Question Time

A

1. Where were the guests waiting?
2. What was happening outside?
3. What was written on the placards?
4. What special event was about to take place?
5. What was so special about the aircraft?
6. Where was it going?
7. Did anyone come to see the aircraft take off?
8. How long was the flight supposed to take?
9. At what speed was the plane travelling?
10. Which ocean was the plane going to cross?
11. Who was talking to the passengers on board the plane?
12. Think of a new title for the story.

B

1. How do you know that the guests were rich?
2. Why were the pilots protesting?
3. Did the guests care about the pilots? How do you know?
4. What does VIP mean?
5. There were no pilots. Do you think there were other crew members on the plane? Why?
6. This was the "first official flight". Do you think there had been other flights? Why?
7. Was there anything unusual about the appearance of the jet?
8. Why, do you think, did the airline invite a group of rich and famous people to be the passengers on the first flight?
9. Who, or what, was talking to the passengers on board the plane?
10. Do some research to find the speed of sound. At how many times the speed of sound was this plane supposed to be travelling?
11. What would have alarmed the passengers?
12. Do you think there was a second official automated flight? Why?

Think and Talk

1. Why is so much time and money spent on the training of airline pilots?
2. Why is the job of a pilot regarded as a very stressful job?
3. What would be the advantages/disadvantages of being an airline pilot?
4. Do you think that, someday, aircraft will be flown by computers instead of pilots? Why?
5. Write a newspaper report covering the event.

Overused Words (1)

Sometimes we use the same word too often when we are writing a story.
It can make our stories very boring to read.

A. Use words from the wordbox to replace the word 'good' in these sentences. Read all the sentences first and then select the most suitable word for each one.

beautiful	wonderful	fabulous	fantastic	delicious	reliable
powerful	brilliant	thorough	great	marvellous	lovely

1. The weather was good while we were on holiday. ____________
2. Carl cooked a good meal for the family. ____________
3. Sally is a good swimmer. ____________
4. The peregrine falcon has good eyesight. ____________
5. Emer's car is good, and it never lets her down. ____________
6. The doctor gave her patient a good examination. ____________
7. I saw some good paintings in the art gallery. ____________
8. The Suzawaki 5000 is a good motorbike. ____________
9. The International Space Station is a good achievement. ____________
10. Marie Curie was a good scientist. ____________
11. Dad gave Mam a good bunch of roses for her birthday. ____________
12. We had a good day on our school tour. ____________

Can you think of any more words that mean 'good'? ____________

B. Use words from the wordbox to replace the word 'bad' in these sentences.

tragic	terrible	horrible	miserable	serious	ridiculous	catastrophic
awful	disastrous	revolting	painful	nasty	dangerous	stupid

1. My Aunt Flo's special octopus stew tastes bad.
2. The Second World War was a bad nightmare for millions of people.
3. Napoleon's army suffered a bad defeat in the Russian winter of 1812.
4. The Roman town of Pompeii was destroyed in a bad volcanic eruption.
5. Samantha's rocket car went too fast around the bad bend in the road.
6. Gilbert knew he was in bad trouble when he saw the lion in his room.
7. Poor Danny had a bad time when he came down with measles.
8. I saw a bad film about a girl who gets chased by giant potatoes – what rubbish!
9. Katherine had a bad scratch on her arm after she tried to get the cat out of the tree.
10. The fire caused bad damage to the building.

Write four more words that can mean the same as 'bad'.

____________ ____________ ____________ ____________

Overused Words (2)

A. Make this boring story come to life by replacing the word 'good' with a more interesting word in each case.

It was a good party. We all had a good time. Jane's dad had set up a really good barbecue in the garden. He cooked good food for us while we chatted and listened to some good music on Jane's stereo. There were good burgers, good fat sausages and good chicken wings. He even prepared some good veggie burgers for Ben and Eva, who are both vegetarians.

The garden looked good too. Jane had hung up lots of good lanterns on trees and bushes, and they made the garden good as they shone in the darkness. We all had a really good time, and we were sad when it was time to go home.

B. Replace the word 'bad' with a more interesting word whenever you find it in this passage.

It was a bad match. The weather was bad. The fog was so bad that we couldn't see either end of the pitch. The referee was bad… no, I mean, really bad. He made the bad decision to start the game despite the bad conditions.

Both teams played a bad game. In the bad visibility, it was hard to see what we were doing. Terry's long kicks were bad. Laura and one of the other team's players had a bad collision when they were going for the ball. She ended up with a bad bang on the head.

In the end, even our bad referee had to call a halt. We were all in a bad mood at this stage. "Play is postponed because of this bad weather," he called. "Back to the changing rooms, everyone." Nice one, Ref. It took us twenty minutes to find the changing rooms! What a bad day!

Write Away!

Functional Essay

- Before writing an essay, it can be helpful to brainstorm the topic. A good way of doing this is to make a 'spider's web', or mind map.

A. Using this web, write a short essay called *The Night Sky*.
Write three paragraphs.
Paragraph one should be about the Moon.
Paragraph two should be about the stars.
Paragraph three should be about the planets.

Planets
Jupiter is the biggest planet.
Mars known as Red Planet. Saturn famous for its rings. Earth is the only planet in our solar system with life. Earth is the third planet from the Sun. Mercury is nearest planet to Sun. 88 days in a Mercury year. Planets don't shine with their own light. Planets shine with reflected sunlight.

THE NIGHT SKY

Moon
Gravity six times less than Earth.
Neil Armstrong first man on the Moon – Apollo 11, 20 July 1969.
Moon's gravity affects Earth's tides.
Orbits Earth once every 28 days.

Stars
So far away they seem like points of light.
Sun is 149·6 million km away.
Sun our nearest star.
Earth orbits Sun once every 365 days.
Made up of very hot gases.
Groups of stars – constellations.
There are 88 constellations in the night sky.

Now make your own spider's web on France. Then write an essay about France.

Write Away!

Edit That!

- Editors use simple symbols to highlight errors (sometimes called 'typos') in manuscripts. This makes it easier to spot the corrections that need to be made before the manuscript is printed. Below is a key to some of the symbols they use.
- Key:

sp	=	spelling error	cap	=	capital letter
.	=	full stop	,	=	comma
?	=	question mark	"	=	quotation marks
^	=	missing word	gr	=	grammar
!	=	exclamation mark	ap	=	apostrophe

A. Read the passage and spot the errors. Put the correct editing symbols in the margin. Rewrite the passage correctly. (The first two lines are already done.)

cap	eddie Dussitt of the E.C. Dussitt School of Motoring had a terrible headache.
sp	He ran a hand over his forehead and up through his sandy brown hare.
	It had been one of those days_Eddie Dussitt was a very good
	driving teacher. the problem was that not all of his pupils were good drivers,
	or ever likely to be. Already today, he had had a close enconter with a truck,
	and his nerves were now shattered. he needed to relax. His hand was still
	trembling as he put_CD into the CD player. He really needed to listen to
	something soothing. As the tape began to play, he turned the car and head
	for home. A voice on the CD began to croon in hypnotic tones,_Breathe
	deeply… Feel the peace around you… You are in compleat control…"
	Complete control? He had nearly being splattered across the front of a
	thirty-ton truck_
	"Clothes your eyes…"
	Close his eyes! For heavens sake, he was driving a car, and the twit on the CD
	wanted him too close his eyes!
	"Feel your spirit spreading outwards…_
	"Feel this, you twit_" snapped Eddie, pulling out the CD and throwing it out
	the_of his car. So much for relaxation CDs!

B. Now try this passage. Write it out correctly when you have edited it.

	"I am the finest cook in all of Madagascarr." Lela paused and thought about
	that. "Probably in all of the world," she corrected herself
	Something was plopped on to to plates from a huge, black pot. The children
	looked the food doubtfully for a moment.
	"Eat!" lela boomed at them. It wasn't an offer they could refuse. Actually, the
	stuff on there plates turned out to be a very tasty vegetable stew with just a
	hint of spice. As finished their second plateful, the children noticed Lela
	tucking into a plate of potatoe crisps and curry-flavoured instant noodles.
	She waved airily at their plates. "That traditional madagascar food is OK,"
	she said as she munched on a crisp, "for tourists.

A Plague of Pets

In 1770, Captain James Cook of the British Navy sighted Australia and claimed the new land for his king. Within a few years, the first European settlements and prison colonies were established along Australia's eastern coast. Ships from Britain and Ireland carried hopeful farmers and desperate convicts to newly formed settlements, such as Sydney and Melbourne.

However, the ships brought more than human cargo. Cattle and sheep were introduced to Australia by the newly arrived farmers. Large areas of bush land were cleared and transformed into rolling pasture. Other animals were also introduced, with devastating consequences for the landscape. Mice escaped from visiting ships, and, in 1859, 24 rabbits were introduced in one village for people to hunt as a pastime.

Within a few short years, there were millions of mice and rabbits in Australia. Both of these species spread rapidly across the country, and their numbers increased dramatically because, among the native Australian animals, there were no natural enemies to prey on them and to control their numbers. Huge plagues of mice and rabbits have been wreaking havoc on crops ever since. In 1907, a rabbit-proof fence running across 1,833km of the Australian continent was completed in order to stop the further spread of the pests.

An even more sinister menace has emerged in the form of domestic cats that have become wild. These feral, or wild, cats are the descendants of pet cats that were abandoned or that strayed from home. They show the great hunting skills that are the hallmark of all cat species. They display none of the affectionate nature that we associate with pet cats. Instead, the feral cat is a stealthy hunter and a vicious predator. The body size of a feral cat is about twice that of an ordinary domestic cat. This extraordinary increase in size seems to be a natural response to the needs of life in the wild.

Millions of feral cats now live across the length and breadth of Australia. Some local authorities have taken steps to hunt down the cats in an effort to protect their vulnerable marsupial wildlife, such as kangaroos.

Question Time

A

1. Who claimed Australia for Britain? In what year?
2. What kind of people went to live in Australia?
3. What changes did the new settlers bring to Australia?
4. Name four animal species that were introduced to Australia.
5. What effect did mice and rabbits have on the lives of Australian farmers?
6. From where did the feral cats come?
7. How do feral cats differ from domestic cats?
8. How long is the rabbit-proof fence?
9. In what year were rabbits introduced?
10. How many rabbits were there at first?

B

1. What is a "marsupial"?
2. Name one marsupial.
3. What steps do you think are being taken to protect the native animals from feral cats?
4. Why were rabbits introduced to Australia?
5. Do you think that the cattle and sheep became a problem? Why?
6. How did the mice arrive?
7. Why did the Australians build a huge fence across the continent?
8. What lessons can we learn from this story about introducing new animal species into a country?

Think and Talk

1. Name some other kinds of animal that farmers might have introduced to Australia.
2. Why, do you think, do we have to be very careful before introducing any new type of plant or animal into the wild?
3. What do you think should be done to protect the native animals of Australia from wild cats?
4. If the Australians could do it all over again, do you think they would change anything? In what way?

Verbs

A verb is a word that describes **action**.
Every sentence needs at least one action word in order to make sense.

Examples: Mahatma Gandhi **was** an extremely wise man.
Brazil **is** the largest country in South America.
Alfie **swerved**, **skidded** and **smashed** the new car into the telegraph pole.

A. Underline the verbs in the following sentences:

1. Lennie built a model of the Eiffel Tower with old matchsticks.
2. The fireman dashed down the corridor and rescued the unconscious child.
3. About a billion billion insects live on Earth at any one time.
4. The faulty firework whizzed over our heads, shot through the hedge, rebounded off the shed roof and exploded with a deafening roar.
5. Thomas Edison invented the light bulb, the first successful record player and the lightning conductor.
6. Tom's model plane turned and then headed straight for us.

B. Put each of the verbs you have underlined into separate sentences.

C. Write the verbs from the wordbox in the correct gaps in the passage below.

wore	slid	hunted	waited	gave
was	ploughed	sailed	listened	judged
travels	happened	watched	shot	accompanied

The submarine __travels__ almost silently through the cold waters of the Atlantic Ocean. On board, one man __wore__ a pair of headphones. He __was__ listening for ships on the surface. Sound __Listened__ well through water, especially the deep throbbing of ships' engines. The submarine __ploughed__ such ships. In 1941, such things __happened__.

Twenty merchant ships __sailed__ steadily through the grey Atlantic waves. Two warships __accompan__ them. The submarine crew ________ and ________ just below the surface. Unaware of the danger, the convoy of ships __shot__ straight towards the trap. The captain of the submarine __watched__ through his periscope and ________ the distance to the targets. He __gave__ the order, and four lethal torpedoes __hunted__ through the water in the direction of the unsuspecting ships.

Write a suitable ending for this story.

Punctuation – . , “ ” ?

Remember:

- A sentence always ends with a full stop or question mark.
- Actual words spoken must be written inside quotation marks.
- A comma is used after the last word that is spoken.

A. Put the correct punctuation marks into these sentences.

1. Tom Dick Harry and Alex are all brothers
2. Did the chicken come before the egg
3. Come over here at once the teacher said
4. Do you want to come to my house asked Susan
5. I had eggs toast grapefruit and tea for breakfast
6. Niall and Henry are really nice fellows Jim told John
7. Did you know that volcanic pumice stone can float on water
8. You are all making a terrible mistake moaned Louise

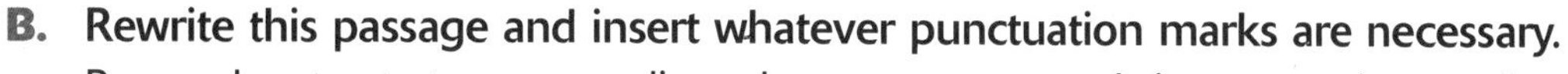

B. Rewrite this passage and insert whatever punctuation marks are necessary.
Remember to start on a new line when you put speech into quotation marks.

Alan saw the huge wave breaking over the wall of the pier He knew it would reach the village The people had to be warned but how All he could do was shout at the top of his voice Run for your lives he screamed People stuck their heads out of doorways and instantly saw why Alan was shouting They dropped everything and ran too The wave came roaring after them

C. Here is another passage for you to write correctly.

I had never seen such a thing before A long ragged battered line of people struggled down the road for as far as the eye could see What is happening I asked one man as he limped by Our town was attacked this morning he told me The look of fear and horror on his face told me more than I wanted to know So this is war I whispered to myself

A Poor Show

Even now, ten years later, I wince when I remember that summer. There was a lot wrong with what we did from start to finish. First wrong thing: We shouldn't have been next or near Smuggler's Cave. It was strictly out of bounds, and swimming into it was considered highly dangerous. Second wrong thing: We should never have borrowed the torch, Pierre's pride and joy.

Pierre was the French student. He was quiet and, to us, seemed surly. "He's just homesick, I expect," decided Mum, and she asked us not to leave him out. To our shame, we didn't heed her. Pierre had an underwater torch, which was just what we needed, so we borrowed it from his suitcase. "We'll put it back safe when we're finished, and he will never know the difference," Greg assured me.

Climbing down the cliff was risky, but neither of us wanted to lose face in front of the other by admitting to being scared. The cave itself was a dark mouth, the sea rushing in and out of it with a gurgling noise. When we jumped into the surging water, an incoming wave seemed to suck us into the cave. The cave was actually quite short, and everytime we dived to search for some underground passage into a hidden cavern, we only came up against rock.

It was only when we were back on the top of the cliff that we noticed that the underwater torch was not waterproof. Its glass had all fogged up. I opened it to dry it out. The spring holding in the battery spun into the air and flew over the edge of the cliff. "You idiot!" yelled Greg, thumping me hard on the arm.

We quietly put the broken torch back in Pierre's suitcase and kept our fingers crossed that he wouldn't check it before he flew home in three days time. No such luck! Pierre was beside himself with rage when he discovered the torch. "You'd swear somebody had died," Greg muttered. "How could you?" Mum asked, her voice full of disappointment. "And he our guest!" Dad was more direct, and we ended our holiday grounded.

Third wrong thing: On the morning of Pierre's departure, Greg and I took his precious camera. We pointed it at the ceiling and clicked and clicked until we had used up the whole film. Then we put it back into his suitcase.

Question Time

A

1. How many years ago did the incident take place?
2. What was "the first wrong thing"?
3. Who owned the underwater torch?
4. What nationality was Pierre?
5. How many days were left in Pierre's holiday to Ireland?
6. Where did Pierre keep his torch?
7. Why did the boys need the underwater torch?
8. What seemed to suck them into the cave?
9. What essential part of the torch did they lose?
10. How did the boys enter the cave?

B

1. Why does the writer still "wince" when he remembers that summer?
2. Why did Greg thump the writer on the arm?
3. What do you think the boys hoped to find in the cave?
4. What is a "smuggler"? Put the word in a sentence to show its meaning.
5. Why did the boys have their fingers crossed?
6. Put these words in separate sentences to show their meanings.

   wince sarcastic surging surly

7. Why was Mum's voice "full of disappointment"?
8. What other "precious" possession did Pierre have?
9. Why did the boys photograph the ceiling?
10. Write a short description of the kind of person you think Greg is.

Think and Talk

1. Write a paragraph from Pierre's point of view, describing his holiday in Ireland to his family.
2. The following summer, it is the turn of the two boys to visit Pierre in France. Pierre has been waiting all year for their arrival, planning and plotting. Write a short account of the boys' French holiday, entitled *Pierre's Revenge*.
3. Smugglers used caves and quiet harbours to bring stolen or illegal goods into a country. Use your imagination to tell how Smuggler's Cave got its name.

Adverbs (1)

- **Adverbs** tell us more about actions (verbs).
  Example: The referee spoke **crossly** to the player.
- **Adverbs** can be made from adjectives by adding **-ly**.
  Example: It was a **rough** game. — rough = **adjective**
  The team played **roughly** in the game. — roughly = **adverb**

A. Change these adjectives into adverbs and put them into the correct sentences.

sad	generous	swift	slow	nervous

1. The good woman ____________ put some money into the charity box.
2. The child cried ______________ when his goldfish died.
3. The bomb disposal expert sweated __________ as he prepared to snip the red wire.
4. The magnificent stallion galloped ______________ through the meadow.
5. The train pulled _______________ out of the station.

B. Turn these adjectives into adverbs by adding -ly.
Remember to double the final 'l'.

thoughtful	_______________	merciful	_______________
beautiful	_______________	tactful	_______________
careful	_______________	powerful	_______________

C. Match answers from B to these clues.

1. showing power _____________________
2. saying something so as not to hurt a person's feelings _____________
3. in a really lovely way _____________________
4. in a way that shows you think about people _________________
5. to show pity _______________________

D. Now change these words to adverbs and put each new word in a sentence to show its meaning.

happy	happily
sleepy	______________
grumpy	______________
angry	______________
lazy	______________
creaky	______________
stormy	______________
speedy	______________
dozy	______________
weepy	______________

Contractions

- A word that is shortened is called a **contraction**.
- **Apostrophes (')** are used to show that letters have been left out.

Example: **She's** the tallest girl in the village.
She is the tallest girl in the village.

A. Write these contractions in their full forms.

you're	I'll	didn't	couldn't	when's	I've
he's	you'll	wasn't	shouldn't	you've	she's
he'll	weren't	wouldn't	what's	we've	we're

B. Now write the shortened versions of these words.
Remember to put in the apostrophe.

she will	will not	had not	could not	they have	they are
we will	is not	here is	should have	it is	you would
they will	are not	there is	would have	cannot	might not

C. Rewrite this passage and shorten the underlined words.

I cannot recall the first time I met Sinead. There is a photo at home of us both when we were toddlers, so I think it is fair to say that we have always known each other. Maybe that is why we are so often mistaken as sisters. Mind you, we both have the same curly hair and big noses.

Anyway, until yesterday, Sinead was my best friend ever. We would spend every day after school hanging out together. We have had arguments, of course, does not everyone sometimes, but not arguments like yesterday! I will never talk to her again! I have never been so humiliated… and by my so-called best friend!

I should have told her exactly what I thought of her, but I could not speak because I was so angry! It is not so much what she did – I might have forgiven that – it is what she said about me! And in front of the whole class! Well I just turned on my heels and walked out the door without saying a word. In my place, you would have done the same! So that is it! I am never speaking to her again, and I am going to ring her up and tell her that right now!

Creative Writing (2)

- When writing a story, it is helpful to make a plan.
- Before you write, it is a good idea to map out your plan.
- You should divide your story into paragraphs.
- Each paragraph should deal with one idea.

This is the first paragraph of a story:

"I can say no to everything except temptation!" I used to say to my friends. Although I only meant it as a joke, I knew in my heart that there was some truth to it. I was easily tempted, and I usually couldn't say no.

This is the last paragraph of the story:

I had learnt my lesson the hard way as usual. Never again would I "borrow without asking". I felt very ashamed, and I only hoped that I would be as forgiving a person as my friend if the shoe was ever on the other foot.

What has happened between the first and last paragraphs?
This is the piece of the story that you have to write.
Here are some questions that might help you to plan the missing section of the story.

Paragraph 2

- What "temptation" does the main character give in to?
- What did "I" borrow without asking?
- Was the thing that "I" borrowed valuable? Old? New? Irreplaceable?
- What happened to the thing that "I" borrowed? Did "I" break it, lose it, damage it or sell it?
- Who did "I" borrow it from?
- Why didn't "I" ask first?

Paragraph 3

- How was "I" caught?
- How did "I" feel when caught?
- How did "I" react when caught?
- Did "I" admit to what I had done? Did "I" deny it?
- Did "I" try and blame somebody else? Did "I" say sorry?
- How did my friend feel about my "borrowing without asking"?
- How did my friend react? Was he/she angry, amused, upset or indifferent?

Now that you have considered all those points, plan your story in note form.

Example: (a) jealous of friend's new Game Boy or PlayStation;
(b) took it from his/her bag without asking first, etc.

When you are happy with your plan, write out the full story, starting with the opening paragraph and finishing with the closing paragraph.

Write Away!

Design an Information Poster or Leaflet

We often need to write clear instructions on a leaflet or poster that will quickly tell people what they need to know. Design a poster or leaflet with clear instructions. You may like to use a computer or you may prefer to use a pen and paper.

Think about the following before you start:

- What will the title of my poster/leaflet be?
- Should I use many words or just a few?
- How should I lay out my information?
- What kind of lettering (font) should I use?
- Would numbered points or 'bullets' be a good way of getting the facts across to the reader?
- Do I need pictures or diagrams as well as words?
- What do I want the reader to learn?
- What colour of paper should I use?
- Who is my poster/leaflet aimed at?

Here are some possible topics for your information leaflet or poster:

- Rules of the school yard.
- How to make a cup of tea.
- Starting up and shutting down a computer properly.
- Safety when crossing the road.
- How to care for a pet.
- What is a bully?
- What to do if you are being bullied.
- Rules of the classroom.
- How to write a letter.

Jailbirds

When Anne Jolly took a last-minute, special-offer holiday to Madagascar, she had had some difficulty finding a minder for her two children, Simon and Kate, at such short notice. Asking Great-aunt Florrie had been her very last resort. If she had been thinking straight, she would never have accepted Great-aunt Florrie's kind offer to take her young offenders into custody for as long as was necessary. In her defence, it had been quite a few years since Anne had met her aunt, and she was quite unaware just how barking mad the old dear had become.

"Mum never mentioned that the house was called Alcatraz!" said Kate forlornly, sitting down heavily on her wooden bed. "Or about the rolls of barbed wire all around the garden!" added Simon. "Or about the bars on the windows!" "Or that the bedrooms are called cells!" "Or that Great-aunt Florrie is about a hundred years old and a skinhead!" wailed Kate. "Did you see her boots? They're Nazi boots," Simon told her, his eyes wide. He was quite impressed. "And the huge bunch of keys chained to her big, black belt..." Kate was beginning to sob. "Mum didn't tell us any of those things."

Great-aunt Florrie was firmly convinced that she was a prison warden and that her happy little home was a high-security jail. All the 'cells' were barred – every door and window had at least seven locks. She rarely spoke – she barked!

"DINNER TIME!" she barked at the two children. "GET INTO AN ORDERLY LINE, YOU LOW-DOWN, NO-GOOD, SCUM-OF-THE-EARTH SLIMEBALLS! DO I MAKE MYSELF CLEAR?" "Yes, Great-aunt Florrie," mumbled the children. "YES, GREAT-AUNT FLORRIE, *SIR*!" roared Great-aunt Florrie, veins bulging in her neck. "Yes, Great-aunt Florrie, *sir*," repeated the inmates, holding up their dinner plates as Great-aunt Florrie slapped an inedible mess of green slime onto them. "NOW BACK TO YOUR CELLS, YOU THIEVING, MURDERING, STEALING, KIDNAPPING LOW-LIFES!" she shouted at the top of her lungs, one hand reaching for her truncheon.

Suddenly, she stood still listening. There were magpies on the roof! "PRISONERS ON THE ROOF!" she barked. "SOUND THE ALARM – IT'S A ROOFTOP PROTEST!" Kate and Simon watched in amazement as their Great-aunt charged down the stairs, flung back the twelve bolts on the hall door and ran out into the garden. There she grabbed a ladder and threw it up against the front of the house, all the while yelling, "THERE WILL BE NO MERCY SHOWN TO PROTESTERS IN THIS JAIL! COME DOWN OFF THE ROOF AT ONCE YOU LOW-LIFE SCOUNDRELS OF THE HIGHEST ORDER!"

"Do you think madness runs in our family?" asked Kate as she followed Simon down the stairs. "It would definitely be madness to stay here a minute longer," replied Simon, making a dash for freedom.

Extract from 'Fowl Deeds' by Jim Halligan and John Newman.

Question Time

A

1. What was the name of the children's mother?
2. Where did she fly to on her holidays?
3. Who did she leave Simon and Kate with?
4. Why did she not know that her aunt Florrie was "barking mad"?
5. What was Great-aunt Florrie's house called?
6. What were the bedrooms called?
7. What kind of boots did Great-aunt Florrie wear?
8. What made the noise on the roof?
9. What did Great-aunt Florrie think was happening on the roof?
10. How many bolts were on the hall door?

B

1. What words did Great-aunt Florrie use that should have warned Anne Jolly that she might not make a very good childminder?
2. List the words that Great-aunt Florrie used to describe the two children.
3. What item of Great-aunt Florrie's clothing impressed Simon?
4. Why, do you think, is practically all of Great-aunt Florrie's speech printed in capital letters? Do you think this is effective? Give a reason for your answer.
5. What food do you think the "inedible green slime" that Florrie serves the children is supposed to be?
6. Put these words in sentences to show their meaning.

   offenders custody inmates inedible

7. List the security measures that Great-aunt Florrie had installed in the house.
8. In your opinion, is Anne Jolly a responsible parent? Give reasons for your answer.
9. In your opinion, was Great-aunt Florrie's house anything like a real prison? Explain your answer.
10. What was "Alcatraz" and where was it located?

Think and Talk

1. What happens next?
   Write about how you think the children escaped and what you think became of them.
2. Anne Jolly rings Great-aunt Florrie from Madagascar to check on the children.
   Write out their telephone conversation.

Adjectives and Adverbs (2)

Adjectives and **adverbs** give more **detail** to a sentence.

Example: The boy licked the ice cream.
(+ *adjectives*)
The **young** boy licked the **raspberry-flavoured** ice cream.
(+ *adverb*)
The young boy **lovingly** licked the raspberry-flavoured ice cream.

A. Add at least one adjective to each of these nouns to give them more detail.

a ________ ship	the ________ cliff	a ____________ wind
the _________ chair	a _________ car	the ________ tree
a __________ flower	a __________ shoe	the __________ hamburger
the _________ lion	___________ hair	___________ cloud

B. Now add an adverb to each of these verbs to give them more detail.

ran _________	sailed _________	galloped _________
looked _________	spoke _________	dived _________
followed _________	danced _________	walked _________

C. Now give these sentences more detail by adding adjectives and adverbs to each one.

1. The tents flapped in the wind.
2. Alex tiptoed up the stairs.
3. The soldier dived for cover under the truck.
4. We saw the mountain ahead of us as we walked down the road.
5. The ship left the harbour.
6. Janet peered over the edge of the wall.
7. The jet landed on the runway.
8. The horse galloped across the meadow.
9. The sun's rays lit up the valley.
10. Sam watched the lifeboat approach.
11. The tortoise walked across the lawn.
12. With a screech, the falcon dived through the air.
13. The clouds gathered on the horizon.
14. A Viking longship sailed up the river towards the town.
15. The shark followed the movement of the diver.
16. Locusts could be seen in every part of the field.
17. The car went over the hill.
18. The snake slithered across the sand.

D. Rewrite this passage and insert suitable adjectives and adverbs in the spaces.

The _________ ship sailed _________ into the port. A _________ sun slipped _________ beneath the waves, bringing the _________ day to an end. The _________ sailors gazed _________ towards the _________ town. On the shore, a _________ but eager crowd waited _________ for the _________ ship to dock.

Homophones (1)

Homophones are words that have the same sound but different meanings or spellings.

Example: They're, Their, There
They're = they are
Their = belongs to them
There = a place; used with 'there is', 'there are', etc.

Example: They're all very annoyed that their team was beaten when they played the match over there.

A. Put in the correct word (they're/their/there) in these phrases.

__________ house

__________ very lazy

__________ are five brothers

__________ legs

__________ great players

__________ is only one correct answer

B. Insert the correct word (they're/their/there) in these sentences.

1. "You should've been __________,"
my starry-eyed sister said when she returned from the concert.
2. Scott and his friends reached Amundsen's marker at the South Pole and __________ spirits fell.
3. __________ hotel was a bit of a dump.
4. "__________ all nice guys really!" Jack told his mother, as she eyed the group of his friends outside the door.
5. __________ are hundreds of man-made satellites in orbit around Earth.
6. Skunks use __________ foul smell to disperse predators.
7. __________ all crazy about basketball in my class.
8. __________ coats are over __________ in the corner.
9. __________ not very happy about the extra work in __________ books.
10. __________ sure that __________ friends will be __________ to meet them.
11. Peter put all __________ shoes in that big, dirty bin over __________.
12. __________ all pretty annoyed with Peter and __________ going to tell him so.

C. Revision of Prefixes

In each line, there are four words.

Write a prefix for each line that will work in front of each word in that line.

1. ______work ______throw ______done ______load
2. ______man ______sonic ______intendent ______vise
3. ______phone ______vision ______gram ______scope
4. ______chute ______site ______glider ______trooper

Unit 16

The Volunteer

It was his own fault. We all knew that.
Deep down, Dad knew that too. He had an awful habit of volunteering for things and then regretting it later. Mam didn't say much. That was a bad sign. She went around with her "he's old and ugly enough to know better" expression on her face. She wasn't going to let him forget this one in a hurry.

He seemed so excited when he came home from work and told us what he was going to do.
"All the lads are going to do it!" he declared.
"It'll be great!" "Huh!" was all Mam said.

As the big day drew nearer, however, it seemed that not quite all of the lads at work *were* going to do it. There were whispers of them coming down with a nasty cough... or a bit of a cold... or a sore shoulder. In fact, all the good excuses were being used up rapidly.

By the time Dad realised that everybody else had pulled out, all the really good excuses had been claimed. There was no way he could give up now. He still put a brave face on it though.
"Your old man will be a hero!" he told Sam and me enthusiastically. "Huh!" was all Mam said.

He managed to keep this up until the night before the jump. Then Mam asked him to get something down from the attic. As he climbed the stepladder, he looked down and then went deathly pale. Our father had suddenly become scared of heights! Sam and I looked at each other.
If the Old Man couldn't cope with six steps on a ladder, how was he going to manage to jump from a ninety-metre crane?

The following day, we arrived at the fairground. We saw the huge sign... **Charity Monster Bungee Jump** ... and we saw the enormous, yellow crane with the elastic rope swinging from its gantry. That's when I felt really, really sorry for Dad.
He stood there, staring up at the crane. He looked deeply, profoundly, extremely, incredibly unhappy and more than a little terrified. He took a step towards the crane...

Question Time

A

1. What bad habit did the children's father have?
2. What had he volunteered for?
3. How did the children's mother react when she heard the news?
4. Did anybody else volunteer?
5. Did these people keep their promises?
6. What excuses did they give for pulling out?
7. What happened to the children's father the night before the jump?
8. How did he seem when he got to the fairground?
9. What was written on the sign?
10. How high was the crane?

B

1. What sort of trouble had Dad made for himself?
2. Why, do you think, was it a bad sign when Mam didn't say much?
3. How did the children's father feel about the idea at first?
4. How do you think his feelings changed when he saw the crane?
5. Do you think he had a good night's sleep before the jump? Why?
6. How do you think he felt about the other people at work?
7. Why did the person telling the story feel so sorry for Dad?
8. Why did the father feel that he couldn't back out like the others had?
9. Do you think he really wanted to back out? How do you know?
10. Do you think he actually jumped?
11. Write sentences to show the meaning of each of these words.

volunteering   regretting   gantry   profoundly

Think and Talk

1. What do you think you should do if you volunteer for something and then want to change your mind?
2. This story is about a charity bungee jump. Can you think of any other exciting or strange ways of making money for charity? Write about them.
3. What do you think it would be like to do a real bungee jump? Write about it in 'real time' – *I feel the rope tight around my ankles. I move to the edge of the drop and look down. Below me, I see…*
4. The story needs to be finished. We don't know if the children's father actually goes through with the jump or, if he does, how he succeeds. Write a short ending for the story.

Spelling Rules (1)

Rule 1: If a word ends in a single **vowel** and a single **consonant** (e.g. **big**, **rub**), double the final consonant when adding an ending to it.
Example: bi**gg**er, ru**bb**ing

A. Write out these sentences and fill in the missing words using words from the wordbox.
Don't forget to make the necessary changes to the words first.

hot	rub	step	slip

1. We made leaf _____________ in art class.
2. Use the _______________ stones to cross the stream.
3. I ____________ on the ice and broke my ankle.
4. Today may be hot, but yesterday was even __________, and the weather forecaster says that tomorrow will be the __________ day yet.

Rule 2: If a word ends in a **consonant + y** (e.g. **try**, **fly**), change the 'y' to 'i' for all endings (except **ing**).
Example: **fly flies** (**flying**)

B. Write out these sentences and fill in the missing words using words from the wordbox.
Don't forget to make the necessary changes to the words first.

marry	sky	cry	carry

1. In winter, the _________ are often overcast.
2. The baby _______________ all last night.
3. For its size, an ant __________________ very heavy loads.
4. The princess is _______________ a frog!

Rule 3: When a word begins with '**all**', only one 'l' is used.
Example: **al**ways, **al**though

C. Write out these sentences and fill the gaps with words that begin with al.

1. _____________ wash your teeth at night.
2. Mam asked Emma to clean her room but she had ________ done it.
3. ____________ Peter trained and trained, he still lost the race.

Rule 4: When words end with '**full**', only use one 'l'.
Example: use**ful**, help**ful**

D. Write out these sentences and fill the gaps with words that end in ful.

1. The pupil was very ____________ for the help that the teacher gave him.
2. The ballerina was very ____________ in all her movements.
3. Tulips are a very ______________ flower.
4. The ______________ boy bought a birthday card for his mum.

Homophones (2)

Remember: **Homophones** are words that have the same sound but different meanings or spellings.

Examples: She is **not** right!
Tie that **knot** tightly.

A. Select the correct words from these homophones to complete each sentence.

mussels / muscles

1. Paul does push-ups to build up his ________________.
2. Molly Malone sold cockles and ________________.

story / storey

1. *The Lord of the Rings* is a great ________________.
2. A bungalow is a single-____________ building.

haul / hall

1. The pupils have their gym class in the school __________.
2. The huskies had to ______________ the sledge over the ice.

reign / rain / rein

1. The jockey held each __________ tightly.
2. The Queen's ____________ lasted forty years.
3. My thin jacket was no protection against the heavy ____________.

sow / sew

1. The farmer will __________ his crops in spring.
2. "I'll have to __________ up the holes in those nets," said the fisherman.

dew / due

1. That library book was __________ back on February 12th.
2. The grass glittered with __________ in the early morning.

B. Write matching homophones for these words.

fair	______________	beach	______________
made	______________	cue	______________
won	______________	pair	______________
know	______________	tale	______________

C. Here are some more homophones. Put each word in a separate sentence to show its meaning.

bridal / bridle   yoke / yolk   chord / cord   bow / bough   sight / site   see / sea

Write Away!

Grabbing the Headlines

Newspapers often use large, bold headlines to get your attention for a story. Look at this:

> **SCHOOLGIRL SETS WORLD RECORD**
>
> A County Sligo girl set a new world record in her school yard yesterday. Ellen Doyle (11) opened 5,428 yogurt cartons in exactly five minutes, shattering the previous world record by a whopping 943.
>
> "It's all in the wrist action," she explained to our reporter moments after her magnificent achievement. Her classmates gave her a rousing cheer as she completed her mammoth task. Ellen calmly says that she won't let this triumph go to her head.

Write your own stories for these headlines. Remember to use paragraphs when writing a story.

Parachutist ruins football final

Goldfish saves drowning kitten

Pet rabbit attacks burglars

Lotto winner blows winnings on monster party

Pensioner (96) robs bank with umbrella

Leitrim win All-Ireland Hurling Final

Write Away!

Creative Writing (3)

Some stories start in the middle. Some even start at the end, and we only find out the beginning as we read through the story. This can be a very good way of bringing the reader right into the middle of the action from the very first sentence.

A. This story starts in the middle. Write the rest of the story.

Here are some things I learned today:
Never steal a pig.
Never feel sorry for one.
Never sneak the runt of the litter out of your father's pigsty and hide it in the laundry basket of your bedroom.
Never let it escape from your room to go absolutely crazy in the kitchen...

Think about the questions below before you start.

1. Who has stolen the pig and why?
2. How did he/she sneak the pig into the house?
3. How did the pig escape?
4. What damage is the pig doing in the kitchen?
5. Will he/she be caught?
6. What happens next?

B. This story starts at the end.
Read the paragraph and the questions and then write the beginning of the story.

Anne looked at herself in the long mirror. She was covered from top to toe in mud. Her hair was sodden and seemed glued to her head. Her clothes were torn and covered with bits of straw and twigs. She grinned – who would have thought that the day would have ended up like this?

Get Started

1. Why is Anne in such a mess?
2. How did her clothes get covered in straw and twigs?
3. Did she expect to be in such a state at the end of the day?
4. Is she upset about it?
5. How did the day start?

Holiday Brochure

New Sizzling Hot Summer Holiday Destination from

Sunny Days Tours

Porto Blanco

on the South Coast of Spain

Villa Del Mar Hotel (****)

Only a 2-hour bus transfer from Malaga Airport, the newly built Villa Del Mar offers the last word in four-star holiday comfort. This beautiful 300-bedroom complex boasts no less than three swimming pools, a golf course, a magnificent leisure centre and two award-winning restaurants. All rooms have en suite bathrooms, and the balcony rooms have breathtaking views of the gorgeous Mediterranean Sea.

So much to see and do!
Golden, unspoilt beaches are only minutes away. Lifeguards patrol all five kilometres of the perfect sandy beach. Why not take a day cruise in one of the many pleasure boats or why not try waterskiing?

Nearby is the lovely old fishing and market town of Santa Cristobel with its ancient castle and stunning cathedral. Learn more about the fascinating history of the area with special guided tours of all the famous sites and landmarks.

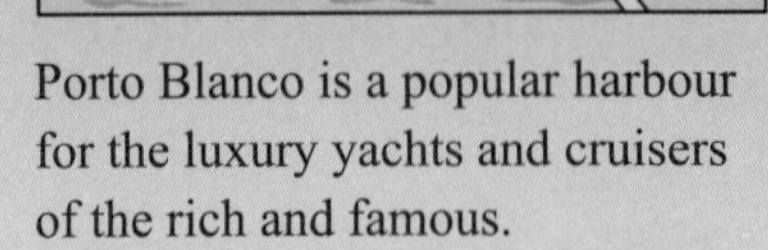

Porto Blanco is a popular harbour for the luxury yachts and cruisers of the rich and famous.

Porto Blanco's lively shopping streets are a shopper's paradise, with fashion, jewellery, cosmetics and electronic goods at bargain prices from the world's leading designers and manufacturers. Why not visit the old market where you can pick up bargains galore from local potters and leather-workers?

And the kids can go for half price!
There are plenty of special family offers for holidays taken in May, June and September.

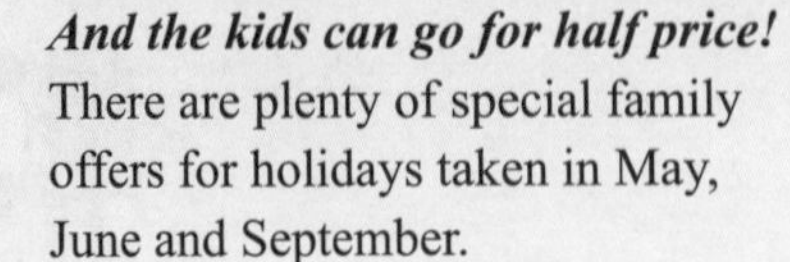

Our Villa Del Mar Kids' Club will keep the children entertained all day with a wide variety of games and activities.

Direct flights from Dublin and Cork.

Rates per person	*7 nights*	*14 nights*
May	€780	€1,150
June	€880	€1,300
July	€1,080	€1,550
August	€1,150	€1,720
September	€850	€1,200

Breakfast and dinner included.

Question Time

A

1. What is this page advertising?
2. What is the name of the hotel?
3. In what country is the hotel?
4. How many bedrooms does it have?
5. What does the hotel have to offer its guests?
6. What can you see from the balconies of the hotel?
7. What sort of shops can be found in Porto Blanco?
8. What can be bought in the old market?
9. What is so interesting about Santa Cristobel?
10. What does the hotel have to keep children amused?
11. What month is the cheapest time to go on holiday?
12. What month is the dearest time to go on holiday?
13. What length is the beach at Porto Blanco?
14. What water sport can holidaymakers try?

B

1. How would you get to the hotel from the airport if you chose this holiday?
2. What has been done to make the beach safer for holidaymakers?
3. What can be done near the beach?
4. Why is Porto Blanco a shopper's paradise?
5. How do you know that Porto Blanco is a very beautiful place?
6. Why, do you think, are July and August the most expensive months to book a holiday?
7. What has Sunny Days Tours done to attract customers during the other months?
8. Where would you visit if you were interested in history? Why?
9. Do you think the hotel would be an attractive place to stay? Say why.
10. How much would a 14-night holiday for two adults and two children cost in July?
11. Which location would appeal to people seeking a quiet holiday? Why?
12. Why, do you think, do the rich and famous like to visit Porto Blanco?

Think and Talk

1. The tourist industry creates many jobs. How many different kinds of job do the local people of Porto Blanco have because of visiting tourists?
2. What would your ideal holiday destination be like?
3. Holiday brochures are always attractive and filled with beautiful pictures. Do you think they tell you the full story about a place you might like to visit? Say why.
4. Design your own page to advertise your perfect holiday.

Overused Words (3)

Some words, such as **said**, are overused. Here are some alternative words for **said**.

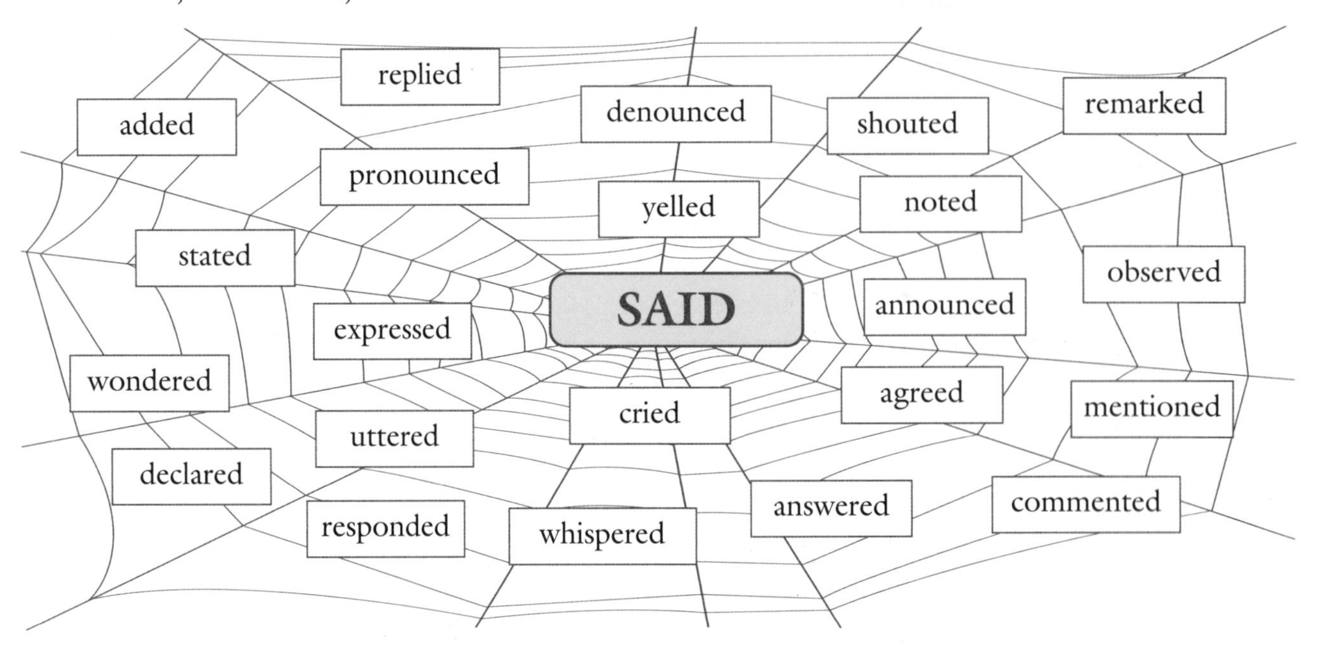

A. Write out these sentences and replace the word said with a more suitable word from the web.

1. "You are quite right, blackberries are full of vitamin C," said the nutritionist.
2. "The 7:40 train for Waterford will depart at 8:15. We apologise for the delay," said a voice from the loudspeaker in the station.
3. "It is going to pour rain in about two minutes!" said Siobhán as she made a dash for the car.
4. "If red is your favourite colour, why do you always wear blue clothes?" said her mother.
5. "Your handwriting leaves a lot to be desired," said the teacher.

B. Now choose five words from the web that you have not used in (a) and write sentences using them instead of said.

C. Went is also overused. There are 11 alternatives to went in this wordsearch.
Find them and write each one in a separate sentence.

C	R	E	T	R	E	A	T	E	D
W	A	L	K	E	D	J	H	O	L
I	O	Q	L	M	E	R	P	D	P
T	J	O	U	R	N	E	Y	E	D
H	P	R	M	O	V	E	D	P	F
D	A	B	M	I	X	L	Z	A	L
R	E	T	I	R	E	D	L	R	E
E	Q	U	O	Y	L	E	F	T	D
W	W	E	F	E	X	I	T	E	D
J	A	D	V	A	N	C	E	D	C

Synonyms

A word that means the same, or almost the same, as another word is called a **synonym**.
Example: terrible – dreadful

A. Write the words from the wordbox beside the correct synonyms below.

sick	completed	every	commotion	harmless	outrage
large	slim	apparent	home	clever	nought
correct	diaper	tongue	lie	powerless	tiny

big	large	right	________
nappy	________	evident	________
language	________	zero	________
intelligent	________	ill	________
hullabaloo	________	anger	________
all	________	finished	________
habitat	________	fib	________
thin	________	helpless	________
minute	________	inoffensive	________

B. Write out these sentences and replace the underlined words with suitable synonyms.

1. The fairytale, *Cinderella*, has been made into a movie 58 times.
2. In every kilogram of peanut butter, there are approximately 1,500 peanuts.
3. When meteorites hit Earth, they make huge hollows in the ground.
4. Their new baby is called Niall.
5. The match will commence at three o'clock sharp.
6. The force of the hurricane destroyed the city of New Orleans.
7. The thief got away with a sack of silverware.
8. The repulsive creature scampered across the kitchen floor.
9. They say that Alexander the Great was buried in a vat of honey.
10. A person sheds a complete layer of skin every month.

Antonyms

A word that means the **opposite**, or almost the opposite, of another word is called an **antonym**.
Example: dark – bright

Write the words from the wordbox beside the correct antonyms below.

lower	fear	despair	virtuous	guilty	mild
courage	strength	sensational	married	melancholy	climb

cowardice	________	weakness	________
unremarkable	________	sinful	________
single	________	bravery	________
higher	________	hope	________
innocent	________	cheerful	________
ferocious	________	descent	________

Poetry Pages

The Sounds in the Evening

The sounds in the evening
Go all through the house,
The click of the clock
And the pick of the mouse,
The footsteps of people
Upon the top floor,
The skirts of my mother
That brush by the door,
The crick in the boards,
And the creak of the chairs,
The fluttering murmurs
Outside on the stairs,
The ring of the bell,
The arrival of guests,
The laugh of my father
At one of his jests,

The clashing of dishes
As dinner goes in,
The babble of voices
That distance makes thin,
The mewing of cats
That seem just by my ear,
The hooting of owls
That can never seem near,
The queer little noises
That no one explains……
Till the moon through the slats
Of my window-blind rains,
And the world of my eyes
And my ears melt like steam
As I find in my pillow
The world of my dream.

Eleanor Farjeon

Question Time

A

1. List all the words in the poem that refer to sounds.
2. What is happening in the house that evening?
3. There are two worlds mentioned in the poem. What are they?
4. Are the people in the poem rich or poor? Give reasons for your answer.
5. Some sounds are outside the house. What sounds are they?
6. Where is the speaker in the poem?
7. Why is it difficult to hear the "babble of voices"?

Your Turn… Write a poem entitled *The Sounds in the Morning*.

Bedroom Blues

Welcome to my bedroom
Do come in!
What? You think it's a tip?
With rubbish enough
To fill a skip?

What's that heap
in the corner?
Beneath all those clothes?
It's a pile of dirty socks
Put a peg on your nose!
If you're hungry, help yourself
To the food on the floor.
I save up cans and bottles and tins
Indeed, much of my decor
Has been recycled from bins!
Don't step on the toadstools
That I'm growing over there
You never said that was
Against the rules!
You're not being fair!

You've seen enough?
Shall I show you some more?
That's a goat's skull
I have nailed to the door.
Oh yes and that's my bed
You've found it at last!
I pretend it's a boat
The sheet is a mast.

What, you're leaving?
So soon?
Are you sure you won't stay?
You'll come back
When I've cleaned it?
NO WAY!

John Newman

Question Time

A

1. What is the visitor's first impression of the narrator's bedroom?
2. Why does the narrator suggest that the visitor should put a peg on his/her nose?
3. What sort of stuff does the narrator save?
4. Where does most of the decor come from?
5. Why, do you think, are toadstools growing in the room?
6. What does the narrator use his sheet for?
7. What does the visitor tell the narrator to do before he/she comes back?

B

1. Do you think the narrator of the story is a boy or a girl? Give reasons for your answer.
2. We do not see the visitor's speech, so what device does the poet use to convey his/her impression?
3. Who do you think the visitor is? Give a reason for your answer.
4. What kind of person is the narrator of the poem? Write a short description of him/her.
5. Does the narrator like or dislike his/her room the way it is? Give a reason for your answer.

Think and Talk

1. Write a short description of your own bedroom.
2. Now write a poem about your bedroom and illustrate the poem with a picture.

Spelling Rules (2) – Plurals

Most plurals are formed quite simply by adding s (dog/dogs).
However, some plurals are more difficult.

Rule 1: Words that end in a **consonant** + **y** – drop the **y** and add **ies**.
Example: baby/babies

A. Write the plural forms of these words.

lorry	____________	daddy	____________	fly	____________
puppy	____________	lady	____________	story	____________
granny	____________	sky	____________	nappy	____________

Rule 2: Most words that end in **ch**, **sh** or **x** – add **es**.
Example: church/churches

B. Write the plural forms of these words.

bush	____________	match	____________	catch	____________
crash	____________	box	____________	beach	____________
brush	____________	fox	____________	church	____________

Rule 3: Most words that end in **z**, **s** or **o** – add **es**.
Example: volcano/volcanoes

C. Write the plural forms of these words.

hero	____________	bus	____________	potato	____________
boss	____________	tomato	____________	loss	____________

**D. Rewrite this passage and put all the underlined words in plural form.
Make any other changes that are necessary.**

Lauren had a vegetable patch. For dinner, she had a home-grown <u>tomato</u>, a <u>potato</u> and lettuce. For dessert, she ate a <u>peach</u>, a <u>strawberry</u>, a <u>raspberry</u> and a <u>gooseberry</u> — all grown in her own garden. After lunch, she intended to dig out a scraggly <u>bush</u> that was taking up a lot of space and replace it with a <u>box</u> of flowers to brighten the place up.

Tenses

Verbs tell us what is happening in a sentence. The **tense** of a verb tells us **when** it happens, whether it be in the **past**, the **present** or the **future**.

Examples: She **saw** horses. = **past tense**
She **sees** horses. = **present tense**
She **will see** horses. = **future tense**

A. This passage is written in the past tense.

Ray turned the key. The engine fired into life. It was beautifully tuned. Ray took his left foot off the clutch and pushed the accelerator to the floor with his right. The van bounced forward and roared down the lane. "Yippee!" yelled Lucy. Ray clutched the steering wheel.

"Watch the gate, Ray!" shouted Lucy, as the van, moving at a steady fifteen kilometres per hour, neared the gate of the estate. "It's very narrow, isn't it?" said Ray nervously, and he closed his eyes tightly.

Most of the van got through the gateway, but the back bumper, unfortunately, was ripped off when it scraped a pillar. "Well done, Ray! You're a born driver!" screamed Lucy. "I am, aren't I?" agreed Ray. He was getting quite excited. "How do I make this thing go faster?"

Rewrite the above passage in the present tense. Start like this: Ray turns the key…

B. Rewrite the passage below in the future tense.

I rode carefully along the mountain trail. The horse knew the way, having to use this trail nearly every day. In the west, the sun was shining low in the sky. I felt pretty tired after such a long day in the saddle, but I thought it was worth it to see such magnificent wild landscapes. In the valley below, the welcoming lights of the cabin twinkled as the sun's last rays faded away.

C. Fill in the blank squares.

PAST TENSE	PRESENT TENSE	FUTURE TENSE
wrote		
	eats	
		will know
	finds	
		will see
drove		

Write Away!

Newspaper Headlines

Newspapers attract readers by using snappy headlines. Are you good at writing headlines?

A. Read these two articles and write suitable headlines for them.

Gardaí in Loretown were today investigating an incident of breaking and entering that occurred in the early hours of Tuesday morning. The home of a local bear family was broken into while the couple, known locally as Daddy and Mammy Bear, were out walking in the woods with their young son, Baby Bear.

The female intruder broke a valuable chair belonging to Baby Bear and stole a small bowl of porridge that also belonged to Baby Bear. The thief was interrupted by the return of the Bear family, and she made her getaway by leaping from an open window and making off on foot.

Gardaí say that the intruder was female with curly, golden blonde hair, that she was about 1·45 metres in height and that she wore white socks.

Kitty Kando, the zany hairdresser who won the nation's hearts with her tantrums and tears on this year's phenomenally successful reality show, BIG SIS, has shocked her fans by announcing her engagement to fellow celebrity Roc the Block.

Bad boy Roc is famous in his own right as the former lead singer of the Wallipops, who stunned their legion of fans early last year when they split up after a ferocious row that led to the arrest of both Roc and his lead guitarist Ed the Head in Silly's Nightclub.

Kitty and Roc met three days ago and, after a whirlwind romance, have announced their intention to be married "at the earliest possible time". *Closet* magazine has learnt that the wedding will most probably take place next Monday at a secret location in Co. Cavan.

B. Now write snappy headlines for articles on these subjects.

1. A whale that gets stranded on a beach.
2. Ireland's first sumo wrestler winning the World Championships.
3. A new cure that has been found for morning grumpiness.
4. Mayor's wig blows off during speech.
5. A football match that ends up in a big brawl.
6. The discovery of an ancient sword that probably belonged to Brian Boru.

Write Away!

The Sea

**The sea, in all its moods, appears in countless stories, ads, poems and films.
Use the wordbox to help you to think about the sea. Think of other words to describe the sea.**

crashing	rolling	splashing	thrashing	glinting	swirling	roaring	lapping
gurgling	emerald	green	turquoise	sapphire	blue	slate	grey
surf	waves	rollers	currents	froth	foam	surging	pulling
rippling							

A. Choose the words you would use to describe…

- a stormy sea; ____________________
- the sea on a calm, moonlit night; ____________________
- waves as they roll up on to a beach; ____________________
- the sea on a dark, gloomy, rainy day; ____________________
- waves breaking over rocks; ____________________
- the sea at sunset on a summer's evening; ____________________

B. Here is a story for you to finish…

The sun was rising, golden and red, over the green, blue and silver sea. We all sat huddled together for warmth, shivering under our towels and blankets. I looked out over the silky, glinting water and thought about what had happened. So much had happened in the last 24 hours…

Revision 1

See if you can answer these questions.
If you get stuck, you can look back through the book to find the answers.
They're all in there … somewhere.
Good luck!

1. What is the world's largest passenger plane?
2. How many insects are alive on Earth at any one time?
3. Where is the Amazon River?
4. Who invented the light bulb?
5. What are the world's smallest mammals?
6. Where were the first Olympic Games held long ago?
7. How long is an adult fox from point of nose to tip of tail?
8. What do you call an animal that has a pouch for its young?
9. Which vitamin is found in oranges and lemons?
10. Who was the first person to reach the summit of Mount Everest?
11. What do pandas eat?
12. Who was the first person to reach the South Pole?
13. What do we call places where traffic accidents happen frequently?
14. How long is the rabbit-proof fence in Australia?
15. When was it completed?
16. What happened to Napoleon's French Army in 1812?
17. When did Captain Cook arrive in Australia?
18. Where do you look if you want to find the addresses of embassies?
19. Who were the first two people to set foot on the Moon?
20. In what year were rabbits introduced to Australia?
21. What does the word 'feral' mean?
22. What happened to the Roman town of Pompeii?

Revision 2

A. Rewrite this passage by adding full stops, commas, question marks and exclamation marks.
Use the capital letters to help you to figure things out.

I knew I was in trouble when the whole building began to collapse around me Bang A piece of the ceiling landed right beside me What was I to do Would I ever get out of there alive Crash Another bit of falling plaster just missed me There was only one thing to do Run I ducked dived dodged and rolled my way past crumbling walls and splintering doors until I found myself safe outside Gosh that was a close one

B. Rewrite this passage by adding quotation marks (“ ”) to show the spoken words, or dialogue, in the conversation.

Who were the first people to fly across the Atlantic? asked Terry.

Two people called John Alcock and Arthur Brown made the first successful flight in 1919, answered Sally.

In a jet? asked Terry.

No. It was a rickety old thing with propellers, said Sally. They took off from Newfoundland in America and crash-landed near Clifden in County Galway.

They must have been very brave men, stated Terry.

That or they were just nuts, sighed Sally.

The New York Times.

ALCOCK AND BROWN FLY ACROSS ATLANTIC; MAKE 1,980 MILES IN 16 HOURS, 12 MINUTES; SOMETIMES UPSIDE DOWN IN DENSE, ICY FOG

GERMANS OBJECTED STRONGLY TO TERMS

Airmen Moving at an 120-Mile Speed Were Unable to See Sun, Moon, or Stars for Hours Owing to Fog.

C. Correct the spellings in this next paragraph.

I was runing down the rode wen I triped and fell. I cut my nee badlee. I whent home hopeing to find a plaster four my knee. My Mam saw me comeing, and she rann out to meat me. We went insid the howse and got sum woter to cleen the cut. Then we put a plasster on it, and I felt a lot beter.

Revision 3

Rewrite this conversation fully.
You have to add one half of it yourself.

Hi. Is that Kate? It's me, Jack.

I'm fine. Look, I was wondering if you could do me a bit of a favour.

Thanks. It's nothing major.
Do you have your copy of *A Way with Words 5* at home?

No – I didn't leave mine in school… The dog ate it.

It's true! I'm not kidding! He really ate it… Years of using that stupid old excuse for not getting my homework done and it actually happens to me! Crazy, huh?

Well, I walked into the sitting room to get my bag and to start my homework, and there was that dratted hound with his nose in my bag… I think he could smell my lunch-box. Anyway, the book was in shreds.

I'm glad you think it's funny! Can I borrow the book? I have to do the exercise on the very last page. I'll only need it for a few minutes.

Thanks! You're a pal!

In Continuing & Gratefu
THE MENIN GATE
VOLUME II

by Paul Foster, FRSA

Published by Minutecircle Services Limited

ISBN 978-1-908345-01-1

from

Dalbiac to Dyer

Second Lieutenant Charles James Shelley Dalbiac

'W' Company, 1st Battalion Northumberland Fusiliers

Died on Wednesday 16th June 1915, aged 19

Commemorated on Panel 12.

Charles was born in 1896 son of Colonel Philip Hugh Dalbiac, CB, and Lilian Dalbiac, of The Elms, Seal, Sevenoaks, Kent. His father had been the Member of Parliament for Camberwell. He was educated at Aldenham School from 1907 to 1912 as a member of Beavers House from where he passed into RMC Sandhurst as a Prize Cadet. Charles was gazetted on Saturday 14th March 1914.

Charles went out to France in March 1915 and joined the Battalion at St Eloi. He was able to visit the medieval town of Ypres, and one of his colleagues who had joined the Battalion at that time wrote: *"Ypres was no longer the undamaged town which the 1st Battalion had entered five months before. None the less, though the cathedral and cloth hall had been shattered by the enemy's shell; and though, as was to be seen a few weeks later, it was in the power of the Germans to reduce the whole town to ruins, it had not in general suffered much as yet, and the inhabitants were still plying a brisk trade with the troops who thronged the town. I had arrived at Ypres during the afternoon, and found the Battalion due to return to reserve from the trenches the same night. While eagerly awaiting their arrival, I passed the time strolling round the town. In the Infantry Barracks I found the upper balconies, which overlooked the square, crowded with troops watching a party of the Liverpool Scottish sounding retreat on penny whistles and tin cans. The air was filled with the chaff and laughter of the men, and it would have been difficult to believe that a war was in progress had it not been for the continuous desultory artillery fire that could be heard in the distance. I could not but shudder at the thought of the havoc that would be wrought by the arrival of a single heavy shell in the midst of this cheery, light-hearted crowd. As darkness fell there came a striking change. Artillery fire died down and was replaced by a ceaseless rattle of musketry fire from the not very distant trenches; while south, east and north the sky was lit by Verey lights rising incessantly from the opposing lines. To one who, so to speak, had not been behind the scenes to witness the simple methods by which these illuminations were produced, the scene was one of beauty and mystery. But, as I watched this narrow semi-circle of rising lights, there came to me a full sense of the peril in which Ypres already stood. Shortly after midnight the Battalion marched into Ypres, and I made my way to the Headquarter billet to greet the friends from whom I had been so long separated. Such meetings are not soon forgotten; but the incident that remains most vividly in my memory is that of being hailed by a strange individual, smothered in mud from head to foot, and whose face was adorned by a week's beard. It was not till I had looked again that I recognised in this fantastic figure an old friend who, in the happier days of peace, had been noted for being one of the smartest and most immaculate mess waiters that the 1st Battalion had ever known But my greatest surprise was still to come. Floundering through mud and slush to take over the line a few nights later, in the belief that I was to enter 'trenches', I found myself in a state of complete bewilderment during the remaining hours of pitch dark night. Dawn revealed to me that the so-called 'trenches' were, in fact, breast-works, which in places had been built up as high as seven feet above the ground and provided with fire steps."*

Charles continued to serve in the sector until Wednesday 26th May when the Battalion was sent to Ouderdom. Working parties for the front line continued to be sent each day, and a further tour of duty was undertaken until at 4.45pm on Tuesday 15th June the Battalion paraded at their bivouac before marching from 5.00pm to the assembly trenches eight miles away. Each of the men were issued with two extra bandoliers of SAA; one day's rations (in addition to iron rations); two empty sand-bags and a water-proof sheet. An extra four hundred Mills bombs and additional shovels were brought up by 'Z' Company. They marched through Vlamertinghe and out via *'Hell Fire Corner'* to their assembly line. At 2.50am the British artillery commenced its barrage including heavy howitzers dropping ahead of the men at Bellewaarde Farm. The assembly trenches were only three and a half feet deep and as a result they suffered several casualties from the British shrapnel as they had insufficient cover. The artillery stopped for the third time at 4.00am and the Germans were convinced the attack was about to take place, so manned their parapet. Ten minutes later a short, sharp barrage opened up and the whistles blew and Charles led his men of 'W' Company forward. Charles did not get very far, despite the distance being so short. However, his men got to the German front and carried it. Charles laid dead in *'No Man's Land'*.

It was written of him: *"... perhaps only those who were with him in the trenches during long night of hard work fully appreciate the value of young Dalbiac on duty; but off duty, back in billets, all who came in contact with him will always hold him in affectionate and grateful remembrance, for in his company it was impossible to be dull or in the dumps."*

In Christ Church, Radlett, Hertfordshire, a brass plaque was placed in his memory with the inscription: *"To the beloved memory of Charles James Shelley Dalbiac 2nd Lieutenant 1st Battalion Northumberland Fusiliers who fell at the head of the leading platoon grenadiers of his regiment in the attack on the enemy's trenches at Hooge On The 16th June 1915. Aged nineteen.*

Right in the van. On the red ramparts slippery swell. With heart that beat a charge to fell forward as befits a man; but the high soul burns on to light men's feet where death for noble ends makes dying sweet."

Charles was recorded in Debretts Obituary — War Roll of Honour published in the 1921 edition.

Corporal Reuben Godfrey Darling

39th Battalion Australian Infantry, AIF

Died on Thursday 4th October 1917, aged 23

Commemorated on Panel 23.

Reuben Darling

Reuben was born on in Sheep Hills, Victoria, on Wednesday 22nd August 1894, son of Edwin and Minnie Jane Darling, of 6 Mackay Street, Essendon, Victoria. He was educated locally from where he joined the Bank of New South Wales on Wednesday 10th January 1912 in Warracknabeal, Victoria, before transferring as a ledger-keeper in Ballarat in January 1915 where he continued to work until enlisting.

On Monday 10th July 1916 he enlisted, and left for Plymouth, from Melbourne on Monday 25th September 1916 on board *HMAT Shropshire*. After training he left for France on Wednesday 20th December and joined the Battalion at Houplines. He remained on tours of duty, with period of rest and training in the Armentières sector until the end of April 1917 when he moved to Ploegsteert where the Battalion repulsed a raid on their line on Monday 30th. He continued to serve in the sector until Sunday 13th May when he was moved to the *'Catacombs'* until the end of the month. From *'Corse Camp'* he took the line at *'Oostrove Farm'* in the southern sector. Reuben was promoted Lance Corporal during June. The first week of July was spent training, resting and participating in various sporting competitions before returning to Wulverghem. He continued to serve in the sector until early September when he was sent to Calais for further training at Zoteau and was promoted Corporal. He spent the majority of the month there before marching 17 miles to Blaringhem on Wednesday 26th September then moving on to Winnezeele. On Wednesday 3rd October Reuben went into the line near Potijze from camp at Vlamertinghe. At 6.00am on Thursday 4th the preliminary barrage commenced and he advanced five minutes later. He was with a comrade in a shell hole sending signals when a shell exploded killing them both.

In the front line

Second Lieutenant Erasmus Darwin

4th Battalion Yorkshire Regiment

Died on Saturday 24th April 1915, aged 33

Commemorated on Panel 33.

Erasumus Darwin

Erasmus was born on Wednesday 7th December 1881, only son of Sir Horace Darwin, KBE, FRS, and Lady Ida, of The Orchard, Cambridge. He was grandson of Charles Darwin and Thomas Henry, 1st Lord Farrer. He was educated at Marlborough College as a member of Cotton from September 1895 and went up to Trinity College, Cambridge, in 1901 with an Exhibition for Mathematics.

Erasmus was employed by Messrs Mather and Platt (Manchester), Cambridge Scientific Instrument Company, followed by Bolckow, Vaughan, & Co Ltd, Middlesborough, where he was remembered by his colleagues for his: *"good judgement and exacting standards of performance: he liked to do things, and to see them done, as well as they could be done."* He was described as having *"strong views about the human side of industry and a sincere sympathy with the man on the shop floor."*

Erasmus volunteered on Saturday 12th September 1914 and was gazetted to the 4th (Territorial) Battalion, Yorkshire Regiment then trained at Darlington and Newcastle. Erasmus entrained at Newcastle Saturday 17th April 1915 for Folkestone from where he sailed for Boulogne two days later. After a short rest period in camp in the hills above the town he took his men to the Pont des Briques Station where they left for Cassel. They marched along the tree-lined roads to the border village of Godeswaersvelde where the Battalion was billeted. The first German gas attack commenced at 5.00pm on Thursday 22nd April against the French colonial troops to the north of Ypres. The line was effectively broken with hardly a soldier defending the line along the French held sector, and the way to Ypres was open. Thankfully the Germans neither realised this nor pressed their home their attack so did not move into Ypres which would have drastically altered the history of the war.

Early on Friday 23rd the Battalion left their billets and marched along the main road to Belgium, crossed the heavily guarded border at Abeele and continued along the road to Poperinghe. The whole area was abuzz with activity, but the Battalion was as yet unaware of the reason or how deadly the gas attack had been and had no protection against any further gas attack. From Poperinghe they were taken by motor bus the short distance to Vlamertinghe where they were accommodated in *'Camp C'* until being sent the Ypres Canal at 1.00am on Saturday 24th. At noon they were ordered to Potijze from where they were sent to assist at St Julien. They managed to reach Fortuin, slightly south of St Julien. As they advanced across the muddy ground to St Julien Erasmus was shot, dying instantaneously after only a few hours at the front.

Colonel Bell wrote: *"Loyalty, Courage, and devotion to duty — he had them all. … He died in an attack which gained many compliments to the Battn. He was right in front. It was a man's death."*

Corporal Wearmouth, of his platoon, wrote: *"I am a section leader in his platoon, and when we got the order to advance he proved himself a hero. He nursed us; in fact, the comment was, 'You would say we were on a field-day'. We had got to within twenty yards of our halting place when he turned to our platoon to say something. As he turned he fell, and I am sure he never spoke. As soon as I could I went to him but he was beyond human aid. Our platoon sadly miss him, as he could not do enough for us, and we are all extremely sorry for you in your great loss."*

His obituary in *'The Times'* read: *"Erasmus Darwin would, if he had lived, have added fresh distinction to the name of his family in a walk of life in which it has never before figured. Between Cambridge and a great iron works in the North there is something of a gulf fixed and one who knew Darwin only in his Cambridge home cannot say anything more than that all those who met him in business conceived a very high opinion of his grasp of his subject, his acuteness and administrative ability. It was, indeed, impossible to know him without realising that he combined with intellectual ability a calm, sound, and practical judgment, and a general capacity for doing things well and thoroughly. He had, too, what must have been invaluable to him in his work, a most genuine sympathy with and affection for working men, and this quality, which, amongst so many other things, had made him love his work at Middlesborough, gave him intense pleasure when soldiering came to him as a wholly new and unlooked-for experience. He delighted in the men, and especially in long expeditions across the moors with his scouts. There is one more quality as to which all his friends would agree, namely, a conscientiousness that was eminently sane and wide-minded and completely unswerving. No one in the world was more certain to do what he believed to be right."*

Erasmus was recorded in Debretts Obituary — War Roll of Honour published in the 1921 edition.

SECOND LIEUTENANT GILES ROBERT DAUBENEY

3rd Battalion attached 1st Battalion
Queen's Own (Royal West Kent Regiment)

Died on Friday 23rd April 1915
Commemorated on Panel 45.

Giles was the son of the Reverend Giles Daubeney, vicar of St Bartholomew's Church, and Lillian Daubeney, of Herne Vicarage, Kent. He went up to Selwyn College, Cambridge, in 1913.

Giles moved from Wulverghem to Vlamertinghe in mid-February and served in the Zwarteleen sector until the end of March. In early April he marched to relieve the French infantry in the line between Broodseinde and Zonnebeke, where they spent their time repairing and building decent trenches. He spent a few days in Vlamertinghe training for the attack that was to take place at Hill 60. Giles marched with his men into the line late on Friday 16th. On Saturday 17th the Royal Flying Corps kept a constant patrol along the area of Hill 60 to stop the Germans for observing the movement and preparations for the attack. At 7.00pm the mines were blown and the artillery barrage opened: *"There was not much noise but the whole ground shook as if there was an earthquake and a few minutes later bricks, Germans and all kinds of débris were hurtling through the air in all directions."* All that remained of the German defenders were sixty men and officers. The infantry charged forward and killed forty of them, most at the point of the bayonet with the rest taken prisoner. The most important work that Giles and his men now undertake was consolidation, it took quite some time scrambling across the craters of the destroyed hill. After a period of time the Germans were able to reorganise themselves and eventually mounted three counter-attacks which the West Kents were able to repulse. The Germans were determined and continued to counter-attack throughout the night. By 9.00am the Battalion was relieved and sent to huts between Ouderdom and Vlamertinghe.

Late on Thursday 22nd April Giles was ordered to the front. It was clear on Friday morning that it was no ordinary day and their work in the line was unusual. From Brielen they manœuvred between the Yser Canal and St Julien to help plug the gap as a result of gas attack. They marched into an artillery barrage towards St Jan and took position on the La Brique to Pilkem road. Everyone escaped injury during the relief. It was impossible to ascertain where the German line was positioned and therefore where to attack. They were able to advance eight hundred yards and until later in the day they consolidated the line one hundred yards behind. Despite not knowing exactly where the Germans were, the fight was intense and Giles was killed.

In 1922 the Bishop of Maidstone dedicated a memorial in St Bartholomew's Church to Giles and his step-brother Captain Henry Hogarth who was killed on Friday 15th September 1916 and is buried in Caterpillar Valley Cemetery, Longueval.

Captain John Robert Davidson

8th Battalion Australian Infantry, AIF
Died on Thursday 4th October 1917, aged 22
Commemorated on Panel 7.

John was born in Creswick, Victoria, son of John and Elizabeth Davidson. He was educated locally and became a carpenter.

At the outbreak of war John volunteered and enlisted, embarking on *HMAT Benalla*, on Monday 19th October 1914 from Melbourne. After serving in the ranks he received a field commission.

He sailed to Egypt and arrived in Alexandria on Tuesday 8th December 1914 and marched to Mena. On Thursday 7th January 1915 he left for Ismailia where he remained until Sunday 4th April, when he returned to Alexandria. On Thursday 8th he sailed for Lemnos, arriving three days later and went to Gallipoli on Thursday 15th. He served in the line until Saturday 11th September when he returned to Lemnos and on Sunday 21st November left Mudros for *'ANZAC Cove'* and bivouacked in *'Shrapnel Valley'*. He continued to serve in the line until Saturday 18th December when he embarked for Mudros. After a period of rest he embarked on *SS Empress of Britain* in Lemnos on Monday 3rd January 1916 and sailed to Alexandria, arriving on Thursday 6th. The Battalion entrained for Tel-el-Kebir before moving to Serapeum and took position along the Suez Canal where they served until 9.00pm on Saturday 25th March. They returned to Alexandria, arriving at 7.00am the next morning and embarked on *HMT Megantic* for Marseilles.

The *Megantic* left at 10.00am on Monday 27th arriving in the afternoon on Friday 31st and they entrained the next day for Godewaersvelde. This was a long tiring journey that took until the morning of Monday 3rd April from where they marched to billets between Bailleul and Steenwerck. Training continued including the use of the new gas helmets and what to do in the event of a gas attack. On Sunday 30th John paraded and set off to Fleurbaix where billets were provided in *'Elbow Farm'*, *'Smith Farm'* and *'Limit Farm'*. General William Birdwood visited the Battalion on Tuesday 2nd May and the next day their billets came under shell-fire. John took the line on the Western Front for the first time on Monday 15th May near Fleurbaix where he remained until Sunday 11th June when he was sent to serve at Sailly for a week. On Friday 19th he crossed the border and went to Neuve Eglise for a week before moving north to Messines. In early July he was sent to *'Bulford Camp'* for a short period of training. The move south to the Somme commenced on Monday 10th July when the Battalion entrained at Bailleul for Doullens, arriving in Rainenville on Friday 14th where they undertook three days' training before moving to Varennes for a week. John arrived in Albert on Thursday 20th July and took the line at Pozières on Sunday 23rd. He took part in the attack on *'Mouquet Farm'*. After ten days the Battalion left for Canaples for a week before moving to Vadencourt on Wednesday 9th August, where the next day HM King George V passed the Brigade in his car during a visit to the front. The Battalion returned to the line at *'Sausage Valley'* and served on the Somme until Saturday 14th October when the Battalion was moved to Eperlecques near St Omer for ten days training prior to returning to the Somme; they were sent to *'Mametz Huts'*. The Battalion took the line at Bernafay and Fricourt. Christmas 1916 was spent in 'Melbourne Camp' from where working parties were supplied to the front. John continued to serve in the sector including at Warloy-Baillon, Bazentin-le-Petit, Flers, and the *'Hindenburg Line'* until Tuesday 22nd May 1917 when the Battalion was sent to Bresle for a month's training. They returned to the line at Mailly Maillet for ten days.

On Friday 27th July John marched with his Company to Aveluy where they entrained for Caëstre and were

Mudros Harbour

sent to billets in Hondghem. He remained in the town until Thursday 9th August when a move was made to Doulieu for five weeks.

On Wednesday 19th John assembled his men at Zillebeke at 8.30pm. The rain had been heavy and the mud was dreadful as the Battalion moved to *'Clapham Junction'*. The initial advance went well; they reached the Red Line where they consolidated the position and used their machine-guns on the German lines for two hours. Shortly before 10.00am they advanced again taking their third objective and moved forward to *'Carlisle Farm'*. The operation was a great success; not only did they capture their objectives but in addition took four officers and sixty men prisoners, and captured their machine-guns.

The Battalion moved from bivouac at 5.40pm on Tuesday 2nd October and moved to *'Anzac Ridge'* with Battalion Headquarters at *'Garter Point'*. On Wednesday 3rd October Lieutenant Leonard Errey, DSO, MC, the Battalion Intelligence Officer, laid out the marker tapes for the men to follow the next day during their attack at Broodseinde. At 1.00am on Thursday 4th John led his men into the assembly positions, arriving at 2.30am. At 5.30am the German artillery opened up — the shell-fire killed John together with Lieutenant Leonard Errey (buried in Menin Road South Cemetery) and Captain Rudolph Kirsch (commemorated on the Menin Gate, see below).

78004 Private Walter James Davidson

7th Battalion Canadian Infantry (British Columbia Regiment)

Died on Saturday 3rd June 1916, aged 24

Commemorated on Panel 24.

Walter Davidson

Walter was born in Leith on Sunday 21st February 1892, son of Charles Britten Davidson and Margaret Anderson Davidson, of 14 Park Avenue, Portobello, Scotland. He was educated at the George Heriot School from 1903 to 1907, leaving aged 14 to join the British Linen Bank in Edinburgh. At 17 he left for Canada and took employment with the Bank of Montreal.

Walter volunteered and enlisted in 1915. As it was going to take too long to get to the front, he resigned, and paid his own way to England where he rejoined on Tuesday 28th September 1915. He was described as a Presbyterian, 5ft 8in tall, with a 36in chest, a medium complexion, brown eyes, dark brown hair, and a scar on the middle finger of his left hand. After training at Shorncliffe he was sent to France in December and joined the Battalion on the Salient.

The Germans launched a huge attack on Friday 2nd June 1916 that had wiped out many Canadians, buried alive by the shelling, or killed during the onslaught. Walter was sent up during the night of Friday 2nd and went into the assembly positions ready for the counter-attack at dawn. It was a difficult march in the pouring rain that added considerably to the weight of their packs, and the officers gave permission for the men to throw them away. The roads were clogged with traffic so many of the men of the 7th, 10th, 49th, 52nd and 60th Canadian Battalions arrived late. The objective was to recapture *'Observatory Ridge'* and Mount Sorrel that had been lost. Communications were poor so the expected preliminary barrage at 2.00am was only partially fired. Zero hour was postponed until 7.00am. The delayed barrage alerted the Germans to the attack. Walter struggled through *'Armagh Wood'* where they came under enfilade fire and the German artillery opened up. Walter was killed when a shell burst close to him.

Captain and Adjutant William Robert Davidson, MC

46th Battalion Australian Infantry, AIF

Died on Thursday 16th August 1917, aged 27

Commemorated on Panel 27.

William was born in Melbourne, on Friday 10th January 1890, son of William Robert and Edith Mary Davidson. He was educated at South Melbourne and King Street State Schools. He was married to Enid L Davidson, of 13 York Street, Glenferrie, Victoria, and they had two sons. He was employed as a grain salesman and served in the Victorian Rifles. He was a member of Melbourne Cricket Club.

On Saturday 27th March 1915 William volunteered, leaving from Melbourne on Tuesday 10th August 1915 on *RMS Persia*, sailing for Egypt. He served in Egypt and was sent to Gallipoli. After the evacuation he returned to Egypt and joined the 46th Battalion as acting Adjutant when it was raised at the end of February 1916 in Tel-el-Kebir. He immediately set about the organisation of the new Battalion, including appointing NCOs. On Wednesday 22nd March HRH The Prince of Wales inspected the new Battalion and congratulated them on their work. On Friday 24th William was promoted Captain and confirmed as Adjutant. On Monday 27th the Battalion marched to Serapeum, arriving on Friday 31st; it was a hard march in the blazing heat across deep sand. Further training continued and they took the line where the first task was to strengthen the defences, and on

General Godley

Monday 8th May General Sir Alexander Godley inspected them in the trenches followed by General Sir Archibald Murray three days later. The Battalion was ordered back to Serapeum on Wednesday 17th, arriving two days later where they relaxed and prepared for the move to France. At 11.00pm on Thursday 1st June he went with the Battalion and entrained for Alexandria where they boarded *HMT Kipanus Castle* the next day. On Saturday 3rd the ship sailed for Marseilles, arriving at 3.00pm on Thursday 8th. By 10.00pm the Battalion had entrained and left for a long, slow journey to Bailleul, arriving at 10.30am on Sunday 11th, from where they marched to billets in Outtersteene. A special service was held on Thursday 15th to the memory of Field Marshal Lord Kitchener who had died on *HMS Hampshire* ten days previously with General Sir Herbert Plumer visiting the Battalion on Monday 19th. Training continued with particular emphasis being given on how to deal with gas, now in general use by both sides.

General Murray

Lord Kitchener

At 5.00pm on Sunday 2nd July the Battalion was ordered to Sailly, seven miles away, where billets were provided. Three days later the Battalion took the line southwest of Fleurbaix where the next morning the gas alarm was sounded although no attack developed. The Battalion was relieved on Tuesday 11th and at 6.30am on Friday 14th entrained at Bailleul for Doullens where they arrived at 12.45pm. A march of thirteen miles was required before the billets in Berteaucourt were reached and they remained there until Thursday 27th. A further march took them fifteen miles to Hérissart where they stayed overnight before marching to huts in Vadencourt.

On Thursday 3rd August William took the line with his men at Pozières, their headquarters at *'Tara Hill'*. He continued on tours of duty with bivouacs at Warloy and billets in Berteaucourt, Talmas, Hérissart and Vadencourt. On Monday 28th General William Birdwood joined them in Vadencourt for Sunday Service and then addressed the Battalion. Later in the day they marched to Albert where they were billeted prior to retaking the line in the pouring rain which continued non-stop for two days. The trenches became flooded, most of them to waist level, and each night their line was bombarded.

General Birdwood

Tours of duty continued until Sunday 3rd September when the Battalion was marched to Warloy and the move north began. On Friday 8th they arrived in Doullens were they entrained for Proven followed by a further ten mile march before reaching *'Kenora Camp'* in Reninghelst. Until Monday 18th William assisted with the reorganisation of the Battalion and training continued when they moved to *'Chippawa Camp'* ready to take the line from Friday 20th. Tours of duty continued until Monday 23rd October when they returned to *'Kenora Camp'* where General Herbert Cox inspected them on Wednesday 25th and presented William with a congratulatory card for his bravery and good work. The next day the Battalion marched to Godeswaersvelde and entrained at 4.00pm for Longpré where they arrived at 3.15am and were sent to billets at l'Étoille. Two weeks later, after further training, the Battalion took the line at Guedecourt, via Bernafay Wood and Delville Wood. Tours of duty continued on the Somme, together with periods out of the line undertaking training.

On Wednesday 11th April 1917 the Battalion undertook an attack on Bullecourt. The attack failed, the village was heavily defended and formed part of the *'Hindenburg Line'*. Four tanks were used but they broke down and did not provide the assistance that was either hoped for or expected. The Battalion took very heavy casualties: three hundred and eighty seven killed, wounded or missing.

The Battalion was sent to Bresle on Monday 30th April where they remained until Monday 14th May when they started to move back to northern France. They arrived in Bailleul on Tuesday 15th at 1.30pm and were billeted in the town. After two weeks they moved to *'Kortepyp Camp'* were they undertook fatigue duties in the front line. During the Battle of Messines they provided Brigade Carrying Parties at *'Gooseberry Farm'* from Thursday 7th June until taking the line at *'Owl Trench'* during the night of Saturday 9th. During the Battle of Messines the Battalion lost two hundred and ninety-four men killed, wounded or missing. On Thursday 14th they were relieved to huts at La Creche for three days before moving to Renescure, St Omer — whilst there he heard that he had been gazetted for the Military Cross. A fleet of buses arrived on Thursday 21st which took them to billets in Doulieu and they went into the line at Hill 63, *'Fort Garry'* where they served until Monday 6th August. They were then sent to a camp on Kemmel Hill. The Battalion served at Wytschaete with their headquarters at *'Derry House'* and there on Thursday 16th William was listed as missing in action.

William was Mentioned in Despatches gazetted on Tuesday 2nd January 1917 and awarded the Military Cross.

SECOND LIEUTENANT
DAVID JAMES DAVIES

Machine Gun Corps
attached 'C' Battalion Tank Corps
Died on Tuesday 31st July 1917
Commemorated on Panel 56.

David was the son of Mr and Mrs Davies. He went up to Trinity College, Oxford, in 1915.

He left University and volunteered on Tuesday 28th December 1915 and was commissioned. David undertook training that included the use of dummy tanks that were constructed of wood and canvas. He and six others practised with the dummies before being given 'the real thing'. The dummies were described: *"They looked for all the world like some drab-coloured prehistoric monster with as many legs as a centipede. A high wind blew during a certain 'action' in March, and made things most difficult. By the time the final objective was reached many of the Tanks were in a state of collapse, the torn canvas revealing the perspiring machinery to the amused gaze of the onlookers. The remains of the tanks were, however, most useful for firewood and the renovation of beds."*

David was based at the tankodrome in Oosthoek Wood that was meant to be a secret headquarters. However it came under German fire and they moved to the area around Château Lovie as: *"The enemy had obtained information of our tankodrome in Oosthoek Wood from a British prisoner, who was either a garrulous fool or a very treacherous knave.*

A soldier belonging to a certain infantry regiment had betrayed every detail of the whereabouts of the Tanks of the 1st Brigade, and of the programme of their movements. A German document was captured setting forth the whole of this creature's evidence and explaining its value and significance. The official account of this murderous piece of treachery was periodically read out on parade to all Tank units, and formed the text of many discourses on the vital importance of strict secrecy and high moral. The name of this man will for ever have a sinister sound for all who served in the Tank Corps."

Careful preparations were made for the Battle of Passchendaele with a model being prepared in Oosthoek Wood that covered more than an acre. Viewing platforms ran around it so that the men could view the whole of the Salient as if they were observing it from a balloon or flying over it.

David's objective was in front of the Steenbeek that was already in a dreadful condition, flooded and covered with deep shell holes. A total of seventy-two tanks were split between 'C' and 'F' Battalions in three groups of twenty-four.

In the mist at 3.50am on Tuesday 31st the British artillery launched the largest barrage of the war and the infantry advanced and the tanks lumbered into action. The mud was thick as a result of the pouring rain over the previous days which slowed the advance. The German line was initially pushed back at some speed, but the tanks were unable to keep up with the rapid advance. An account of David's 'C' Battalion for day from the Battalion history: *"At 11.30 a.m. message was received that a Battalion of Argyll and Sutherland Highlanders were held up on the right. Tank' Canada' moved in this direction and silenced enemy machine-guns in the Railway Embankment, assisted by the Tank 'Cuidich'n Rich.' When patrolling in front of the infantry whilst they were consolidating, Tank bellied.*

At the same time enemy barrage came down, and both Tank 'Canada' and Tank 'Cuidich'n Rich' received direct hits. Five of the crew remained with the infantry, and assisted in repelling a counter-attack, two of the men being wounded.

... Tank 'Cape Colony' arrived at Low Farm and proceeded in front of the infantry. Came under heavy shell-fire and bellied. Whilst unditching, Tanks 'Cyprus' and 'Culloden' were observed under heavy fire from anti-Tank guns, which were in position on the high ground beyond. Both 'Cyprus' and 'Culloden' were seen to be hit.

'Cape Colony' then came under heavy M.G. fire from both flanks. On request of infantry 'Cape Colony' proceeded to a wood on right flank, where they were held up.

Although not fired upon from the Tank, several enemy machine gunners surrendered to the infantry, on seeing the

Tank approach. 'Cape Colony' now turned N.E. towards Beck House, where a good view of anti-Tank guns, which had been shelling 'Cyprus' and 'Culloden,' was obtained. Whilst manœuvring to take these guns in flank or rear, the Tank sank in a swamp, water rising to the engine cover. Boche aeroplanes circled low overhead whilst unsuccessful attempts were made to unditch. Enemy shelling then became very heavy, so Lewis guns were taken out and Tank locked up.

... Flag Tank 'Cumbrae' was delayed half an hour by bellying in a trench near Bill Cottage, went in front of the infantry towards second objective. Opened fire on enemy who were disappearing in direction of Delva Farm. Ground was quite water-logged, and Tank bellied in a borrow pit. Whilst digging out was fired at by a sniper, and by an aeroplane flying low overhead. Time was then zero plus 9 hours (i.e., 12.50 p.m.).

... Tank 'Caithness' came under sniper and machine- gun fire near Beck House. No bullets penetrated armour- plating. Proceeded in company with Tank 'Carstairs,' which silenced enemy M.G. fire. Cameron Highlanders then advanced, and Tank followed, bellied near Zonnebeke Stream. Mud was up to floor level and door of sponson was pushed off its hinges. Enemy aeroplane circled over head, and fired on them whilst attempting to unditch. Eventually Tank' Carstairs' came to the rescue, and Tank was got clear.

... Tank 'Culloden' had her unditching gear carried away by barbed wire near Hill Cottage. Unditching beam was recovered, but again broke loose, until secured with rope. Just west of Frost House shell burst under front of Tank. Whilst crossing light railway half-way between Frost House and Square Farm, a second shell hit roof door and killed one gunner. Tank stopped, and it was found petrol pressure pipe was cut. Time 9.15 a.m. A third shell struck behind right sponson. Crew were with drawn from Tank, and took up a position in shell-holes near Square Farm. Tank was still being shelled, undoubtedly by an anti-Tank gun, about ten shells being fired at it in five minutes, six of which hit the Tank.

Tank 'Cyprus' was then seen to be hit by the same anti-Tank gun. At 10.15 a.m. survivors of Tanks 'Culloden' and 'Cyprus,' together with undamaged Lewis guns, with drew to Battalion Rallying Point, after pigeon messages had been despatched reporting the situation.

... Tank' Carstairs' arrived at Black Line near Beck House, but infantry had not then arrived.

Tank soon bellied in boggy ground, but was unditched successfully. Just west of Borry Farm Tank 'Caithness' was found badly bellied, and with unditching gear lost.

Having been informed by 6th Cameron Highlanders that the second objective had been captured, Tank 'Carstairs' hitched on to Tank 'Caithness' and towed it out. Enemy shell-fire was extremely heavy, and an aeroplane flew over, firing at crew with machine-guns during the operation.

Instructions were then received to return to Battalion Rallying Point."

Lieutenant George Herbert Davies

3rd Battalion attached 1st Battalion
King's Shropshire Light Infantry
Died on Monday 9th August 1915, aged 26
Commemorated on Panel 47.

George Davies

George was born at home on Friday 16th November 1888, sixth son of the Reverend John Bayley Davies (Rector of Waters Upton) and Mrs Davies, of Waters Upton, Wellington, Salop. He was educated at Hereford Cathedral School, and went up to Glasgow University from 1910 to 1914 where he was the Sergeant Major in the OTC. George studied to be a civil engineer and worked for John Brown & Co Ltd, Glasgow.

George volunteered at the outbreak of war and was gazetted on Saturday 15th August 1914, leaving for France in December and promoted Lieutenant on Sunday 21st March 1915.

He was invalided to England in February 1915, returning to the front in April, joining the 1st Battalion in May. Throughout the summer the Shropshires were mainly based in the area around Wieltje and undertook some good work. On Saturday 3rd July they were relieved and went to billets in Poperinghe. On Friday 7th Field Marshal Lord Kitchener inspected the Battalion in Poperinghe town square after which a message was sent to the Battalion: *"I am directed by Field Marshal Earl Kitchener to express to the battalion under your command his satisfaction at being able to inspect the battalion and his appreciation of the smartness of the turn out and the efficiency and fitness of the battalion after nine months' hard campaigning."*

On Sunday 11th July George took his men back into the line in the area of Hooge. On Monday 9th August they were still in at Hooge when an attack was launched at 3.15am and they advanced over a thousand yard front. The attack was successful, however, casualties were heavy, including George, three other officers and forty-one other ranks, one hundred and sixty-nine were wounded and eighteen listed as missing. As a result of bravery during the attack three Military Crosses and six Distinguished Conduct Medals were awarded to the men of the 1st Battalion.

Major Edward Luard, DSO, (later promoted Lieutenant Colonel, who died on Monday 24th April 1915 and buried in Lijssenthoek Military Cemetery) wrote: *"He was in charge of the machine-guns, and was most gallantly getting one into position when he was shot dead. He is a very great loss to the regiment."*

His brother, 2nd Lieutenant Walter Llewellyn Davies, died on Saturday 15th July 1916 and is buried in La Neuville British Cemetery, Corbie.

Second Lieutenant Ivor Theophilus Davies

5th Battalion Oxford and Bucks Light Infantry

Died on Tuesday 22nd June 1915

Commemorated on Panel 37.

Ivor was the son of Mr and Mrs Davies and went up to Gonville and Caius College, Cambridge, in 1913.
He gave up his studies and volunteered. Ivor was sent for training and was commissioned. He left with the Battalion for France, landing in Boulogne on Friday 21st May 1915 and was sent to northern France for training. After only a few days in the front line Ivor was killed in action.

86654 Sapper John Henry Davies

171st Tunnelling Company Royal Engineers

Died on Sunday 20th June 1915, aged 35

Commemorated on Panel 9.

John was born in Newcastle-on-Tyne, on Thursday 1st April 1880, eldest son of Charles and Ellen Davies, of 1 Mount Gardens, Northampton. He was educated locally and then employed at one of the local mines near Barnsley. At Morcott, Uppingham, Rutland, on Monday 13th April 1903, John married Esther Ann Davies, of 15 Vernon Street North, Barnsley. They had three sons, John born on Tuesday 12th July 1904, Charles on Thursday 7th May 1908 and George on Sunday 18th September 1910.
At the outbreak of war John enlisted and was transferred to the Royal Engineers with his skills as a miner. He was engaged in action at Hill 60 when he was killed and was buried where he fell.
Sapper Roberts wrote: *"We have lost one of the finest men who came out of Newall Camp, Silkstone ... There was not a more willing or better man in the camp. A man who did his duty thoroughly, and everyone thought the world of him, and all that we can say is that he died a noble death."*

10141 Private William Davies

'B' Company, 1st Battalion

King's Shropshire Light Infantry

Died on Monday 9th August 1915, aged 16

Commemorated on Panel 49.

William was born at home son of John and Margaret Davies, of 3 Southall's Buildings, Willow Street, Oswestry, Salop. He was educated locally.
He enlisted at Shrewsbury and was sent for training. William joined the Battalion in the field with a draft. On Saturday 31st July 1915 the Battalion was relieved from the line at Hooge and sent to a camp near Vlamertinghe before being billeted in Poperinghe. On Thursday 5th August William marched into the line to relieve the 6th Somerset Light Infantry. Due to the recent fighting the trenches were badly damaged and some work was undertaken to make them usable. On Friday 6th a British bombardment began which brought a massive retaliatory bombardment that was so heavy that the proposed attack was postponed and throughout Sunday 8th reconnaissance was undertaken over the German lines. At 3.15am on Monday 9th William went forward and they advanced over a thousand yard front. The attack was successful but casualties were heavy, including William amongst forty-one other ranks. One hundred and sixty-nine were wounded and eighteen listed as missing.

Second Lieutenant Wilfrid Allen J Davis

4th Battalion attached 1st Battalion

East Surrey Regiment

Died on Wednesday 21st April 1915, aged 21

Commemorated on Panel 34.

Wilfrid Davis

Wilfrid was born in 1894 son of Walter Lance Davis and Rosita Davis, of 82 Worple Road, Wimbledon, London. He was educated at Wimbledon College followed by Stonyhurst from October 1911. Wilfrid went up to Jesus College, Oxford, in 1913 with an Open Mathematical Scholarship rowing for the College VIII and a member of the College Tennis Team.
Wilfrid volunteered and was gazetted on Saturday 15th August 1914 leaving for France on Tuesday 26th January 1915.
At the beginning of April 1915 Wilfrid was in the front line close to Kemmel. They were billeted at Locre and Zevecoten before marching up to Ypres that was under fire, and they lost three men wounded. The next day a cheer went up when the men of the 2nd Battalion marched passed them in front of the Cloth Hall *en route* to the front. The next day Wilfrid was in the line close to the Verbrandenmolen and on Tuesday 13th Brigadier General Frederick Stanley Maude was inspecting them and their front line when he was severely wounded. The Royal Engineers blew the mines on Hill 60 on Saturday 17th and the Hill was captured. At 5.00am on Monday 19th Wilfrid moved in front of Hill 60. They were under particularly heavy fire, late on Tuesday Wilfrid and his platoon were virtually cut off with only the communication trenches

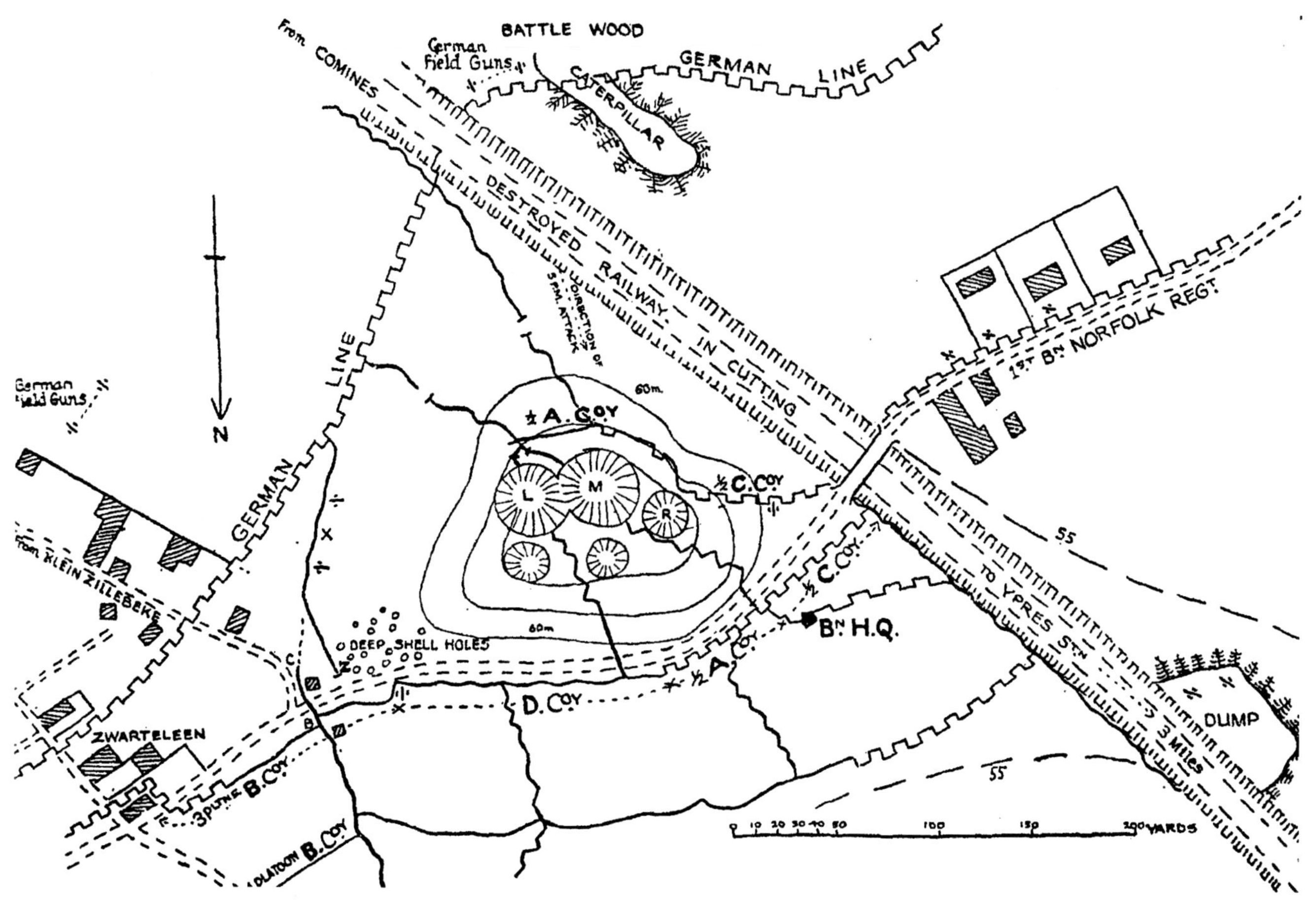

1st Battalion East Surrey Regiment, Hill 60, April 1915

being kept open connecting him with the Battalion. The German artillery increased in strength and their infantry kept the British defenders under pressure. A German counter-attack was expected on Wednesday 21st but it did not come in force. The Battalion was withdrawn from the line later in the day but during the relief Wilfrid was killed. It had been a costly tour of duty with seven officers and one hundred and six other ranks killed, eight officers and one hundred and fifty-eight other ranks wounded.

His Company Sergeant Major wrote: *"He went during the night at the head of a few men right up the hill to see how many Germans were holding it. He came almost face to face with the Germans, bombed them, and returned without a scratch. When the East Surreys took the hill next morning they found the defences in a very bad state. The parapet was broken, and dead and wounded lying about it. Lieut. Davis selected for himself the most dangerous place beside the huge crater and began to build a parapet in full view of the Germans. They fired on him and several bullets caught him in the chest. He fell into the crater dead, right on the crest of the hill. That is his grave at the present moment, for the Germans recaptured the hill. Had he been spared he would be wearing the V.C."*

His Commanding Officer wrote: *"Your son was hit by a shell, and death was instantaneous; he led his men brilliantly, and was killed in action in which this gallant regiment distinguished itself more than words can say. It achieved wonders, and withstood a most terrible bombardment which some men had reported was impossible. I can only add your son has a full share of the honour, and his loss will be deeply felt in the regiment. He had made himself very dear to all — officers and men."*

A brother officer wrote: *"I can never repay the kindness he showed me when I was hit; he came and covered me up with his coat, and cheered me when I thought I was going to die. Afterwards I saw him going about, fearlessly disregarding the perfect hail of shells and bullets which swept round him. Several times I tried to get him to take the ordinary precautions, but he only laughed, saying 'I was born to be hanged, not shot!'. He seems to have done exceptionally well. When I went down he was the only unwounded officer on the hill in our Company."*

Lieutenant Thomas Gordon Davson

Royal Horse Guards

Died on Thursday 13th May 1915, aged 26

Commemorated on Panel 3.

Thomas Davson

Thomas was born on Thursday 31st May 1888 the fourth and youngest son of Sir Henry Katz and Lady Anne Helen Davson, of 20 Ennismore Gardens, London SW.

In January 1915 Thomas was sent for training in the Hazebrouck area with billets in Lynde that were described: *"Lynde is on rather high ground and the fields are comparatively dry. It is quite*

a grassy country, and the only place where I have seen stake and bound fences which would do credit to Leicestershire. Michael Wymyss and Phillipps have made it easier to ride about by larking over the country every day and making gaps in the all the fences." On Wednesday 27th January Field Marshal Sir John French visited them in camp and undertook an inspection. After crossing the border back into Belgium Thomas went into the line, taking over a series of dreadful trenches from the French infantry. He commenced a series of tours of duty on the Salient before being sent to northern France during the Battle of Neuve-Chapelle that was followed by further training around Merville. By the end of March he returned to the trenches with billets being mostly provided in Vlamertinghe from where he was sent into the line at 8.30pm on Wednesday 12th May. Thomas went through the dark eerie ruins of Ypres, out via the Menin Gate and along the Menin Road, taking position between Verlorenhoek and Hooge. He arrived to an ominously quiet line. At 3.30am shelling commenced that became an immense barrage at 4.00am Which lasted until 7.00am when the German infantry poured forward. Their weight of numbers overwhelmed the position; by 8.30am the line was straightened and reorganized. At 2.30pm Colonel Lord Tweedmouth ordered the advance and during the counter-attack Thomas was killed leading his men forward.
Thomas was recorded in Debretts Obituary — War Roll of Honour published in the 1921 edition.

Captain
John Kearsley Dawson-Scott

5th Field Company Royal Engineers

Died on Thursday 29th October 1914, aged 31
Commemorated on Panel 9.

John Dawson-Scott

John was born in London on Friday 18th May 1883, third son of General Robert Nicholl Dawson-Scott, JP, (Colonel Commandant of the Royal Engineers), and Grace Mansel C Dawson-Scott (née Nicholl-Carne), of Brent House, Penrith. He was educated at Tonbridge School from 1896 to 1900. He passed into RMA Woolwich and passed out fourth. He went to the School of Military Engineering, Chatham in July 1902. John was musical, playing the 'cello, enjoyed sketching and was a good sportsman. He won many cups for shooting and received his colours in hockey at Woolwich. John also won many other cups and prizes for polo, cricket, tennis and croquet. John was engaged to the daughter of Colonel T Bigge, RE.
John was gazetted on Thursday 31st July 1902, promoted Lieutenant on Monday 26th December 1904, and Captain on Thursday 31st July 1913. From 1902 to 1906 he served at home and the following five years in Egypt, returning to Chatham where he was Assistant Instructor in Fortifications.
At the outbreak of war John went out to France on Saturday 15th August 1914 and served at Mons, Le Cateau and the Aisne. He was awarded the Chevalier of the Legion of Honour *'for special gallantry'* between Friday 21st and Sunday 30th August. John was in making a reconnaissance in the front trenches when he was killed by a high-explosive shell near Zonnebeke.
His Commanding Officer wrote: *"I write a few lines to tell you of your son's death. He was looking through a loophole in a house just behind the firing line, when a German high explosive shell came into the room and burst. Death must have been instantaneous.*
He was one of those who the gods love: able, energetic, quick to grasp, rapid and thorough in action, a charming personality. He was the most able assistant a Company Commander could hope for, and he did so much for me that I feel lost without him."
Brigadier General Spring Robert Rice *"We R.E. of the 1st Army have had many severe losses during the battle near Ypres, but none that we deplore more than that of your boy. He was a most brave and particularly efficient officer. He did particularly good work on the Aisne in designing a bridge which proved a great success, being much admired by the French engineers. His fine work from the very beginning of the campaign gave great promise for the future."*
In Christ Church, Penrith, Cumbria, a brass memorial was placed in his memory with the inscription: *"In loving memory of John Kearsley Dawson-Scott, Captain Royal Engineers, Chevlr. Legion of Honour. Youngest son of General Dawson-Scott Colonel Commandant R.E., who was killed in action near Ypres 29 Oct. 1914. Aged 31 years."*

2088 Lance Corporal
Arnold Ellis Day

1st/5th Battalion West Yorkshire Regiment (Prince of Wales's Own)

Died on Tuesday 13th July 1915, aged 26
Commemorated on Panel 21.

Arnold Day

Arnold was born in Dewsbury on Sunday 19th May 1889, only son of Edward Joseph and Adah Day, of 10 South Drive, Harrogate. He was educated at Woodhouse Grove School, Leeds, and then worked for the *'The Bradford Daily Telegraph'* in the literary department.
Arnold volunteered on Friday 28th August 1914. On Wednesday 7th

July 1915 Arnold returned from a couple of days rest and went back into the line to the northeast of Ypres where they were under attack from gas, mortar shells, rifle grenades and whizz-bangs. The British replied with 56lb trench mortars and Hales bombs, amongst others, that had their effect. At 10.00pm on Saturday 10th July the Germans mounted an attack and took two lines of trenches. However, the King's Own Yorkshire Light Infantry undertook the counter-attack and retook the lost trenches. Then gas shells were sent over: *"... gas hung about the trenches for a considerable time."* On Tuesday 13th a further gas attack was mounted soon supplemented by shrapnel and general artillery. Arnold was killed in action and was buried at *'Tucos Farm'*.

2nd Lieutenant Allen wrote: *"He was in my platoon and a most promising N.C.O. He was shot in the head while carrying out his duties, and died a little afterwards."*

One of his comrades wrote: *"I wish you could have seen Arnold with the children out here; how they loved him. It was common to see him with a crowd around him, all talking to him at once, all of them adoring him. It was the same with the old people."*

Lieutenant Calvin Wellington Day

No 1 Company, 2nd Battalion Canadian Infantry (Eastern Ontario Regiment)

Died on Friday 23rd April 1915, aged 24

Commemorated on Panel 10.

Calvin Day

Calvin was born at home on Sunday 19th April 1891, son of Sidney Wellington and Adelaide Isabella Day, of Kingston, Ontario. He attended local schools before graduating from the Collegiate Institute of Kingston and the Collegiate Institute of Coburg. In 1911 Calvin gained an MA from Queen's University, Kingston, Ontario. He was also a graduate and research assistant of Harvard University, America, appointed Witing Fellow in 1913 and was preparing his thesis for a doctorate. Calvin was a member of the Kingston Yacht Club and the Harvard Canadian Club. His interests included swimming, boating, canoeing and walking.

From 1907 to 1910 Calvin was a member of the Coburg Garrison Artillery, winning first prize for gun laying. From 1911 to 1914 he joined the Princess of Wales's Own Rifles (14th Regiment), Kingston. He was gazetted Lieutenant in April 1912.

Calvin volunteered at Valcartier on Tuesday 22nd September 1914. His attestation papers describe him as 5ft 7in tall, with a 35in chest, fair complexion, blue eyes, light brown hair, a single vaccination mark on his left arm, and a large white birthmark between his right shoulder and his spinal column.

Calvin left Gasepé Bay on Saturday 3rd October 1914 and arrived in Portsmouth on Wednesday 14th October when he was sent to *'Bustard Camp'*, Salisbury Plain for training. On Monday 19th he wrote from the camp: *"Last night at 9.15 we fell in and marched on to the pier, leaving our home of twenty-four days. As modern sea-voyages go it was quite long in point of time. We made off from the pier at 10 p.m. and marched through the narrow, paved streets of the Navy Yard between the towering stone walls. The tramp, tramp, tramp sounded even above the singing. When we struck town I understood what 'Merry England' meant. In spite of the lateness of the hour, the streets were crowded and every window as we passed had its occupants. The old women and the young girls crowded into the road, and the lucky fellows on the outer flanks kissed everyone they liked. Mother, father, and daughter would be standing there together, and a soldier would stop to shake hands with the old people, to talk to them and kiss the young daughter, and the parents would not think anything of it all. There was laughing and singing everywhere. The old ladies kissed the boys and wished them a safe return, and our company, thanks to my watchful care perhaps, was more orderly than the others. We didn't allow any girls being brought into the ranks, nor did any of our men fall out of the ranks and walk along the street with girls (except — till I saw him). But apart from that there was no interference. They exchanged souvenirs and everybody was happy and good natured, and as one very nice-appearing man to whom I was speaking said, in all the merriment there wasn't an objectionable word or suggestion to be hear. Merry England!"*

Calvin Day

Calvin enjoyed visiting London and recorded one of his visits: *"In the afternoon we (Mac and I) went to Prince's Club, of which we are honorary members, and had a fine time skating. I never saw so much good skating at one time before. Mac was Canadian champion figure skater for two years. There's always an old fogy in a club. We were going a little fast and he stopped us and asked if we were Canadians, etc., and said the ice was like Europe, and was full of little Belgiums, and that they didn't violate one another's neutrality. We caught on and didn't need to be told any more. We had crossed his little 'area'. After a time Mac remarked to him and some others were waltzing about and infringing a bit, and the old gentleman remarked, 'Yes, but they're good skaters'. Mac was dumfounded. I nearly laughed out loud."*

He left for France on Thursday 11th February 1915,

sailing through a horrendous gale that killed many of the horses and injured a number of the men. Calvin landed on Sunday 14th in St Nazaire where he entrained to Hazebrouck, via Rouen, Abbeville, and Boulogne. Calvin marched with his men to billets in the area of Caëstre. For a week he continued training before taking the line in the Houplines sector. Here Calvin gave the constant order of *"Steady! aim low! shoot your man first and bayonet him afterwards"* as the Germans advanced towards them. He was in reserve during the Battle of Neuve-Chapelle where he remained until Wednesday 7th April when he was moved to Cassel, marching some twenty-five miles. On Saturday 10th the Division was inspected by General Sir Horace Smith-Dorrien and five days later he marched across the border into Belgium at Abeele. He was taken by London bus via Poperinghe towards Ypres marching to billets in Brielen.

On Sunday 4th April he wrote: *"Father's Birthday. Cold and windy with a sprinkling of rain in the morning. Church parade at 10 a.m. with Holy Communion. It was a very impressive service. I won't forget it soon. The communion rail was made of scaling ladders which the engineers had devised and made for getting over barbed wire entanglements in an assault. A large number of men took communion, considerably over 100. I took the communion also. The last time was in Salisbury Cathedral about two months ago."*

Wednesday 14th April: *"About 5 p.m. I got a wheel from Hdqrs., and started over the sticky up-hill road to Cassel. It is eight kilometres, but I got there before six. The road winds about on its way up the hill, and as one rises the level surrounding country unfolds itself like a map. It is the first time I ever saw a level country from a height, and in this thickly populated and highly developed country is a very striking sight. On the way up I passed an auto coming down the broad level pavé, and in it was General Foch readying his daily papers. To enter the town one has to pass through an old, covered gateway. Inside all the ground is paved. There was the usual square with the usual collection of motor transports. The town is old and quaint, streets at different levels and twisting about. Some very venerable looking buildings. I pushed my bike up to the highest point where there is a little park, an old château, and a wireless station. Here I was agreeable and intensely surprised. The only other soldier up there was Brokenshire, Harvard '16. I hadn't seen him since we left England. It was very strange and pleasing to me. We sat in one of the stone bastions, very like those at Fresh Pond in Cambridge which I remember so well, overlooking the level plain three hundred feet below with its great straight roads losing themselves like endless white ribbons in the mist and gathering darkness — the road to Dunkerque and the sea and the road to Ypres and the British wedge, from which direction the occasional report of an extra heavy gun was heard indistinctly. Here we talked of Harvard and Cambridge and the places and the girls we had known. It was a pleasing and impressive sight in the setting sun and a very pleasant experience, and I was very sorry to leave it to him."*

On Thursday 15th April Calvin wrote to his sister: *"We're going to Ypres. They can't make us mad that way. We're all sick and tired of this inaction."*

On his birthday, Monday 19th, he went with the Battalion for a 'bathing parade': *"We had a dandy swim and ran about the grounds and summer houses and caves and bridges in our bare feet like a company of fairies. I had a gorgeous time."*

On Thursday 22nd he was in billets with orders to go into the line. Calvin was killed in action near St Julien.

It was written of him: *"Creeping up in the early morning to within fifty yards of the German trenches, they charged. Major Bennett, who led the charge, fell badly wounded and died later. Lieutenant C. W. Day fell dead with other officers and men. The regiment was decimated, but won the trenches, driving the Germans out. The 2nd Battalion held this position till relieved, though suffering from wounds and lack of food and water."*

A Memorial Service was held at Sydenham Street Methodist Church where every seat was taken, including in the galleries.

Calvin is commemorated in the Memorial Church of Harvard University.

Captain Charles Edward Mary De La Pasture, (Count de la Pasture)

1st Battalion Scots Guards

Died on Thursday 29th October 1914, aged 35

Commemorated on Panel 11.

Charles de la Pasture and his family coat of arms

Charles was born at Caley Hall, Otley, Yorkshire, on Monday 15th September 1879, eldest son of Gerard Gustavis Ducarel, 4th Marquess de la Pasture of Cefn, Usk, Monmouthshire and his second wife Countess Georgiana Mary (the title is French, its origins dating back to the 1304).

He was educated at St Edmund's College, from 1890 to 1892, followed by Downside from September 1892 to December 1895, then the Jesuit College, Wimbledon. On Monday 20th April 1914 Charles married Agatha, second daughter of Alexander Mosley, CMG, of Gibraltar. He held memberships of the Guards' and Travellers' Clubs.

Charles was gazetted from the

Militia in April 1900, promoted Lieutenant in April 1903, Captain in June 1907 and from that date until August 1910 he was ADC to General Sir Frederick Forestier Walker, Governor and Commander-in-Chief, Gibraltar.

Charles served in the South African War where he received the Queen's Medal with two clasps.

Charles left Farnborough on Thursday 13th August 1914 for Southampton and sailed for Le Havre on *SS Dunvegan Castle*, from where they were sent to a camp at Harfleur. The Battalion was entrained to northern France and took position overlooking the Mons battlefield. They did not become involved in any action with Sunday 23rd August was described as *"a day of rest"*! Before being ordered to move forward and take part in the battle, orders to retire were received. They continued to march southeastward until Sunday 6th September where they turned to engage the enemy.

He first saw real action at the Battle of Marne and whilst on the Aisne on the road to Vendresse on Friday 25th September a shell burst nearby knocking him off his feet (he was uninjured) — at the same time three others were blown to pieces by another shell. They did not leave the Aisne until Friday 16th October. The next day they marched to Fismes and entrained for the Ypres Salient.

Charles arrived at Hazebrouck on Sunday 18th October, marching to Poperinghe on Tuesday 20th into their billets for a night's rest. The next day they picked their way along the clogged roads of refugees through Elverdinghe and Boesinghe to Pilkem in support of the line in front of Langemarck. Here they had their first casualties on the Salient: four men killed and five wounded. On Sunday 25th Charles was sent with the Battalion to Zillebeke to help support the line south of Gheluvelt, arriving at 5.30am the next day. Each day the intensity of the battle increased, as did the casualties. Throughout the night of Tuesday 27th he was pinned down by shell fire, incessant rifle fire and very accurate sniping. On Thursday 29th the situation became dire with the British line being broken and the right flank badly beaten up. Reinforcements arrived and counter measures started immediately. The Scots Guards held on and repulsed an attack but at great cost — two hundred and forty casualties in a single day, including Charles who was killed between Becelaere and the Menin Road; he was first posted as missing then his death was confirmed.

Charles was Mentioned in Despatches that were gazetted on Thursday 14th January 1915.

Charles was recorded in Debretts Obituary — War Roll of Honour published in the 1921 edition.

His relation Captain Cecil Twining is commemorated on the Menin Gate, see below.

CAPTAIN THOMAS CECIL DE TRAFFORD

4th Battalion Royal Fusiliers

Died on Tuesday 10th November 1914, aged 33

Commemorated on Panel 8.

Thomas de Trafford

Thomas was born on Monday 3rd January 1881 son of the late Augustus Henry de Trafford and Gertrude Mary de Trafford (née Walmesley), of Haselour Hall, Tamworth, Staffordshire. He was cousin of Sir Humphrey de Trafford, Baronet. Thomas was educated at Stonyhurst College until 1899, where he played for the Football XI. He went to study engineering. In September 1914 he married Mary Winifrede Teresa de Trafford, (daughter of Sir Joseph Edward Radcliffe, 4th Baronet), of Rudding Park. Thomas was a keen sportsman, particularly enjoying polo, racing and hunting.

He had wanted to join the Navy and make it his career but was rejected due to poor eyesight. In 1901 Thomas was gazetted from the Militia to the Royal Fusiliers and went to join them in Bermuda. He served in Egypt, South Africa and India. During the Delhi Durbar he was part of the Guard of Honour to HM King George V and Queen Mary and was awarded the Durbar Medal.

At the outbreak of war Thomas was at the depôt in Hounslow and was sent to the Duke of York's School in Dover to help with training. On Monday 2nd November 1914 he went out to France and from there to the Salient. Just as Thomas arrived, on Wednesday 4th November, the Battalion was inspected at Bailleul by General Sir Horace Smith-Dorrien and in his speech to the men said: *"Now I must say a few words about your Colonel, who stands here with us. Of course you know quite well that he has recently been promoted to a brigade, but the work he has done with the regiment has been so valuable, and so well done, that we cannot spare him to take up the position he ought to be now occupying, and therefore, I am here to tell you — and I'm afraid it will be a great disappointment to you — that, instead of the seven or eights days' rest you were looking forward to at Bailleul, I am very much afraid that in another twenty-four or forty-eight hours you will find yourselves back in the trenches again."* On Friday 6th the Battalion, sure enough, found themselves back in the line a little east of Hooge on the Menin Road on the edge of Harenthage Wood. To their left were the Zouaves with the Northumberland Fusiliers on their right. On Saturday 7th the Zouaves came under heavy artillery fire and were destroyed. On Sunday 8th the barrage continued and various small penetrating

attacks were made against their line — all were repulsed. As the attacks continued Thomas was mortally wounded in Nonne Bosschen.
Thomas was recorded in Debretts Obituary — War Roll of Honour published in the 1921 edition.
In St Michael and St James Roman Catholic Church, Haunton, Staffordshire, a stained glass window was placed in his memory with the inscription: *"In loving memory of my dear husband Capt. Thomas Cecil De Trafford, Royal Fusiliers, wounded and missing November 11th. 1914. R.I.P."*
His brothers, Captain Henry de Trafford, died on Saturday 25th September 1915 and is commemorated on Loos Memorial and Lieutenant Augustus de Trafford, DSO, had died in the South African War.

2nd Battalion Duke of Wellington's, from Mons to the Aisne

LIEUTENANT DOUGLAS FENTON DE WEND

'A' Company,

2nd Battalion Duke of Wellington's (West Riding Regiment)

Died on Wednesday 11th November 1914, aged 24

Commemorated on Panel 20.

Douglas de Wend

Douglas was the twin son of Colonel Douglas Campbell de Wend (1st Battalion Duke of Wellington's Regiment) and Alice Woodroffe de Wend, of Poyle Park, Tongham, Surrey and Aislaby Hall, Slieghts, Yorkshire. He was educated at Wellington College from 1904 to 1908 and was a member of the Shooting VIII. He passed into RMC Sandhurst in 1908. Douglas was a keen footballer, enjoyed hunting and was a member of the Public Schools Club.
Douglas was commissioned in December 1909, promoted Lieutenant in January 1914.
On Thursday 13th August 1914 Douglas embarked on *HMT Gloucester* and sailed for Le Havre, arriving on Sunday 16th. He marched his men in the pouring rain to Bellville Camp, led by a local boy scout to show them the way. When they arrived they found a sea of mud and half the tents had collapsed in the storm. On Tuesday 18th he entrained for Landrecies, arriving at 6.00pm. Major General Sir Charles Fergusson, CB, MVO, DSO, visited the Battalion on Thursday 20th and addressed them. They marched through the Forêt de Mormal to Bavai and onward to the Belgian border, crossing it south of Athis. Captain Ozanne wrote: *"I shall always remember crossing the frontier line where many Belgians had collected, to greet us as it were, and who showered upon us boxes of matches, chocolates, and fruit etc. Being ahead of the Battalion I presume I came in for more than my share of these attentions; matches were particularly welcome as French matches were scare and of very bad quality."* They took the line on the Mons to Condé Canal where they engaged the Germans who, at one point, were able to cross the Canal at Lock 5. Douglas and the Battalion were able to drive them back. One of his fellow officers wrote: *"It was, I think, early in the afternoon when we saw the masses of German Infantry advancing on us, into which we poured as much rifle fire as we could, and it was not until I saw the platoon on my right retiring in extended order, just as one might see it on a field-day at home, that I realized that something was up. Very shortly one or two men came to our position running hard, saying that they had received orders to pass the message to retire."* At 11.00pm orders were received that a retirement was imminent. In the early hours they left the Canal and started to march south. On Monday 24th a short, sharp, fight took place lasting 90 minutes causing significant casualties to the Germans. The march to Le Cateau continued where they were in the rear-guard. Their next action took place at Néry on Tuesday 1st September where they captured a number of German cavalry — 'Death Head Hussars'.
On Sunday 6th the Retreat ended and they turned eastward, Lieutenant Ince wrote: *"I remember, Sunday, September 6th, was our turning point and a red-letter day, as it was on this day that we received orders to turn around*

and advance against the enemy instead of continuing our retreat. I remember Capt. Tidmarch and I walking up to the top of some ground near by, and having a glimpse of Paris some 15 kilometres to the south-west of us. We had an excellent view of the Eiffel Town and the dome of Nôtre Dame. I think it struck us somewhat forcibly then as to the distance we had covered since Mons in so short a time, and the fact that we had approached so near Paris. At 12 noon, on 6th we had a Church Parade in the square of Villeneuve, and in the afternoon we moved off in pursuit of the enemy."

On Thursday 15th they crossed the Aisne at Missy under artillery fire. He remained on the Aisne until Sunday 25th when the Battalion was withdrawn from the line and sent to Sermoise until Friday 2nd October.

On Friday 9th they arrived in Béthune and were sent into the line at La Bassée. On Thursday 22nd the Germans broke through and they remained under heavy artillery fire and constant attack, with the Germans coming within four hundred yards of their trenches. On Thursday 29th the Black Watch relieved them but it did not last long as they were required to support the Sikhs who were coming under pressure at Festubert. On Monday 2nd November Douglas left the line and marched to Estaires where he was taken by bus to Bailleul. From there he marched into Belgium, arriving in Ypres on Thursday 5th November at 5.00pm and took billets in *'Hermitage Château'*. Colonel Harrison recorded: *"Marched 6.45 a.m. Were delayed three-quarts of an hour at Dranouter, where a French Cavalry Division passed us. About noon heavy artillery fire was going on in front of us, so the whole Brigade turned left-handed and we spread ourselves out over a largish area behind some woods and hedges, where we stayed for two hours, when the shelling ceased. Roads very bad and knee-deep in mud except on the pavee. Arrived Ypres 5 p.m. As we passed the fine old Town Hall and Cathedral it looked splendid in the twilight, and though a few shells had been dropped in various buildings in the town there had actually been no damage done to these buildings. Later on, however, I believe the greatest part of this pace has been destroyed. Marched on till 7.30 p.m., and took over the trenches from the General Commanding 22nd Brigade, of which only some 900 men remained. An attack about 10 p.m. died out, and the fire trenches were taken over by the Bedfords and Cheshires. We remained in support in edge of wood."* From 9.00am on Sunday 8th the Battalion came under heavy shell fire and the Germans counter-attacked, retaking some lost trenches until they were ordered to retire. On Monday 9th, at 4.30pm, he was sent to support the Lincolns and on Tuesday 10th he was in reserve with 'A' Company and was then sent into the fray against the Prussian Guard when he was killed.

Colonel Harrison recorded for the day: *"Exceptionally heavy shelling started 7 a.m., practically all shrapnel, covering the whole position from the firing line to the reserves, continuing the bombardment till 8 a.m., when it abated. At this time a message came to me by an orderly from Lieut. R. O. D. Carey, saying; 'Am very hard pressed but will hang on as long as possible.' I then advanced with the rest of my force. We found the Germans had advanced past the Veldhoek Château, but we managed to repulse them, gaining back the ground, being nearly as far as our old firing line, which Lieut. R. O. D. Carey with D Company had been driven out of. We could have actually regained these trenches if the troops on the right and left of us had been up, but in this position behind a small rise in the ground our right rested on the Ypres to Menin Road, the next troops being 300 yards in rear on the south side of the road. On our left a company of the Zouaves occupied a position between us and the next British troops on our left, but immediately after the advance, in which they materially assisted, they vacated the position, thus leaving both our flanks exposed. At 10 a.m. I sent back a message saying I could retake my original trenches if I had another company in support, but got no reply till 3 p.m. I also sent two more messages, which, however, were never received. By this time we had dug ourselves in under a small bank some 60 yards from the Germans, who were occupying our old trenches. During the action, lasting the whole day, Lieut. Thackeray had command of the reserve company, and owing to his energy and gallantry in pushing forward, not only his own men but also a number of Zouaves who were on our left, contributed to our success. Capt. H. K. Umfreville, my Adjutant, although wounded, continued for several hours looking after the left flank."*

In Beverley Minister, Humberside, a brass plaque was placed in his memory with the inscription: *"To the glory of God and in loving memory of Lieut. Douglas Fenton De Wend of the 2nd Batt. Duke of Wellington Regt. who after serving through The Battles of The Marne, The Aisne and Bethune fell mortally wounded whilst leading his company against The Prussian Guard in the 1st great Battle of Ypres 10th November 1914, aged 21 years. Dulce Est Pro Patria Mori.*

In dear memory also of Cyril George De Wend twin brother of the above who died at sea off Southampton on August 18th 1902, aged 12 years."

In York Minster a wooden chair was placed in the Duke of Wellington's Regimental Chapel with a brass plaque inscribed: *"Lieut. D. F. De Wend, 11th November 1914."*

In St Margaret's Church, Aislaby, North Yorkshire, a brass plaque was placed in his memory with the inscription: *"To the glory of God & in loving memory of Lieut. Douglas Fenton De Wend of the 2nd Duke of Wellington's Regt. who, having served through The Battle of The Marne, The Aisne & Bethune was killed in action at the first great Battle of Ypres on November 11th 1914. The tower clock, given by his mother and sisters, was started on the anniversary of his death 1915."*

Lieutenant Colonel Edmund 'Ned' Deacon

Essex Yeomanry formerly 1st (King's) Dragoon Guards
Died on Thursday 13th May 1915, aged 43
Commemorated on Panel 5.

Ned Deacon

Ned was married to Sybil Deacon, of Sloe House, Halstead, Essex. He was educated at Malvern College from 1888 to 1890. Ned was the Master of the Essex Foxhounds.

He joined the King's Dragoon Guards in 1892, he was appointed Adjutant from 1897 to 1899 and then retired from the Army. Ned joined the Militia in 1901 where he commanded 'B' (Halstead) Squadron, promoted second in command in November 1908 and Lieutenant Colonel in February 1909.

On Friday 7th August 1914 Ned sent out telegrams to all his officers, it contained one word: *"Mobilise"*. He mobilized the Essex Yeomanry at Ipswich where they were also billeted. They were part of the Eastern Mounted Brigade under Brigadier General Hodgson, CVO. Ned moved their billets to Melton where they were inspected on Tuesday 10th November by HM King George V and two days later he received the orders for taking his men to France. They entrained on Sunday 29th November at Woodbridge for Southampton embarking for Le Havre. Upon arrival they marched into a muddy camp. After the men settled down he and the officers were invited for a dinner by Colonel Harry Cooper, CMG, Vice Chairman of the Essex County Territorial Force Association, who was based in the town.

On Thursday 3rd December Ned entrained his men for St Omer and were greeted by snow, sleet and rain as they marched to Wardrecques. After a week of further training they marched through Hazebrouck to Grand Sec Bois. Three days later the Regiment got close to the front line when they went into support at Locre during an attack at Wytschaete but did not see any action.

On Wednesday 27th January 1916 Ned ordered the men to 'stand to' as it was the Kaiser's birthday and it was thought an attack was be launched but it did not materialise. In the afternoon Ned, with pride, paraded the Yeomanry for inspection by Field Marshal Sir John French who was accompanied by HRH The Prince of Wales. The next day they moved billets to Mount Croquet. However, before they left Grand Sec Bois a farewell dinner was held with the local dignitaries where Ned thanked the local population for their kindness and help since they had based in their village.

On Wednesday 3rd February the Regiment went to Ypres by motor bus, via Hazebrouck, Steenvoorde, Poperinghe and Vlamertinghe. They were billeted in a school along the Menin Road. Ned sent Major Hill with 'A' Squadron into the line immediately where some of the German lines were only twelve yards apart. Whilst in their billets in the school a periscope was constructed from an old downpipe. It was over twenty foot long and when finished was camouflaged with bark to look like a tree. It was taken into the line where it was a popular and useful addition to them and those who followed them in the line.

HRH Prince Arthur of Connaught

The Battle of Neuve-Chapelle commenced and the Essex Yeomanry was ordered to 'stand to': however, they were not called upon to go into the line. HRH Prince Arthur of Connaught organised a Brigade Marathon that the Yeomanry won, Ned was presented with a silver cup by the Prince. During the last week of the month HRH The Prince of Wales was attached to the 10th Hussars and Ned was invited to dine with him.

On Friday 23rd April orders were received to move into the Salient. The next day they went up to the area of Vlamertinghe. On Wednesday 5th May Ned led his men to Brielen, arriving at 7.30pm. He took a party to the Yser Canal and organised the digging of trenches that was completed by 1.30am — they had dug under light emanating from Ypres that was in flames. On Friday 7th the Yeomanry returned to their old billets at Mount Croquet. On Wednesday 12th Ned took the men to construct a communication trench near Potijze. They managed to undertake the majority of the work as digging could only take place under the cover of darkness and even then heavy machine-gun and rifle fire poured down on them.

At 4.00am on Thursday 13th a German preliminary barrage commenced; Ned and his men were in the support trenches on the northeastern edge of the gardens of Potijze Château. By 9.00am the line was beginning to give way and retirement was the only option. At lunchtime Ned received orders to move forward and relieve the Blues and 10th Hussars who had been able to move forward. Ned, together with the squadron leaders, met Brigadier General Charles Bulkeley Johnson*, in his Brigade HQ in the château gardens. (* General Bulkeley Johnson was killed on Wednesday 11th April 1917 and is buried in Gouy-en-Artois Communal Cemetery Extension). It was agreed that a counter-attack would be mounted at 2.15pm. Ned sent Major Buxton with two scouts to report to Lieutenant Colonel Robert Shearman of the 10th Hussars (who was killed on Saturday 15th May 1915 and is buried in Vlamertinghe Military Cemetery) that his men were coming up on his right flank. As the Yeomanry advanced, at the point of the bayonet, they were being mown down. Lieutenant Colonel Shearman ordered them to halt and lay down, which they did. Shortly afterward the Germans were seen leaving their post and retiring so the Yeomanry advanced at speed taking heavy casualties. During the attack Ned was killed and his body was never found.

Second Lieutenant Frank Dean

2nd Battalion King's Royal Rifle Corps

Died on Saturday 31st October 1914, aged 38

Commemorated on Panel 51.

Frank was born at home on Monday 28th August 1876, son of Francis and Sarah Dean, of Widnes, Cheshire. He was educated locally. Frank was married to Ada L Dean, of 47 Surrenden Road, Folkestone, Kent. He was a good shot and a cross-country runner.

Frank enlisted in October 1898, eventually becoming Colour Sergeant in September 1910. He served in the South African War including the Relief of Ladysmith.

Frank was sent out to Le Havre, arriving on Friday 14th August 1914 and entraining the next night for Le Nouvion. He was sent south of Mons where the Battalion could see and hear the action but were not themselves engaged in any action. On Monday 24th the Battalion retired via Le Cateau and the march south continued until Sunday 6th September when the retreat stopped and at last they were ordered to turn east to face the Germans. Frank saw his first real action on the Chemin des Dames, close to Moussy, where the Battalion took considerable casualties although they repulsed a strong German counter-attack. Whilst on the Aisne Frank received a field commission on Thursday 1st October 1914 only a few days before they were relieved and entrained for the Ypres Salient.

He arrived in Cassel on Sunday 18th followed by Ypres on Wednesday 21st where they were sent to billets in Boesinghe. He went into the line and assisted in a push to recapture lost ground. On Thursday 29th Frank was in front of Gheluvelt when they attacked the village, the Battalion taking heavy casualties. The Germans attacked in force on Saturday 31st and during the fierce battle Frank was killed.

Frank was Mentioned in Despatches on Monday 7th September 1914.

Lieutenant Denis Deane

'C' Company, 2nd Battalion

Royal Warwickshire Regiment

Died on Saturday 24th October 1914, aged 18

Commemorated on Panel 8

Denis Deane

Denis was the son of Major A Deane (Royal Warwickshire Regiment) and Mrs Deane, of Ellerslie, Fleet, Hampshire. He was educated at Wellington College from 1910 to 1913 and passed into RMC Sandhurst. He played in the First XV at both School and Sandhurst.

Denis was based in Malta at the outbreak of war and the Battalion was ordered home, arriving on Saturday 19th September 1914. After a period of training and re-equipping he sailed to Zeebrugge, arriving on Tuesday 6th October. Denis entrained for Ghent on Friday 9th where they supported a battalion of French Marines four miles outside the city. With the cover for the retreat of the Belgian Army complete, orders to withdraw and march south-east were received.

Late on Sunday 11th they commenced a hard series of route marches via Thielt and Roeselare to Ypres, arriving on Wednesday 14th. Two days later Denis was moved with the Battalion to take the line at Zonnebeke. On Sunday 18th they moved forward to Becelaere and Kruiseik where the next day an attack on Menin commenced. They passed through Dadizeele, on to Kezelberg and were advancing upon Klijthoek. The advance was progressing well when news came that large numbers of Germans were advancing from the direction of Iseghem. Orders for a retirement were issued and they returned to billets in Zonnebeke, suffering several casualties from shell fire. During the morning of Tuesday 20th Denis marched his men to Harenthage Château where he was in reserve. During the afternoon the Germans launched an attack to the east of Zonnebeke and the 2nd Battalion was ordered to support the line. The Coldstream Guards relieved them at midnight and Denis returned to billets in Zonnebeke. Another attack took place the next day and the Battalion was again called to take the line, this time at the cross-roads on the main road east of Zonnebeke. Throughout Thursday 22nd they consolidated their trenches but were not able to put them to good use as they were sent on Friday 23rd to Polygon Wood where the Germans had broken the line. Early on Saturday 24th a counter-attack was mounted and Denis was killed leading his men against a small farmhouse.

Lieutenant James Owen Cunninghame Dennis

12th Battery 35th Brigade Royal Field Artillery

Died on Saturday 24th October 1914, aged 26

Commemorated on Panel 5.

James was born on Sunday 5th August 1888 son of the late Colonel and Mrs Dennis, of Cumberland Mansions, London W. He was educated at Malvern College from 1903 to 1907 where he was a Prefect, Head of House, a member of the Shooting VIII and the House XV. He passed into RMA Woolwich.

James was gazetted Friday 23rd July 1909 and promoted Lieutenant on Tuesday 23rd July 1912.

James went out with the BEF to Zeebrugge landing on Tuesday 6th October. Before they could be deployed to defend Antwerp the city had fallen. He rode with his guns to take part in the First Battle of Ypres. After only a week of service in the sector James was killed in action whilst in the front line directing his battery.

In December 1914 *'The Malvernian'* wrote: *"Owen Davies was killed by a shell when he was directing his battery fire from the infantry trenches. His Major states that he considered him to be his smartest officer. Throughout the time that he was at the front, he displayed unflinching bravery This was quite in accordance with what we noted in him at school."*

Captain Harry Stuart Dennison

Princess Patricia's Canadian Light Infantry (Eastern Ontario Regiment)

Died on Saturday 8th May 1915, aged 30

Commemorated on Panel 10.

Harry was the son of Ralph Abercrombie Dennison and E Helen E McTaggart Dennison, of 90 Warrior Square, Street, Leonards-on-Sea, Sussex. He was married to Blanche Dennison (née Darcy).

Harry joined the Regiment in November 1914. The Princess Patricia's were inspected by HM King George V and Field Marshal Lord Kitchener on Wednesday 16th December before leaving for Southampton on Sunday 20th embarking on *SS Cardiganshire* at 7.00pm for Le Havre. After a night in camp they entrained for Arques and marched to Blaringhem. From Christmas Eve, for ten days, they dug trenches between Mount Croquet and Steenbeek. On New Year's Day Field Marshal Sir John French visited them in their camp and wished them well for their future battles and taking the line. On Tuesday 5th they marched to Méteren moving onto Dickebusch the next day from where they relieved the French at Vierstraat. Until the end of March he remained on tours of duty in the southern sector until he was sent into reserve at Poperinghe. On Monday 5th April he marched

A postcard of Méteren in 1915

via Vlamertinghe to billets in Ypres where he remained for two days before being sent to Bellewaarde Lake. On Friday 9th he moved to Polygon Wood for a further two days before being sent to Vlamertinghe into reserve. On Monday 12th the camp was bombed by a Zeppelin and the next day General Plumer visited them and took the opportunity of inspecting the bomb damage. On Wednesday 14th he returned to Polygon Wood and relieved the Rifle Brigade where he remained for three days and following relief he was sent to the Infantry Barracks until Tuesday 20th. The Germans launched their gas attack on Thursday 22nd and any thought of relief from the line was put to one side. Over the next eight days in Polygon Wood they came under heavy artillery fire and more than eighty casualties were taken. On Tuesday 4th May they returned to Bellewaarde Ridge at 3.00am and occupied a series of newly dug trenches that were attacked by the Germans at dawn. On Saturday 8th the Battle of Bellewaarde Ridge commenced. The Germans demolished the front line but could not advance any further. The battle was intense and during the day Harry was killed, the Regiment taking three hundred and ninety-two casualties during the action.

His only brother, Lieutenant Ralph Dennison was killed the next day, Sunday 9th May 1915, and is commemorated on the Le Touret Memorial.

177873 Private Russell Smith Deuel

87th Battalion Canadian Infantry (Quebec Regiment)

Died on Thursday 28th June 1917, aged 19

Commemorated on Panel 30.

Russell Deuel

Russell was born at Des Rivières Station, Quebec, on Wednesday 6th October 1897, son of William R and Mary Ann Deuel, of Cowansville. He was educated at the Cowansville Academy, Quebec. He joined the Commerce Bank on Wednesday 8th October 1913 from St John's Branch in Quebec.

Russell volunteered in Montreal on

Monday 8th November 1915 where he was described as a Congregationalist being 5ft 10¾in tall, a chest, dark complexion, blue eyes and dark brown hair. When he enlisted he was suffering with an ingrowing toe nail that was *"operated on with success, now fit"* on Monday 29th November.

Russell arrived in England was sent for training at *'Bramshott Camp'*. On Friday 11th August 1916 the Battalion let for Southampton and embarked on *SS Archangel* and sailed to Le Havre. They arrived at 7.15am on Saturday 12th and marched to No 4 Rest Camp. At 6.30am on Tuesday 15th they entrained for Houpre, arriving at 9.00am the next morning and were sent to *'Connaught Camp'* for three days when they moved to *'Alberta Camp'*. From Saturday 19th the Battalion started instruction in the front line attached to the 26th Battalion near Voormezeele. They continued to serve in the sector until Sunday 17th September when they were relieved and after moving via a series of route marches from *'Ontario Camp'* to *'Victoria Camp'* they were sent to Hazebrouck, followed by Arques, and Zouafques. They entrained for Doullens and were billeted at Hemp arriving at 4.30pm on Tuesday 3rd October. The Battalion marched to the Brickfields in Albert from where they went to bivouac at *'Tara Hill'*. On Tuesday 17th they relieved the 54th Battalion in the trenches in front of Courcelette at *'Regina Trench'*. At 12.06pm on Saturday 21st they attacked across a front of three hundred and seventy-five yards and by 12.15pm *'Regina Trench'* was captured. They consolidated the position and remained in the line until 10.30pm on Monday 23rd when they were relieved by the 75th Battalion and took the dug-outs at Pozières. After a week they returned to billets in Albert.

Russell continued on tours of duty until mid-March 1917 when the Battalion was sent for training at *'St*

Lawrence Camp' at Château de la Haie. The took part in the Battle of Vimy Ridge, part of the Battle of Arras that commenced on Monday 9th April. Following the battle they returned to Château de la Haie and *'Niagra Camp'* for further training. On Thursday 10th May the Battalion returned to the line at *'Zouave Valley'* where they came under attack throughout the night. Throughout Saturday 12th Russell and his comrades dug in and consolidated their position whilst under constant observation by the German aeroplanes. During Monday 14th the Germans reduced the intensity of their artillery barrage and took the opportunity of collecting their dead under a Red Cross flag. Late on Monday 21st Russell was relieved and returned to *'Niagra Camp'* where they were all able to have a hot bath and were issued with clean clothes. Throughout Tuesday 22nd they rested and from Wednesday 23rd commenced training. From Wednesday 6th June they returned to the line around Lens and prepared for an attack that commenced against Coulotte and Fosse 7 on Friday 8th. The attack was successful and they captured two machine-guns, a Lewis gun, two Granatenwerfers and more than one hundred prisoners. On Tuesday 12th the Battalion was relieved and returned to Camp for further training until Tuesday 19th when they went into Reserve at *'Coburg Street'* and relieved the 46th Battalion. Russell was on a working party when he was badly wounded and taken prisoner. He died as a prisoner of war in a German hospital.

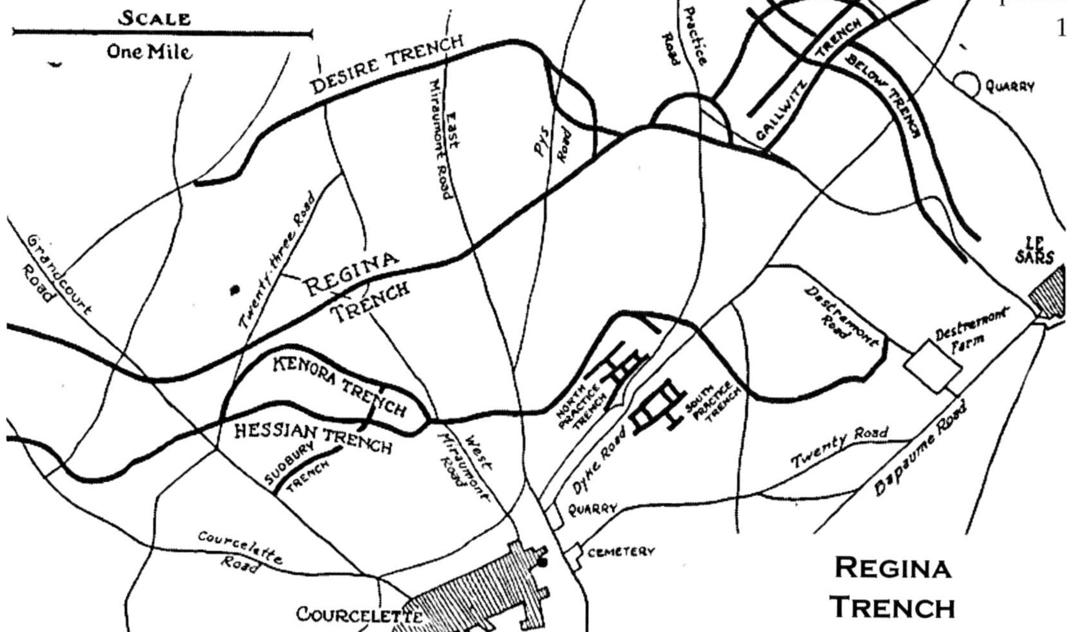

8562
Company Quarter Master Serjeant John Charles Monro Devis

2nd Regiment (Infantry) South African Infantry
Died on Saturday 20th April 1918, aged 36
Commemorated on Panel 15.

Charles was married to Bessie Lavinia Devis, of 18 Kingsbury Street, Marlborough, Wiltshire.
His son, Private John Devis, died on Friday 24th September 1915 and is commemorated on the Menin Gate, see below.
Charles served in Egypt before sailing to Marseilles in early 1916. He trained intensively in trench warfare for two months before taking the line. He saw action and survived The Battle of the Somme, The Butte de Warlencourt, The Battles of Arras and Third Ypres. On Saturday 1st December 1917 Charles was moved to Gouzeaucourt when he was involved in some intense fighting. On Sunday 17th February 1918 he attended the unveiling of the wooden cross at Delville Wood and a drumhead service was held. The *'Ludendorff Offensive'* started to push the Regiment back from Friday 22nd March 1918. On Wednesday 27th March he was sent to Candas to entrain for Abeele, arriving on Tuesday 2nd April. On Monday 8th Charles was sent to hutments near La Clytte from where he took the line at Messines to Wytschaete that was under severe pressure. They came under heavy attack on Tuesday 16th that pushed them back from the villages. During a counter-attack Charles was killed.

11057 Private John Albert Devis

1st Battalion Wiltshire Regiment
Died on Friday 24th September 1915, aged 21
Commemorated on Panel 53.

John was the son of John Charles and Bessie Lavinia Devis, of 18 Kingsbury Street, Marlborough, Wiltshire.
The Battalion was sent out to France at the outbreak of war, landing in Rouen on Friday 14th August 1914. They proceeded to Mons from where they took part in The Retreat, the Battles of the Marne and Aisne. They transferred north and took part in the battles in October 1914 around La Bassée before crossing the border to take part in the defence of the southern sector of the Salient around Messines. John served on tours of duty until Spring 1915 when he became involved in the Second Battle of Ypres, taking part in the Battle of Bellewaarde and Battle of Hooge. John was in the line at Bellewaarde, prior to the battle that would commence the next day, when he was killed.
His father, Company Quartermaster Serjeant, Charles Devis, died on Saturday 20th April 1918, see above.

Second Lieutenant
Guy Francis Ormand Devitt

7th Battalion Rifle Brigade
Died on Friday 30th July 1915, aged 23
Commemorated on Panel 46.

Guy was born in Harrow on Thursday 28th July 1892, son of Andrew and Jane Dales Devitt, of Coldshott, Oxted, Surrey. He was educated at Marlborough College from September 1906 as a member of Littlefield, and went up to Gonville and Caius College, Cambridge, in 1912.
Guy trained at Aldershot and Elstead. He arrived in Boulogne on Wednesday 19th May 1915 and was sent to Watten for further training. Guy led his men into the line for their first tour of duty and remained in and out of the line without being involved in any major action until mid-July. On Thursday 22nd July a mine was blown in front of Hooge, Guy went into the line on Friday 23rd, the relief being delayed by a day due to the blowing of the mine. The Battalion spent their first twenty-four hours rebuilding the line that was completely undone when the Germans blew their own mine on Saturday 24th! The Germans followed the blowing of their mine with an attack that Guy and the men repulsed with support from the British artillery. Shortly before midnight on Friday 29th the 8th Battalion arrived to relieve the 7th who wearily marched to Vlamertinghe, arriving at 3.45am. The Battalion was exhausted after the particularly difficult tour and gratefully collapsed into their beds. It did not last long as an hour later they were roused. The Germans had mounted a terrific attack against Hooge, against the 8th in particular, and the 7th were needed for a counter-attack. Without food or any proper rest Guy and the Battalion returned from whence they had only just arrived. *En route*, Colonel Heriot-Maitland halted them whilst he attended headquarters in the ramparts of Ypres to receive his orders for the counter-attack. The Battalion had left Vlamertinghe at 7.00am but did not reach their lines until 1.30pm, so difficult was their move forward during the raging battle. At 2.45pm they moved forward against the German lines. The battle was fierce, the plans were sketchy in the extreme and not well thought through. As Guy led his men forward from *'Zouave Wood'* he found the wire uncut and progress was impossible: orders were received for them to dig in and hold their position. German machine-gun fire was tremendously fierce from their high position on the ridge. In the infernal mêlée Guy was killed.
In St Swithun's Church, East Grinstead, West Sussex, an altar screen was created in his memory with the inscription:
Left-hand screen: *"To the glory of God and in the memory of 2nd Lieut. Guy Francis Ormond Devitt, Rifle Brigade, aged 23."*
Right-hand screen: *"Who was mortally wounded at Hooge in Flanders whilst leading his platoon July 30th 1915."*

Lieutenant Henry Lyman Devlin

75th Battalion Canadian Infantry
(Central Ontario Regiment)
Died on Saturday 9th September 1916, aged 20
Commemorated on Panel 30.

Henry was born in Stayner, Ontario, on Saturday 18th January 1896, son of Samuel L and Margaret J Devlin, of 71 Delaware Avenue, Toronto. He was educated at Stayner Public School followed by St Andrew's College from 1911 to 1912. He studied at University College, University of Toronto, and at the same time worked as a journalist with the *'Toronto Star'*. Henry was a Lieutenant in the 9th Mississauga Horse, the 35th Regiment of the local Militia.

Henry Devlin

Henry left his studies and work to volunteer in Toronto on Thursday 29th July 1915. After training he sailed to England in March 1916 and was sent for training at *'Bramshott Camp'*. Training continued until 3.25am on Friday 11th August when he paraded with his men to march to Liphook railway station. They entrained at 5.30am for the Western Station in Southampton where they embarked on *HMT Mona's Queen* bound for Le Havre. They started boarding at 5.00pm and the ship left at 8.00pm arriving at 5.00am the next morning. By 10.15am disembarkation was completed and the Battalion was marched to *'Halle No 3'* where they arrived at 11.47am and remained there for twelve hours. They marched to the station and left for Hopoutre at 3.00am on Sunday 13th, arriving at 5.00am the next morning. After a short march they were billeted in farm buildings along the Poperinghe road where they rested for the rest of the day. During the afternoon of Tuesday 15th they marched to the area close to where Lijssenthoek Military Cemetery is today and rested in a field close to an estaminet. During the evening buses arrived and took some of the men to *'Café Belge'* at Dickebusch where they went into the line near Voormezeele. During the Wednesday 16th their first casualty was taken, Private W E Reed was wounded, and the next day Private G S Rowe was invalided with a self-inflicted wound. Henry continued on tours of duty until he accompanied Lieutenant Howard and a party on a night raid; they were spotted and he was killed by machine-gun fire — Lieutenant Francis Howard was mortally wounded and is buried in Pont-du-Hem Military Cemetery, La Gorgue. Initially both officers were listed as wounded and missing, however they were both buried by the Germans.

Café Belge

489796 Private Christian Fraser Dick

Princess Patricia's Canadian Light Infantry
(Eastern Ontario Regiment)
Died on Tuesday 30th October 1917, aged 25
Commemorated on Panel 10.

Christian Dick

Christian was born at Brookville, St John County, New Brunswick, on Tuesday 10th May 1892, son of Elizabeth W Dick, of 980 Dougall Avenue, Windsor, Ontario, and the late John Montgomery Dick. He was educated locally. On Monday 22nd November 1915 he joined the Commerce Bank, Saskatoon Branch.

Christian volunteered at Saskatoon on Wednesday 29th March 1916 where he was described as Presbyterian, 5ft 5in tall, with a 35in chest, a medium complexion, brown eyes, dark brown hair, three vaccination marks on his left arm, a mole on this back and a scar on his head.

Christian was sent for training before sailing for England where he continued to train until he left to join the Regiment with a draft. He trained for the Battle of Arras which commenced on Monday 9th April 1917. The Regiment attacked La Folie Wood: they came under heavy attack from Hill 145 with the Regiment taking heavy losses after the initial advance. During the next day the 4th Canadian Division took Hill 145 which helped relieve the pressure for the rest of the day. Late on Wednesday 11th the Regiment relieved to *'La Motte Camp'* at Villers-au-Bois. Training commenced on Sunday 15th at Gouy-Servins for five days until being sent Vimy Ridge. After a further period of training they were sent to *'Pylones Shelters'* at Vimy on Monday 7th May where Christian was wounded in the hand on Thursday 10th. Tours of duty and training continued in the sector until early October when the move north began.

On Tuesday 16th October they marched to Savy and entrained for Caëstre and were billeted at Le Peuplier.

On Saturday 22nd HRH The Duke of Connaught inspected the Battalion at Borre, the day before they entrained to Ypres and were billeted in the ruins. During the night the Germans made a number of sorties over the town and bombed it continuously for the next thirty-six hours. Christian was employed on working parties until Sunday 28th when the Regiment was sent to Gravenstafel at 3.00pm ready for their attack that would

Passchendaele - the Canadians attack

take place against Meetscheele Ridge. At 5.50am on Tuesday 30th the advance moved forward from *'Snipe Hall'* and *'Bellevue'*. *'Duck Lodge'* was captured and during the day Lieutenant Hugh McKenzie and Sergeant George Mullin were each awarded the Victoria Cross for the capture of a pill-box. The battle was particularly heavy, made worse by the terrible muddy conditions, and Christian was killed. (Lieutenant Hugh McKenzie is commemorated on the Menin Gate, see below.)

Sergeant Mullin, VC

Lieutenant George Bairnsfather Dickinson

3rd Battalion East Lancashire Regiment

Died on Monday 3rd May 1915, aged 29

Commemorated on Panel 34.

George was born on Monday 4th January 1886 son of the late William and Helen Isabella Dickinson.

George was sent for training before leaving for France and joining the Battalion with a draft. George was killed in action at Wieltje.

A cross was raised at All Saints Church, King Weston, Somerset that reads: *"Pro Patria. The churchyard cross was restored to the memory of Lieutenant Colonel Hugh C. Dickinson, Somerset Light Infantry and King's African Rifles, died at Dar-es-Salaam British East Africa, December 18th 1918 aged 34 and of Lieutenant George B. Dickinson, East Lancashire Regiment, fell at Ypres, May 3rd 1915 aged 29."*

His brother, Lieutenant Colonel Hugh Dickinson, is buried in Dar es Salem Cemetery, Tanzania.

637 Private Leonard Taylor Dickinson

North Somerset Yeomanry

Died on Tuesday 17th November 1914, aged 28

Commemorated on Panel 5.

Leonard was the son of Mr and Mrs J L Dickinson, of Weston-Super-Mare, Somerset. He went up to Queen's College, Oxford, in 1903, graduating with a BA. He was admitted as a solicitor in April 1911 and joined J L Dickinson & Sons of Weston-super-Mere.

On Wednesday 12th August 1914 he volunteered and enlisted being sent for training prior to leaving for France. Leonard was killed by a shell whilst at Vlamertinghe.

Captain Ronald Francis Bickersteth Dickinson

'C' Company, 10th Battalion

The King's (Liverpool Regiment)

Died on Wednesday 16th June 1915, aged 27

Commemorated on Panel 6.

Ronald Dickinson

Ronald was born at 23 Abercromby Square, Liverpool, on Thursday 19th January 1888, second son of George and Mary Florence Dickinson, of Red How, Lamplugh, Cumberland. He was educated at Rugby School from 1901 to 1905 as a member of Steel. Ronald was admitted as a solicitor in 1910 with Hill, Dickinson & Co, of Liverpool. He was commissioned to the Liverpool Scottish in 1906 and promoted to Captain in 1912.

At the outbreak of war Ronald was mobilized and went to Southampton where the Battalion embarked on *SS Maidan*, sailing for Le Havre on Sunday 1st November. They went by train to St Omer, a journey that took twenty-seven hours! At Abbeville their Medical Officer, Lieutenant Noel Chavasse, who was to win the Victoria Cross and Bar, shocked the locals when he took a cold bath in the water tank that supplied the locomotives! They moved onto St Omer and marched the three miles to Blendecques where they were billeted, and went into training. On Tuesday 17th November the Battalion had the sad honour of providing an officer and twenty men to line the Place Gambetta, leading to the Hôtel de Ville, where Field Marshal Lord Robert's body was taken for a memorial service before being returned to England.

Noel Chavasse

On Tuesday 20th November they moved to Hazebrouck and on Wednesday 21st to Bailleul. The march to Bailleul was a difficult one over frozen roads and many men slipped on the ice injuring themselves due to the weight of their packs, and many motor vehicles slipped off the road into ditches and had to be pulled out. However, when they arrived at the town they were given good billets and everyone enjoyed being in a busy town with a sufficiency of amusements for all! On Wednesday 25th Ronald marched out of the town with his men to be paraded in front of HRH The Prince of Wales and General Sir Horace Smith-Dorrien who addressed them. Two days later Ronald was in the line at Kemmel. On Thursday 3rd December he paraded his men again for a Royal Inspection at Westoutre, this time by HM King George V accompanied by HRH The Prince of Wales. They continued to serve in the front line which was not a happy prospect for anyone as they were standing knee-deep in freezing water, one of Ronald's men was asked by Serjeant Ferguson: *"Well, Barker, are you the sentry here?"*, the reply being; *"No, I'm a bulrush!"*. At Christmas they were out of the line, so did not participate in the Christmas Truce but on New Year's Eve they were back in the line. They remained in the Kemmel area — whilst at rest in Bailleul, on Thursday 28th February 1915, the 6th Kings arrived in the town and they had the opportunity to meet up.

HRH The Prince of Wales

In early March Ronald was moved into the Ypres Salient, serving at Zillebeke. Whilst in action on Hill 60 on Monday 15th March 1915 Lance Corporal Rawlins went out putting up barbed wire when he was mortally wounded by a sniper. (Lance Corporal Bertram Rawlins is buried in Ramparts Cemetery, Lille Gate.) Ronald, commanding 'X' Company, went to fetch the wounded NCO but was forcibly held back by his men; so four of his men went out and successfully brought him in, Private Howarth was awarded the Distinguished Conduct Medal for the action, the first to be awarded in the Battalion. Ronald and his men were under murderous artillery fire on *'Slaughter Hill'* the section of Hill 60 near the *'Spoilbank'*, suffering eight killed on Thursday 1st April. Two days later he was relieved and sent into the line at St Eloi.

At 4.00pm on Tuesday 15th June Ronald marched with his men from Busseboom and took position in *'Cambridge Road'*, ready for the attack and The Battle of Hooge. The Germans, aware that an attack was imminent, shelled them remorselessly. The British artillery opened up at 2.50am on Wednesday 16th and continued until 4.15am (although some pauses were included to confuse the enemy as to when the attack was to commence). Ronald was commanding 'X' Company, fighting in the front line near Hooge and assisted in the capture of four German trenches but reinforcements were not forthcoming and the Germans were preparing a counter-attack. Ronald was wounded in six places during the German attack and he was captured by them, by the small pond at Bellewaarde Farm, dying shortly afterwards. His men insisted on remaining with him but just before he was captured Ronald ordered them to retire and not be captured too.

His Colonel wrote: *"He was absolutely lion-hearted, and I think all will agree that he was pre-eminent in a battn. which I am proud to say numbers many brave men in its ranks. It was my duty on many occasions during the winter months to tramp round the front line trenches at night, and invariably Ronald was to be found wherever a dirty or dangerous job had to be done."*

One of his men wrote: *"Time and again when any of his men were lying wounded outside the trench, he ordered his men to keep under cover while he himself ran the greatest risk in bringing the wounded in. If anyone deserved the V.C. it was Capt. Ronald Dickinson; he had won it over and over again. He was a little god to his men."*

One of his fellow officers wrote: *"The finest man that ever set foot on French soil. I, and in fact all the men of X Company, would have followed the Captain to the end of the earth."*

He was buried by the Germans near Bellewaarde.

Ronald was Mentioned in Despatches on Monday 31st May 1915.

In St George's Memorial Church, Ypres, a brass plaque in his memory has been erected that reads *"In memory of Capt. Ronald F B Dickinson, Kings Liverpool Regt., Liverpool Scottish, killed in action at Bellewaarde, 16 June 1915"*.

Two almshouses were named after Ronald and his brother, a plaque is placed on each house with their name and details of the battle in which they were killed.

His brother, Captain, Alan Dickinson, died on Saturday 1st June 1918 and is buried in Houchin British Cemetery.

Lieutenant Alan James Dickson

2nd Battalion Highland Light Infantry

Died on Saturday 14th November 1914, aged 22

Commemorated on Panel 38.

Alan was born at Laurencekirk on Sunday 28th February 1892, son of Mr Patrick Dickson, JP, and Mrs R I Dickson, of Sunnyside House, Montrose. He was educated at Carigfield Preparatory School and Fettes College from 1906 as a member of Carrington then went up to Merton College, Oxford, graduating with a BA in 1914.

Alan was commissioned in July 1914 and promoted Lieutenant in November. Alan left Aldershot at 3.30am on Thursday 13th August 1914 and sailed to Boulogne

where he entrained for northern France. On Monday 24th he saw action near Paturages during the Battle of Mons. Alan marched with his men two hundred and thirteen miles south for the next thirteen days. On Sunday 6th September he was ordered to turn and engage the Germans. Two days later, after crossing the Petit Morin, he was involved in a brief skirmish taking fourteen prisoners. On Sunday 13th he crossed the Aisne and from Monday was in action on the Chemin des Dames.
He remained on the Aisne until Tuesday 13th October when he was sent to Flanders. He marched across the border and onto Poperinghe where he was billeted. On Tuesday 20th October the Battalion took the line near Poelkapelle for three days before being relieved to Langemarck. During their three days in the line they had repulsed a major attack where they were outnumbered five to one.
Alan went with his men to Polygon Wood where he was involved in heavy and ferocious fighting, much of it hand-to-hand. Alan survived a sustained artillery barrage and attack on Friday 13th November but the next day he was killed by a sniper near Zonnebeke whilst out reconnoitring to put the sniper out of action!
Alan is commemorated on the Hillside War Memorial.

Lieutenant Averell Digges-La Touche

5th Battalion attached 2nd Battalion Royal Irish Rifles
Died on Saturday 25th September 1915, aged 30
Commemorated on Panel 40.

Averell was the son of Major Everard N and Mrs Clementine Digges-La Touche, of 56 Highfield Road, Rathgar, Dublin.
On Thursday 13th August 1914 the Battalion left Tidworth for Southampton where it embarked on the *SS Ennisfallen* bound for Le Havre and *SS Sarnia* bound for Rouen. The Battalion reformed at a camp at Mont St Aigan, three miles from Rouen. On Sunday 16th they entrained for Aulnoye. From the town they marched north and eventually arrived in Nouvelles, east of Ciply. At 2.30pm on Sunday 23rd they moved forward and relieved the 2nd Royal Scots who had suffered heavy casualties. At 4.00pm the German artillery opened fire on their lines and at 6.00pm the German infantry mounted an attack which was repulsed by rapid fire. At 2.00am on Monday 24th they started to retire reaching Nouvelles by 5.00am. The march continued, passing General Sir Horace Smith-Dorrien in his Headquarters

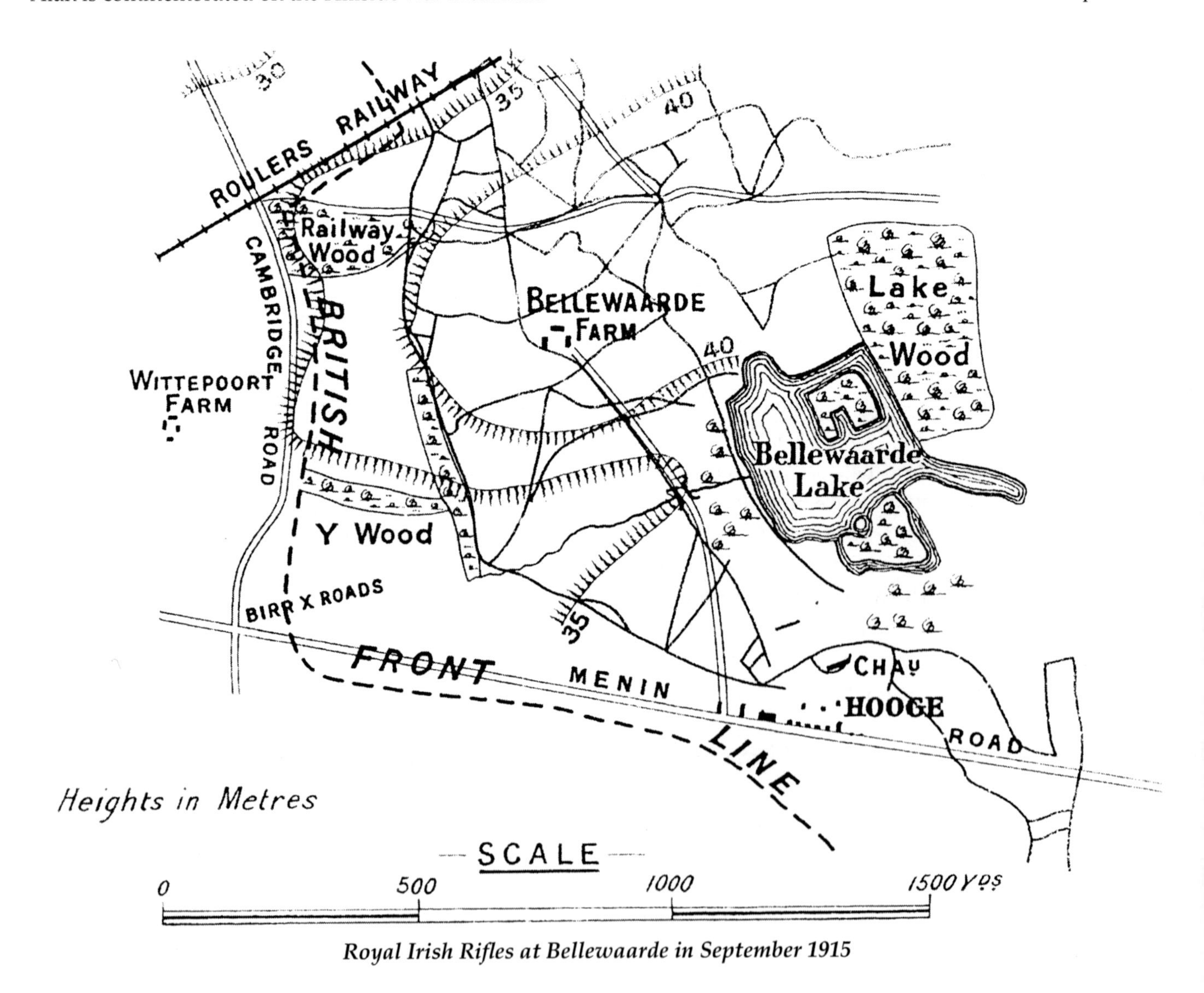

Royal Irish Rifles at Bellewaarde in September 1915

who complimented Colonel Bird on the smartness of the men. The Battalion dug in north of Montigny from where they mounted an attack on Caudry and drove the Germans out. The expected counter-attack did not come and the Battalion was relieved, marching south to Beaurevoir where they met up again with the rest of the 7th Brigade. At 2.00am on Thursday 27th, the Battle of Le Cateau completed, the march continued southward. The Marne was crossed on Thursday 3rd September at Meaux, the bridge being blown immediately after they crossed. On Sunday 6th the Battalion turned to face the enemy. The Retreat was at an end. In the early hours of Monday 14th the Aisne was crossed and they took position at Rouge Maison, near Vailly.

The Battalion remained on the Aisne until Friday 2nd October when they were withdrawn and the move north began. After two weeks they arrived on the La Bassée sector and took the line, seeing action throughout the Battle of La Bassée until the end of the month.

On Friday 30th the Battalion was marched to Merris from where they went up into Belgium and northward to Hooge becoming involved in the Battle of Nonne Bosschen on Wednesday 11th November. On Friday 27th they moved to the Wytschaete sector where they remained for several months, their billets being provided in Locre, Westoutre and Dranouter. On Thursday 3rd June 1915 Averell marched with the men into bivouac south of the Poperinghe to Vlamertinghe road. For the next week he arranged working parties taking barbed wire to the line before moving into the line at Hooge on Wednesday 9th. After three days they were relieved until 5.30am on Tuesday 15th when they paraded and marched to their assembly positions ready for the attack on Bellewaarde. Due to the mist the attack was delayed and eventually he went forward at 3.35pm; in the attack two hundred and fifty yards was gained but they suffered heavy losses. Averell remained on tours of duty, mainly around Hooge, but also at St Eloi and Wieltje. At 7.10pm on Friday 24th September he paraded with his platoon and marched to Hooge to relieve the Honourable Artillery Company. At 3.50am a huge bombardment commenced against the German lines which was followed by the blowing of four mines, in two pairs, at 4.19am and 4.21am along the Bellewaarde Ridge. As soon as the second pair of mines were blown the attacking infantry poured forth. The German machine-gunners were particularly active and accounted for so many of the casualties. Averell was killed leading his men forward.

His brother 2nd Lieutenant Everard Digges-La Touche died between Friday 6th and Sunday 8th August 1915 and is buried in Lone Pine Cemetery, Anzac, and his cousin, Captain Denis Digges-La Touche died on Friday 8th August 1915 and is commemorated on Helles Memorial.

Captain and Adjutant Edward Charles Dimsdale

Rifle Brigade

attached 1st Battalion Monmouthshire Regiment

Died on Saturday 8th May 1915, aged 31

Commemorated on Panel 50.

Edward Dimsdale, family coat of arms

Edward was born on Thursday 20th December 1883, eldest son of Charles Robert Southwell, 7th Baron Dimsdale, and Baroness Alice Dimsdale (daughter of Charles James Monk, MP). His ancestors were Knights of the Realm dating back to the middle ages and Robert Dimsdale accompanied William Penn to America in 1684. Dr Dimsdale, in 1745, was on the medical staff of the Duke of Cumberland when he marched into Scotland to suppress the Rebellion. The good doctor was a pioneer in small-pox inoculation and was invited by HIM Empress Catherine of Russia in 1762 to inoculate her and the Imperial Family. He made quite an impression on the Empress and she created him a Councillor of State and on Tuesday 13th February 1759, a Baron of the Russian Empire with an annuity of £500 per annum (she also gave him £12,000 for his services and a number of valuable gifts). The black wing in the centre of the coat of arms is taken from the Russian Imperial coat of arms by special request and permission of the Empress.

Eton College

Edward was educated at Eton College, as a member of Remington Walter White-Thomson's House, leaving in 1901 when he passed in to RMC Sandhurst. On Wednesday 12th October 1910 he married Katharine Joan Dimsdale (daughter of Edward Exton Barclay of Brent Pelham Hall, Hertfordshire), and they had two sons, Thomas Edward, born on Wednesday 11th October 1911 (who succeeded to the title on Sunday 6th December 1928 on the death of his grandfather) and John Robert on Thursday 16th October 1913.

Edward was on the Frezenberg Ridge during the first gas attack and saw at first hand the appalling results. After a few days in Brielen, on Thursday 6th May he took the men back into the line, arriving in the early hours the next morning where they had to repair the badly damaged trenches before dawn. They came under heavy shell fire followed by fierce machine-gun attack from a farm house. Edward tried to organise an attack to silence the machine-gun but

Unsere Gefangenen

A German advert showing how many prisoners of war they had claimed to have captured by Friday 1st January 1915
French — Russian — Belgian — English
(numbers of other ranks quoted first, followed by officers)

the Germans advanced, taking a farm to their right. Edward called on his men to follow him, bayonets fixed, and was leading his men forward when he was killed early on Saturday 8th.

Edward was recorded in Debretts Obituary — War Roll of Honour published in the 1921 edition.

In St Mary's Church, Meesden, Hertfordshire, a plaque was placed in his memory with the inscription: *"In memory of Captain Edward Charles Dimsdale, Rifle Brigade, killed in action while serving as Adjutant of 1st Monmouthshire Regiment May 8th 1915 aged 31. Also of Lieutenant Reginald Thos. Dimsdale, R.N. killed in action while in command of Submarine E22 April 25th 1916 aged 30. Sons of Charles Seventh Baron Dimsdale of Meesden Manor, Herts. For God and King and Country."*

His brother, Lieutenant Reginald Dimsdale, died on Tuesday 25th April 1916, and is commemorated on Portsmouth Naval Memorial.

Second Lieutenant Samuel Eric Ditchfield

4th Battalion attached 7th/8th Battalion
King's Own Scottish Borderers
Died on Tuesday 31st July 1917, aged 22
Commemorated on Panel 22.

Samuel Ditchfield

Samuel was born at Moston, Manchester, on Sunday 14th July 1895, only son of Percy and Alice Barlow Ditchfield, of Holmgarth, Menston-in-Wharfedale, Leeds. He was educated at the Ilkley Grammar School and then worked for Scottish Widows Assurance in Leeds.

On Friday 3rd November 1916 Samuel joined the Inns of Court OTC, trained at Berkhamsted and Catterick, being gazetted in April 1917. Samuel left for France and joined the Battalion in the field. He was killed on the Frezenberg

Redoubt. The attack took place at 3.50am on Tuesday 31st July 1917, Samuel leading his men forward after a well placed artillery barrage. By 9.00am a heavy fight took placed around the ruins of *'Frost Farm'*, as they advanced to take the final objectives Samuel was killed by a sniper.

His Commanding Officer wrote: *"He had not been with us very long, but he was so keen on his work and quick, and a most promising officer, that we are all deeply grieved with his loss. He died gallantly going forward with his men."*

One of his fellow officers wrote: *"Though he was not in my platoon here, I got to know him well, as he was one of my chief helpers in the production of the 'Bancroft Magazine'. I shall always remember his great keenness and unselfishness in that work, and, indeed, in everything he took up when he was here. He was one of our best cadets, and the Army can ill afford to lose him."*

Another wrote: *"I feel I must write and tell you how sorry we are at the death of your son; he and I were very good friends, and he was liked by everybody. He was doing fine work when unfortunately he got killed by a sniper, shot through the heart, and his death was instantaneous. Please accept my deepest sympathy in your loss."*

24713 Private Thomas Charles Dixon

13th Battalion Canadian Infantry (Quebec Regiment)

Died on Thursday 22nd April 1915

Grave reference Panel 24.

Thomas Dixon

Thomas was born in Newcastle-upon-Tyne, in 1892. He was educated in Alnmouth and Tynemouth. In March 1913 he joined the Bank of British North America in Montreal, followed by a temporary appointment in Hamilton, Ontario.

At the outbreak of war he volunteered and left with the First Canadian Contingent for England on Friday 25th September 1914, arriving on Friday 16th October on board *HMTS Alaunia*. He continued his training and left for France on Friday 12th February 1915 from Avonmouth. On Tuesday 16th he arrived in St Nazaire from where he entrained to Hazebrouck. Whilst in camp at Flêtre, on Saturday 20th, the Battalion was inspected by Field Marshal Sir John French and four days later tours of duty by company commenced near Armentières.

On Saturday 3rd April an officer wrote: *"Today we received our marching orders for a long move to another part of the line. The proposed movement of the troops in this district has been called off. ... At present we cannot tell what may be in store for us. We are diligently learning new methods of attack never before laid down in any book. It reminds me of the pictures one used to see of the storming of castles in the Middle Ages. Ladders are carried, bridging material, explosives, etc. Whilst practising today I fell into a ditch of slimy water up to the waist, which did not add to my comfort. We throw live bombs, and they seem to be about as dangerous to the throwers as to anybody else. A large piece of iron flew very close to my head, and I am surprised that no one was hurt. It was not bad fun, and the men liked it. We have had several football games, and this afternoon we hold sports. The men show fine condition, and no ill effects from trench life."*

A couple of days later they marched seventeen miles into Belgium into billets.

On Friday 16th April Thomas was sent to St Jan which was initially relatively quiet whilst they remained in reserve. The took the front line during the night of Wednesday 21st under heavy artillery duel. The trenches were in poor condition and they had to step over many corpses that had not been removed from the battlefield. In the late afternoon on Thursday 22nd a huge barrage opened from the German lines and shortly afterwards the yellowish-green cloud of gas was seen. Shortly afterwards the French colonial troops were streaming back through St Julien. Thomas was killed by shell fire during the bombardment.

Captain William Cary Dobbs

'D' Company, 2nd Battalion Middlesex Regiment

Died on Tuesday 31st July 1917, aged 46

Commemorated on Panel 49.

William was born on Friday 14th October 1870 son of Robert Conway Dobbs, JP, and Edith Juliana Dobbs, of Camphire, Cappoquin, County Waterford. He was educated at Winchester College from 1884 to 1889 and went up to Trinity College Cambridge, from 1889. William was a partner in Broadwood & Sons, piano makers from 1894 to 1901.

William was commissioned in 1915 to the 3rd Battalion and joined the 2nd Battalion in the field.

After seeing considerable action on the Somme the Battalion left on Sunday 3rd June 1917 and arrived in Bailleul at 4.00am on Monday 4th. Two weeks later they were in Ypres billeted in the Cavalry Barracks and at the Lille Gate. From Monday 25th to Saturday 30th June they undertook a tour before returning to camp where they spent the majority of July in training. At 9.00pm on Monday 30th they moved into the assembly trenches in *'Railway Wood'*. Zero Hour was 3.50am on Tuesday

31st July 1917 and William's objective, and that of the Battalion, was the Black Line on the Westhoek Ridge. William was on the right flank of the attack and as soon as they reached the objective: *"... the enemy stopping running away and then opened fire with machine-guns from an enclosure on the railway and from the neighbourhood of Sans Souci. Gradually also his snipers crept closer and began their deadly work."* At 8.00am a German aeroplane flew over their position and dropped a flare after which the German artillery opened up on them. During an attack William was killed.

8200 Rifleman James William Dodd, DCM

'D' Company, 3rd Battalion King's Royal Rifle Corps

Died on Monday 10th May 1915, aged 27

Commemorated on Panel 53.

Citation for the Distinguished Conduct Medal, London Gazette, Wednesday 30th June 1915:

"For gallant conduct and ability as a scout. One day during February this man, on his own initiative, crept out close to the German trench beyond St Eloi and took some compass bearings. Private Dodd always volunteers for dangerous work and has set a very good example under heavy shell fire, and on other occasions."

James was born in Lambeth the son of Henry and Jane Dodd. He was educated locally.

James was living in Kennington when he enlisted in Tidworth. James went out to France shortly before Christmas 1914. He was sent to northern France where they went into training and small groups of men went to the front line in turn to experience trench warfare. When the Battalion took the line they found the trenches were in very poor condition and were flooded with freezing cold muddy water. The communication trenches did not exist so going in and out of the line could only take place at night; similarly supplies of ammunition, food and water could only be taken up at night. On Sunday 14th February James went into the attack at St Eloi with the objective of recapturing a line of trenches and in the action he was awarded his Distinguished Conduct Medal. During March James was relieved from the line and was sent into reserve at Poperinghe. In mid-April he was sent into the line at Polygon Wood, and in early May to Hill 60. On Sunday 9th the Germans laid down a massive barrage and undertook a series of counter-attacks that were repulsed: however James was killed.

Lieutenant Philip Walter Rudolph Doll

Machine Gun Officer, 1st/8th Battalion
The King's (Liverpool Regiment)

Died on Saturday 31st October 1914, aged 24

Commemorated on Panel 6.

Philip Doll

Philip was born on Wednesday 28th May 1890, fourth son of Charles Fitzroy Doll, FRIBA, FSI, JP, (London and Hertford), and Emily Frances Doll (née Tyler), of Hadham Towers, Much Hadham, Hertfordshire. He was educated at Charterhouse from 1905 to 1907 as a member of Verites where he was in the cricket XI an then passed into RMC Sandhurst. Philip was in the Sandhurst football team and then played both cricket and football for the army. He won The Lord Roberts' Gold Cup at Aldershot in 1914 with his guns.

Philip was gazetted on Saturday 6th November 1909 and promoted Lieutenant on Wednesday 10th April 1912.

Philip embarked on the *SS Irrawaddy* sailing for Le Havre, arriving on Thursday 13th August 1914. He marched with his men to camp at St Adiesse. The next morning the Battalion went to the coast and everyone enjoyed bathing in the sea. The following day they entrained for Busigny from where they marched to Hannapes. On Friday 21st the march towards Belgium commenced, arriving on the Mons battlefield at 11.00am on Sunday 23rd taking position close to the chalk pit at Givry. In the early evening they came under artillery fire: *"As far as we were concerned we were perfectly safe and had, so to speak, front seats for a particularly good firework display. But the noise was appalling and the sight of these puffs of smoke which were breaking over the ground less than 800 yards away, and the knowledge that each of them was showering lead far and wide, the whole thing was bound, just for a moment, to have a paralysing effect. It was not fear, but the terror of amazement. Very soon, however, as nothing happened to us, we were regarding it with interest."*

At 4.45am on Monday 24th the Battalion was ordered to retire. The next day they engaged the enemy near Houdain and caused significant casualties amongst the Germans. The retirement continued and on Tuesday 1st September at Villers-Cotterêts they acted rearguard. On Sunday 5th their long march of two hundred and thirty-six miles southwestward came to an end at Chaumes where a good deal of supplies were purchased, Lieutenant Synge recorded: *"My Captain and I started off, followed by my servant armed with a canvas bucket. The shops were few, but, such as they were, full of every kind of commodity. We bought tins of sardines, rice, tapioca, sugar,*

coffee, etc., and some sweets. I bought a pair of woollen slippers for myself at the same shop, there being nothing left to buy, we moved on elsewhere. The next shop was practically cleared out, but the good lady had a huge earthenware jar of honey, which she was dishing out with a large wooden ladle. This was too good to miss and so we stepped in and bought the whole outfit, ladle and all, much to the disgust of the piecemeal purchasers. I then went on to the ironmonger's where I bought a very cunning collapsible lantern. The people were only too glad to let things go cheap, as they fully expected the Germans to arrive next day and there would be no paying then. My Captain was very worried because he could not buy any chocolate, but later we discovered that another company had made a corner in chocolate, as we had in honey, and we effected a partial exchange." All ranks were delighted with the orders received at 5.15pm: *"The Army will advance eastwards with a view to attacking. The left will be covered by the Sixth French Army also marching east, and the right will be linked to the Fifth French Army marching north."*
At 6.30am on Sunday 6th the Battalion set off in search of the German army that were found four days later when a short sharp action took place at Hautevesnes. By Monday 14th they had arrived on the Aisne and took position on the Chemin des Dames. For the next month the Battalion

... capturing Germans during the Battle of the Aisne

remained engaged until 2.00am on Thursday 15th October when they were ordered to Fismes where they entrained at 7.00pm. After a long and tiring rail journey via Paris, Calais and St Omer they arrived at Strazeele from where they marched into billets at Hazebrouck.
At 6.00am on Tuesday 20th October Philip marched with his men to the Ypres Salient via, Reninghelst and Vlamertinghe. After being billeted in St Jan, at 4.00am on Thursday 22nd the Battalion was ordered to Zillebeke, arriving in the early evening. The expected German attack did not materialise therefore they were marched back to St Jan. Saturday 24th brought the Battalion into action; they took position at Westhoek but were sent almost immediately to attack Molenaarelsthoek. They cleared the village, house by house, at the point of the bayonet. Over the next five days the Battalion attacked, repulsed counter-attack and attacked again, with heavy shell fire pounding their line all the time. On Thursday 29th the Battalion moved to Polygon Wood for twenty-four hours before returning to their old positions. On Saturday 31st October 1914 Philip was resting at Westhoek. At 5.30am he was ordered into the line; the mist had started to clear. At 6.00am the Germans attacked in large numbers against the line east of Gheluvelt. At 11.30am he was ordered to help support the position at the southeastern corner of Polygon Wood but due to such heavy shell fire they did not arrive until 1.00pm. Philip went out alone to reconnoitre the position. He did not return and his body was not recovered.
Philip is commemorated on The Lord's Members War Memorial.

5304 Lance Sergeant
Donald Gordon Douglas

4th Regiment (Infantry) South African Infantry
Died on Thursday 20th September 1917, aged 31
Commemorated on Panel 16.

Donald Douglas

Donald was born on Friday 21st May 1886, son of Richard Maginis Douglas, of Portballantrae, Bushmills, County Antrim, Ireland, and the late Julie Douglas. He was educated at Moravian School, Ballymena, and at Foyle College, Londonderry.
In 1901 Donald enlisted and served in the South African War, receiving the Queen's Medal with two clasps, followed by service in the Natal and Zulu Rebellions, receiving the Medal with clasp.
At the outbreak of war Donald initially served in the West African Campaign after which he returned to England for training at *'Borden Camp'*. He went out to Egypt and then to France where he served during the Battle of the Somme at Delville Wood and at the Butte de Warlencourt. Following serving through the Battle of Arras Donald transferred to Flanders and commenced training for the forthcoming offensive. Donald was north of the Ypres to Roeselare railway when he was sent into the assembly positions on Wednesday 19th September 1917. The next day they attacked *'Beck*

House', *'Borry Farm'* and lastly *'Mitchell's Farm'* where he was killed and buried in the field.
His Commanding Officer wrote: *"It is my painful duty to advise you that your son was fatally wounded at my side this morning. He fell to a sniper's bullet when the position was captured and victory complete for the moment. Your son was my right arm in the taking of the objective that fell to the lot of my platoon. A moment or so previously I had a marvellous escape myself, being struck by a bullet on the steel helmet. It was your son's great boldness and bravery that took him to the fatal spot to reconnoitre the resistance so as to deal with it. He was struck in the stomach and died almost immediately, but not before we had brought him into safety. Your son was buried in the neighbourhood of the 'strong point' and a cross put up bearing his name and that of his regiment."*

SECOND LIEUTENANT SIDNEY HAROLD LIONEL DOUGLAS-CROMPTON

1st Battalion attached 5th Battalion Royal Fusiliers
Died on Thursday 7th June 1917, aged 21
Commemorated on Panel 8.

Sidney Douglas-Crompton

Sidney was born in Lisbon on Tuesday 2nd June 1896, only son of Sidney Douglas Crompton and of Kathleen Louise Douglas Robertson (formerly Douglas-Crompton), of Lisbon, Portugal. He was educated at Sir Will Borlase's School, Great Marlow.
Sidney enlisted on Monday 15th March 1915 and was recommended for a commission in July, after training in the Cadet School at General Headquarters, being gazetted on Friday 27th August 1915.
He was wounded on Sunday 30th April 1916 and was sent to the hospital in Caniers for three weeks before being sent to recover in England. Sidney went back to the front in early September and continued to serve at the front until he was transferred to the Royal Naval Air Service in June. After training at Crystal Palace he joined *HMS Lightfoot* for a month before he went for nine months training, but it did not suit him.
Sidney returned to the Royal Fusiliers and was killed at Messines. At 3.10pm Sidney led his men of 'A' Company forward under the barrage to attack a strong point held by the Germans when he was killed.
One of his fellow officers wrote: *"His end was as fine as it could possibly be. He tied a blue handkerchief to his stick, and told him men to follow it. He was perfectly splendid, and seemed to forget there was any danger."*

LIEUTENANT ARCHIBALD WILLIAM JOHN JOSEPH DOUGLAS-DICK

1st Battalion Scots Guards
Died on Sunday 8th November 1914
Commemorated on Panel 11.

On Friday 9th October 1914 Archibald joined the Battalion on the Aisne shortly before its conclusion. On Saturday 17th he marched with the Battalion to Fismes and entrained at 8.30pm for Hazebrouck, arriving the next day. After twenty-four hours in billets they marched to Poperinghe.
At 4.35am on Wednesday 21st they marched via Elverdinghe and Boesinghe towards Langemarck. They were in the line for two days when at 1.00pm on Friday 23rd the Germans mounted a heavy attack that they repulsed inflicting heavy casualties. After a further thirty-six hours they were relieved by the French and sent to Zillebeke from where they were sent to Gheluvelt to reinforce the line. The Germans were shelling the position heavily when orders were received to attack Poezelhoek. They got within two hundred yards of the German line and dug in, holding onto the position for the rest of the day; it was a costly action with the Battalion taking one hundred and thirty casualties. Late in the evening they took over the trenches from the Bedfords. At 5.30am on Thursday 29th the Germans launched a major attack that was brought to a standstill by the rapid fire inflicted from the defenders. However, the Battalion took very heavy losses of two hundred and forty officers and men. On Saturday 31st the Germans increased their artillery fire and were making headway, and Archibald went forward with the Battalion to support the situation. Shortly after noon the German infantry moved in strength against Gheluvelt and took the village by 2.30pm. The situation was rescued in the afternoon when the Worcesters charged and the Scots counter-attacked regaining some lost ground. Despite the tiredness of the men, new trenches were dug between Gheluvelt and Veldhoek. For the next six days Archibald and the men dug in and held the line under heavy shell fire. On Wednesday 4th and Thursday 5th much needed reinforcements arrived. On Sunday 8th the Germans renewed their attack and broke the line held by the Zouaves and Loyal North Lancashires on their right, allowing the Germans to enfilade Archibald's trenches. A counter-attack was mounted and drove the Germans from most of the captured trenches. During the attack Archibald was killed, initially listed as missing.
The other officer casualties who were with Archibald were: Lieutenant (later Captain) Sir John Dyer was wounded (to be killed on Tuesday 31st July 1917 and is buried in Canada

Farm Cemetery); Lieutenant Bernard Winthrop Smith was mortally wounded, he had only just arrived a few days before with a draft and is buried in South Wingfield (Park) Burial Ground, Derbyshire; and Lieutenant John Stirling-Stuart died of wounds the next day and is commemorated on the Menin Gate, see below.

Lieutenant The Honourable Alan George Sholto Douglas-Pennant

1st Battalion Grenadier Guards

Died on Thursday 29th October 1914, aged 24

Commemorated on Panel 9.

Alan Douglas-Pennant, family coat of arms

Alan was born on Wednesday 11th June 1890, the son and heir of Edward Sholto, 3rd Baron Penrhyn and Blanche Georgiana, Lady Penrhyn (daughter of Lord Southampton), of Wicken Park, Stony Stratford. He was educated at Eton College as a member of the Reverend Henry Thomas Bowlby's House, leaving in 1908 and passing into RMC Sandhurst.

Alan was gazetted in February 1910 and promoted Lieutenant May 1911. In April 1914 he was appointed extra ADC to Lord Carmichael, GCIE, KCMG, the Governor of Bengal.

On Sunday 4th October Alan embarked with the Battalion at Southampton for Zeebrugge. They sailed on *SS Armenian* and *SS Turcoman*, arriving on Wednesday 7th, he was a member of No 3 Company under Captain Lord Richard Wellesley (killed on the same day as Alan and buried in Hooge Crater Cemetery). Twenty-four hours after they arrived they marched south to Ostend where the Battalion entrained for Ghent. Despite remaining there until the early hours of Monday 12th they did not engage or see the enemy. A long and tiring march via Thielt and Roeselare followed until they arrived in Ypres on Wednesday 14th. They marched out of the town along the Menin Road to Zandvoorde and set up a line that ran for a mile in a half-moon back to the Menin Road. On Sunday 25th Lieutenant Colonel Earle sent a platoon from Alan's Company to help clear the houses to the rear. That night the Germans mounted an attack, coming forward crying: *"Don't shoot! We are the South Staffords"*. The burning buildings silhouetted them, their German helmets gave them away and rapid fire bore down on them before they retired. On Tuesday 27th Alan and the Battalion went into bivouac in *'Sanctuary Wood'*. On Thursday 29th October, Alan, with his men and fellow officers were in an exposed position supporting the Scots Guards. The Germans advanced under the cover of fog, only being spotted at fifty yards range. They could contend with the fierce German attack, but not coupled with their faulty equipment — the ammunition did not fit the rifles and the machine-guns jammed — it was a total disaster. It was, therefore, hardly surprising that the German attack succeeded and all eleven officers were killed, wounded or listed as missing. Those killed with Alan were Major The Hon Leslie Hamilton, Captain Gordon Brown, Lieutenant Geoffrey Campbell, Lieutenant Granville Smith, 2nd Lieutenant Vere Boscawen (all of whom are recorded on the Menin Gate), and 2nd Lieutenant Charles Williams-Wynn, the only one to have a grave, who is buried in Perth Cemetery (China Wall). Lieutenant F W Gore-Langton was wounded and Lieutenant Wavell-Paxton who was wounded and taken prisoner; Captain Gibbs and 2nd Lieutenant Alison were also taken prisoner. In addition, one hundred and eighty other ranks were either killed, wounded or captured.

Lord Wellesley

Alan is commemorated on the House of Lords War Memorial, on the Llandegai War Memorial, Carnarvonshire and a plaque was placed in the Guards' Chapel, Birdcage Walk, London, which was destroyed during the Blitz in the Second World War.

His brother Lieutenant The Hon Charles Douglas-Pennant was killed on the same day (buried in Perth Cemetery (China Wall), and another, Captain The Hon George Douglas-Pennant died on Thursday 11th March 1915 and is commemorated on Le Touret Memorial.

10840 Serjeant Thomas Victor Dôvey (served as Seymour)

5th Battalion Oxford and Bucks Light Infantry

Died on Friday 6th August 1915, aged 30

Commemorated on Panel 37.

Thomas was born at Bridlington, Yorkshire, on Monday 16th February 1885, son of Thomas and Esther Dôvey, of Vine Cottage, Barley Mow Lane, Catshill, Bromsgrove, Birmingham. He was educated at the Denis Road Public School, Moseley, and was employed as a foreman in the art metal industry. Thomas was the Scoutmaster for the second troop at St Michael's Parish Church, Haworth. At the outbreak of war Thomas volunteered and enlisted on Wednesday 26th August 1914, leaving for France in May 1915. Whilst on a tour of duty on the Salient Thomas was killed in action and buried where he fell.

Captain Noel Darwell wrote: *"I used to be Second in Command of the company of which your son was a member, and, indeed, was originally his Platoon Officer and knew him very, very well. ... At the time of your son's death I had been called from the company to take over the command of A Company, or I should have written. I am now brought back to my old company to take Capt. Sanderson's place. I have, however, got all the facts concerning your boy's death, and these I will give you, saying now what is in my heart to say — that he death was a personal grief to all of us who knew him. Of his abilities I will speak later. You will have heard that he had taken over the command of No. 15 Platoon when my duties as 2nd Captain made it impossible for me to carry on with the work. He and a part of the platoon occupied a small redoubt, and had experienced very few casualties there (indeed, Capt. Sanderson made his headquarters there for some days), when on 6 Aug. a large enemy shell entered the dug-out where your son and two others were resting, and (though not exploding) dealt two of them injuries from which they died almost immediately."*

In the *'St Michael's Magazine'* published: *"He is a splendid example of what the Boy Scouts have done in preparing our young men for England's great task. He loved boys and tried to do his duty."*

Captain
Geoffrey Charles Walter Dowling

7th Battalion King's Royal Rifle Corps

Died on Friday 30th July 1915, aged 23

Commemorated on Panel 51.

Geoffrey was born in Melbourne, Australia, on Wednesday 12th August 1891, only son of Rose Dowling and the late Joseph Dowling. His mother remarried to Colonel Foster Cunliffe of The Nunnery, Rusper. He was educated at Charterhouse from 1905; he captained the cricket XI and played in the football XI. He went up to Trinity College, Cambridge, in 1910. An excellent cricketer Geoffrey played for Sussex County Cricket Club.

The 7th Battalion was formed in Winchester at the outbreak of war and after a period of training left for France on Wednesday 19th May, landing in Boulogne the next day. He entrained for northern France then crossed into Belgium. Geoffrey organised the training of the men for the tours of duty they were about to commence. The Battalion did not have much time in the line before the major action at Hooge was undertaken. On Thursday 22nd a huge mine was blown creating a large crater. The Germans kept the crater under constant fire and it was impossible to make use of it. Late on Thursday 29th Geoffrey took the line in front of *'Sanctuary Wood'*. At 3.15am the ominous silence was broken by the shattering explosion at the ruined stables of Hooge Château and thereafter mortar shells poured down on them coupled with heavy machine-gun fire. The night sky was illuminated by a crimson light as the Germans advanced using *'Flammenwerfer'* (flame throwers or 'liquid fire') for the first time under a cover of shrapnel and high explosive shells. In the mayhem, Geoffrey was killed.

He is commemorated on Rusper War Memorial.

9884 Serjeant
Robert Drinkall, DCM

3rd Battalion Worcestershire Regiment

Died on Monday 7th June 1915, aged 23

Commemorated on Panel 34.

Citation for the Distinguished Conduct Medal, London Gazette, Thursday 3rd June 1915:

"For conspicuously gallantry in the assault on the enemy's position at Spanbroek Molen on 12th March, 1915. Was one of the first to enter the German trench and by marked determination and ability succeeded in holding the right end for nearly three hours, not-withstanding the bombardment with grenades and machine-gun fire by the enemy."

Robert was born in Woodhall, Horncastle, Lincolnshire, son of John and Ellen Drinkall, of North End, Coxhill, Hull. He was educated locally.

Robert enlisted in Lincoln and was a professional soldier. From Thursday 4th to Thursday 11th March 1915 Robert was in billets at Locre and heard the roaring of the guns on Wednesday 10th, the barrage announcing the beginning of the Battle of Neuve-Chapelle. They were sent to the front and marched through the night and took position at dawn on Friday 12th. The Germans had been counter-attacking at Neuve-Chapelle and up the line, along the Messines Ridge. The British artillery were particularly active but due to the mist and fog it could not be ascertained what was being achieved, nor could the movements of the Germans in the trenches ahead of them be seen. A message came through indicating that the Germans were reinforcing their position at Neuve-Chapelle and therefore the British attack was made to capitalise on the now more weakly defended positions. At 2.30pm the British artillery opened up and the men who had been in the partially completed assault trenches which were knee-deep in water and affording little cover, were sent 'over the top' at 4.10pm. A terrible toll was taken by the Battalion but Robert, with his men, managed to break through the wire and took a short section of front line trench. To his right some of his men had broken through and taken a few very badly damaged buildings — only to be killed later in the day by British artillery who got their positioning co-ordinates wrong! The Germans mounted a counter-attack again. The Worcesters, at

The Worcesters clearing a house during the Battle of Neuve-Chapelle

the point of the bayonet moved forward, throwing bombs as they went. Corporal Mansell was sent back to report on the terrible position the Battalion were in, being wounded three times *en route* to HQ. He returned to join Robert and the men in line under heavy fire — he was awarded the Distinguished Conduct Medal for this action. Robert and Sergeant Ince created a temporary sandbag block and held onto the position under seemingly impossible fire; for this action both men were awarded the Distinguished Conduct Medal. Robert remained in the area for the next few weeks, only going back to La Clytte and their billets at the end of the month.

During May the 3rd Battalion did not see much intense action, as an officer wrote: *"Though we have put in a tremendous lot of work in this part of the line and though we are bound to have a thoroughly unpleasant time of it in the Salient, I am almost glad that we are going up there. Lately one has felt has been just out of the big fight, and, though we have had the fag ends of the bombardments and occasional wiffs of gas, we have been having a comparatively easy time, while the people on our left have been having a wretched time of it. We shall now be at the point of honour."*

They left the St Eloi trenches and went into their billets at Vlamertinghe late on Thursday 3rd June. They had a day of rest before being sent through Ypres, along the Menin Road to Hooge where they were to serve for four days. Robert was destined never to return — he was killed in action on the third day in the line.

Lieutenant
David Robert Drummond

2nd Battalion Scots Guards

Died on Tuesday 3rd November 1914, aged 30

Commemorated on Panel 11.

David Drummond

David was born at 14 Belgrave Square, London, on Thursday 30th October 1884, second son of George James and Elizabeth Cecile Sophia Drummond, of Swaylands House, Penshurst, grandson of the Duke of Rutland. He was educated at Harrow School from 1898 to 1903 as a member of Druries. On Tuesday 10th September 1907 David married Hilda Margaret Drummond (née Harris), they had three daughters, Joan Cecile born in 1909, Violet Hilda on Sunday 30th July 1911 and Winifred Pansy on Wednesday 3rd June 1914. David was a member of the Carlton, Guards', and Royal Automobile Clubs. He was a good cricketer and shot.

David was commissioned to the Militia (Black Watch) in 1903 and transferred to the Scots Guards in 1904, being promoted Lieutenant in 1907, and joined the Reserve of Officers in 1911.

At the outbreak of war he rejoined the 2nd Battalion, Scots Guards, at the Tower of London. He went out to the front on 5th September with his Battalion sailing on *SS Lake Michigan* and *SS Cestrian*, stopping in Dover due to the presence of German submarines in the Straits of Dover and disembarking in Zeebrugge. They were to aid the defence of Antwerp although it was basically lost. They entrained for Ghent and served in its abortive defence from where they were sent on a thirty-two mile march over the cobblestones of Flanders to Thielt and from there to Roeselare, Moorslede and onward to the Ypres Salient.

David saw fierce fighting within a short space of time of arrival on the Salient. Initially he was in the line at Zillebeke. Whilst there HRH Prince Arthur of Connaught visited them and a badly wounded Uhlan was captured. On Friday 16th October, in thick fog, they moved to Gheluvelt. For the next two weeks they were very much in the midst of defending the line and stopping the Germans driving through to the coast. On Saturday 31st a huge artillery barrage was launched against them that was followed by a numerically superior infantry attack on their lines. Gheluvelt Château was more or less surrounded and the village was being systematically occupied. The Worcesters came through and helped relieve the perilous situation with the Germans being pushed back. That night David assisted in digging the Battalion in on the lines between Gheluvelt and Veldhoek. Sunday 1st gave them some respite and was, in comparison to previous days, quiet. On Monday 2nd the Germans laid down an accurate barrage that destroyed their meagre trenches, Captain Stacy was buried alive, being rescued after an hour and half, barely alive. David and his men clung on and by the evening the line was consolidated. Tuesday 3rd brought further heavy bombardments and costly sniping. David was shot in the head by a sniper near Gheluvelt, being buried near Veldhoek, one of thirteen to be killed that day from the Battalion.

His Captain wrote: *"Just a hurried line on the march to tell you about poor old David; he was shot through the head by a sniper, and thank God, suffered no pain. We buried him that night. I got a parson to say a few words over his grave, and I put up a rough cross I cut out of the wood, with his name and regiment on it. We can ill spare him — one of the best officers I had, and the most unselfish fellow I have met; however tired and hungry, he was always the first to volunteer to do anything, or to help others. I am simply miserable about him. He was a very gallant gentleman."*

The wife of a brother officer wrote to Hilda Drummond: *"... The same night there was a wounded man in the trench a little way off. They heard him moaning, and during the night Mr. Drummond managed to go to him with some morphia. The poor man died in the night, so his last hours were painless owing to Mr. Drummond's act. Another day they passed a wounded many lying on the ground in the cold, waiting to be picked up. Mr. Drummond took his Burberry and covered the man with it and left it there. Considering what coats mean to them out there, it was a splendidly kind and noble action."*

David was recorded in Debretts Obituary — War Roll of Honour published in the 1921 edition.

In St John The Baptist Church, Penshurst, Kent, a black marble and brass tablet was placed in his memory with the inscription: *"In most loving memory of David Robert Drummond 2nd Scots Guards. The dearly loved son of George and Elizabeth Drummond, and beloved husband of Hilda Margaret Drummond. Born October 30th 1884. Died for his King and Country at Ypres November 3rd 1914. This tablet is erected by his family. Greater love hath no man than this, that a man lay down his life for his friends."*

Captain Spencer Heneage Drummond

7th Battalion Rifle Brigade

Died on Friday 30th July 1915, aged 31

Commemorated on Panel 46.

Spencer was born on Tuesday 12th August 1884, third child and second son of Captain Algernon Heneage and Mrs Margaret Elizabeth Drummond, of Preston House, Colebrook Street, Winchester and was related to the Earls of Perth. His brother, Lieutenant Commander Geoffrey Heneage Drummond, won the Victoria Cross at Ostend in May 1918.

Geoffrey Drummond, VC

Spencer arrived in Boulogne on Wednesday 19th May 1915 and was sent to northern France. After a period of training he was sent into the line. On Friday 23rd July the Battalion relieved the Gordon Highlanders in the line at Hooge after the mine had been blown. As they arrived the Germans were bombarding the line and the newly created crater. The next day the Germans blew a mine of their own, to the left of the British one, and commenced to sap towards the British line. The British artillery opened up and Spencer, with his men, counter-attacked with bombs and the German attack was repulsed. The 8th Battalion came up to relieve the 7th during the night of Thursday 29th, arriving in camp at Vlamertinghe at 3.45am. After only an hour orders were given for the men to 'stand to' and at 7.00am they wearily marched back towards Ypres. The Germans had launched an attack on the lines they had so recently left where *'Flammenwerfer'* (flame throwers or 'liquid fire') was used for the first time. They halted near the Asylum whilst their Colonel, Heriot-Maitland, went to the Ramparts to received his orders. The Battalion was to support the 8th Battalion in a counter-attack that was to commence with an artillery barrage at 2.00am, and forty-five minutes later the advance. It took until 1.30pm before the Battalion reached *'Zouave Wood'*. The Brigade Commander wrote: *"In my opinion situation precludes counter-attack by day. Counter-attack would be into a re-entrant and would not succeed in face of enfilade fire."* As Spencer led his men forward from *'Zouave Wood'* they found that the wire was uncut and came under heavy machine-gun fire. In the early stages of the move forward Spencer was shot and killed.

Spencer was recorded in Debretts Obituary — War Roll of Honour published in the 1921 edition.

11116 Private Charles Dryden, DCM

2nd Battalion Duke of Wellington's (West Riding Regiment)

Died on Wednesday 5th May 1915

Commemorated on Panel 20.

Citation for the Distinguished Conduct Medal, London Gazette, Thursday 3rd June 1915:

"For conspicuous gallantry, initiative and ability on the evening of the 19th April, 1915. During the attack on 'Hill 60' Private Dryden, with another man, became separated from their company, and they at once attacked a German trench by themselves, killing three men, capturing two and dispersing the remainder."

Charles was born in Bradford where he volunteered. From early April 1915 Charles trained with his comrades preparing for the battle on Hill 60. For two days, from Friday 16th, he carried supplies up to Zillebeke and helped dig dug-outs. He was in billets in Ypres when the British blew three mines at 7.00pm on Saturday 17th. Ypres came under sustained artillery fire in retaliation for the attack on Hill 60. It was not a pleasant or safe move from the town up to support the attack. They reached the lip of the craters between 3.00am and 6.00am on Sunday 18th. Charles was awarded his Distinguished Conduct Medal posthumously for action on the Hill, see citation above.

Lieutenant Ince wrote: *"About 4.30 p.m. an order was received from Brigade Headquarters that the battalion was to attack and dislodge the Germans from that portion of the Hill they had regained during their counter-attacks made the previous night. Colonel Turner at once issued orders for the remainder of the Battalion to move up into the craters in readiness, whilst the 2nd Battalion K.O.Y.L.I. occupied the trenches they vacated in readiness, and joined in to support that tack as the second wave.*

B Company was given the right section of the attack, C the centre, and D the left section, whilst A Company, which had suffered so heavily during the day, was held in reserve. Battalion was in the centre crater.

Under supporting artillery fire, with bayonets fixed, at 6 p.m. the Battalion went over the top. B Company reached their objective without much difficulty, but lost Lieut. R. H. Owen, who was killed during the advance.

C Company had to charge over some 50 yards of open ground and suffered very heavily, Capt. Barton and a few men only reaching the objective. They, however, captured the trenches allotted to them, killing and capturing a number of the enemy.

Ptes. Behen and Dryden of this Company particularly distinguished themselves in this operation, and took charge after their platoon officers and sergeants had been killed or wounded. Both of these brave fellow received the Distinguished Conduct Medal."

He also wrote: *"At the time we sometimes wondered what it was all for, this attack on what was called a 'hill' but which to us at the time was merely a system of muddy trenches, shell-torn ground, and a haunt of death. The place was practically a cemetery, and hundreds must have been buried on the ground, it proving impossible, when digging trenches, not to disturb some poor fellow in his last long sleep."* On Tuesday 20th he was sent for three days rest at Zevecoten. After a tour of duty at Potijze on Tuesday 4th May he returned to Hill 60 relieving the Devons at 3.30am the next morning. At 8.00am the Germans launched a chlorine gas attack that killed a good many of his comrades and the German counter-attacked succeeded in recapturing their line of trenches, and Charles was killed.

Lieutenant Ince wrote: *"Alas, what would have happened under natural circumstance was impossible under supernatural ones. At 8 a.m. the Germans, aided by a favourable wind, sent over asphyxiating gas with disastrous effects, a proceeding rightly described by the Commander-in-Chief in his despatch of June 15th as 'a cynical and barbarous disregard of the well-known usages of civilized war, and a flagrant defiance of the Hague Convention'. Gas had been first employed by the enemy on April 22nd at the commencement of the Second Battle of Ypres and fully effective counter-measures had not yet been established. We had not received gas masks yet, only a piece of gauze soaked in a preparation prepared by the medical authorities. This solution after a few minutes required renewing, a procedure absolutely impossible, of course, in action. On came this terrible stream of death, and before anything could be done, all those occupying the front line over which it swept were completely overcome, the majority dying at their posts — true heroes. By this foul means the Germans quickly got possession of trenches 40, 43, 45, there being practically no one left to hold them. Capt. G. W. Robins, East Yorkshire Regiment, attached to the Battalion was the last man to leave of the few who managed to crawl away, and he, poor fellow, died in agony that night from the effects of the gas.*

Our support trenches 38, 39, some 100 yards in rear, were held secure, also a small portion of the front line trench 40 on the lower slopes of the crest line was reoccupied. The few holders of these, assisted by strong reinforcements from the Dorset Regiment, counter-attacked and regained some of the lost trenches, but the actual crest of the hill remained in the enemy's hands.

The Battalion suffered over 300 casualties that morning, large numbers dying as a result of this barbarous gas. The writer will never forget the sight of men writhing in agony and slowly dying from the asphyxiating effects of the chlorine, nor the feeling of helplessness at being unable to do anything for them."

2076 Private James Duchart

1st/7th Battalion Argyll and Sutherland Highlanders

Died on Sunday 25th April 1915, aged 16

Commemorated on Panel 44.

James was born at home, son of Alexander and Elizabeth Sorley Duchart, of 16 Church Square, Grahamston, Falkirk. He was educated locally.
He enlisted in Falkirk and was sent for training. James left for France on Wednesday 16th December 1914 from where he entrained for northern France. James's training continued and it included being attached to troops in the front line for practical experience before his Battalion took the line for the first time.
On Thursday 22nd April 1915 the Germans launched a gas attack on the French colonial troops and Ypres was under threat. James was sent with the Battalion to assist in the defence and counter-attack at St Julien. He was in the assembly positions on Saturday 24th awaiting the order to move against *'Kitchener's Wood'* (Bois des Cuisiniers). The counter-attacks commenced at 3.30am. As James was led forward the Germans in the heavily defended *'Kitchener's Wood'* poured their machine-guns and rifle fire into the attacking troops. Despite moving forward at speed the attack failed and during the fierce battle James was killed.

Lieutenant Walter Joseph Dudley

4th Battalion Royal Fusiliers

Died on Wednesday 16th June 1915, aged 35

Commemorated on Panel 8.

Walter Dudley

Walter was born in Dundalk, Ireland, on Thursday 22nd January 1880, fourth son of Henry Christopher Dudley, of Appleton, Park Road, South Farnborough. His father was Quartermaster Sergeant in the Royal Engineers and the family moved from one station to another depending on his posting. He was educated at local military schools wherever his father was based. Walter was married to Annie (née Raison) and they had a daughter Sybil Grace who was born in 1910.
Walter enlisted in the Royal Fusiliers in 1894 rising through the ranks to Company Sergeant-Major in 1905. He was serving with the London Regiment (Territorial Force) in 1914 in Malta and France. Walter received the Long Service and Good Conduct Medals.
In February 1915 Walter was commissioned in the field into the Royal Fusiliers. During the action at Bellewaarde, at 4.50am, he led his men from the parapet in the direction of the Bellewaarde Lake. Walter was leading his men forward when he was badly wounded and subsequently killed by shell fire.
His Commanding Officer wrote: *"He was with us during the most difficult part of our work, and his magnificent character made him beloved by us all. He died, as he always lived, a fine example of the British soldier."*
A brother officer wrote: *"We were all most awfully fond of him, and it was a great shock to me when I heard the news of his death, as I had heard, earlier in the day, that he was wounded and coming back. He was a very brave and a very capable officer. I looked on him as one of my best platoon commanders, and I was always sure that anything he had to do would be very well done; and if there was a bit more he could do, it would be done. Only the day before the fight he did a very brave thing. He was coming back with Rogers when the latter was hit by a sniper. They were outside of the communication trench. Your husband dressed Rogers' wound under very heavy snipers' fire, absolutely in the open, without assistance, and remained with him until he died."*

260166 Private Alfred Duffy

1st/5th Battalion Gordon Highlanders

Died on Tuesday 31st July 1917

Commemorated on Addenda Panel 59.

Alfred was born in Barony, Lanarkshire, and was educated locally.
He enlisted in Glasgow, his Battalion, known as the Buchan and Formartin Battalion, was formed in Peterhead in August 1914. After training it was sent to France in May 1915.
Alfred was given extensive training, like his brother John, in July 1917 in preparation for the attack they would make on the first day of the Third Battle of Ypres. He was sent into the assembly positions near the Pilkem Ridge and they were to advance to the right of Pilkem in the direction of Poelkapelle. The British artillery pounded the German defences, concentrating in particular on the various concrete pill-boxes that dotted the battlefield. Despite their best efforts the Germans were able to maintain strong defensive positions and poured fire down on the advancing men. Despite the hail of lead flying in the air, the Battalion was able capture *'François Farm'* and *'Varna Farm'* and took a large number of prisoners and equipment. The Battalion pressed on with considerable success but they lost one officer and fifty-eight men killed including Alfred, a further seven officers were wounded and one hundred and seventy-one men wounded with seven listed as missing.
His brother, Private John Duffy, was killed on the same day and is commemorated on the Memorial, see below.

... a successful attack on a German strong point during Third Ypres

19227 Private John Duffy

6th/7th Battalion Royal Scots Fusiliers
Died on Tuesday 31st July 1917, aged 37
Commemorated on Panel 19.

John was born in Anderston, Glasgow. He was educated locally. John was married to Grace Duffy, of 9 Cavendish Place, South Side, Glasgow.

The 6th and 7th Battalions were formed in Ayr in August 1914 as part of Kitchener's New Army. The 6th Battalion landed in France in May 1915 and the 7th in July. On 13th May 1916 the two Battalions were combined to become the 6th/7th Battalion. The Battalions had served through the Battle of Loos and the combined Battalion through the Battles of the Somme and Arras before being transferred to Flanders where they prepared for the Third Battle of Ypres throughout July. John was sent to take position between Potijze and the Roeselare to Ypres railway line. The Division's objective was to take and secure the German front and support lines, followed by the German second line and finally the German third line with its defensive positions, a total distance of more than two thousand yards. At 3.50am on Tuesday 31st the main attack began in a thin mist. John did not being to advance until 10.18am to support consolidate the second objective and then move forward on the third. Unfortunately the second objective was not secured and they were held up at the wire in front of the *'Bremen Redoubt'*. At 2.00pm the first German counter-attack began in an attempt to recapture their second line. John's Battalion took very heavy losses and his body, with so many of his comrades was lost in the thick mud and never recovered.

His brother, Private Alfred Duffy, was killed on the same day and is commemorated on the Memorial, see above.

Major Francis Taylor Duhan

19th Punjabis attached
57th Wilde's Rifles (Frontier Force)
Died on Monday 26th April 1915, aged 42
Commemorated on Panel 2.

Francis Duhan

Francis was born in Calcutta, India, on Friday 3rd January 1873, fourth and youngest son of the late Harry Reilly Duhan. He was educated at Victoria College, Jersey, from 1881 to 1884, followed by Bedford Grammar School — where he was Head Boy in 1892 — and passed into RMC Sandhurst. Francis was a good cricketer and enjoyed fishing.

Francis was gazetted in the Indian Army in October 1894, promoted to Lieutenant in January 1897, Captain in October 1903, and Major in October 1912.

Indian troops in action, 1915

Francis served on the North West Frontier, seeing action at the Relief of Malakand and Chakdara, at Landakai, in Bajaur and in the Mamund country, he received the Medal with two clasps. In 1903 he served in Tibet, receiving the Medal, and in 1908 he was in Mohmand Country where he received the Medal with clasp.
Francis arrived in Marseilles and entrained for Flanders and took the line between Wytschaete and Messines. He continued to serve in the Salient and following the gas attack on Thursday 22nd April was ordered to support the line along the Ypres to Langemarck road. On Monday 26th was on the left flank as they advanced under heavy shell fire and reached within ninety yards of the German line when he was killed.
In Bedford School Chapel, a wooden plaque was placed in his memory with the inscription: *"In memory of Frank Taylor Duhan Major 19th Punjabis 1885-1892 Head of the School 1892. Killed in action near Ypres on 26th April 1915 aged 41."*

Lieutenant Barry Pevensey Duke

3rd Battalion attached 2nd Battalion
Royal Sussex Regiment
Died on Tuesday 3rd November 1914, aged 27
Commemorated on Panel 20.

Barry Duke

Barry was born on Thursday 5th September 1889, the eldest son of Blanche Duke, of 84 Bouverie Road West, Folkestone, and the late Colonel O T Duke. He was educated at Wellington College from 1900 to 1904 and passed into RMC Sandhurst. Barry was commissioned in October 1906 and promoted Lieutenant in December 1909.
At the outbreak of war Barry was sent out to France. The Battalion saw action during the Battle of Mons, the rearguard action at Etreux during the early part of The Retreat, and served throughout the Battles of the Marne and Aisne. In early October Barry had been sent north to Flanders and participated in the Battle of Ypres. On Saturday 31st October their Divisional (First) Headquarters at Hooge took a direct hit severely wounding Major General Samuel Lomax, and Colonel Frederic Kerr, DSO, was killed (he is buried in Ypres Town Cemetery). As the battle raged Barry was killed in the front line.
He is commemorated on Folkestone Town War Memorial.

Light railway, similar to the one that ran along the Menin Road

Lieutenant John Duncan

10th Battalion Highland Light Infantry
Died on Tuesday 31st July 1917, aged 31
Commemorated on Panel 38.

John was born on Tuesday 11th May 1886, eldest son of John and Mary J Duncan, of 25 Buccleuch Place, Edinburgh. He was educated at George Watson's College from 1891 to 1902 where he won prizes in both German and art. John was an apprentice architect with Cousin, Ormiston & Taylor whilst he attended the School of Art and Heriot Watt College where he twice won the Bronze Medal. He went to work for the British Aluminium Company.
In September 1914 John volunteered and enlisted in the Royal Scots and was gazetted in November, promoted Lieutenant in January 1916.
John went to France on Thursday 1st July 1915 and fought on the Salient. He was invalided home the same month with shell shock.
He returned to the front in January 1917. During March he trained for the forthcoming Battle of Arras. At 5.00am on Wednesday 11th April John took his men forward to attack Monchy le Preux and the Battalion was credited with being the first to enter the village. On Monday 23rd John was in the line between the River Cojeul and Guémappe. The next evening at 6.00pm the Battalion advanced but unfortunately due to communication difficulties, they were not informed that the preliminary barrage had to be delayed by half an hour and therefore their advance too should be delayed. Heavy losses were taken by the Battalion as they walked straight into the British barrage. At the end of April the Battle of Arras was concluded and the Battalion was refreshed with new drafts before they were sent to Flanders. He trained for the Third Battle of Ypres where he was in the line on the Ypres to Roeselare railway. The Battle of Pilkem Ridge commenced on Tuesday 31st July and the Battalion was supported by a couple of slow, lumbering tanks on each flank. Alan was killed leading his men towards the second objective, east of Frezenberg, by heavy machine-gun fire.
One of his officers wrote: *"His work has at all times born the stamp of excellence. He was beloved by us all. I feel his loss deeply."*

S/5634 Serjeant Robert Duncan, DCM

8th/10th Battalion Gordon Highlanders

Died on Tuesday 31st July 1917

Commemorated on Panel 38.

Citation for the Distinguished Conduct Medal, London Gazette, Monday 26th March 1917:

"For conspicuous gallantry and devotion to duty during a raid on the enemy's trenches. He led his party quickly forward, and rushed two enemy posts in quick succession. He set a splendid example of courage and determination throughout."

Robert was born in Falkirk son of Mr and Mrs Duncan. Robert served on the Somme without being involved in any particular action until Thursday 14th September when he marched to Contalmaison where he remained overnight until moving to *'Gunpit Road'* northwest of Martinpuich. The attack on Flers and Courcelette was the first battle in which a tank was used. The attack was successful although by Monday 18th, when they were relieved, four officers were wounded and one hundred and twenty-five men were killed or wounded. On Monday 6th November Robert was sent to a camp in Bresle for rest, it was comfortable and dry much to the delight of the Battalion. Various work parties were organised and from Monday 20th a period of concerted training commenced for a week. From Bresle the Battalion was sent to Albert where they undertook road cleaning!

In early January 1917 the Battalion prepared and trained for a raid on the German lines at the Butte de Warlencourt. On Monday 29th January they were in the line at Le Sars when at 1.45am the attack commenced. All the men wore white smocks and white-washed helmets that provided camouflage against the thick snow. As the men advanced the machine-guns poured fire on them until it was silenced. They captured seventeen prisoners and caused considerable damage to the German defences. Those Germans who did not take the opportunity to surrender were bombed in their dug-outs and tunnels, so the true number of their dead is not known.

From the Somme Robert moved north to participate in the Battle of Arras. Their objective lay more than two thousand yards ahead and they moved forward under cover of a barrage which they walked into, together with the Black Watch and were forced to halt for forty minutes to reorganise. At 7.50am they continued to advance but were checked by machine-gun fire from *'Railway Triangle'*. A tank was brought up in support and the machine-guns were silenced so the advance to their objective was then completed. During the attack on Guémappe, on Monday 23rd April Robert was engaged in supplying ammunition and stores to the font line coming under constant fire that caused fifteen to be killed and one hundred and thirty-eight wounded (of all ranks).

Following the Battle of Arras Robert was transferred up to the Ypres Salient to participate in the Third Battle of Ypres. On Tuesday 31st July 1917 at 3.50am Robert went forward, the Battalion being a leading one, and attacked across three hundred and fifty yards of line. Their second objective was over a mile ahead of them — the Frezenberg Ridge. The Germans launched an artillery barrage on them; luckily they had passed through the area targeted. It was a fierce hand-to-hand battle, particularly around *'Wilde Wood'* and by 4.25am the first objective was taken and by 6.00am the second. They held their position to allow their artillery to move forward and support them. At 10.18am they recommenced their attack but only achieved five hundred yards before a German counter-attack commenced. During the early afternoon Robert was killed and buried in the field.

Captain Stuart Duncan

Gloucestershire Regiment attached

2nd Battalion South Lancashire Regiment

Died on Friday 13th November 1914, aged 49

Commemorated on Panel 22.

Stuart Duncan

Stuart was born in London on Thursday 25th May 1865, the youngest son of Dr James and Mrs Duncan, of 24 Chester Street, Grosvenor Place, London. He was educated at Marlborough College from January 1878 to 1882.

Stuart was commissioned in 1884 and promoted Captain on Thursday 31st December 1891. He retired on Saturday 16th April 1904 and joined the Reserve of Officers.

He served in the South African War and received the Queen's Medal with three clasps.

At the outbreak of war Stuart volunteered and rejoined his regiment. He saw action on the Aisne from where he was sent north; on Monday 12th October he was in the line at Givenchy and spent two weeks around La Bassée. He was moved to Neuve-Chapelle where on Monday 26th the Battalion recaptured the village.

In early November he moved to the Ypres Salient where at 2.00am on Friday 6th November he went into the line at Zwarteleen, Hooge. On Wednesday 11th November 1914 the Prussian Guard started their attack against *'Shrewsbury Forest'* and Polygon Wood. Their artillery opened up in the fog and mist, and at 9.00am the Prussian Guard advanced towards the Menin Road.

At 10.00am the Gloucesters moved towards Hooge Château and then advanced an hour later towards Westhoek. In the afternoon Stuart was in the front line that now stretched from *'Inverness Copse'* to Verbeck Farm and here they stayed for four days under heavy shell fire. It was whilst here that Stuart was killed leading his men forward.

Second Lieutenant Christian Dalrymple Hamilton Dunlop

10th Battalion The King's (Liverpool Regiment)

Died on Wednesday 16th June 1915, aged 34

Commemorated on Panel 6.

Christian Dunlop

Christian was born at Southsea, on Tuesday 29th June 1880, the only son of Mrs Julia Robina Dunlop, of 23 Murrayfield Avenue, Edinburgh, and the late Captain Hamilton Dunlop, RN. He was educated at Winchester College from 1894 to 1897. After leaving school Christian worked in the shipping business for Messrs John Warrack & Co, Leith. He worked for five years in India before returning to England and was employed as a stockbroker in Liverpool for Messrs Pilkington and Dunlop. Christian was a member of the Royal Liverpool Golf Club and Secretary of the Liverpool Rugby Football Club.

At the outbreak of war Christian volunteered, enlisting with the Liverpool Scottish until he was gazetted in November 1914. After training he went out to join the Battalion in the field at Ypres in January 1915. At the opening of the Battle of Hooge, he was leading his platoon against the German trenches at Bellewaerde Farm when he was shot through the heart.

... the barbed wire in front of the line

A Memorial Service in the memory of both 2nd Lieutenant Christian Dunlop and Lieutenant William Turner* his great friend was held at Sefton Park Church, Liverpool on Monday 5th July 1915, when eloquent tribute was paid to the young officers' gallantry, loyalty and devotion to duty. (* Lieutenant Turner is commemorated on the Menin Gate, see below.)

William Turner

435613 Private John Burt Dunlop

49th Battalion Canadian Infantry (Alberta Regiment)

Died on Friday 2nd June 1916, aged 16

Commemorated on Panel 30.

John was the son of Daniel and Annie Dunlop, of Frank, Alberta. He was educated locally.

John volunteered on Wednesday 25th August 1915, in Blairmore, Alberta, where he claimed to have been born in Calmarnock, Scotland, on Wednesday 25th August 1897, therefore he volunteered on his '18th' birthday, was employed as a labourer, and a Presbyterian, 5ft 4in tall, a 33in chest, fair complexion, blue eyes and dark hair.

John sailed to England with the Battalion and was sent to train at *'Shorncliffe Camp'*, Folkestone. He marched through the town to the docks and embarked on *HMT Golden Eagle* bound for Boulogne on Saturday 9th October 1915. He was marched to *'Ostrohove Camp'* where he remained for three days and then returned to the town to entrain at La Brique Station for Caëstre. The Battalion was sent to billets at *'English Farm'* in Belgium where their training continued. At the beginning of November the Battalion was sent to *'Westhof Farm'* and Locre where John served on tours of duty until Monday 20th December. He was marched to Berthen where the Battalion was billeted and remained out of the line for both Christmas and New Year.

Troops marching through Folkestone

On Sunday 9th January 1916 John was paraded and marched from his billets at 8.30am to Dranouter and went into reserve for three days. He moved the short distance and took the line at Wulverghem and remained on tours of duty until Tuesday 8th February when they moved into reserve at *'Kemmel Shelters'*.

A pre-war postcard of Poperinghe

John was sent with his comrades on working parties during the day until the Battalion relieved the Princess Patricia's Canadian Light Infantry in front of Kemmel. On Monday 20th March John left the southern sector and marched at 8.30am from Locre via Boeschepe and Wippenhoek to Poperinghe, arriving at 11.00am. He was able to spend twenty-four hours in the town and enjoy the cafés, shops and general relaxing activities that were provided. In the early evening of Tuesday 21st John was entrained to the Asylum at Ypres and was marched out to relieve the 1st Battalion Royal Fusiliers close to *'Warrington Avenue'*, *'Vigo Street'* and *'Cumberland Dugouts'*. By the end of March John had been sent into the front line between *'Maple Copse'* and *'Railway Dugouts'*. On Monday 1st May the line occupied by John came under heavy fire and later in the day the Battalion came under attack, Lieutenant Wilhelm Binder of the 121st Württembergers was captured together with an NCO, both badly wounded and the NCO died shortly after being captured. On Wednesday 31st May the Battalion was relieved by the Princess Patricia's Canadian Light Infantry for a short period of well earned rest.

At 1.00pm on Friday 2nd orders were received to 'stand to' and march to *'Belgian Château'* an hour later. They came under very heavy shell fire and the Battalion was forced to proceed in small groups to Ypres ramparts. John was mortally wounded by shell fire and was buried in the field, his body being lost in subsequent shelling.

Captain Julian Silver Strickland Dunlop

'B' Company 1st Battalion
South Staffordshire Regiment

Died on Saturday 24th October 1914, aged 38
Commemorated on Panel 35.

Julian Dunlop

Julian was born on Friday 15th September 1876, son of Dr Andrew Dunlop, MD, and his wife, Alice, of Belgrave House, Jersey, Channel Islands. He was educated at Victoria College, Jersey, from 1886 to 1894, playing for the First XV. Julian was a good polo player and Secretary to the Garrison Beagles at Lichfield.

Julian was gazetted from the Militia in 1895, promoted Lieutenant in 1898, and Captain in 1904. From 1899 to 1903 he served as ADC to Sir Frederick Fryer, KCSI, Lieutenant Governor of Burma, and from 1905 to 1910 was Adjutant of the 4th (Special Reserve) Battalion South Staffordshire Regiment. In 1911 Julian attended the Coronation Durbar and received the Medal.

At the outbreak of war Julian was in Pietermaritzburg, Natal, and was ordered to return to England. The Battalion sailed to Southampton from where they marched to camp in Lyndhurst on Saturday 19th September 1914. After a period of mobilisation, training and re-kitting they returned to Southampton to embark for Zeebrugge, arriving on Tuesday 6th October. The Battalion was to be sent to assist with the defence of Antwerp, but it was being evacuated as they landed and the Belgian and French armies were retreating towards the coast. Julian was ordered to march with his Company to Ypres where they arrived a week later. He took position along the Menin Road around Westhoek. Julian was killed in action leading a bayonet charge.

A description of the action was recorded: *"In the morning B Company, under Captain Dunlop and Lieutenants Bartlett and Hume, went out to reinforce the Northumberland Hussars, who were in the wood on the right of the Battalion Headquarters. We had just advanced to reinforce them when an order to retire was given. The company retired on the road until the artillery had finished shelling the wood: when they advanced again they joined on to the Worcester Regiment. They then got the order to prepare to charge. The company charged the farm house, which was in a sort of clearing in the middle of the wood, after which we advanced into the wood again and drove out the Germans, about 50 of them, who had a machine-gun and were firing at our party. Captain Dunlop led the Company in the charge. He said 'Come on, men' and the men would have followed him anywhere and*

... a motorised ambulance coming under fire in 1914

through anything. He was killed by the fire of the gun while leading the charge. He was a clever, thoroughly reliable officer, smart and efficient in every way, and no regiment ever possessed an officer more universally beloved. He was kindness personified."

Julian was Mentioned in Despatches.

His brothers Captain Frederick Dunlop, died on Sunday 8th November 1914 and is buried in Royal Irish Rifles Graveyard, Laventie; 2nd Lieutenant Kenneth Dunlop, died on Sunday 26th September 1915 and is buried in Vermelles British Cemetery. Two other brothers served: one, Lieutenant W H S Dunlop, was severely wounded on Sunday 25th April 1915.

1538 Lance Corporal Alfred James Dunn, DCM

58th Battalion Australian Infantry, AIF

Died on Tuesday 25th September 1917

Commemorated on Panel 29.

Citation for the Distinguished Conduct Medal, London Gazette, Wednesday 30th October 1918:

"For conspicuous gallantry and devotion. He tended and dressed the wounded, under very heavy fire, with great courage and determination."

Alfred lived in Dun, Landsborough, Victoria, where he was employed as a butcher.

On Tuesday 1st December 1914 Alfred volunteered and enlisted, leaving on Tuesday 19th February 1916 from Melbourne, embarking on *HMAT Runic*. He arrived in Egypt and joined the Battalion at *'Ferry Post'* for two weeks before moving to the *'Hogs Back'*. He remained alternating between the two until June when he was sent to Moascar in preparation for the move to the Western Front. On Saturday 17th the Battalion embarked in Alexandria on board *HMT Transylvania* arriving in Marseilles on Wednesday 23rd. They entrained for northern France, arriving in Steenbecque at 4.00am on Monday 26th. After a short period of training the Battalion took the line near Fromelles from billets in Estaires and they started to take casualties from the first day, mainly from shelling. They remained in the sector on tours of duty until Wednesday 18th October when they marched to Bailleul and entrained for Longpré at 1.00am, arriving at 4.15am. On Saturday 21st a fleet of buses collected them and took them to Ribemont from where they marched to Becordel. They bivouacked overnight in very cold and poor conditions. The next morning they marched to *'Montauban Camp'* where they provided working parties for the front line. Alfred remained on fatigues until Thursday 2nd November when the Battalion was ordered to Dernancourt, a march that took six hours to complete. After arriving at 8.00pm the mobile kitchen arrived and provided them with a hot meal before they went to their billets, again being considered to be very poor. The Battalion trained in the camp until Wednesday 8th when they were moved to Flesselles to continue the training. Hot baths and showers were provided, men were provided with clean clothes and issued with sheepskin jackets and woollen gloves. Part of their programme included:

Day	*Forenoon* 9.30 - 11.30	*Afternoon* 2.30 - 4.00
Thursday 9th.	Physical exercises Issue of clothing etc. Lecture - Order and Cleanliness in Billets, etc.	Setting up drill
Friday 10th.	Short route march Lecture - cleaning trenches etc.	Setting up drill
Saturday 11th.	Physical exercises Lecture - subject matter of list of questions issued.	Strong point to be stated on the ground. All details to be explained and men organised on the work as if the work was to actually done.
Sunday 12th.	Church Parade.	Nil.
Monday 13th.	Short route march Lecture - system of barrage fire.	Advancing under cover of barrage at rate of 50 yards per minute. Lifts to be shown by flags. Men to be in marching order and will carry shovels and picks.
Tuesday 14th.	Physical exercises. Lecture - construction, conversion of trenches.	Liaison with aircraft. Method of indication by flares on reaching successive positions. Organisation of system.

Note:-

Officers will emphasize strongly during lectures the urgent necessity of not taking in to the firing line any document likely to give information to the enemy and also will remind the men that, if captured, they only need give their No., name and unit. Any other information given by them may be the cause of the death of many of their comrades.

Brigade Staff Officers are available to assist C.O.'s in connection with the working of the programme.

On Friday 17th the Battalion went back to Dernancourt until Tuesday 21st when they returned to Montauban and took the line. He continued on tours of duty. Christmas was spent at Ribemont where a Church Parade was held in the Church followed by a roast beef dinner and by plum pudding, washed down with beer for everyone.

The Battalion marched to St Vaast on Wednesday 3rd January 1917 for further training for ten days when they returned to the front at Fricourt then served at Delville Wood.

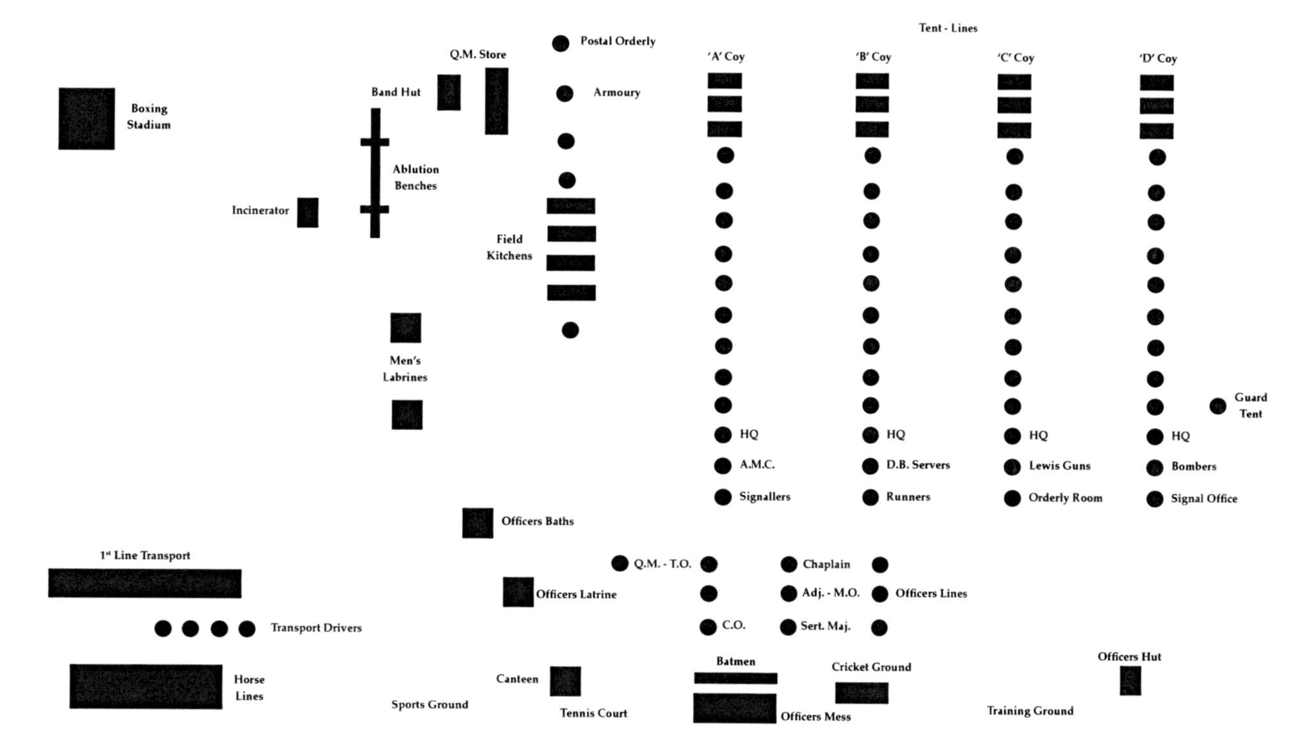

Layout of a typical camp, based on one used by the 58th Australian Battalion whilst near Bapaume in June 1917

At the commencement of the Battle of Arras the Battalion was at Beaulencourt remaining in readiness in preparation to support the line if required. The Battalion was relieved by the 6th York and Lancashires and sent to *'Mametz Camp'*. The Battalion served at Bullecourt — opposite the *'Hindenburg Line'*, moved to Beugny to Ytres Line, then trained at *'Bienvillers Camp'* from Monday 21st May until Thursday 14th June when they marched to Contay. The Battalion was led from the Camp by their band on Friday 6th July to Hérissart for ten days training and then moved to *'Bolton Camp'* near Mailly. They remained in the Camp until Monday 30th when they entrained for Steenbecque and were billeted near Sercus. Intensive training was provided for the next seven weeks in preparation for the Third Battle of Ypres in which they were about to participate.

On Monday 17th September Alfred marched to *'Dominion Camp'* via Steenvoorde, arriving the next day. Final training and preparation for the battle was completed. On Saturday 22nd the Battalion moved to *'Château Segard'* and took the line at 10.00pm on Sunday 23rd near Polygon Wood towards *'Glencorse Wood'*. Alfred's first task was to improve the trench he was allocated as patrols were sent out during the night. At 5.15am the German artillery fire increased in intensity that continued for an hour. At 6.00am the enemy infantry was seen massing for an attack which they launched at 6.40am. The attack was successfully repulsed although a foothold was taken in the line to the Battalion's right. At 2.00pm Alfred took part in the counter-attack, which was his last action; it drove the Germans from their captured position towards *'Cameron House'*, but Alfred was killed and did not live to see the success.

Second Lieutenant Wilfrid Mervyn Dunnington-Jefferson

7th Battalion attached 3rd Battalion Royal Fusiliers

Died on Tuesday 27th April 1915, aged 23

Commemorated on Panel 8.

Wilfrid Dunnington-Jefferson

Wilfrid was born at Middlethrope Hall, York, on Sunday 2nd April 1893, youngest son of the late Captain Mervyn and Louisa Dorothy Dunnington-Jefferson, of Thicket Priory, York. He was educated at Radley College from 1906 to 1910 and went up to Christ Church, Oxford, with a history scholarship, graduating in 1913 with BA Hons. He was called to the Bar, Inner Temple.

Wilfrid volunteered at the outbreak of war and was gazetted on Saturday 15th August 1914. He arrived at the front on Tuesday 20th April 1915 and moved into the line at s'Gravenstafel just as a German attack was imminent. The Germans were pounding Ypres that destroyed the heart of the medieval town. As the battle intensified the Germans launched the first gas attack that particularly affected the French and Canadians. Lieutenant Colonel Birchall who was a Royal Fusilier, however, was commanding the 4th Canadians and was on the left flank of the Fusiliers when he was killed (he is commemorated on the Menin Gate, see above). At 3.30am on

Colonel Birchall

Saturday 24th the Germans launched a second gas attack against St Julien and Wilfrid took his men up to support and their machine-guns wrecked havoc. On Monday 26th the Germans continued their attack and were able to get into part of the rear of the Battalion but were driven out, the position being described: *"... absolutely plastered with shell and every other kind of fire from three sides at once the whole time, with practically no assistance at all from our guns, and nothing could exist or move over the ground in rear, as every yard of it was plastered without ceasing by enormous shells."* The effect of the attacks was to force the Battalion to retire over the next couple of days. Wilfrid was mortally wounded and buried in the field at s'Gravenstafel.

In St Helens Church, Thorngamby, North Yorkshire, a brass plaque was placed in his memory with the inscription: *"To the glory of God and in memory of Wilfred Mervyn Dunnington-Jefferson. Youngest son of Capt. Mervyn Dunnington-Jefferson. 2nd Lieut. 7th Batt. (attached to 3rd Batt.) Royal Fusiliers killed in action at the 2nd Battle of Ypres on April 25th 1915 aged 23 years. Crux Christi Nostra Corona."*

36606 Private
Albert Edward Durham

'D' Company, 11th Battalion
West Yorkshire Regiment (Prince of Wales's Own)
Died on Wednesday 18th July 1917, aged 27
Commemorated on Panel 21.

Albert Durham

Albert was born at home at Wednesday 2nd October 1889, youngest son of Emma Durham, of 25 Willow Street, Burley, Leeds, and the late William Durham. He was educated at Burley Lawn Council School then went to work at an iron foundry in Hunslet.

On Saturday 11th December 1915 Albert enlisted and was sent for training. He joined the Battalion in the field in France.

He was involved in the Battle of the Somme where in the early hours of Tuesday 4th July 1916 the Battalion participated in the attack on *'Horseshoe Trench'*, the Battalion Diary recording: *"Attacked the enemy's lines during the afternoon and obtained our objective. We were forced to retire, so fell back on our own lines."* A further attack took place the next morning and by 6.45am reports were being sent back that they had taken *'Points 35'* and *'56'*. They were able to consolidate the position for the ensuing two hours whilst under constant counter-attack which forced them to retire to *'Scots Redoubt'*. At 4.30pm the Battalion counter-attacked and *'Horseshoe Trench'* was captured, taking more than eighty prisoners, the section of line being taken by 10.00pm. Albert and the Battalion were relieved by the 8th Yorkshire Regiment and sent to bivouac in Bécourt Wood. The Brigade Diary recorded: *"The perseverance and tenacity shown by the 11th West Yorkshire Regiment, and by the 10th West Riding Regiment in their ultimately successful efforts to gain ground, displayed very high qualities and both Battalions, though exhausted physically, were in the highest spirits, and full of devotion up to the time of their relief."*

On Monday 10th July Albert participated in the attack on *'Bailiff Wood'* and Contalmaison. The preliminary bombardment began at 4.00pm for half an hour when the assault began. Despite the effective defence of the Wood with a machine-gun nest, the attack was pressed home and it was captured. They came under repeated counter-attack but they were able to hold on, their Lewis machine-gun cutting down the attackers. The main, and successful, attack on the village commenced at 4.50pm. Later in the evening the Battalion was relieved by the Cameron Highlanders and sent to rest at Albert.

Albert's next main action was on Sunday 6th August and the attack on *'Munster Alley'*. After the position was consolidated they came under heavy counter-attacks which they repulsed. More than thirty prisoners were taken, the majority were killed by German shell fire as they were being sent back. The Regimental History records: *"By this time Torr Trench, Munster Alley and the surrounding ground were hardly recognisable. Shell fire had tumbled and blown the defences to bits and all around lay*

An attack by the West Yorkshires on a German trench

German dead. In many places the bodies were half buried and trodden under foot during the progress of the attack." Brigadier General Lambert wrote: *"Much credit is also due to the 11th west Yorkshire Regiment and other troops under Lieut.-Col. Barker for the skilful manner in which fresh men were brought up to relieve exhausted troops, to carry up bombs, ammunition and food and to defeat constant counter-attacks which continued throughout the night."*

The Battalion was sent to billets in Bresle from where they moved to Bellancourt before returning to 'normal' front line tours of duty. During Wednesday 4th October the Battalion moved from Martinpuich to Le Sars into trenches that were virtually non-existent due to the

Cleaning up after a hard march following relief

terrible weather conditions and constant bombardment. At 2.05pm on 7th the whistles blew and Alfred was led forward to attack their objective which was taken. They moved forward to the left of Le Sars from *'Destremont Farm'* under heavy artillery bombardment, rapid rifle fire and constant machine-gun fire. The battle was particularly furious and more than a hundred prisoners were taken by the Battalion. Following the capture of a significant portion of the line Albert was relieved and marched to billets in Albert. After a period of rest he continued on tours of duty without being involved in any particular action before moving to Ypres before the end of the year.

Albert spent the first half of 1917 in the southern sector of Belgium and undertook considerable training. He left Boeschepe and marched to a camp near Busseboom on Friday 1st June 1917 for two days when they moved to *'L Camp'* and on Monday 4th into the Zillebeke Bund. The attack that Alfred would participate in was against *'Windy Corner'* and *'The Snout'* around Hill 60. During the night of 6th he was sent forward to his assembly position and by 2.30am the next morning the Battalion was ready for the attack. At 3.10am the nineteen mines were detonated along the line from Hill 60 to Messines and it appeared to everyone present as if an earthquake was taking place. Alfred moved forward with his comrades and they captured the line between *'Imp Avenue'* and *'Impartial Lane'*. The Battalion Diary records: *"At 3.10 a.m. simultaneously with the explosion of the mines at Hill 60 and the Caterpillar, the attack was launched and proceeded entirely according to plan. By 4.30 a.m. it was reported that the whole of the Red, or first objective, had been taken, and by 5 a.m. the three companies in the front line, were consolidating the Blue Line. By 7 a.m. the 12th D.L.I. had passed through our blue line to assault the Black Line. Up to now casualties, though very heavy amongst officers, had been comparatively reasonable amongst 'other ranks' and remained at the same figure for the rest of the 7th. ... Up to the Blue Line the advance was comparatively easy, and all units consider that, had there been no pause there, the Black Line would have been reached without difficulty, the Germans being demoralised. The halt for three hours on the Blue Line enabled the enemy to recover from his surprise and loss of morale."* During the attack the Battalion captured two Granetenwerfer and one was sent as a gift to the Mayor of Leeds. On 8th the Battalion was relieved but 'D' Company remained in the line for a further twenty-four hours. They remained at *'Battersea Farm'* before marching to *'P Camp'* at Ouderdom.

... taking the wounded to the CCS

The Battalion returned to the line at *'Battle Wood'*, and Alfred continued on tours of duty at the front whilst resting at *'Micmac Camp'* until he was killed during a tour of duty.

His Commanding Officer wrote: *"I am sorry to tell you of the death of your son, who was killed whilst we were in the trenches this last tour. I know that any words of mine can be of little comfort to you when confronted with such a loss, for he has been in my platoon several months, and I could tell he would be as good a son as he was a soldier. As a soldier he was everything one could ask: brave and cheerful under the worst circumstances, and out of the line always clean, tidy and steady. I am certain there wasn't a better lad in the company. He was killed by a shell wound in the head and suffered no pain, and was buried behind the line. Several of his chums and comrades attended his funeral."*

Captain Richard Selby Durnford

9th Battalion King's Royal Rifle Corps

Died on Saturday 31st July 1915

Commemorated on Panel 51.

Richard was the eldest son of Richard Durnford, CB, MA, and Mrs Beatrice Mary Durnford of Hartley Wespall House, Basingstoke, his paternal grandfather was the Bishop of Chichester. Richard, like his father, was educated at Eton College a member of Mr Hubert Brinton's House. He also followed his father by going up to King's College, Cambridge, in 1904. Richard then returned to Eton College as an Assistant Master.

Eton College

Richard landed in Boulogne in May 1915 and entrained for northern France crossing into Belgium. After a period of training the Battalion undertook a series of tours of duty at the front, but were not involved in any significant action until Hooge. On Thursday 22nd July a huge mine was blown by the British at Hooge but despite rushing it and manning the lip, they were forced to retire. Any movement was sniped and would come under machine-gun fire. During the night of Thursday 29th Richard led his men along the Menin Road and took the line in front of *'Sanctuary Wood'* together with the 7th Battalion. After a short period of rest they returned to the line during the night of Thursday 29th. At 3.15am on Friday 30th the Germans launched an attack on their lines using liquid fire, a terrifying new weapon. The two Battalions were forced to retire and consolidated their position. Counter-attacks were mounted, Richard and his men were able to recapture some of the line, however during fighting he was killed.

An attack at Hooge

Richard is recorded in Debretts Obituary — War Roll of Honour published in the 1921 edition.

In St Mary's Church, Hartley Wespall, Hampshire, a marble plaque was placed in his memory with the inscription: *"Alleluia to the beloved and honoured memory of Richard Selby Durnford Captain 9th Battalion King's Royal Rifle Corps. Killed in action at Hooge in Flanders 30th July 1915, aged 30, and of Robert Chichester Durnford D.S.O. Capt. 4th Battalion Hampshire Regiment, killed in action 21st June 1918, aged 22, buried at Resht in Persia. Eldest and youngest sons of Richard Durnford, C.B., of Hartley Wespall and Beatrice his wife, who gave their lives for country and freedom in The Great War. They were lovely and pleasant in their lives and in their deaths they were not divided."*

Also in the Church a figure of Christ was donated with the inscription: *"The figure of our Saviour was placed upon The Rood Cross by the parishioners in honour of our Redeemer and in proud and reverent memory of Capt. Richard S. Durnford, 9th Batt. K.R.R.C., and of Capt. Robert C. Durnford, D.S.O., 4th Hampshire Regt. and of Rifleman Thomas Elliott, 12th Batt. K.R.R.C., who were killed in The Great War."* (Rifleman Thomas Elliott, died on Tuesday 19th September 1916 and is buried in St Mary's Churchyard.)

Another tablet with the same inscription as above was placed in St Augustine's Church, Queen's Gate, Kensington.

His brother, Captain Robert Durnford, DSO, died on Friday 21st June 1918 and is buried in Tehran Military Cemetery.

Second Lieutenant Cecil Macmillan Dyer

6th Battalion attached 4th Battalion Rifle Brigade

Died on Friday 9th April 1915

Commemorated on Panel 46.

Clifton College

Cecil was the son of Louis Dyer, of Chicago and Oxford, and his wife Margaret Anne, daughter of Alexander Macmillan, and grandson of the publisher Macmillan. He was educated at Clifton College from 1908 to 1912 and went up to Christ's College, Cambridge, in 1912.

Cecil volunteered in August, joining the Battalion in Winchester when they returned from India in November 1914. On Wednesday 16th December he paraded with his men for the traditional pre-overseas inspection by HM King George V; the Battalion marched to Southampton on Sunday 20th where they embarked for Le Havre. They disembarked from the ship directly onto the train, arriving in St Omer on Wednesday 23rd where they marched to billets in Blaringhem. They continued with training and helped strengthen the defences around St Omer. On Wednesday 6th January 1915 Cecil took his men into the line at St Eloi; the regular troops so recently returned from India suffered particularly in the cold, wet conditions. During February the Battalion received a large draft from England that replaced the large number of casualties they had suffered. On Sunday 14th March Cecil was in camp at Reninghelst when at 5.00pm the Germans blew a mine under *'The Mound'* at St Eloi and rushed forward, took the lip but did not press on further. Cecil and the Battalion moved off marching via Voormezeele and St Eloi using the roads as the cross-country conditions were impossible. They reached *'Bus House'* where they awaited the arrival of the Princess Patricia's Canadian Light Infantry who were to join them on the left flank. They had been held up in Voormezeele, so by 5.15am the Battalion had to undertake the counter-attack alone. Captain Hugh Pryce and 'D' Company stormed *'Rifle Brigade Trench'* surprising the Germans who fled, but Captain Pryce was killed (he is buried in Bailleul Communal Cemetery Extension (Nord)). Captain Miles Selby-Smith charged through the village where he was killed (he is buried in Dickebusch New Military Cemetery Extension) whereupon Colonel George Thesiger (later promoted Major General who died on Sunday 26th September 1915 and is commemorated on the Loos Memorial) urged the men forward and cleared the first barricade. The battle continued as they pushed on towards *'The Mound'* — Colonel George Thesiger wrote: *"Repeated efforts were made by individual officers and men to rush forward, but the sting had gone out of the attack."* Despite more men coming up to support the line by 6.00am *"It was almost broad daylight and there was a confused mass of troops by the St Eloi crossroads."*, the village had been taken but *'The Mound'* remained in German hands. From Wednesday 24th Cecil had a well-earned rest in Poperinghe before being sent to Polygon Wood in front of Polderhoek. Whilst in the line, during a 'normal' tour of duty he was killed.

George Thesiger

Cecil had written home: *"I've never felt fitter in my life. I'm quite enjoying things."*

Cecil is commemorated on Castleton War Memorial, Whitby and on the War Memorial in Danby Parish Church.

THE MENIN GATE - A HYMN

Oh symbol of the Power o'er-shadowing,
No boasting triumph with an archway spanned
the road that passaged an immortal host —
The ramparts in supreme endurance manned.
For right, triumphant through the scourge of war,
Oh Majesty of God, we Thee adore!

Oh wide-flung gate, fast held against the foe,
Valour and sacrifice here barred the way:
The army of indomitable souls
Is filing down an open road to-day.
In they high service where the brave have trod
Grant us to follow unafraid, Oh God.

Oh, tragic road, with pain and glory paved,
None treads this way, but he must pass between
The muster of their close engraved names,
Whose ashes earth has garnered all unseen.
Because our love may tend no sacred sod
They watch alone we plead for these, Oh God!

Oh road, and gate, and archway: word and sign
Of memory — in hope more glorious they
Call forth our souls to march that hallowed route
And steadfast bear the standard till that day
When Thou, Oh King and Captain call us home
And, ranked once more with our beloved, we come!

Beatrix Brice

Orders issued in 1917 regarding kit to be carried during an attack:

"The fighting kit to be carried will be as follows: Steel helmet, haversack on back, water bottle filled, entrenching tool, waterproof sheet, one large tool on back of every other man in proportion of five shovels to two picks, tube helmet, box respirator, field dressing, two sand-bags per man, two grenades, one in each top pocket of jacket to be collection by Section Commanders on reaching objective and used to form a reserve, S.A.A., 120 rounds, two flares every other man, one in each bottom pocket of jacket, one iron ration, one day's preserved meat and biscuits.

All infantry officers must be dressed and equipped the same as their men. Sticks are not to be carried."

First Trooper (coming upon Boche who has been lying for hours on the wrong side of the parapet)
— Wot's he yelling for, Charley?
Second Trooper — Search me! Sounds like 'Vasser! Vasser!'
First Troops (shareholder in Chesebrough) —M—m! Try him with some Vasserline.

from

Eagle to Eykyn

1616 Corporal Horace Frederick Eagle, DCM

11th Brigade Australian Field Artillery

Died on Thursday 11th October 1917, aged 36

Commemorated on Panel 7.

Citation for the Distinguished Conduct Medal:

"For conspicuous gallantry and devotion to duty and consistent good work. He has rendered valuable service, particularly in two important engagements, and has always set a splendid example of coolness and determination. He frequently attended to wounded men under heavy shell fire."

Horace was born in St Ives, Huntingdonshire, son of Sarah and the late Thomas Eagle. He was educated locally. Before leaving for Australia he served for nine years in the Marine Artillery.

On Thursday 20th August 1914 Horace volunteered and left from Brisbane on Friday 25th September on board *HMAT Rangatira* sailing for Egypt. He served in the Gallipoli Campaign from Sunday 4th April 1915 and was wounded in May, invalided to Alexandria before returning to the front in December. Following the evacuation Horace was sent to the Western Front on Thursday 1st June 1916. Whilst in Belgium he was slightly wounded on Sunday 10th June 1917, and again on Tuesday 31st July when he was sent to hospital in Etaples, returning to the front on Saturday 15th September. Horace was killed in action.

Captain Hubert James East

1st Battalion York and Lancaster Regiment

Died on Monday 10th May 1915, aged 30

Commemorated on Panel 55.

Hubert East

Hubert was born on Wednesday 28th May 1884 second son of Mr and Mrs W H East, of East Lee, Maison Dieu Road, Dover, Kent. He was educated at Dover College from 1899 to 1901. In August 1914 Hubert married Mary Vera Hyde Upward (formerly East, née Stewart-Brown), of 111 Victoria Drive, Eastbourne and they had a daughter, born after his death.

Hubert was gazetted from the Militia in July 1903, promoted Lieutenant in February 1906 and Captain in July 1912.

He served in the South African War receiving the Queen's Medal with two clasps.

Hubert Was in Jubbulpore, India, at the outbreak of war. The Regiment was recalled to England, arriving on Wednesday 23rd December 1914. On Friday 15th January 1915 he sailed to Le Havre. During the Second Battle of Ypres Hubert was killed leading a charge.

His batman wrote: *"He was leading his men into action when he received his first wound, which was in his leg, and he was leaving the line when he saw his Subaltern lying very badly wounded. He went to his assistance, and was helping some men to attend to him, and it was when raising him from the ground to give him a drink of water that he received his fatal wound, and only lived a few moments. His last words were: 'Get him away — I'm done for!' He was a hero all through, and I am proud of having had such a master."*

Chaplain 4th Class The Reverend Herbert Hinton East

Army Chaplains' Department

attached 13th Battalion Cheshire Regiment

Died on Sunday 5th August 1917, aged 30

Commemorated on Panel 56.

Herbert was the son of Emma Jane East, of 284 Kew Road, Kew, Surrey, and the late Francis Hyde Hinton East. He studied for Holy Orders and was a priest in Govan before leaving for Canada where he continued his ministry.

In 1917 he was commissioned as a Chaplain and went out to France. The 13th Battalion was in support at the beginning of the Battle of Passchendaele, where their objective was Zonnebeke. Despite the success they had, casualties were heavy. Herbert was killed while attending to the wounded.

Lieutenant Frank Molyneux Eastwood

1st Battalion The Queen's

(Royal West Surrey Regiment)

Died on Friday 30th October 1914, aged 21

Commemorated on Panel 11.

Frank Eastwood

Frank was born in November 1892, fourth son of John Edmund and Ethel Eastwood, of 14 Chichester Terrace, Brighton. He was educated at Eton College as a member of Mr Robert Penrice Lee Booker's House, left in 1910 and passed into RMC Sandhurst. Frank was a member of the Conservative Club.

Frank was gazetted in September 1912 and promoted

to Lieutenant in September 1914.
At the outbreak of war Frank was in *'Rushmoor Camp'*, Aldershot, training, from where he was mobilized for overseas service. On Wednesday 12th August 1914 the Battalion left for Southampton and embarked on the *SS Braemar Castle* where they were *"packed like herrings"*. They arrived in Le Havre the next day and left for Le Nouvion via Rouen. They marched through the villages of northern France into Belgium. On Sunday 23rd the Battle of Mons commenced although the Battalion did not engage the enemy. In the early hours of Monday 24th the Battalion covered the retirement and for the first time came under shell fire. At 8.15am a small Uhlan patrol came close to their lines and all were despatched bar one. The Battalion continued to march southwestward for over two hundred miles when they reached Rozoy on Sunday 5th September and orders were received to turn east and engage the enemy. On Wednesday 9th the Marne was crossed at Nogent and by Monday 14th the Battalion had arrived on the Chemin des Dames and the Aisne. They came under fire as they took position at Paissy then mounted a counter-attack with the Battalion taking considerable numbers of casualties. After serving on the Aisne in the sodden cold trenches orders were received to move north on Wednesday 14th October. However they did not leave for a further two days.
The journey to Ypres was undertaken by train, bus and marching. On Tuesday 20th they had arrived in Elverdinghe where they rested. At 2.45 am they moved off to take the line northeast of Langemarck towards Poelkapelle station. After a long day's engagement and heavy bombardment, the French infantry relieved them to return to billets in Langemarck. During the morning of Thursday 22nd Frank organised his platoon to dig in. During the afternoon they came under attack and were forced to retire before mounting a successful counter-attack. Friday 23rd was a particularly difficult day for the Battalion; at 10.15am the line was bombarded with *'coalboxes'* and *'Black Marias'*. Despite the deluge at 11.30am they advanced against the Inn, north of Pilkem. At 5.30pm a group of Germans advanced on their lines claiming to be British; however, the ruse was spotted and rapid fire brought them to a standstill. At 11.00pm on Saturday 24th the Battalion was relieved and during Sunday they had the opportunity to meet with their friends from the 2nd Battalion. On Thursday 29th October they left their bivouac in a field near Bellewaarde Farm to help hold the line between Gheluvelt and Kruiseik to the south. They were ordered to take a German trench which failed. The Germans counter-attacked but were successfully repulsed, so they dug into new positions near the windmill. In this action Frank was killed.

Second Lieutenant Wilfred Ebery

10th Battalion Sherwood Foresters
(Notts and Derby Regiment)
Died on Monday 14th February 1916, aged 21
Commemorated on Panel 39.

Wilfred was the son of John and Elizabeth Ebery, of 12 Salisbury Street, Darlaston, Wednesbury, Staffordshire. He went up to Jesus College, Oxford, in 1914.
In March 1915 he volunteered and was commissioned being sent for training. Wilfred entrained to Folkestone where he embarked for Boulogne on Wednesday 13th July. He entrained for St Omer from where he marched with his platoon to Zudausques where they were provided billets in the early hours of Friday 16th. On Sunday 18th they set off on a route march that took two days before arriving in Caëstre. After further rest he arrived at Reninghelst on Sunday 25th where he remained until Sunday 1st August when he moved to Kruisstraat. The Battalion was in support at *'Sanctuary Wood'*, a sector he served in until late October before moving the short distance to serve in front of *'Railway Wood'*. From Thursday 6th January 1916 the Battalion was sent for rest and training to Houlle and Moulle, near St Omer. They returned to Salient, arriving in camp at La Clytte on Tuesday 8th February for rest and further training and were issued with the newly designed tin helmets. During the night of Sunday 13th they relieved the 7th Lincolnshires on the *'The Bluff'*. The small mound had been created from spoil when the Ypres to Comines Canal was dug; the Germans were at the foot of *'The Bluff'* and for once the British lines looked down on their lines. At 8.30am on Monday 14th the German artillery commenced a bombardment: from 2.30pm it increased in intensity until 5.30pm when they blew a mine under *'The Bluff'* that was followed by an infantry attack. Wilfred was defending the line and rallying his men when he was killed.
Wilfred is commemorated on Darlaston War Memorial.

It is too late now to retrieve
A fallen dream, too late to grieve
A name unmade, but not too late
To thank the gods for what is great:
A keen-edged sword, a soldier's heart,
Is greater than a poet's art,
And greater than a poet's fame
A little grave that has no name.

France Ledwidge
(buried in Artillery Wood Cemetery)

Lieutenant The Honourable William Alfred Morton Eden

4th Battalion King's Royal Rifle Corps

Died on Wednesday 3rd March 1915, aged 22

Commemorated on Panel 51.

William Eden and his family coat of arms

William was born on Wednesday 15th June 1892, eldest son and heir of William, 5th Baron Auckland, and Lady Sybil, of Gate Burton, Lincoln and related to Lieutenant General Sir Edward Hutton, KCB, KCMG. He was educated at Eton College, a member of Mr de Haviland's House leaving in 1908. William was an all-round sportsman enjoying in particular hunting, shooting, hawking, rowing, football and golf.

He was gazetted in January 1914 and promoted Lieutenant in November 1914.

At the outbreak of war William was based in India and in mid-October 1914 returned to Plymouth on board *SS Ionian*, arriving on Wednesday 18th November. He was sent into camp at Winchester. After a month of foul weather in a camp that resembled the Western Front after a heavy barrage, they were sent to France, arriving shortly before Christmas 1914.

After entraining to northern France they undertook short tours of duty to gain experience of the line in small groups. Their first tour of duty in the southern sector of the Belgian front lasted only three days and they were relieved to Dickebusch, the next morning six officers and five hundred men reported sick because they were unable to walk as a result of standing in more than two feet of freezing cold liquid mud. On Monday 1st March he was in the line at St Eloi when they undertook an attack to regain captured ground. During a night attack on German trenches he was listed as missing, his death being confirmed at a later date. Probate was granted in May 1916, William was the fifth heir to a peerage to be killed in the war. On his death his brother, Frederick, became the heir to the barony.

William is commemorated on the House of Lords War Memorial.

William was recorded in Debretts Obituary — War Roll of Honour published in the 1921 edition.

Lieutenant Richard Fayrer Arnold Edgell

3rd Battalion King's Own Scottish Borderers

Died on Wednesday 5th May 1915, aged 19

Commemorated on Panel 22.

Richard was born in Warwick in 1896, the elder son of the Reverend and Mrs Richard Arnold and Mrs Edgell, of The Rectory, Beckley, Sussex, who had been Headmaster of Meamington College, and grandson of Sir Joseph Fayrer, Baronet. He was educated at home until he attended Tonbridge School from 1911 to 1914 as a member of Hill Side. He was appointed a House Præposter and served as Corporal in the OTC.

At the outbreak of war Richard volunteered and was about to be commissioned when the authorities realised that he had lost an eye as a child but his good work, and the determination of his Colonel, plus others, persuaded Lord Kitchener to intervene personally to ensure he was gazetted. He went out to Belgium on Wednesday 21st April 1915. Richard was in a wood close to Hill 60 on Wednesday 5th May 1915 when the Germans launched a gas attack that was followed by an infantry advance that retook the Hill. At 10.00pm the Battalion advanced in a counter-attack and with artillery support they bombed their way forward. Despite their best efforts Richard and his men were forced back into their trenches. Casualties were heavy: Richard and three fellow officers were killed and one hundred and thirty casualties were recorded amongst the other ranks.

Richard was recorded in Debretts Obituary — War Roll of Honour published in the 1921 edition.

He is commemorated on the Beckley War Memorial, Sussex.

11553 Private Joseph Edwards

2nd Battalion King's Own Scottish Borderers

Died on Wednesday 18th November 1914, aged 15

Commemorated on Panel 22.

Joseph was born in Everton, Liverpool, and was the nephew of Elizabeth Hardwick, of 38 Smollett Street, Kensington, Liverpool. He was educated locally.

He enlisted in Bedford and was sent for training before leaving for France with a draft and joining the Battalion in the field.

On Tuesday 10th November 1914 Joseph was in the line at Nonne Bosschen when they came under heavy shell-fire with the line being attacked on Wednesday 11th. After a fierce fight the Germans were repulsed killing or wounding more than sixty of the enemy. For nine hours on Friday 13th he was under sustained bombardment. On Tuesday 17th the Germans launched another attack that was again repulsed by rapid fire. The next day the *'minenwerfers'* poured down on his line and the King's Own were assisted by the Royal Engineers in digging a section of new trench. During the work Joseph was killed.

LIEUTENANT CHARLES VIVIAN DE GRETE EDYE

2nd Battalion Duke of Cornwall's Light Infantry

Died on Friday 30th October 1914, aged 28

Commemorated on Panel 20.

Charles was born on Thursday 25th November 1886, younger son of Ernest and Kate S Edye, of Syon House, East Budleigh, Devon. He was educated at Bradfield College and passed into RMC Sandhurst where won several competitions for topography. Charles was Secretary of the Hong Kong Polo Club and a member of the Junior United Services Club.

In August 1905 Charles was gazetted, promoted Lieutenant in January 1900. He served at several different posts abroad and in 1910 his Commanding Officer wrote: *"Commands his section well, is a good leader and instructor, a good horseman and horsemaster, has a very good eye for country, has tact, judgment, energy and self-reliance; is quite reliable, has plenty of common sense, has influence over officers and men, lives quietly, is fond of sport, is a very good scout officer, and has done very well."*

In July 1913 he was appointed ADC to Major General Francis Henry Kelly, CB, General Officer Commanding in China. Charles was invalided to England in July 1914 with pleurisy and fever. General Kelly wrote: *"We shall miss him very much. I found him a first-rate A.D.C. — neat, methodical, and always smart as paint."*

At the outbreak of war Charles went out with the Royal Welch Fusiliers arriving in Zeebrugge at 9.00am on Wednesday 7th October 1914. He entrained to Oostcamp, Brugge, before being sent to Oudenburg, southeast of Ostend. On Friday 9th they moved to Ostend, Lieutenant Hindson recorded: *"... we halted for several hours on a piece of waste land near a canal: this proved very unpleasant on account of smells. Many refugees passed us here, on carts, bicycles, and on foot, carrying as much as they could. A few of the Royal Naval Division wounded also passed us from Antwerp. Both refugees and wounded were very pessimistic and said Antwerp was bound to fall."* He was sent by train to Ghent, arriving at 6.30pm, marching to their bivouac in the pouring rain. At 2.00am on Saturday 10th he was moved to Melle and joined the Royal Warwickshires. The next day they were ordered to cover the retirement of the French and Belgian troops. They did not engage the German army before orders were received to retire, arriving in Hansbeke at 7.00pm where they rested until 2.00am then continued their march to Roeselare. Some of the offices and men (one hundred and fifty per company) were taken to Ypres by train, the rest marched. Billets were provided in the barracks from where they were sent to Zillebeke during the day on Thursday 15th. After two days at Zonnebeke they went into reserve on Sunday 18th at Veldhoek until late in the evening when they marched to billets in Becelaere. Orders were received to advance and attack the German infantry at Klijthoek. The Welsh had considerable success, but the Germans were marching in force on the left flank and the Battalion was ordered to withdraw and support the line at Broodseinde. Early in the morning of Wednesday 21st a German aeroplane flew low over their lines and shortly afterwards the German artillery opened up on their position before mounting an attack. The Battalion, behind Polygon Wood, remained under heavy shell fire for the next three days before moving back to Veldhoek. From Saturday 24th they were slightly east of Zandvoorde village as the Battle of Gheluvelt commenced. The battle intensified each day until Friday 30th when most of the Battalion was wiped out. Lieutenant Wodehouse wrote: *"We were holding a line about three-quarters of a mile long, A Company on the right, then B, D, and C on the left. Battalion H.Q. was in a dugout about 600 yards to the rear. The trenches were not well sighted for field of fire. So far as I know, no one was on our right; some 'Blues' were supposed to be there, but I did not see them. It was foggy in the early morning, so that the Germans could not shell us much, which was lucky, as they had two batteries on Zandvoorde Ridge. About 8 a.m. the shelling increased, and we saw large numbers of Germans advancing down a slope about 1,500 yards to our front. Also I believe large numbers were seen coming round our exposed right flank. The batteries on the ridge were now firing point blank into our trenches, so that it was difficult to see what was happening, and the rifle fire also increased from our right rear. No orders were received, so it was thought best to stay where we were, and about midday the whole battalion was either killed, wounded, or taken prisoners."*

General Capper

General Sir Thompson Capper (who was later killed and is buried in Lillers Communal Cemetery) wrote: *"On 19th October the Battalion attacked Klijthoek with much gallantry and dash, and later on the same day acted with coolness ad discipline under trying conditions. On the 20th and 21st October, at Zonnebeke, the battalion held the left of the line under very heavy enfilade fire and enveloping attack of the enemy's infantry, until withdrawn by orders of the Brigadier. During these two days' fighting the battalion lost three-quarters of its strength in offices and men.*

On the 30th the battalion occupied the right of the division line. Owing to troops on their right being driven back, the battalion became very exposed, and was subjected to an enveloping attack by the enemy. The battalion, however, held on and lost nearly all its effectiveness, including the Colonel and all other officers, only 90 men rejoining the brigade. This battalion has fought nobly and has carried on its best traditions by fighting until completely overwhelmed. As a battalion it had for the time ceased to exist."

Lieutenant Dudley Sinclair Elliot

35th Battalion Australian Infantry, AIF

Died on Friday 12th October 1917, aged 27

Commemorated on Panel 25.

Dudley was born in Plymouth, England, on Tuesday 14th January 1890, son of Captain Charles Elliot, RN, and Florence Louisa Elliot, and was related to the Earl of Minto. He went to Australia in his late teens where he continued his education at The King's School, Parramatta, Sydney, followed by the Hawkesbury Agricultural College, New South Wales. Dudley was married to Annie Caroline Elliot.

At the outbreak of war he volunteered and enlisted, serving in New Guinea until early 1916. Dudley was commissioned and embarked on *SS Ascanius* on Wednesday 25th October 1916 and sent to England. He continued his training before proceeding to France, joining the Battalion in the line.

After undertaking tours of duty in the line Dudley undertook training for the Battle of Messines, the first major battle he participated in. He continued to serve in the sector until the end of July where the latter month was described as being one of the most strenuous that the Battalion had been involved in bar the Battle of Messines itself — with long tours of duty in trenches that were in poor condition due to the rain and the constant artillery fire. During this time Dudley was billeted in Neuve Eglise and *'Douve River Camp'*.

From Wednesday 15th August Dudley served in the line at Wismes until the end of September when they left their billets in Winnezeele for Zonnebeke. On Thursday 4th October the Battalion was relieved and sent back to their billets until Wednesday 10th when they were collected by a fleet of buses and taken to *'Cavalry Camp Farm'* where they arrived at 9.00pm. After a short period of rest Dudley formed with his Company and led them to their assembly positions at 3.30am on Friday 12th along a muddy track under constant shell-fire. At 5.25am, Zero Hour, Dudley struggled to lead his men forward, their rifles clogged with mud; he and most of the men became casualties due to machine-gun fire — more than a one hundred men from just over five hundred were killed or wounded.

Dudley was recorded in Debretts Obituary — War Roll of Honour published in the 1921 edition.

Lieutenant Kenward Wallace Elmslie

4th Dragoon Guards (Royal Irish)

Died on Wednesday 4th November 1914, aged 27

Commemorated on Panel 3.

Kenward Elmslie

Kenward was born Tuesday 31st May 1887, the second son of Mr and Mrs Kenward Wallace Elmsie, of May Place, Hampton Wick, Middlesex. He was educated at Cheltenham College from September 1901 to July 1906 as a member of Newick House where he was a Prefect and won Ladies' Prize in 1906. He went up to King's College, Cambridge, in 1906 where he studied law and graduated with an LLB, and was called to the bar, Inner Temple.

In May 1909 Kenward joined the Special Reserve and was promoted Lieutenant in May 1914. At the declaration of war the 4th Dragoons were at Tidworth on Salisbury Plain in Assaye Barracks. On Saturday 15th August 1914 they left Southampton on *SS Winifredian* for Boulogne, where they went to camp until entraining for Haupmont, arriving on Wednesday 19th. They were marched to the Bois la Haut, south-west of Mons before moving forward to St Denis. During the night of Saturday 22nd patrols were sent out and the Germans were seen massing in the area. Captain Hornby came across a party of Uhlans and chased them out. The Brigadier sent the following order: *"The Brigadier desires to congratulate the 4th Dragoon Guards on the spirited action of two Troops of the Squadron on reconnaissance, which resulted in establishing the moral superiority of our cavalry from the first, over the German cavalry."* After the short engagement the Retreat commenced: on Monday 24th they came under heavy shell fire at Audregnies. They marched south to Le Cateau and onto St Quentin to Le Plessis. Here, in the early hours, the Germans launched an attack and rear-guard action commenced that repulsed them. By Thursday 3rd September they had reached the Marne when two days later they were ordered to confront von Kluck's advance in the direction of La Ferte Gaucher on the Petit Morin. On Wednesday 9th they encountered the German infantry at Sablonnières where they took the first bridge and eventually, with support, took the second. They continued to advance to the Aisne. On Monday 14th September they were ordered to march on Troyon and came under heavy shell fire at Vendresse. By the Saturday 19th they were on the Chemin des Dames, remaining on the Aisne until early October when they were sent north.

On Monday 12th they were at Bailleul opposing the German front line. On Tuesday 20th they were involved in action at Ploegsteert Wood where Captain Hornby (see above) was badly wounded. Kenward was in the line in front of Messines until Wednesday 28th October when they were ordered to support the Second Corps at Neuve-Chapelle where they joined the Indian Division at Richebourg St Vaast. On Friday 30th October he returned to Messines to help support the line that was under heavy attack. They were forced to retire to a new line south of the Wulverghem to Messines Road where howitzers opened on their line causing many men to buried alive. Kenwood, commanding his machine-gun section, was killed in action.

Second Lieutenant Gerard Gordon Clement Elrington

East Yorkshire Regiment attached 2nd Battalion Duke of Wellington's (West Riding Regiment)

Died on Saturday 31st October 1914, aged 20

Commemorated on Panel 21.

Gordon Elrington

Gerard was born in Brugge, Belgium, on Saturday 28th April 1894, son of Mary Tilly Miles (formerly Elrington), of 103 Belgrave Road, London SW1, and the late Captain Gerard Gordon Elrington, and step-son of General John Miles. He was educated at Cranleigh School from 1908 to 1911, where he was a Corporal in the OTC, and then passed into RMC Sandhurst.

On Friday 1st October 1912 Gerard was commissioned to the 3rd Battalion East Yorkshire Regiment and in August 1914 transferred to the 1st. He went out to France attached to the Duke of Wellington's. Gerard saw action at La Bassée in mid-October. From Monday 19th they came under heavy shell fire for four days before the Germans mounted an attack on Thursday 22nd where they broke the line. Colonel Harrison wrote: *"A very heavy day, being shelled practically without ceasing. Extended our firing line right along the Violaines road. At midnight got orders to retire about a mile and to dig in a new line of trenches. We did not get into position until 4.30 a.m. in the open ploughed field and had great luck not to lose one company, but owing to the good management of the company officer who got into his place just before daylight very few hit and none killed."* At 8.00am on Friday 23rd the Germans attacked again and Gerard was under high-explosive and shrapnel shell fire from 7.00am until 4.00pm. The Germans advanced to within 400 yards of their line but no further. On Thursday 29th he was relieved and sent to billets. Their rest did not last long as on Friday they were ordered to prepare to support the Sikhs at Festubert. Gerard was leading his men forward when he was killed.

Colonel Harrison wrote: *"... after saying that this young officer had on previous occasions during the fighting on the Aisne and north of Arras shown conspicuous gallantry, cheerfulness, and disregard of danger. ... Near Festubert, on the night of the 30th to 31st, a company of this battalion was ordered to co-operate with the Sikhs in recovering a trench captured by the Germans the previous night. 2nd Lieutenant Elrington was leading his platoon in this attack, and was shot through the head within a few feet of the trench. The trench was not taken, but I assured myself later that he was quite dead, and his burial was carried out by the officers of the Sikh (58th Rifles) Company in the trench later on."*

Captain Umfreville, wrote: *"During the time I commanded the battn., during the Aisne fighting and the later operations north of Arras, 2nd Lieut. Elrington has shown conspicuous gallantry, and his company commander repeatedly expressed to me his admiration of the cheerfulness and carelessness of danger displayed of this officer."*

Captain Robert Ernest English

North Somerset Yeomanry

Died on Thursday 13th May 1915, aged 31

Commemorated on Panel 5.

Robert English

Robert was born in South Africa on Tuesday 6th November 1883, second son of Robert and Mary English. He was educated at Harrow School from 1897 to 1901 as a member of West Acre and in 1902 went up to Magdalen College, Oxford, graduating with a BA. Robert worked in insurance as a member of Lloyds. He was a Member of the Bath Club, enjoyed shooting and fishing. Robert went out to West Africa in 1913 for big-game hunting. Robert was gazetted in 1909, promoted Lieutenant in August 1912 and Captain in September 1914.

At the outbreak of war Robert was mobilized, leaving for France in November 1914. During the Second Battle of Ypres he was in action at Hooge when he was killed during a German artillery bombardment.

The President of Magdalen wrote: *"Robert Ernest English was certainly one of the most pleasant and popular of the many pleasant and popular men Harrow has sent to this College in the last dozen years. Without any special or specialized ability, either in athletics or in the Schools, he soon became a leading man in the College, known and liked by all, and exercising an undemonstrative but valuable influence. His healthy, sensible, pleasant, and very kindly disposition, and unselfish love of his fellows, displayed itself no less when he went down. He devoted himself with much ardour and readiness to the College Mission, and in particular to the Boys' Clubs, for which no one ever did more. When the War came he gave up business to join the North Somerset Yeomanry. Every Magdalen man knew what a good officer he would make, but, alas very little scope was given him, for the end came almost directly he had got abroad. Simple, unselfish, good-hearted, no one was ever more ready to sacrifice himself. For none will there be more unqualified regret, among those who knew him here."*

Captain & Adjutant Henry Etlinger

9th Bhopal Infantry

Died on Tuesday 27th April 1915, aged 35

Commemorated on Panel 2A.

Henry Etlinger

Henry was born at home on Tuesday 27th April 1880, son of Edmund and Charlotte Etlinger, of 27 Cavendish Road West, London NW. He was educated at Durnford School and Marlborough College from May 1894 where he was Captain of the School XI in 1897 and went up to Trinity College Dublin in 1899 where he played in their XI. Henry was married to Muriel Etlinger (née Jelf). He was a good sportsman winning a selection of cups and shields for football, tennis and cricket whilst serving in India. Henry was a member of the Junior Army and Navy Club.

Henry was gazetted to the North Staffordshire Regiment from the Militia in January 1902, promoted Lieutenant in April 1904, Adjutant from October 1909 to October 1912, and Captain in November 1912 in 9th Bhopal Infantry. He served in the South African War receiving the Queen's Medal with two clasps. He went to India in 1902 where he served for ten years.

At the outbreak of war Henry sailed with the Lahore Division, landing in Marseilles. He entrained to Flanders and fought in the front line through the winter at Ypres and northern France. Following the German gas attack on Thursday 22nd April 1915 Henry was ordered into the line taking part in an advance at 12.20pm on Tuesday 27th. As he took his men forward he was killed on his 35th birthday, one of one hundred and twenty Battalion casualties.

A brother officer wrote: *"I knew him for the past two years, but never knew a better. I am unable to give you exact details of his death, but he was found in the trenches by one of our men, and an officer was on the spot immediately and applied first aid. He was quite unconscious, as the bullet struck him in the head. He died right nobly in the attack. I am seeing to his grave, and am having a cross to mark the spot."*

Lieutenant Hilary Gresford Evan-Jones

1st Battalion Welsh Regiment

Died on Tuesday 16th February 1915, aged 26

Commemorated on Panel 37.

Hilary Evan-Jones

Hilary was born at home on Sunday 22nd January 1899, younger son of the Reverend Canon Richard and Mrs Evan-Jones, of Llanllwchaiarn Vicarage, Newtown, Monmouthshire. He was grandson of Edward Evan, JP, DL, High Sheriff of Denbighshire, nephew of Sir Edward Evan, KCVO, CB, RA. His brother was Reverend Basil Evan-John, MA, sub-editor of the Powysland Collections. Hilary was educated at Charterhouse from 1902 to 1906 as a Hodgsonsite and went up to Hertford College, Oxford, in 1907 where he was Williams Prizeman, served in the OTC and graduated with a BA in 1910. He was a keen sportsman, boxer, good shot, polo player, a horseman and Master of the Hunt.

He was gazetted on Wednesday 5th October 1910, promoted Lieutenant in November 1911. Hilary served in England, India and in the Mediterranean.

At the outbreak of war Hilary was on his way from Chakrata, India, to Cyprus where he was to marry Miss Nancy Bolton, daughter of Major Bolton, Commissioner of Kyrenia. Orders received *en route* meant he was unable to marry his fiancee and he sailed directly to England, arriving in December 1914.

Hilary left for Le Havre on Monday 18th January 1915 arriving the next morning where the lady volunteers provided refreshments to the troops. The Battalion entrained for Hazebrouck and marched the seven miles to billets in Merris. They commenced training for the front line and were inspected by General Sir Horace Smith-Dorrien on Tuesday 26th and two days later by Field Marshal Sir John French.

General Smith-Dorrien

On Tuesday 2nd February the Battalion was transported by motor bus to Vlamertinghe from where they marched along the cobbled road towards Ypres. During the march rations were issued and at Ypres they were met by guides that took them to the lines at Hill 60 and relieved the French infantry: *"They were small men, and seemed very agitated at our being a little behind time. We knew it was only about an hour's march from Ypres to our support positions, and as there were still several hours of darkness, we were rather inclined to think that they had got the wind up. They were of course anxious to get well clear by daylight, to say nothing of wanting to get out to rest, but as we had not yet been in the trenches, we were a bit unsympathetic. To our surprise they were dressed in the old blue overcoat and baggy red trousers of the French infantryman of peace time, and must have made very conspicuous targets. During the next three months we were to see hundreds of dead Frenchmen lying out in No Man's Land, between our front and support trenches and to realise what gallant hearts those theatrical garments had covered. Eventually Battalion H.Q. and two Companies arrived at some brick fields (Tuileries) where the men got into shelters of sorts, and Battalion H.Q. were uncomfortably installed in a kiln, at least so we thought at the time. We little knew what a palace it was! When day dawned we looked out on our new world, which appeared to be uninhabited. The French had warned us to keep under cover by day, but with true British scorn we did not do so, and got some fairly heavy shelling during the next few days which set 'B' Company's farm, the Moated Grange, close to the Tuileries alight, and killed one man, and wounded seven, besides destroying most of the men's equipment."* The area was strewn with the French dead who had not been removed from the field, with a large number of the corpses having been built into the trench walls — and sanitary arrangements did not exist!

On Thursday 11th February the Battalion was relieved and sent to huts in Vlamertinghe where Hilary wrote home: *"We have just finished our first eight days — divided between the supports and the firing line. I had the worst bit of trench to look after with my platoon and did all right, but had a good few casualties, considering the 96 hours I was actually up — two killed and nine wounded. I made two night expeditions by myself with some bombs, which I successfully dropped into the German trenches. During my first I met a German gentleman apparently at the same job as myself. My revolver accounted for him all right, as we were only two feet apart. The trenches are from 30 to 75 feet apart in most places and sometimes closer. We are now off on a four days' rest, which is absolutely ripping. It is splendid to get out of the noise and to get some proper food and sleep. I think, if anything I am rather enjoying myself. Cold feet are the worst part of the show, but my men are such rippers, it makes up for lots. I hate having them hit, though otherwise it is quite cheery. I had a sing-song in my trench the other evening, which did not please the Germans. I sat in a chair, which collapsed, and I went straight to sleep where I lay. The strain is fairly big up there."*

On Sunday 14th February Hilary returned to the line at *'The Bluff'* however they were not required but relieved the line the next day.

'Recollections of a Field Officer' records: *"It was a miserable, rainy, cold day, and we arrived at Lankhof Chateau at dusk to find it crowded with officers from all sorts of units, including Belgian artillerists, who kindly gave us some tea, as of course we had nothing but iron rations on us. Guides appeared for the Company Commanders, but none for Lieutenant-Colonel Marden and Captain Westby (Adjutant), who set out to get to Battalion H.Q. in pitch darkness and driving rain, and soon lost their way. They were fortunately rescued by a N.C.O. of the 3rd R.F., returning to the trenches, who walked along running a telephone wire through his hand, or he too would have lost the path. Eventually we arrived at a broken down farm, where we descended into a cellar, the H.Q. of the 3rd R.F., whom we were to relieve. Here we found the C.O., Lieutenant-Colonel Du Maurier, the author of that well-known play, 'An Englishman's Home,' which had depicted the realities of a German invasion of England, and had had a great run shortly before the war. His forecast of what would happen was more than fulfilled by the Germans, when they took possession of B and put civilians up against the wall and shot them on the slightest pretext. Du Maurier, who was killed a few days later by a shell just outside this farm, was picturesquely attired in semi-civilian kit, which appeared to be much more suited to the climate than our military garments, and he wore a very hand some beard. The cellar was so low that one could just sit upright, and could not stand at all, but at any rate it was dry and warm, though airless. Having been informed of the horrors of the situation we struggled back to the Chateau to hear that C.S.M. McCarthy, who had won the D.C.M. in the South African War, and was one of our stoutest fighters, had been very badly wounded as he was leaving 'Y' trench. He died the next day. 'Annie' Lloyd (Lieutenant G. Lloyd), his Company Commander, said that he knew he would suffer the same fate when he took over' Y 'trench, and sad to say, his premonition was right. We rode back to Mile Kapellen Farm, where the Battalion was billeted, and had not been in an hour or so when we were ordered out again, and at 330 a.m. the Battalion was on the move to Ypres and the Lankhof Chateau. Half-way we met the N.C.O.s who had been reconnoitring, marching back—we were dead tired, and they must have been even more so. However, we got some hours sleep on some corn sacks in an outhouse at Lankhof during the 15th inst., all except the C.O., who had to go to a Brigade Conference, and then do another reconnaissance."*

In the short time he spent at the front Hilary had a reputation as a bomb-thrower and had written home: *"I have been favourable reported on for going out and throwing those bombs. It was really quite a simple thing to do, and I think people are making rather an unnecessary fuss about it all."*

When the Battalion finally took the line, relieving the 3rd Royal Fusiliers, the Battalion Diary recorded: *"The track to the trenches was over a mile long, and deep in holding mud. 'T' trench (Major Hoggan), was on a sort of hillock (The Bluff), but there was a good deal of dead ground in front and to the north of it. It was regularly and accurately shelled twice a day by the enemy. 'X' trench was only a series of small dugouts under a bank with a 40 yards view. It protected 'T' from small parties creeping in under the hillock. 'Y' trench (Lieutenant C. Lloyd) was merely a ditch with a very weak parapet, and under close fire (40 yards) of the very strong German line. There were also ruined houses in advance of both flanks which gave trouble. The trench was knee deep in water, and casualties always occurred when entering and leaving the trench, It was not properly supported by fire from either 'T' or 'Z', and was untenable, 'Z' trench (Major Toke) had been strong once, but was now only partially held. It was subject to enfilade fire from one of the cottages. The parapets were not bullet proof, and sand bags were shot down as soon as placed. 'B' Company (Captain Montgomery) and the Grenadier platoons had better trenches on the south of the Canal."*

Hilary was in 'Z' Trench, in the wood, but had no field of fire. The German had captured a section of it and were able to attack at very close quarters, from a small cottage: the position was under constant sniper and enfilade fire. Whilst in the line Hilary was killed.

His Commanding Officer wrote: *"I regret most deeply having to inform you of the death on the 16th inst., in the trenches, of your gallant son Hilary. As far as we can ascertain, his death was instantaneous from a rifle bullet, but many of his platoon were shot down at the same time, and there was no one in the trench who could give accurate information as to what happened. He is a great loss to us, as he was such a good soldier, and so popular with all ranks. As you know, probably, he was selected to lead the second Grenadier Platoon, and had behaved so gallantly during his former tour of duty in the trenches, when he kept the spirits of his whole platoon up by his energy and enterprise, that I had brought his name specially to the notice of the Brigadier. He crept out of the trenches alone on several occasions and threw bombs into the enemy's trenches. All his brother officers wish me to express to you and Mr Evan-Jones out sincerest sympathy for the loss of your very gallant son."*

The *'Oxford Magazine'* published the following *"While at Oxford Lieutenant Hilary Gresford Evan-Jones, B.A., devoted himself with whole-hearted enthusiasm to military affairs. At the end of his first year the old Volunteers gave way to the O.T.C. He fathered the change in Hertford and multiplied the strength of the College detachment by ten. He was Colour-Sergeant of 'D' Company in 1909 and 1910, and in the latter year on the Williams Prize, which is given to the most efficient non-commissioned officer in the corps. He was a great leader, and when not on military duty was usually organising some very healthy 'rag'. Everyone who was at Hertford with him has lost a friend, and the Army has lost one of its best junior officers."*

He was Mentioned in Despatches, gazetted on Monday 31st May 1915.

On Sunday 28th February 1915 a Memorial Service was held in Llanllwchaiarn Parish Church that was conducted by his father and elder brother with Canon Williams, the Rector of Newtown, delivering the sermon.

Second Lieutenant Charles Heyland Evans

2nd Battalion Border Regiment

Died on Monday 26th October 1914, aged 23

Commemorated on Panel 35.

Charles was born on Monday 4th May 1891 son of Warren Edward and Helen Lloyd Evans, of Henblas, Llangefni, Anglesey. He was educated at Mill Mead School followed by Haileybury from 1905 to 1909 as a member of Hailey and went up to Pembroke College, Cambridge, in 1910.

William left Lyndhurst Camp at 10.00pm on Sunday 4th October 1914 for Southampton; the Battalion was transported to Zeebrugge on the *SS Turkoman* and *SS Minneapolis*. The intention was to defend Antwerp but by the time they arrived it was too late so they were sent to assist with the defence of Ghent. They were in the line for a couple of days before they were sent on a forced march to Thielt and then onward to Ypres, arriving on Thursday 15th. On Sunday 18th he marched to Kruiseik along the Menin Road, arriving at 5.00pm. On Monday 19th the Battalion Diary records: *"The Brigade advanced in artillery formation on Menin, which was occupied by the enemy. On arrival at a village, America, the Brigade was subjected to a heavy shrapnel fire from enemy guns firing from direction of Menin. Two men of the Battalion were wounded. At 3 p.m. the Battalion fell back and entrenched on Kruiseik Hill leaving 'D' Company at America as support."*

Charles served in the Zandvoorde to Gheluvelt sector until his capture. From Wednesday 21st to Saturday 24th they came under heavy shell fire, with more than one hundred and fifty shells an hour falling on their lines. He was severely wounded in action and taken prisoner. Charles was shot by the Germans later the same day whilst trying to defend one of his men who was being ill-treated by them.

G/16521 Private Roger MacDonnell Evanson

7th Battalion Queen's Own (Royal West Kent Regiment)

Died on Tuesday 31st July 1917, aged 25

Commemorated on Panel 45.

Roger was born on Wednesday 26th August 1891 son of Arthur MacDonnell Evanson and Katherine Mary Evanson, of Chilverton Elms, Dover, Kent. He attended the Royal College of Music from May 1912 to July 1914 where he studied singing and piano. Roger was employed as a schoolmaster in the Dover area.

For the majority of June 1917 Roger was in training and rest in Coigneux; on Tuesday 3rd July he entrained for Doullens and onward to the Ypres Salient. He went into the line near Zillebeke where the Battalion took a number of casualties. On Tuesday 31st July Roger was in support, carrying material forward to supply the 1st North Staffordshires and the 8th Queen's who were consolidating their position in *'Jehovah Trench'*, Zillebeke, when he was killed in action.

3001 Private John Birnie Ewen

'D' Company, 4th Battalion Gordon Highlanders

Died on Saturday 25th September 1915, aged 22

Commemorated on Panel 38.

John Ewen

John was born at home on Tuesday 21st February 1893, son of James and Helen Ewen, of 37 Hosefield Avenue, Aberdeen. He was educated at Robert Gordon's College and went up to Aberdeen University in 1910, graduating in 1914 with a Second Class Honours in Classics. He played football for the College and won his Blue for tennis.

At the outbreak of war he volunteered but was rejected on medical grounds. He tried again in October 1914 and this time was accepted. He trained in Aberdeen until March 1915 when he was sent out to France. He could have remained in Scotland as he had won an open competition under the National Health Insurance Commission but after some persuasion the authorities gave him leave for the front, joining the Battalion at La Clytte. After further training and short trips to the line he was sent on tours of duty.

He remained at the front until he was killed in action at Hooge when he advanced at 4.10am which was countered by a German barrage at 4.30am. He came up against uncut wire where John and many of his colleagues perished.

Captain and Adjutant Gilbert Davidson Pitt Eykyn

Royal Scots

attached 4th Battalion Yorkshire Regiment

Died on Sunday 25th April 1915, aged 33

Commemorated on Panel 11.

Gilbert was born at France Lynch Parsonage, Gloucestershire, on Monday 22nd August 1881, the only son of the late Reverend Pitt and Charlotte Elizabeth Eykyn, of 82 Prince of Wales Mansions, Battersea Park, London. He was educated at Haileybury College for two terms in 1895 as a member of Melvill, followed by Clayesmore School, Iwerne Minster, Dorset. On Friday 28th November 1902, in Bombay Cathedral, Gilbert married Constance Eykyn (née Norton) and they had a son, Duncan Arthur Davidson, born on Saturday 11th August 1906.

Gilbert joined The Loyal North Lancashire Regiment Militia in March 1899, being promoted Lieutenant in June 1900. He studied under Colonel Bosworth at Roehampton before serving in the South African War where he received the Queen's Medal with three clasps. Gilbert returned to England and passed into the Army, being gazetted in the Manchester Regiment in May 1901, promoted Lieutenant in December. From 1904 he served in the Indian Army and in February 1905 he transferred to the Royal Scots Regiment. He was appointed Adjutant in February 1913 and was promoted temporary Captain, confirmed in June. He passed his examinations in both Russian and Hindustani and qualified in gymnastics. Gilbert was an accomplished speaker and often was employed as a spokesman for the National Service League, greatly assisting in their recruitment drives.

Gilbert entrained in Newcastle at 9.00am on Saturday 17th April 1915 for Folkestone. The Battalion embarked for Boulogne and were marched out to camp at St Martin's before entraining to Cassel. They marched to Godeswaersvelde into billets remaining for four days; training was to follow. However, the Germans launched the first gas attack on Thursday 22nd April and late that evening the Battalion was ordered to 'stand to'. The next morning they marched from the village to Poperinghe where they were taken to *'Camp C'* at Vlamertinghe. At 1.00am on Saturday 24th they marched to the Ypres Canal where they remained until noon when orders arrived for them to move forward to Potijze. The Battalion had crossed the pontoon bridge across the Canal when it received a direct hit and was destroyed and their machine-guns, limbers and Medical Officer's cart were marooned on the west bank. Shortly after arriving they were sent assist in resisting the German advance at St Julien and marched to Fortuin where they consolidated their position. Gilbert arrived at HQ to report that the senior officers had been killed and requested orders. Two companies of the Battalion, together with two of the East Yorkshire Regiment were sent to support the line. As they moved forward across the open ground he was killed by a sniper and buried in the woods close to the reserve trenches.

His Commanding Officer wrote: *"Remember this, he trained the battalion, and the General has personally thanked us for our behaviour at a critical moment. His is the credit."* His Brigadier General wrote: *"He will be sadly missed, not only in the regiment, but in the brigade. He died like a gallant gentleman."*

In Clayesmore School Chapel, Iwerne Minster, Dorset, a stained glass window was placed in his memory with an inscription: *"G. D. P. Eykyn. Esse Quam Videri."*

Punch cartoon — UNCONQUERABLE
The Kaiser: "So, you see — you've lost everything".
The King of the Belgians: "Not my soul".

from

Faber to Fyson

Second Lieutenant Cecil Valdemar Faber

9th Battalion King's Royal Rifle Corps

Died on Friday 30th July 1915, aged 19

Commemorated on Panel 51.

Cecil was born on Tuesday 20th December 1895, the youngest son of Johan Valdemar and Emma Maude Stanley Countessa Vivian Faber, of The Links, Worplesdon, Surrey (his father was Danish). He was educated at Cottesmore School, Hove, followed by Eton College as a member of Mr John Hugh Montague Hare's House, where he was Head of House, and a member of the OTC. He matriculated for Oriel College, Oxford, in 1914 and was to have gone up in 1915.

Cecil volunteered after leaving School, enlisted in the Royal Fusiliers, was subsequently commissioned, and arrived in Boulogne on Friday 21st May 1915. The Battalion entrained for northern France from where they marched across the border into Belgium; after a period of training they were sent into the line. For the next few weeks they undertook tours of duty but did not participate in any significant action until Hooge. The Germans launched a fierce attack at 3.15am on Friday 30th and used *'Flammenwerfer'* (flame throwers or 'liquid fire') for the first time. The British line was forced to retire and Cecil and the 9th Battalion mounted a series of counter-attacks. As Cecil led his men forward he was shot and killed instantaneously.

1329 Rifleman Arthur West Fairbairn

'C' Company 1st/6th Battalion

The King's (Liverpool Regiment)

Died on Wednesday 5th May 1915, aged 19

Commemorated on Panel 6.

Arthur was the son of George E and Jessie F Fairbairn, of Rowallan, Blundellsands, Liverpool.

Arthur and his brother William (see below) enlisted together in Liverpool and they had consecutive service numbers. Following training they left for France from Canterbury, Kent, arriving in Le Havre on Thursday 25th February 1915. After a night in *'No 6 Rest Camp'* they entrained for Bailleul and sent to billets in l'Ecole-des-Jeunes-Filles. Here they prepared to move into the line and on Wednesday 3rd March crossed the border into Belgium and to camp at Ouderdom then onto Vlamertinghe. The brothers only had a short wait before their baptism of fire attached to the Dorsets. A Captain wrote: *"Imagine the company, in Indian file, feeling its way in the pitch dark, burdened with ammunition boxes and stores, in addition to pack, goatskin coat and rifle, stumbling into shell-holes, checking at every ditch and hedge and running to catch up between, bogged in mud like treacle, with guides ignorant of the way and an utter uncertainty of what lay before. Now and then the flash of a bursting shell or the flare of a star-light would show up a ruined farm house and the great shell-holes on every side, filled to the brim with slimy water. Presently bullets begin to whistle, and one can hear their flick into the mud. A man is hit — there is a call for the stretcher-bearers. Never mind, press on, it is worse than useless to halt. Another is hit, then another. At length, it seems ages (it is, in fact hours), we see before us, in a low rise among some splintered trees, a few lights, apparently coming from burrows in the earth facing towards us."*

Arthur and William undertook fatigues carrying ammunition to the front following the gas attack on Thursday 22nd April and remained on such duties until the Battalion was ordered to take the line on Wednesday 5th May. The Germans had launched a gas attack and the British position was becoming increasingly difficult. At 10.45am they marched from bivouac in a wood near Kruisstraat Château to Zillebeke where they halted. The officers went forward to reconnoitre the route to be taken into the line. The men were taken out of the village towards the front line unnoticed by the Germans. As the Battalion undertook a counter-attack the heavy German machine-guns poured their lead and shrapnel shells burst continuously over them.

As the afternoon the losses taken by the Battalion mounted and by the end of the day both Arthur and William lay dead on the battlefield.

1330 Rifleman William Ritchie Fairbairn

1st/6th Battalion The King's (Liverpool Regiment)

Died on Wednesday 5th May 1915, aged 25

Commemorated on Panel 6.

William was the son of George E and Jessie F Fairbairn, of Rowallan, Blundellsands, Liverpool.

See his brother, Rifleman Arthur Fairbairn, above.

... in action at Hill 60

Captain Frank Fairlie

2nd Battalion Royal Scots Fusiliers

Died on Friday 23rd October 1914, aged 36

Commemorated on Panel 33.

Frank Fairlie

Frank was born on Thursday 17th January 1878. He was educated at St Paul's School from 1893. He married Annesley Pollock (formerly Fairlie), of Newcastle House, Kingscourt, County Cavan.

Frank was gazetted in October 1901 after serving with the 3rd Battalion, Scottish Rifles from February 1901, promoted Lieutenant in June 1903 and Captain in January 1912. Frank served in the South African War where he received the Queen's Medal with four clasps. From 1911 to 1913 he served with the West African Frontier Force.

Frank sailed to Zeebrugge on Tuesday 6th October 1914 to assist in the campaign at Antwerp, but they arrived too late as the city was being evacuated. The Battalion spent some time going round in circles in West Flanders before arriving in Roeselare on Tuesday 13th. They marched to Ypres and went into the line at Wieltje before being moved between Reutel and Poezelhoek. The Germans advanced on Wednesday 21st and they held their ground in the Château. Orders were received to clear the village of Poezelhoek, which proved too much. However, a group of thirty Germans offered to surrender and Frank went forward to accept it when one of them shot him dead.

Third Battle of Ypres, the Line of Advance

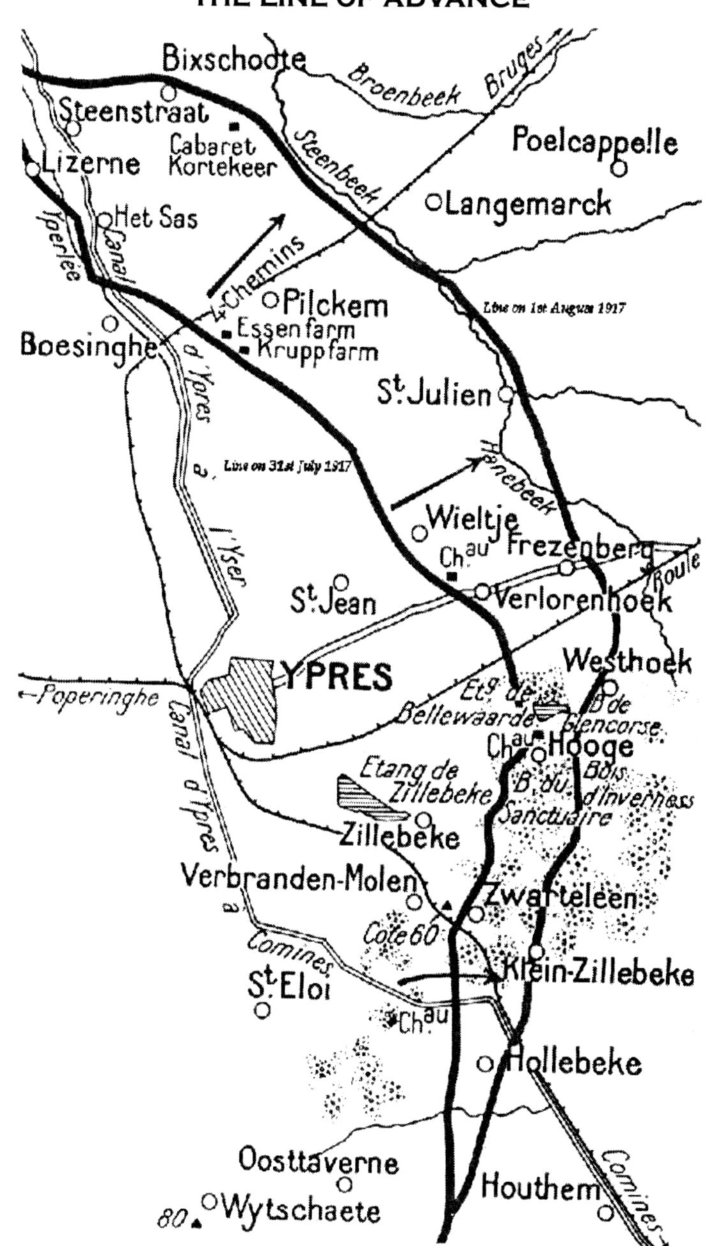

Lieutenant John Keith Falconer

Hampshire Yeomanry (Carabiniers)

Attached 14th Battalion Hampshire Regiment

Died on Tuesday 31st July 1917, aged 20

Commemorated on Panel 5.

John was born on Tuesday 15th June 1897 son of John Arthur Keith Falconer and Mabel Falconer, of Calmsden Manor, Cirencester. He was educated at Winchester College from 1911 to 1915.

John and his men left the line on *'Observatory Ridge'* on Wednesday 25th April, entraining for rest at Arques, St Omer. Over the next three weeks they were able to clean up and catch up on sleep, but with the usual round of training interspersed with sporting competitions and events. On Thursday 17th May they moved to Wormhoudt for ten days training from where they went back into the line near Wieltje. During June they were given the duty of digging a series of new trenches including one that went out into *'No Man's Land'*, close to the German wire. On Thursday 21st June the Battalion went for training at Houlle, near Watten, in preparation for the Battle of Passchendaele, remaining there until Sunday 15th July when they moved closer to the line. On Sunday 29th they were back at the front, in the second line. At 3.50am on Tuesday 31st July 1917, *'Zero Hour'*, the Hampshires advanced under the heaviest barrage so far

George V and King Albert review Belgian troops

of the war — or so it was then described. John advanced in conjunction with the 11th Royal Sussex on *'Kitchener's Wood'* (Bois des Cuisiniers), to the 'Black Line', the second objective. They were held up by the various German pill-boxes that were only taken when the Hampshires were able to work round them and take them from the rear, resulting in heavy casualties. In this action, 2nd Lieutenant Hewitt won his Victoria Cross (commemorated on the Menin Gate, see below), and John was killed.
In All Saints Church, Long Sutton, Hampshire, a stained glass window was placed in his memory with the inscription: *"To the glory of God and in loving memory of John Keith Falconer Ltn. Hants. Yeo. Killed in action 31 Jul. 1917. Age 20."*

624308 Private Robert Frank Fane

10th Battalion Canadian Infantry (Alberta Regiment)
Died on Sunday 11th November 1917, aged 19
Commemorated on Panel 24.

Robert Fane

Robert was born in Surbiton, Surrey, on Friday 30th April 1897, son of Sidney Lee and Annie Ellen Fane, of 11 Hilsea Street, Lower Clapton, London. He was educated in Brighton and was a member of the OTC. He left for Canada and on Monday 15th February 1915 he joined the Commerce Bank being employed in the Vermilion Branch, Alberta. Whilst living in Vermilion he was appointed an instructor with the local OTC.
Robert volunteered Friday 7th January 1916 in Vermilion and was described as a Methodist, 5ft 7¼in tall, a 35in chest, fair complexion, blue eyes, light coloured hair a small pimple on the side of his left nostril and he weighed 140lbs. Robert enlisted in the 151st Overseas Battalion before being transferred to the 10th Battalion, Canadian Infantry.
He was sent for training before leaving for England and onward to France where Robert joined the Battalion in the field. On Monday 28th August 1916 the Battalion was sent to the Somme. Whilst in the line at *'Mouquet Farm'* on Sunday 10th September the Germans raided them on five occasions but did not break into the their line and were comprehensively repulsed. Five days later the Battalion took part in the successful attack that took Courcelette; vicious action was seen at the *'Zollern Redoubt'*, *'Stuff Redoubt'*, and the *'Hessian'* trench system.
From the beginning of November Robert served in the Lens-Vimy sector until mid-March 1917. He was sent for training in preparation for the part he would play during the Battle of Arras. He went into the assembly position on Sunday 8th April and at 5.30am he went over the top and within an hour had captured the German front line that was their first objective. He fought on towards Farbus Wood where he consolidated his position. Robert was relieved to billets at Mont St-Eloi on Saturday 21st April and returned to normal

... the ruins on Mont St-Eloi

tours of duty until mid-July. He moved north and took part in the successful attack on Hill 60 on Wednesday 15th August. He remained in the Sector until early November when he moved to Flanders.
Robert was in the line on Saturday 10th November, during the Battle of Passchendaele. The 7th and 8th Battalion thought they were also being relieved by the 10th Battalion and withdrew from the line. This meant that Robert had to cover a much wider area in the trenches than expected. The German artillery was pounding their line and counter-attacking and during one such attack Robert was killed.

Lieutenant Leighton Dalrymple Fanshawe

7th Company Machine Gun Corps (Infantry)
Died on Friday 3rd August 1917, aged 21
Commemorated on Panel 56.

Leighton was the second son of Captain Frederick Bradford Fanshawe and Marianne Fanshawe, of Hartwell, 18 Coley Avenue, Reading. He was educated at Marlborough House, Reading, followed by Tonbridge School from 1910 to 1913 as a member of Park House where he was a House Præposter and a Lance Corporal in the OTC. Leighton was an Apprentice of the Worshipful Company of Vintners.
At the outbreak of war Leighton was at *'Rugeley Camp'* with the School OTC and he applied for a commission. Whilst waiting to be gazetted he enlisted in the Honourable Artillery Company on Tuesday 8th September 1914, resigning his commission so he could get to the front, leaving for France on Boxing Day 1914

and serving in Belgium. He received a field commission on Wednesday 27th January 1915 to the Royal Berkshire Regiment (his father's regiment) and was sent to England for further training in February, transferring to the Machine Gun Corps on Monday 3rd January 1916. He returned to France in April 1916 and served through the Somme, serving with distinction at Guillemont and Guinchy. In January 1917 he was appointed Second in Command of the 7th Company, Machine Gun Corps. Leighton was killed in action and buried close to where Perth (China Wall) Cemetery is now situated.

LIEUTENANT
FREDERICK BRIAN ARTHUR FARGUS

1st/9th Battalion London Regiment
(Queen Victoria's Rifles)

Died on Friday 1st January 1915, aged 27

Commemorated on Panel 54.

Frederick Fargus

Frederick was born at Strawberry Hill, Middlesex, on Wednesday 8th June 1887, younger son of Henry Robert and Helen Mary Fargus, of 169 Queen's Gate, London. He was educated at Rugby School from 1901 to 1904 as a member of Brooke, and then studied to be a solicitor. In 1911 he joined Messrs Clayton, Sons & Fargus, 10 Lancaster Place, Strand. Frederick was a good sportsman, playing cricket, football, golf and tennis, he also enjoyed motoring and fishing, and was Master-Elect of the Felix Masonic Lodge.

In 1911 Frederick was gazetted in the Queen Victoria Rifles and was promoted to Lieutenant in 1912. At the outbreak of war he was mobilized leaving on Wednesday 4th November 1914 on *SS Oxonian* for Le Havre commanding the machine-gun section. He marched with the men to *'No 1 Rest Camp'* and the next day entrained for a twenty-six hour rail journey to St Omer. They undertook training when on Saturday 14th he accidentally let off his revolver that passed through the upper part of his boot and the bullet lodged in his sole — he only suffered bruising! On Thursday 19th the Battalion marched to Hazebrouck and after a night's rest continued to Bailleul. Two days later a Taube bombed the area close to their billets near a hospital that took the brunt of the attack. Frederick marched across the border into Belgium and were billeted in Neuve Eglise on Friday 27th before taking the line at Wulverghem where he organised his two machine-guns. Frederick undertook a series of duties in the area without being involved in any particular action. Christmas was spent out of the line and a good time was had by all in the Battalion. New Year was spent in the line and all was relatively quiet until early on New Year's Day when the Germans commenced shelling them, a barn where a good number of men were resting was hit and eleven men were killed and thirty-six wounded. Shortly afterwards Frederick was sniped, the first officer of the Battalion to be killed.

Captain Woodruff Cox wrote: *"'B' Company's sector was situated in front of a semi-ruined farmhouse known as the Petite Douvre Farm, and the actual trench of which I had command was close to the Douvre River. The trench consisted of a high command parapet of very indifferent construction and in a bad state of repair and in only a few places raised to the height of a man's shoulder. One of our machine-guns under Lieut. Fargus was placed near the centre. The trench at that time was in a very muddy state and most of the men were squatting on the fire-step or on wooden boxes, sheltering behind the parapet. I was seated on one of these boxes just below the parapet near the Douvre River end of the trench. I noticed Brian Fargus inspecting the gun position, and with his usual disregard for personal safety he exposed himself once or twice and a sniper hidden in the Petite Douvre Farm had one or two shots at him. When Fargus bad finished his inspection he came along the trench in my direction, the sniper potting at him from time to time as his head showed over the parapet. On reaching me I warned him that he had been spotted and got him to sit beside me on the box, and we discussed the situation generally. At the end of five minutes' conversation Fargus found his position somewhat cramped and shifted slightly. At that moment I raised myself so as to see over the parapet from behind some sandbags. Brian Fargus put his hand on my shoulder saying something about getting along and raised himself to practically a standing position. Almost at once a shot was heard from the direction of the farm and poor Fargus dropped dead behind me shot right through the centre of the forehead. He was buried at night close behind the trench he was in when he was hit, at a place called 'the willows,' it being practically impossible in those days to carry the body to the rear owing to the awful condition of the track across the fields."*

His Commanding Officer wrote: *"Your son Brian was in the trenches yesterday and was shot dead by a German sniper. One and all of us will miss his cheerful, bright presence, and his devotion to his duties has been an example to us all. Your son had endeared himself to us one and all, and as for his gun team they absolutely worshipped him. He was so devoid of fear that he was invaluable in patrolling and reconnoitring."*

One of his NCOs wrote: *"He was absolutely a man after our own hearts, and we are proud to know that he died in wandering about his infantry, putting courage into them under shell fire."*

One of his men wrote: *"Not only have we lost a man who was an ideal officer and a good soldier, but we have lost a personal friend, for he was never so happy as when he was with the section or doing something for us."*

Lieutenant Montague Lewis Farmar-Cotgrave

2nd Battalion Canadian Infantry
(Eastern Ontario Regiment)

Died on Tuesday 6th November 1917, aged 25
Commemorated on Panel 10.

Montague was born in Bedford on Friday 23rd December 1892, youngest son of Richard de Malpas Farmar-Cotgrave and Amelia Farmar-Cotgrave, of 13 Staverton Road, Brondesbury Park, London, late of San Stefano, Narnamead, Plymouth. He was educated at King's College, Taunton, after which he left for Canada in 1912, and lived at 2 Herrick Street, Saulte Ste Marie working in the paper mills as a clerk. Montague was a keen footballer and a member of the *'Sons of Scotland'* football team.
Montague had served for two years with the Royal West Kent Regiment and nineteen months in the 2nd Battalion, Canadian Infantry.

Montague volunteered at Valcartier on Tuesday 1st September 1914 where he was described as 6ft ½in tall, with a 32½in waist, a swarthy complexion, hazel eyes, dark brown hair and a mark on his neck as a result of an operation.
The Battalion sailed to Devonport *on SS Cassandra,* arriving at 8.00am on Thursday 15th October. He remained on the ship until Monday 26th when it docked and entrained to Amesbury from where he marched to *'Bustard Camp'* on Salisbury Plain for training. His training continued until Sunday 7th February 1915 when the Battalion returned to Amesbury and entrained for Avonmouth and embarked on *SS Blackwell*, sailing at noon the next day for St Nazaire. They arrived on Thursday 11th and entrained for Strazeele, marching to billets in Merris. Montague first saw the front line trenches on Wednesday 17th when the Battalion was sent for practical experience with the North Staffordshires and the King's Royal Rifle Corps near Armentières. Following a tour of duty he returned to Merris and was sent to Sailly des Lys. General Edwin Alderson inspected the Battalion on Monday 1st March before they relieved the Royal Warwickshires at Bois Grenier. Following a further tour of duty at Fleurbaix the Battalion was sent to Neuf Berquin for rest and training. On Tuesday 6th April they moved to Winnezeele where General Edwin Alderson and General Sir Horace Smith-Dorrien inspected them on Friday 9th and Monday 12th respectively.
At 9.26am on Sunday 18th April Montague formed up with his platoon and marched to billets northwest of Poperinghe prior to moving closer to the line and camp at Vlamertinghe on Tuesday 20th. The German gas attack commenced at 5.00pm on Thursday 22nd and the Battalion was ordered to 'stand to' and went into the line. They mounted a counter-attack that was unsuccessful due to the number of machine-guns defending the position. He remained in the line mounting attacks and repulsing counter-attacks until 1.10am on Monday 26th when the Battalion was relieved to La Brique for three hours. Orders were received to march back to Vlamertinghe, when the roll was called the Battalion had suffered sixteen officers and five hundred and twenty-eighty casualties, killed, wounded and missing. After a night's rest he returned to the line for a further tour of duty.
The Battalion marched to Bailleul on Tuesday 4th May for ten days when they were sent to Calonne for two days rest before moving to Hinges. On Thursday 20th he was sent to Béthune from where he was sent into the line near Festubert. He served in northern France until Thursday 1st July when he was sent to Ploegsteert and served in the southern sector, including Wulverghem, with billets in La Creche and Neuve Eglise. Whilst in the line during autumn 1915 he was wounded and invalided to Canada. Whilst in Canada he was promoted Captain and Adjutant, returning to England in February 1917 and onward to the front at Bouvigny. He went back into the line at Souchez from Friday 2nd March for a tour of duty, before going to Camblain l'Abbe to train until returning to the trenches at the end of the month. From Sunday 6th May he moved to Barlin for four weeks training, retaking the line at Bois des Alleux on Sunday 3rd June. In August he went to camp at Mazingarbe and trained at Ruitz before being sent to the front at Les Brehis. He served at Magnicourt and Fosse 10 during September. On Monday 22nd October the Battalion was sent to St Marie Cappel from where they went into the Salient.
On Thursday 1st November everyone had the opportunity of having a bath in Staple and were issued with clean underclothes. The next day he entrained at Bavinghove Station at 6.00am and arrived at Ypres at 9.30am. They marched out to Wieltje and took position at 11.45am where they cleaned up their line which was flooded due to the rain. On Sunday 4th they moved forward into the front line and came under intermittent shell fire. They prepared for the attack that would commence at 6.00am on Tuesday 6th. At 3.50am the German artillery laid down a heavy barrage, but this did not delay the attack that commenced on time. By 9.30am the final objective had been taken. However, Montague was killed and buried near *'Valour Farm'*.
Lieutenant Colonel McLoughlin wrote: *"His gallantry and utter disregard for his own life were in a very large measure the factors which made for the great success of the engagement ... your son fought bravely and conducted himself well in the battle."*
Montague was recorded in Debretts Obituary — War Roll of Honour published in the 1921 edition.

20479 Private
Alexander Crosbie 'Aleck' Farmer

10th Battalion Canadian Infantry (Alberta Regiment)

Died on Thursday 22nd April 1915, aged 27

Commemorated on Panel 24.

Aleck Farmer

Aleck was born in Liverpool, on Wednesday 13th July 1887 the son of John Harvey Farmer and Euphemia Copeland Farmer, of Liverpool, England. He was educated at Birkenhead School from 1902 to 1903 and went up to Liverpool University to study architecture. He was a member of the London Scottish Territorials whilst working as a architect in Liverpool prior to leaving for Canada in 1910. He continued to work as an architect whilst living in Canada and joined the 103rd Calgary Regiment.

Aleck volunteered at Valcartier on Saturday 5th September 1914 where he was described as 6ft 1in tall, with a 40in chest, a ruddy complexion, blue eyes, medium auburn hair, two vaccination marks on his left arm and three gold crowns.

Aleck arrived in England with the First Canadian Contingent in October and was sent initially to *'Pond Farm Camp'* on Salisbury Plain for training. At 8.00am on Wednesday 10th February 1915 he left from *'Lark Hill Camp'* and entrained at Amesbury at 9.30am for Avonmouth. He embarked on *SS Kingstonian* and sailed at 5.00am the next morning bound for St Nazaire. After a delay due to the ship being blown onto a sandbank, he disembarked and marched to the station. After arriving in Hazebrouck they marched to billets in Borre on Wednesday 17th where he remained for three days when they moved to Strazeele and were inspected by Field Marshal Sir John French. On Sunday 21st he marched to Romarin, arriving at 5.15pm going into the line the next day for the first time for practical training and experience with the Royal Dublin and Royal Irish Fusiliers.

The Battalion was ordered to Bac St Maur, via Armentières, on Monday 1st March. The next afternoon General Edwin Alderson visited the Battalion and spoke to all ranks that was followed by a parade. At 5.05pm they marched to Fleurbaix arriving in their billets at 7.00pm where Aleck remained until 6.00pm on Friday 5th when he went into the line near La Boutillerie. His first tour of duty lasted until 9.15pm on Monday 8th when he was relieved and returned to his billets. Whilst resting on Tuesday 9th they came under shellfire and throughout Wednesday 10th the Battalion was 'stood to' during the opening of the Battle of Neuve-Chapelle. At the end of March Aleck was moved to Estaires for rest and training.

General Alderson

He moved to Abeele, via Caëstre, on Monday 5th April, arriving at 3.00pm. General Edwin Alderson visited again on Saturday 10th an inspected them with a further inspection by General Sir Horace Smith-Dorrien the next day. On Wednesday 14th Aleck marched to Vlamertinghe and on to Wieltje from where the Battalion relieved a French Regiment on the Gravenstafel Ridge. Their lines came under heavy shellfire that continued until being relieved to Ypres on the night of Monday 19th as part of the Divisional Reserve. The town came under shellfire the next day and a number of his comrades were wounded.

General Smith-Dorrien

At 4.40pm on Thursday 22nd the German artillery could be heard bombarding the line between Elverdinghe and Brielen. At 5.15pm Aleck's officers held a meeting as the town was being pounded and a 6.00pm the Battalion moved towards St Jan from where they took the line to help with the defence of the line that was under extreme pressure. A counter-attack was being prepared and by 11.10pm the Battalion was in position ready for the attack. The Germans were defending their positions stoutly as Aleck advanced at 11.48pm. The night was well lit by the moon that made the attackers easier targets for the German machine-gunners and infantry. Aleck was shot and killed during the initial advance.

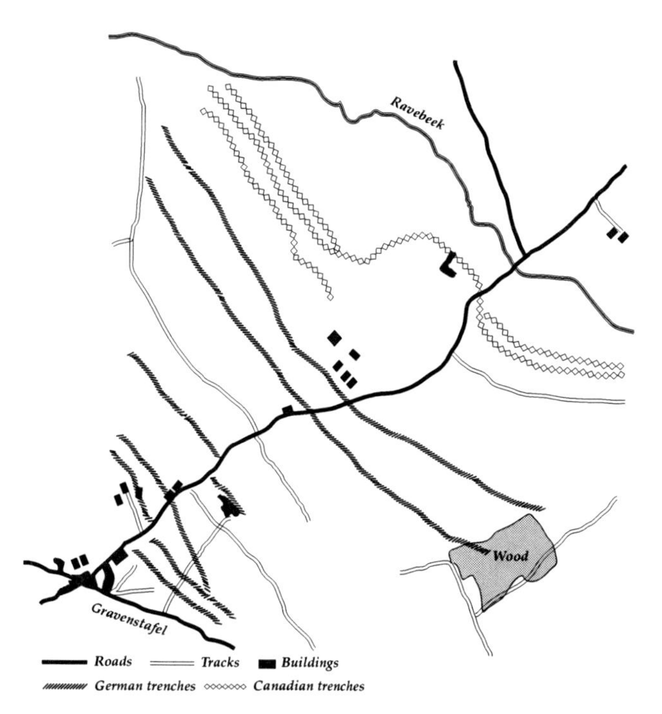

10th Battalion, Canadian Infantry at Gravenstafel on Wednesday 14th April 1915

Second Lieutenant Henry Charles McLean Farmer

6th Battalion attached 4th Battalion
King's Royal Rifle Corps
Died on Monday 10th May 1915, aged 22
Commemorated on Panel 51.

Henry Farmer

Henry was born at Arundel Vicarage, Sussex, on Tuesday 8th August 1882, younger son of the Reverend James Edmund Gamul and Margaret Farmer, of Yeardsley Cottage, Furness Vale, Cheshire. He was educated at Summer Fields from in 1902 to 1906 followed by Eton College as a member of Mr Allen Beville Ramsay's House, leaving in 1911 and went up to Trinity College, Cambridge.

Henry volunteered at the outbreak of war and enlisted with the 3rd Dragoon Guards on Thursday 3rd September 1914 whilst waiting for a commission which he received on Tuesday 22nd September. He went to train at Sheerness with the 6th Battalion King's Royal Rifle Corps. They were sent to northern France from where they crossed into Belgium. They took the line in January 1915 for the first time in the water-logged and sodden fields between Messines and Kemmel. After a tour of only three days the freezing, waist-deep water, took a heavy toll on the Battalion and when they were relieved and sent to Dickebusch six officers and more than five hundred men were invalided, unable to walk. On Monday 1st March the Battalion was ordered to attack a section of line at St Eloi; it was a fierce and costly engagement with one hundred and thirteen of the three hundred who saw action becoming casualties. In early May Henry was on Hill 60 and in the thick of the action but was able to withdraw as the Battalion Diary records: *"It was arranged that the withdrawal should begin at the extreme end of the salient after dark, and that the remaining parts of the line should withdraw in rotation. First, half the garrison were withdrawn, then half the remainder, and then the whole of the remainder, with the exception of three or four men per trench under 2nd Lieutenant D. Morton, who remained firing rifles and Verėy pistols until the last moment.*

The withdrawal was carried out with complete success, and the enemy were apparently in ignorance of the movement until after daylight." On Saturday 8th they were back on Hill 60 and came under heavy fire and the next day the German artillery obliterated their line. A series of counter-attacks were mounted during which Henry was killed. He was buried on the east of Bellewaarde Wood.

Colonel Brownlow wrote: *"He worked hard down here and was very keen to get to the Front."*

Henry is commemorated on Waddesdon War Memorial.

In St Michael and All Angels Church, Waddesdon, Buckinghamshire, a figure of St Michael was placed to his memory by his surviving brother together with a stained glass window in the Lady Chapel with the inscription: *"We pray you remember Henry Charles Maclean Farmer, 2nd Lieut. K.R.R.C. killed in action near Ypres, the 10th day of May 1915. In being recollection of whom this window, in honour of the Holy Incarnation of Our Lord Jesus Christ, is dedicated by his parents."*

Second Lieutenant James Douglas Herbert Farmer

9th Battery 41st Brigade Royal Field Artillery
Died on Wednesday 4th November 1914, aged 21
Commemorated on Panel 5.

James was born on Friday 2nd December 1892, second son of James Herbert and Edith Gertrude Farmer, of Fairfield, Mundesley, Norfolk, grandson of Alderman Sir George Harris, JP, LCC. He was educated at St Paul's School where he was in the First XV and XI, followed by the Army College at Farnham and passed into RMA Woolwich.

James was gazetted in July 1913. He went out with the BEF in August 1914 and was deployed at Mons. The Retreat began towards Paris where on Tuesday 1st September they came under heavy attack between Puisieux and Vivers on the edge of the Forest of Mormal. The excellence of the British artillery silenced their opposite numbers but the German infantry attempted to capture the guns. A desperate dash by the drivers saved them and two of their number were awarded the Distinguished Conduct Medal. James served on the Aisne for the rest of the month before he was sent north with his guns to the Ypres Salient. The artillery duels continued with increased intensity as the First Battle of Ypres came to its climax. James and the battery were supporting front line from Westhoek and attempting to hold off the ever-pressing German infantry. He was killed in action and was buried in the grounds at Eksternest Chapel in Westhoek that was, at the time, being used as Brigade Headquarters.

Artillery and limbers on the move

434511 Private James Farquhar

10th Battalion Canadian Infantry (Alberta Regiment)

Died on Saturday 3rd June 1916, aged 38

Commemorated on Panel 24.

James was born on Wednesday 10th November 1880, the son of the late James and Elizabeth Farquhar. He worked as a labourer and spent five years with the Sutherland Highlanders.

His brother, Private William Farquhar, died on the same day and is commemorated on the Menin Gate, see below. James volunteered in Calgary on Monday 25th January 1915, where he was described as a Presbyterian, 5ft 8½in tall, with a 38in chest, a fair complexion, blue eyes and dark hair. Following a period of training James and William were sent to England to continue with their training before leaving for France to join the battalion in the field.

James and William were in the line between Wulverghem to St Eloi from September 1915 where they remained until Thursday 25th November on six-day tours of duty in the water-logged trenches. They were sent to Bailleul for training and rest before returning to the line. After Christmas lunch they were sent out on support duties in the rain. They were pleased, after a few days, to be sent to *'Bulford Camp'* to train for a raid on German lines. Returning to the Salient, on Friday 4th February 1916, parties were sent out to cut the German wire at 6.30am, finishing their work at 2.30pm. That night the raiding party set out in three groups. Unfortunately, as they cleared the gaps in the wire, a German working party was encountered and whilst they waited for them to disperse a German patrol met them. A ghastly hand-to-hand fight took place between the two groups that alerted the German front line who fired indiscriminately on them all. The German patrol was dealt with, the raiding party continued to the front line using bombs and hand grenades. When they returned to their line, an officer and four men had been killed and fifteen men wounded, and their estimate for German dead was in excess of fifty. Throughout March, April and May, James and William saw considerable active service on the Salient, including several tours on Hill 60.

On Tuesday 2nd June the Germans commenced a severe bombardment from 10.00am covering the sector from *'Observatory Wood'* to Hill 60. At 1.00pm the German infantry emerged from their trenches and advanced on the British front line. James and William, 'resting' in the reserve trenches were rushed up the support lines from *'Armagh Wood'* to Mount Sorrel to take part in the counter-attack. The fighting was ferocious and in the early hours of the morning the brothers were killed.

434397 Private William Farquhar

10th Battalion Canadian Infantry (Alberta Regiment)

Died on Saturday 3rd June 1916, aged 34

Commemorated on Panel 24.

William was born on Thursday 26th March 1885, son of the late James and Elizabeth Farquhar. He worked as a salesman and spent five years in the Territorials.

He volunteered in Calgary on Thursday 21st January 1915, his attestation papers describe him as a Presbyterian, 5ft 6in tall, with a 36½ in chest, a fair complexion, blue eyes and dark brown hair.

His brother, Private James Farquhar, died on the same day and is commemorated on the Menin Gate, for their story, see above.

153571 Private Donald Farquharson

27th Battalion Canadian Infantry (Manitoba Regiment)

Died on Tuesday 6th November 1917, aged 31

Commemorated on Panel 26.

Donald was born at home on Saturday 3rd April 1886, son of Alexander and Helen Farquharson, of Aberdeen, Scotland. He was employed as a crane operator and served in the Militia, 79th Cameron Highlanders.

On Saturday 31st July 1915 Donald volunteered in Winnipeg where he was described as a Presbyterian, 5ft 5in tall, with a 34in chest, a fair complexion, blue eyes, fair coloured hair, with tattoos on his right arm and wrist. Donald was sent for training before being sent to England and onward to join the Battalion in the field with a draft on the Ypres Salient where his tours of duty began in the front line.

In August 1916, after a tour of duty at St Eloi that included a raid on the German lines, the Battalion was relieved to *'Chippawa Camp'*. On Friday 18th they attended a YMCA concert in Reninghelst and two days later marched to billets in Steenvoorde then onto Hazebrouck for training. Whilst at camp the Battalion was issued with Lee-Enfield rifles to replace their Ross rifles. At the end August an eleven miles march took them to billets in Leulinghem for rest and training. On Monday 4th September they marched to St Omer to entrain for Candas. Following a night's rest they moved to Vadencourt, then onto bivouac at the brickfields near Albert. On Monday 14th the marched to their assembly positions from where they would attack Courcelette the next morning. A preliminary artillery barrage was laid down then the Battalion moved forward, within only a few minutes had overwhelmed the German front line and taken a large number of prisoners. On Thursday 17th the Battalion went into reserve at the brickfields. Their next tour of duty took them through *'Sausage Valley'* to La Boisselle from where they continued to attack the Germans lines. October took them to the line at the Lorette Spur followed by Noulette Wood in the Souchez sector close to Vimy Ridge. Christmas 1916 was spent in the front line before they were relieved to spend New Year's Eve bathing and re-equipping. Tours of duty recommenced until Saturday 20th January 1917 when they moved to Comté for training until the end of the month when they marched to Rambert for a further

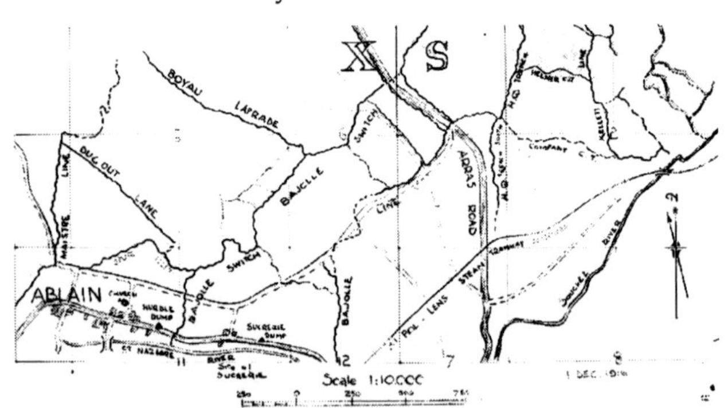

The Lorette Spur, December 1916

two weeks training. They relieved the 31st Battalion in trenches at Mont St Eloi on Sunday 18th February and served in the sector for three weeks. Two weeks of training at Maisnil-Bouche commenced on Wednesday 7th March from where they went into the line at Neuville St-Vaast where they prepared to take part in the Battle of Arras. At 11.30am on Monday 9th April the Battalion was in its assembly positions and a hour later their attack began but immediately came up against fierce German machine-gun fire; the machine-gun was bombed into silence. The advance continued and they reached the ruins of Farbus, and despite heavy counter-attacks they held on. The Battalion captured three officers and over three hundred men together with nine artillery pieces. Following relief and a day of rest they returned to the line at the Bois des Arleux and remained on tours of duty in the sector until the end of May when they were sent for training and spent June in Ruitz. On Tuesday 3rd July they relieved the Sherwood Forresters in Noulette Wood. Tours of duty continued in northern France until the end of August. After six weeks of training at Estreé Cauchie they marched to Camblain l'Abbé and relieved the 24th Battalion at the *'Crater Line'*, Vimy. October was spent in the Chaudiere sector until Tuesday 23rd; the battalion marched to Savy where they entrained for Cassel to be billeted in Hazebrouck.

Intensive training began for the part the Battalion would play in the Third Battle of Ypres that was raging a few miles to their north and the stories of the horrific conditions were well known to all. On Saturday 3rd November the Battalion paraded and moved via Caëstre to *'Lake Erie Camp'*, Brandhoek. The next morning they moved through Ypres to Potijze where all ranks were equipped for the front line. They passed Hill 47 and went into position in front of Passchendaele village. At 5.00am on Tuesday 6th the assault on the village began and by 7.40am all the objectives had been achieved with those who survived spent the rest of the day consolidating their position. Donald was one of those who remained in the mud and whose body would not be recovered.

Donald is commemorated on the Archiestown and Aberdeen City War Memorials.

One of four brothers who died: Private James Farquharson died on Thursday 2nd March 1916 and is buried in RE Farm Cemetery; Private Nathaniel Farquharson died on Wednesday 31st May 1916 and is commemorated on Plymouth Naval Memorial; Trimmer J Farquharson died on Friday 15th February 1918 and is buried in Aberdeen (Allenvale) Cemetery.

Lieutenant John Charles Lancelot Farquharson

14th Battalion London Regiment (London Scottish)

Died between Saturday 31st October and Sunday 1st November 1914, aged 33

Commemorated on Panel 54.

John Farquharson

John was born on Monday 16th May 1881, seventh son of Mrs Emma Farquharson, of Glengarry, The Grove, Woking, Surrey, and the late Colonel M H Farquharson, RMLI. He was educated at Dulwich College from 1894 to 1900 where he was in the First XV and First XI. He went up to University College,

Hill 60, September 1916

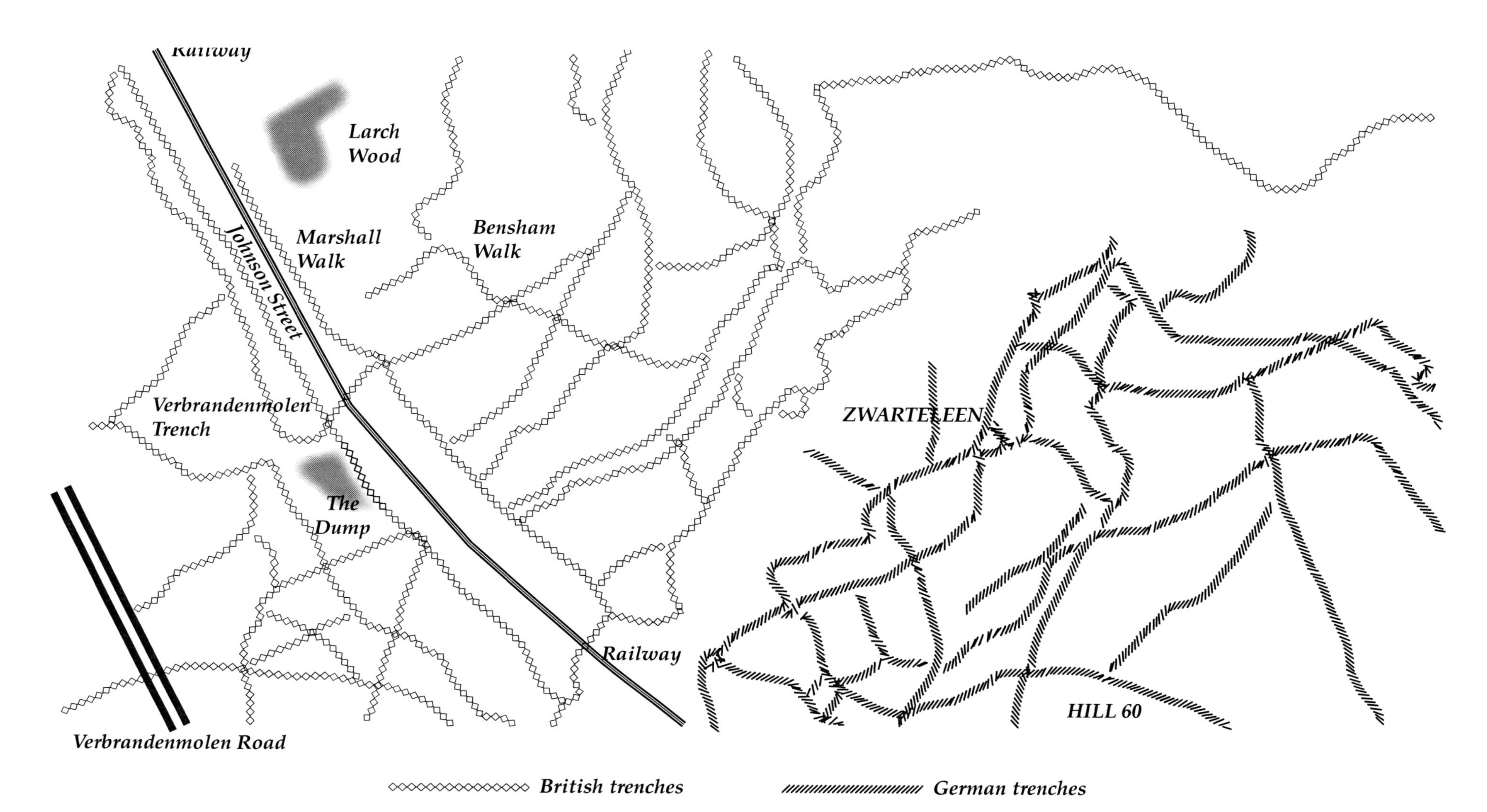

Oxford, and in 1903 he won his Blue for rugby. John was appointed Captain of the Old Alleynian Football Club from 1904 to 1907.

As a member of the London Regiment (London Scottish) Territorial Force John went out to France on Tuesday 15th September 1914 embarking on *SS Winifredian* from Southampton and sailed for Le Havre. It was a smooth crossing although the boat was considered to be poor transport even for cattle! Upon arrival they marched through the town to camp, their pipers leading the way. From Le Havre they were dispersed to various duties in support including Orleans, Le Mans and La Fere-en-Tardenois (where they provided Guard for Field Marshal Sir John French at Headquarters).

Field Marshal Sir John French

Their work continued for a month before they were ordered to meet in St Omer from Sunday 25th October — virtually everyone had arrived within three days. John paraded his men and marched out of the town to meet a fleet of London buses on Thursday 29th which took them on a gruelling nine hour journey to Ypres. The buses struggled on the cobbled roads which were slimy and covered with mud. Many of the omnibuses slipped off the road or simply became bogged down in the mud — the men jumped out and pushed them back onto the road.

... boarding buses for the front

The Battalion arrived in Ypres town square at 3.00am in the morning where John organised the men to rest in the Cloth Hall. Breakfast was provided at 6.00am followed by parading in the square at 8.00am amongst the milling throng of refugees and other groups of soldiers. Colonel Malcolm led the men out of the town, through the Menin Gate and along the Menin Road. They stopped at *'Hellfire Corner'* and the Colonel met General Sir Douglas Haig who was in his Headquarters at *'White Château'*. John took his men further along the Menin Road to Hooge. Before they could be deployed orders were received to form up and they were to move to another sector. Motor buses arrived and drove them through Ypres to St Eloi where they arrived at 7.00pm. After arrival they had their first square, and hot, meal but no billets were provided so everyone had to do their best to find shelter. At midnight they were to be paraded, but the Colonel was able to persuade General Gough to allow them to rest for a few more hours. At 4.00am on Saturday 31st they paraded again and marched to a wood where they started to dig in; again new orders were received and they were sent to Wytschaete.

General Gough

The route to Wytschaete was under heavy artillery fire and they took the line in front of *'Hun's Farm'* and the windmill, plugging a gap that was opening up. They immediately set about digging in. Throughout the day they came under sustained machine-gun fire and artillery fire. Despite the din of battle, at 9.00pm John and his men heard the sound of soldiers singing and their band playing as the German infantry advanced towards them in close formation. He ordered the men to rapid fire which halted the advance and caused very heavy casualties. At midnight they attacked again and in the fierce fight that took place John was killed.

Captain Bede Farrell

4th Battalion East Yorkshire Regiment

Died on Saturday 24th April 1915, aged 33

Commemorated on Panel 21.

Bede Farrell

Bede was born on Tuesday 28th June 1881, eldest son of Thomas Frederic and Monica Farrell, of Brookside, Newland Park, Hull. He was educated at Ushaw and Hymers College, Hull, and then became articled to his father, was admitted as a solicitor in January 1905, and became a partner in Rollit & Sons, of Hull.

Bede was gazetted to the Territorials on Wednesday 7th February 1900, promoted Lieutenant on Wednesday 19th June 1901 and Captain on Sunday 24th November 1907. At the outbreak of war Bede volunteered, he was commissioned and sent for training. He went out to the front on Sunday 18th April 1915.

On Thursday 22nd April, The Official Despatch read: *"From Steenstraate to the east of Langemarck as far as the Poelcapelle road, a French Division. Thence, in a south-easterly direction towards the Passchendaele-Becelaere road, the Canadian Division. Thence a Division (28th) took up the line in a southerly direction east of Zonnebeke to a point west of Becelaere, whence another (27th Division) continued the line south-east to the northern limit of the Corps on its right."* That

night, at 10.00pm, orders were received that they were required at the front. At noon on Friday 23rd twenty-four motor buses took them to Poperinghe. They marched to *'Camp A'* beyond Vlamertinghe. At 1.40am on Saturday 24th they marched eastwards towards the Yser Canal. Captain Sharp wrote: *"The march to our line was a queer one. We knew not where we were going, nor what to, and the men's anticipations were not brightened by seeing a dressing station in a very busy state. We crossed over a pontoon over a small canal — a piece of the Yser Canal but not actually it. The banks were very high and we were on the further one which commanded the other side. It was provided with trenches and dug-outs and, after much scrambling in the dark and moving further down and forth, we got into our position, holding partly some dug-outs and partly a trench. This was about 2 or 3 in the morning of 24th. When day broke we found that there was an old, small factory with a chimney on our right and several cottages and farms still occupied along out front. There were some Canadian Scottish in the factory who kindly gave the men some beef and tea."* At 10.00am they moved off towards Potijze Château, Battalion Headquarters. They went into the line and immediately were under very heavy artillery fire, howitzers that made huge craters 30ft by 10ft, throwing up vast quantities of mud that rained down on Bede and his men. Bede was shot through the heart between Wieltje and St Julien and was buried where he died.
One of his brother officers wrote later: *"… Then a hell of a machine-gun fire swept the place. All I could do was to lie 'doggo' — as small as possible. When it was over I went on and found two platoons of 'C' Company who couldn't advance further. An order then came down to stay where we were till dusk. The enemy's fire ceased and we, after some time, collected up and returned to trenches. Poor Farrell was shot through the heart close to me, and Theilmann* in the body and he died on the way back."* (* Major Carl Theilmann is commemorated on the Menin Gate, see below.)
Another wrote: *"I gather that Bede was so conscientiously looking after his men that he took no care of himself."*

1440 Private Matthew Farrell

1st/5th Battalion King's Own
(Royal Lancaster Regiment)
Died on Wednesday 14th April 1915, aged 16
Commemorated on Panel 12.

Matthew was born in Scotforth, Lancashire, son of Mrs Farrell, of 6 Little John Street, Lancaster.
He enlisted in Lancaster and was sent for training. He sailed for Le Havre, arriving on Monday 15th February 1915. He was sent to northern France for further training before crossing the border into Belgium. He had not been serving in the front line very long before he was killed during a tour of duty.

Second Lieutenant Charles Reginald Fausset

3rd Battalion attached 1st Battalion
Royal Irish Regiment
Died on Sunday 2nd May 1915, aged 36
Commemorated on Panel 33.

Charles Fausset

Charles was born in 1880 the second son of Mrs Ellen F O Fausset (née Lane) and the late Reverend Charles Fausset. He was educated at Rathmines School and went up to Trinity College, Dublin, and graduated with a BA, in 1902 and LLD in 1907. He captained the College Cricket XI and played in a match against W G Grace in 1903. Charles was the mile and quarter-mile Champion of Ireland and played for Durham County Cricket Club. He lived at 3 Ferrers Road, Oswestry.
At the outbreak of war Charles volunteered, enlisted on Saturday 19th September 1914 being gazetted into the 3rd Royal Irish Regiment in October. On Friday 23rd April 1915 he left for France to join the Battalion in the field on the Salient. He immediately went into the line and during his first short tour of duty was killed.
He was in the line at St Julien when on Sunday 2nd May the German launched a series of attacks. During the morning the Battalion was badly shelled and at 5.00pm they sent over gas. Charles was the only officer to be killed that day, and during the tour.

Lieutenant Cecil Frederick Featherstone

3rd Battalion attached 2nd Battalion
East Surrey Regiment
Died on Sunday 25th April 1915, aged 18
Commemorated on Panel 34.

Cecil Featherstone

Cecil was born at Lewisham on Saturday 13th February 1897, eldest son of Frederick and Minnie Elizabeth Featherstone, of Mount Pleasant, Plough Lane, Purley, Surrey. He was educated at Holmwood School, Bexhill-on-Sea, from 1906 to 1910. In 1907 he joined the Cadet Corps and shot for the School VI winning both the Sheffield Trophy and the Holman Cup. In 1911 Cecil attended Dover College, where he was promoted Sergeant in the OTC, shooting for the school at Bisley in 1913, and

was in the Ashburton Shield team in 1914. He played for their First XV and various cricket teams.
Cecil was gazetted in December 1914, whilst he was still at school, joining the Battalion in January 1915, leaving for France in March. At the end of March Cecil was in the line at St Eloi being relieved from the line on Tuesday 30th. The next day they were inspected by General James Haldane. For the next two weeks they went in and out of the lines at St Eloi before moving to Château Rosenthal on Wednesday 14th April. Whilst marching through Ypres they met the 1st Battalion who were marching in the opposite direction and each gave the other a rousing cheer. They went into the line close to Broodseinde. On Saturday 24th April at 1.00pm the Battalion was attacked with gas. The next day Cecil was assisting in repulsing a German attack when he was killed and was originally buried in the officers' graveyard at Zonnebeke.

General Haldane

His Adjutant wrote: *"Your son was in No. 15 Platoon, and Sergeant Lower was with him at the time of his death. The Germans attacked us on the 25th April, and your son was killed by a bullet-wound in the head whilst defending his trench, which was successfully held by us. Like all our young officers, he carried out his duty to the end, and by his example the men remained steadfast and the trenches were held in spite of poisonous gases and rifle and shell fire. We have been so fortunate in having such good officers that the battalion has earned special praise from all, and General French thanked us yesterday for the work of 25th April, during which your son fell."*
A fellow officer wrote: *"2nd Lieutenant Featherstone was killed during the German attack on April 25th under circumstances which proved him a very brave officer. The enemy having got all round us, our men were firing in all directions, generally at no particular object, as often happens in times of excitement. It was in trying to stop the men wasting their ammunition that Lieutenant Featherstone was twice wounded. He still continued, however, to calm his men till he was shot in the heart by a stray bullet. His death was instantaneous, and, apart from the slight wounds he had previously received, could have suffered no pain."*
In Christ Church, Purley, a stained glass window was dedicated in his memory with the inscription: *"Be thou faithful unto death and I will give thee a crown of life study to show thyself approved unto God I have fought the good fight put on the whole armour of God. To the glory of God and in loving memory of Lieutenant Cecil Frederick Featherstone 3rd Battn. (attd. 2nd Battn.) East Surrey Regt. Born 13th January 1897, killed in action 25 April 1915, this window is erected by Frederick and Minnie Elizabeth Featherstone, his parents."*

2809 Private Robert Albert Featherstonehaugh-Wooster

43rd Battalion Australian Infantry, AIF
Died on Thursday 4th October 1917, aged 31
Commemorated on Panel 27.

Robert was born in Adelaide in 1886, son of Henry and Annie Cora Featherstonehaugh-Wooster, of 200 Rowe Street, Railway Town, Broken Hill, New South Wales. He enlisted in October 1916 and was described as 5ft 4½in tall. Robert left on *HMAT Berrima* on Saturday 16th December 1916 from Adelaide. He was sent to Flanders and served initially in the Armentières sector. On Wednesday 23rd May 1917 Robert was marched towards Belgium and served at Le Bizet until Friday 1st June when he moved to Ploegsteert Wood. At the Battle of Messines Robert supplied ammunition and assisted with his comrades in making up a digging party. He continued to serve on fatigues until 10.00pm on Tuesday 10th when he took the line as the Battalion relieved the 44th Battalion. He was immediately involved in attacking the *'Pottery'* trenches and consolidated the position. The next day the 16th Battalion arrived at 11.00pm and Robert was relieved to *'St Andrew's Drive'* and onto Neuve Eglise on Tuesday 12th. After twenty-four hours of rest he was marched to Steenwerck for rest and training until Thursday 21st when he returned to Neuve Eglise. After two days the Battalion was sent to Messines and served on tours of duty until Wednesday 11th July when Robert was sent for training at *'Camp T2'* near Neuve Eglise. Church Parade was cancelled on Sunday 29th due to heavy rain and the next day Robert left camp by motor bus for the front line at Messines for a tour of duty, and returned for training at *'Camp T2'*. On Tuesday 7th August the Battalion moved to Steenwerck for training at *'Jesus Farm'* until they moved to Abrouzt at 5.00pm on Wednesday 22nd where their training continued. General Sir Douglas Haig inspected the Division on Saturday 22nd September and four days later marched they to Steenvoorde where they were

... crossing the mud of Passchendaele

billeted overnight. The next morning Robert marched on towards Poperinghe where he was sent out on working parties until Tuesday 2nd October when he was sent to Ypres by train at 2.45pm. He remained in camp until 9.00pm on Wednesday 3rd when the march to the assembly positions began, arriving at 2.00am the next morning. At 6.00am, Zero Hour, Robert moved forward and during the day he was killed at Broodseinde and buried on the field.

LIEUTENANT
CHARLES MAGRATH FENDALL

Royal Field Artillery

Died on Tuesday 14th December 1915, aged 23

Commemorated on Panel 5.

Charles Fendall

Charles was born on Monday 29th August 1892, elder son of Colonel Charles Pears Fendall, DSO, RA, and Mrs Rose E Fendall (née Lane-Ryan), of Wokingham, Berkshire. He was educated at Downside from September, 1905 to July 1908. Following School Charles worked in London and then emigrated to Alberta, Canada, where he worked on a ranch.

At the outbreak of war Charles returned to England and was commissioned, leaving for France in early 1915 to join his battery in the field.

He was killed by a shell fire which hit the office where he was working: *"It happened by the merest chance — if there be such a thing as mere chance — that it occurred to me to go round the Cameron Highlanders' trenches on the morning of December 14th. There was really no reason why I should have done so, as I had been with the Camerons almost daily. In passing your son's battery I saw the medical officer, whom I knew pretty intimately, and stopped to chat with him. Your son joined us, and subsequently I asked him about the Catholics of the battery. He knew them all well, so I ventured to ask if he were not a Catholic himself. We talked for some time, and he made his confession while we walked to the little wood where his battery was. It was a great shock to me when I heard early in the afternoon that he had fallen. It must have been within an hour of my leaving him."*

German artillery moving to the front

His Captain wrote: *"... He was the subaltern on duty in the battery, and usually sat in the office. At about 2.15 p.m., just as I had returned from the trenches, four or five German shells came straight into the battery, one going through the office roof. On rushing there I found your son had been killed, and the brigade doctor, who was also sitting there, very badly wounded; he has since died. I can't tell you what a gloom it has cast over us all, as we were all so fond of him. He was buried at 10 a.m. the following day, a Roman Catholic chaplain officiating, the Brigade Commander and all the officers attending."*

LIEUTENANT
JAMES ARTHUR ROSS FERGUSON

3rd Battalion Royal Sussex Regiment attached

1st Battalion King's Own Yorkshire Light Infantry

Died on Sunday 9th May 1915, aged 17

Commemorated on Panel 20.

James was born in Thornton Heath, Surrey, on Wednesday 12th May 1897, son of Dr Robert James Ferguson, MD, and Mrs Gertrude K Ferguson, of 10 St George's Place, Canterbury, Kent. He was educated at the Abbey Preparatory School in Beckenham and Durston House Preparatory School in Ealing before attending The King's School Canterbury, from January 1911 to July 1914. In December 1912 he was awarded a Junior Scholarship. James was a good sportsman being a member of the XV and the rowing IV, and was appointed captain of both in 1914. He was an active member of the OTC, rising to Serjeant, and James was appointed a School Monitor.

When the war broke out James was with the OTC on annual camp and he immediately volunteered and commissioned to the Royal Sussex Regiment. Following training he was sent out to France. He was confirmed in his rank from probation on Tuesday 16th March 1915 and was attached to the King's Own Yorkshire Light Infantry on Wednesday 31st March. James joined the KOYLI in Belgium. On Thursday 1st April marched with his platoon through Ypres and out to the front via the Menin Gate to relieve the 2nd Battalion, East Yorkshire Regiment, in the woods near Zonnebeke. The war was yet to reduced every tree to matchsticks and stumps and they found the trenches in poor condition with German snipers making life more difficult. The British attack at Hill 60 began on Saturday 17th April and on Thursday 22nd the German launched their gas attack to the right of James line that opened the Second Battle of Ypres. One of the NCOs, later Lieutenant F K Lambert, serving with James and the Battalion wrote of the gas attack: *"In the early afternoon a greenish-yellow cloud was seen to be approaching the French Colonial Div. line from the Boche trenches. Men looked at it in wonderment, such a phenomenon had never before been seen, and nobody realised what it was until the French Colonials were seen leaving their trenches.*

The enemy with his terrible ingenuity had selected a junction of two armies composed on the one hand of native troops of simple mind, and a worn-out British division on the other. There was no doubt that he meant the full force of his new and horrible weapon to fall on the simple-minded Africans, to whom witchcraft and magic were dreadful and fearsome things to be avoided. These poor fellows had suffered terrible bombardments and attacks, but in this new weapon there was something uncanny. Men gripped their throats as the terrible gas went to their lungs, and writhed in agony as they slowly succumbed to its effects. The rain of shells and machine-gun bullets poured unceasingly and pitilessly amongst them, but these did not account for the effects of the yellow-green cloud about them. It was some unseen hand, some new and terrible 'white man's magic' brought against them, it was too much for their simple minds to grasp, and they fled terrified from it. The whole of the French Colonial Div. streamed off in panic back across the fields to Vlamertinghe

and Poperinghe, leaving a tremendous gap in the line. The 84th Bde., which was holding the extreme left of the British line, was also caught by the gas cloud. They hung on to their trenches. men dipped handkerchiefs or socks in filthy water and put them over their mouths and nostrils, and stuck to their rifles until the deadly gas overpowered them.

It was not until about six days after the first gas cloud that any preventive measures were received. Then small respirators made of a strip of muslin enclosing a wad of tow soaked in chemicals began to arrive. Two came at first to the battalion with instructions that they were to be issued to the front line sentries, then half-a-dozen, each day bringing a larger number, until every man in the battalion had one. As the supply increased a second one per man was issued.

These respirators were worn with the wad of tow over the mouth and packed round the nostrils and tied behind the head with the muslin strip. The taste and smell were horrible and at first many men were averse to using them. They soon learnt their value and took great care to protect them. These respirators were superseded by the flannel helmet with mica eyepieces about a month later, and these in their turn gave way to an improved pattern, which was eventually replaced by the small box respirator of the present day."

Due to collapse of the line to his left James' sector was becoming dangerously exposed and the line was ultimately untenable. A plan was devised for the reorganisation of the line: on Tuesday 4th May James led his man back towards Ypres to their new front line at Frezenberg. Late that night the Battalion was relieved but it was short-lived as the Germans mounted an attack on the position they had occupied and the Battalion was needed to support the line. The German attacks became heavier by the day, Saturday 8th brought a storm of high-explosive shells on James' trench and he rallied his men to counter three separate infantry attacks. James was shot and wounded in the head late on Saturday evening and he died the following day.

James is recorded on Canterbury War Memorial.

LIEUTENANT KENNETH MOUNTNEY JAMES FERGUSSON

2nd Battalion Lincolnshire Regiment

Died on Tuesday 31st July 1917, aged 23

Commemorated on Panel 21.

Kenneth was born on Sunday 25th February 1894, son of Mr J Fergusson, of 23 Sumner Place, London SW. He was educated at Marlborough College from 1907 to 1909.

In 1915 Kenneth volunteered and was commissioned. Following training he was sent to join the Battalion in the field. He served through the Battle of the Somme and was promoted to Lieutenant. In August and September he served in the Loos sector before returning to the Somme on Tuesday 10th October. On Monday 23rd Kenneth took his men forward in an attack on *'Zenith Trench'*; the Battalion took very heavy losses and failed to take their objectives. At the end of the month the Battalion was sent to *'Citadel Camp'* in Méaulte where they reorganised, rested and trained. The Battalion returned to the front line in France where they served until mid-1917 when they moved to Belgium. Kenneth trained his men in preparation for the Third Battle of Ypres. At 9.00am on Tuesday 31st July 1917 Kenneth was in the assembly position waiting for the order to advance. Many of the men were affected by the gas and as they advanced they came under heavy machine-gun fire — the British barrage had failed to silence the German forward positions, their shells had landed long. As Kenneth came close to *'Jabber Trench'* he was shot and killed.

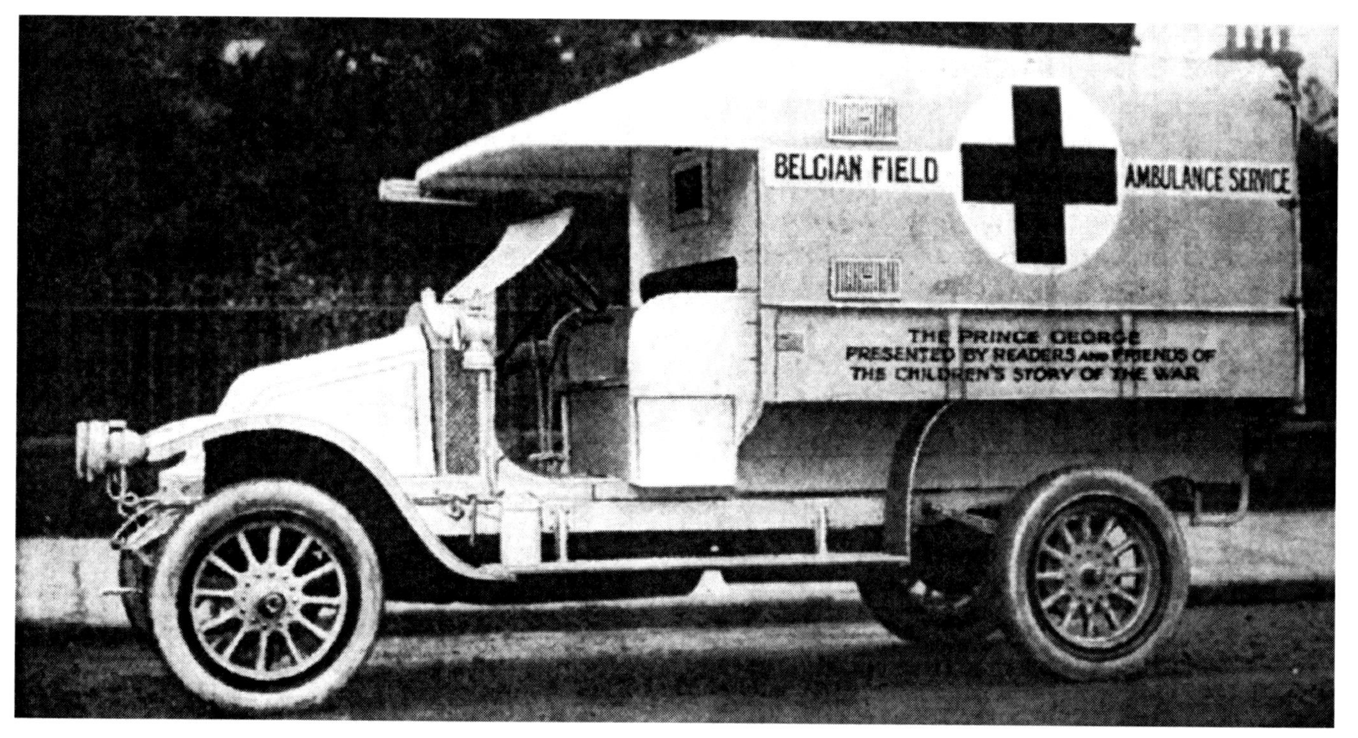

The Prince George Motor Ambulance

Lieutenant Philip Tregenwell Fetherstonhaugh-Frampton

Royal Warwickshire Regiment attached
2nd Battalion The Buffs (East Kent Regiment)
Died on Monday 3rd May 1915, aged 18
Commemorated on Panel 8.

Philip was born on Sunday 15th November 1896, son of Henry Rupert and Violet Edith Millicent Fetherstonhaugh-Frampton, of Moreton, Dorset. He was educated at Wellington College from 1910 to 1913.

Wellington College

On Saturday 16th January 1915 Philip marched to Southampton and embarked for Le Havre from where he marched to camp. He entrained for Hazebrouck where in early February, after training, they battalion relieved the French close to the Ypres to Comines Canal. Many of the men had only returned from India shortly before Christmas and suffered badly in the cold and wet conditions. During the evening of Monday 15th Philip took his men into assembly positions, bayonets fixed, and at 9.00pm led his Platoon against *'O Trench'*. The German machine-gunners opened up on the advancing troops who were, however, able to reach their objective and occupied part of the trench. The Germans continued to bomb from the section of the trench they still held until they were cleared out. By midnight the promised relief had not yet arrived and many of the rifles were jammed with mud, and holding onto the position was difficult. Eventually they were relieved from the line and went to the Cavalry Barracks in Ypres to rest before marching to billets at Reninghelst. On Friday 19th Philip marched his men to Westoutre where baths were

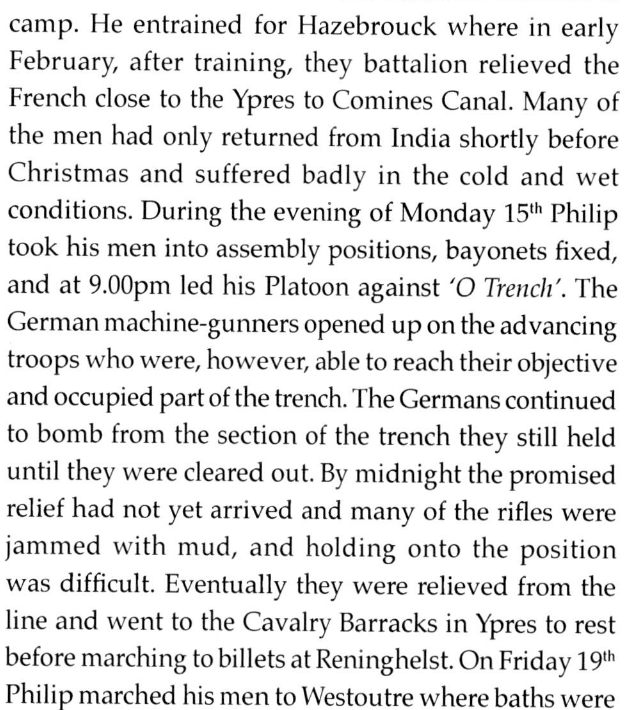

provided and clean, dry clothes replaced the mud-caked uniforms they arrived with. Until Tuesday 23rd March Philip served in the Kemmel sector when he transferred the short distance north to St Eloi. After a couple of tours of duty they moved in the Salient at Zonnebeke on Saturday 10th April where the Battalion relieved the French close to the Broodseinde crossroads — part of the front line ran within five feet of the German front line. They came under fire from heavy trench mortars that caused considerable damage and during their four day tour five officers and eighty-four men were casualties. On Thursday 22nd April the Battalion was bivouacked at St Jan when the Germans launched the first gas attack. The German fire was so intense that even in St Jan, supposedly safe, machine-gun bullets flew about. At 3.30am on Friday 23rd the Battalion was ordered to Wieltje, taking the line some eight hundred yards to the north. They took part in the counter-attack and served in the line until Tuesday 27th when they were relieved to St Jan; the village came under heavy shell fire, and late on Wednesday 28th Philip led his men to Verlorenhoek. Initially the line was relative quiet, but on Monday 3rd May the Germans commenced a bombardment at dawn which was followed by an attack. During the day Philip was killed and buried in the field.

In St Nicholas of Myra Church, Moreton, Dorset, a tablet was placed in his memory with the inscription: *"In loving memory of Philip Tregenwell 2nd Lieut. 3rd Batt. Royal Warwickshire Regt. Eldest son of Henry Rupert and Violet Edith Millicent Fetherstonhaugh-Frampton, of Moreton in the county of Dorset. Born November 15th 1896, killed in action at Ypres May 3rd 1915. Faithful Unto Death."*

CAPTAIN FREDERICK FIDLER

1st Battalion Hampshire Regiment

Died on Monday 26th April 1915, aged 24

Commemorated on Panel 35.

Frederick Fidler

Frederick was born on Wednesday 23rd March 1881, second son of Mr J Fidler of Romsey, Hampshire. He was educated at Romsey School. In April 1904 Frederick married Bessie Fidler (née Cook), and they had four children: May born in August 1906, Frederick in August 1908, Freda in December 1911 and George in May 1913.

Frederick was a good sportsman, playing cricket, hockey and football, and was appointed Secretary of the Regimental Football Club.

In February 1899 Frederick enlisted and rose through the ranks to Sergeant Major in June 1912 and finally Regimental Sergeant Major. He was gazetted on Thursday 1st October 1914 and promoted Captain in February 1915.

He served in the South African War receiving the Queen's Medal with two clasps.

Frederick embarked in Southampton for Le Havre, arriving on Saturday 22nd August 1914, and marched to one of the camps outside the town. The Battalion entrained for Le Cateau at 4.00am on Tuesday 25th, arriving twenty-four hours later. *'The Retreat'* was already under way, and they were ordered to Solesmes

... artillery bursting during 'The Retreat'

to help cover the retiring BEF. The Battalion engaged the enemy on Wednesday 26th taking over two hundred casualties. Whilst on the Aisne he was given a Field Commission in mid-September, gazetted two weeks later. On Sunday 11th October the Battalion entrained via Amiens to Wizernes, arrived at 10.00pm and went into billets. The next day they went close to Méteren in reserve but did not see action as the Germans were driven off the Mont de Cats and back beyond Bailleul.

In the evening on Wednesday 28th October Frederick went into the line near Le Gheer, east of Ploegsteert Wood. At 6.30am on Friday 30th the Germans launched a massive barrage which continued for most of the day. At 4.30pm the grey hordes came forward in close formation and were met by rapid fire and as a result took very heavy casualties, as one of the men wrote: *"They came on so thick you couldn't miss them. It was just like shooting rabbits on Shillingston Hill."* In the centre an isolated trench was taken from Lieutenant Trimmer who had defended it to the last man (he is buried in Ploegsteert Churchyard). Frederick led his platoon to stop the Germans from breaking through despite being attacked in the rear and on both flanks. They stopped the advance and shortly thereafter the Somersets recovered the captured trench. The Battalion remained in the line until Spring 1915.

On Monday 26th April Frederick was attacking *'Berlin Wood'* when he was killed returning after taking a platoon from 'B' Company to assist the Battalion on

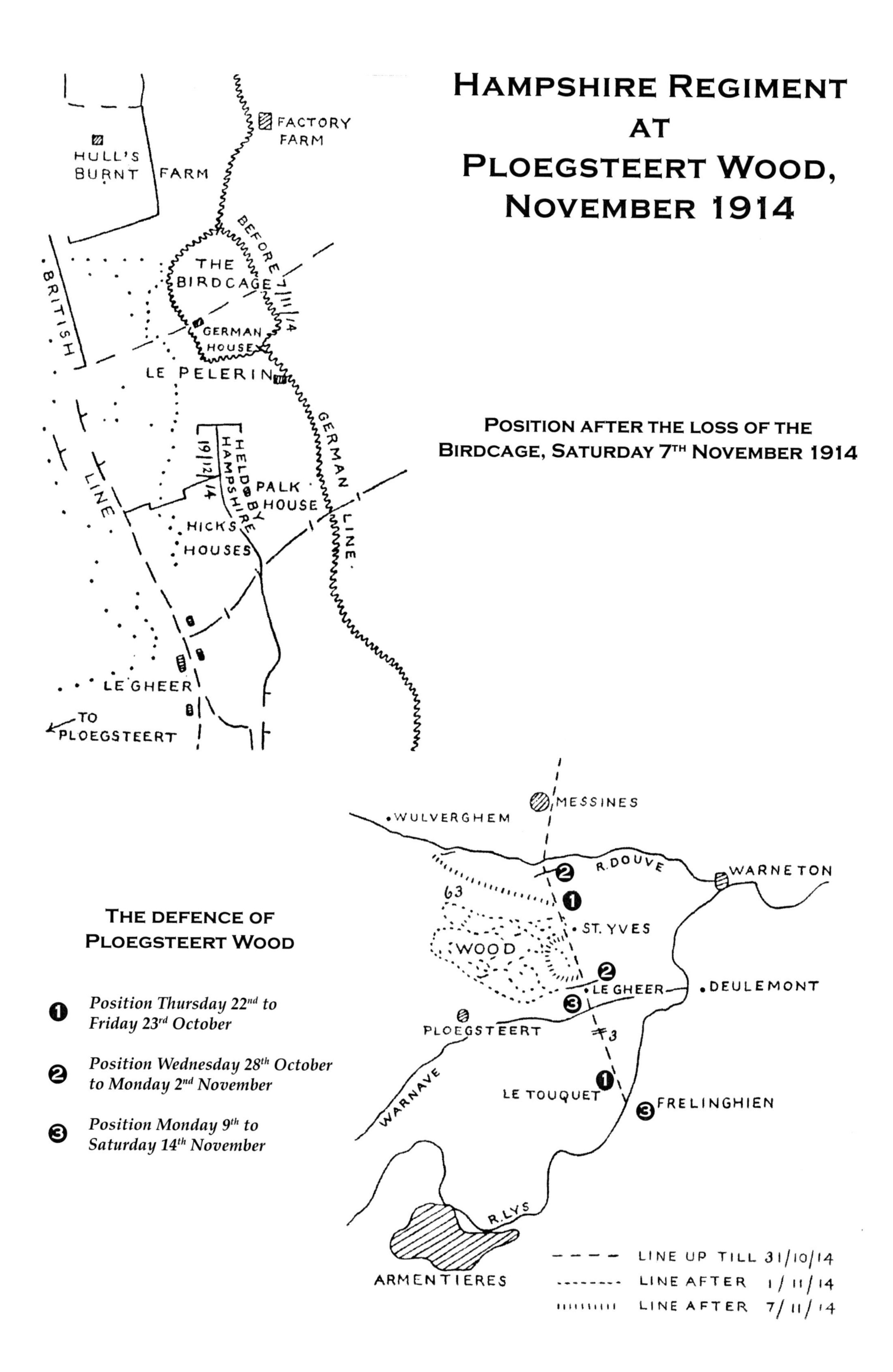
HAMPSHIRE REGIMENT AT PLOEGSTEERT WOOD, NOVEMBER 1914
FACTORY FARM
HULL'S BURNT FARM
BRITISH LINE
THE BIRDCAGE
BEFORE 7/11/14
GERMAN HOUSE
LE PELERIN
HELD BY HAMPSHIRE 19/12/14
PALK HOUSE
HICKS HOUSES
GERMAN LINE
LE GHEER
TO PLOEGSTEERT
POSITION AFTER THE LOSS OF THE BIRDCAGE, SATURDAY 7TH NOVEMBER 1914
MESSINES
WULVERGHEM
R. DOUVE
WARNETON
63
ST. YVES
WOOD
LE GHEER
DEULEMONT
PLOEGSTEERT
3
WARNAVE
LE TOUQUET
FRELINGHIEN
R. LYS
ARMENTIERES
LINE UP TILL 31/10/14
LINE AFTER 1/11/14
LINE AFTER 7/11/14
THE DEFENCE OF PLOEGSTEERT WOOD
1 Position Thursday 22nd to Friday 23rd October
2 Position Wednesday 28th October to Monday 2nd November
3 Position Monday 9th to Saturday 14th November

the left flank. He was hit while standing on the parapet bringing his men into the trench and safety.
His Commanding Officer wrote: *"There is not an officer or man in the regiment who has done better work during these awful eight months of war, and his name would certainly have been mentioned again for distinguished service. He is a real loss to the regiment, and his memory will always be honoured by us. I was close by when he was killed. It was early on the morning of the 26th … A rumour came up that the Germans were getting round our left in the mist. I told Captain Unwin to take half his company and go for them. It turned out to be a false alarm, so Captain Unwin sent your husband and his platoon back to the trench. The mist was clearing then, and the enemy's riflemen began sniping at them. Your husband called out to his men to hurry and get down into the trench, but he himself stayed up, urging them on bravely, though unwisely, a bullet hit him in the head. He was killed instantly. … I hope it will be a consolation to you to know what a splendid reputation your husband has left behind, and what a grand example he has given to all of us and to the whole country. Not only was he brave in battle and a gallant leader, but he loved by all his men for his pluck and cheerfulness in the most miserable circumstances. I never saw him depressed: he was always cheering us up."*
Frederick was Mentioned in Despatches and was awarded the French Médaille Militaire for services in the field.

Lieutenant Dare Hamilton Field

2nd (London) Heavy Battery Royal Garrison Artillery
Died on Thursday 22nd April 1915, aged 22
Commemorated on Panel 9.

Dare was the son of Belle Hamilton Field, of The Cedars, Langley, Buckinghamshire, and the late Henry Kearns Hamilton Field. He was educated at Wellington College from 1906 to 1908 where he played in the XI.
Whilst serving with his guns the Germans advanced and over-ran his battery, Dare was killed whilst defending his guns and firing at the Germans with his revolver shortly after the first gas attack.
In St Mary's Church, Langley, Berkshire, a copper plaque was placed in his memory with the inscription:

… an officers dugout

"In loving memory of Dare Hamilton Field Lieutenant Royal Garrison Artillery (T). Killed in action in France on the 22 April 1915, aged 23. R.I.P."

Second Lieutenant Samuel Hatten Field

4th Battalion South Lancashire Regiment
Died on Tuesday 31st July 1917, aged 20
Commemorated on Panel 37.

Samuel was the son of Mr and Mrs Henry H Field, of Tattenhall, Cheshire. He was educated at Uppingham School from September 1911 to December 1915 with a scholarship. He gained a scholarship and the Johnson Exhibition at Clare College, Cambridge.
Samuel gave up his studies and was sent for officer training. Following his commission he went out to France and joined the Battalion in the field. During the night of Thursday 12th and Friday 13th July 1917 between three to four thousand mustard gas shells were fired on Ypres. By the end of the day eleven officers and two hundred and fifty-five men of the Battalion were hospitalised, one officer and seven men died. Samuel was fit for the opening of the Battle of Passchendaele but was killed in action on the first day.
Samuel is commemorated on the Tattenhall War Memorial.

Second Lieutenant Leonard Amauri Filleul

Somerset Light Infantry attached
2nd Battalion Oxford and Bucks Light Infantry
Died on Wednesday 21st October 1914, aged 26
Commemorated on Panel 21.

Leonard Filleul

Leonard was born at St James's Lodge, Bath, on Monday 6th February 1888, son of the Reverend Philip William Girdlestone Filleul, Rector of Devizes and Elizabeth Filleul, of The Homestead, Combe Down, Bath. He was educated at Cleveland House Preparatory School, Weymouth, Monkton Combe School, followed by Trent College, Derbyshire, and won the National Service League gold medal for proficiency whilst serving in the school cadet force, and received a book prize from Field Marshal Lord Roberts. Leonard then went up to Lincoln College, Oxford, in 1907 graduating with an MA. He rowed in the winning

Oxford trial VIIIs in 1910 and served as the Secretary and Captain of Lincoln College Boat Club. Leonard worked at Chatham House School, Ramsgate before he joined Monkton Combe School, Bath, as an Assistant Master in 1911 where he developed the rowing club.
On Friday 14th August 1914 he volunteered and went out with the BEF. On Wednesday 21st October Leonard was fighting near St Julien. During an attack in the early morning he was leading his men across open ground when he was shot through the heart.
His Colonel wrote: *"It was a great disappointment to learn on my arrival here that Filleul had been appointed to another regt., and was not coming out to join us at the Front, for he was a most capable officer and very popular with his brother officers."*
His former Colonel wrote: *"Filleul was my subaltern in two separate years, and of all the young fellows who were attached to the battn. he was far and away the best soldier. And not only the best soldier but one of the pleasantest and most delightful companies I have ever met. Always willing, keen and cheery, I loved having him with me, and I placed more reliance upon his judgment and ability than on many a more experienced man."*
The *'Oxford Magazine'* wrote of him: *"He was one of the very best of his time, an inspiring leader, devoted to the College, and enthusiastically beloved."*

1573 Lance Corporal Alexander Findlater

4th Battalion Gordon Highlanders
Died on Saturday 25th September 1915, aged 19
Commemorated on Panel 38.

Alexander Findlater

Alexander was born in Edinburgh, on Wednesday 1st April 1896, son of Alexander and Margaret Findlater, of Mill of Sauchen, Aberdeen. Alexander was a nephew of Piper Findlater, VC. He was educated at Fordyce Academy where he was awarded five prizes in his last year before going up to Aberdeen University in 1913 where he won first prize in Latin and came fifth in Greek.
At the outbreak of war he volunteered and enlisted and was sent for seven months training in Bedford before leaving for France. He embarked on *SS Archimedes* in Southampton bound for Le Havre on Friday 19th February and entrained for northern France. He was marched to La Clytte, arriving on Wednesday 27th where for two weeks he continued to train and was sent into the line for front line experience.
In mid-March he undertook his first tour of duty. By May the Battalion had moved along the Menin Road; they were in reserve when the Germans launched a gas attack at Hooge on Monday 24th May, and saw fierce action at Bellewaarde. On Saturday 25th September Alexander went forward at 4.10am at Hooge and was killed shortly afterwards when caught on the uncut wire.

24066 Lance Corporal Fred Fisher, VC

13th Battalion Canadian Infantry (Quebec Regiment)
Died on Saturday 24th April 1915, aged 20
Commemorated on Panel 24.

Citation for the Victoria Cross, London Gazette No 29202, dated Tuesday 22nd June 1915:

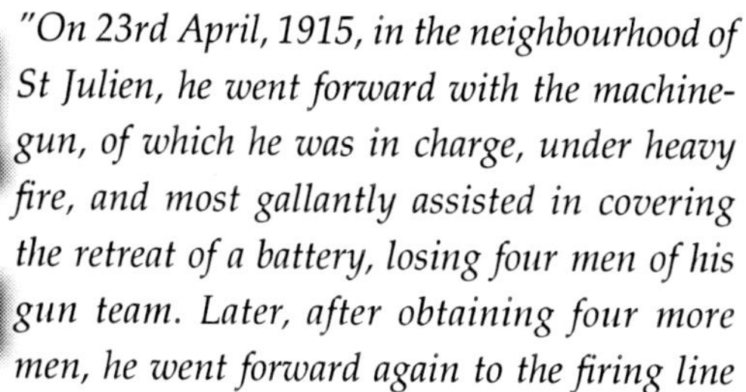

"On 23rd April, 1915, in the neighbourhood of St Julien, he went forward with the machine-gun, of which he was in charge, under heavy fire, and most gallantly assisted in covering the retreat of a battery, losing four men of his gun team. Later, after obtaining four more men, he went forward again to the firing line and was himself killed while bringing his machine-gun into action under very heavy fire, in order to cover the advance of supports."

Fred Fisher

Fred was born in St Catherine's, Ontario, on Friday 3rd August 1894, third son of Mr William H Fisher, of 100 Fort Street, Montreal. He was educated at Westmount Academy and went up to McGill University, Montreal, to study engineering, where he served in the OTC and was a member of the Alpha Psi of the Zeta Psi Fraternity. He excelled at all sports, in particular football, shooting, tennis and swimming.
Fred left University and volunteered on Saturday 29th August 1914 at Valcartier. His attestation papers describe him as a student, 5ft 9½in tall, with a 36in chest, a fair complexion, hazel eyes, light brown hair, a freckled forearm and large moles on the left side.
In October Fred left for England on *RMS Alaunia*, commanded by Captain Rostron, RNR, who had been the Captain of the *RMS Carpathia* which rescued the survivors from the *RMS Titanic*. On arrival in England, and after being read a letter of welcome from Field Marshal Lord Kitchener, he went to Salisbury Plain for training. On Friday 12th February 1915 the Battalion left for France on *SS Novian* from Avonmouth; the ship was somewhat crowded with the men crammed in like sardines. It was a rough crossing and many of the men suffered with sea

sickness, and it was difficult to get them up on deck for fresh air and some relief. They arrived in St Nazaire on Monday 15th. William disembarked and went to the station where they entrained spending the next two days and two nights winding slowly up to the front (via Nantes, Rouen, Boulogne, Calais, St Omer and Hazebrouck). Upon arrival a seven mile march was required before arriving in Flêtre where he was billeted for four days. At 8.00am on Tuesday 23rd February he marched to Armentières, three miles behind the front line. From Thursday 25th the Battalion began tours of the front line proper.

In early April 1915 Fred moved from Terdeghem, to Abeele — a march of six miles — where they encamped for the night. The next day he was taken through Poperinghe to Vlamertinghe by London bus. The Battalion was sent through the damaged city of Ypres to St Jan where they remained in reserve. During the evening of Wednesday 21st they took the line under heavy shell fire, adjacent to the French colonial troops. They were put under great pressure by the Germans, including a foray by some Germans dressed in French uniforms shouting *"Don't shoot, we are French"* but were soon unmasked and shot down. The Germans had the Canadians pinned down with enfilading fire and well placed shell-fire, directed by aeroplane. On Thursday 22nd the Germans launched their gas attack on the French colonial troops who came streaming back through St Julien to where the Battalion had moved to protect the village. Throughout Friday 23rd he was under a continuous barrage. Fred set up his machine-gun to cover the retreat of Major King's 18-pounder guns, but four of his six colleagues were killed. Fred returned to St Julien and found four men to accompany him, but these four were killed. He held on until he was shot dead.

Field Marshal Sir John French wrote in his despatch of the effort made by the Canadians: *"In spite of the danger to which they were exposed, the Canadians held their ground with a magnificent display of tenacity and courage; and it is not too much to say that the bearing conduct of these splendid troops averted disaster which might have been attended with most serious consequences."*

In the park on St Paul Street, St Catharine's, a plaque was place in his memory with the inscription: *"Born in St. Catharine's, Fred Fisher abandoned his studies at McGill University when World War I broke out and served with the 13th Battalion, First Division, Canadian Expeditionary Force. Fisher was awarded the Victoria Cross for his exceptional courage in action near St. Julien, Belgium, on April 23rd, 1915, during the second battle of Ypres. Under very heavy fire he led a machine-gun detachment covering the withdrawal of an artillery battery. Though his crew fell to enemy attack, Fisher held their position. He then returned to the garrison for more men and advanced again to the firing line. Killed in action the next day, Fisher has no known grave."*

8633 Private Frank Fisher

1st Battalion Wiltshire Regiment

Died on Friday 12th March 1915, aged 26

Commemorated on Panel 53.

Frank was born at home the son of Frederick and Elizabeth Fisher, of Southton Cottages, Collingbourne Ducis, Marlborough, Wiltshire.

He enlisted in Devizes, Wiltshire. The Battalion landed in Rouen on Friday 14th August 1914 and served through the Battle of Mons, The Retreat, the Battles of the Marne and Aisne before transferring north to serve at La Bassée before moving to the Ypres Salient. Whilst on a tour of duty Frank was killed in action.

His brother, Private Herbert Fisher, died on Tuesday 31st July 1917 and is commemorated on the Menin Gate, see below.

8327 Private George Fisher, DCM

9th (Queen's Royal) Lancers

Died on Monday 24th May 1915

Commemorated on Panel 5.

Citation for the Distinguished Conduct Medal:

"For conspicuous gallantry. Hearing a wounded man of another regiment calling for help, he, in company with another private, went out of the trench under a heavy fire, and carried the man in through the wire entanglement."

George was born in Grantham, Lincolnshire. He was living in Hoddingham when he enlisted in Lincoln.

George embarked for France on Monday 16th September 1914. He arrived as the Battle of the Aisne was drawing to a close. The Queen's Royals moved north to Flanders and took part in the First Battle of Ypres.

He was in the line at Wieltje on Wednesday 12th May 1915 when they came under very heavy shellfire from 5.00am. The fighting in the sector continued and after being relieved he was sent on Sunday 23rd to relieve the 15th (The King's) Hussars in front of Hooge. Shortly after the relief was completed in the early hours of Monday 24th the Germans launched an attack on their line. Considerable quantities of gas fell on their lines with the 9th Lancers taking the brunt of it and George died in the most awful conditions.

... 9th Lancers in action

32197 Private Herbert Leonard Fisher

2nd Battalion Wiltshire Regiment
Died on Tuesday 31st July 1917, aged 19
Commemorated on Panel 53.

Herbert was born at home the son of Frederick and Elizabeth Fisher, of Southton Cottages, Collingbourne Ducis, Marlborough, Wiltshire.
He was living in Marlborough when he enlisted in Devizes, Wiltshire. He was sent for training before going to France where he joined the Battalion in the field.
On the opening day of the Third Battle of Passchendaele Herbert was killed and his body was never recovered.
His brother, Private Frank Fisher, died on Friday 12th March 1915 and is commemorated on the Menin Gate, see above.

Brigadier General Charles FitzClarence, VC

General Staff,
Commanding 1st Guards Brigade, Irish Guards
Died on Thursday 12th November 1914, aged 49
Commemorated on Panel 3.

Citation for the Victoria Cross, The London Gazette, Friday 6th July 1900:

"On the 14th October 1899, Captain FitzClarence went with his squadron of the Protectorate Regiment, consisting of only partially trained men, who had never been in action, to the assistance of an armoured train which had gone out from Mafeking. The enemy were in greatly superior numbers, and the squadron was for a time surrounded, and it looked as if nothing could save them from being shot down. Captain FitzClarence, however, by his personal coolness and courage inspired the greatest confidence in his men, and, by his bold and efficient handling of them, not only succeeded in relieving the armoured train, but inflicted a heavy defeat on the Boers, who lost 50 killed and a large number wounded. The moral effect of this blow had a very important bearing on subsequent encounters with the Boers. On the 27th October 1899, Captain FitzClarence led his squadron from Mafeking across the open, and made a night attack with the bayonet on one of the enemy's trenches. A hand-to-hand fight took place in the trench, while heavy fire was concentrated on it from the rear. The enemy was driven out with heavy loss. Captain FitzClarence was the first man into the position and accounted for four of the enemy with his sword. The British lost 6 killed and 9 wounded. Captain FitzClarence was himself slightly wounded. With reference to these two actions, Major-General Baden-Powell states that had his Officer not shown an extraordinary spirit and fearlessness the attacks would have been failures, and we should have suffered heavy loss both in men and prestige. On the 26th December 1899, during the action at Game Tree, near Mafeking, Captain FitzClarence again distinguished himself by his coolness and courage, and was again wounded (severely through both legs)."

Charles Fitzclarence and his family coat of arms

Charles was born at Bishop's Court, County Kildare, on Monday 8th May 1865, the eldest twin son of the late Hon George FitzClarence and his wife Lady Maria Henriette. Charles was great-grandson of HM King William IV and grandson of the Earl of Munster. Charles' twin brother was killed in action at Abu-Hamed on Saturday 7th August 1897.
Charles was educated at Eton College as a member of Mr John Coles' House leaving in 1879 followed by Wellington College and passing into RMC Sandhurst.
On Wednesday 20th April 1898 Charles married at The Cididal Church, Cairo, Violet FitzClarence, the fourth and youngest daughter of Lord Alfred Spencer Churchill, MP, and grand-daughter of John, 6th Duke of Marlborough. They lived at 12 Lowndes Street, Belgrave Square, London, and had two children, Edward Charles born on Tuesday 3rd October 1899 and Joan Harriet on Monday 23rd December 1901.
Charles was a member of the London Territorial Force Association, holding memberships of the *I Zingari*, Guards' and Naval and Military Clubs.
Charles was gazetted from the Militia on Wednesday 10th November 1886, promoted Captain on Wednesday 6th April 1898, Brevet Major on Thursday 29th November 1900, Major on Monday 2nd May 1904, Lieutenant Colonel on Wednesday 14th July 1909, Colonel on Thursday 6th March 1913, and Brigadier General on Wednesday 5th August 1914.
Charles served in the South African War and during the Defence of Mafeking he was wounded twice. He was Mentioned in Despatches on Friday 8th February 1901, received the Queen's Medal with four clasps and the Victoria Cross (see citation above). Upon returning from the war he was appointed Brigade Major of the 5th Brigade at Aldershot from April 1903 to March 1906.
Charles went out to France on Thursday 3rd September 1914 where he was given command of the 1st Guards Brigade. He directed the counter-attack of the 2nd Worcesters that recaptured Gheluvelt and was killed

at 4.25am near Polygon Wood against the Prussian Guard.

"The counterattack had for its objective the recovery of some trenches taken by the enemy in Polygon Wood, and the operation was to be carried out by the Grenadier Guards … and by the Irish Guards … The General himself decided to show his old regiment the way. It was an awful night, and in the darkness the Irish Guards moved out along a country road and then struck across the open country. Suddenly the moon emerged from drifting clouds, and in the momentary brightness the Germans fired from the trenches ahead. Gen. Fitzclarence flung up his hands and fell dead."

Field Marshal Sir John French wrote in his Despatch of the order given by Charles: *"I regard it as the most critical moment in the whole of this great battle. The rally of the 1st Division and the recapture of the village of Gheluvelt … was fraught with momentous consequences. If any one unit can be singled out for special praise it is the Worcesters."*

Field Marshal Sir John French wrote of Charles: *"Another officer whose name was particularly mentioned to me was that of Brigadier-General FitzClarence, V.C., commanding the 1st Guards' Brigade. He was unfortunately killed in the night attack of the 11th November. His loss will be severely felt."*

He Wrote further: *"It was not until some time after the battle that I ascertained that the original moving spirit had been Brigadier-General FitzClarence, V.C., Commanding the 1st Guards Brigade (1st Division)."*

Captain Thorne, who was Staff Captain of the 1st Guards Brigade on Saturday 31st October, made the following statement: *"On October 31st, 1914, the 2nd Batt. Worcester Regt. were in reserve to the 2nd Division who were on our left. About 8 a.m., finding the 1st Brigade rather pressed and having no reserve of our own, General FitzClarence got the loan of one company of the Worcesters, and this was placed along the railway line to Becelaere, just north of Gheluvelt, to cover our right flank and to catch any Germans emerging from the village. This they did most successfully. Then a little later, when General FitzClarence found out how badly things were going on the right of the Scots Guards, he at once decided that an immediate counter-attack was to be made, and sent me off with orders to get hold of the remaining three companies of the Worcesters, and instruct the C.O. to counter-attack on the Scots Guards' right; the latter were holding the château. The three companies then went up through the company lining the railway, through the château garden, drove the Germans out of the village north of the main road, and re-established the line. It was undoubtedly entirely on General FitzClarence's initiative that this counter-attack was made, as he gave me the order personally.*

Major Hankey, who was commanding the 2nd Battalion of the Worcester Regiment on that day, fully corroborated Captain Thorne's account. He wrote: *"I feel perfectly certain that by shoving us in at the time and place he did, the General saved the day. If he had waited any longer, I don't think I could have got the battalion up in time to save the South Wales Borderers, and fill up the gap. This most distinguished Irish Guardsman, FitzClarence, was killed a week or two later in the same part of the field, and his loss was most deeply felt."*

Charles Fitzclarence's medals

Charles was Mentioned in Despatches on Monday 30th November 1914.

In the Guards Chapel, Birdcage Walk, Westminster, a plaque was placed in his memory, but it was destroyed during the Blitz in the Second World War.

His cousin, Captain Arthur FitzClarence, died on Monday 28th June 1915 and is commemorated on the Helles Memorial.

German artillery moving through Belgium

Captain Gerald Gadsden Fitze

'C' Battery Royal Horse Artillery

Died between Wednesday 28th and Saturday 31st October 1914, aged 28

Commemorated on Panel 5.

Gerald Fitze

Gerald was born at 56 Kensington Park Road, London, on Monday 11th January 1886, elder son of Ada E Fitze, of Kiln Meadow, Kingsley Green, Haselmere, Surrey, and the late Samuel Fitze. He was educated at Marlborough College from September 1899 as a member of Cotton and passed into RMA Woolwich. Gerald enjoyed hunting and held memberships with the Junior Army and Navy, and Marlborough Clubs.

Gerald joined the army in July 1906 and was gazetted in the Royal Field Artillery, promoted Lieutenant in 1912 and joined the Royal Horse Artillery and promoted Captain on Friday 30th October 1914 which was gazetted posthumously.

Gerald sailed to Zeebrugge with his battery, arriving on Tuesday 6th October 1914. He was sent south to participate in the First Battle of Ypres. Whilst in position at Zandvoorde Gerald was killed whilst reconnoitring.

Lieutenant
Dudley Thomas Francis Fitzpatrick

3rd Battalion attached 2nd Battalion
South Staffordshire Regiment
Died on Tuesday 27th October 1914
Commemorated on Panel 35.

Dudley Fitzpatrick

Dudley was born in India in 1893, son of Mr and Mrs Fitzpatrick of Poona. He was educated at Stonyhurst College from 1909.
At the outbreak of war Dudley volunteered and was commissioned. After training he joined the Battalion in the field and was killed during the Battle of Langemarck in his first engagement.
The Adjutant wrote: *"It is with the deepest grief that I have to write and tell you that we were never able to recover your poor brother's body. He was shot dead whilst gallantly leading an attack on an advanced post of the enemy's which was causing heavy casualties to the men of the battalion. The position could not be held, and very few of the gallant little party got back after dark, and could neither bury him nor bring his body back. Eventually we had to retire from the position."*
One of his School friends, and fellow officer, wrote: *"Fitzpatrick died as a Stonyhurst boy should. He wasn't up in the firing line twenty-four hours. He came up overnight, and went straight to his company, which, together with mine, took part in an attack on a very strongly concealed position — a ruined farm and hidden trenches. One of his men who was wounded, but managed to get back, told me that he was sent with a platoon to strengthen the firing line. He was hit before getting there, but got up and tried to go on; he was hit a second time, but got up again and tried to go on, to be finally hit again and killed."*

Captain
Hamilton Maxwell Fleming

No 2 Company, 16th Battalion Canadian Infantry
(Manitoba Regiment)
Died on Saturday 24th April 1915, aged 39
Commemorated on Panel 26.

Hamilton was born at Homewood, Chislehurst, Kent, on Saturday 4th March 1876, the eighth son of the late John Fleming, CSI, and Mary Fleming. He was educated at Dulwich College from 1889 to 1895, where he became a Lieutenant in the OTC, played for the First XV and XI, winning the Public Schools' Fencing Competition at Aldershot in 1895. Hamilton presented a silver bowl to the School as a Fencing Prize which still bears his name.

Hamilton Fleming

Hamilton was based in Argentina when the South African War broke out and he immediately volunteered, leaving for Cape Town and working his passage on a cattle boat. He enlisted in Brabant's Horse, rising through the ranks to Quartermaster Sergeant within a year. He was invalided from the war due to rheumatic fever, and he received the Queen's Medal with three clasps. He returned to South Africa where he was a farmer in Cape Colony and made three trips across the Kalahari Desert with mules in the German South African War. Hamilton served as a newspaper correspondent in the Russo-Japanese War. In 1910 he emigrated to Vancouver where he joined the Seaforths as a Lieutenant subsequently promoted Captain, commanding 'A' Company.
At the outbreak of war Hamilton volunteered at Valcartier on Wednesday 23rd September 1914. His attestation papers describe him as a Presbyterian, 5ft 9½in tall, with a 41½in chest, a fair complexion, brown eyes and hair, and vaccination marks on his left arm.
Hamilton sailed on Wednesday 30th September for Plymouth which he reached on Saturday 17th October. He was sent for training on Salisbury Plain and one of his colleagues wrote: *"It is a camp of bell tents, beside a bluff on a big plain; and for miles around, these plains stretch far into the distance. Thousands of blankets were distributed on arrival. Some of them are lengths of rough tweed, others soft, fleecy, woollen blankets. It looks as if the country has been scoured for anything in the way of cover, regardless of cost."*
Life in the camp was not pleasant: *"The ground is awful, the mud, inches deep, of soft watery stuff, is awful too, in and all around the camp."* During the night of Wednesday 4th December a fierce storm destroyed their tents and camp so they were sent to huts at Lark Hill. The huts were not considered to be particularly good: *"A fearful lot of sickness here in these huts. Flue reigns supreme in the shape of sore heads, sore throats and racking coughs. At night it sounds like hell with all those graveyard coughs around."*
He was sent ahead to France, acting as Landing Officer and made the arrangements for the Canadians' arrival. The Battalion sailed for St Nazaire on Friday 12th February, arriving after a rough crossing on Monday 15th. He entrained for Hazebrouck from where he marched to Caëstre where billets were difficult to find: *"It was raining, we sat down at the side of the street for over an hour, then marched out into the darkness over a muddy road to a farmhouse. We were kept waiting there for over half an hour and marched back to town. Again marched out to another*

The Canadian Scottish troops cheering HM King George V on Salisbury Plain

farmhouse, but no room there, so back to the starting point, and into a hayloft some time this side of midnight." On Thursday 24th February he accompanied his fellow officers and NCOs from No 2 Company to visit the line prior to the Battalion taking the line at Bois Grenier. On Wednesday 4th March the Battalion relieved the 2nd Border Regiment near La Cardonnerie Farm, Rue Petillon, Fleurbaix.

He remained on tours of duty until Wednesday 7th April when he left for Cassel. On Saturday 10th the Battalion paraded for an inspection by General Sir Horace Smith-Dorrien.

General Sir Horace Smith-Dorrien

On Thursday 15th he marched to Steenvoorde where he was billeted overnight before being taken by motor bus to Vlamertinghe. At 2.30pm the Battalion formed up and marched the five miles along the *pavé* to Wieltje; at 8.00pm they relieved the French 79th Division on the St Julien to Poelkapelle road. After three days in the line Hamilton was relieved to reserve with billets being provided in north Ypres.

Hamilton's commander, Captain Rae, had noticed during the tour of duty that the German front line had been altered, but no-one at Headquarters could understand why this might be. Hamilton was able to take advantage of strolling around Ypres in the relative quiet before the storm broke. On Thursday 22nd the explanation for the changes in the German parapets became clear — at 5.00pm the first gas attack was launched.

At 5.30pm the Battalion was 'stood to' and they formed up along the canal at 6.00pm until 7.40pm. They marched via La Brique to St Jan, however, at Wieltje they were held up by the clogged roads. One of the men recorded: *"I heard Major Markham say 'Damn this Staff, we are only two days out of the trenches and now they are blanking us around on night manœuvres'."* Whilst waiting to move forward many of the men suffered the effects of the gas blowing in the wind, leaving them with dry throats and streaming eyes.

Orders were received to participate in a counter-attack on *'Kitchener Wood'* (Bois des Cuisiniers). Hamilton's company led the way as the attack commenced at 11.45pm. He was shot in the leg but refused to go back and continued until he was shot through the head, dying instantaneously.

One of his men wrote: *"I tied up his leg and wanted him to go back to the dressing station, but he was too good an officer and too brave a gentleman to do that, as he thought the boys needed him."*

8356 Private George Fletcher

1st Battalion Lincolnshire Regiment

Died on Sunday 1st November 1914, aged 60

Commemorated on Panel 21.

George was born in St Mary's, Nottingham. He was educated locally. George enlisted in Lincoln.

George left Victoria Barracks, Portsmouth, at 6.15am on Thursday 13th August 1914 and entrained for Southampton. He embarked for Le Havre on *SS Norman*, arriving the next morning. After two days in a swampy camp outside the town he entrained for Landrecies. He marched to Mons and took the line at Cuesmes, but he did not see action. Late in the afternoon of Sunday 23rd he was ordered with the Battalion to retire. At 10.00pm on Monday 24th the Battalion arrived at Frameries where

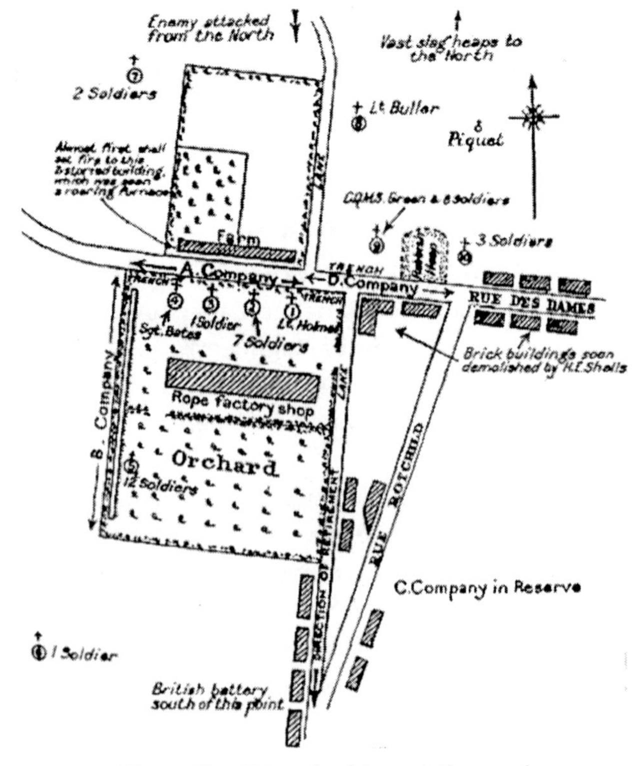

1st Battalion Lincolnshires at Frameries

they took part in a fierce engagement that lasted for four hours.
The march south continued and they did not receive a square meal until Saturday 29th, as over the previous days each time food was to have been provided it had not been dropped off, or there were no cooking facilities. The Retreat did not end until they had marched two hundred and thirty-seven miles, when at Liverdy on Saturday 5th they were ordered to turn and engage the enemy. At 6.00am on Sunday 6th September they commenced their march in search of the Germans and had reached the Grand Morin by 11.00pm. The march through the Marne continued onto the Aisne which was reached by Saturday 12th and two days later they had crossed the river and taken position at Vailly. The Battalion remained on the Chemin des Dames until 7.00pm on Friday 2nd October when they were relieved and sent to billets in Servenay. The next day a series of long forced marches commenced after seventeen continuous days in the wet sodden trenches of the Aisne. It was small wonder that George and his comrades suffered badly with their feet and were totally exhausted by the time they entrained for Abbeville at La Croix St Ouen.
A fleet of motor buses were sent to Hesdin which collected them at 9.00am on Saturday 10th October and transported them to the La Bassée sector. As George was led through Richebourg St Vaast they came within range of the German artillery and shells started dropping close to them. At 2.30am on Friday 16th they relieved the 2nd Royal Irish Regiment near Rouge Croix where they entrenched their position at the crossroads. The advance continued through Pietre and took part in the

Rouge Croix, 1914

capture of Herlies. George went forward and covered fifteen hundred yards before attacking the German lines at the point of the bayonet. After a fierce fight the German lines and the village were taken. At 3.30am on Monday 26th George was relieved and sent to billets in Croix Rouge. At 3.30pm George was being sent back into action and served at Neuve-Chapelle until Thursday 29th.

At 6.45am on Saturday 31st George paraded and marched north, crossing the Belgian border, moving through Neuve Eglise and Lindenhoek to Kemmel. They were sent into the line and at midnight the Germans commenced a preliminary barrage. An hour later German infantry poured from their trenches to attack Wytschaete with overwhelming superiority in numbers. Within two hours the village was taken. George was marched to within a quarter of a mile of the village, where they were fired upon by what they thought could be Indian 'friendly fire'. Lance Corporal King went out to reconnoitre the position, and called out to the attackers who claimed to be Indian soldiers so he advanced and was shot dead. Another NCO undertook the same duty and suffered the same fate. The Lincolnshires were forced back and were then reinforced by the Northumberland Fusiliers. The combined forces launched an attack on Wytschaete, and George was one of the many who were killed or wounded that day.

200388
Company Quartermaster Serjeant James Fletcher, DCM

'D' Company, 1st/4th Battalion
The Loyal North Lancashire Regiment
Died on Tuesday 31st July 1917, aged 23
Commemorated on Panel 41.

Citation for the Distinguished Conduct Medal, London Gazette, Thursday 5th August 1915:

"For conspicuous gallantry and devotion to duty on 15th June, attending on the wounded under very heavy fire, continuing at that work after he had been twice wounded, and even after his battalion had withdrawn."

James was the son of Alexander Edward and Mary Alice Fletcher, of 9 Maynard Street, Preston.
At the outbreak of war James was at camp at Kirkby Lonsdale when the Battalion was recalled to Preston. The Battalion paraded in Preston's Market Square as they presented their colours to the Mayor for safe keeping whilst they were at the front. On Saturday 22nd August 1914 they moved to camp at Swindon where they trained and guarded the Great Western Railway. In March 1915 they moved to Oxted and assisted in the London defences.
On Sunday 2nd May 1915 James entrained at Ballast Pit Siding, Bedford, for Folkestone. The Battalion sailed to Boulogne on *SS Onward* and they marched to a camp at Ostrohove. They were sent by train to Lillers arriving on Thursday 6th and they undertook training until

Tuesday 25th. Their opportunity of serving in the front line arrived. They were in the line near Locon, with only shallow trenches (just two feet deep) to occupy. The whole area had a dreadful aroma, from the corpses of the Scots Guards and the Germans that had been killed during the Battle of Festubert. James remained in the line until Wednesday 2nd June when they were relieved and went to Cornet Malo, Locon. On Sunday 13th June they returned to the line from which they had only been relieved the previous Friday. James and 'D' Company were in the support trenches: all they could do was await the attack. The preliminary bombardment commenced and lasted for forty-eight hours; the German artillery replied, mainly with shrapnel. From 5.30pm on Tuesday 15th the British artillery increased its fire power considerably and the Germans, realising that they had to reply properly as an attack was imminent, started to shell the British lines with some force. The attack commenced on time and James helped guide the men up the damaged communication trenches where they supported the centre. James and the Company were in the thick of the fighting and for bringing in the wounded during the attack he was awarded the Distinguished Conduct Medal. Despite the initial success and capture of the German front line, they could not hold onto them and were forced to retire when counter-attacked by the Prussians.

The British report of the attack read: *"Yesterday evening, we captured the German front line of trenches east of Festubert, on a mile of front, but failed to hold them during the night against the strong counter-attacks delivered by the enemy."*

The German report read: *"Again influenced by Russian defeats, the French and English yesterday attacked with strong forces of men at many points on the Western front. On the other hand, two attacks of four English Divisions between the roads of Estaires-La Bassée and La Bassée Canal completely collapsed. Our brave Westphalian regiments and reinforcements, consisting of portions of our Guard, repulsed the attacks after desperate hand-to-hand fighting. The enemy suffered heavy losses. We captured several machine-guns and one mine-throwing howitzer."*

The Battalion was taken out of the line and organised themselves at Le Touret where they had breakfast, a tot of rum followed by a roll call which confirmed the high casualties they had taken.

James served in the area until Sunday 27th June when they entrained at La Gorgue and were sent to Corbie via Calais, Abbeville and Amiens. On Monday 31st they were sent to Martinsart for a weeks training. On Friday 6th August they went into the line at Aveluy Wood. The Battalion remained on the Somme until October 1916. On Wednesday 2nd February 1916 the Earl of Derby visited the Battalion at Vieulaine. James served through The Battle of the Somme from the outset, and served at Guillemont on Saturday 1st July. They saw action at Delville Wood from Saturday 9th September and ten days later they served at Fricourt before returning again to Delville Wood.

On Sunday 1st October James left with the Battalion entraining for Poperinghe arriving the following evening. The next day they marched the short distance to Brandhoek where they undertook training. Two weeks later they were billeted on the ramparts at Ypres and on Thursday 19th they went into the line at *'Railway Wood'*. They served in and out of the line until the end of the year, and were relieved from the line on Christmas Eve. Christmas Day was recalled: *"Out of the trenches! Came out last night and forthwith had a shave and partial wash. We sent an Officer on, and when we landed here the men found candles lit and fires going in their billets, and we had ditto in ours. To-day we gave the men a decent Christmas dinner, and are now about to have one ourselves, a roaring fire, plenty of candles, turkey stuffed with the stuffing, beer, vin ordinaire, pudding and sundries have the promise of a very pleasant evening in them, if the Boche will refrain from throwing stuff over — he peppered this place some to-day! To-morrow, work — pulling things together — refitting, cleaning, reorganising; to-night, Christmas Day, home thoughts, comfort and God bless everyone, especially those at home, who are always with us in thought — what we owe to their prayers no man knows."* They remained at 'C Camp' until Saturday 6th January 1917 when they marched back to Ypres and to *'Railway Wood'* the next day.

James remained on the Salient until he was killed. For a considerable period of time they were often billeted in Ypres. They had regular visits to Poperinghe, undertook training and had tours of duty throughout the Salient. One account of being under shell fire was written after James and 'D' Company had gone into the line at Potijze: *"It is curious to notice the different effects intermittent and concentrated shelling have on one — intermittent shelling takes people different ways — on the whole it makes you angry; concentrated shelling, such as a barrage, you rise above altogether by some curious effort of will. I think it is that in the first case one hears each one coming hissing along in a descending scale, and speculates where it will fall, while in the second there is simply a terrific medley of bangs and crashes which you can only accept as a perfect inferno of noise, and leave it at that."*

"To be within two or three yards of a big shell when it bursts sounds like sudden death, but it isn't necessarily; it happens daily to lots of people who survive; I have been several times as close as that, closer in one case; the shock and noise absolutely deafen one for some minutes afterwards, but it seems to pass off; but there must be a good solid bulwark of earth between you and the shell! if there isn't, well shell-shock is the best you can hope for!"

On Saturday 26th May James and the men moved to the

front, however, James and 'D' Company remained for twenty-four hours in Ypres as a digging party before going into the reserve trenches behind 'B' who were in support of 'A' and 'C' at Potijze. On Friday 1st June the British launched a gas attack, releasing five hundred drums of gas towards the German trenches. One Company was poisoned by their own gas; the Germans then launched a heavy reply. The next day more gas was sent over but very little damage was caused. The Germans replied by launching a further large gas attack on Ypres during the night of Sunday 3rd.

James was in Poperinghe on Saturday 28th July and the next day they started to prepare for the attack and went to Vlamertinghe. The weather changed completely and a violent thunderstorm burst over the salient, turning the mud to thick glue and filling every shell hole with water. *"The succeeding days were dull and heavy, making the completion of the artillery preparation peculiarly difficult, and typical Flanders weather prevailed on the morning of the 31st — the moment chosen for the attack. Low-lying clouds which made aerial observation and co-operation as difficult as could be imagined; a dampness of atmosphere, threatening rain at any moment; a half-sodden ground, greasy and depressing — such was the luck of the weather when the barrage opened."* At 9.25pm on Monday 30th they moved off along the Ypres road, passing the water tower and assembled at *'Congreve Walk'*, surprisingly arriving without any casualties. From 10.00pm until 2.00am gas was launched at the German lines who in turn replied with mustard gas. At 10.00am on Tuesday 31st James and the Battalion were ordered to move forward, taking heavy casualties amongst the officers from machine-gun fire. The Battalion captured *'Somme Farm'* — a collection of concrete dug-outs, where they captured sixty prisoners — followed by *'Keir Farm'* and *'Gallipoli'*, similarly constructed and further prisoners were taken. The advance continued and more casualties were taken, including James.

Captain
Roland Sackville Fletcher

'W' Company, 1st Battalion Northumberland Fusiliers

Died on Sunday 1st November 1914, aged 32

Commemorated on Panel 12.

Roland Fletcher

Roland was born in London on Friday 24th March 1882, second son of Lionel and Eleanor Mary Lionel Fletcher, of Elmscroft, West Farleigh, Maidstone, Kent. He was educated at Charterhouse from 1895 to 1900 as a Saunderite. He was of a literary bent, contributing articles relating to his experiences in Northern Nigeria in *'Blackwood's Magazine'*, and published *'Hausa Sayings and Folk-lore'*. Roland was keen on all forms of sports and was a member of the Wellington Club.

Roland was gazetted in January 1901 from the Militia, promoted Lieutenant in February 1902, Captain in 1912. He was a qualified, first class interpreter in Hausa and served with the West African Frontier Force from November 1904 to January 1910.

Roland, commanding 'W' Company, went out to the front on Thursday 29th October 1914. Two days later he marched the twelve miles with his men to Lindenhoek from where they went into billets for a short period. At 1.45am on Sunday 1st November orders were received that reinforcements were urgently required to support the front at Wytschaete which was under very heavy attack. Despite their march being in the middle of the night, the route was well illuminated by the exploding shells, burning woods and houses. At 4.30am a counter-attack was ordered and as they advanced they came across uncut wire which impeded them. After only a very short period of time Roland was killed together with most of his men. Captain St John, of 'X' Company went to look for Roland to discuss the position but only found broken bodies — no trace of Roland was ever found.

Roland was recorded in Debretts Obituary — War Roll of Honour published in the 1921 edition.

Second Lieutenant
Reginald William 'Reggie' Fletcher

118th Battery 26th Brigade Royal Field Artillery

Died on Saturday 31st October 1914, aged 22

Commemorated on Panel 5.

Reggie Fletcher

Reggie was born in Oxford on Saturday 19th March 1892, the third and youngest son of Charles Robert Leslie, MA, and Katharine Fletcher (née Leslie), of Norham End, Oxford (his father was a Fellow of both All Souls' and Magdalen Colleges and an author). Reggie and his brother, George, were close with their careers mirroring each other. Reggie was described as a *'Viking'* and *'Homeric hero'* with his athletic build, wavy yellow hair and clear-cut features. Reggie educated at The Dragon School from 1900 to 1903 followed by Durnford School, Langton Matravers, Dorset. He went to Eton College from 1905 to 1910 as a member of College and a scholar, then went up as a Commoner of Balliol College, Oxford, graduating with a BA in 1914. He enjoyed literature and poetry, and often wrote Greek and Latin verse. He rowed for their

VIII and IV; Leander IV for Stewards' 1913; stroked Oxford University Boat Club trial eights 1911 to 1913; and received his Oxford Blue 1914 — and could often get upset when things went badly, his Master wrote: *"... however fiercely he had been growling in the barge in the afternoon, there was not a room in College where he would not have been the most welcome guest of all an hour or two afterwards."* Reggie was second in command of the artillery section of the Oxford OTC, becoming Second in Command. Reggie enjoyed the outdoor life and spent holidays in Iceland, Norway, Ireland and Scotland. He was an ardent Freemason.

Reggie was gazetted with a University Commission on the day war was declared. He sailed for France on Thursday 20th August 1914 and served at the Battle of the Aisne with 116th Battery. He was then sent to Belgium with the 118th with his horse *'Playboy'*. He was killed when hit by the bursting of a shell during the First Battle of Ypres at Veldhoek whilst returning from observation duty.

His Major wrote: *"I have lost a very charming and cheery comrade and a Verey gallant and capable officer. From a military point of view his death is a great loss to the Battery and from a personal point of view it has been a great shock and grief to his brother officers."*

The *Oxfordian* wrote: *"He had in him the qualities which make a first-class mountaineer, ad the fascination of the rocks caught him during his last two summers when he was with his brother in Skye. What his friends will always remember about him was the whole-heartedness which was in all that he did and felt; the intense enjoyment with which he would wander about the wilds of Iceland or sit by the fireside repeating by heart innumerable lines of poetry. When the boat was not going well he could be depressed almost beyond the limits of tragedy. One who knew him for many years says of him that 'there was something about him which the Ancient Greeks called δαιμονιος, compact of light and fire'. It was a fire that could burn others. He was not tolerant of all opinions, nor yet of all men. He had prejudices which he cherished as precious possessions; but even those who suffered from them often realized that they were only possessions, not part of himself. Given a hard task to do, ad they would fall off him. The task was put upon him; he bore it for some ten weeks (he had only six weeks at the front) in a way which won the admiration and affection of his brother officers; then the end came. What his old friends have lost they would, like all old friends, find it difficult indeed to express."*

In the Chapel of Eton College a red marble plaque was erected with the inscription: *"Remember with thanksgiving two brothers both scholars of this College, Walter George Fletcher, Captain of the School 1906. Assistant Master 1913-1914. Second Lieutenant Royal Welch Fusiliers. Killed at Bois Grenier, March 20th 1915 aged 27. Reginald William Fletcher, Second Lieutenant Royal Field Artillery, killed at Gheluvelt October 31st 1914 aged 22."*

His brother, 2nd Lieutenant Walter George Fletcher, is buried in Bois Grenier Communal Cemetery.

Second Lieutenant Edgar Reginald Folker

3rd Battalion attached 'A' Company
1st Battalion York and Lancaster Regiment
Died on Saturday 20th February 1915, aged 30
Commemorated on Panel 55.

Edgar Folker

Edgar was born at 106 St George's Avenue, Tufnell Park, London, on Thursday 23rd October 1884, second son of Alfred Henry and Hannah Maria Keevill Folker, of 12 Park Road, Harlesden, London (agent for the Royal Crown Derby Porcelain Company). He was educated at St Paul's College and Willesden High School.

Edgar was apprenticed to the Vauxhall Engineering Company followed by the Rover Company before starting his own company in the Haymarket where he designed and raced many different cars.

Edgar was a big man standing 6ft 4in, weighing nearly 14 stone. A keen sportsman and a member of the Thames Rowing Club, he rowed for the VIII and IV in the Thames Cup of 1908 and 1910. He was also a member of the Twickenham Rowing Club, the Remenham Club and The Motor Club.

In August 1914 Edgar joined the York and Lancaster Regiment and went into training. On Friday 15th January 1915 he sailed to Le Havre from where he went up to northern France for further training before proceeding to Belgium. He was in trench No 37 close to the Verbrandenmolen in Ypres when he was killed by poisonous fumes when investigating damage to a connecting trench.

Colonel Isherwood wrote of him (commemorated on the Menin Gate, see below); *"Although your son had only been with us a comparatively short time, yet he had endeared himself to us all; and we very much miss him in the regiment. I feel that nothing I can say will be able to alleviate your sorrow, but I am sure you will be glad to hear what an excellent officer he was and could very ill be spared. He was so keen on everything he had to do and did it so well, and the men of his company were so fond of him."*

On Saturday 13th March 1915 a memorial service was conducted by Canon A E Humphreys at St Michael's Church, Stonebridge Park, where Edgar had been a choir boy. (His younger brother suffered severe head injuries shortly after his Edgar's death.)

Lieutenant Donald Keith Forbes

1st Battalion Suffolk Regiment

Died on Monday 15th February 1915, aged 23

Commemorated on Panel 21.

Donald Forbes

Donald was born at Bridgewater, Somerset, on Saturday 30th January 1892, son of William Alexander Forbes, Barrister-at-Law, Inner Temple, and Margaret Forbes, of Amraoti Camp, Berar, India. He was educated at Bedford School where he excelled at all sports including football, and hockey, and won many cups for running. In 1910 Donald passed into RMC Sandhurst.

Donald was gazetted in September 1911 and promoted Lieutenant in February 1914.

He joined his regiment in Alexandria, Egypt, in September 1911, from where Donald was sent to Cairo and onward to Khartoum as a member of the Camel Corps.

Shortly after the outbreak of war Donald sailed from Egypt for Liverpool on board *HMT Grantully Castle* arriving October 1914, from where he went to camp at Lichfield before being sent to Winchester. On Saturday 16th January 1915 he sailed to Le Havre, embarking on *SS Mount Temple*. He entrained for Hazebrouck and marched to Merris where the Battalion was billeted. For the rest of the month they trained and prepared for front line duty — on Thursday 28th they were inspected by Field Marshal Sir John French. On Tuesday 2nd February Donald went by motor bus to Vlamertinghe and then marched to Ypres. Two days later they undertook their first tour of duty on the Salient between the Canal and Hill 60. He was in action on the Ypres Salient when he was accidentally guided to within seven yards of the German trenches. His friend, Lieutenant Francis Wood-Martin*, was shot and in going to his aid, Donald too was mortally wounded. (* Lieutenant Francis Wood-Martin is commemorated on the Menin Gate, see below.)

1661 Private Gilbert Forbes

'B' Company, 4th Battalion Gordon Highlanders

Died on Saturday 25th September 1915, aged 19

Commemorated on Panel 38.

Gilbert was the son of James and Elizabeth Forbes, of Bleachfield House, Persleyden, Woodside, Aberdeen. He was educated locally.

Gilbert volunteered and was sent for training. He left from Southampton on board *SS Archimedes*, arriving in Le Havre on Friday 19th February 1915. He was sent to northern France before marching to La Clytte on Wednesday 27th were he remained for training. Until mid-March he undertook short trips into the line before being sent on tours of duty. In May he was in reserve near Zillebeke when on Monday 24th the Germans launched a gas attack at Hooge and he took part in the attack on Bellewaarde. On Saturday 25th September a feint on the Salient was launched to cover the real attack further south, at Loos. At 4.10am Gilbert *'went over the top'* and headed towards the German lines, at 4.30am the Germans opened a barrage that destroyed the front line trenches. As Gilbert went forward he was held up by the uncut German wire where he was mown down by machine-gun fire.

His brother, Private Walter Forbes, died on Friday 2nd June 1916 and is commemorated on the Menin Gate, see below, and another brother, Joseph, was also killed.

2820 Serjeant John Keith Forbes

4th Battalion Gordon Highlanders

Died on Saturday 25th September 1915, aged 32

Commemorated on Panel 38.

John Forbes

John was born in Aberdeen, on Thursday 12th April 1883, son of Alexander Forbes, FEIS, and Jessie Forbes (née Keith), of Glenaden, Mintlaw Station, Aberdeenshire. He went up to Aberdeen University where he graduated with an MA. He was employed at Rathven Public School from 1905 until 1912 before he studied divinity at Aberdeen United Free College where he was awarded the Foote Scholarship in Hebrew and the Eadie Prize in New Testament Greek. John enjoyed walking, mountaineering, and was an accomplished musician.

At the outbreak of war John volunteered and enlisted in October 1914. After training he sailed to Le Havre on Friday 19th February 1915. He arrived in camp in La Clytte on Monday 27th where his training continued for two weeks.

John was offered the opportunity of a commission but preferred to remain in the ranks. As a first class marksman whilst on the Salient he organised groups of snipers and undertook valuable reconnaissance for which he received a letter of thanks from the Divisional General. Initially he served in the southern sector with billets in La Clytte. He was killed by a sniper on the Bellewaarde Ridge during the feint for the Battle of Loos.

109342 Private Walter Grant Forbes

4th Canadian Mounted Rifles
(Central Ontario Regiment)
Died on Friday 2nd June 1916, aged 23
Commemorated on Panel 32.

Walter was born on Saturday 26th August 1893, son of James and Elizabeth Forbes, of Bleachfield House, Persleyden, Woodside, Aberdeen. He went out to Canada where he was employed as a machinist and was a member of the Militia.

On Sunday 8th November 1914 Walter volunteered in Toronto where he was described as a Presbyterian, 5ft 5½in tall, with a 38in chest, a dark complexion, dark grey eyes, dark brown hair, with a tattoo, three vaccination marks and a scar on his right arm.

Walter left for Folkestone on Sunday 24th October 1915 from where the Rifles went into camp and 36 hours later they landed in Boulogne. On Tuesday 2nd November he moved to *'Aldershot Huts'* at Neuve Eglise from where he went into the line on the Messines Ridge near St Yves. His first 'serious' tour took place on Wednesday 1st December at Hill 63 and Walter remained in the sector until the end of the year; Christmas being spent in billets. January 1916 was spent in training before returning to tours of duty, first on the Wulverghem to Messines road and from Sunday 19th March at Zillebeke. Walter was sent to the front in various sectors of the Salient over the ensuing weeks by which time he was familiar with Ypres and the various battlegrounds that created the Salient. On Tuesday 16th May he was relieved from the line at *'Sanctuary Wood'* and went for rest and training, remaining in reserve until the evening of Wednesday 31st. Walter paraded with full kit and gas-masks and sent by train to Ypres and onto Mount Sorrel. The trenches were good — deep, clean, well constructed with elephant-shelters. Thursday 1st June passed uneventfully, however, at 6.00am the next morning Lieutenant Colonel Ussher toured the line in preparation for an inspection by Major General Malcolm Mercer. Shortly after 8.00am as the senior officers were making their way forward, the Germans launched a massive bombardment which lasted four and half hours. Most of the senior officers were killed, the Canadian trenches were destroyed, trees became little more than matchsticks and the area had become a mass of shell-holes. At 1.00pm the barrage ended and a mine was blown after which the German infantry advanced. The toll on the 4th Canadians was colossal, only seventy-three out of six hundred and eighty answered the roll call on Sunday 4th.

Colonel Ussher

General Mercer

Walter's brother, Private Gilbert Forbes, died on Saturday 25th September 1915 and is commemorated on the Menin Gate, see above, and another brother, Joseph, was also killed.

110167 Private Eric Allan Ford

Princess Patricia's Canadian Light Infantry
(Eastern Ontario Regiment)
Died on Friday 2nd June 1916, aged 24
Commemorated on Panel 10.

Eric Ford

Eric was born at home on Wednesday 27th January 1897, son of Joseph and Mary Jessica D Ford, of Portneuf, Province of Quebec. He went up to McGill University, graduating with a BA in 1914.

Eric volunteered on Wednesday 3rd March 1915 in Montreal where he was described as a Presbyterian, bring 5ft 7in tall, with a 38in chest, a medium complexion, grey eyes, light brown hair, with a mole close to his ear and a large vaccination mark on his left arm. He enlisted in the 5th Mounted Canadian Rifles prior to transferring to the Princess Patricia's Canadian Light Infantry on Friday 7th April 1916.

In July 1915 Eric sailed to Plymouth, arriving on Wednesday 28th, from where he went by train to London and onward to Shorncliffe, Kent, where his training continued. He was mainly based at *'Cæsar's Camp'* from where he left for *'St Martin's Camp'* on Sunday 24th October and then to the dock in Folkestone. He sailed Boulogne, arriving in the early hours of Tuesday 26th; they immediately entrained for Bailleul. The train pulled out of the station at 8.15am and they arrived at 12.45pm and went to billets in Méteren in intermittent rain. On Tuesday 2nd November Eric moved through Bailleul to *'Aldershot Huts'* to the east of the town where final preparations were made to undertake work in the trenches when they were attached to more experienced troops and undertook fatigues. He returned to Méteren before taking to the line for the first time at Hill 63. Christmas was spent out of the line at Méteren and the Regiment remained there in training and on fatigues until Tuesday 1st February 1916 when they returned to front line duties in the Messines-Wulverghem sector. Following a further period stationed in Méteren Eric

moved to Ouderdom, via Locre, where he was prepared to take to the line in the Salient. He went via *'Belgian Château'*, through Ypres and the Menin Gate, via *'Hellfire Corner'* to *'Yeomanry Post'* where he came under heavy fire from the *'Birdcage'*. Following a series of duties in the *'Maple Copse'* sector Eric was relieved on Wednesday 5th April and sent to *'Camp A'* when he transferred to the PPCLI and joined his brother, William.
For his the rest of his story, see his brother, Private William Ford, who died on the same day and is also commemorated on the Memorial, see below.

3250 Rifleman Percy Gordon Ford

1st/9th Battalion London Regiment
(Queen Victoria's Rifles)
Died on Saturday 24th April 1915, aged 24
Commemorated on Panel 54.

Percy Ford

Percy was born in Hornsey on Friday 11th September 1891, second son of John William Fletcher and Catherine Ann Ford, of The Grange, Roydon, Essex. He was educated at Tollington School and Christ's College, Finchley, after which he was employed as a commercial traveller. Percy was a junior sidesman in the Methodist Church, Finchley.
At the outbreak of war Percy volunteered and enlisted, leaving for France on Sunday 14th February 1915, joining the Battalion ten days later. Percy was sent into the line at Wulverghem where he undertook a series of tours, coming under increasingly heavy fire as the month progressed. At the end of the month Percy was slightly wounded.
His story was written by a comrade: *"He was in hospital when we went up to Hill 60, but joined us up there in the dug-outs when we had been relieved from the firing line. I remember him, Claude, coming up to me and saying, as we shook hands, 'By Jove, Ashford, old man, I'm glad to see you; you fellows had a rough time'. Not a word about the narrow escape he had had with out transport in Ypres. We left on the Thursday morning, 10 men at a time; they were shelling us and it was dangerous to offer too large a target. We assembled outside the hospital at Ypres and Smith-Dorrien inspected us. We marched back to huts as we thought to a well-earned rest. The huts were not complete and we had to bivouac. About 6.30 p.m. we saw the French coming pell mell across country, a regular rout, we spoke to them and found they were retreating. We had to fall in and dig ourselves in by hedges in some fields near. We did not know which way the Germans were supposed to be coming, and had to change our position three times during the night. We were fagged out and had no proper sleep since the Saturday previous — we couldn't get much at Hill 60. At about 2.30 a.m. we had orders to stop digging; marched back some way and spent the remainder of the night in a field. In the morning we had to sit in ditches along the road, in order to be out of sight of aeroplanes, awaiting orders. The cookers came up and we had some tea, I remember as well as if it were yesterday; Percy gave me some of his condensed milk, and I sat down beside him and we laughingly arranged to go to Golders Green in the afternoon. Shortly afterwards we had to march off with the rest of the 13th Brigade, to which we were attached. We were in support on the banks of the Yser. The Canadians had driven the Germans back after the French retreat. During the night we had to go up to the firing line, but only for a few hours. The morning of Saturday found us on the banks of the Yser, awaiting orders. We had dug ourselves in as a protection against shrapnel. We moved off about 11 o'clock in single file along the banks of Yser, towards Ypres, then we cut inland and gradually wound our way forward, moving in zig-zag manner, taking as much advantage of hedges, etc., as we could. Shells were flying all around, but Percy was there then and that was Saturday. Amy tells me you were told Friday; I feel certain that it was Saturday. Well, we must have marched about 3 to 4 miles and we then got right into the thick of it, it was raining shells. We deployed and were told to take shelter behind some semicircular parapets. The Germans seemed to have them taped and dropped shells right in amongst us. It was flat country and evidently they could see us approaching and shelled us very heavily indeed, the air was thick with shells. We advanced by short stages about 100 yards, and then I got hit by a shell in the right shoulder, and missed Percy then; he was in the right half of our platoon and I was in the left half, so that we got separated. Those that were comparatively lightly wounded were the fortunate ones, Claude. I am sorry that I cannot give you more news of Percy; the last I saw of him was coolly smoking a cigarette as we marched along over those fields in that awful hail of shells."*

McG/166 Lance Corporal William Dalgleish Ford

Princess Patricia's Canadian Light Infantry
(Eastern Ontario Regiment)
Died on Friday 2nd June 1916, aged 26
Commemorated on Panel 10.

William was born on Sunday 20th April 1890, son of Joseph and Mary Jessica D Ford, of Portneuf, Province of Quebec. He went up to McGill University, graduating with a BA in 1913 and became an agricultural instructor. William had served in the Militia prior to the war.
William volunteered on Monday 7th June 1915 where he was described as a Presbyterian, being 5ft 10in, a 35½in chest, fair complexion, blue eyes, brown hair, a mole

William Ford

under his right armpit and a scar on the crown of his head. After training he joined the Regiment in the field with the Second University Draft on Wednesday 1st September at *'Petit Moulin Farm'* in northern France. He had a relatively easy introduction to the Western Front including at Brigade Horse Show on Sunday 10th. William marched to Hazebrouck and entrained for Guillancourt, arriving the next day and marched to Méricourt. After moving to Froissy, Cappy and Éclusier he first went into the line at Frise. He remained in the sector on tours of duty and on fatigues until marching to Pont Rémy on Thursday 25th November and entrained for Caëstre where the Regiment was met by General Edwin Alderson and the band of the 2nd Canadian Brigade. William marched to billets at Flêtre and General Alderson inspected them on Tuesday 30th. He returned to the line at Kemmel where he continued to serve in the sector until then end of March 1916. On Wednesday 5th April William was sent to *'Camp C'* and two days later his brother, Eric, joined him, the same day the camp receiving a direct hit from a heavy shell! They went together into the line at Hooge on Wednesday 12th and they continued to on tours of duty at *'Sanctuary Wood'* until their death during the Battle of Mount Sorrel. At 1.00pm on Friday 2nd June the Germans attacked their line after a four hour heavy bombardment and casualties amongst all the Canadian troops were particularly high.
His brother, Private Eric Ford, died on the same day and is commemorated on the Memorial, see above.

Contemporary propaganda drawing showing a captured German soldier sneering at the British soldiers wounded by gas

2204 Private Robert Clive Forrest

1st/14th Battalion London Regiment
(London Scottish)

Died on Sunday 1st November 1914
Commemorated on Panel 54.

Robert Forrest

Robert was born in Cardiff, the only son of Mr Robert Forrest, JP, DL, and his wife of Calderhead, Lanarkshire. He was educated at Harrow School as a member of Druries from 1909 to 1914. He was to have gone up to New College, Oxford, but the war intervened. On Thursday 6th August 1914 Robert volunteered in London and enlisted. He was sent for training until orders were received to embark overseas. He marched to Watford Station and entrained for Southampton, Robert sailed on the *SS Winifredian* for Le Havre. After a month on a series of support duties, orders were given to report to St Omer on Sunday 25th October, and within three days the Battalion had arrived. After parade he was marched out of the town to meet a fleet of more than forty London buses that set off in convoy for Ypres. They left at 6.00pm in the dark, the buses were not able to use lights for the last part of the journey and as a result many of them slipped off the muddy cobbled roads. They had three hours rest in Ypres before breakfast, followed by parade. An abortive mission to Hooge followed and after an hour Robert was boarding a motor bus to be taken south to St Eloi. After a hot meal he had to find a convenient place to sleep as billets were not provided. Early the next morning Robert paraded on the road before marching off to take up a position a mile south. Just after he had started to dig in he was ordered to form up and move to the next village, Wytschaete. He took position in front of the windmill where again he dug in. The Battalion was under heavy fire throughout the day. At 9.00pm the Germans advanced on their lines in close formation, bands playing, soldiers singing and walked into the rapid fire from Robert and his comrades. The Germans fell like

dominoes due to their close formation and their advance was checked. At midnight they attacked again and Robert was badly wounded in the leg during the famous charge. He was last seen lying with other wounded in a farmhouse before it was overrun by the Germans.
Robert is commemorated in St Mary's Church, St Fagans, Glamorgan.

Captain Herbert Cyril Forster

3rd Battalion Royal Fusiliers

Died on Tuesday 25th May 1915

Commemorated on Panel 8.

Herbert was the son of Mr and Mrs Forster. He was educated at Eton College as a member of Mr Francis Batten Cristall Tarver's House, leaving in 1895. On Tuesday 16th February 1904 he married Edrica Alice Forster.
On Tuesday 25th May 1915 Herbert was with his men south of the Ypres to Roeselare railway line. They were under heavy attack, including gas, and from 5.00pm the night before communication had been mainly cut off with headquarters and was under constant repair. Counter-attacks were ordered which were not successful and matters went from bad to worse. The Germans advanced and manœuvred around *'Ridge 44'* and were able to enfilade the Fusiliers. On Tuesday 25th they lost their fire trenches and were forced back to the third line, the Fusiliers had already lost seven hundred and thirty men killed or wounded. Casualties mounted further and by the end of the day only Major Baker survived. Herbert and sixteen other officers were lost.

Lieutenant Samuel Sanford Forsyth

Royal Field Artillery

Died on Saturday 25th September 1915, aged 30

Commemorated on Panel 5.

Samuel was the son of Mrs Ellen Sanford Forsyth, and the late Colonel Frederick Aitken Forsyth. He was educated at Wellington College from 1899 to 1904, and went up to Hertford College, Oxford.
On Wednesday 5th August 1914 Samuel volunteered and was commissioned. Following training he left for France. He was killed in action at Hooge during the feint for the Battle of Loos.
Samuel was Mentioned in Despatches and had acted as an ADC.
His brother Lieutenant John Forsyth, died on Tuesday 22nd September 1914 and is buried in Braine Communal Cemetery.

17362 Private John Leonard Forsyth-Ingram

2nd Regiment (Infantry) South African Infantry

Died on Thursday 11th April 1918, aged 15

Commemorated on Panel 16.

John was the son of J Forsyth-Ingram, of 381 Loop Street, Pietermaritzburg, Natal. He was educated locally.
John volunteered and was sent for training. He joined the Regiment with a draft in the field following the Ludendorff Offensive that began on Thursday 21st March 1918. He arrived in camp in the *'Ridgewood'* area in early April and the whole Brigade was reorganised until General Tanner. The German offensive was slowing and grinding to a halt at Amiens and their attention was turning towards Flanders.
On Monday 8th April John marched to hutments on the Locre to La Clytte road and the next morning Ludendorff's offensive was launched against the La Bassée sector and around Ploegsteert. The latter village was lost as was Messines. Around *'Pick House'* the line was breaking and the South African troops were sent to counter-attack to stem the tide. By the evening of Wednesday 10th the Germans had succeeded in establishing a new line from Hollebeke, along the Messines Ridge, to west of Ploegsteert. Throughout the night John and his comrades held on in front of Messines. During the afternoon on Thursday 11th a further offensive was launched by General von Arnim that took Hill 63 and drove the 2nd Regiment back more than six hundred yards towards *'Hell Farm'*. During the counter-attacks John lost his life.

Captain Lawrence Fort

'A' Company, 2nd Battalion The Buffs (East Kent Regiment)

Died on Tuesday 16th February 1915, aged 33

Commemorated on Panel 14.

Lawrence Fort

Lawrence was born at Oswestry, Shropshire, on Thursday 8th September 1881, son of John and Ianthe Fort, of 48 Earlsfield Road, Hythe, Kent. He was educated at Cheltenham College from 1891 to 1899 as a Day Boy then as a member of Southwood House and passed into RMC Sandhurst. His main interests were all types of shooting and he was a keen big game hunter. It was his intention to leave the Army and pursue his hobby but the war intervened.
Lawrence was gazetted in August 1900, promoted

Lieutenant in September 1903, and Captain in October 1911. He served in the South African War receiving the Queen's Medal with five clasps. He later served in India.

At the outbreak of war Lawrence returned from India with the Battalion, embarking on *SS Ultonia* arriving in Plymouth on Wednesday 23rd December 1914. Lawrence was sent to camp in Winchester where very little was provided for the Battalion in the way of blankets, cooking pots or any form of comfort. On Wednesday 6th January 1915 the Battalion was provided with billets in Winchester where they remained until Saturday 16th when they marched to Southampton and embarked for Le Havre. He entrained for Hazebrouck from where Lawrence marched with his company to be billeted at Rouge Croix where training continued until early February, when he went into the line on the Salient close to the Ypres to Comines Canal. During the night of Sunday 14th February the Battalion was relieved and sent the short distance to Château Rosenthal (now Bedford House Cemetery). At 4.30pm on Monday 15th the Battalion was ordered to support the East Surrey's and Middlesex during an attack. At 9.00pm the advance against 'O Trench' commenced, five minutes after the preliminary bombardment. Sadly the British artillery alerted the Germans to the probability of an attack and so they were therefore fully prepared. As the advance went forward the German rifles, machine-guns and trench mortars poured forth and their flares lit up the battlefield. Despite the heavy fire Lawrence and the men reached their objective, the German firing trench, and took possession of part of it. The Germans threw bombs from their section of the trench and tried to bomb the attackers out. Eventually Lawrence with Captain Tomlinson and 2nd Lieutenant Strettell went forward to demolish a sandbag wall and clear the Germans from the trench, but in this action, Lawrence was killed and 2nd Lieutenant Strettell was badly wounded and taken prisoner.

The ruins of Château Rosenthal

Lieutenant Colonel Augustus Geddes* wrote: *"Your son met his death in a very gallant manner. He had previously distinguished himself by leading a very daring reconnaissance. For this he was mentioned in Despatches, and I feel sure he would have been awarded at least the D.S.O. had he survived."* (* Colonel Geddes subsequently died and is buried in Ypres Reservoir Cemetery.)

Lawrence was Mentioned in Despatches gazetted on Monday 31st May 1915 and had been twice recommended by his officers.

Captain Thomas Brittain Forwood

'B' Company, 2nd Battalion King's Own
(Royal Lancaster Regiment)
Died on Saturday 8th May 1915, aged 28
Commemorated on Panel 12.

Thomas Forwood

Thomas was the only son of Thomas Brittain and Edith Anne Forwood, of Courtbourne, Farnborough, Hampshire. He was educated at Northaw House followed by Harrow School from 1900 to 1903 where he was a member of Rendalls, then passed into RMC Sandhurst. In 1912 Thomas married Constance M Forwood (née Fairlie), of Mon Plaisir, La Haule, Jersey, Channel Islands, and they had a daughter.

In 1905 Thomas was commissioned and promoted Captain in 1915.

In January 1915 Thomas left for France. Thomas took his men from their rest camp up into the line in front of the Frezenberg Ridge on Tuesday 4th May. On Saturday 8th May the Germans commenced a huge barrage at 5.30am using both high explosive and shrapnel shells, which lasted for four hours. Within an hour the front line was practically destroyed and the Monmouths were being wiped out. Lieutenant Colonel Aylmer Martin ordered Thomas and his men to go up and help re-establish the line and defend the position. In the centre was the command dug-out that had been, only a couple of hours before, five hundred yards behind the line! The Germans came forward in a further attack but were checked. At 10.50am they recommenced their barrage and attack. Thomas was leading the men forward to counter-attack when he was shot through the head, dying instantaneously.

One of his fellow officers wrote: *"I have taken over T. B. F.'s old Company and assure you that I have a very hard task, if I am in any way to fill his position and keep up the standard of its last Company Commander. On all hands I am told by the N.C.O.'s and men of what was done when he commanded the Company, and can only say they make me feel very small. They were absolutely devoted to him and would have done anything for him."*

Lieutenant Colonel Aylmer Martin wrote: *"The Regiment has lost one of its best Officers, and one who was not only an officer but a gentleman, in the best sense of the word; while I personally have lost a friend for whom I had the greatest liking and respect. Everyone in the Regiment is sharing his family's sorrow, for he was one of the best."*

In St Andrew's Church, Sturt Road, Frimley Green, Surrey, a brass plaque was placed in his memory with the inscription: *"To the glory of God and in loving memory of Thomas Brittain Forwood, Captain 2nd Battn., The King's Own Royal Lancaster Regiment. Killed in action near Ypres in Flanders May 8th 1915 - aged 28. Only son of Thomas Brittain & Edith Forwood of Fernhurst, Frimley Green. Pro Patria."*

Second Lieutenant Herbert Knollys Foster

1st Battalion Gloucestershire Regiment

Died on Friday 30th October 1914, aged 19

Commemorated on Panel 22.

Herbert Foster

Herbert was born at All Saints' Vicarage, Gloucester, on Friday 18th October 1895, son of Canon Herbert Charles and Mrs Edith Susan Foster, of St Thomas' Vicarage, Groombridge, Kent. He was educated at Glyngarth Preparatory School followed by Marlborough College from September 1909 until December 1912 from where he passed into RMC Sandhurst.

Herbert was gazetted on Saturday 8th August 1914 and left with the Battalion on Wednesday 12th from Southampton for Le Havre on board the *SS Gloucester Castle*. Upon arrival a long and tiring train journey took him via Rouen to Le Nouvion. A series of hard marches took him to the Mons battlefield and the Battalion was deployed near Haulchin. As the battle raged ahead of them, Herbert was unable to participate but just hold onto his position. After a short period of confusion, made worse by contradictory orders late on Sunday 23rd and early Monday 24th, Herbert formed up with his men and began to march south. Their ordeal ended at Rozoy-en-Brie on Saturday 5th September when orders were received to turn and move towards the German armies. Herbert marched with his men across the Petit Morin, the Marne and finally the Aisne where he served until Friday 16th October when the move towards Flanders commenced.

On Tuesday 20th October the Battalion arrived in Poperinghe where they rested for a short period of time before marching to Langemarck via Elverdinghe. They arrived at the front to be greeted by a German bombardment that continued as they dug in. After five days they were ordered to move toward Hooge, via Wieltje: the Germans were pressuring the British front line. Herbert and his men were successful in repulsing the attacks but as he was giving orders to his men he was shot and killed.

In All Saints Church, Gloucester, a marble plaque was

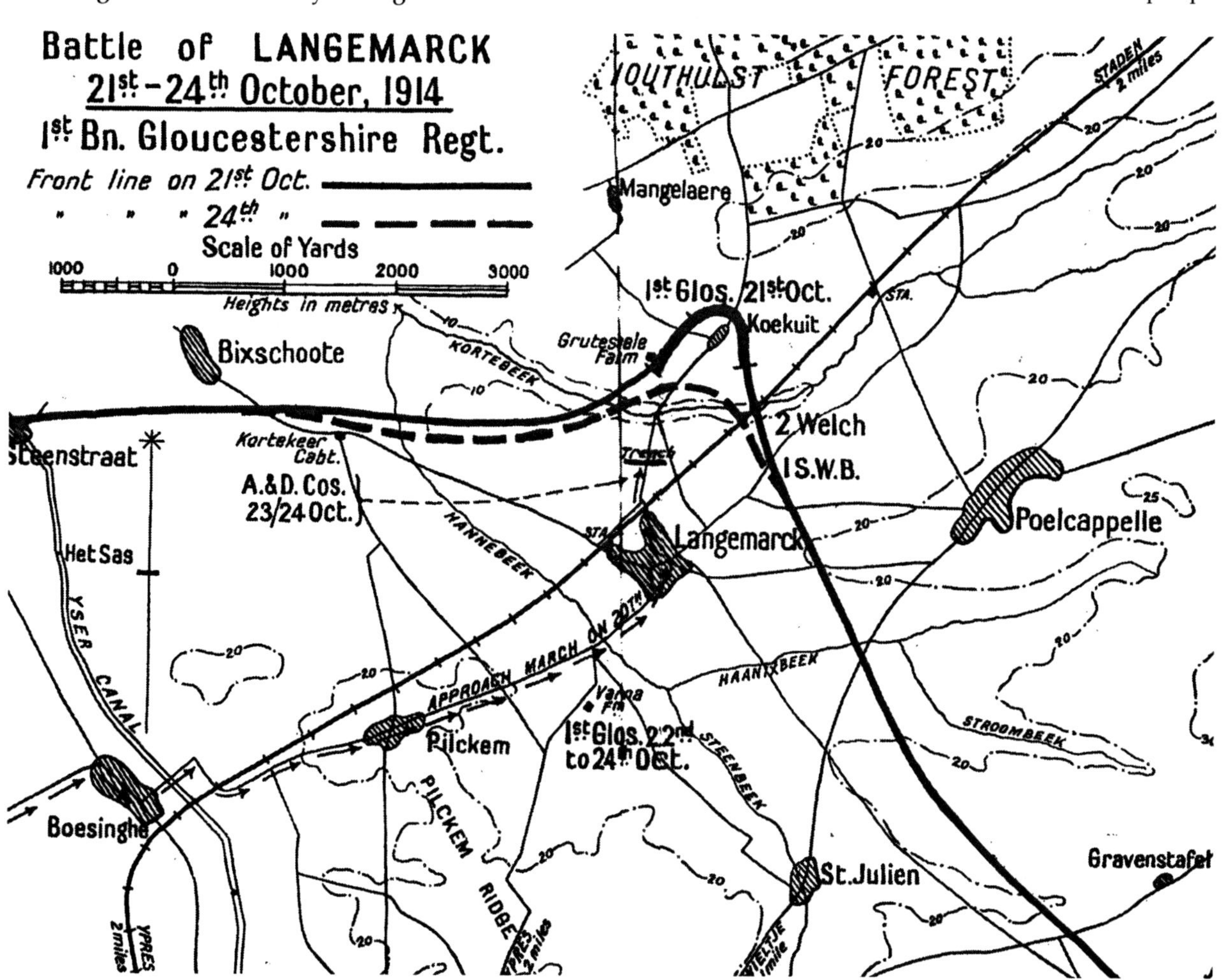

placed in his memory with the inscription: *"To the dear memory of Herbert Knollys Foster, 2nd Lieut., 1st Bn. Gloucestershire Regt. killed in action near Ypres in Flanders, 29th Oct. 1914. Aged 19 years.*

Second Lieutenant Brendan Joseph Fottrell

3rd Battalion Royal Irish Regiment

Died on Monday 15th March 1915, aged 29

Commemorated on Panel 33.

Brendan Fottrell

Brendan was born on Monday 12th October 1885, only son of John George and Lily Fottrell, of Richelieu, Sydney Parade, County Dublin. He was educated at Downside from January 1899 to April 1902 where he was a member of the soccer XI, the Abingdon Society and a member of the Sports Committee. He went up to Trinity College, Dublin, to read law, graduating with a BA in 1906. He was employed as a solicitor in Dublin. Brendan was married to Antoinette Fottrell.

At the outbreak of war Brendan volunteered and was gazetted on Saturday 15th August 1914. He was sent for training and left for France in February 1915.

At 5.00pm on Sunday 14th March the Germans blew a mine under *'The Mound'* at St Eloi. At 5.30pm the Battalion, together with 1st Leinster Battalion, were ordered to the line. At 8.30pm the Battalion attacked *'The Mound'*, but by the early hours of the next morning their attack had been brought to a standstill.

His father wrote of his death: *"He was called up at 2.30 in the morning of March 15th to take part in an attack on the 'Mound' near St. Eloi. While leading his men, coming out of the village, he was shot dead by a machine-gun which the Germans had installed. His body could not be recovered for several days, but finally it was brought in and buried at a spot nearly opposite where he fell."*

Brendan is commemorated on the Solicitors' Memorial, Inns Quay, Dublin, that has the inscription:

"This Tablet Is Erected To The Memory Of
The Irish Solicitors And Apprentices To
Irish Solicitors Who Gave Their Lives For
Their King And Country In The Great War
Who ventured life and love and youth
1914 For the great prize of death in battle 1918"

Captain Alan Arthur Fowler

'B' Company 2nd Battalion, Cameron Highlanders

Died on Wednesday 28th April 1915, aged 28

Commemorated on Panel 38.

Alan Fowler and his family coat of arms

Alan was born at Inverbroom, Lochbroom, on Tuesday 22nd February 1887, youngest son of the late Sir John Arthur Fowler, 2nd Baronet, and Lady Alice Janet Clive (daughter of Sir E Clive Bayley, KCSI), of Braemore, Ross-shire, grandson of Sir John Fowler, Engineer-in-Chief of the Forth Bridge. He was educated at Harrow School from 1901 to 1905 as a member of Elmfield and went up to Trinity College, Cambridge, in 1910. He then passed into RMC Sandhurst. In 1912, at Bankipore, India, Alan married Alice Mary Fowler (daughter of Sir Charles Stuart Bayley, GCSI, Lieutenant Governor of Bihar and Orissa) and they had a daughter, Marjorie Mary, born at Bangalore, in September 1913. Alan was a keen sportsman and hunter.

Alan was gazetted in May 1907, promoted Lieutenant in April 1911, and Captain in February 1915. He served in South Africa, China and India.

In November 1914 Alan returned to England, arriving on Monday 16th in Devonport. He went for training in Winchester from where he left for Southampton, arriving in Le Havre on Sunday 20th December. Initially he was appointed Transport Officer and then served on the Staff. In mid-April he was sent to help relieve the situation on Hill 60 and moved into the front line trenches on the lip of one of the huge craters created by the blowing of a mine. Alan was killed at noon, together with many of his men, by a minenwerfer.

Brigadier General Duncan Macfarlane wrote: *"He was a first-rate soldier and a dear good fellow, for whom I had a great regard, and I always wished I had him on my Staff. He will be dreadfully missed, both in his Regiment and in the Brigade."*

Colonel John Campbell wrote: *"He died a soldier's death about 12 noon to-day, when holding a trench in a difficult and important position. I cannot speak too highly of the truly gallant way in which he has behaved and kept his men together and cheerful."*

A brother officer wrote: *"During the week on Hill 60 he was never once depressed, though all of them, and his Company in particular, were having a very rough time."*

Alan was recorded in Debretts Obituary — War Roll of Honour published in the 1921 edition.
In Argyle Street, Ullapool, Highland, a lamp was erected to the memory of Alan, his father, and his brother, John. It has four panels with the following inscriptions:
East: *"In memory of Sir J. Arthur Fowler (2nd Baronet) of Braemore who died March 25th 1899 aged 44. 'Ready To Do Good, Kind To Man, Steadfast, Sure' Wisdom 7.23."*
North: *"Also in memory of Sir Arthur Fowler's second son Captain Alan Fowler 2nd Battalion Queen's Own Cameron Highlanders. Born Inverbroom, Loch Broom on 22nd February 1887. Killed while commanding a Company in the front trench of Hill 60 in Flanders on 28th April 1915. His Colonel wrote 'He died a soldiers death today when holding the trench in a difficult and important position. I cannot speak too highly of the truly gallant way in which he had behaved.' The General wrote of him 'He was a first rate soldier, a good comrade, popular with officers and men alike'."*
West: *"This clock is erected by Sir Arthur Fowler's Friends in remembrance of his unfailing devotion to the interests and welfare of the people of Loch Broom."*
South: *"Also in memory of Sir John Edward Fowler Third Baronet of Braemore, Captain 2nd Battalion Seaforth Highlanders, Adjutant of the 4th Battalion Seaforth Highlanders. Born at Inverbroom, Loch Broom on 21st April 1885. Killed by shell fire in trenches at Richebourg l'Avoue in France 22nd June 1915. He was Mentioned In Dispatches. His Brigadier General writes 'He was one of the very best young officers I ever met and an example to all others'. One of his Non Commissioned Officers wrote 'He endeared himself to all whether under him or over him. He was the guide, adviser & helpmate of every individual in the Battalion'."*
His brother, Sir John Edward Fowler, is buried in Foich Burial Ground, Ross and Cromarty.

Lieutenant John Dudley Fowler

5th (Royal Irish) Lancers
Died on Monday 30th November 1914
Commemorated on Panel 5.

John was educated at Eton College as a member of Mr Richard Stephen Kindersley's House, leaving in 1910.

At the outbreak of war John was mobilized and he sailed from Dublin to France in early September 1914. He fought through the Battle of the Aisne before being sent to northern France. In October he was in action on the French-Belgian border and assisted in the retaking of the Mont des Cats. John fought northward and took part in the actions at Messines at the end of October and early November. He continued in the front line until he was killed in action.

21600 Private William Henry Fowler

7th Battalion Canadian Infantry
(British Columbia Regiment)
Died on Saturday 24th April 1915, aged 21
Commemorated on Panel 18.

William Fowler

William was born in Cork, on Monday 7th August 1893, second son of Mr John B Fowler, of Belle View Park, Cork. He was educated at Cork Grammar School and went up to the National University, Cork. He joined the Commerce Bank on Wednesday 6th March 1912 and was employed in the Herbert Branch. Two of his brothers were also employed by the Bank and served in the war: Regimental Sergeant Major Richard Fowler with the Princess Patricia's Canadian Light Infantry, and Sergeant John Gerald Fowler with 5th Canadian Battalion.

William volunteered on Thursday 10th September 1914 in Valcartier where he was described as 5ft 9in tall, with a 33in chest, a fair complexion, blue eyes, light brown hair and a small mole on his left shoulder.

William marched from *'Lark Hill Camp'* on Salisbury Plain for Amesbury Station and entrained for Avonmouth. He embarked on *HMT Cardinganshire* and sailed to St Nazaire where he disembarked at 6.30am on Monday 15th. He entrained for Strazeele where training continued until he was sent to Ploegsteert for front line instruction and practical experience until Monday 1st March. From Friday 5th he served in the trenches for three weeks until sent to Estaires. Training continued for a further three weeks when the Battalion marched to Steenvoorde.

A fleet of motor buses arrived on Wednesday 14th April and collected the Battalion and drove them to Vlamertinghe where they had a short period of rest. William marched along the cobbled road through Ypres, out to St Julien and took the line on the Gravenstafel Ridge. Following a tour of duty he was relieved to reserve in Wieltje, when the Germans launched their gas attack at 5.00pm on Thursday 22nd April. William was 'stood to' and later in the evening marched to St Julien to assist with the defence of the line. He dug in and consolidated the position. At 4.00am on Saturday 24th, the wind came up and ensured that the gas had little effect. At 5.00am the German bombardment fell on William's line and during the bombardment he was killed.

His father, John Fowler, wrote to the Commerce Bank of his three sons: *"It was on the 24th May, 1915; that my son Gerald was wounded somewhere near Ypres, where his brother William was killed just a month before. On 25th he wrote: 'I have been admitted to hospital, wounded, and am being sent down to the base'. On 2nd June he wrote me a long letter from the Anglo-American Hospital, Wimereux, near Boulogne, and in this he stated that a shrapnel bullet had entered his head underneath the temple and came out father down the right side of his face, after breaking his jaw and four or five teeth. He had then, for some time, to live on liquid nourishment, and made light of his wound, but I had a letter from the Chaplain and from a friend in the army, who visits him twice daily, and, from what they say, the wound must have caused him much suffering, while he himself says that it was 'just a bit uncomfortable'. Since the, he has undergone three operations, and is under the care of one of the best surgeons in France, who says he will not allow him to leave hospital until he has made a proper job of the jaw. We hear from him frequently, and his letters take but two days in the post. In his last, dated 28th July, he says: 'I had a lovely afternoon yesterday. One of the nurses gave a picnic in my honour, and Lady Hadfield, who finances this hospital, very kindly lent her motor car for the occasion. We went about five miles into the country, and had our meal in a very nice spot. I am feeling ever so much better, and all the bandages have been taken off, but my face is still swollen, and I don't suppose it will go down for some time. When I came here, I was under the impression that only my lower jaw was smashed, but since I have found out that it was both upper and lower, also the roof of my mouth. This all sounds much worse than it really was. I don't think it will be very long now before they send me to England.'*

... Accept my best thanks for your kind sympathy in the loss of my second son, and convey my thanks to your staff. We miss him sorely, for he was a good son and a devoted and affectionate brother. I had a personal letter from general Sam Hughes, in which he speaks as my splendid son, William H. Fowler, who, as 'a brave soldier, did his duty fearlessly and well, and gave his young life in the cause of liberty and the upbuilding of the Empire'."

His youngest brother, 2nd Lieutenant Francis Fowler, died on Wednesday 18th October 1916 and is commemorated on Thiepval Memorial.

12613 Lance Corporal Andrew Thomson Fowlie

'D' Company, 4th Battalion Gordon Highlanders

Died on Wednesday 16th June 1915, aged 26

Commemorated on Panel 38.

Andrew Fowlie

Andrew was born on Monday 9th July 1888 son of Mr and Mrs Patrick Fowlie, of The Cottage, Strichen, Aberdeenshire. He was educated at Glaslaw and New Pitsglo Public School before going up to Aberdeen University in 1906 to study agriculture, obtaining the University Diploma, National Diploma and finally the National Diploma in Dairying in 1910. From 1909 to 1912 Andrew was appointed an Assistant Lecturer in Agriculture for Inverness, Ross and Cromanty, and he was then appointed County Organiser for Orkney.

At the outbreak of war he volunteered and enlisted in September 1914. Andrew was sent to Ripon for training before leaving for Southampton on Thursday 18th February 1915 and the next day he embarked on *SS Archimedes* bound for Le Havre. He entrained to northern France from where he marched across the border to La Clytte, arriving on Wednesday 27th. Until mid-March he was trained for the front line and was sent with small groups to the front before being sent on a tour of duty. Andrew was killed in action on the Bellewaarde Ridge during an attack on German lines close to the wood at Hooge.

Captain Leslie William Fox

10th Battalion The King's (Liverpool Regiment)

Died on Tuesday 31st July 1917

Commemorated on Panel 6.

Leslie Fox

Leslie was the only son of the late Robert John Fox of Birkenhead. He was educated at Birkenhead Preparatory School from 1901 and joined the Senior School from 1905 to 1911. He was employed in a shipping office in Liverpool. His main interest was supporting the School Mission and the Boys' Brigade.

Leslie volunteered and was commissioned. He was sent for training and joined the Battalion in the field.

The Battalion saw considerable action in the Battle of the Somme and during the attack at Guillemont Captain Noel Chavasse won his first Victoria Cross (he died on

Wreathes laid on the Menin Gate on Remembrance Day

Saturday 4th August 1917 and is buried in Brandhoek New Military Cemetery). The Battalion remained on the Somme until October 1916 when they transferred to the Ypres Salient.

They initially served close to *'Wieltje Farm'* and over the next few months undertook a series of tours of duty without being involved in any particular action. They participated in various raids including one on Wednesday 29th November against the German trenches named *'Kaiser Bill'*. The Battalion Diary recording: *"... as arranged the raid took place on 29th inst. After a preliminary bombardment by the field artillery, the heavy artillery opened up and first on the objective — Kaiser Bill — for about twenty minutes. At 4.50 p.m. the raiding party (which was divided into two parties) advanced to the assault and entered the German trenches at Kaiser Bill and proceeded to carry out the programme previously arranged. The raid was a great success and much useful information and identifications were obtained."*

Leslie and his Company were intensively trained for the forthcoming offensive at Ypres. He visited the large model of the battlefield and studied the attack with his fellow officers and NCOs. A few days before the attack he took his men into their assembly positions east of Wieltje. Leslie led his men forward and met with little opposition until he had crossed the Steenbeek. Fierce machine-gun fire was poured onto them from *'Capricorn Trench'* that was silenced with the aid of tanks. During the advance Leslie was killed.

His Colonel wrote of him: *"Your son was killed while advancing at the head of his men, and was leading them with the utmost determination. For a long time he had been in charge of the Battalion Scouts, for which work his extraordinary coolness and courage particularly fitted him. He was marked out for early promotion, and his death is a great loss to the battalion."*

His Sergeant wrote: *"I was Mr. Fox's servant for a time, and I must say Mr. Fox was a real good friend to me, and there is no one will miss him more than myself. ... All the boys in the platoon send their deepest sympathy to you, and all of them admit what a real good friend they have lost."*

The President of West Cheshire Boys' Brigade said of him: *"... many a poor boy in Birkenhead will have good reason to bless his memory."*

7992 Private Reginald Clement Francis, DCM

2nd Battalion Suffolk Regiment

Died on Wednesday 16th December 1914, aged 22

Commemorated on Panel 21.

Citation for the Distinguished Conduct Medal, London Gazette, Thursday 1st April 1915:

"For conspicuous gallantry on 15th December 1914, near Kemmel, in voluntarily taking a message over very dangerous ground. His destination was 150 yards in front and he was killed after covering 80 yards of this distance."

Reginald was born in Bradfield, Essex, the son of Benjamin and Mary S Francis, of Hall Cottage, East Donyland, Rowhedge, Colchester, Essex.

Reginald went out to Le Havre at the outbreak of war and entrained for Le Cateau. He marched to Mons where they held the line along the Mons to Condé Canal. Orders were received for a retirement late in the evening and they marched south to Le Cateau. At 6.00am on Wednesday 26th the German patrols were sighted and No 15 Platoon opened fire on them. The German artillery replied and landed amongst them and during the bombardment Lieutenant Colonel Brett was mortally wounded (he is commemorated on La Ferté-sous-Jouarre Memorial). By 11.00am the German attack was pressing home on the Battalion's line and their ammunition was running low. The Battalion held on despite taking heavy losses. Major General Sir Charles Fergusson wrote: *"Anybody who held*

... a German attack

out to the end under the circumstances deserves all the honour that can be given, and did his duty nobly, and no words can express the value to the division and corps of such self-sacrifice."
Following Le Cateau Reginald marched south, reaching Favieres on Saturday 5th September where The Retreat ended. The next day the Battalion turned northeastward to engage the enemy. On Wednesday 9th they recrossed the Marne where later in the day, at Montreuil, they came under rifle fire. They continued to the Aisne crossing on Sunday 13th where they were shelled as they approached Ste Marguerite. After serving at Missy the Battalion was sent to billets in Le Carrier on Thursday 24th from where they were sent to GHQ at Fere-en-Tardenois taking over the duties from the Gordon Highlanders. On Thursday 8th October the Battalion entrained for Abbeville and were sent to St Omer with GHQ. The line at Neuve-Chapelle was coming under pressure and the Battalion was collected by motor buses to be taken to Vieille Chapelle on Sunday 25th. During the night of Monday 26th they moved forward to relieve the 2nd Royal Scots. German snipers were particularly active and the Colonel asked for artillery assistance to silence them. After three weeks in the sector they moved across the border to serve near Wulverghem relieving the French infantry on Sunday 15th November. After two weeks they moved the short distance to the Sherpenberg with billets in the nearby village of Locre. On Monday 30th Reginald paraded for an inspection by General Sir Horace Smith-Dorrien at Locre and four days later paraded along the road as HM King George V visited the area. He remained on tours of duty in the area of Kemmel, where on Tuesday 15th December a group of eighty men were seen coming towards them. They were dressed in khaki and it was thought they were engineers, but it became clear they were Germans when they called out that they wished to surrender. Two parties went to bring them in when they were fired upon by the Germans from both flanks; rapid fire from the Suffolks soon put paid to the deception. Reginald volunteered to take a message to the machine-gun officer who was one hundred and fifty yards away across a meadow. After eighty yards he was hit and killed and for this act of bravery he was awarded the Distinguished Conduct Medal.
Reginald is commemorated on Fordham War Memorial.

... collecting the post

Major The Honourable Hugh Joseph Fraser, MVO

2nd Battalion Scots Guards

Died on Wednesday 28th October 1914, aged 40
Commemorated on Panel 11.

Hugh Fraser and his family coat of arms

Hugh was born on Monday 6th July 1874 at Phoiness, Beauly, son of the late Simon Fraser, 13th Baron Lovat of Beaufort Castle, Beauly, and 38 Grosvenor Gardens, London, Lord Lieutenant of Inverness, Hon Colonel of the 2nd Battalion of the Queen's Own Cameron Highlanders and ADC to HM Queen Victoria, and his wife, Lady Alice Mary (the title dating back to the mid-15th century). Hugh was educated at St Benedict's Abbey School, Fort Augustus.
Hugh was gazetted from the Militia on Wednesday 12th December 1894, promoted to Lieutenant on 15th November 1897, Captain on Saturday 16th March 1901, Adjutant from Wednesday 1st April 1903 to Wednesday 31st July 1907 and Major on Wednesday 12th June 1907.
Hugh served in the South African War where he was Mentioned in Despatches on Tuesday 10th September 1901, received the Queen Medal with three clasps and the King's Medal with two clasps. He was appointed ADC to the Viceroy of India from 1910 to 1913. Hugh was created a Member of the Royal Victorian Order in 1912.
Hugh embarked for Zeebrugge on Saturday 5th September 1914. As the convoy entered the Straits of Dover it was ordered to return to Dover due to possible U-boat activity. They spent Sunday, until the evening, in Dover before leaving again for Zeebrugge. Upon arrival the Battalion had to await orders as the intention of leaving to support Antwerp had been abandoned because the city was already being evacuated. They were sent to Ghent and took the line for its defence but did not engage the enemy. Orders were received for them to march to Ypres. A long and tiring slog over the cobbled roads commenced, their route taking them through Thielt, Roeselare and Moorslede.
Hugh arrived at Ypres on Thursday 15th October and shortly after their arrival HRH Prince Arthur of Connaught visited them to wish the Battalion well for the battle ahead. The next day he was sent into the line near Kruiseik, and on Saturday 17th October the Battalion was ordered to clear a wood but was forced to withdraw under fire from the German Horse Artillery. The whole line also retired towards Gheluvelt. On Thursday 22nd October the Germans laid down a rolling barrage at 6.00am and advanced. The Scots Guards were called to support the

2nd Gordons and the Grenadiers, Hugh went round to the right of the south-east end on the Vervicq road to reconnoitre the situation and found more than a thousand Germans advancing on Gheluvelt — a shock for anyone to discover! He took forty men and contacted Captain George Paynter to inform him that Lieutenant Holbech's trench had been taken. Hugh and Lieutenant Holbech went off to recapture the lost trench, but as they were about to charge Hugh was shot dead and Lieutenant Holbech was badly wounded. The attack was successfully concluded and two hundred prisoners were taken including officers.

Captain Paynter wrote: *"Our trenches were tremendously shelled all day, some of the trenches being blown in; Dummond and Kemble, being buried in their trench, had to be dug out. A lot of cheering was heard in the distance when it became dark, and it was passed down the trenches that the French were attacking on our right. Then we noticed masses of troop advancing on our trenches. It was extremely dark and raining in torrents. Some got as far as our trenches and were shot down, others lay down in front calling out 'We surrender', and 'Don't shoot; we are Allies', 'Where is Captain Paynter 'G' Company?' Parties got through the line on my right and left and commenced firing at us from behind, others got into houses. We shot at and silenced all these. Fresh lots kept coming on; but, as our fire was pretty heavy, they seemed to make for the places where others had got through. After about a couple of hours all was quiet. I was very relieved to hear Major Fraser's voice, about 11.30 p.m., calling to me that we would be relieved by R.F. and L.F. Companies at dawn on 26th."*

Hugh is commemorated on the House of Lords War Memorial and was recorded in Debretts Obituary — War Roll of Honour published in the 1921 edition.

Lieutenant James Howie Fraser

2nd Battalion Gordon Highlanders

Died on Thursday 29th October 1914, aged 26

Commemorated on Panel 38.

James Fraser

James was born in Blackheath, London, on Wednesday 4th April 1888, the only son of Edward Cleather Fraser, CMG, and Mary Josephine Fraser, of The Castle, Beau Bassin, Mauritius. He was educated at Summer Fields from 1896 followed by Rugby School from 1901 to 1906 as a member of Steel and passed into RMC Sandhurst where he won prizes for tactics and military engineering.

He was gazetted on Wednesday 9th October 1907 and promoted to Lieutenant on Saturday 20th March 1909. He served in India and Egypt.

James embarked in Southampton on Monday 5th October 1914 and sailed for Zeebrugge arriving on Wednesday 7th. He entrained for Brugge but was immediately sent to Ostend to help cover the arrival of the 3rd Cavalry Division. On Friday 9th they took part in the defence of Ghent and whilst in the city the Colonel presented the Mayor with Battalion drums for safe keeping. It was not until 1933 that the drums were returned to the Battalion by General Sir Ian Hamilton after a visit to Berlin. On Sunday 11th they were sent southeast and marched through Thielt to Roeselare. On Wednesday 14th the Battalion arrived in Ypres and was sent to Voormezeele. On Sunday 18th he advanced towards Amerika before being sent into reserve in front of Reutel. They moved to the Gheluvelt-Kruiseik sector where they came under heavy attack which they repulsed, and for his bravery in the action, Drummer Kenny was awarded his Victoria Cross. In the fog at 7.30am on Thursday 29th the Germans laid down a preliminary barrage; at 7.30am they advanced *en mass* toward his line. Shortly afterwards James was killed during an attack on Zillebeke Farm House and buried at Klein Zillebeke.

His Colonel wrote: *"He was one of the very finest officers I have ever met, absolutely fearless, a splendid leader, always cool, and every soul in the Battalion admired him for his splendid soldierly qualities, and loved him for his character, which was an ideal one. I cannot tell you what his loss is to me personally, and from a military point of view the Army has lost one of its very best Officers."*

James was Mentioned in Despatches, gazetted on Wednesday 17th February 1915.

Second Lieutenant The Honourable Simon Fraser

3rd Battalion attached 2nd Battalion Gordon Highlanders

Died on Thursday 29th October 1914, aged 26

Commemorated on Panel 38.

Simon Fraser's family coat of arms

Simon was born on Friday 7th September 1888 third son of Alexander William Frederick Fraser, 18th Baron Saltoun and Lady Mary Saltoun, of Philorth, Fraserburgh, Aberdeen. He was educated at Winchester and Charterhouse from 1902 to 1905 before embarking on a career in the City with Greenwell & Co, and became a member of the Stock Exchange in 1912.

Simon was gazetted on Monday 7th September 1914 and was sent to Lyndhurst. Simon's story is the same as Lieutenant James Fraser, see above. Simon was in the front line when he was he was killed by a shell whilst talking to a brother officer. His men carried him back three miles to headquarters. His younger brother, William, who was also serving in the Gordon Highlanders, helped bury him. Simon is commemorated on the House of Lords War Memorial and was recorded in Debretts Obituary — War Roll of Honour published in the 1921 edition. He is also commemorated on The Stock Exchange War Memorial.

1201 Rifleman Geoffrey William Freeman

1st/5th Battalion London Regiment (London Rifle Brigade)

Died on Thursday 13th May 1915, aged 18

Commemorated on Panel 54.

Geoffrey Freeman

Geoffrey was born in Narabri, New South Wales, on Friday 11th September 1896, eldest son of William Edward Freeman, LDS, RCS Eng, and his wife Maud, of 77 North Side, Clapham Common, London. He came to England with his family in 1903. He was educated at Manor House School, Clapham, and was studying medicine at Guy's Hospital when the war broke out.

Geoffrey enlisted on Wednesday 4th November 1914 and was sent for training at Crowborough and Haywards Heath. He left for France on 12th March 1915 joining his Battalion in the field at Ploegsteert. On Friday 23rd April he was moved to Poperinghe in preparation to taking the front line at Wieltje on Monday 26th. On Thursday they moved to relieve the 4th East Yorkshire Battalion. The Germans attacked in force against his position on Sunday 2nd May which they stopped despite gas being used. At 12.45am on Tuesday 4th he was relieved from the line and sent to Elverdinghe Château, arriving at 5.00am. Whilst

Elverdinghe Château and its grounds in 2009

resting in the grounds of the château their post was delivered and General Plumer visited to congratulate them on their successes during their last tour of duty. On Sunday 9th he was sent to camp at Vlamertinghe Château from where they went up to the Yser Canal in working parties. On Tuesday 11th he was sent to relieve the French

Sergeant Douglas Belcher winning his Victoria Cross, Thursday 13th May 1915

close to *'Essex Farm'* where they came under heavy shell fire and were able to see the bombardment of Ypres which lit the night sky as the town was in flames. On Thursday 13th they were defending their position close to the Wieltje to St Julien Road under heavy bombardment and the combined efforts of the men prevented the Germans from breaking through. Geoffrey volunteered to take a message to Captain John Somers-Smith (died on Saturday 1st July 1916 and commemorated on Thiepval Memorial), and after he had delivered it he was killed by a shell. Geoffrey was one of the men with Sergeant Douglas Blecher when he won his Victoria Cross.

2nd Lieutenant A Sharp wrote: *"He was always popular wherever he went, and everyone who came in contact with him, liked him. During the whole time I knew him I never met one person who had anything but good to say of him. In his last term at Manor House he won the Gold Medal, and everyone who was with him during his short but glorious career in the Army says that they have lost in him a great pal. During his whole life he upheld the traditions of his school, which was very dear to him, and he died as every Manorian would wish to die. Truly when one thinks of him one is convinced that Manor House makes no idle boast when she says that all her sons are 'Sportsmen and true gentlemen'."*

6396 Private James Freemantle

1st Battalion Scots Guards

Wednesday 11th November 1914

Commemorated on Panel 11

James was born at home, son of William and Sarah Freemantle, of Easton, Winchester. He was educated locally. James enlisted in the Scots Guards from Monday 15th January 1906 to Tuesday 14th January 1913 when he took employment as a moulder. On Saturday 15th March 1913 he joined the Surrey Police and served in Ripley rising to the rank of 1st Class Constable.

James and his brother, Thomas, joined the Army in Winchester, serving and dying together, their stories are,

Scots Guards – Mons to the Aisne, 1914

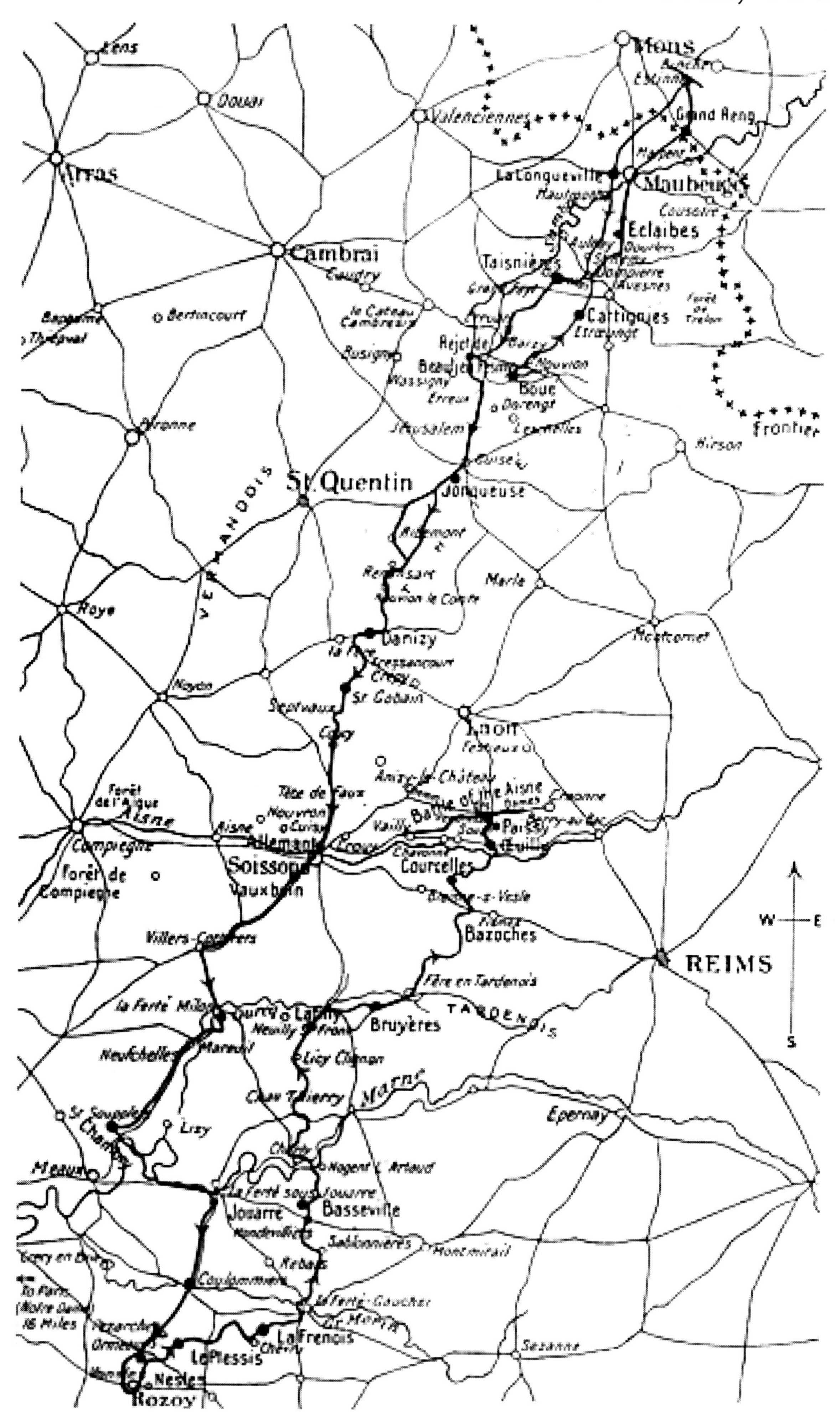

therefore, almost identical. His brother, Private Thomas Freemantle, died on the same day and is commemorated on the Menin Gate, see below.

At the outbreak of war James and Thomas rejoined the Colours and were marched out of Farnborough Camp for Southampton and embarking on *SS Dunvegan Castle* for Le Havre on Thursday 13th August. They marched to Harfleur and into camp and after a short rest they entrained to Nouvion (via Rouen, Amiens, Arras and Cambrai). Eventually they marched through Maubeuge, crossed the French-Belgian border but were held in reserve a few miles short of Mons and did not see action there — an officer of the Battalion described Sunday 23rd August as *"a day of rest"*! Before the expected order to advance and support the attack at Mons was given the contrary order was received and they were ordered to retreat. Hard marching over cobblestones in the summer heat was their enemy and saw their first real action during the Battle of the Marne. They marched onward to the Aisne and the Chemin des Dames. Here they saw considerable action in the sodden trenches with little respite until mid-October when they left the Aisne for the Ypres Salient. They entrained at Fismes bound for Hazebrouck. James and Thomas were assembled and marched to Poperinghe where after a night in billets they saw action on the Salient until they were killed.

From Poperinghe they marched along the narrow roads connecting it with Ypres passing, as they did, the streams of Belgian refugees who were fleeing the ever advancing

A pre-war photograph of the Menin Gate

German armies. They were sent through the medieval town of Ypres with its beautiful Cloth Hall still intact and vibrant town square, marching through an innocently named *'Menin Gate'* out to the farmland and villages beyond. It would not be long before the Menin Gate had a more sinister reputation, a small crossroads would become *'Hell Fire Corner'*, the unknown villages and hamlets household names and its fields their grave.

They took the line in front of Langemarck: their first few days in the line were hard and they were constantly being moved. On Sunday 25th October James and Thomas were sent to Zillebeke, at 5.30am they marched forward towards Gheluvelt via Hooge. They were subjected to heavy shell fire and were ordered to attack Poezelhoek. The Germans continued to advance in large numbers and took heavy casualties, Major Sir Victor Mackenzie, MVO, said: *"God knows how many we killed"*, just before he was wounded and taken back to the dressing station at Gheluvelt Château.

The Germans laid down a ferocious barrage on Saturday 31st the most terrible barrage yet laid down on the defenders of the Salient. At 11.00am the German grey hordes appeared from their positions and started to attack. Despite the onslaught the Battalion initially were able to hold onto the village of Gheluvelt, but being numerically vastly outnumbered, by 2.00pm it was captured by the Germans. James and Thomas found themselves 'fighting for their lives' as the Château was now almost completely surrounded but relief came with the famous 'charge' by the Worcesters (see map on following page), and some ground was retaken. The situation was however untenable and James and Thomas, with their remaining pals from the Battalion, were ordered to retire to the ridge behind the village and consolidate the position. Field Marshal Sir John French wrote of that fateful day: *"All said and done, however, the main element of success was to be found in the devoted bravery, and the stern unyielding determination to 'do or die' displayed by the rank and file of the 'contemptible little army' and its reinforcements."*

Sunday 1st November provided some relative respite from the heavy fighting of the previous few days. Monday morning opened with a heavy barrage on their trenches causing great damage and many casualties. One of their officers, Captain Stacey, was buried alive for an hour and half before he was dug out. They were now being fired upon from the front, flanks and rear; they were ordered to dig a new line from the Menin Road to Veldhoek. For the next three days no attack on their position took place although constant artillery fire was an ever present danger. On Sunday 8th November the German assault was renewed and to the right they took the communication trenches: James and Thomas helped drive them out and the German attack petered out for two more days. From 6.30am to 9.30am on Wednesday 11th a furious barrage opened up and the Prussian Guard attacked in strength as the 1st Scots Guards were based around a burnt-out farm, close to Gheluvelt Wood. Captain Stacey (who had been buried alive) held on with great tenacity in the orchard until he too was overwhelmed. The attack took the lives of James and Thomas, who died first will never be known, and the effect of learning that two sons were killed at the same time would have been devastating. At the end of the battle the 1st Battalion Scots Guards virtually ceased to exist so heavy were their losses.

Gheluvelt, Saturday 31st October 1914
The counter-attack by the Worcesters

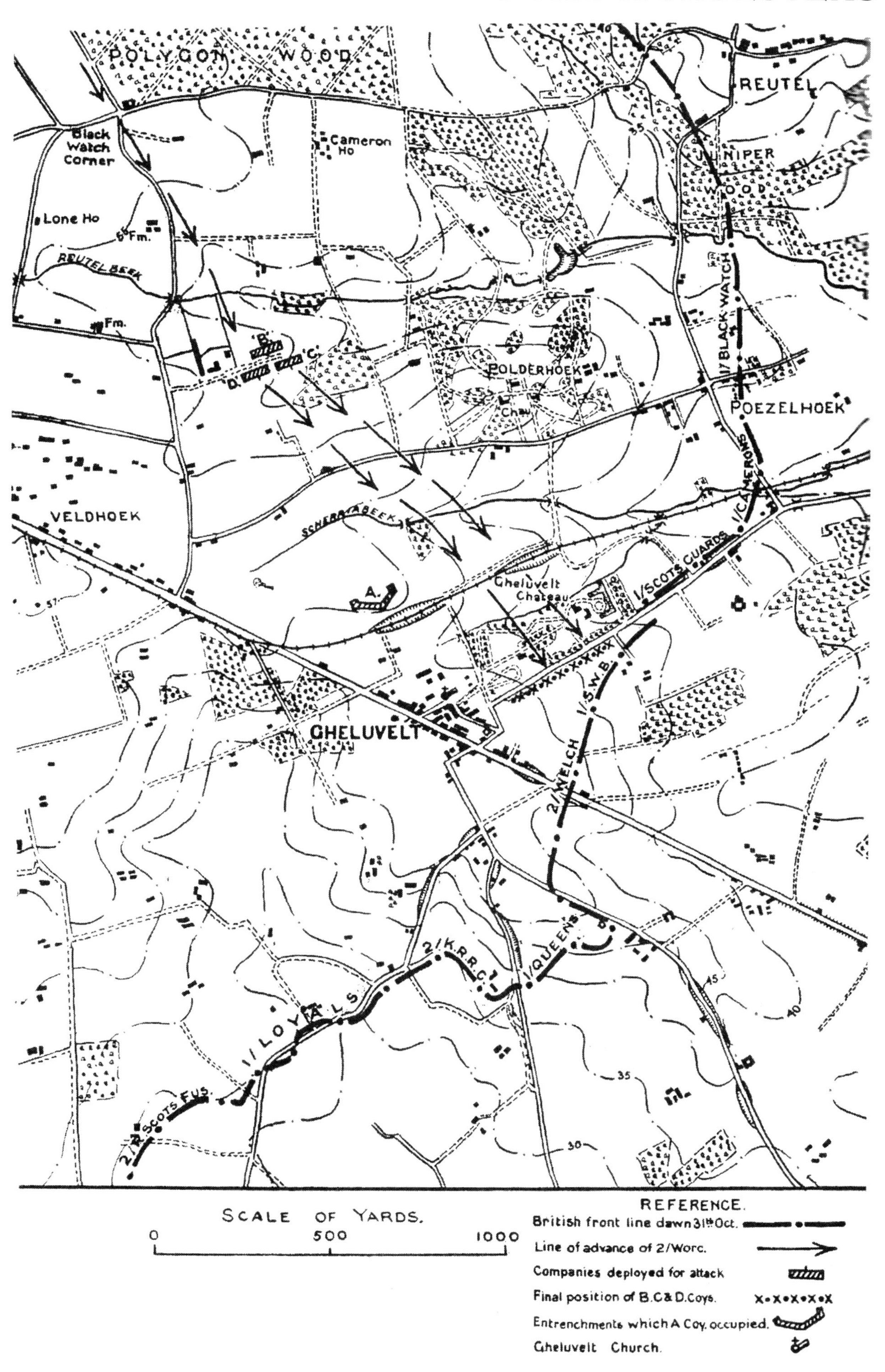

6268 Private Thomas Freemantle

1st Battalion Scots Guards

Wednesday 11th November 1914, aged 26

Commemorated on Panel 11

Thomas was born at home, son of William and Sarah Freemantle, of Easton, Winchester. Thomas served in the Army before joining Surrey Police in 1913 being stationed in Horley.

His brother, Private James Freemantle, died on the same day and is commemorated on the Menin Gate, for their story, see above.

... horses panic as the shells begin to fall

Lieutenant Charles Stockley French

2nd Battalion Royal Dublin Fusiliers

Died on Sunday 25th April 1915, aged 22

Commemorated on Panel 44.

Charles was the son of John Alexander French, LLD, and Elizabeth Mary French (née Stockley), of St Ann's, Donnybrook, County Dublin. He was educated at Shrewsbury School from 1905 to 1910 and went up to Trinity College, Dublin, being awarded his BA in 1915.

Charles was gazetted on Wednesday 26th August 1914 and went out to the Ypres Salient. He was wounded near Armentières in December 1914, and invalided from the line, returning to the front on 23rd March 1915 joining the Battalion near Messines. He was killed in action at St Julien at *'Shell Trap Farm'* where they faced a terrific bombardment of gas shells, followed by shrapnel, fierce machine-gun and rifle fire.

Captain Dickie wrote: *"Captain Tobin Maunsell, with Corporal (now Sergeant) Lalor and a few men, got into the village up a ditch, but the rest of the company under me was mopped up trying to get there in extended order. Young French and Salvesen were killed next me and Elsworthy wounded, close to the village."*

Charles is commemorated at St Mary's Church of Ireland, Anglesea Road, Dublin.

His brother, Captain Claude French, died on Tuesday 1st June 1915 and is buried in Wimereux Communal Cemetery.

Captain William Sigismund Friedberger

5th Battalion attached 3rd Battalion Royal Fusiliers

Died on Monday 24th May 1915

Commemorated on Panel 8.

William Friedberger

William was the son of Joseph Friedberger. He became a partner in his father's firm working in the Stock Exchange where he elected a member. William was married.

William served in the South African War, commanding a Battalion of the Royal Fusiliers, and was Mentioned in Despatches. William subsequently retired from the Army with the rank of Major.

At the outbreak of war he volunteered and was offered a commission as a Captain. Following a period of training he joined the 3rd Battalion when they returned from Lucknow, India, in December 1914.

William left with the Battalion and landed in Le Havre during January 1915. The were sent for further training prior to taking the line for the first time.

He served in the front on tours of duty without being involved in any significant action until Monday 24th May William was south of the Ypres to Roeselare railway where they came under heavy shell fire and the Germans launched a further gas attack which drifted across the lines on the warm summer breezes. The fighting was particularly fierce and the Fusiliers took very heavy casualties. By 8.00am the Germans had captured the fire trenches and during the defence of the position William was killed. At the end of the attack only one officer, Major Baker, remained and casualties totalled five hundred and thirty-six for the Battalion.

The Adjutant wrote: *"He was deeply respected and loved by his company and brother officers. I never met a man who was better fitted to command men, in fact a born soldier."*

A brother officer wrote: *"He did quite enough for his country during the South African War without risking his life again. ... He was a keen officer and good comrade; his kindness to me in South Africa and at home I can never forget."*

A Colonel under whom he served wrote: *"We soldiered in South Africa together and I knew what a good soldier he was. He was most popular with all ranks, both officers and men, and I feel I have lost a friend whom it is impossible to replace."*

William is commemorated on the Stock Exchange War Memorial.

Lieutenant Edmund Lionel Frost

1st/4th Battalion South Lancashire Regiment

Died on Wednesday 16th June 1915, aged 24

Commemorated on Panel 37.

Edmund Frost

Edmund was born at Laswade, Midlothian on Saturday 30th May 1891, only son of Dr Edmund Frost, MD, of Chesterfield, Meads, Eastbourne. He was educated at Uppingham from 1904 to 1909 as a member of Fircroft. He was the boxing heavyweight champion, Captain of Games, Captain of the Hockey XI, Captain of the Football Team, Captain of Fircroft House and a Præposter. Edmund passed his entrance examinations for Cambridge aged 16 but remained at school until he was old enough to go up. In 1909 he left for Trinity College, Cambridge, and graduated in 1912 with a BA in the Natural Sciences Tripos. Edmund won two Half-Blues for boxing and shooting, was the Captain of the Cambridge Revolver IV, rowed for the College and was a member of the OTC winning numerous awards at Bisley. In 1912 Edmund joined his uncle, Mr F A Frost of Grappenhall Hall, in his file and tool business, Peter Stubs Limited of Warrington. He was well travelled in Europe, speaking French fluently; he had also travelled to Canada and the Far East. Edmund was a member of the Hawks' Club, Cambridge, and the Warrington Club.

In November 1912 Edmund joined the Warrington Territorials being promoted Lieutenant in September 1914. He won a number of the officers' trophies for rifle and revolver shooting.

On Friday 12th February 1915, Lieutenant Colonel Fairclough led his men to Southampton where they boarded *SS Queen Alexandra* and *SS Trafford Hall* bound for Le Havre. Edmund took his men to No 2 Rest Camp where they stayed for two days. He marched to the station where the Battalion entrained for Bailleul and were billeted in the *'Grapperies'*. On Friday 21st March he led his men out along the cobbled road that took him across the border into Belgium, passing through the village of Locre to camp at the hamlet of La Clytte. After a further three days training he undertook his first tour of duty. He marched down the straight road connecting the hamlet with Kemmel and onward to the lines on the other side of the village. Over the next four weeks he undertook tours of duty at Kemmel before being sent to St Eloi, a grim area. The only view from the parapet was decomposing bodies, some having been there for months. On Thursday 1st April he was relieved but returned on tours of duty until moving to Elzenwalle Château on Saturday 1st May. A gas attack on Hill 60 took place the next day and some of gases drifted onto their lines causing eye irritation to many of the men. The rest of May was a repetitive tour of duties without any particular action taking place. On Wednesday 16th June Edmund was in action at Hooge — he was leading his men in successfully capturing two German trenches on the Bellewaarde Ridge at the point of the bayonet, when he was shot through the head.

Major Crossfield wrote: *"I was speaking to him only ten minutes before, and, though we were then in the thick of it, he was just a bright and cheery as ever. The whole battalion mourns his loss. All ranks deplore his loss, as he was such a fine, straightforward, kindly disposed man, and a perfect British gentleman in every sense of the word, the world being the poorer by his loss."*

The Reverend W Bracechamp, Chaplain, wrote: *"When the Battalion left to make the charge he was thoroughly cheery and said to me, 'Good-by Padre. We shall soon meet again.' Your son was one of the finest characters it has ever been my privilege to meet. He was beloved by officers and men alike. His fine physique, his noble character, endeared him to everybody. He was one of the noble cause for God, King, and Country."*

2902 Rifleman Edwin Samuel Fryer

1st/9th Battalion London Regiment (Queen Victoria's Rifles)

Died on Tuesday 18th December 1914, aged 27

Commemorated on Panel 54.

Edwin Fryer

Edwin was born on Thursday 20th January 1887, son of Mary Anne Fryer, of Harvest Home, Bury Goss, Gosport, Hampshire, and the late Samuel Fryer. He was educated at Archbishop Tenison's Grammar School, London, and served until the age of 21 in the Civil Service before working in the private sector. In 1912 Edwin was elected Worthy Master of the Equitable Friendly Society and was a an ardent Freemason.

Edwin volunteered on Wednesday 2nd September 1914, left for France on Wednesday 4th November on board the *SS Oxonian* and arrived in Le Havre the next day. After a night in camp he entrained for St Omer, an uncomfortable twenty-six hour journey. He continued his training until Friday 27th November when he was marched from Bailleul crossing the border to Neuve Eglise. He was sent into the line at Wulverghem. Sergeant Crossthwaite described their first action 'going over the top': *"In the late afternoon we started for the trenches, most of us armed then with the long rifle and short bayonet, with a heavy pack and certain comforts not detailed in Army Orders; 150 rounds, and a stout heart, although I think we had the look of men who were about to pierce the fog of war and face the yet unknown horror of it. Our company — Capt. Flemming in command — and a very gallant gentleman he was — got to Wulverghem, as the night, dark and wet, had settled down. It was a village ruined, dead and deserted, and the battered church tower loomed up ghostlike. Passing through we left the road and struggled ankle-deep over beet fields sodden with water, platoon after platoon plodding along in silence. Guides from the trenches met us hereabouts and soon, slopping along like spectres, we wheeled half left and came under long-range rifle and machine-gun fire. This, our first baptism of fire, I shall never forget; the 'ping 'of the bullets, seemingly near and just overhead, the mystery of the night, the soft 'slosh' of marching men, the whispered command passed on. The going became worse as we neared the line, the beet fields being here intersected by deep gulleys crossed by narrow planks, slimy with mud, off which many a man slipped to the ditches below. Suddenly there loomed up in the darkness what seemed like a long irregular ditch and here and there a black head bobbed up, and from near the heads flashes from rifles lit out, but all else was silent, dark, and sinister. The column extended along the line of the ditch and waited, and then out crawled objects that looked like men — black, muddy and utterly exhausted. Platoon leaders took over, and our line stumbled through patches of mud and rubbish plump into a foot of black water with a wet wall of sandbags in front. Sentries were posted and the relieved garrison crawled out, slipping away into the gloom like grim shadows. I don't think we were very miserable that first night, the novelty of it all was so obsessing, but the iron entered our souls later, and the time came when we got to know trenches to which these were a home of rest. In this part of the line, beneath the Messines Ridge, there were no shelters, no dug-outs, no trenches even, but merely a shallow ditch with a sandbag rampart in front, held together by rude revetments, black mud below, bullets overhead, the smell of death and the horror of blackness—but we kept our tails up! On the left of our sector was a barn reputed to be occupied at times by a sniper, and right in front, as we observed when dawn broke, was the low skyline of the Messines Ridge topped by the German trenches. Between their line and ours, and distant only about 200 yards, was a gully, evidently the haunt of snipers—indeed these gentry seemed to be everywhere, as bullets would repeatedly enfilade a sector and not infrequently come from the rear.*

To clear up the front a volunteer patrol was sent out under myself for two nights in succession, and, acting on Brigade instructions, we searched the gully. There was a bright moon and we were fired on from some dense bush in front, but we managed to crawl back without a casualty and with information that proved useful to the Brigade Artillery. This was our first adventure 'over the top' and I should like to mention the cheerful bravery of my companions, Lce.-Cpls. W. R. Gittens and L. Jolly. We got some souvenirs from a dead German, who smelt most horribly, but the papers found on him were not of much use."

On Sunday 16th Edwin took to the line for the last time, one of the officers describing the advanced trenches: *"... a dirty ditch about 3 feet deep and 10 feet broad, on top of a hill, with no shelter of any kind and up to your knees in mud and water."* During the tour of duty Edwin was one of three killed with five others wounded.

His Commanding Officer wrote: *"He always did his duty well and cheerfully under often very trying conditions, and showed a fine spirit, setting a splendid example to the rest of the men, by whom he was much liked and respected, and who, in common with myself, will feel his loss very much."*

Lieutenant
Bernard Vincent Fulcher, MC

2nd Battalion South Lancashire Regiment

Died on Tuesday 17th November 1914, aged 22

Commemorated on Panel 37.

Bernard Fulcher

Bernard was born at Lorne House, Great Yarmouth on Friday 22nd January 1892, son of William and Alice Popplewell Fulcher, of Walton, 85 The Hill, Wimbledon, London. He was educated at King's College School, Wimbledon, where he was Captain of the Shooting VIII and the First XV. He was a member of the OTC and gained his 'A' Certificate. Bernard passed into RMC Sandhurst in 1910, being gazetted on Wednesday 20th September 1911 and promoted Lieutenant on Wednesday 16th July 1913.

Bernard assisted in mobilising the Battalion at the outbreak of war: they gathered at Tidworth before embarking at Southampton. The Battalion sailed to Le Havre on Friday 14th August 1914. On Thursday 20th they entrained to northern France from where they marched into Belgium, crossing the border at 8.00am on Friday 21st and arriving at Frameries in late-afternoon on Saturday 22nd. They took the line at Ciply: Lieutenant Colonel Wanliss wrote: *"That evening before dark I went round the whole of the position held by the Battalion and was more impressed than ever that our chief weakness lay on our left flank, where the railway embankment would afford excellent cover for the enemy's infantry, only some 500 yards from the left of our line. I therefore told Travis-Cook, commanding 'D' Company, to throw back his left and ordered the two machine-guns to support that flank. The whole of the night we continued improving our trenches and head-cover, before daybreak I sounded my whistle and had the trenches manned. ... Almost immediately afterwards the enemy's artillery opened a tremendous fire on Frameries and after some time the whole place was in a blaze. Our artillery, although outnumbered 5 to 1, did magnificent work. At one time a Germany battery took a position on a hill about 1,200 yards to the left of our line, and in prolongation of it, and began to enfilade our trenches and several shrapnel bullets dropped into my portion. However, almost immediately one of our batteries switched on and dropped two shelling bang into the middle of it and the German battery disappeared."* Late in the day the orders arrived for a retirement and The Retreat began.

Bernard saw action at Le Cateau and continued the march south. At 5.00am on Sunday 6th September they stopped retreating and turned eastward to attack the German army. On Wednesday 9th they crossed the Marne and the Aisne on Sunday 13th September. He remained at Vailly from Tuesday 15th to Monday 21st where they came under attack in their shallow trenches. Bernard remained on the Aisne until early October when the Battalion was transferred to northern France.

On Monday 12th he left Hinges at 7.00am and marched to the trenches in the La Bassée sector. After two weeks heavy action the Battalion moved to Neuve-Chapelle where they attacked the village.

In early November Bernard moved to the Salient going into the line at 2.00am on Friday 6th at Zwarteleen. On Wednesday 11th and Friday 13th the Prussian Guard advanced on them at Nonne Bosschen. The German attacks continued with intensity and Bernard was killed in a dugout by a shell, together with Lieutenant Colonel Malcolm Green who had taken command only five days beforehand. (Colonel Green is commemorated on the Menin Gate, see below.)

Colonel Green

Bernard was Mentioned in Despatches twice, gazetted on Monday 19th October 1914 and Wednesday 17th February 1915. He was awarded the Military Cross in November 1914.

Major Baird wrote: *"I wish to tell you how nobly your boy was doing his duty when he met his death ... Your son was quite indefatigable in doing his duty under conditions the difficulties of which can never be fully realised except by those who were there. ... Often I used to feel that he was destined to go far in our profession. ... None of us who served together in those fifteen strenuous days will ever forget his splendid work. As officer commanding that particular section of the trenches, I have officially brought to notice the very splendid way in which his conduct was distinguished."*

The Headmaster of King's College School wrote: *"He was with us just the best kind of English boy, straight and loyal and keen, ... with a healthy influence with his friends and all the school."*

Second Lieutenant Frank Fullerton

'D' Company, 1st/4th Battalion
The Loyal North Lancashire Regiment
Died on Tuesday 31st July 1917, aged 21
Commemorated on Panel 41.

Frank was born in Altrincham, Cheshire, in 1896, son of Hugh and Ada Fullerton, of Brackenhoe, Sale, Manchester. His father had been the Member of Parliament for the Egremont constituency in Manchester. Frank was educated at Manchester Grammar School from 1910 to 1912 and became a salesman.

Frank was attached to Manchester University OTC where he undertook his military training from May to October 1916 when he was commissioned. On Monday 2nd April 1917 Frank left for France, joining the Battalion in the field whilst they were serving in the front line at La Brique on the Ypres Salient, allocated to 'D' Company.

On Saturday 28th July the Battalion was in camp at Poperinghe and preparations for the opening of the Third Battle of Ypres were well under way. On Sunday 29th they moved off at 9.00am for Vlamertinghe where the next day they were visited by the Brigadier and the Divisional Commander. On Friday 30th they moved to their assembly positions close to *'Congreve Walk'*.

At 10.00am the Battalion moved forward and were successful in taking *'Gallipoli'* a series of concrete pill-boxes: *"Two snipers who caused trouble near Gallipoli were captured. The Platoon consolidated the Green Line until 2.30*

Billets in a farmhouse

p.m., when the enemy counter-attacked on the right. The Scots on the right were seen to withdraw, and Second Lieutenant Fullerton, who had taken over command of the whole line, shouted to us to hang on. He himself established a defensive flank on our right, but was shortly afterwards killed.
On reaching our objective we dug in under machine-gun fire from our left. About 1.15 p.m. we saw the smoke of an engine on the other side of the ridge. About half an hour after this the enemy appeared over the ridge, and advanced towards us. We opened on him with Lewis guns. He was covering his advance with machine-guns on the left. The 6th Camerons were seen retiring, and took up a position in a strong point about 150 yards behind our trench. We hung on to our trench for 20 minutes or half an hour. Second Lieutenant Fullerton acted with great gallantry during this trying period. He persuaded the whole of our line to hang on — he was the only Officer left in the Green Line —and it was a great loss when he was killed, just before we withdrew.
Twenty minutes previous we had seen the smoke of a train. For a time he was disorganised by our machine-guns and Lewis gun fire; then he advanced on the front of the Battalion on our right, which withdrew immediately, and the enemy followed. Second Lieutenant Fullerton ordered us to line the hedge on our right, and we held on there for half an hour. Meanwhile the enemy tried to get round behind us, and to a certain extent succeeded."
A bursary was established at Manchester Grammar School in Frank's memory.

Captain Frederic Furze

5th Battalion London Regiment
(London Rifle Brigade)
Died on Thursday 20th September 1917, aged 36
Commemorated on Panel 52.

Frederic Furze

Frederic was born in Beckenham, Kent, on Friday 29th April 1881, elder son of Frederic and Helen E Furze, of 10 Chiswick Place, Eastbourne, Sussex. He was educated at Charterhouse from 1895 to 1899 as a Robinite then a Hodgsonsite. On Tuesday 27th October 1908 in Beckenham, Frederic married Alice Duthie Furze (née Trimmer). He was employed as a clerk at the Stock Exchange.
At the outbreak of war Frederic volunteered and enlisted, being commissioned in late August 1914. He was promoted Lieutenant in 1915, served as Adjutant from Thursday 17th June 1915 to Saturday 23rd July 1917 and appointed Captain in 1916.
After seeing action on the Somme, in the summer of 1917, on Friday 24th August he entrained for Godewaersvelde from where he marched to Poperinghe. He went into training for ten days at 'Reigersburg Camp' before going into the line at *'Kitchener Wood'*. Great care had to be taken navigating along the duckboards at the front as the mud was deep and many men drowned falling off them. After a four day tour of duty they were sent to *'Dambre Camp'* Vlamertinghe, for training and Lieutenant General Sir Ivor Maxse, KCB, addressed Frederic and the officers: *"Gentlemen, you lead your men creditably, but you are too polite. The spirit of the attack I have just witnessed savours more of the Sunday School than of the sanguinary battle. Far too gentle and kind. Your commands should be short and sharp: less 'if you please' about them, more calculated to exact instant automatic obedience from the soldiers brain, half paralysed by noise and*

... preparing the bombs at Passchendaele

shock. Swear, gentlemen, swear: the men like it so long as you don't repeat yourselves. Cultivate a vocabulary." At 10.45am on Wednesday 19th he led his men to assembly positions ready to attack *'Von Tirpitz Farm'* and *'Stoppe Farm'*. At 5.40am the next morning he took his men *'over the top'* and advanced under a creeping barrage. Progress was slow due to German machine-gun fire. After a long and difficult fight they took their objectives, when the Brigade were asked to assist the Post Office Rifles at *'Hubner Farm'*. In the attack Frederic was wounded twice, both quite severely, but refused to leave his men. Frederic continued to fight on and lead the men until he was killed by a sniper and buried at *'Hubner Farm'*.
His Commander wrote: *"His behaviour during the attack was splendid, and it is due to his fine example and great gallantry that the attack was the great success it was. He was shot three times, but still carried on, and was finally killed by a sniper at the final objective. His loss to us is immense be was most popular with all ranks."*
Frederic is commemorated on The Stock Exchange War Memorial.

29546 Private Oliver Fyson

'D' Company, 16th Battalion Canadian Infantry (Manitoba Regiment)

Died on Friday 23rd April 1915, aged 30

Commemorated on Panel 26.

Oliver was born on Tuesday 28th October 1884, twin son of the Right Reverend Bishop Philip Kemball Fyson, DD, (formerly Bishop of Hokkaido, Japan), and of Eleanor Fyson, of Elmley Lovett Rectory, Droitwich, Worcestershire. He was educated at Loretto School from 1897 to 1904 where he was a Prefect and played in the First XV. Oliver emigrated to Canada, where he was a clerk, a member of the Militia and captain of the British Columbian Rugby Team.

Oliver volunteered at Valcartier on Monday 7th September and enlisted, where he was described as 5ft 9½in tall, with a 41in chest, grey eyes, brown hair and a slight scar on his left shoulder.

After training he was sent to board *SS Andania* on Monday 28th September 1914, sailing on the Wednesday, arriving in Plymouth on Saturday 17th October. He entrained for Salisbury Plain where he continued to train until Thursday 11th February 1915. He entrained for Avonmouth sailing for St Nazaire on Friday 12th, arriving three days later. He was sent to Hazebrouck from where he marched to Caëstre where, after a lot of marching about, billets were finally provided in a hayloft. After a further period of training he was sent into the line near Bois Grenier at the end of the month. He served in the Fleurbaix sector until Friday 26th March when he was marched to reserve in Estaires on Wednesday 7th April. Three days later he was paraded for an inspection by General Sir Horace Smith- Dorrien. On Thursday 15th he moved to Steenvoorde where after being billeted overnight he was taken by motor bus to Vlamertinghe. After a short rest and lunch, Oliver paraded and at 2.30pm marched along the cobbled roads to Wieltje. At 8.00pm the Battalion relieved the French 79th Division along the St Julien to Poelkapelle road. His tour of duty lasted three days before being sent into reserve in northern Ypres and along the Canal. Life was relatively quiet for Oliver and his comrades; he was able to bathe in the Canal and visit the town. At 5.00pm on Thursday 22nd the much anticipated German attack commenced. What was not known was that the attack would be supported by poison gas. At 5.30pm he was ordered to 'stand to' and within half an hour the Battalion was assembled along the Canal where they remained until 7.40pm. Whilst guarding the line along the Canal some of the French colonial troops who had been gassed started to flee passed them. No-one could understand why they were so panicked or in such distress. At Headquarters the information coming in was confusing but it was known that the French line had collapsed and Ypres was exposed to a German attack. Oliver was marched via La Brique to St Jan, which was under shell fire. When they reached Wieltje the village was clogged with men, limbers and refugees. Whilst they halted the effects of the gas blowing on the gentle breezes affected most of the men: their eyes started to stream, their throats dried up and became sore. They continued their march toward St Julien where a counter-attack was to be mounted. At 11.45pm the attack commenced; it was dark as they advanced, the moon had gone in but flares put up by the Germans turned night into day. The German infantry was well entrenched in the small wood and poured rapid fire onto the advancing Canadians. They were in close formation and casualties were heavy. Oliver was killed in the fierce battle which successfully took *'Kitchener's Wood'* (Bois des Cuisiniers).

... German mount an attack on the Canadian line

His twin brother, Lieutenant Geoffrey Fyson, died on Wednesday 4th September 1918 and is commemorated on the Doiran Memorial.

... the Menin Road in 1915

Serjeant Major —I dunno wot to do with 'im sir. 'e ain't been a casualty, an' the M.O. says 'ain't a defective, an, 'e says 'e comes o' fightin' stock. My God, sir, look 'im —ain't 'e a fair champion for the Corkscrew Cuirassiers?

from
Gamack to Gwyn

2306 Private
Bruce Macquarie Gamack

36th Battalion Australian Infantry, AIF

Died on Saturday 21st July 1917, aged 24

Commemorated on Panel 25.

Bruce was born in Rolland's Plains, New South Wales, son of James and Mary Elizabeth Gamack, of Kempsey, New South Wales. He was educated locally. Bruce was married to Janet C Gamack, of Ferry Street, East Kempsey, New South Wales, and was employed as a teamster.

On Tuesday 23rd May 1916 he volunteered and embarked on *HMAT Borda*, on Tuesday 17th October from Sydney. He continued training and joined his Battalion in the field.

In February 1917 he served in the Armentières sector followed by Houplines in March before returning to Armentières on Tuesday 3rd April. After a period of training at Wizernes and rest at Arques and Erquinghem, Bruce was sent into the line at Le Touquet where he remained throughout May before moving the short distance to Ploegsteert Wood. As the Battle of Messines opened their lines were attacked with gas and heavy artillery fire. The Battalion undertook an advance in the Wood that captured a reasonable amount of ground. In July he was moved to the Messines sector where on Wednesday 18th a number of early morning patrols and raids on the their lines were repulsed which the Germans followed by a gas attack where they were bombarded with mustard gas. From Thursday 19th to Saturday 21st a constant barrage was aimed on their lines with further gas being sent over at 2.30am on Saturday 21st. Bruce was killed when a shell burst close to him at mid-day.

His brother, Private Wilton Gamack, died on Tuesday 6th November 1917 and is commemorated on the Menin Gate, see below.

3806 Private
Wilton Campbell Gamack

19th Battalion Australian Infantry, AIF

Died on Tuesday 6th November 1917, aged 22

Commemorated on Panel 23.

Wilton was born in Port Macquarie, New South Wales, son of James and Mary Elizabeth Gamack, of Kempsey, New South Wales. He was educated locally and then worked as a clerk.

Wilton had served in the Militia and volunteered for active service on Monday 19th April 1915, leaving from Sydney on board on *HMAT Runic* on Thursday 20th January 1916 and joined the Battalion in the field in Egypt.

An Australian camp in the shadow of the pyramids

The Battalion was sent to the France to serve on the Somme and saw action at Pozières where he served in the line for nineteen days continuously.

Wilton entrained on Tuesday 5th September 1916 for Poperinghe where he was sent to billets until 9.00pm on Saturday 9th, when he marched to the Salient and into reserve. On Thursday 14th he took the line at *'Observatory Ridge'* and Mount Sorrel where he served until Wednesday 20th. After five days in billets in the ruined town of Ypres he returned to the line. Wilton continued on tours of duty until Friday 6th October when the Battalion entrained for Steenvoorde.

After a week in billets the Battalion was entrained for Tatinghem on Sunday 15th for eight days. A route march took them to Tournehem on Monday 23rd where they rested for two days before entraining to Pont Remy and

Café Belge

I'm going back to dear old Zillebeke,
That's the hottest place I know
Can't you hear the busmen calling,
'Café Belge, Bedford House, Zillebeke and Vint Street?'
I won't hesitate to duck my head
When a shell is coming near.
Oh, find me a shelter anywhere —
Dug-out, shell-hole, I don't care,
There's a Red Cross car awaiting there,
In dear old Zillebeke.

Bedford House

were taken by motor bus to Ribemont.
Wilton marched to Mametz where he was in reserve for five days before taking the line at Flers on Thursday 9th November. On Tuesday 14th he was involved in the attack on Flers where he assisted in taking the German defences called *'The Maze'*. From Tuesday 21st he was sent to *'Fricourt Camp'* where the Battalion undertook Corps fatigues until Sunday 26th after which they returned to Ribemont. Training continued from Friday 1st December until Saturday 16th when a series of route marches took them back to the line on the Somme. He continued serving in the sector including at Martinpuich, Flers, Le Sars, Bazentin, Fricourt until July 1917 when he was sent to Bienvillers for a month of training.

On Sunday 29th July he was sent to Arques, remaining there or in Alquines until Wednesday 12th September when he marched to Steenvoorde. The next day Wilton crossed the border at Abeele and went into *'Pioneer Camp'* at Dickebusch. On Monday 17th he took the line on the Bellewaarde Ridge before moving to Westhoek Ridge on Wednesday 19th until Saturday 22nd, when he returned to *'Halifax Camp'* in Dickebusch. After two days rest Wilton was sent to *'Patricia Camp'* where the Battalion was reorganised before moving back to the line at *'Railway Wood'* on Thursday 4th October. From Friday 12th he was sent to Steenvoorde for further training which lasted until Tuesday 16th when a fleet of buses arrived and took the Battalion to Ypres where they worked on the light railway. The work continued until Thursday 1st November when they went into reserve in huts close to *'Café Belge'* before taking the line at Westhoek Ridge. Wilton was moved forward at 4.15pm on Monday 5th and relieved the 18th Battalion on the Broodseinde Ridge which was completed two hours later. Patrols and reconnaissance was undertaken. To the Battalion's left, the Canadians attacked Passchendaele that brought a retaliatory bombardment from the German artillery, and Wilton was killed.
His brother, Private Bruce Gamack, died on Saturday 21st July 1917 and is commemorated on the Menin Gate, see above.

"The Return of the Goth"

Major Ernest Gardiner

1st (South Midland) Field Company
Royal Engineers
Died on Tuesday 2nd March 1915, aged 34
Commemorated on Panel 9.

Ernest was the son of Thomas Chapple Gardiner and Sarah Bishop Gardiner, of Waratah, Beaufort Road, Clifton, Bristol. He was educated at Clifton College from 1889 to 1896 where he was an enthusiastic rugby player. Ernest was married to Kathleen Eleanor Wellesley-Bigsworth (formerly Gardiner).

Ernest went out to France with the BEF and whilst in action at St Eloi he was killed by shell fire.
He was Mentioned in Despatches.

Major Robert MacGregor Stewart Gardner

'D' Company, 1st Battalion Gloucestershire Regiment
Died on Saturday 31st October 1914, aged 44
Commemorated on Panel 22.

Robert Gardner

Robert was born on Thursday 25th August 1870, second son of Mr and Mrs William Gardner of Thorpe, Surrey, and nephew of General Sir Robert Stewart, GCB. He was educated at Bath College. On Tuesday 25th October 1910, in Clifton, Robert married May Gardner (née Wasbrough). They had two daughters, Stella Mary Bridget born on Sunday 19th November 1911 and their youngest born after Robert's death on Thursday 11th February 1915.
Robert was gazetted from the Militia in February 1891, promoted Lieutenant in May 1892, Captain in February 1900 and Major in July 1914.
Robert served in the South African War and was present at the Relief at Mafeking. He was Mentioned in Despatches gazetted on Tuesday 10th September 1901 and received the Queen's Medal with four clasps.
At the outbreak of war Robert embarked on *SS Gloucester Castle* for Le Havre, arriving on Thursday 13th August 1914. They marched to a stubble field and took over one hundred bell tents which were blown down the next night during a thunderstorm, soaking everyone. In the wet and clinging mud, at 4.00am on Saturday morning the Battalion was pleased to move to the station and entrain for Le Nouvian where they arrived at 7.00pm on Sunday evening. They rested in camp before marching to the Mons battlefield via Maubeuge. After the short Battle of Mons they were ordered to retire but they were soon back in action. The Battalion took position on the Le Favril to Landrecies road with Robert's 'D' Company on the right, with his machine-guns being brought into play. Germans were spotted advancing in numbers and after stiff resistance they were forced to retire. The Retreat continued to Le Cateau and southwest, a march of two hundred miles. On Sunday 6th September orders were received to stop marching south and turn to face the German Army. They re-crossed the Marne and on to the Aisne where, near Vendresse, a shell burst close to where Robert was standing with a group of fellow officers and was knocked off his feet. He continued to serve on the Aisne until early October when the Battalion was ordered north.
By mid-October he had arrived on the Ypres Salient, reaching Poperinghe on Tuesday 20th. Early the next morning Robert marched his men through Elverdinghe, Boesinghe and Pilkem, moving in front of Langemarck; 'D' Company taking the right flank next to The Queen's. At 4.00pm Robert and his company came under heavy machine-gun fire which was followed by hordes of German infantry advancing at seven hundred yards distance. The attack was repulsed by three bursts of rapid fire to which the German artillery replied accurately and killed several men.
By the end of October the Battalion had been moved in front of Gheluvelt. On Thursday 29th the German attack commenced at 5.30am under the cover of a thick mist. Robert led his men forward along the Menin Road to within three hundred yards of the Kruiseik crossroads. They were under heavy pressure from the Germans and Captain Robert Rising (who was killed on Saturday 7th November and buried in Zillebeke Churchyard) came up with 'A' Company to help relieve Robert and then covered his retreat. Sergeant Warwick and Corporal Birley of 'D' Company were cut off and taken prisoner - Corporal Birley escaped from Germany and returned to England, and was subsequently commissioned. Eventually Robert was able to get his men back to the east of Gheluvelt Church before rejoining the

Captain Rising

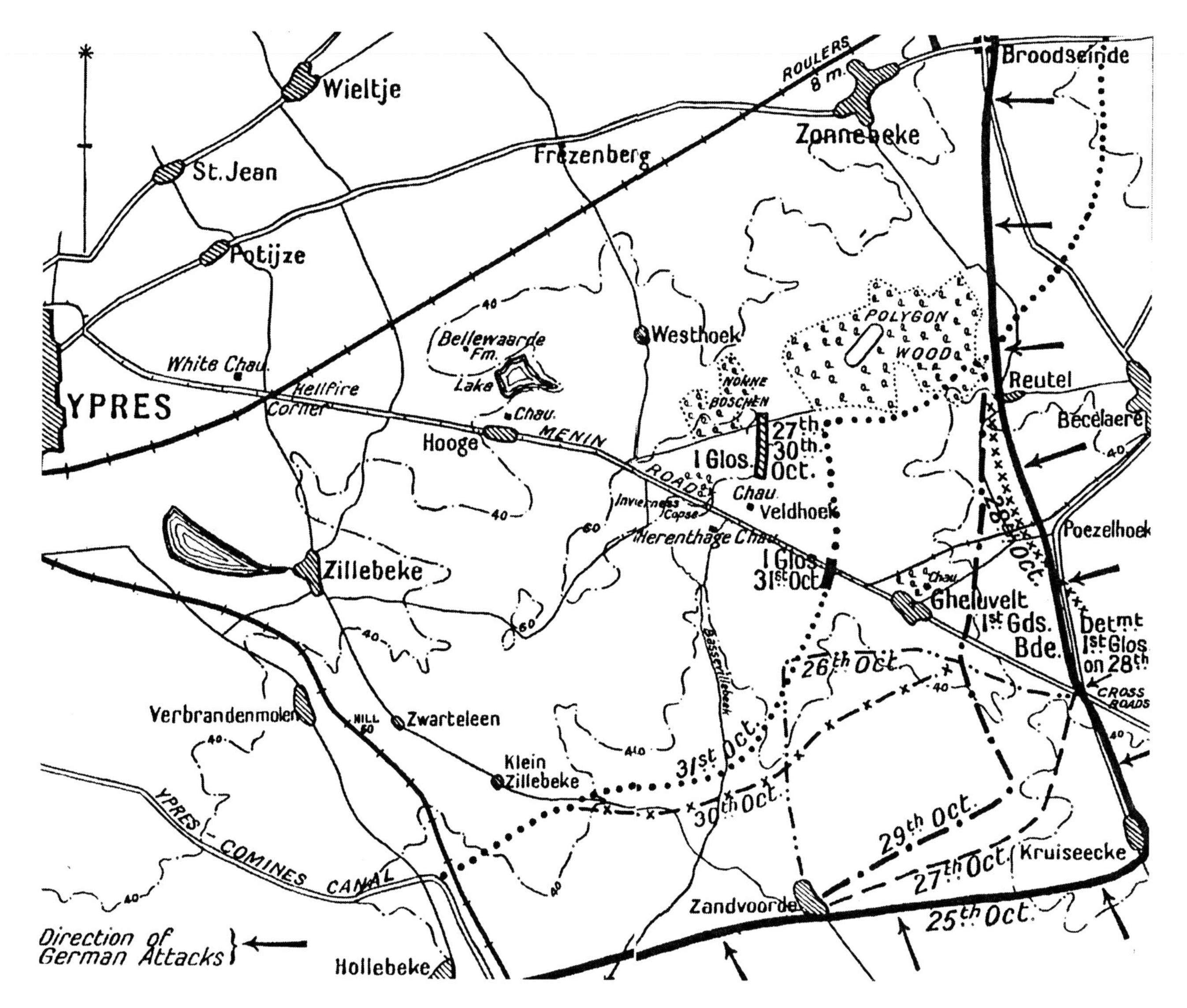

Gloucestershire Regiment at Gheluvelt in October 1914

Battalion near Veldhoek. On Saturday 31st Gheluvelt came under very heavy artillery fire with most of the village and its windmill destroyed. At 5.30am the Gloucesters advanced and took heavy losses. At mid-day Robert ordered a charge against the German trenches and was first out of the trench — almost immediately he was mortally wounded in both the side and arm.

The Official History records: *"'D' Company, now only eighty strong, was ordered up at about mid-day and told to recapture the trench which had been lost, immediately to the north of the Menin Road. The Company, under Major Gardner, advanced under a terrific shell fire until they came in sight of the front-line trenches. Those immediately in front were safely in British hands, and it was evident that the break had occurred more to the south. Accordingly Major Gardner led the Company across a stretch of extremely open ground to a sunken road where the few remaining men rallied. There were only thirty left. Knowing the urgency of the situation, Major Gardner decided he could not wait for the possible arrival of any more men and so ordered a further advance to the attack. Within a few yards he and fifteen men fell and the remainder, under Lieutenant J. Caunter, were forced to remain in a sunken lane where they gallantly held out until the Germans swarmed over the position and took prisoners of the few who remained alive. It seems highly probably that 'D' Company had somehow pushed forward at a point where there was a gap in the attacking line of the enemy. The British front line here had been almost wiped out and the enemy had pushed on. This would account for the fact that no British troops were visible and that the Germans who were encountered later were advancing in small columns and to attack the first line."*

His Colonel wrote: *"We were heavily engaged on Oct. 31, and had to go to the assistance of the remainder of the Brigade. He dashed to the front with his company and was hit badly while leading them most gallantly. The previous day he also displayed the greatest bravery in penetrating to the front in making a counter-attack."*

In St Mary's Church, Thorpe, Surrey, a brass plaque was placed in his memory with the inscription: *"In loving memory of Robert MacGregor Stewart Gardner. Major in the 1st Gloucester Regiment who was killed in action near Gheluvelt on 31 October 1914 while leading his Company, aged 44 years."*

230911 Company Serjeant Major Walter Evershed Gardner

2nd/2nd Battalion London Regiment (Royal Fusiliers)

Died on Saturday 15th September 1917, aged 29

Commemorated on Panel 52.

Walter Gardner

Walter was born at Rotherhithe on Sunday 14th March 1888, eldest son of John and Eleanor Charlotte Gardner, of Hatfield Grange, Harlow. He was educated at Ardingly College.

At the outbreak of war Walter joined the London Regiment. After training at Epsom Downs and Tonbridge he was sent to Malta before moving to Egypt on Friday 27th August 1915. After a further period of training he arrived at Cape Helles on Wednesday 13th October. After the evacuation he was returned to Egypt and continued to serve there until April 1916. The Battalion embarked at Alexandria for Marseilles and served on the Western Front.

Walter was sent to serve on the Salient where during the Third Battle of Passchendaele, he was killed by a shell. His Commanding Officer wrote: *"It is with great regret that I have to inform you that your son was killed while we were in the line last. On Saturday night, the 15th inst, he was in charge of a party laying a duck-board track, when a shell landed near and killed him outright, wounding several others. A wood cross in a neighbouring valley marks where he was buried. Everyone regrets that his long service with the battalion has ended so abruptly. The position of Acting Regtl. Sergt.-Major, which he filled so ably, can hardly be replaced."*

One of his comrades wrote: *"At no time out here did he attempt to shelve responsibility and notwithstanding the fact that he was offered a Base billet, he preferred to rejoin the battalion and go forward."*

Second Lieutenant Alec Mansel Gaselee

15th (The King's) Hussars

Died on Monday 24th May 1915, aged 21

Commemorated on Panel 5.

Alec was born on Saturday 12th May 1894, son of Henry and Alice Esther Gaselee, of 75 Linden Gardens, Bayswater, London. He was educated at Summer Fields from 1905 to 1907 followed by Winchester College from 1907 to 1912 then went up to King's College, Cambridge.

Alec volunteered at the outbreak of war and was commissioned in August 1914. Following a period of training Alec was sent out to France and joined his Squadron in the field.

The Germans launched the first gas attack at 5.00pm on Thursday 22nd April 1915. The King's were in billets near Hazebrouck when at 7.45am on Friday 23rd orders were received to saddle up. Rumours abounded for the reason for the move and as they rode towards Poperinghe they learned about the horrors of the gas attack. As they arrived in the town it was coming under shellfire and they continued out along the Elverdinghe road and bivouacked for the night. The next day they moved to Woesten Wood where they remained until the next morning in the pouring rain. At 8.30am on Sunday 25th they moved to support the Belgians close to Oostvleteren but were not required so were sent to Eikhoek. Until 9.30am on Wednesday 28th they remained in reserve when they were sent to Herzeele arriving at 11.00pm, a slow move due to heavy traffic of men and materials. On Sunday 2nd May they were sent to Esquelbecq then Hondeghem for four days. The Regiment provided working parties at Ypres, riding backwards and forwards until Sunday 9th May when they were ordered into the line at Wieltje.

At 5.00am on Thursday 13th May the Germans laid the largest barrage experienced at that time on the line occupied by Alec and the whole 1st Cavalry Division. Many of the trenches were obliterated and all communication was lost. At midnight Alec ordered his men to fix bayonets and advanced through the pouring rain against the German lines. At 2.00am orders were received for the line to retire to west of *'Crump Farm'* near Verlorenhoek where he organised his men to dig in with tools supplied by a group of Royal Engineers. Throughout Friday 14th they continued to construct their new line without much interference from the Germans until 9.00pm when they were relieved by the Royal Scots Greys and went to Vlamertinghe. On Sunday 16th Major General Henry de Lisle inspected them and addressed them: *"I have striven to get the Regiment under my command, and you have now fully justified my hopes; you have well maintained the high traditions of the Regiment has gained in the past. The British cavalry are the best in the world, and the 15th Hussars stand out as one of the finest regiments of our cavalry."*

General de Lisle

Their period of rest ended at 6.45pm on Tuesday 18th May when they rode to Hooge and relieved the Argyll and Sutherland Highlanders and the Cameron Highlanders. It was not until 4.00am that the relief was complete and their line stretched from the stables of Hooge Château to *'Sanctuary Wood'*. The situation in the trenches was poor, they had been badly damaged and the area was flooded to a depth of two feet. Alec

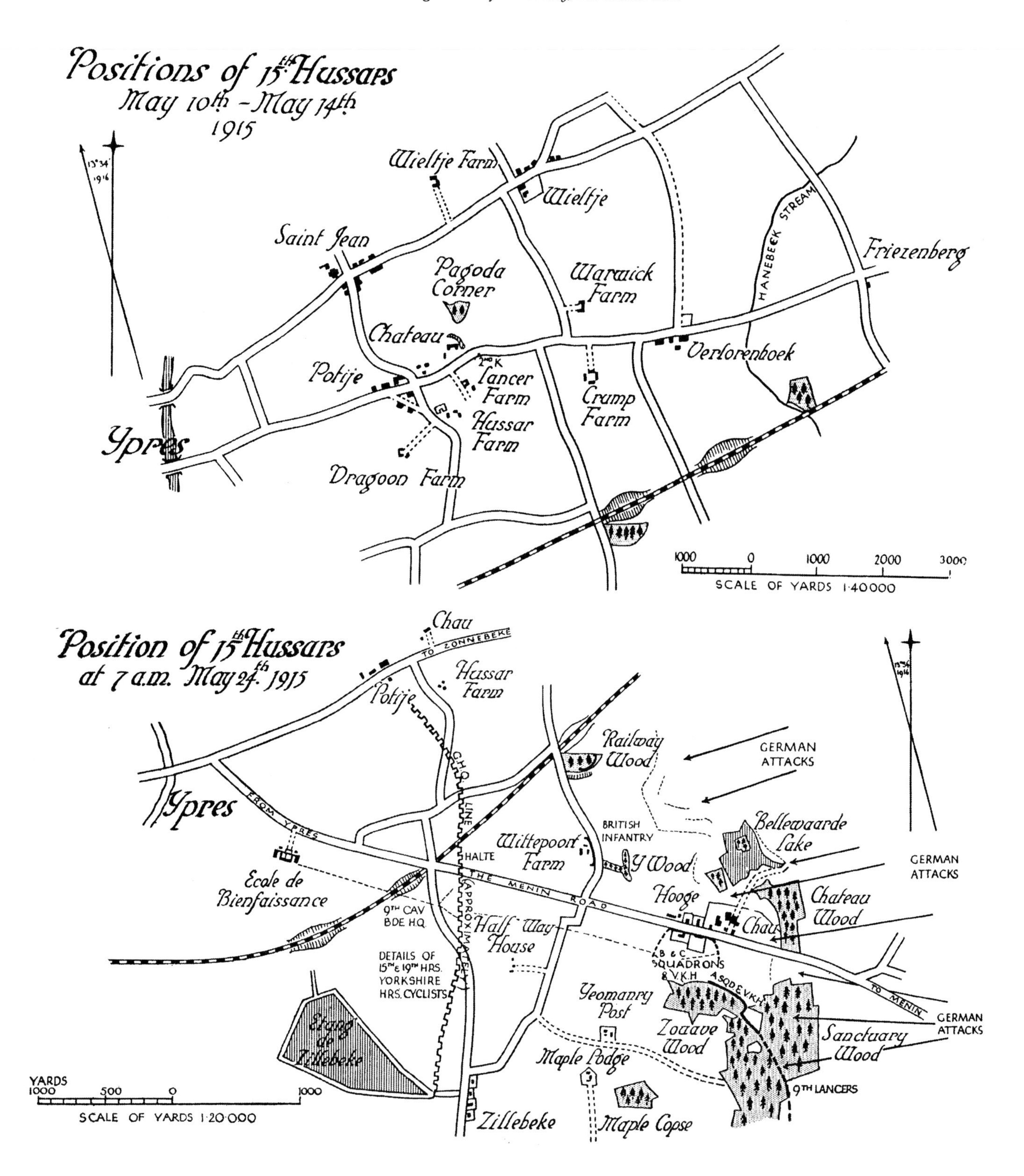

immediately commenced strengthening the parapet and repairing the trenches: most of the work had to take place at night. The Germans put up star shells that illuminated the working parties who had to swiftly dive for cover as machine-gun and rifle fire was brought to bear on them. The 9th Lancers relieved them during the night of Sunday 23rd and they moved slightly to the rear for a period of rest. Alec and his squadron were sent to the École de Bienfaisance.

Shortly after the relief the Germans mounted a severe gas attack which was aimed on the lines they had just left and the 9th Lancers suffered terribly as a result. The gas continued to drift down towards the GHQ line where 'C' Squadron was resting and they too suffered badly. Alec together with 'A' and 'B' Squadrons, had sufficient time to fix their primitive gas masks before the gas reached them and only a few minor casualties were suffered. Alec was ordered to replace 'C' Squadron on the GHQ line as they had gone to reinforce the Lancers. At 5.00am 'A' and 'B' Squadrons were ordered to reinforce the Lancers; their route was difficult, they came under continuous shell fire and without communication trenches the move was made across the open ground. At 6.20am Captain Francis Grenfell, VC,

Captain Grenfell

(who died later that day and is buried in Vlamertinghe Military Cemetery) ordered Alec and 'A' Squadron to counter-attack where the line was breaking. As Alec took his men forward it was clear that the Germans were in vastly superior numbers and Captain Grenfell countered the order. Sadly Alec did not hear the new instruction and was killed moments later.

LIEUTENANT ROBERT FITZAUSTIN GAVIN

2nd Battalion Royal Irish Rifles

Died on Saturday 25th September 1915

Commemorated on Panel 40.

Robert was the son of Captain and Mrs G Fitzaustin Gavin. He was educated at Wellington College from 1901 to 1907 where he played in the XV. He passed into RMC Sandhurst from where he was commissioned in 1909.
Robert served on the Aisne until Friday 2nd October 1914 when he transferred north. On Tuesday 13th he was in the line at the commencement of the Battle of La Bassée. As they advanced on Croix Barbée the German machine-gunners held up their progress. Advances were attempted each day until Sunday 18th when the Battalion was relieved to Pont Logy for a few hours rest before returning to the line. From Tuesday 20th the Germans counter-attacked in force, succeeding in some part. On Thursday 22nd the Battalion was in front of Neuve-Chapelle where they came under heavy artillery fire. At 5.00pm their line came under attack which took an hour to repulse, at the point of the bayonet. During the morning of Tuesday 27th the left flank of the Battalion was turned in the fierce hand-to-hand fighting that took place moving from one house to another in the village. After ten days in the line they were relieved and sent to Richebourg St Vaast. On Friday 30th the Battalion was withdrawn for the last time in the sector and sent to Merris then onward across the Belgian border to Locre. After a period in billets they took the line on Thursday 5th November at Hooge to participate in the Battle of Nonne Bosschen on Wednesday 11th. On Friday 27th the Battalion moved to the Wytschaete sector, remaining there for several months, with billets provided in either Locre, Westoutre or Dranouter.
On Thursday 3rd June Robert and the Battalion marched to bivouac to the south of the Poperinghe to Vlamertinghe road. The Battalion was engaged for the ensuing week organising working parties taking barbed wire up to the line. On Wednesday 9th he marched along the Menin Road and went into the line at Hooge. After a three day tour followed by three days in camp he returned to the line to prepare for the attack on Bellewaarde. The attack was successful with 250 yards being gained. Tours of duty continued, mainly around Hooge, St Eloi and Wieltje. On Friday 24th September Robert took the line, this time in preparation for another attack on Bellewaarde. At 3.50am on Saturday 25th the British preliminary bombardment commenced; at 4.19am and 4.21am two pairs of mines were blown along the ridge. Immediately after the second pair of mines were blown Robert led his men forward and he was killed by machine-gun fire.

SECOND LIEUTENANT THOMAS FRANCIS GAWAN-TAYLOR

2nd Battalion York and Lancaster Regiment

Died on Monday 9th August 1915, aged 22

Commemorated on Panel 55.

Francis Gawan-Taylor

Francis was born in Darlington on Saturday 27th August 1892, second son of His Honour Judge Henry and Mrs Rachel Gawan-Taylor, of Croftlands, Heads Nook, Carlisle. He was a scholar of Rossall School from 1907 to 1912 and a member of the OTC before he went up to Sidney Sussex College, Cambridge, as a scholar. Francis was a keen athlete running the mile for the college. He was engaged to Alyson Boucher.
Francis was gazetted on Saturday 16th January 1915 and went to France on Tuesday 1st June 1915, joining the Battalion in the field on the Ypres Salient. Late on Monday 2nd August Francis took his platoon into the line at Hooge and prepared for an attack which would take place a week later. At 3.15am on Monday 9th he led his men forward in a swift and successful charge against the German lines under the cover of a creeping barrage. The German trenches were taken and a large number of prisoners taken. Francis was killed whilst consolidating the position.
His commanding officer wrote: *"Your son was one of my subalterns; he was a very promising young officer and was doing very well. We had to take some German trenches… It was while directing the consolidating of their trenches that he was hit by a bullet through both temples. The men of his platoon greatly regret his loss, as they had learned to love him."*
He is commemorated on Hayton War Memorial and in St Cuthbert's Church, Darlington.
His brother Norman, also of the York and Lancaster Regiment, was killed on Tuesday 24th April 1917 and is buried in Zantvoorde British Cemetery.

CAPTAIN JOHN GEDDES

16th Battalion Canadian Infantry
(Manitoba Regiment)
Died on Saturday 24th April 1915, aged 37
Commemorated on Panel 26.

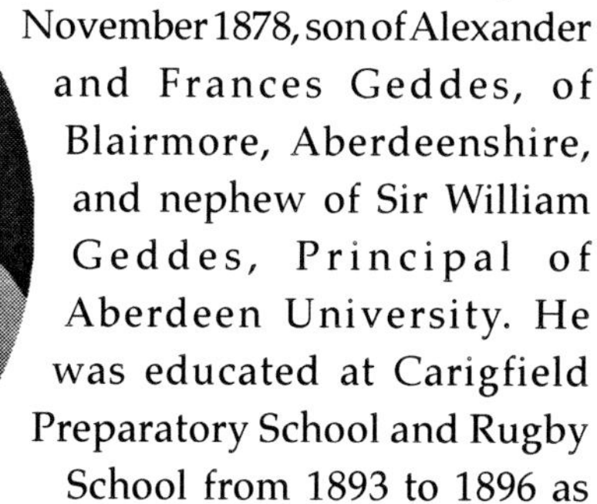

John Geddes as a young man and during the First World War

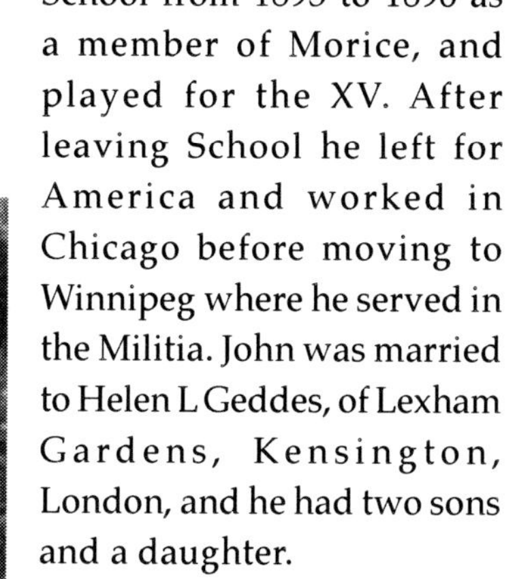

John born on Wednesday 6th November 1878, son of Alexander and Frances Geddes, of Blairmore, Aberdeenshire, and nephew of Sir William Geddes, Principal of Aberdeen University. He was educated at Carigfield Preparatory School and Rugby School from 1893 to 1896 as a member of Morice, and played for the XV. After leaving School he left for America and worked in Chicago before moving to Winnipeg where he served in the Militia. John was married to Helen L Geddes, of Lexham Gardens, Kensington, London, and he had two sons and a daughter.

Following the outbreak of war John volunteered for overseas service on Monday 7th September 1914 in Valcartier where he was described as Presbyterian, 5ft 11in tall, with a 39¼in chest, a fresh complexion, grey eyes, light hair, an appendix scar, vaccination mark on his left arm and a damaged second finger on his right hand.

John left Canada on Monday 28th September 1914 and sailed on *SS Andania* bound for Plymouth, landing on Thursday 15th October. John went with his men to Salisbury Plain for training for the Western Front. He left Avonmouth on Thursday 11th February 1915 for St Nazaire, arriving on Monday 15th.

... on Salisbury Plain with Stonehenge in the background (see Lieutenant Antrobus, above)

The Battalion was sent by train to Caëstre where final training was completed before being sent into the line at Bois Grenier.

At the end of March John marched to Estaires where the Battalion undertook training and rest until moving to Cassel on Wednesday 7th April. General Sir Horace Smith-Dorrien inspected the Battalion on Saturday 10th then General Edwin Alderson addressed them. On Friday 16th he marched to Steenvoorde where a fleet of buses collected the Battalion that took them to Vlamertinghe where they stopped and had lunch. At 2.30pm they paraded and marched to Ypres where they were met by guides that took them to Wieltje. At 8.30pm they moved to Poelkapelle into support trenches and immediately came under shell fire. On Tuesday 20th John was relieved and sent to billets in Ypres. During the afternoon of Thursday 22nd the town came under heavy shell fire and in the early evening the Battalion was ordered to parade along the canal as a major attack had commenced to the north. The saw French Zouaves fleeing the battlefield in confusion and agony — the results of the first gas attack. John took his men forward to support the line and prepared to counter-attack. The Battalion formed up in four lines, single rank, with thirty yards between them, behind the 10th Battalion. Shortly before midnight the counter-attack began and took over thirty prisoners, killing more than one hundred and wounding over three hundred and fifty. John and his men moved forward into a wood where they found four French artillery pieces. Furious fighting continued and reinforcements came to collect the guns. The Battalion was able to hang onto their position despite coming under heavy attack until John was killed leading his men.

One of his friends wrote: *"... he was one of the very first Officers of the 79th to volunteer. 'If they have any use for me, I am ready,' he said; and for the rest of his life he was a soldier."*

One of his School friends wrote: *"He was an absolutely fearless man. At School he never knew what fear was, and his one idea was to do things in a way to bring credit to his House. I have talked to several men who were at School with him, and we always remarked on his pluck, because it had stuck in our memories."*

One of his fellow officers wrote: *"Even after he was hit, and while dying, he kept crawling onwards, calling, 'Go on, boys, you'll win, you'll win!' He was a true born Highland gentleman; every single man in the Regiment felt that, and his death is indeed a heavy blow."*

His only brother, 2nd Lieutenant Alistair Geddes, died on Wednesday 16th June 1915 and is commemorated on Le Touret Memorial.

Liquid fire

Second Lieutenant William Purdon Geen

9th Battalion King's Royal Rifle Corps

Died on Saturday 31st July 1915, aged 23

Commemorated on Panel 51.

William was born in Newport, on Saturday 14th March 1891, son of Mr and Mrs W R Geen. He was educated at Northern Place, Potters Bar, followed by Haileybury where he played for the First XV and First XI. He went up to University College, Oxford, reading Classics, graduating in 1910 and was awarded his Rugby Blue. William played for the Barbarians, Blackheath, and Newport Rugby Football Clubs and was a Welsh Rugby International. In addition he was a good cricketer and played for Monmouthshire Minor Counties Cricket Club.

On Thursday 6th August 1914 William volunteered and enlisted, being sent to Petworth for training before he was gazetted.

He left for France on Thursday 20th May 1915. William took his men into the line on Thursday 29th July where at 3.15am the next morning a major attack took place on his line at Hooge. *'Flammenwerfer'* (flame throwers or 'liquid fire') was used against them, the first time it was used in the war and their line was forced back. Counter-attacks were made and the Battalion was able to recapture a short part of their trenches but William was killed in process.

L/9490 Private Charles Richard George

2nd Battalion The Buffs (East Kent Regiment)

Died on Sunday 14th February 1915, aged 23

Commemorated on Panel 14.

Charles was born in Stratford, London, on Monday 21st August 1893, eldest son of Charles and Catherine M George, of 26 Littlewood Road, Lewisham, London. He was educated at the Ennersdale Road School, Lewisham.

Charles became a professional soldier, enlisting in January 1910, joining the 1st Battalion The Buffs and served with them in Ireland for two years. After transferring to the 2nd Battalion he left with them to serve in India from January 1912.

At the outbreak of war Charles was in Wellington, India, and the Battalion was recalled to England. He sailed from Bombay on board *SS Ultonia* arrived in Plymouth on Wednesday 23rd December, and marched to camp in Winchester. Christmas was pretty dismal for Charles and his comrades; the camp was little more than a swamp, no provision was made for them, only some thin blankets to keep them warm — after years of warmth in India it was an unpleasant home-coming. It was a great relief when the Battalion was moved into billets in the town on Wednesday 6th January 1915. Prior to their departure for France HM King George V, accompanied by Field Marshal Lord Kitchener, inspected the Battalion on Tuesday 12th. Charles was paraded on Saturday 16th and was marched to Southampton where he embarked for Le Havre the next day. Upon arrival he was sent to camp prior to entraining for Hazebrouck where his training for the front line continued.

Prior to taking the line Field Marshal Sir John French, accompanied by HRH The Prince of Wales, inspected the Battalion on Thursday 28th. A few days later Charles was sent across the border into Belgium and undertook his first tour of duty close to the Ypres to Comines Canal where they relieved the French. Conditions in the trenches were dreadful, they were flooded with two feet of freezing water and many of his comrades suffered from frostbite or 'trench foot'. On his second tour of duty Charles was killed not long before the Battalion was relieved.

Germans mount an attack

His brother, Private Ernest George, died on Tuesday 24th October 1916 and is buried in Euston Road Cemetery, Colincamps.

LIEUTENANT HARRY VERNON GERRARD

2nd Battalion Border Regiment

Died on Monday 2nd November 1914, aged 36

Commemorated on Panel 35.

Harry was born in Dublin on Thursday 18th April 1878, son of Thomas Gerrard and was Crown Solicitor for Queen's County and Carlow. He was educated at King's School, Warwick, and Tipperary Grammar School where he excelled in athletics at both schools.

Harry was gazetted in August 1902 from the Militia, appointed Adjutant from May 1904 to July 1905, promoted Lieutenant in July 1905, and Captain in October 1914 (although not recorded as such by CWGC).

Harry embarked from Southampton on Monday 5th October and sailed to France with the Battalion on *SS Turkoman* and *SS Minneapolis* and went up to the Ypres Salient. Two days after arrival he entrained to Ghent where he assisted in its defence. The French Marines relieved them and the Borders marched to the Ypres Salient, arriving on Thursday 15th. After two weeks of serving in the line near Zandvoorde, at 10.00am on Monday 2nd November the German artillery opened up a violent barrage that continued until 3.00pm when their infantry commenced their assault. The German attackers came forward and were almost on top of the British lines before the machine-guns and rapid fire was unleashed on the attacking infantry. The result was devastating and piles of German dead lay in front of their parapet. Harry was killed by shell fire, one of the very many casualties taken by the Battalion.

Harry was Mentioned in Despatches gazetted on Thursday 14th January 1915.

His brother, Captain Percy Gerrard, was killed in the riots at Singapore on Monday 15th February 1915.

SECOND LIEUTENANT JOHN HARDIE GIBB

18th Battalion King's Royal Rifle Corps

Died on Tuesday 31st July 1917, aged 19

Commemorated on Panel 51.

John Gibb

John was born on Thursday 17th March 1898 son of William Doig Gibb and Mary Gibb, of 166 East Dulwich Grove, London. He was educated at Dulwich College from 1910 to 1916.

He joined the Officers Cadet Battalion in Oxford after leaving School and in January 1917 he was commissioned. He left for France in May 1917 joining the Battalion in the field in Belgium.

He and his men first saw major action on Thursday 7th June during the Battle of Messines where he was involved in supplying the front line under heavy fire. On Thursday 14th he took part in a successful attack on *'Olive Trench'*. On Tuesday 31st July John led his men forward at 3.50am under the cover of a barrage. The first objective was taken but the second, *'Forret Farm'* remained in German hands as the Battalion lost its bearings. John was mortally wounded by a sniper; shot through the lung whilst leading his men against the Farm in the early afternoon, near Hollebeke, and died an hour later.

SECOND LIEUTENANT RONALD CHARLES MELBOURNE GIBBS

'F' Company, 2nd Battalion Scots Guards

Died on Wednesday 28th October 1914, aged 21

Commemorated on Panel 11.

Ronald Gibbs and his family coat of arms

Ronald was born in Salisbury, Melbourne, Australia, on Sunday 26th August 1894, the second and younger son of the late Honourable Henry Gibbs and Alice Mary Gibbs, of 25 Cadogan Square, London, grandson of Henry, 1st Baron Aldenham (Governor of the Bank of England, previously Member of Parliament for the City of London) and General Charles Crutchley. He was educated at Wellington House, Westgate-on-Sea, Kent, followed by Eton College from 1908 to 1913 as a member of Mr Philip Vere Broke's House and was a member of the OTC obtaining his 'A' Certificate. Ronald was a keen rower and was part of the team that rowed for HM King George V and HM Queen Mary when they visited the school on Monday 16th June 1913. Ronald was a member of the Guards' Club.

Ronald was gazetted on Saturday 27th September 1913 and passed his Army exam in 1914.

Ronald was sent out to Zeebrugge on Sunday 4th October 1914. He entrained to Ghent where he assisted with its defence just before it fell. He marched with the Battalion via Thielt and Roeselare to the Salient with 'F' Company.

The Battalion had not been on the Salient for thirty-six hours before they went into the line. One week later Ronald was killed in action and was initially buried in Gheluvelt Château but the grave was subsequently lost. At 11.00pm Ronald was marching with his men

along the Menin Road when two shells were launched in their direction from close by. The first shell burst killing him, six men and two pack animals, the second burst harmlessly.
Lord Esmé Gordon-Lennox wrote: *"He was a splendid young officer... He had a charming disposition and showed such keenness and ability as an officer that the blow was all the harder. Liked by everybody he came in contact with, both officers and men, his death as been a great loss to the Regt."*
Roland was recorded in Debretts Obituary — War Roll of Honour published in the 1921 edition.
In St John The Baptist Church, Aldenham, Hertfordshire, a marble tablet was placed in his memory with the inscription: *"Remember in the Lord, Ronald Charles Melbourne Gibbs, Lieut. Scots Guards. Born 26th August A.D. 1894. Killed in action at Ypres 28th October A.D. 1914. Buried at Chateau Gheluvelt."*

Captain Robert 'Bob' Gibson

2nd Battalion King's Own Scottish Borderers
Died on Wednesday 5th May 1915, aged 26
Commemorated on Panel 22.

Bob Gibson

Bob was born on Monday 9th February 1891 elder son of James and Grace Gibson, of 28 Victoria Park Gardens North, Broomhill, Glasgow. He was educated at Glasgow High School and went up to Glasgow University where he graduated with a First Class Honours degree in Classics in 1908. Bob was awarded the Snell Exhibition and Newlands Scholarship and went up to Balliol College, Oxford, in 1907 where he graduated with a First Class Degree in Moderations and the Greats, he won prizes in Organic Chemistry and Civil Law and was then elected a Fellow, Tutor and Bursar. Bob was a member of the Oxford University OTC, as he had been at School and Glasgow University and President of the Arnold Society.
Bob was gazetted on Saturday 15th August 1914, leaving for France in September, and was appointed the Battalion Scout Officer. He was promoted in November and Mentioned in Despatches. Bob described wrote how, whilst in Ploegsteert Wood, he made bombs made from jam tins and about the hand-to-hand fighting that took place. On Sunday 25th April he took over the duties of Adjutant. He was killed at Hill 60, that was described as *"an irreparable loss to the College teaching staff"*.
One of his contemporaries from Balliol wrote: *"Bob Gibson had a fiery contempt for shams, that sort of white-hot*

Recipe for a Jam Pot Bomb

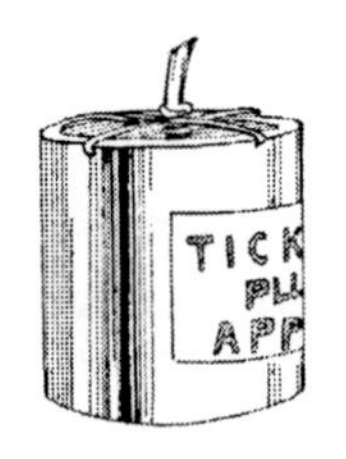

Take a jam pot.

Fill it with shredded gun-cotton and ten penny nails, mixed according taste.

Insert a No 8 detonator and short length of Bickford's fuze.

Clamp up the lid.

Light with a match, pipe, cigar or cigarette and throw for all you are worth.

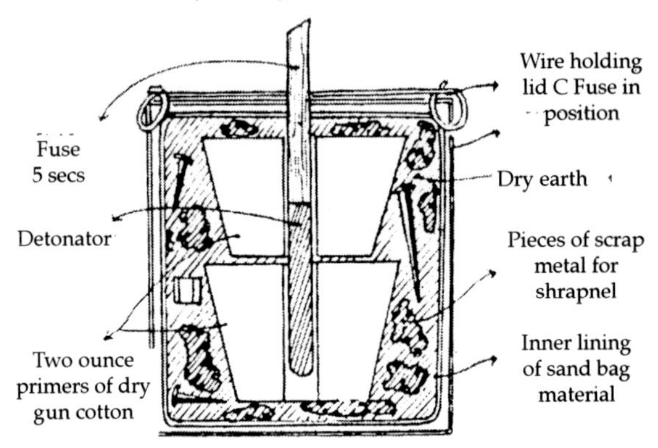

Hairbrush Grenade

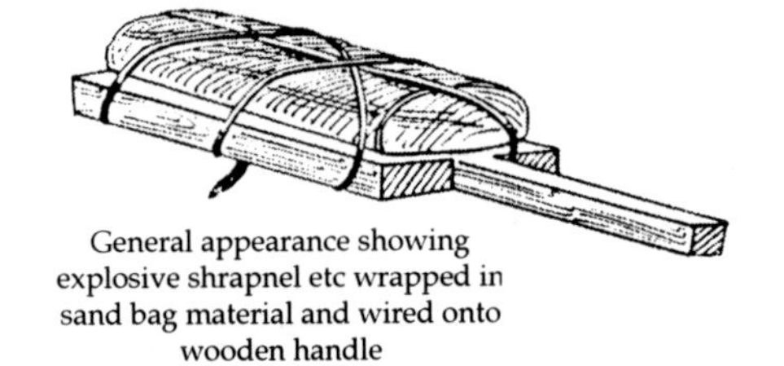

General appearance showing explosive shrapnel etc wrapped in sand bag material and wired onto wooden handle

Gas Pipe Grenade

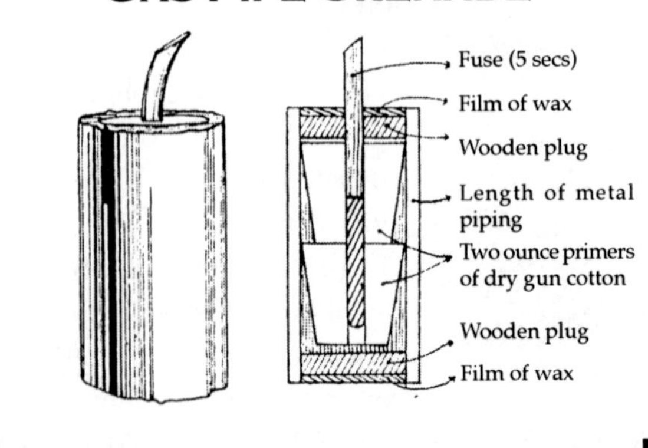

sincerity, before which accidents shrivel and only essentials remain. To spend a day or two with him was to have no illusions left about oneself. I have never know a man before whom one felt so mentally and morally naked — a wholesome experience, no doubt, but it meant that, while we all admired him, only some knew him well enough to realize that his heart was a warm as his brain was ruthless, and so learned to as they admired. To spend a day or two with him was to have illusions about oneself."

1957 Rifleman Geoffrey Gillate

London Regiment (Queen Victoria's Rifles)
Died on Thursday 29th April 1915, aged 22
Commemorated on Panel 54.

George was born in Camberwell, son of Mr E Unwin Gillate, of 57 Venner Road, Sydenham, London. He was educated at the Aske School, Hatcham, and after leaving school was employed by Messrs Pawsons & Leaf Limited.

Geoffrey volunteered and enlisted in London and was sent for training. He was sent out to join the Battalion with a draft. Geoffrey was trained during April 1915 for the attack that was to take place on Hill 60. At 7.00pm on Saturday 17th mines were blown which destroyed the top of the Hill and the Royal West Kents charged and captured the top. The Germans mounted a series of counter-attacks and by 6.00pm on Sunday 18th they had recaptured part of their lost lines. The Battalion was ordered to support a counter-attack. Captain George Culme-Seymour (commemorated on the Menin Gate see above) wrote: *"We've got the hill all right but we've lost a lot and I only hope and believe that they lost more. ... I went to the Lille Gate this evening to see the party off which was taking up rations to our machine-gun team and all the time wounded men kept passing us, chiefly hit in the head, judging by the bandages. Tremendous bombardment again this evening, and we got notice a few minutes ago to be ready to move off at short notice to support. The Prussians are against us and, of course, pretty tough fighters, but they're up against the best crowd in the whole world and I believe we'll do them all right. Nichols is doing Staff Captain and had a very narrow escape to-day I hear. The brigade staff are in our dug-out where we were the other day, and he was standing just outside with a lot of men. He left them and was just stepping inside when a big shell burst outside and killed the whole lot. One shell went on top of the dug-out and burst up one of the beams, but no one was hurt. The whole cutting is full of men killed and wounded, and of course it's the same in the trenches. We've got lots of men though and are quite all right. Everything will probably quieten down to-morrow. They made continuous counter attacks all last night, and two companies of them which were attacking at one time were wiped out by our machine-guns."*

The involvement of the Battalion at Hill 60 was substantial and their Memorial to the contribution remains to this day where so many of the men were killed.

On Sunday 25th April Geoffrey was serving at Wieltje when they were relieved and sent to Elverdinghe where he and his comrades were able to sleep and rest in the warm sun. At 6.00pm on Thursday 29th Geoffrey was ordered to parade and they returned to the line at Wieltje. Shortly after his arrival in the line he was killed.

Lance Corporal Norman Bell wrote: *"It was after the Canadians had been driven back and we were advancing again. A party of us had to go out to dig a trench right in advance of our lines, at night-time of course. After digging in one place we had to cross over some open ground right in front of the German position to get to another part of the trench. We ran across and some of our men jumped down into the trench, when we found that one named Clarke had been hit. Gillate immediately dropped his spade and ran out to try and help him, only to be hit himself. We got them both in and found that Clarke was dead, and that Gillate had three bullets in his body and only lived about twenty minutes. I was so struck by the manner of his death that I thought I would like his people to know, otherwise he will remain one of the 'nameless heroes' of this terrible war."*

8622 Company Quartermaster Serjeant Leonard Gillborn, DCM

1st Battalion Northumberland Fusiliers
Died on Sunday 15th November 1914, aged 29
Commemorated on Panel 12.

Citation for the Distinguished Conduct Medal:

"For conspicuous gallantry and devotion to duty, he led a party of fifty men and recaptured a stable and two trenches lost earlier in the day. On numerous occasions he exhibited fine courage and ready resources."

Leonard was born at home the son of Mrs Maria Gillborn, of 30 Norton Street, Radford, Nottingham.

Leonard enlisted in Nottingham and at the outbreak of war held the rank of Sergeant. Leonard embarked on *SS Norman* for Le Havre where he arrived at 3.00am on Friday 14th August 1914. A tiny Boy Scout led the Battalion from the docks to their camp at Eprémesnil six miles away. In the early hours of Sunday 16th he marched back into the town entraining to Busigny thence to billets in Landrecies. Following a series of marches they arrived on the Mons battlefield and took position along the Canal. Following the Battle the Battalion was ordered to take up defensive positions at Frameries where they engaged the Germans, inflicting heavy losses. Orders were given to retire and for the next

Northumberland Fusiliers from Mons to Ypres, 1914

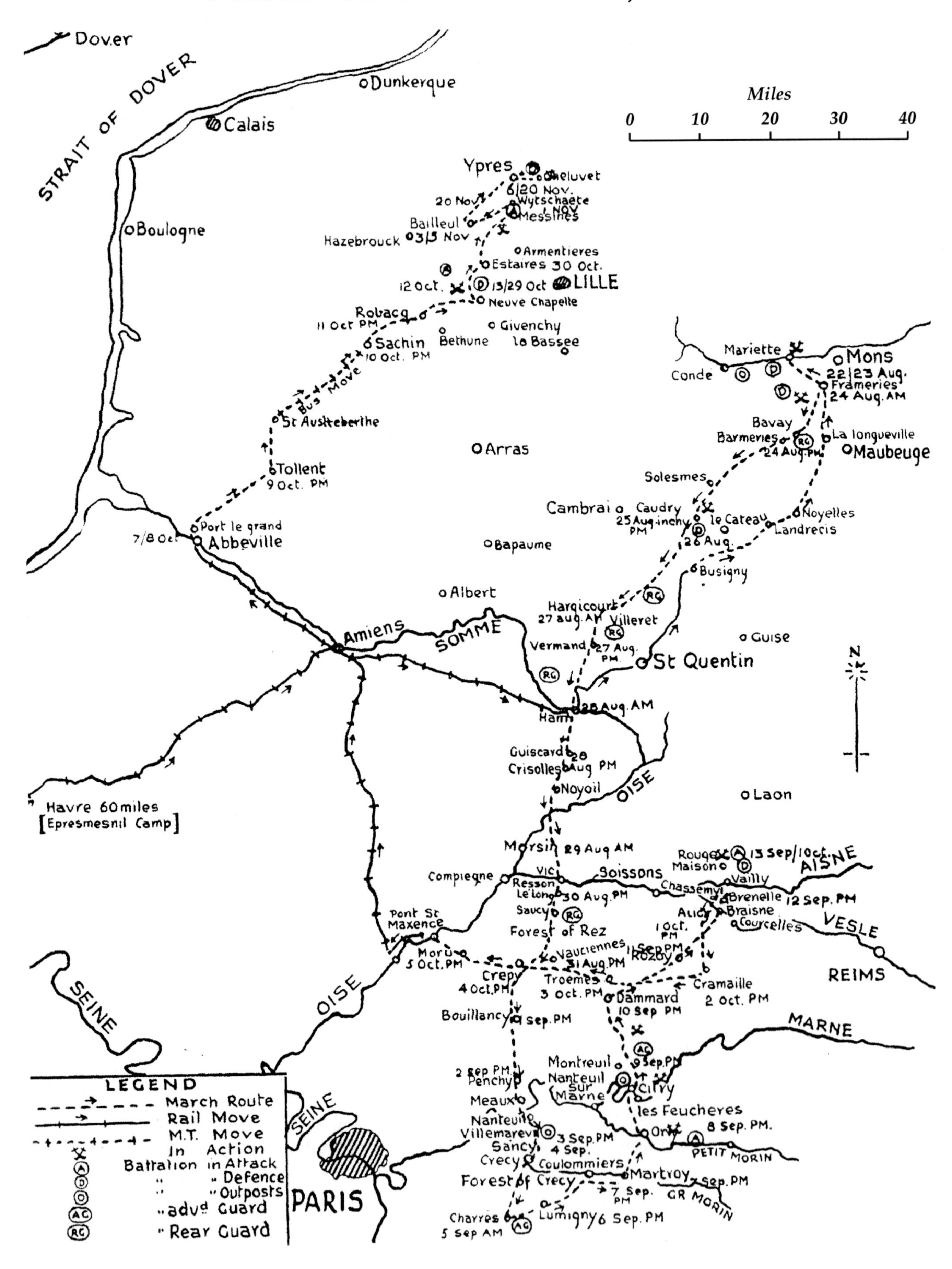

few days the Battalion acted as rearguard. Their march southwest continued until Saturday 5th September when orders were received to turn and engage the enemy. The next morning they left Châtres and advanced towards the Marne where on Tuesday 8th they were involved in a short skirmish at Orly. They continued to advance and fight their way to the Aisne which was reached on Monday 14th, at Vailly, when they came in range of the German artillery. To this point only three officers of the Battalion had been wounded: within seven days six were killed. Leonard continue to serve on the Aisne until Saturday 3rd October, arriving at Pont Maxence on Tuesday 6th where he entrained for Abbeville.

The Battalion arrived the next day and were sent to billets at Port le Grand for a rest of twenty-four hours. On Friday 9th he started a series of route marches and with a section being covered by motor buses that brought him to Mount Bernechon close to the La Bassée Canal on Monday 12th. The next day the German cavalry were advancing from Bout Deville and were pushing the Gordon Highlanders back. At 3.00pm the Battalion deployed to assist in countering the attack. Throughout the Wednesday 14th they continued the attack and took the village of Bout Deville. As they advanced on Thursday 15th Pont du Hem was taken however Croix Barbée remained in German hands. On Saturday 17th they participated in the successful attack on Herlies where they came under heavy artillery fire from Fromelles. On Monday 26th the Battalion was moved to Neuve-Chapelle to relieve the 1st Battalion, Lincolnshire Regiment. At 2.50pm the German laid down a barrage and attacked that was repulsed at the point of the bayonet and rapid fire accounted for a large number of the attackers. After sixteen days of continuous action the Battalion was relieved during the night of Thursday 29th to billets around Estaires where ten days rest was promised. Their rest lasted until 6.45am on Saturday 31st when they were marched across the border via Neuve Eglise to Kemmel. At 1.45am on Sunday 1st November they were ordered to support the line at Wytschaete and paraded within fifteen minutes. At 4.45am they were back in action mounting a counter-attack. In the fierce fighting that took place during the day and night the line moved forward and backwards, prior to being relieved they had been pushed back but had stopped the Germans from breaking through. The Official History recording: *"In the few hours' fighting, the Lincolnshire had lost 8 officers and 293 other ranks, and the Northumberland Fusiliers 5 officers and 93 other ranks, total representing 30 per cent. of the men present; but they had put up a fight worthy of the best traditions of the British Army."* The Battalion spent a day in their billets at Kemmel before marching to Bailleul where three nights of comfortable billets were provided. Leonard was able to have his first hot bath in weeks and was also provided with a clean uniform.

... Bailleul in 1914

On Friday 6th November Leonard paraded and marched along the cobbled roads to Ypres and took the line at Hooge close to Harenthage Château. On Sunday 8th Leonard was in the line when at 1.00pm the Germans launched an attack that was repulsed at the point of the bayonet. The Germans made a further attack at 5.30pm where they reached the British front line and had some initial successes but were again repulsed. A daily battle of nerves between the two front line trenches continued over the next couple of days. Leonard was one of the noted marksmen of the Battalion and he had particular success picking off large numbers of the enemy. On Wednesday 11th November the German artillery opened up just after dawn with the infantry pouring out of their trenches at 8.30am where they gained considerable ground. At 1.00am on Thursday 12th a counter-attack was launched without success and later in the evening the Germans launched a further attack however they were not able to advance any further. At 5.45am on Sunday 15th Leonard led fifty of his men against a farm building that had been hit by the British artillery, they gained the objective. In the action he was mortally wounded and awarded the Distinguished Conduct Medal for his bravery.

426190 Private Reuben George Gillespie

28th Battalion Canadian Infantry
(Saskatchewan Regiment)

Died on Tuesday 6th June 1916, aged 24
Commemorated on Panel 28.

Reuben was born in East Garafaxa, Ontario, on Sunday 11th September 1892, son of Mr and Mrs Andrew Gillespie, of Mawer, Saskatchewan. He was employed as a carpenter and was a member of the Militia.

On Tuesday 29th December 1914 he volunteered in Moose Jaw where he was described as a Methodist, 5ft 6in tall, with a 35½in chest, a fair complexion, blue eyes and brown hair. His brother, Private William Gillespie, died on the same day and is commemorated on the Menin Gate, see below.

Reuben and William were sent for training at Winnipeg until May 1915 when they sailed from Montreal to England. From June to September they trained at Shorncliffe where several inspections were carried out, the final one by HM King George V, accompanied by Field Marshal Lord Kitchener and Major General Sir Sam Hughes. They sailed to France where they entrained for northern France, taking the line for the first time on Saturday 25th September at Kemmel. They marched passed the Château with its graveyard in the grounds to the front. The sector was relatively quiet except for the Germans blowing two mines under their lines on Friday 8th October on their second tour of duty! The Germans advanced expecting to find the area undefended but the Battalion put up a good show and drove the Germans back. On Monday 31st January 1916, after a period of training, the Battalion took part in a successful raid on the Spanbroekmolen. Their tours of duty remained in the southern sector, mainly around Kemmel until early April when they were in front of St Eloi. On Monday 27th March the British blew a series of mines but an attack to follow did not take place for a further week. Reuben and William were in reserve at Dickebusch. It was a grim time at the front as described by one of the Staff Officers: *"... our front line is no line at all. The men are unprotected and in mud and filth, and have to be relieved every twenty-four hours."* From the beginning of April the brothers were at Voormezeele and when the Germans attacked in the early morning on Thursday 6th they came under heavy shell fire. During the evening reconnaissance parties went out to investigate the craters and the German front line. Teams of bombers went out and eventually established a presence on the craters. The situation for the Battalion was untenable. Colonel Embury wrote: *"I told Captain Styles he was to come round north of the craters. He started off at 11.30 and left part of his men with Major Daly. It was dark and raining hard, and we had never seen the ground before. The craters looked just like the ordinary ground (a morass). Styles went up and found Lieut. Murphy at 4 o'clock, but had no time to fix up for an attack. The men were all in; they had only had three hours' sleep in forty-eight."*

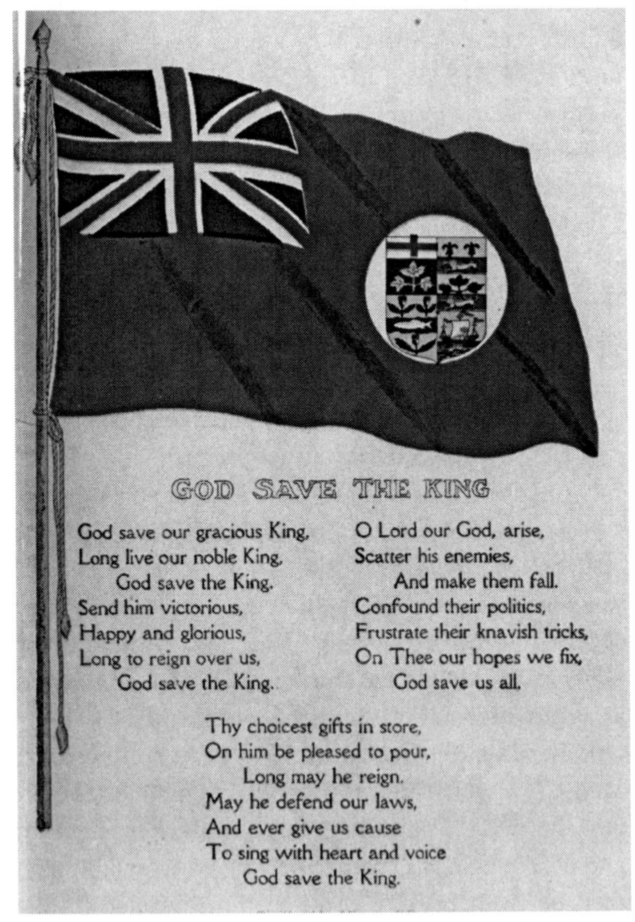

The Canadian Flag and National Anthem

For the next six weeks they undertook a series of tours into the line without being engaged in any particular action. On Tuesday 6th June Reuben and William were in the line at Hooge when the Germans attacked in force which almost annihilated the Battalion, and during the attack the brothers were killed.

426117 Private William James Gillespie

28th Battalion Canadian Infantry
(Saskatchewan Regiment)
Died on Tuesday 6th June 1916, aged 28
Commemorated on Panel 28.

William was born in East Garafaxa, Ontario, on Saturday 2nd June 1888, son of Mr and Mrs Andrew Gillespie, of Mawer, Saskatchewan. He had spent six months in the Militia.

On Monday 21st December 1914 he volunteered and enlisted in Moose Jaw where he was described as a Methodist, 5ft 8in tall, with a 35½in chest, a fair complexion, blue eyes, light brown hair and a scar on his left knee. His brother, Private Reuben Gillespie, died on the same day and is commemorated on the Menin Gate, for their story see above.

Lieutenant Arthur Gilliat-Smith

26th Field Company Royal Engineers
Died on Sunday 1st November 1914, aged 26
Commemorated on Panel 9.

Arthur Gilliat-Smith

Arthur was born in Blackheath on Tuesday 3rd July 1888, the only surviving son of Harold and Laura Sybil Gilliat-Smith, of 37 Kenilworth Street, St Leonards-on-Sea, Sussex. He was educated at St Paul's House, St Leonards, at Hillside, Godalming, followed by Rugby

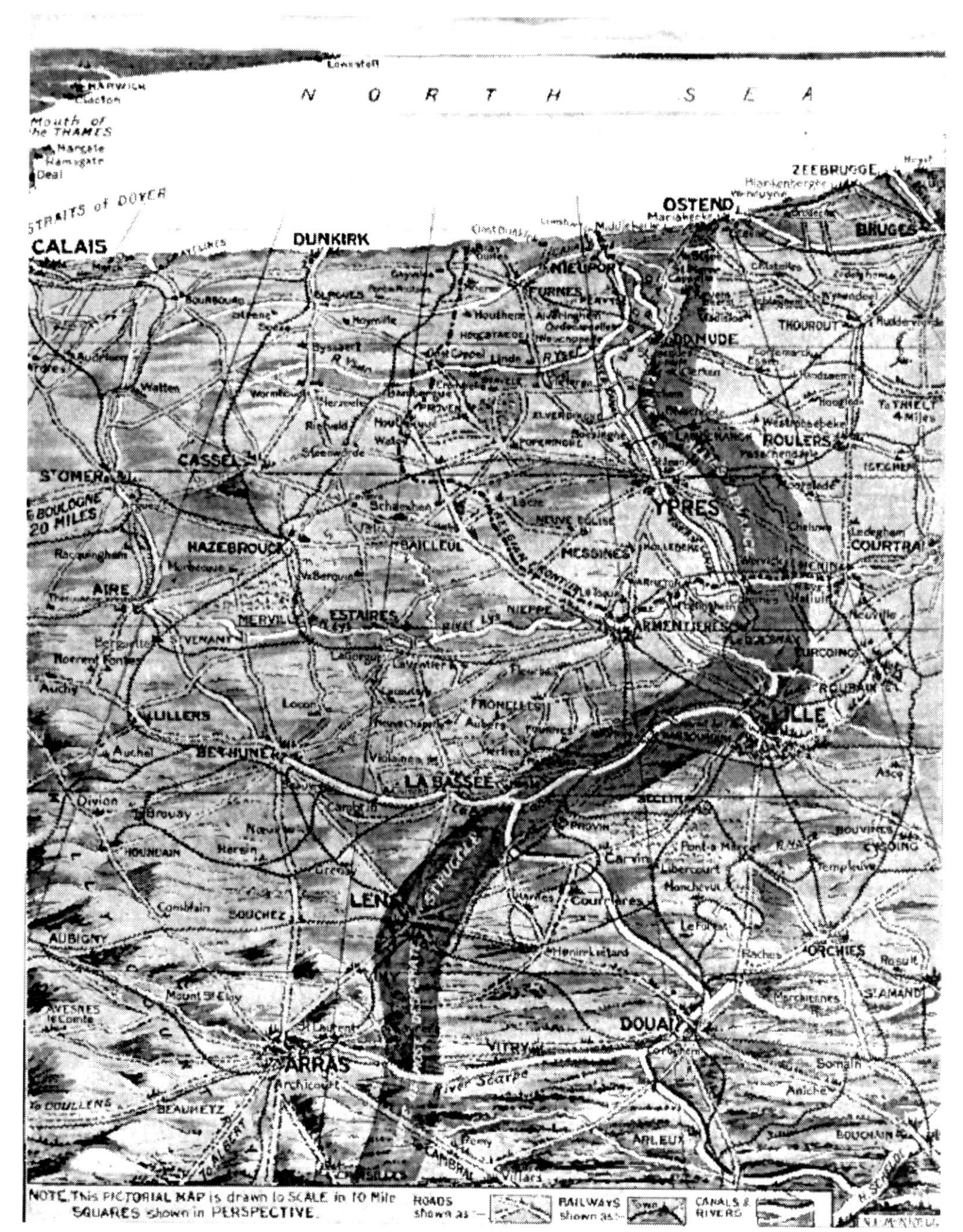

Flanders and northern France, 1914

School from 1902 to 1906 as a member of Whitelaw and passed into RMA Woolwich. He was a good horseman and won several point-to-point races and enjoyed skiing.
Arthur was gazetted to the Royal Engineers in December 1908 and promoted to Lieutenant in February 1911. He served in England until August 1914.
At the outbreak of war Arthur left with the BEF and landed in France and was sent to serve at Mons. Following the Battle of Mons he took part in the Retreat, the Battles of the Marne and Aisne. In early October Arthur was sent north to serve in the Ypres Salient. On Sunday 1st November Arthur was in reserve when ordered forward to reinforce the line that was coming under intense pressure. As he took his men across open ground Arthur was shot and killed.
His Commanding Officer wrote: *"A most keen and efficient Officer, who died gallantly leading his section."*

Captain Valentine Knox Gilliland

2nd Battalion Royal Irish Rifles

Died on Saturday 8th May 1915, aged 25

Commemorated on Panel 40.

Valentine Gilliland

Valentine was born on Friday 15th February 1889 son of George Knox Gilliland and Frances Jane Gilliland, of Brook Hall, Londonderry. He went up to Trinity College, Cambridge, in 1907.
Valentine left with the Battalion from Tidworth for Southampton. The Battalion split into two sections, one embarking on the *SS Ennisfallen* bound for Le Havre and the other on *SS Sarnia* bound

for Rouen. The Battalion reformed at a camp at Mont St Aigan, three miles from Rouen. On Sunday 16th they entrained for Aulnoye. After a period of training and rest Valentine marched north, crossed the Belgian border and was positioned east of Ciply at Nouvelles. From four o'clock on Sunday 23rd the Battalion came under heavy shell fire prior to the infantry attack which commenced at 6.00pm and which was repulsed by rapid fire. At 2.00am the next morning their retirement commenced, although the Battalion became separated from the rest of the Brigade. After a fierce and costly engagement at Caudry the retirement continued, now rejoined with the 7th Brigade. A long and tiring march was ahead of the Battalion. On Thursday 3rd September they crossed the Marne at Meaux and the bridge was blown by the Engineers immediately after they had crossed. The Retreat ended for Valentine and the men on Sunday 6th September when they turned to chase the German army. The Aisne was crossed on Monday 14th when he took position at Rouge Maison, Vailly. He remained on the Aisne until Friday 2nd October when he started the move north. Valentine was sent La Bassée where he saw considerable action until the end of the month when he was sent to Ypres.

Valentine's first taste of the Salient was at Hooge; after billets in Locre he marched north passing Messines and Wytschaete on his right. The Prussian Guard mounted a major attack on Wednesday 11th November at Nonne Bosschen where he and the Battalion assisted in repulsing them. On Friday 27th the Battalion moved to the Wytschaete sector where they served for several months with billets mainly in Locre, Westoutre and Dranouter. On Thursday 3rd June 1915 Valentine marched with the men into bivouac south of the Poperinghe to Vlamertinghe road. For the next week he arranged working parties taking barbed wire to the line. Valentine marched with his Company to Hooge on Wednesday 9th to undertake a three day tour of duty. After three days rest he returned and participated in an attack on Bellewaarde which captured two hundred and fifty yards of ground and was considered a great success. Trench life returned to normal with tours of duty in the Hooge sector, and he also served a tour at St Eloi and at Wieltje. At 7.10pm on Friday 24th September he paraded with his platoon and marched to Hooge to relieve the Honourable Artillery Company taking position ready for the attack on Bellewaarde. The British preliminary bombardment opened up at 3.50am, two pairs of mines were blown at 4.19am and 4.21am, after which the attack commenced. The wire had not been adequately cut and the German machine-gunners put up a good show and accounted for many of the men, including Valentine.

Valentine left £4,152 8s 5d in his will.

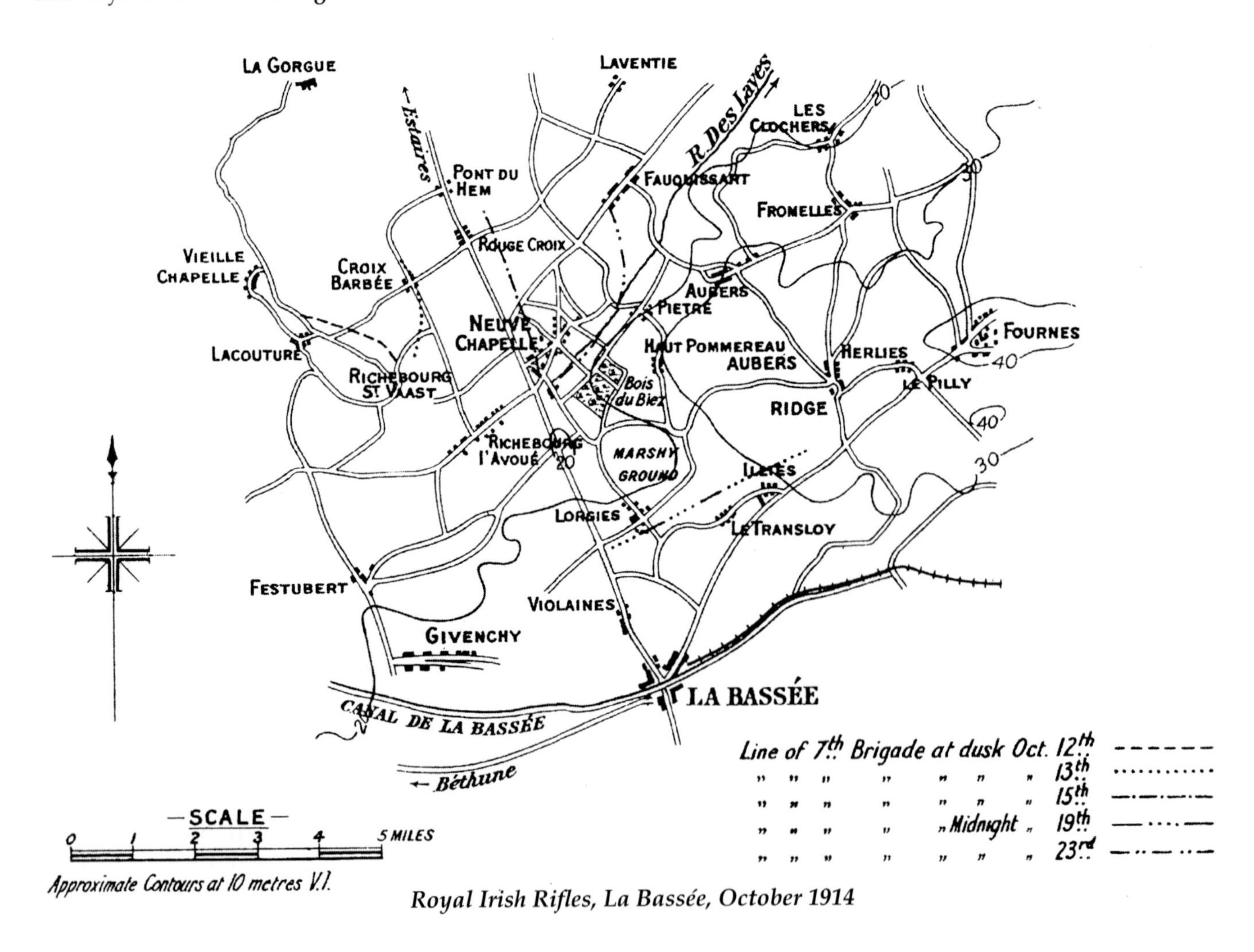

Royal Irish Rifles, La Bassée, October 1914

Lieutenant James Scott Elliot Gillon-Fergusson

5th Battalion attached 'A' Company, 3rd Battalion Middlesex Regiment

Died on Tuesday 27th April 1915

Commemorated on Panel 49.

James was the son of the late Mr and Mrs J Gillon-Fergusson, of Isle, Dumfriesshire.

James joined the Battalion at *'Mornhill Camp'*, Winchester, just before New Year 1914. On Tuesday 12th January 1915 the Battalion paraded for HM King George V who inspected them before they embarked for France. On Monday 18th they left Southampton for Le Havre arriving the next day. After a long and exhausting train journey they arrived in Hazebrouck and went into camp at Flêtre. Following a period of training they moved into Belgium to continue training at Ouderdom whilst being billeted a short distance away in Reninghelst. James' first experience of the front line and being under enemy fire was on Saturday 6th February at St Eloi. It was freezing cold (some of the men soon suffered with frostbite), they were on a lower slope with the German lines perched above them and their trenches were filled with freezing water. They were under heavy artillery fire and could be easily spotted by the German snipers. They remained in the line, except for one day, until Monday 15th. For the majority of March they were in the line at Rossignol waiting to support the line when required at St Eloi, but the call did not come. In April they went through Ypres and were sent to St Jan. During the evening of Friday 23rd April the Battalion entrenched across the crossroads in St Jan. They came under heavy shell and gas-shell fire before the Germans opened up with heavy machine-gun fire and wiped out the majority of the platoon of 'A' Company, including James.

Lieutenant Reginald Nigel Gipps

1st Battalion Scots Guards

Died on Saturday 7th November 1914, aged 23

Commemorated on Panel 11.

Reginald was born in London on Sunday 22nd November 1891, son of the late General Sir Reginald Gipps, GCB, and Lady Evelyn Charlotte Gipps, of Sycamore House, Farnborough, Hampshire, and 11 Chester Street, London SW — his grandfather had been the Governor of New South Wales. He was educated at Wellington College from 1905 to 1909 as a member of Bevir and passed into RMC Sandhurst in 1910. Reginald was a keen polo player, and was in the battalion team. He held memberships of the Guards' and Boodle's Clubs.

Reginald Gipps

Reginald was gazetted on Saturday 4th February 1911, promoted to Lieutenant on Sunday 19th January 1913, and served in Egypt from 1913.

Reginald left for Le Havre on Thursday 13th August from Southampton on *SS Dunvegan Castle,* and proceeded from there to the Battle of Mons where he was in reserve and did not see any action. He took part in the Retreat and marched over two hundred miles until Sunday 6th September when orders were received to turn and engage the enemy. He fought in the Battle of the Marne where he first saw action before moving forward to the Chemin des Dames and the Battle of the Aisne. He remained in the ghastly sodden trenches until Saturday 17th October when he entrained for Hazebrouck.

Reginald marched with his men to Poperinghe into their billets for the night. The next day they went through Elverdinghe and Boesinghe to the trenches in front of Langemarck. From here he was sent along the Menin Road to see action until his death in the front line in the area of Gheluvelt. On Sunday 1st November Reginald organised his men to dig a new line in between Gheluvelt and Veldhoek. The next day the German barrage opened up again with even greater ferocity than before. After a couple of days of sharp action he took a position around a burnt-out farm house at the edge of Gheluvelt Wood; he was killed during shelling of their position.

The Battalion Diary records for the period: *"The 4th was a comparatively quiet day, on which a point d'appui was made at a burnt farm-house near Gheluvelt. In this position the line remained till the 7th, suffering from German artillery fire on each day. On the 4th and 5th reinforcements of 110 men arrived, and Lieutentants R. N. Gipps and F. A. Monckton were killed on the 7th."* (Lieutenant Francis Monkton is commemorated on the Menin Gate, see below.)

Francis Monckton

Reginald was recorded in Debretts Obituary — War Roll of Honour published in the 1921 edition.

A memorial was placed in his memory in Victoria Road Cemetery Chapel, Farnborough with the inscription: *"To the honour of God and in dear memory of Reginald Nigel, Lieutenant Scots Guards, elder son of General Sir Reginald R. and Evelyn C. W. Gipps. Born Novr. 22nd 1891. Killed in action in Flanders Novr. 7th 1914. 'Give rest, O Christ, to Thy servant with Thy saints: where sorrow and pain are no more: neither sighing, but life everlasting.' - Russian Contakior. 'A good soldier of Jesus Christ' 2.Tim.II.3."*

7774 Private Robert George Girbow

2nd Battalion Suffolk Regiment

Died on Wednesday 16th December 1914, aged 22

Commemorated on Panel 21.

Robert was born at home, son of John Girbow, of 8 Alms Row, Bridewell Lane, Bury St Edmund's.
Robert had arrived in the front line at Wulverghem on Sunday 15th November 1914. At the end of the month he moved to the Sherpenberg and was billeted in Locre where General Sir Horace Smith-Dorrien inspected them and four days later paraded along the road as HM King George V visited the area.
Robert was in the front line near Kemmel when his Captain, Arthur Temple, was shot dead who fell and died in his arms (he is commemorated on the Menin Gate, see below). Robert was killed twenty-four hours later at the same spot.

Captain Temple

Second Lieutenant Albert Øle Moller Gjems

5th Battalion attached 2nd Battalion Royal Fusiliers

Died on Wednesday 8th August 1917, aged 22

Commemorated on Panel 8.

Albert was the son of the late Andreas and Kathinka Gjems. He was to have gone up to Oriel College, Oxford, but the war intervened.
Albert served during the Battle of Arras, on Tuesday 24th April 1917 he led his men forward from *'Shrapnel Trench'* at Zero Hour, 4.00am. German resistance was still and the Battalion took particularly heavy casualties, although the Germans lost more.
Following the Battle of Arras Albert continued on tours of duty until he was sent to Flanders where he trained for the forthcoming offensive. The Royal Fusiliers were heavily involved during the Battle of Passchendaele where Albert was killed.

266426 Serjeant Joseph William Gladding, DCM

Hertfordshire Regiment

Died on Tuesday 31st July 1917, aged 34

Commemorated on Panel 54.

Citation for the Distinguished Conduct Medal, London Gazette, Friday 26th January 1917:

"For conspicuous gallantry in action. He led his platoon with great gallantry, and himself accounted for many of the enemy. He set a splendid example throughout."

Joseph was born in Ponders End, Middlesex, son of George and Elizabeth Gladding, of 3 Wades' Mill, Ware, Hertfordshire. He was married to Emily Elizabeth Gladding, of 4 Railway Street, Norwich.
Joseph enlisted in Hertford. On Thursday 5th November 1914 he entrained from Bury St Edmunds and sailed on the *SS City of Chester* for Le Havre. After two days in a rest camp they entrained for St Omer and on Tuesday 10th November Field Marsh Sir John French visited them and undertook an inspection. The next day they were taken by motor bus to Vlamertinghe, sent through Ypres and along the Menin Road to Hooge. They remained in the sector until the end of the month when they were sent to Méteren for training. On 8th January 1915 they were ordered to Richebourg St Vaast and two days later relieved the Irish Guards. He spent the rest of the year in the northern France sector, mainly using Béthune for billets. Joseph saw action during the Battle of the Somme and in late 1916 was in front of the *'Schwaben Redoubt'*. Towards the end of November he was sent back to the Ypres Salient, arriving on Tuesday 28th in Poperinghe. The next day he took the line on the Ypres to Comines Canal and spent Christmas in the line. On Sunday 7th January 1917 Joseph came under heavy artillery fire which was followed by a raid where the Germans captured three of his colleagues. Until March he was in the line either on the Canal or in the Wieltje sector. In March and April he served on *'Observatory Ridge'* before returning in May to trenches on the Canal. On Monday 27th May he was relieved from the line and two days later went to camp at Wormhoudt. On Sunday 3rd June a special parade was held to celebrate HM King George V's birthday. After training and a series of route marches the Battalion arrived in Watten where they entrained for Poperinghe on Friday 29th June and were sent into the line on the Canal once more, relieving the Cambridgeshire Regiment. On Tuesday 17th they were sent back to Watten for further training ready for the offensive at the end of the month. On Monday 30th Joseph was sent to his assembly position in the *'Hill Top'* sector. At 3.50am on Tuesday 31st he moved forward toward Langemarck. They charged

a German strong point which they captured. As they advanced further the German wire remained uncut and very deep and here Joseph was killed.

6859 Private
Frank Glasspool, DCM

1st Battalion Hampshire Regiment

Died on Sunday 9th May 1915, aged 29

Commemorated on Panel 35.

Citation for the Distinguished Conduct Medal, London Gazette, Thursday 1st April 1915:

"For gallant conduct on the night of 16th-17th December 1914, in going within fifteen yards of the enemy's lines and locating the position of a machine-gun."

Frank was born at home, son of Mrs A Glasspool, of Steventon Warner, Overton, Basingstoke, Hampshire. Frank enlisted in Winchester.
Frank was awarded the Distinguished Conduct Medal whilst in the line at Le Gheer, when he went out with Lance Corporal Alfred Irish (commemorated on the Menin Gate, see below) reconnoitring and Frank reported the position of a particularly troublesome machine-gun.
After serving in the Ploegsteert area from mid-October 1914 until the Spring of 1915, Frank was in the line at the heart of the Salient. They supported the line after the first gas attack and were in front of *'Mouse Trap Farm'* in a particularly weak position. Each time trenches were hastily dug they were destroyed by German artillery; Frank was killed by shell-fire in one such attack.

2585 Private
Tom Hatcher Godfree

1st Battalion Honourable Artillery Company

Died on Wednesday 16th June 1915, aged 25

Commemorated on Panel 9.

Tom Godfree

Tom was the son of Alfred and the late Kate Godfree, of Kingswood, Burnt Ash Road, Lee, London. He was educated at Colfe's Grammar School from 1903 to 1905.
Tom volunteered and enlisted on Wednesday 18th November 1914 and left for France on Monday 25th April 1915. On Tuesday 15th June he marched to Ypres through the Lille Gate, leaving via the Menin Gate. They marched along the Menin Road to Hooge and took position in the front line awaiting the attack the next day. At 2.30am the British artillery opened up which lasted until 4.15am when the whistles blew and he charged towards the German front line. They were under continuous fire and heavy casualties were suffered, including Tom.
His brother, Private Reginald Godfree, died on Thursday 15th March 1917 and is buried in Gommecourt British Cemetery, No 2, Hebuterne.

Second Lieutenant Alan Godsal

7th Battalion Rifle Brigade

Died on Friday 30th July 1915, aged 21

Commemorated on Panel 46.

Alan Godsal

Alan was born at Hawera, New Zealand, on Friday 4th May 1894, second son of Edward Hugh and Marion Grace Godsal. He was educated at Oundle School from May 1905 to 1913 as a member of Berrystead and subsequently of School House. At the outbreak of war Alan volunteered and was gazetted on Tuesday 22nd September 1914. On Wednesday 19th May 1915 he sailed from Folkestone to Boulogne with his Battalion on the *SS Queen*. After a short period he was sent to the Ypres Salient and went into training at Dranouter. In July he was appointed Battalion Machine Gun Officer.
After a particularly difficult tour of duty in front of Hooge he was relieved by the 8th Battalion shortly before midnight and returned to camp at Vlamertinghe, arriving at 3.45am the next morning. Just as Alan and the men flopped down onto their beds the Germans launched their attack on Hooge using *'minenwerfer'* in their preliminary barrage, followed by an attack using *'Flammenwerfe*r' (flame throwers or 'liquid fire') for the first time. An hour later Alan was roused and ordered to get the men to 'stand to'. At 7.00am they marched off, unfed and without any rest to return along the cobbled road to Ypres. They were halted whilst their Colonel, Heriot-Maitland, received orders from Headquarters in the Ramparts of the town. The movement out to the line was difficult and it was not until 1.30pm that they arrived at their assembly position at *'Zouave Wood'*. He led his men in the advance and was able to recapture one of the machine-guns, and was last seen firing his revolver at the enemy who were using liquid fire. He was killed when a shell burst and struck him in the face. Private Frank King* went to pull him in but was killed in the attempt, and he was subsequently buried in *'Sanctuary Wood'*. (* Private Frank King is commemorated on the Menin Gate, see below.)

Colonel Heriot-Maitland wrote: *"... quite my most promising officer"*.

A brass plaque was erected in his memory in St Nicholas Church, Hurst, with the inscription: *"In honour of our Lord Jesus Christ and in memory of Alan Godsal 2nd Lieut: and Batt: Machine Gun Officer 7th Bn. Rifle Brigade: younger son of Edward Hugh & Marion Grace Godsal and nephew of William Charles Godsal of Haines Hill. Born at Hawera, New Zealand, May 4th 1894. Killed in action at Hooge, Flanders July 30th 1915. Be thou faithful unto death and I will give thee a crown of life."*

5322 Private Albert Edward Goldsworthy

1st Battalion Lincolnshire Regiment

Died on Sunday 1st November 1914, aged 33

Commemorated on Panel 21

Albert was the son of William and Ann Goldsworthy, of 2 Result, Frizington. He was educated locally. Albert was married to Mary Ellen Goldsworthy, of 1 Jane Street, Frizington, Cumberland.

On Thursday 13th August 1914, at 6.15am, Albert marched from Victoria Barracks, Portsmouth, and entrained to Southampton. They sailed to Le Havre on board *SS Norman*, arriving at 2.30am the next morning. They remained in camp six miles outside the town that had become a swamp due to the continuous rain, for a couple of days before being sent to Landrecies where they billeted in the Dupleix Barracks. Albert was marched to Mons along the cobbled roads, through the villages and hamlets where they were greeted by the local inhabitants. Throughout the march gifts were exchanged, the men received flowers, food, beer and other presents and in return they gave their cap badges, buttons and other miscellaneous kit! As they camped overlooking the old battlefield of Malplaquet, Lieutenant Colonel Smith wrote: *"You will find outposts to-day on the general railway to Riez de l'Erelle, both inclusive, connecting with the outposts of the 8th and 13th Brigades respectively on your flanks."* They went into the line from Jemappes towards the Bois de Boussu on the canal from where they were sent to Cuesmes.

The Battle of Mons passed without incident for Albert and at 6.00pm on Sunday 23rd he was ordered to get ready to march — the Battalion retired to Frameries. They took a position in an orchard where they came under heavy shell-fire. Lieutenant Colonel Smith wrote: *"It was undoubtedly the steady and accurate fire of the Lincolnshires which enabled them to maintain their position. The Germans seemed quite non-plussed. They no doubt expected to get close up to our position without serious loss and then rush it. The enemy also probably exaggerated the effect of the intense shell-fire, which our night-long preparations had seriously discounted. Whilst in action our machine-guns did great execution; but in such a cramped position it was inevitable that they should be quickly located and knocked out."* They had to retire at speed and the wounded were taken to the local convent: only the walking wounded escaped captivity. The Germans entered the village and the German Battalion History recorded: *"Up to all the tricks of the trade from their experience of small wars, the English veterans brilliantly understood how to slip off at the last moment."*

Frameries in 1914

The retirement continued and on Tuesday 25th a Taube appeared over them and they opened rapid fire. A British machine appeared and was able to bring it down and it crash-landed close to them: the pilot and observer were taken prisoner. They took a position at Le Cateau where the Battalion took a few casualties; from there The Retreat commenced. The march seemed endless as QMS North recorded: *"At daybreak they were still marching. The rain ceased and as the sun rose in the heavens its rays became hotter and hotter. No one kept count of time. No one bothered about which villages were passed through. The only village that mattered was the one in which the battalion would billet wherever it might be, as there would be a chance of getting some sleep and perhaps some rations."*

In sixteen days Albert had marched two hundred and thirty-seven miles by the time they arrived on the Marne at Bezu where they saw their first action since Le Cateau. They were under heavy shell fire which was returned, Captain Hoskyns recalled: *"Never have I had such big gun hunting. We first started in file, not knowing if the Germans were in the wood or not — we never knew when machine-guns would open on us unawares as we crossed the many sides tracks in the wood. At last, after some time, we came to a broad ride and felt that here at least the Bosche must surely have someone, as the reports of his guns seemed quite close. A minute's anxiety as we pushed a few men across at intervals, and as no horrid 'phut, phut' came, I got my Company over and formed them into line, C company doing the same on my right, to beat through the wood. I went ahead with my Sub, Thruston — and as we got near to the further edge we went warily and silently, followed by our men, who had thoroughly entered into the spirit of our hunt. As Thruston and I got near to the edge we distinctly saw the German artillery in line, firing at right angles to our advance on their left, and nearest gun about one hundred and fifty yards from the wood, and to our horror, we also saw a few yards off a Bosche sentry looking in our direction. I now felt that the game was up and called to Thruston, who was carrying a rifle to 'down him'. No sooner said than the Bosche was shot and our men, who were level with us, opened fire on the German gunners: these, taken entirely by surprise, tried to turn their guns round on us, but long before this was done we had shot them down."*

The onward march continued and they soon reached Soissons which was followed by the Battle of the Aisne that Albert fought through until Friday 2nd October when the Battalion was relieved from the line, entraining for Abbeville on Tuesday 6th. The Battalion Diary records: *"The men were in a very exhausted condition. Seventeen days in the wet and mud of the trenches with no time to take off their clothing and only one day on which they would take their boots off had made their feet in a very bad state. Following this were three forced marches. These abnormal conditions accounted for their exhaustion. After a four hours wait, during which the men were able to cook and make hot tea, the Battalion entrained and proceeded via Amiens to Longpré, where we arrived about 8.00 p.m., and halted there till 11.00 a.m. on the following day, when we went on to Abbeville, where we detrained."*

They moved to La Bassée and took a position on the canal. On Saturday 17th they attacked Herlies, the Battalion Diary records: *"The village of Herlies, looking at it from the point of view of our attack, was situated at the foot of a long and gentle slope, perfectly open and at the time covered with beet. On our side the village was defended by strong entrenchments, further protected by barbed-wire entanglements. The enemy was in considerable force of infantry and was supported by machine-guns and a horse battery. The distance to be crossed was 1,450 yards. Battalion advanced in lines to within 1,000 yards of position, when we commenced to return the heavy fire poured into us. From thence we worked our way by short rushes to within five hundred yards of the forward trenches. At this point an urgent order was received that the village must be carried before dusk. Whereupon Colonel Smith gave the order to 'cease fire'."*

By the end of the month they moved to Armentières and from there to Kemmel where they arrived on Saturday 31st and went into the line on the Messines Ridge. The Germans attacked in great strength at Wytschaete and reinforcements were needed. Albert and the Battalion was sent to assist. The fight was intense and he was killed during the day.

His brother, Private Alfred Goldsworthy, died on Friday 30th April 1915 and is commemorated on the Menin Gate, see below.

18194 Private Alfred Ernest Goldsworthy

1st Battalion Canadian Infantry
(Western Ontario Regiment)

Died on Friday 30th April 1915, aged 27
Commemorated on Panel 10.

Alfred was born in Cleaton Moor Cumberland, on Saturday 10th December 1887, son of William and Ann Goldsworthy, of 69 Result, Frizington, Cumberland. He went out to Canada on Monday 18th March 1907 and was employed as a miner. On Sunday 3rd January 1915, in Laxey, Isle of Man, Alfred married Ellen Elizabeth Goldsworthy (née Joiner).

On Sunday 23rd September 1914 he volunteered and enlisted at Valcartier where he was described as a Wesleyan, 5ft 5in tall, with a fair complexion, blue eyes, brown hair, four vaccination marks on his left arm, and scars on his left elbow and on his neck.

Alfred was sent for training prior to joining the Battalion in England at *'Bustard Camp'* on Salisbury Plain. He continued to train until Sunday 7th February 1915 when the Battalion started its move to Avonmouth and embarked on *HMT Architect*, leaving at 11.45pm the next evening bound for St Nazaire. At 8.00am on Friday 12th the ship docked and he entrained for Strazeele from where he marched to billets in Merris. Training continued until Wednesday 17th when he marched to Armentières where he undertook his first visit to the trenches attached to the 2nd York and Lancashire Battalion for practical experience which lasted until Tuesday 23rd. Alfred returned to Merris for five days rest and training from where he was sent to Fleurbaix.

He continued on tours of duty and training until he moved to Oudezeele on Tuesday 6th April, arriving at 2.30pm where he remained training until Sunday 18th: he was then sent to Proven via Watou for two days before being sent to *'Camp B'* in Vlamertinghe. Whilst in camp the Germans launched the first gas attack at 5.00pm on Thursday 22nd. The Battalion was ordered to 'stand to' and at 1.40am on Friday 23rd marched to Brielen, together with the 4th Battalion leading the way. At 5.00am they were ordered to attack Pilkem village and by 9.30am they had advanced to within five hundred yards of the crest of the ridge where they halted and entrenched. At 3.45pm the French infantry

Furthest point reach during the afternoon
Line by 7.15pm
Shrine
British line
German front line
Cut willows
Roads
Tracks
Buildings

Plan of the action on Friday 23rd April
1st Battalion Canadian Infantry

advanced to his left and Colonel Augustus Geddes, of The Buffs, took his men through Alfred's line and went forward capturing some of the of the advanced trenches (the Colonel was killed in action and is buried in Ypres Reservoir Cemetery). At 11.30pm Alfred was led forward and relieved the troops in the forward position. He remained in the line until 7.00pm until Saturday 24th under intensive artillery, machine-gun and rifle fire. They received little support from the British artillery, only one battery was engaged. When relieved from the line he marched via Wieltje to Fortuin and supported an attack on St Julien. At 8.00pm on Sunday 25th Alfred was withdrawn and sent to the west bank of the Yser Canal where he assisted in digging a series of trenches before returning to Vlamertinghe. At 8.00pm on Wednesday 28th he returned to the line where he was mortally wounded during the action. His brother, Private Albert Goldsworthy, died on 1st November 1914 and is commemorated on the Menin Gate, see above.

Colours of the 4th Battalion Canadian Infantry

Lieutenant Henry William Goodden

Royal Army Medical Corps
attached 2nd Battalion Royal Irish Regiment
Died on Sunday 9th May 1915, aged 31
Commemorated on Panel 56.

Henry was born on Tuesday 11th September 1883, son of Dr Wyndham C Goodden, of 5 Park Place Villas, Paddington, London. He was educated at Clifton College from 1892 to 1899. He attended Bristol Royal Infirmary to study medicine, as well studying in Paris and Vienna.

He went out at to France with the BEF and was wounded at the Battle of the Aisne.

Henry was attached to the Royal Irish Regiment, joining them in the field at Le Bizet in mid-March 1915. He served in the sector until the end of April when the Battalion was sent to La Brique. Henry was in the line at St Julien when on Monday 3rd May the Germans sent over poison gas, the first time that he had to deal with such an attack or with its consequences. From Saturday 8th the Battalion came under heavy artillery fire and it continued throughout the next day when Henry was killed by a shell.

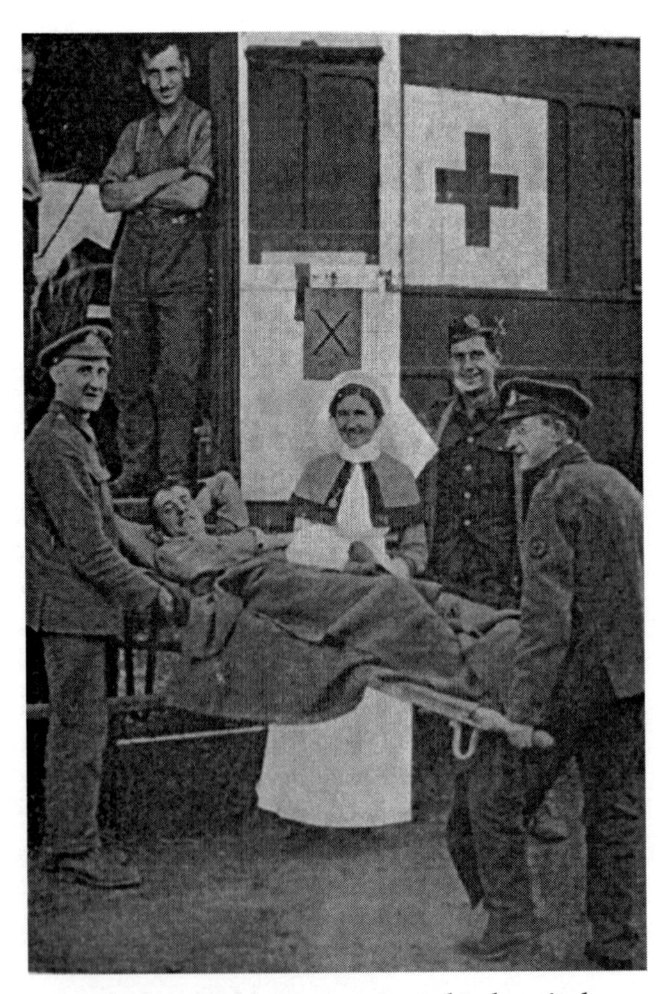

The wounded being transported to hospital

B/3022 Lance Corporal Godwin Blade Gooding

7th Battalion Rifle Brigade
Died on Saturday 24th July 1915
Commemorated on Panel 46.

Godwin was the son of Mr and Mrs Gooding. He went up to Christ Church, Oxford, in 1902.
He volunteered and was sent for training. On Wednesday 19th May 1915 he sailed from Folkestone to Boulogne with his Battalion on *SS Queen*. He was sent to Watten for further training and spent a week attached to the Lincolnshires and Leicestershires for front line experience from Friday 28th May. Godwin undertook a series of duties until Friday 23rd July 1915 when he was sent into the line at Hooge, the day after the British had blown their mine. The line was under very heavy shell fire as he arrived which destroyed much of the trenches and the night was spent repairing the damage. At 8.00am the next morning the Germans blew a mine of their own to the left of the British one, destroying all the work that Godwin had undertaken throughout the night. The Germans sapped their way forward, Godwin and his comrades countered with bombs. The fight was fierce and during the action he was killed.

8930 Lance Corporal Francis Rueben Gorbey

1st Battalion Royal Irish Regiment
Died on Friday 23rd April 1915, aged 25
Commemorated on Panel 33.

Francis Gorbey

Francis was born in Villerstown, Waterford, on Wednesday 13th November 1889, the son of Mrs Ellie Gorbey, of 9 The Terrace, Tranmore, County Waterford, and the late Mr John W Gorbey.
Francis joined the Army on Thursday 22nd March 1906.
Francis landed at Le Havre on Sunday 20th December 1914 from where the Battalion entrained for Arques, arriving at 5.50pm the next day. On Thursday 7th January 1915 they marched to Merris and after a night resting in the village, they continued to Mount Kokereele on Friday 8th. From Monday 11th the Battalion commenced a relief at Vierstraat and remained in the line until Saturday 16th. After a short period of rest they returned to the trenches at St Eloi where the first man of the Battalion was killed.
The daily routine was described: *"... began with the "stand-to" for an hour before daylight, during which time the parapets were manned in anticipation of a possible surprise attack. When day broke the order was passed along to "stand down" and officers and men had hot tea or coffee. Little was done during the day. Rations, letters and home parcels came up from the dump in the evening. At night sentries watched in the corners of the bays and patrols and working parties went out. Officers and men not on duty slept as best they could on the fire step, which was just broad enough to permit a man lying down on it — at this date there were no dug-outs. The Commanding Officer paid a daily visit to the trenches of his unit."*
During the morning of Thursday 28th January the Germans targeted *'The Mound'* with high explosive shells. After more than sixty large shells had crashed down onto the lines, orders were sent for the men of Platoon of 'C' Company to withdraw. During the night the Battalion was relieved to Dickebusch. After further tours of duty at 4.15pm on Sunday 14th February orders were received for the Battalion to be sent in support of the Fusiliers at St Eloi and mount a counter-attack. The machine-guns on *'The Mound'* were rendered useless as they were clogged with mud and therefore were unable to provide covering fire for the advance. The Germans covered them with withering fire and a number of casualties were taken. The attack was halted until such time as more support would be provided. After another attack the Battalion was relieved and sent to huts at Zevecoten overnight before being sent to billets in Westoutre, arriving on Friday 19th. They remained in the village training for two weeks. He was promoted Lance Corporal on Monday 15th February 1915.
On Friday 2nd April Francis marched to Ypres and saw it in its medieval glory before the shelling reduced it to

Gas attack!

a ruin. The cafés and shops remained open, although many of the inhabitants had already left their homes which were now used as billets. He was sent along the Menin Road and took position at Hooge for a three day tour. On Friday 23rd he moved close to the lake at Hooge Château and they came under heavy artillery fire. Some of the shells landed in the lake which blew the fish onto the bank: these were collected and provided a pleasant meal for the men! The next day the Battalion was moved to Fortuin via Potijze Château to support the line that was under threat of breaking. They were ordered to advance against the ridge and deny it to the Germans who were also intent on its capture. They consolidated their position on the ridge until nightfall when they withdrew to Potijze Wood. During the engagements Francis and thirteen of his comrades were killed.

One of his comrades wrote: *"A braver soldier or truer comrade never lived. He died as a brave man, with a smile on his face, and was mourned by his regt. as a true comrade."*

His brother-in-law, CQMS Charles Abbott, died on Monday 24th May 1915 and is commemorated on the Menin Gate, see above.

Lieutenant Alexander Maurice Gordon

1st Battalion Royal Fusiliers

Died on Thursday 20th January 1916, aged 21

Commemorated on Panel 8.

Alexander was born on Tuesday 28th August 1894, son of Alice Elise Gordon, of Woodlands, Chalfont St Giles, Buckinghamshire, and the late Alexander Duncan Gordon. He was educated at Repton School from 1908 to 1912 as a member of Hall, his Housemaster wrote of him:

1908 — December
Heavy and lethargic. Very much overgrown. Has some wits.
1909 — March
Lacking in life rather. Reports satis.
November
Poor report. Lifeless and dull.
December
Improved considerably since half term. Overgrown.
1910 — February
Poor reports from P.G.E. Heavy.
June
Improving: still rather sluggish.
November
Gone over to Modern side where he continues to be sluggish. Very big. They speak well of him in the House.
December
Very poor reports. All agree that he is slack.
1911 — March
Better on the whole. A good fellow I think.
June
Doing pretty well.
November
Working hard for Smalls. Just failed in September having had mumps just before.
December
Went home rather before his exam, because rather overworked. Failed again.
1912 — April
Got through Smalls at last.
July
A highly satisfactory last term. Leaves for Queen's College, Oxford.

Alexander went up to Queen's College, Oxford, in 1912 and was a member of the OTC.

At the outbreak of war Alexander volunteered and was gazetted in August 1914, and promoted Lieutenant in February 1915. Alexander landed at St Nazaire on Saturday 12th September 1914 and was sent to the Aisne where he remained until Tuesday 6th October when the slow move north began. It took over a week for them to arrive in northern France; they participated in the Battles of Armentières and La Bassée before crossing into Belgium to take the line in the Ploegsteert sector. He was in the line during the *'Christmas Truce'* opposite the Saxons who are said to have called out: *"Let's have a truce for today. We don't want to kill you fellows. Why should we kill each other? We are to be relieved by the Prussians tomorrow night. You can kill them if you like. We don't care. We are Saxons."* After a few months the Battalion moved to the Salient itself and were involved in the action on Wednesday 29th September 1915 when a mine exploded under the German lines and they undertook a fierce bombing battle. Alexander continued serving on the Salient until he was killed in action.

Captain Colin Gordon

2nd Battalion London Regiment (Royal Fusiliers)

Died on Thursday 16th August 1917, aged 23

Commemorated on Panel 52.

Colin was born on Friday 6th October 1893 son of the late Bertha Gordon, of 55 Albert Bridge Road, Battersea, London, and the late William Edward Gordon. He was educated at Winchester College from 1907 to 1911. He then attended Wye College and passed his Surveyors Institute Examination winning the Beadle Prize.

Colin was sent to Malta in September 1914 and remained there until Wednesday 6th January 1915 when he arrived in Marseilles and was sent to serve on the Western Front. He was wounded in March 1915 and was Mentioned in Despatches. In 1916 he was sent to the Somme area where they trained for the forthcoming major battle. During the Battle of the Somme he saw action at Gommecourt, Ginchy and Flers. He was sent to Arras seeing action at *'Cavalry Farm'*. During the summer he transferred to the Ypres

Salient. On Thursday 16th August a second attack to the west of *'Glencorse Wood'* began under very heavy fire but the Battalion was able to take their first objectives. One of their officers managed to get as far as the racecourse in Polygon Wood but was surrounded when he sent a pigeon with the following message: *"Ammunition and bombs exhausted. Completely surrounded. Regret no course but to surrender"*. Despite their hard efforts the Battalion was forced back to its original trenches by the end of the day. In the attack and counter-attacks Colin was killed.

LIEUTENANT GEOFFREY GORDON

12th (Prince of Wales's Royal) Lancers

Died on Friday 30th April 1915, aged 34

Commemorated on Panel 5.

Geoffrey was born at home on Saturday 15th October 1881, son of the Reverend Alexander Gordon, MA, and Mrs Clara Maria Gordon (née Boult), of 35 Rosemary Street, Belfast. He was educated at Grafton House School, Manchester, and went up to Aberdeen University graduating in 1903 with an MA followed by Gonville and Caius College, Cambridge, in 1904. Geoffrey was employed in the Indian Civil Service and appointed Assistant Commissioner in the Punjab. He was commissioned in the Punjab Light Horse and promoted to Captain.

At the outbreak of war Geoffrey was in England and volunteered. He joined the Regiment in the field on Tuesday 10th November 1914. After fighting through the very heavy action at Wytschaete, and taking very many casualties, the Regiment was sent for rest and reorganisation. The Regiment remained in support for the rest of November and in December was sent to Steenwerck until early January 1915. From there they moved to Fauquembergues and were billeted in the villages of Wandonne and Audinchthun which provided roomier billets for the men and provision for the horses. After a month he was sent to Merville for bomb and mortar training. On Sunday 13th February a fleet of motor buses collected the regiment and took them to Ypres, from where they took the line in Zillebeke Wood for a tour of duty lasting seven days. A mine was blown under the 16th Lancers on the left of Geoffrey's line; the German infantry rushed the newly created crater and consolidated their position. Geoffrey took part in the unsuccessful counter-attack. The Lancers were billeted in Ypres where most of the properties were intact and thus were popular billets. In early March he returned to Fauquembergues before being sent to Estaires on Wednesday 10th March, although they were held back in case they were needed to attack Aubers Ridge. In the event the orders were cancelled during the evening of Friday 12th. The next day the Regiment was sent to Caudescure where they remained until Friday 23rd April. The first gas attack had taken place the day before and pressure on the Salient was intense. Geoffrey and the Regiment arrived in Vlamertinghe where they left their horses and marched to Ypres. The closer they got to the town the noise of shell fire grew louder as the Germans were pounding the whole area. In small groups they circumnavigated the burning town and went out to Potijze. The trenches were in poor condition and until he was killed in the front line, Geoffrey organised the men in deepening, strengthening and improving them.

CAPTAIN ROBERT NORMAN GORDON

2nd Battalion Border Regiment

Died on Wednesday 28th October 1914, aged 39

Commemorated on Panel 35.

Robert was born at Rio de Janeiro, Brazil, on Friday 18th June 1875, son of John and Harriet Gordon, of Didmarton, Tunbridge Wells, Kent. He was educated at a Prep School in Frant followed by Repton from 1889 to 1892 as a member of Mitre. Robert married Rhoda (née Jefferson) and they had a son born on Sunday 5th May 1912.

Robert was gazetted on Saturday 28th September 1895, promoted Lieutenant on Saturday 23rd April 1898, and Captain on Friday 1st April 1904. He served in India, Burma and South Africa.

Robert left Lyndhurst Camp at 10.00pm on Sunday 4th October 1914 for Southampton and the Battalion was transported to Zeebrugge on the *SS Turkoman* and *SS Minneapolis*. Robert was sent by train to Ghent were he went into the line to help defend the city. His line was taken over by the French Marines and he was sent on a route march to the Ypres Salient. After arriving in Ypres he took the line at Zillebeke on Thursday 15th October. The Battalion moved forward along the Menin Road towards Gheluvelt and took position in the area of Zandvoorde were he remained under constant attack. Robert was killed when a shell exploded as he was leaving the trenches near Kruiseik.

1446 PRIVATE ROBERT PATRICK GORDON

4th Battalion Gordon Highlanders

Died on Saturday 19th June 1915, aged 19

Commemorated on Panel 38.

Robert was born at home on Monday 5th August 1895, son of James Adam and Jeannie Gordon, of Christkirk, Insch, Aberdeenshire. He went up to Aberdeen University in 1912 where he was a member of the OTC

Robert Gordon

and the Territorials.
At the outbreak of war Robert was with the Gordon Highlanders at the annual summer camp at Tain and he was mobilized. After a period of training he went out to Le Havre from Southampton on the *SS Archimedes* on Friday 19th February 1915. After a long and winding journey by train they marched to La Clytte, arriving on Wednesday 27th. Robert undertook further training and was sent with a small group into the line to train in front line duties. In mid-March he undertook his first tour of duty near Kemmel. In April Robert was invalided with influenza to Boulogne, then sent to a hospital in Rouen, returning to the Battalion at the earliest opportunity. He rejoined his comrades in Brandhoek where the battalion was encamped, before being sent to Hooge and seeing action at Bellewaarde where they were bombarded with both artillery and gas shells. After surviving some very heavy fighting he was the only man to be killed on Saturday 19th June (by shell-fire) with the 4th Battalion just before they were to leave the line and return to camp. He was buried by his comrades who erected a small cross, but his grave was subsequently lost.
Robert was described as: "*... the fall of the unripened fruit*".
His brother, Private George Gordon, died on Friday 4th June 1915 and is commemorated on the Le Touret Memorial.

Captain
Ronald Steuart 'Jock' Gordon

No 2 Company, 57th Wilde's Rifles (Frontier Force)
Died on between Thursday 29th October and Monday 2nd November 1914, aged 37
Commemorated on Panel 1A.

Ronald was born at home in Elgin, Morayshire, on Friday 24th November 1876, fifth son of John Lewis Gordon, of Colombo, Ceylon, and West Park, Elgin, Scotland. He was educated at Elgin Academy followed by Trinity College then Glenalmond College, Perthshire, and passed into RMC Sandhurst. Whilst at Sandhurst Ronald won the bronze medals for cricket, rugby and Association football. Ronald was married on Thursday 6th August 1914 at St Peter's, Melbourne, Australia, to Ruby Mary Gordon (née Moore). The day after his marriage he left for India to rejoin his regiment.
Ronald was gazetted into the Indian Army in January 1897, and promoted Captain in January 1906. Ronald served in China during the Boxer Rebellion in 1900, serving in the Relief of Pekin, and was awarded the Medal with clasp, the Military Order of the Dragon and the Bronze Medal. He then served on the North West Frontier of India where in 1908 he was awarded the Medal and clasp and was Mentioned in Despatches on Friday 14th August 1908. He was awarded the Durbar Medal. Whilst serving in India he won many cups for polo, football, golf and cricket, playing for the City Cricket Club and in India. He was a member of the Caledonian Club, London, and was a keen shot and fisherman, and enjoyed playing tennis.
At the outbreak of war he was drafted with his men to France and during the First Battle of Ypres he was killed in action at Wytschaete.
General Sir James Willcocks, GCMG, KCB, wrote in his book *'With the Indians in France'*: "*No. 4 Company of the 57th was bearing the weight of a strong attack at the same time, and Captain R. S. Gordon, commanding No. 2 Company at once led them to its assistance. As the Highlander leaped from the trench he was killed; and thus passed away an ideal soldier. 'Jock' Gordon was a very uncommon man, loved by all who knew him, of a nature that knew no guile, literally worshipped by his men, on that cold October morn he found his place in the Valhalla of his northern land.*"
An fellow officer wrote: "*He did the most gallant thing I have ever seen; he took a platoon and went forward to check the advance of the Germans to cover the retirement of the rest of his company, though he must have known it was certain death. While advancing he was shot through the head and died instantaneously.*"
Another wrote "*He was the best officer I have ever known. He was extraordinarily popular with the men, and I have never seen them so cut about anything as they were when they came in.*"

Lieutenant
Sidney Eustace Laing Gordon

4th Battalion Royal Fusiliers
Died on Saturday 13th March 1915, aged 22
Commemorated on Panel 8.

Sidney Gordon

Sidney was born at Witheridge, Devon, on Sunday 5th June 1892, son of Henry Laing Gordon, MD, and Maud Laing Gordon, late of Florence, Italy and of 7 Egerton Mansions, Chelsea, London, grandson of Judge Gates, KC, Recorder of Brighton. He was educated at Pelham House, Folkestone followed by Harrow School from 1906 to 1911 as a member of Druries where he became Head of House, a

Monitor, Captain of the House Football Team, and was a member of the Phil-Athletic Club. Sidney went up to Brasenose College, Oxford, in 1911 with a Scholarship, graduating with Third Class Honours in 1914 and had been a member of the OTC.

At the outbreak of war Sidney was holidaying in the northwest of France with his family and he returned to England at once, arriving in the early hours of Wednesday 5th August 1914. Sidney immediately went to volunteer, arriving at the War Office in London at 6.00am — according to the policeman on the door: *"He was the very first young gent to apply"*. He was gazetted as a University entrant in August 1914 training in Dover, Kent, and leaving for the front in December, joining the Battalion in the field in the Armentières sector. He was promoted Lieutenant in February 1915. Whilst in the front line Sidney was giving orders to his platoon when he was hit by a bullet that glanced off a sandbag and went into his right lung. He was buried close to the Headquarters dug-out at Verbrandenmolen.

His Colonel wrote: *"He was indeed a natural soldier. Such charming gentleman are now becoming rare, and his loss will be felt very much by the Regiment. He was greatly loved by his men, and had a happy tact in dealing with them that does credit to his Harrow education."*

His Major wrote: *"He was always cheery and bright. He had no fear of anything, and whatever work he had to do there was no fuss about it, and he went off and did it. I looked on him as one of my most experienced young officers."*

His Captain wrote: *"He was an ideal subaltern in every way; always willing and reliable. Your son was a man without fear and on one or two occasions I had to check his wishes to do something which might have cost him his life."*

Sidney is commemorated on St Jude's Church War Memorial, South Kensington, London.

Captain
Walter Leslie Lockhart Gordon

2nd Battalion Canadian Infantry

(Eastern Ontario Regiment)

Died on Friday 23rd April 1915, aged 24

Commemorated on Panel 10.

Walter was born at home on Tuesday 30th September 1890, fourth son of William H Lockhart Gordon and Emily Gordon of 221 George Street, Toronto. He was educated at St Alban's Cathedral School and Bishop Ridley College. He passed into the Royal Military College, Canada, where he won the Sword of Honour. He was commissioned and served for the three years. Walter was a member of the Royal Canadian Yacht Club and the University Club of Toronto.

Walter volunteered at Valcartier on Tuesday 22nd September 1914, his attestation papers describe him as 5ft 8½in tall, with a 33½in chest, a fair complexion, blue eyes and brown hair.

After he was commissioned he was sent for training before sailing to England to join the Battalion at *'Bustard Camp'* on Salisbury Plain. Walter entrained at Amesbury for Avonmouth and embarked on *SS Blackwell*, sailing at noon the next day for St Nazaire. They arrived on

... defending the line

Thursday 11th and entrained for Strazeele, marching to billets in Merris. Walter took his men into the line at Armentières, with the North Staffordshires and King's Royal Rifle Corps, for front line training from Wednesday 17th. The Battalion undertook a tour of duty before returning for further training at Merris and went to serve at Bois Grenier and Fleurbaix. More training was provided at Neuf Berquin before being sent to Winnezeele, from where they were sent to Poperinghe.
On Thursday 22nd April the Battalion was ordered to 'stand to' after the German gas attack. Walter paraded with his company and marched into the line near St Julien where he was killed in action.
One of his Sergeant Major's wrote of the action and his death: *"On the morning of Friday, the 23rd of April, at about 3.30 a.m., we were about one hundred and fifty yards from the enemy trenches when we received an order to charge (this applies to No. 1 Double Company only). As we commenced to charge, the Command of my platoon, Lieutenant Day, was killed, and Captain Gordon at once took his place. Owing to the intensity of the enemy fire, we had to advance on our knees, Captain Gordon in front, encouraged the men by voice and gesture. We managed to get within thirty yards of the German trenches, and it was then Captain Gordon was hit through the neck and through the top of the head. At the time he died I was about six feet from him to the left rear."*
One his men wrote: *"Just a line to let you know how Captain Gordon died a hero's death. He was the bravest officer I saw in the engagement at Ypres. He went in front of his men and led them into action. He certainly did his duty well. He was shot through the neck. Every man in the company thought the world of him for his bravery and skill. Where he went, the men followed."*

2007 Private Horace Leslie Gough

36th Battalion Australian Infantry, AIF

Died on Friday 12th October 1917, aged 26

Commemorated on Panel 25.

Horace Gough

Horace was born at Bathurst, New South Wales, on Sunday 23rd December 1890, son of Henry Alexander Gough and Amy Margaretta Gough, of Jesmond Dene, Centennial Avenue, Chatswood, New South Wales. He was educated at East Maitland School from where he joined the Bank of New South Wales in Armidale on Thursday 4th April 1907 moving to other branches, finally appointed a teller in the Forbes Branch in January 1916.

On Monday 20th November 1916 he volunteered and was sent to England for additional training before leaving for France to join the Battalion in the field.
At the beginning of June 1917 Horace was in the line at Ploegsteert near *'Prowse Point'*. The Battle of Messines was to begin on Thursday 7th only a few miles to the north. He remained in the line until Thursday 14th when he was marched to Vieux Requin and the Battalion was reorganised. After a week of training tours of duty recommenced followed by employment in working parties around Messines. On Tuesday 17th July he returned to the front line where he came under mustard gas attacks and violent shelling from the German artillery.
At the end of the month he was relieved to *'Douve River Camp'*. The Battalion was totally exhausted from the work and trench duties they had undertaken. For a week Horace and his comrades were allowed to rest without route marches or training. Throughout their time in the camp it poured with rain and the River Douve flooded and their bivouac had to be moved to billets in Steene on Friday 3rd August. On Wednesday 8th he moved to *'Wakefield Camp'* and from the next day some light training commenced. General Sir Herbert Plumer visited the Battalion on Sunday 12th and inspected them. Horace was marched to the training area at Ledinghem, arriving at 6.30pm on Wednesday 15th and from the next morning a full programme of training began. Some light relief was given on Saturday 1st September when a Brigade Sports Day took place at Le Mesnil Boutry.

General Plumer

Training for the Third Battle of Ypres continued until Wednesday 26th September when he was paraded to be marched fifteen miles to Heuringhem, a further twenty miles the next day to Eecke, followed by six miles the following morning when he arrived in Winnezeele. After a short period of rest they marched into the line at Passchendaele where they relieved the Royal Fusiliers at 5.00am on Sunday 30th. Horace was in the line at *'Bremen Redoubt'* which came under sustained shell-fire and constant sniping from *'Levi Farm'*.
Throughout Wednesday 3rd October considerable aerial activity was seen above both sides of the lines and the Battalion snipers 'bagged' three of the enemy at *'Levi Farm'* and *'Jacob's House'*. An attack took place through his lines early the next morning and he watched as groups of German prisoners were sent back. The Battalion was relieved on Saturday 6th and marched through Ypres, Vlamertinghe to Winnezeele for a complete rest.
On Wednesday 10th a fleet of buses arrived and collected the Battalion which took them to *'Cavalry Farm'*, east

of Ypres. At 7.00pm on Thursday 11th he marched in single file to *'Potsdam'* under shell-fire; from the ruins of Zonnebeke railway station the artillery became heavier. As they advanced the Corporal in charge of his platoon was killed and Horace took over, despite being wounded. Very heavy machine-gun fire was being directed on them from *'Crest Farm'* and Passchendaele. Horace was hit again and fell into a flooded shell-hole, was rescued by a comrade, being left for stretcher bearers to collect. He was never seen again.

1839 Private
Fred Raymond Goulding, DCM

42nd Battalion Australian Infantry, AIF
Died on Thursday 4th October 1917, aged 23
Commemorated on Panel 27.

Citation for the Distinguished Conduct Medal, London Gazette, Saturday 25th August 1917:

"For conspicuous gallantry and devotion to duty whilst acting as a company runner. Four times he successfully carried messages through a heavy barrage from an isolated portion of the line, a distance of half a mile, on the last occasion returning exhausted and shaken by an explosion. In spite of this, he volunteered to take another message, and through his wonderful courage and determination his battalion was able to deal successfully with a difficult situation."

Fred was born in Lismore son of William and Mary M Goulding, of Baillie Street, North Lismore, New South Wales. He was educated locally and became a farmer. On Thursday 27th January 1916 he volunteered and enlisted, leaving from Brisbane on Sunday 16th August 1916 embarking on *HMAT Boorara*. After six weeks training in England he left for France on Sunday 26th November to join the Battalion in the field.
On Saturday 23rd December 1916 Fred went into the line for the first time at Armentières until New Year's Eve when they were relieved. He continued to serve in the sector until Friday 16th March 1917 when he served at Pont de Nieppe and at Ploegsteert from where he was invalided with influenza for three weeks. He rejoined the Battalion in Alquines where they were undertaking training for two weeks.
Fred returned to tours of duty in the line at Ploegsteert on Wednesday 23rd May and served at Pont de Nieppe, *'Bunhill Row'*, and the *'Catacombs'* until Thursday 14th June. He was awarded his Distinguished Conduct Medal at *'Schnitzel Farm'*. The Battalion was sent to Bailleul for a period of rest in the bustling town. The shops, cafés, brothels and entertainment were very

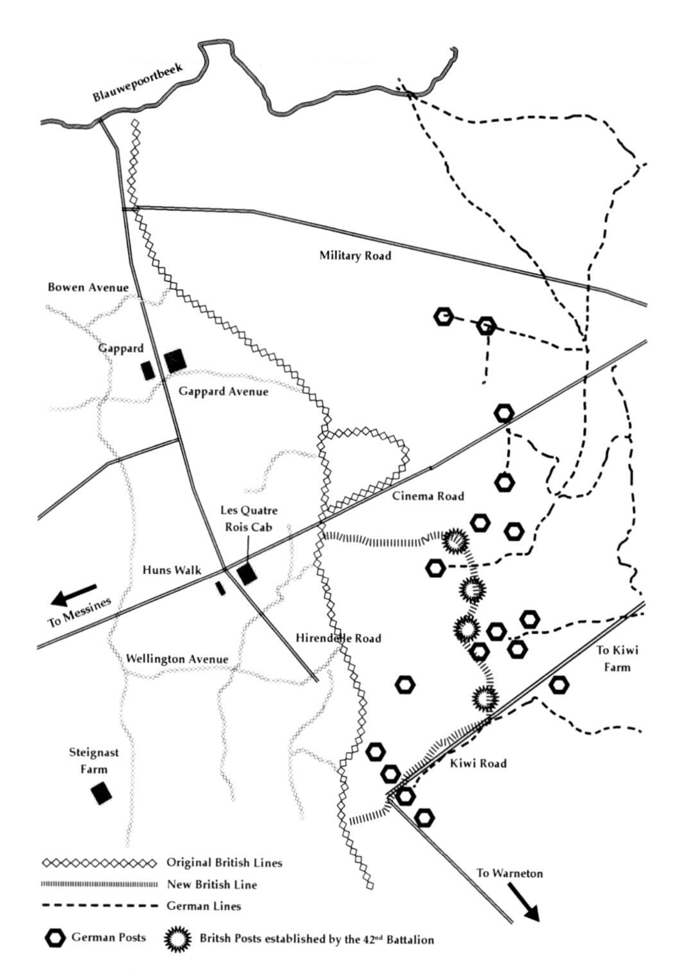

42nd Battalion, AIF, at Messines in July 1917

popular with all ranks. The opportunity to have a hot bath and change of clothing was also much appreciated. After resting and training Fred returned billets in Neuve Eglise and served in the Messines sector until Wednesday 11th July when he was sent for a period of rest until the end of month. On Tuesday 31st the Battalion returned to the line at Messines with billets in *'Douve Camp'* before moving to *'Woodlands Farm'* for training that continued at Remilly-Wirquin.
On Thursday 27th September he arrived in Poperinghe where he stayed in billets until Tuesday 2nd October. The Battalion entrained and was sent to the asylum at Ypres where they bivouacked near the town cemetery. During the night of Wednesday 3rd he marched into the line at Zonnebeke near Hill 40. At 6.00am Fred charged the German line and during the attack he was killed and was buried in the field.

... a German mobile bread kitchen

The Front Line, May to September 1917

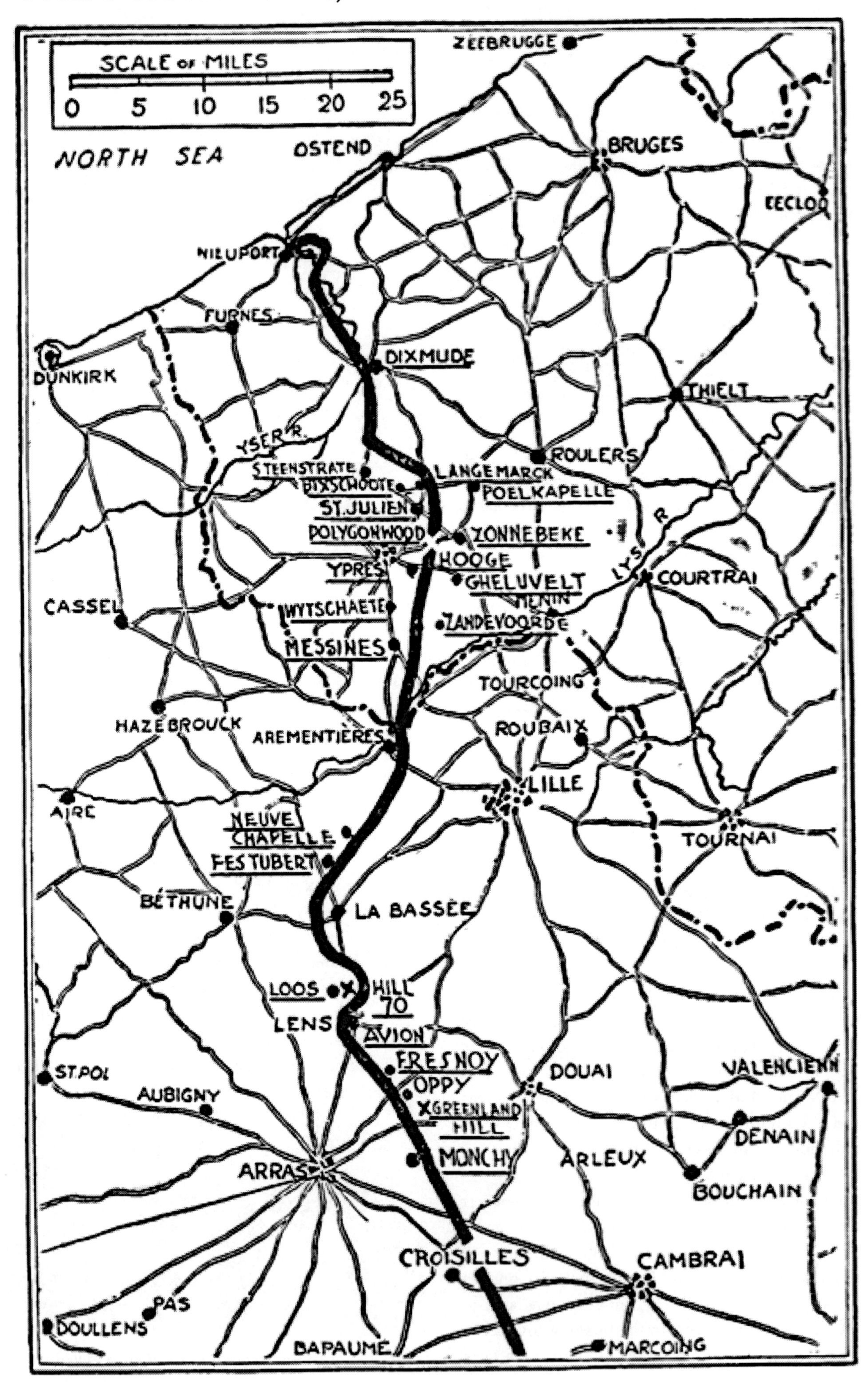

Second Lieutenant Walter Henry Grady

6th Battalion attached 3rd Battalion Royal Fusiliers

Died on Sunday 25th April 1915, aged 28

Commemorated on Panel 8.

Walter Grady

Walter was born in Sheffield on Thursday 9th September 1886, eldest son of the late Mr and Mrs W Grady, of Sheffield. He was educated locally and went up to the University of Sheffield studying metallurgy, also joining the University OTC. Walter was employed as an analytical chemist in Sheffield. He married Ida Grady (née Bateman), of 26 Thorney Hedge Road, Gunnersbury, London. Walter was a Scoutmaster at St Mark's Church, Sheffield, where he also sang in the choir. He was a keen gymnast and cricketer.

In February 1914 Walter was gazetted into the Reserves. At the outbreak of war he was mobilised. Walter left for France in January 1915 arriving in Le Havre. In March he was in the line at Kemmel coming under heavy fire when the Battalion headquarters were destroyed and his Colonel, Guy du Maurier, DSO, was killed by shell fire (he is buried in Kemmel Château Cemetery). On Tuesday 20th April the Battalion moved back into the trenches at Gravenstafel just as the German preliminary bombardment began. At 5.00pm on Thursday 22nd the Germans launched their gas attack which put the battalion under great pressure. Two days later the second gas attack was launched with a further heavy attack which was repelled by the Battalion machine-gunners.

Arthur Conan Doyle wrote: *"Great slaughter was caused by a machine-gun of the 3rd Royal Fusiliers, under Lieutenant Mallandain."* Walter was killed in his dug-out when a shell landed and blew him to pieces.

Lieutenant Archibald Stuart Bulloch Graham

2nd Battalion Gordon Highlanders

Died on Saturday 31st October 1914, aged 23

Commemorated on Panel 38.

Archibald was born on Tuesday 28th April 1891, son of Archibald Bulloch Graham, of 3 Park Gardens, Glasgow. He was educated at the Glasgow Academy followed by Rossall School from 1902 to 1909 and passed into RMC Sandhurst.

Archibald was gazetted on Saturday 25th March 1911 and in October he went out to Cawnpore, India. In December 1912 he left for Egypt and was promoted to Lieutenant in July 1914.

In September 1914 Archibald left Cairo for Southampton, and he was sent to camp at Lyndhurst for a few days before leaving for Zeebrugge on Monday 5th October, arriving two days later. He immediately entrained for Brugge and was sent straight back to cover the arrival of the 3rd Cavalry Brigade. He was sent by train to Ghent where they helped cover its defence before, on Sunday 11th, he marched with his men via Thielt to Roeselare. The Battalion arrived in Ypres on Wednesday 14th and was sent to Voormezeele. On Sunday 18th they had moved along the Menin Road and were ordered to advance on Amerika and by the end of the day they had been sent into reserve at Reutel. On Wednesday 21st Archibald took his men to south of Kruiseik where his Company repulsed some minor raids on his line. On Friday 23rd he was in front of Kruiseik when they came under sustained attack but were able to repulse the oncoming Germans. On Thursday 29th the Germans attacked in greater numbers but the Gordon Highlanders did not yield and during the evening he was relieved from the line for the night. The next morning the Germans attacked again and at 6.45am Archibald led his men forward to support the line at Zandvoorde. The attack on Saturday 31st was even heavier and he was killed. By 2.30pm the remnants of the Battalion were forced to retire.

He was killed in action and his batman wrote: *"At the time of his death he was one of three officers left with the remains of the battalion, which after the recent severe fighting had been largely reduced in numbers. They were ordered to take a wood, and this they did in such a manner that the enemy thought they were over-powered by numbers, and threw up their hands to surrender. While the officers were seeing that the enemy's arms were given up a wounded German officer, pretending to Be dead, Waited till Lieutenant Graham was close in front of him, and then shot him in the back of the head with his revolver. Our men were so enraged that they gave the German no quarter."*

Archibald was Mentioned in Despatches.

Captain John Graham

10th Battalion The King's (Liverpool Regiment)

Died on Wednesday 16th June 1915, aged 38

Commemorated on Panel 6.

John Graham

John was born on Tuesday 3rd April 1877, elder son of the late John and Mary Gilkison Graham of Aigburth Drive, Liverpool and The Croft, Hoylake. He was educated at Marlborough College from January 1891 as a member of Littlefields. John was Captain of the Cricket XI, played for the school in racquets, hockey and football. John was an excellent amateur golfer, winning many medals and awards (including the St George's Vase at Sandwich in 1904 and 1914). He was a partner of Macfie & Sons of Liverpool, sugar refiners. John held memberships of the Royal Liverpool Golf Club, the Royal and Ancient Golf Club of St Andrews and the Walton Heath Golf Club, he was also a member of Liverpool Cricket Club. John played for Scotland from 1902 to 1911. He won the St George's Vase, was in the semi-finals of the Amateur Championship five times and frequently was in the lead during the Amateur Open Championships.

John served in the Liverpool Scottish Volunteers from 1900 rising to the rank of Captain.

At the outbreak of war John volunteered and was gazetted in late August, promoted Lieutenant in September and Captain in April 1915.

On Sunday 1st November 1914 John went with the men to the station at Royal Tunbridge Wells, Kent, and entrained for Southampton. He embarked on *SS Maidan* for Le Havre; after a night in *'No 1 Rest Camp'* they entrained for St Omer and took billets in Blendecques. They had the sad duty of lining the route for the cortege for Field Marshal Lord Roberts, VC, on Tuesday 17th. On Friday 20th they undertook a series of route marches to Bailleul, arriving on Wednesday 25th. Two days later they had crossed into Belgium and taken the line at Kemmel. They remained in the sector until early Spring 1915 when they moved north to the Salient itself.

Although he was not involved directly in the first gas attack in April, the Battalion Diary records: *"On the occasion of the enemy using poisonous gases on 22nd inst. in the north, the fumes could be detected in our trenches and in Voormezeele. The men in the trenches complained of a smarting and watering of the eyes. Ypres was shelled for days on end with very heavy shells, and the noise of them was heard clearly by all ranks. The town must have been knocked into ruins and great fires were seen every now and then."*

At 2.00am, Thursday 27th May, John was relieved from the line and sent to Dickebusch until Wednesday 2nd June, when they relieved the East Yorkshire Regiment on the eastern edge of *'Armagh Wood'*, undertaking a four day tour of duty. John took his men to Busseboom for rest, re-kitting and training. At 4.00pm on Monday 14th they went up through Ypres to *'Railway Wood'*. Just after midnight the Germans started a heavy barrage on their lines where a number of men becoming casualties and the opposing front lines were one hundred and fifty yards apart. In the early hours of Wednesday 16th the British wire was taken down which assisted in the advance, and the German wire had been cut by effective artillery fire. They took the first and second line trenches at speed but as they advanced and consolidated the position John was killed.

'The Times' wrote of him: *"Not only was he one of the very finest of amateur golfers, but his most delightful and modest nature had endeared him to everyone who ever met him. 'Jack' Graham will be remembered in golfing history as the one really great player who never won a championship. It would not be right to call him an unlucky golfer. He had good chances and a natural genius for the game, but there was something in his temperament that prevented him from playing his best game in the crucial rounds towards the end of a championship. It was certainly not lack of courage in the ordinary sense of the word. No one who knew him could doubt that, and he has given the finest and most conclusive proof to the contrary. But the strain of hard matches day after day always proved too great a strain on his powers of endurance, and though he five times reached the final of the Amateur Championship he never got any farther. He was more successful as a score player than a match player. Only last year at Sandwich he won the St. George Vase at Sandwich by truly magnificent golf; his record in the Hoylake medals was one of many successes and he several times finished first amateur on the list of the Open Championship. On one occasion in particular at Muirfield he finished immediately after the great 'triumvirate' and gave Taylor, who, was drawn with him, one of the most agitating days of his long career. Capt. Graham was a great golfer. He could not but have been sometimes disappointed on account of his comparative lack of success, and he knew that his friends at Hoylake were more bitterly disappointed on his behalf than he ever was on his own. Not only did no word of complaint or excuse ever escape him, but he never for one moment fell into the opposite error of pretending that he did not care. He took his ups and downs with perfect modesty and quietness, and was always interested in the play and the success of others. At Marlborough he distinguished himself at football, cricket and racquets, and if he had had time to play might have made a name for himself as a cricketer, but he always worked very hard at his business. Indeed he played comparatively little golf, but it was remarkable how he could so constantly play a very fine game with so little practice — an occasional Saturday afternoon and perhaps an evening walk on the links with two clubs under his arm, being apparently all the practice that he needed."*

John was Mentioned in Despatches on Monday 31st May 1915.

Second Lieutenant Duncan Grant

'B' Company, 2nd Battalion Cameron Highlanders

Died on Wednesday 28th April 1915, aged 34

Commemorated on Panel 38.

Duncan Grant

Duncan was born at home on Thursday 8th July 1880, eldest son of Archibald and Annie Grant of Distillery Buildings, Fort William, Inverness. He was educated locally then employed by the Scottish Meteorological Society at the Ben Nevis Station.

Duncan joined the army in November 1899 and via Gibraltar went out to serve in the South African War where he received the Queen's Medal with five clasps. He returned with his regiment and served for two years in the British Isles before again going abroad, to Natal, China and India where he was awarded the Durbar Medal.

At the outbreak of war Duncan was in Poona with the rank of Company Serjeant Major. He was ordered back to England with the Battalion, landing in Devonport on Monday 16th November. He was commissioned on Monday 14th December, leaving for France where he arrived in Le Havre on Sunday 20th. Duncan was killed in action by a shell during a bombardment on Hill 60. Duncan was Mentioned in Despatches.

Hill 60 before the mines were blown in April 1915

Lieutenant Richard Charles Graves-Sawle

No 4 Company, 2nd Battalion Coldstream Guards

Died on Monday 2nd November 1914, aged 26

Commemorated on Panel 11.

Richard Graves-Sawle and his family coat of arms

Richard was the eldest child and only son of Rear-Admiral Sir Charles Graves-Sawle, MVO, 4th Baronet, and Lady Constance Mary Graves-Sawle (daughter of Major General Charles Daniell, CB), of 60 Queen's Gate, London and Penrice, Cornwall, nephew of Colonel Sir Francis Graves-Sawle, MVO, Baronet, one-time commander of the Coldstream Guards.

He was educated at Harrow School from 1903 to 1907 as a member of Druries and passed into RMC Sandhurst. In 1914 Richard married Muriel Cecil Harriott Graves-Sawle (daughter of Lieutenant Colonel Sir Charles Henry Brabazon Heaton-Ellis) on Thursday 6th August 1914. The wedding had been brought forward from October due to the outbreak of war. Richard was a keen yachtsman and big-game hunter. He was a member of the Guards' Club.

Richard was gazetted in 1908 and promoted to Lieutenant in 1910, and from 1913 to August 1914 was Assistant Adjutant.

Richard left Victoria Barracks, Windsor, on Wednesday 12th August 1914, under Lieutenant Colonel Pereira, entrained for Southampton where the Battalion embarked on the *SS Olympia* and *SS Novara*, Richard being a member of No 4 Company. They arrived in Le Havre and marched for five miles out to camp in the summer heat, including a rather difficult section up a long steep hill! In the early hours of Saturday 15th August they went to the station but were left hanging around for five hours in the pouring rain until they could set off at 7.00am. They arrived at Vaux-Andigny at midnight and spent the night there, before continuing on foot to Grougis where they camped with the Irish Guards for four days. Richard arrived at Mons on Sunday 23rd, taking up position at Harveng, although he was not involved in any particular engagement. At 2.00am the next morning the retirement began, ending on Sunday 6th September at Rozoy, when

they turned to face the enemy. A member of the German General Staff wrote of the actions taken by Richard, his men and those of the British Army at Mons and Le Cateau: *"The Englishman is cool, indifferent to danger. ... He is good at bayonet attack ... and it is during these bayonet attacks when luck is against him that he is at his very best. ... It was General French's army that had stayed the retreat. We ordered the English lines to be stormed. Our troops dashed into them with fixed bayonets, but our best efforts to drive the English back were in vain. ... The English are a cool lot! ... Even the sight of the wounded surprised us and commanded our respect. They lay so still and scarcely ever complained."*
The Marne was re-crossed on Wednesday 9th September and the Battalion engaged the Germans at Soupir on Monday 14th as they crossed the Aisne and took position on the Chemin des Dames. Richard remained in the cold and sodden trenches of the Aisne until mid-October when he entrained to Hazebrouck. After Church Parade on Sunday 18th October he was taken by London motor bus to Ypres via Reninghelst and Vlamertinghe. The town was alive with activity, local inhabitants were continuing to run their cafés and shops which were doing a roaring trade. Refugees continued to filter their pathetic way through the town fighting for space with troops who were marching in both directions. The town square was filled with activity and noise — troop resting, horses feeding, the continuous tramp of marching feet and the sound of battle echoing in their ears.
After being fed in the town with a hot meal the Battalion marched to St Jan from where they took the line along the Zonnebeke to Langemarck road. The First Battle of Ypres began in earnest with the Germans desperately attempting to break through to the coast. For the next ten days Richard was involved in defending the line against one onslaught after another, coupled with counter-attack following counter-attack. Throughout this time Richard served between Gheluvelt and Polygon Wood.
At 10.00pm on Sunday 1st November, Richard moved with his men in front of Veldhoek and came under heavy fire. The next morning the Germans made a series of attacks during which his Captain was killed. Richard took charge whilst in an advance trench — a mere eighty yards from the Germans who were continuously sniping their position. The French had mounted an attack which had been repulsed, and as they retreated, they required cover in the British communication trenches. Richard climbed onto the parapet to go forward to his men when he was picked off by a sniper and died two hours later in a casualty clearing station.
The stretcher bearer wrote: *"We did everything in our power to bring him back to life, as we loved him so much, and he was an example to us all of the wonderful bravery and unselfishness."*
Richard was recorded in Debretts Obituary — War Roll of Honour published in the 1921 edition.
He is commemorated on a family memorial in St Michael's Chapel, St Austell.
In St Giles Church, Wyddial, Hertfordshire, a plaque was placed in his memory with the inscription: *"To the glory of God & the loved memory of Richard Charles Graves-Sawle Lieutenant 2nd Battalion Coldstream Guards. Only son of Admiral Sir Charles Graves-Sawle, Bart., of Penrice, Cornwall and Barley Exeter and husband of Muriel eldest daughter of Lieutenant Colonel Heaton-Ellis of Wyddial Hall who fell in action near Ypres on the 2nd Nov. 1917 in his 27th year. Faithful and true. Rev XIX II."*
In the Guards Chapel, Birdcage Walk, Westminster, a memorial was placed in his memory (subsequently lost during the Blitz in the Second World War) with the inscription: *"In memory of Richard Charles Graves-Sawle, Coldstream Guards, 1908-14. Born 10th August, 1888. Killed in action at Polygon Wood, near Ypres, 2nd November, 1914."*

113261 Private David Beatt Gray

4th Canadian Mounted Rifles Battalion

Died on Friday 2nd June 1916, aged 26

Commemorated on Panel 32.

David was born at home on Monday 17th June 1889, son of the late Henry and Helen Gray, of 3 Queens Road, Aberdeen. He was educated at Aberdeen Grammar School from 1895 to 1898. David was employed at a fur station Fort McMurray, Athabasca, Canada, from 1905 to 1908, followed by Malaya working for the Oriental Tea and Rubber Company on the Sungei Makang Estate, Negri Sembilan. He returned to the fur trade in London with Messrs William Gordon & Company before returning to Fort McMurray. David was living in Toronto employed as a cigar clerk in 1914.
On Thursday 22nd July 1915, in Toronto, David volunteered and was described as a Presbyterian, 5ft 6¾in tall, with a 34in chest, a fair complexion, grey-brown eyes, light brown hair and a scar on his middle right finger.
David was sent for training and was then sent to England where it continued. In May 1916 he sailed with a draft for France and entrained for Ypres. He joined the Battalion at *'Camp B'* in Vlamertinghe and was prepared to go into the line the next day. At 7.45pm on Wednesday 31st May David marched from the camp and entrained at 8.19pm for the Ypres Asylum. Following a route march he manœuvred along the communication trenches to the front line where the Battalion relieved the 52nd Battalion near *'Maple Copse'*. Thursday 1st June passed relatively quietly for the Ypres Salient; the

Germans sent a few trench mortars over that caused a couple of casualties, perhaps they were the lucky ones being sent from the line with what was about to befall their friends and comrades. At 4.00pm a large German working party was spotted digging a shelter, it was soon stopped following a few rounds from a Stokes mortar and the Lewis gun being brought into play. The night passed without incident but at 7.00am between twenty and thirty trench mortars were fired into their trenches that was a quiet herald to the bombardment that would commence at 8.30am. Thousands of shells rained down together with trench mortars and as the front line was destroyed David was killed.
His brother, Private William Gray, died on Thursday 22nd April 1915 and is commemorated on the Menin Gate, see below.

317231 Private Frederick Arthur Gray

'D' Company, 1st Battalion Gordon Highlanders
Died on Monday 14th December 1914, aged 29
Commemorated on Panel 38.

Frederick Gray

Frederick was born in 1884, second son of the late Mr and Mrs James Gray, of 29 Polworth Gardens, Edinburgh. He was educated at George Heriot's School from 1896 to 1900. He was initially employed by the Clydesdale Bank, George Street, Edinburgh, and was elected a Member of the Institute of Bankers. He went to work for the Bank of South America in Buenos Aires followed by Montevideo. Frederick had been a Private in the 4th Royal Scots (QERVB) prior to the war.
At the outbreak of war he returned from Uruguay to volunteer and enlisted, becoming a member of 'D' Company. Frederick was sent out to join the Battalion in the field with a draft.
In early November the Battalion was in the line near Hooge and *'Shrewsbury Forest'*. At dawn on Wednesday 11th the Germans laid a preliminary barrage and at 9.00am attacked along the line from Messines to Polygon Wood. The Gordons were able to repulse the attack by the Pomeranians and continued in the line until Friday 20th when they were relieved. He marched from Ypres to Westoutre for rest and re-kitting. On Monday 14th December he was on the Messines to Wytschaete road, in front of Maedelstede Farm and took part in the attack on Messines. At 7.45am the advance began but it came up against heavy resistance and by 4.00pm only a few men had managed to get within fifty yards of the German lines. As they advanced Frederick was killed.

7137 Serjeant Joseph Gray, DCM

'D' Company, 2nd Battalion
York and Lancaster Regiment
Died on Monday 9th August 1915, aged 29
Commemorated on Panel 55.

Citation for the Distinguished Conduct Medal, London Gazette, Wednesday 30th June 1915:

"For conspicuous ability as a platoon commander. Serjeant Gray has distinguished himself in the carrying out of many valuable reconnaissances."

Joseph was born in Gainsborough, the son of Mr J and Mrs M Gray, of 7 Bell's Terrace, Stevenson Road, Attercliffe, Sheffield. He was educated locally.
He enlisted in Manchester. On Wednesday 9th September 1914 Joseph landed in St Nazaire from where he entrained to Coulommiers where he was billeted. From Sunday 13th September he marched to the Aisne where he served until Tuesday 6th October. On Friday 9th he entrained for northern France where he served in the Armentières until Sunday 14th March 1915. On Monday 15th he was sent to Vlamertinghe were he remained for a day before being sent back to serve again in the Armentières sector. On Monday 31st May he returned again to the Ypres Salient, this time to remain there. On Wednesday 2nd June Joseph took the line between Wieltje and the Ypres railway line. On Sunday 20th June the Germans launched an attack on their lines using gas, the first horrific experience of this weapon. On Friday 30th July the Germans mounted an offensive against Hooge and drove the line back; as a result the Battalion was sent on Monday 2nd August to Hooge where they would participate in a counter-attack a week later. At 3.15am on Monday 9th Joseph charged forward and the German lines were quickly captured. As the position was consolidated they came under heavy shell and machine-gun fire, and Joseph was killed.

7969 Private William Gray

2nd Battalion Canadian Infantry
(Eastern Ontario Regiment)
Died on Thursday 22nd April 1915
Commemorated on Panel 18.

William was born at home on Sunday 1st January 1882, son of the late Henry and Helen Gray, of 3 Queens Road, Aberdeen. He was educated at Aberdeen Grammar School Preparatory School from 1886 and returned to the Senior School from 1895 to 1899 and went up to Aberdeen University. In 1903 David left for Canada and was employed first as a stockbroker and estate agent then as a publisher and he was a member of the

William Gray

Royal Field Artillery (Militia) for twenty months prior to the outbreak of the war.

On Wednesday 23rd September 1914 in Valcartier William volunteered and was described as a Presbyterian, 5ft 7in tall, with a 36in chest, a fair complexion, grey eyes and brown hair.

William sailed for Devonport on *SS Cassandra*, arriving on Thursday 15th October 1914 from where he entrained for Amesbury and marched to *'Bustard Camp'*. William trained on Salisbury Plain until Sunday 7th February 1915 when the Battalion when they entrained for Avonmouth and embarked on *SS Blackwell*. They sailed for St Nazaire, arriving Thursday 11th then entrained for Strazeele and marched to billets in Merris. William was sent for practical experience in the front line near Armentières. From Monday 1st March the Battalion took the line in their own right at Bois Grenier where they remained on tours for three weeks. On Wednesday 7th April they left for training at Winnezeele before moving to Vlamertinghe. Following the German gas attack at 5.00pm on Thursday 22nd April William was paraded at 9.00pm and marched from camp toward Ypres to the sight and sound of battle. William was sent into the line four hundred yards west of the St Julien to Wieltje road to help in countering the German attack and take part in a hastily constructed counter-attack. The German machine-guns cut up the Canadians and William was killed.

His brother, Private David Gray, died on Friday 2nd June 1916 and is commemorated on the Menin Gate, see above.

719 Sergeant Walton Robert Grayson, DCM

XXII Corps Australian Light Horse

Died on Friday 26th April 1918

Commemorated on Panel 7.

Citation for the Distinguished Conduct Medal:

"For conspicuous gallantry and devotion to duty. After a severe fall with his horse into a shell hole, from which he was extricated with great difficulty, he went on after his detachment carrying his Kotchkiss rifle, which he brought into action in time to stop a hostile field gun from being withdrawn. He was badly bruised and shaken, and showed a fine example of pluck and determination."

Walton was born in Williamstown, Victoria, son of Thomas Walton Grayson and Lilly Elizabeth Grayson, (née White), of Central Wharf, Millers Point, New South Wales. He was educated locally and was employed as a labourer.

On Saturday 24th October 1914 Walton volunteered and enlisted, leaving from Melbourne on Wednesday 3rd February 1915 on board *HMAT Katuna*.

He arrived in Egypt where he served with the 4th Light Horse Regiment. Following the evacuation after the Gallipoli Campaign and deployment to France, the 4th Light Horse Regiment provided two squadrons and joined a squadron from the Otago Mounted Rifles (from New Zealand) which formed the Second ANZAC Mounted Regiment. In November 1917 a further reorganisation occurred and it was renamed the XXII Corps.

Major General Alexander Godley, Commander of the XXII Corps

Walton saw considerable action when the German armies retired to the *'Hindenburg Line'* in early 1917, but he then returned to the normal duties of reconnaissance, escorting prisoners, traffic control and other necessary duties behind the lines. From the Somme Walton was sent to Flanders where he served through the Battle of Messines in June 1917. He remained on the Salient and saw action at Broodseinde and Passchendaele during the Third Battle of Ypres.

... Uhlans on the Hindenburg Line

In April 1918 Walton was serving at Kemmel when it came under heavy attack and he was killed. During the fighting at Kemmel more men from the XXII Corps were killed than in all other actions of the war combined.

460795 Lance Corporal Robert 'Bobby' Felix Grech

13th Battalion Canadian Infantry (Quebec Regiment)

Died on Sunday 4th June 1916, aged 25

Commemorated on Panel 24.

Bobby was born in Malta on Saturday 5th July 1890, the son of the late Professor Salvatore Grech, MD, and Mrs Jane Grech (née Shillinglaw) of St Aloysius College, Malta. His mother died when he was very young then his father just after Bobby went to school. He was educated at Stonyhurst College from 1901 as a member of Hodder and was a member of the OTC. After leaving College Bobby emigrated to Canada where he worked as a clerk and was a member of the 90th Regiment (Militia).

Bobby enlisted in Winnipeg in the Royal Highlanders of Canada on Wednesday 2nd June 1915. His attestation papers describe him as a Roman Catholic, 5ft 7in tall, with a 43in chest, a fair complexion, brown eyes and light brown hair. After a period of training Bobby was sent to England, then onward to join the Battalion on the Western Front.

Christmas 1915 was spent out of the line before returning to the line near *'Red Lodge'* at La Plus Douve in the southern sector of Belgium close to the French border. From Sunday 2nd February 1916 the Battalion was sent to rest billets near Bailleul where training commenced the next day. They remained training and resting for the next three weeks before returning to *'Red Lodge'* and the line.

At 8.00am on Friday 2nd June the Germans opened up their artillery barrage over the Canadian line, Bellewaarde Beek to Mount Sorrel (including *'Sanctuary Wood'*/Hill 62, Hill 61, and *'Armagh Wood'*). The casualties over the next forty-eight hours were particularly high and included senior officers Major General Malcolm Mercer (buried in Lijssenthoek Military Cemetery), Lieutenant Colonel Alfred Shaw (commemorated on the Menin Gate, see below), Lieutenant Colonel George Baker (buried in Poperinghe New British Cemetery) and Lieutenant Colonel Buller (buried in Voormezeele Enclosure No 3). The whole of the Canadian front line was pulverised and rendered unrecognisable. At 1.45pm the German assault commenced and advanced with little difficulty, but when they reached *'Sanctuary Wood'*, *'Armagh Wood'* and Mount Sorrel they were stopped and a counter-attack commenced. At 7.30pm on Friday night Bobby paraded and was force marched to Ouderdom where Lieutenant Colonel Buchanan ordered him and the men to leave their packs behind and move quickly into the front line. When they arrived at the bridge across the Ypres to Comines Canal the shrapnel started to fall and the shelling became heavier and more dangerous. They managed to get up to *'Zillebeke Trench'*, along the edge of Zillebeke Lake. The area was a total quagmire with men sinking up to their waists in the mud. At 7.10am, Bobby and his comrades counter-attacked in an attempt to retake the ground from Mount Sorrel to *'Observatory Ridge'*. They managed to advance some five hundred yards. On Saturday 3rd June the 13th Battalion hastily dug new trenches with the rain still falling heavily. Bobby died the next day whilst they continued to dig in and hold onto their hard-won ground.

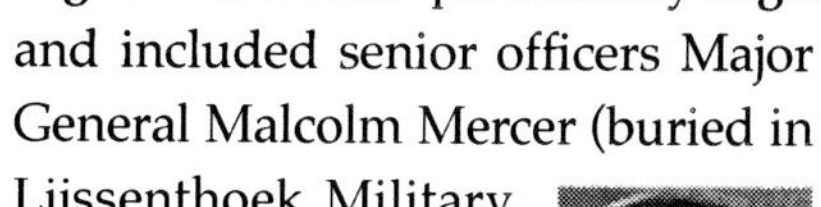

General Mercer

Colonel Shaw

Colonel Buller

Colonel Baker

2623 Private Arnold John Green

'B' Company, 1st/7th Battalion Durham Light Infantry

Died on Monday 24th May 1915, aged 22

Commemorated on Panel 36.

Arnold Green

Arnold was born on Saturday 27th June 1908, younger son of John and Isabella Elliot Green, of 41 Otto Terrace, Sunderland. He was educated at the Ackworth Friends' School, near Pontefract and then went to work for the North Eastern Railway and continued his studies. Arnold received a first class pass in *'Railway and Commercial Geography'* and a second class pass in *'Railway Operating'*. He was a prominent member of the YMCA in York. Arnold wrote many articles for the magazine of the North Eastern Railway including *'Bonnie Blanchland'* and *'A Peep At Durham'*.

Arnold volunteered and enlisted in September 1914 and went to train at Gateshead. He arrived in Boulogne on Saturday 17th April 1915 and continued his training in northern France.

On Sunday 23rd May he marched to Steenvoorde from Cassel where he was taken by bus via Poperinghe to Vlamertinghe. He marched to Potijze where he was bivouacked. Arnold went into the line and was killed near Hill 60.

German PoWs in 'The Cage'

Captain
Edward Unsworth Green, MC

9th Battalion The Loyal North Lancashire Regiment

Died on Friday 10th August 1917, aged 37

Commemorated on Panel 41.

Edward Green

Edward was born on Friday 27th August 1880, son of Edward Unsworth Green and Annie Louisa Green, of 112 Church Road, Richmond, Surrey. He was educated at Dulwich College from 1895 to 1896 where he played for the Second XV. He became the Captain of the Old Alleyians XV from 1903 to 1905 and was responsible for the School Mission from 1905 to 1914.

On Monday 19th February 1900 Edward enlisted in the Honourable Artillery Company and rose to the rank of Sergeant Major.

At the outbreak of war Edward immediately volunteered and went out with the BEF on Friday 18th September 1914 as Company Quarter Master Serjeant with No 3 Company, joining the 1st Battalion in the field near Troyon. He continued to serve on the Aisne until 2.30am on Thursday 15th October when the French relieved them and he marched to Fismes where he entrained the next day for Cassel arriving over forty-eight hours later. After a period of rest Edward marched across the border into Belgium from Steenvoorde to Poperinghe and onward to Boesinghe. He took part in an action in front of Langemarck which retook lost ground; General Edward Bulfin produced the following Brigade Order on Wednesday 28th October: *"In spite of the stubborn resistance offered by the German troops, the object of the engagement was accomplished, but not without many casualties in the Brigade. By nightfall the trenches captured by the Germans had been re-occupied, about 600 prisoners captured and fully 1,500 German dead were lying out in front of our trenches.*

General Bulfin

The Brigadier-General congratulates the 1st Loyal North Lancashire Regiment, the 1st Northamptonshire Regiment, and the 2nd King's Royal Rifle Corps: but desires specially to commend the fine soldier-like spirit of the 1st Loyal North Lancashire Regiment, which, advancing steadily under heavy shell and rifle fire, and aided by its machine-guns, was enabled to form up within a comparatively short distance of the enemy trenches. Fixing bayonets, the Battalion then charged, carried the trenches, and then occupied them, and to them must be allotted the majority of the prisoners captured.

The Brigadier-General congratulates himself on having in his Brigade a battalion which, after marching the whole of the previous night without food or rest, was able to maintain its splendid record in the past by the determination and self-sacrifice displayed in this action." Edward continued to serve in the line including at Hooge towards the end of the First Battle of Ypres. He was relieved from the line and sent to Merris, and billeted in Hazebrouck, where much needed rest was provided.

On Saturday 21st December Edward organised the men to go to the line when urgent orders were received and they boarded a fleet of motor buses for Le Touret, arriving at 3.00pm. The Battalion was immediately sent into the line next to the Indian Regiments and successfully counter-attacked at 7.20pm, retaking the lost trenches.

Edward spent Christmas 1914 in Essars, one of the officers wrote: *"To-day, Christmas Day, has been celebrated in the time-honoured way, carols have been sung and there is not a man who has been forgotten by those has left behind. Relatives and friends and charitable organizations have combined to make our Christmas as festive and happy as it possibly could be; plum puddings have been received, tobacco and cigarettes have been literally showered upon us in almost staggering quantities; whilst warm clothing, gloves, mufflers and many other personal comforts have been distributed with a lavish hand. The gratitude of the men who have received these gifts is profound, far more so than words can tell. The Christmas card which Their Majesties the King and Queen graciously sent to each man made a cheery opening for the day and the Royal message 'May God protect you and bring you home safely' roused lusty cheers which were repeated again and again."*

On Tuesday 5th January 1915 he took the line at Cambrin and served in the Festubert and the La Bassée sector until the Battle of Loos. At 9.45pm on Friday 24th September he moved into the line from Marles-les-Mines. At 6.34am the British released their gas attack, but the wind direction changed and a considerable amount floated back into their lines causing many casualties, which resulted in the Battalion being forced back to its original trenches. Various attempts to restart the attack failed; despite not achieving very much the losses to the Battalion was heavy, sixteen officers and four hundred and eighty-nine men killed, wounded or missing. Edward continued to serve in the Loos sector until Thursday 30th December 1915 when he was gazetted, and joined 9th Battalion near Le Bizet.

In January 1916 the 9th Battalion took part in its first attack supporting the 2nd Battalion Royal Irish Rifles at Le Touquet. Throughout February Edward was based in Steenwerck in reserve; from March to May he moved around the sector, and was slightly wounded in the front line, until being sent to Ostreville for the first two weeks of June. The Battalion was then sent to Warloy until early on Tuesday 4th July when they moved south to Bouzincourt where they would participate in the Battle of the Somme. The Battalion History records:

"On the morning of 7th it participated in an attack by the 12th Division on Ovillers and the trenches to the right across the Pozières road. The attack was carried out by the 9th North Lancashire and 13th Cheshire, with the 2nd Royal Irish Rifles and 11th Lancashire Fusiliers in support. The attacking battalions, after an intense bombardment from massed artillery of all calibres, moved forward at 8.5 a.m. and successfully reached their first objectives after heavy fighting. Mainly owing to the heavy losses, great difficulty was experienced in reaching the second objective the same day, but, during the night of 7th-8th and the following morning, bombing parties eventually established themselves in the enemy's line just south of the Pozières road."

During action on the Ancre he was awarded the Military

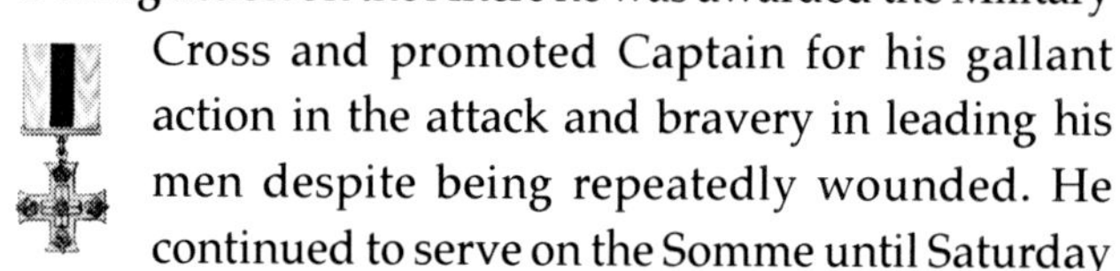

Cross and promoted Captain for his gallant action in the attack and bravery in leading his men despite being repeatedly wounded. He continued to serve on the Somme until Saturday 21st October when he participated in an attack on Thiepval. The Battalion Diary records: *"... at 12.6 p.m. the Battalion got out of Hessian Trench in three lines and crossed No-Man's-Land immediately behind the barrage, very few casualties occurring until we reached the enemy's wire, when a considerable amount of trouble was caused by an enemy machine-gun and snipers. This machine-gun was outside a dug-out in the Sunken Road and was put out of action by 2nd Lieut. G. M. Jones and three bombers, the gun being captured. Many prisoners were taken, chiefly from the Sunken-Road dug-outs, not many of the enemy being in the front line. About two hundred prisoners were taken, including one officer who said that he was a battalion commander. As soon as they had taken the trench the men did remarkably good work consolidating, and an outpost line was immediately organized and put out by 2nd Lieut. G. M. Jones. On the 22nd the Battalion was relieved and proceeded to the Rest Camp."* During the action he was wounded again.

After a period of rest the Battalion entrained north and marched into Belgium, taking the line at Ploegsteert from Tuesday 31st October until mid February 1917. Christmas Day was spent in the line at Ploegsteert but there was no repetition of the truce that had taken place two years previously. From Saturday 24th February to Wednesday 21st March he was sent for training near St Omer before going into reserve near Merris. Edward went back into the line at Wulverghem where he remained until The Battle of Messines on Thursday 7th June. The part played by the Battalion was successful as they achieved their objectives within an hour and forty minutes. He was relieved on Saturday 9th returning to the front before being sent for training and rest near Bomy, St Omer.

On Saturday 4th August he was sent into the line between Westhoek and Bellewaarde, taking part in the attack on Friday 10th August. The Divisional History records: *"To complete the capture of Westhoek Ridge was now, the task allotted to the 74th Brigade. On the right the 55th and 54th Brigades of the 18th Division had as their objective the capture of Inverness Copse and Glencorse Wood. The 74th Brigade attacked with all four battalions in the front line, along a front of about 2,000 yards, with its left flank on the Ypres-Roulers railway.*

The assembly of the assaulting troops was complete by 3.25 a.m. on the 10th August. At 4.25 a.m. the whole line moved forward to the attack and was well clear of our line when the enemy's barrage came down a few minute later. ... The attack was a complete success in every way, and notwithstanding some severe fighting, particularly on the right, the whole Brigade was firmly established on its objectives by 5.30 a.m. Several strong points, pill-boxes and fortified houses garrisoned with machine-guns, offered considerable opposition, but were quickly rushed and captured by assaulting troops. ... The Irish Rifles rushed Westhoek, together with the two strong points, and took the garrison before the enemy realized they were being attacked. The 9th Loyal North Lancashire advanced in three waves. The first company was held up by a strong point which they quickly surrounded, capturing a machine-gun and its detachment. The Battalion had many casualties from snipers, especially on the right flank. German aeroplanes flew low and fired on any bodies of troops moving in the open." In the action Edward and the three other Company Commanders were killed.

His brother, Lieutenant Vivian Green, died on Monday 26th March 1917 and is commemorated on Jerusalem Memorial.

Second Lieutenant Frank Clifford Green

1st Battalion Lincolnshire Regiment

Died on Wednesday 16th June 1915, aged 25
Commemorated on Panel 21.

Frank was born in East Ham on Sunday 4th May 1890, third son of Mr and Mrs John Green, 193 Browning Road, Manor Park, Essex. He was educated at Hartley University College, Southampton, and was a member of the OTC then joined the Territorials. He was employed as a teacher in East Ham. Frank was a member of Ilford Wanderers' Rugby Club, and Chairman and Captain of the Teachers' Swimming Club. He received two medals from the Royal Life Saving Society and was an Honorary Instructor.

At the outbreak of war Frank enlisted in the Artists Rifles in August 1914 with service number 2452, initially stationed at the Tower of London and afterwards in Watford. He went out to France in October and was promoted Lance Corporal, and gazetted on Friday 23rd April 1915.

An attack was planned for Wednesday 16th June by General Edmund Allenby with the aim of straightening the line at Bellewaarde Ridge, Hooge, and of taking the high ground away from the Germans. Frank, with his men, had been in training from Sunday 6th June for this action, with special anti-gas respirators and helmets being issued, although in reality they gave precious little protection. The respirator formed a hood coated in hyphosulphate of soda with a celluloid window that fitted over a helmet and tucked into the top of the tunic. On Tuesday 15th June they left their bivouac at Brandhoek and went into assembly trenches at *'Cambridge Road'* via Kruisstraat, *'Hell Fire Corner'* and

Birr Cross Roads

Birr Crossroads (four men were killed during the march to the line). From 2.30am to 4.15am a bombardment opened up on the German lines. Frank was with his men in the second line and were rushed forward to support the Royal Fusiliers who were leading the attack. At 4.30am the Lincolnshires advanced at the point of the bayonet and took the second objective. Sadly, during the action Frank was mortally wounded by rifle fire.

A Captain wrote: *"Your son was standing with me in a hail of shell and rifle fire, and we decided to jump into a trench captured from the Germans, close by. He jumped in while talking to me, and suddenly said 'On! I'm hit'. After a short pause he added, 'I'm finished'. I cut off his equipment and clothes and did my best to bandage the wound, which went right through the chest, but could not stop the bleeding. I left him in the hands of the stretcher-bearer with instruction to do the best he could. I regret to say that your son was unconscious then, and the stretcher-bearer is missing."*

Later he wrote: *"I asked a doctor afterwards if there was anything I could have done to have saved him, and he told me nothing. I made every effort to stop the bleeding, but could not do so. I handed him over to a stretcher-bearer who belonged to another regiment; your son was alive then, but unconscious, and I am afraid very near the end. It was in the German second-line trench where your son was hit, and that night we were ordered to evacuate the trench owing to the line not being straight."*

28972 Lance Corporal Herbert B Green

16th Battalion Canadian Infantry
(Manitoba Regiment)

Died on Friday 23rd April 1915, aged 34
Commemorated on Panel 26.

Herbert was born in Farnham, on Thursday 21st April 1881, son of the late Mr and Mrs Herbert E B Green, of Ellesmere, Worthing. He was educated at Eton College as a member of the Reverend Thomas Dalton's and the Reverend Francis Johnson Tuck's Houses, leaving in 1896.

He served in the South African Campaign with 4th Battalion King's Shropshire Light Infantry and held a commission in Northumberland Fusiliers until 1908.

Herbert emigrated to Canada and became a rancher. He volunteered at Valcartier on Monday 7th September 1914, his attestation papers describe him as 5ft 6¾in tall, with a 34in chest, a fair complexion, grey eyes, brown hair, a tattoo of a flag and anchor on his left forearm and a scar on his right forearm.

He came to England with the first Canadian Contingent and was sent for training at *'West Down South'* followed by *'Larkhill'* on Salisbury Plain. On Thursday 4th February 1915 HM King George V and Field Marshal Lord Kitchener undertook an inspection prior to their departure to France. At 6.00am on Thursday 11th Herbert left camp and entrained at Amesbury for Avonmouth where he boarded *SS Maidan* bound for St Nazaire. He arrived on Monday 15th and entrained for Hazebrouck where he arrived two days later and marched to Caëstre. Training continued until Tuesday 23rd when the

Battalion was ordered to parade and march to Flêtre, Bailleul, Steenwerck, Bac St Maur and Erquinghem where they were billeted. Herbert had his first taste of the trenches when he was sent in for twenty-four hours attached to experienced troops for practical training.

On Wednesday 3rd March the Battalion paraded and was addressed at 11.15am by General Edwin Alderson and that evening they relieved the Border Regiment at Rue Petillon for a three day tour of duty. On Sunday 7th a bath parade was held in their billets at Rue de Sur, followed by a service held in the canteen led by Major Scott, the Chaplain. After three days Herbert went back into the line to continue on tours of duty until Friday 26th when he was sent to Estaires. The Battalion moved to Cassel on Wednesday 7th April where General Sir Horace Smith-Dorrien inspected them on Saturday 10th, together with General Edwin Alderson.

General Alderson

At 9.00am on Friday 16th April a fleet of twenty-five buses arrived to collect the Regiment and drove to Vlamertinghe which they reached at 11.45am. After a period for rest and food, at 2.30pm Herbert was paraded and marched towards Ypres. They went around the town to the north and arrived in Wieltje where they rested until 8.30pm. The Battalion was moved to St Julian and took a position near Poelkapelle where they were warned of a potential German attack. On Monday 19th they came under high explosive shell-fire which destroyed the telephone wires. Late on Tuesday 20th the Battalion was relieved by the 48th Canadian Battalion and was sent to billets in Ypres. Wednesday 21st was a the lull before the storm: it was passed quietly at rest in the town. During the afternoon of Thursday 22nd the German bombardment of the northern sector and Ypres began and Herbert was ordered to parade along the Canal. The local inhabitants started to panic as the shells began to land in the town. Herbert watched as streams of Zouaves ran passed him and it was clear that the French had been routed to their north. At 7.40pm he was marched to St Julien where additional ammunition was issued to him and he was prepared to mount a counter-attack. At 11.30pm he was in position along the main road and a thousand yards from the German lines. Shortly after midnight he moved forward and got to within three hundred yards of the German lines when they opened with rapid rifle fire coupled with their machine-guns. Flares were sent up and Herbert fell flat to the ground and then charged the German lines where many of the defenders were bayoneted and some were able to surrender. The Battalion moved on towards a small wood and during the advance Herbert was killed.

Lieutenant Colonel Malcolm Charles Andrew Green

Commanding 2nd Battalion
South Lancashire Regiment

Died on Tuesday 17th November 1914, aged 43
Commemorated on Panel 37.

Malcolm Green

Malcolm was born in St George's Road, London, on Sunday 2nd July 1871, son of the late Colonel Malcolm S Green, CB, 3rd Scinde Horse, grandson of Admiral Sir Andrew Pellet Green who commanded *HMS Collingwood* at Trafalgar. He was educated at Oxford Military College and passed into RMC Sandhurst. Malcolm married Elsie Green (née Bisdee), they had three sons who were aged two, three and five at the time of his death. He was a member of the United Services Club, Pall Mall.

Malcolm was gazetted on Saturday 5th December 1891, promoted to Lieutenant on Wednesday 1st August 1894, Captain on Sunday 1st April 1900, Major on Sunday 16th May 1909 and Lieutenant Colonel on Thursday 12th November 1914. He served in the South African War receiving the Queen's Medal with four clasps.

At the outbreak of war Malcolm assisted with the mobilisation at Tidworth after he relinquished command of the Depôt in Warrington. He went with the Battalion to Southampton and embarked for Le Havre, arriving on Friday 14th August 1914 where they entrained for northern France. Along the route into Belgium they were cheered by the local population and were given small gifts and souvenirs. They crossed the border at 8.00am on Friday 21st, arriving at Frameries in late-afternoon on Saturday 22nd, taking the line at Ciply. Lieutenant Colonel Wanliss wrote: *"That evening before dark I went round the whole of the position held by the Battalion and was more impressed than ever that our chief weakness lay on our left flank, where the railway embankment would afford excellent cover for the enemy's infantry, only some 500 yards from the left of our line. I therefore told Travis-Cook, commanding 'D' Company, to throw back his left and ordered the two machine-guns to support that flank. The whole of the night we continued improving our trenches and head-cover, before daybreak I sounded my whistle and had the trenches manned. … Almost immediately afterwards the enemy's artillery opened a tremendous fire on Frameries and after some time the whole place was in a blaze. Our artillery, although outnumbered 5 to 1, did magnificent work. At one time a Germany battery took a position on a hill about 1,200 yards to the left of our line, and in prolongation of it, and began to enfilade our trenches and several shrapnel bullets dropped into my portion. However, almost immediately one of our batteries switched on and dropped two shells bang into the middle of it and the German battery disappeared."* Late in the day the orders arrived for a retirement and the long march south began which did not stop until Sunday 6th September. At last the retreat had ended and the battalion turned northeastward towards the Germans. Three days later Malcolm crossed the Marne and the Aisne was reached on Sunday 13th. From Tuesday 15th he occupied the shallow trenches in front of Vailly which they defended until Monday 21st coming under sustained attack. Malcolm continued to serve on the Aisne until early October when the Battalion was relieved and entrained for northern France.

At 7.00am on Monday 12th October Malcolm took his men from Hinges to Lacouture from where they attacked Givenchy. The next day he saw action at Richebourg St Vaast before moving to the water-logged trenches at Le Transloy, La Bassée, where they repulsed a major attack on Tuesday 20th. The next morning the Germans attacked again and the Battalion was forced to retire taking heavy losses of seven officers and two hundred men. In the evening they were withdrawn and sent to billets near the Bois de Biez. After a short rest they were sent to Neuve-Chapelle where again Malcolm saw action on Monday 26th.

In early November he was sent to the Ypres Salient taking the line at Zwarteleen, at 2.00am on Friday 6th. The Prussian Guard attacked them on Wednesday 11th whilst in front of Nonne Bosschen, which they repulsed. The next day he took command of the Battalion, remaining under heavy fire and the pressure of constant attack. He was killed five days later, together with Lieutenant Bernard Fulcher when a shell landed in their dug-out (Lieutenant Fulcher is commemorated on the Menin Gate, see above).

Bernard Fulcher

12553 Serjeant James Greenan, DCM

6th Battalion Border Regiment

Died on Thursday 7th June 1917

Commemorated on Panel 35.

Citation for the Distinguished Conduct Medal, London Gazette, Saturday 25th November 1916:

"For conspicuous gallantry in action. He carried out a daring reconnaissance under heavy fire. Later, he held an isolated post against numerous enemy attacks, displaying great courage and determination."

James was born at Cleator Moor, Cumberland.

He enlisted at Maryport, Cumberland. The 6th Battalion was in training until Wednesday 30th June 1915 when they were ordered to prepare for overseas service. They entrained for Liverpool and were sent out to Gallipoli. The hulk of the *River Clyde* provided their route onto the beaches. He was evacuated to Egypt where, after rest and further training, he was sent to Alexandria on Friday 30th June 1916 to embark on the *SS Scotian* to Marseilles. They entrained on Thursday 6th July and eventually arrived in Arras in which sector they remained until September when orders were received to move to Ovillers.

During May 1917 James was with the Battalion in France on the old Somme battlefields. On Tuesday 15th May they left and went to a camp at Caëstre where they trained for the forthcoming battle until Wednesday 6th June. They went to Westoutre from where they marched into the line at Messines, arriving about 2.00am; at 3.10am the British mines were blown. It was not until lunchtime that they received orders to move to the *'Vierstraat Switch'*. By early evening they were attacking *'Van Hove Farm'* which objective was achieved only after taking several casualties, including James.

"The German front line skirted the W. foot of the ridge in a deep curve from the River Lys, opposite Frelinghien, to a point just short of the Menin Road. The line of trenches then turned N. W. past Hooge and Wieltje, following the slight rise known as the Pilckem Ridge to the Yser Canal at Boesinghe. The enemy's second-line system followed the crest of the Messines-Wytschaete Ridge, forming an inner curve. In addition to these defences of the ridge itself, two chord positions had been constructed across the base of the salient from S. to N. The first lay slightly to the E. of the hamlet of Oosttaverne and was known as the Oosttaverne line. The second chord position, known as the Warneton line, crossed the Lys at Warneton, and ran roughly parallel to the Oosttaverne line a little more than a mile to the E. of it."

James was awarded the Serbian Gold Medal for Bravery.

Second Lieutenant Francis Pemberton Greener

2nd Battalion East Surrey Regiment

Died on Monday 15th February 1915, aged 29

Commemorated on Panel 34.

Francis was the son of Maria E Greener, of 18 Albert Road, Southport, Lancashire, and the late W J Greener. He was educated at Christ's Hospital, Horsham, from 1898 to 1902.

On Monday 22nd March 1909 Francis joined the Inns of Court OTC, rising to the rank of Sergeant.

He was gazetted to the East Surrey Regiment from Inns of Court OTC on Saturday 15th August 1914. The 2nd Battalion returned from India on Christmas Eve and he joined them in Winchester before the end of the year. On Tuesday 12th January 1915 Francis paraded with the Battalion when they were inspected by HM King George

V; the next day he left Winchester for Southampton. The battalion embarked on *SS Maidan* and at 6.30pm sailed for Le Havre. Within twenty-four hours he entrained for Hazebrouck — a long, winding and tiring journey. They went into camp at Caëstre and Flêtre. On Thursday 28th the Battalion was inspected by Field Marshal Sir John French. On Tuesday 2nd February they marched the thirteen miles to a camp in Ouderdom. Their first sight of the Germans was the next day when an aeroplane flew low over the camp at which many of the men took pot-shots. After about thirty-six hours of training they marched to Ypres and went into the line for a few hours before being ordered to return to Ouderdom. A further twenty-four hours were spent at rest before Francis marched to St Eloi into pretty poor trenches, many of them were only two feet deep. A good number of the men had to lie flat in the line and as a result their rifles became clogged in mud and unusable. Francis remained on tours of duty and periods of rest and training until he was killed. On Sunday 14th February Francis and the Battalion were ordered to Trois Rois where Brigade Headquarters were based, *en route* collecting additional ammunition for their front line duties. They marched into the line under heavy artillery fire, but no losses were sustained; it soon became a day of fierce close fighting with heavy casualties. At 3.30am on Monday 15th Francis was relieved, marching to Kruisstraat and into their billets at 6.00am: only two hundred officers and men from the Battalion arrived. At 5.15pm they were called up to the front just north of St Eloi. At 9.00pm the whistles blew and they advanced. However, the Germans put up flares and opened up with strong rifle, machine-gun and artillery fire and during the attack Francis and eleven men were killed.

Lieutenant Campbell Greenhill, MC

3rd Battalion Worcestershire Regiment

Died on Friday 10th August 1917, aged 34

Commemorated on Panel 34.

Citation for the Military Cross, London Gazette, Thursday 26th July 1917:

"For conspicuous gallantry and devotion to duty during a raid upon enemy trenches. Finding his party suddenly attacked by a machine-gun, he attacked it with bombs down the flank and front, putting it out of action and saving his company from many casualties."

Campbell Greenhill

Campbell was born at Garelochhead, Argyll, on Wednesday 4th November 1885, son of Dr Robert Greenhill, of 1 Rodger Drive, Rutherglen, Glasgow. He was educated at The High School of Glasgow and became a commercial traveller, a member of the Glasgow University OTC, Scout Master of the 113th Scout Troop (Burnside) and a member of the Lanarkshire Field Artillery, Territorials. Campbell enjoyed playing tennis and was Secretary of Burnside Tennis Club.

On Monday 14th September 1914 Campbell enlisted at Rutherglen and served as a driver until he was commissioned on Friday 14th May 1915. He left France on Tuesday 14th March 1916, joining the Battalion in the field.

At the end of May 1917 Campbell marched with his men from a camp at Dranouter to Kruisstraat Cabaret near Wulverghem prior to the Battle of Messines. At 10.45am on Saturday 2nd June a raid took place on *'Nutmeg Avenue'* and *'Nutmeg Support'*. A German machine-gun opened up causing havoc. Campbell drove away the crew and captured the gun by bombing his way forward by himself. For this action he was awarded his Military Cross, gazetted on Thursday 26th July 1917.

On Friday 10th August Campbell blew his whistle and led the men forward at dawn under cover of a tremendous artillery barrage. The attack went up the Westhoek Ridge taking the crest but they could not progress much further. The German artillery opened on them on the Ridge, his colleagues in *'Glencorse Wood'* were being driven back. On their right the Cheshire's were very badly cut up, by 11.00am all senior officers had been killed and the 3rd Battalion Worcestershires took command. From the direction of the Hannebeek Germans could be seen advancing in their direction which was countered time and time again. During one of the attacks Campbell was killed by machine-gun fire.

Lieutenant John Francis Bernal Greenwood

1st Battalion King's Own (Royal Lancaster Regiment)

Died on Sunday 2nd May 1915, aged 30

Commemorated on Panel 12.

John Greenwood

John was born in Limerick, Ireland, on Sunday 22nd March 1885, eldest son of the late Lieutenant Colonel Joseph Greenwood and Mrs Greenwood, of 212 Haverstock Hill, London NW3. He was educated at the Military College, Plymouth. On Friday 29th July 1910, at Lucknow, India, John married Frances Mary Georgina Greenwood (née Anderson), of Evelyn Court, Cheltenham, and they had a son, Henry Vincent Bernal, born on Wednesday 16th August 1911.

John enlisted in the Royal West Surrey Regiment and was gazetted to the King's Own in January 1908, serving in India for five years. He undertook considerable training and obtained a wide range of certificates. John also passed examinations in Hindustani, Pushtu, Persian and was a qualified French interpreter. In 1910, at Lucknow, he won the Cup as the *'Best Officer-at-Arms'*. He was promoted Lieutenant in May 1911. In January 1913 he served at Warley, Essex, in the Army Pay Department.

John rejoined his regiment in January 1915 and went out to the front in April 1915. During the Second Battle of Ypres he was hit in the head by machine-gun fire and killed instantaneously whilst repelling a German attack at St Julien. The Germans buried him in the field.

One of his Corporal's wrote: *"On the 2nd May, at about 3 p.m., the enemy used gas, and under cover of it they advanced, abut 700 strong, against a farmhouse held by ten men of 'C' Company. Lieutenant Greenwood, the Corporal (also called Greenwood), and three men of the same company rushed about 200 yards to the farmhouse to assist the small party holding it. The enemy continued their advance under rifle and machine-gun fire, getting to within 300 yards. During the attack, Lieutenant Greenwood with his revolver, and later, when his ammunition was finished, with a rifle, and the men with rifles, accounted for a good many of the enemy. After firing a few rounds from the rifle, Lieutenant Greenwood was shot in the head, his death being instantaneous. The small party had to retire, leaving the officer's body behind with those of ten of the men."*

22565 Private Leonard Greetham

14th Battalion Hampshire Regiment

Died on Tuesday 31st July 1917, aged 27

Commemorated on Panel 35.

Leonard was the son of Henry and Helen Greetham, of Mayfield House, Stratfieldsaye, Hampshire. He was educated locally. He was married to Gertrude L Greetham of Virginia Cottages, Hurst, Berkshire.

Leonard enlisted in Godalming, Surrey, and trained at *'Witley Camp'* before leaving from Southampton to Le Havre on Sunday 5th March 1916.

In May Leonard moved from near St Omer, where the Battalion had been undertaking training, towards the Belgian border, continuing their training at Wormhoudt (to be made infamous in the Second World War where a group of British soldiers were massacred). On Saturday 26th May 1917 they were in the line at Wieltje on the Salient, followed by the Yser Canal and then *'Hill Top Farm'*, and remained in the front line for a month. The Battalion was sent to the rear where they continued training ready for the Battle of Passchendaele. On Sunday 29th they moved to a second line position ready for Zero Hour. They attacked from *'Bilge Trench'* towards St Julien, their objective. They were supported by tanks but hampered by driving rain. In this action Leonard died, together with 2nd Lieutenant Denis Hewitt (who won his Victoria Cross) and 2nd Lieutenant John Falconer, both of whom are commemorated on the Menin Gate, see below.

Lieutenant Hewitt

Captain Reuben Henry Gregory, MC

9th Battalion Sherwood Foresters (Notts and Derby Regiment)

Died on Saturday 9th June 1917

Commemorated on Panel 39.

Reuben was educated at Christ's Hospital, Horsham, and went up to Hertford College, Oxford, in 1910.

In September 1915 Reuben volunteered and was commissioned, leaving for France with the 10th Battalion in July 1915. He had not been in the front very long when he was wounded in the foot late on Friday 27th August 1915. He joined the 9th Battalion when they arrived in France after serving in the Gallipoli Campaign. On Sunday 18th June 1916 he took the line near Arras where he served for two months before being sent to the Somme. They went into training before taking the line. He took part in various actions including the Battle of Thiepval from Tuesday 26th to Thursday 28th

September. He continued to serve on the Somme in the front line as well as undertaking a series of training and rest until Friday 18th May 1917, when they entrained at Albert for Caëstre from where they marched to billets in Godeswaersvelde.
After a short period of rest they marched for two hours to reach their new billets in Westoutre on Thursday 24th where they were able to have a bath and were issued with clean uniforms. Initially Reuben organised his men into working parties before undertaking last minute training for the Battle of Messines. Together with his fellow officers and NCOs he carefully studied the model of the battlefield. At 10.00am on Wednesday 6th June Reuben was called to a conference with the Colonel to finalise the plans for the next day. At 11.30pm Reuben marched to the line, arriving two hours later. The Battalion was held in reserve at the commencement of the Battle. The use of mines was a well kept secret and so when they were blown the terrific noise came as a shock to all the men. At 1.30pm they were ordered to move forward and reached Messines Ridge with little difficulty, then onto the *'Mahieu Farm'* without the support of the creeping barrage which had been promised. The Battalion consolidated the position and remained in the line with the British artillery opening a large barrage late in the evening. Shortly after midnight rations arrived which cheered everyone. Whilst at *'Forester Post'* Reuben was killed in the late morning of Saturday 9th June.

Second Lieutenant The Honourable Gerald William Grenfell (known as 'Billy')

8th Battalion Rifle Brigade

Died on Friday 30th July 1915, aged 25

Commemorated on Panel 46.

Billy at School

Billy was born on Saturday 29th March 1890, son of William Henry, 1st Baron Desborough, KG, GCVO, and Ethel Anne Priscilla, Lady Desborough (Lady of the Bedchamber to HM the Queen), of Taplow Court, Clivedon Road, Taplow, Buckinghamshire, grandson of John, 11th Earl of Westmorland.

Lord Desborough

He was educated at Summer Fields from 1899 where he was a good athlete and held four School records. He then attended Eton College from 1903 to 1909 where he won an entrance Scholarship and the Newcastle Scholarship (one of the few Oppidans to be so awarded) as a member of Mr Arthur Christopher Benson's and Mr Arthur Murray Goodhart's Houses. He was one the editors of the *'Eton College Chronicle'* from 1907 to 1909. Billy went up to Balliol College, Oxford, in 1909, and was awarded the Craven Scholarship in 1911. He won a Real Tennis Blue and boxed for the College. Billy had intended to read for the Bar but the war intervened.

Billy Grenfell's family coat of arms

Billy and Julian with their mother

Billy volunteered at the outbreak of war and was gazetted on Saturday 12th September 1914. He was sent for training until Saturday 22nd May 1915 when he sailed for France. He entrained for Watten in northern France to continue training; from Friday 28th he was attached to the North and South Staffordshires for training in the front line on the French-Belgian border. On Saturday 29th Major Billy Congreve, VC, DSO, MC, wrote: *"I rode off to look for Ronnie who is now out here commanding the 8th Battalion which is in the 14th Division. Eventually found him in a farm between Neuve Eglise and Bailleul. I much admired the general appearance of the good riflemen. They may be new but they look splendid and have such a fine lot of officers."* (Major Congreve was killed on Thursday 27th July 1916 and is buried in Corbie Communal Cemetery Extension.)

Major Congreve

On Monday 7th June Billy went into the line for the first time at St Eloi for a three day tour of duty after which they were relieved by the 7th Battalion. On Monday 5th July the Germans bombarded their lines and twenty of them managed to enter the trenches. The North Staffordshire's Bombing Officer rushed in and helped mount the counter-attack which cleared them out. On Friday 30th July Billy was leading his troops from a trench in *'Zouave Wood'*, near Hooge, at 3.00pm when he was killed by machine-gun fire. He spoke to the men of his platoon and urged them: *"Remember, you are Englishmen. Do nothing to dishonour that name."* Due to the fierce battle that raged, Billy's body was not recovered until Sunday 15th August when it was buried but the grave was subsequently lost. He had written: *"Death is such a frail barrier out here that men cross it smilingly and gallantly every day."*
Lieutenant Carey (later Lieutenant Colonel Carey, DSO) wrote a comprehensive account of the action:

"The 8th Battalion left Ypres by the Lille Gate something after 10 p.m. on July 29. 'A' Company was commanded by Lieutenant L. A. McAfee, an old Cambridge Rugger Blue, beloved of both officers and men; he was also in charge of No. 1 Platoon (we lost our original company commander a week or so earlier at Railway Wood — the first officer of the Battalion killed). I commanded No. 2 Platoon, Lieutenant M. Scrimgeour No. 3 and 2nd Lieutenant S. C. Woodroffe No. 4. 'A' Company was to hold the line on the left of the crater, with my platoon on the right of our sector holding up to the left edge of the crater. No. 4 Platoon was on my left, and Nos. 1 and 3 in a trench running parallel to No. 4's bit, a few yards in rear of it. 'C' Company (Captain E. F. Prior) was to hold the line on the right of the crater; Keith Rae commanded a platoon in this company and I'm pretty sure his platoon's sector was that nearest the right-hand edge of the crater. 'B' Company (Captain A. L. C. Cavendish) and 'D' Company (Captain A. C. Sheepshanks) were in support, in trenches at the near edge of the wood.

I remember having a strong presentiment as I plodded up to the line that night that I should never come back from it alive; in the event I was the only officer in my company to survive the next twenty-four hours.

The relief was complete shortly after midnight. It has been rather a tiring business, for we had two miles to cover before the line was reached, with the delays inevitable to troops moving over strange ground in the dark; and the difficulty of getting our men into the broken-down trenches while the 7th Battalion were getting out of them was even greater here than we had found elsewhere. I had warned my men of the need for silence, owing to the nearness of the Boche, and I remember when the time came feeling certain that the tramp of feet and the clatter of rifles must have given the show away (I need not have worried — we knew afterwards that the Boche learned from more reliable sources when a relief was to take place). Indeed, the night was ominously quiet. There had been very little shelling on the way up — for which we were duly thankful; but the absence of the sniper's bullet as we filed up the communication trench from Zouave Wood was something more surprising. The continued silence after we got into the line became uncanny. About an hour after we were settled in and the last of the 7th Battalion had disappeared into the darkness, I decided that a bomb or two lobbed over into the Boche trench running close to mine near the crater might disturb him if he were up to mischief there. (It should be mentioned here that in these early days of bombs there was only a limited number of men in each battalion who could use them, and these were organized as a squad under a single officer. Their disposition over the battalion sector and their supply of bombs was under the supervision of the Battalion bombing officer, who on this night had begun his rounds on the 'C' Company sector and had not yet reached mine. I had in the meanwhile posted a few bombers attached to my platoon at what I considered the vital spots, the point where my trench joined the crater, and Point B. Our supply of bombs was small, though more were expected to be up before daylight.) Accordingly I got one of the bombers to throw over a hand grenade; it looked to carry about the right length and it exploded well. We waited; no reply. At short intervals he sent over two more. 'This ought to rouse them,' we said; again no reply. There was something sinister about this.

It was now about half an hour before dawn, and just then the order for the usual morning 'stand-to' came through from the Company Commander. I started on the extreme right of my bit of the line, to ensure that all my men were lining the trench, with their swords fixed. Working down gradually to the Point B, I decided to go on along the stretch of trench which bent back from the German line almost in the form of a communication trench; there were servants and some odd men from my platoon in so-called shelters along here, and I wanted to make sure that these people, who are apt to be forgotten at 'stand-to,' were all on the alert. Just as I was getting to the last of these (Point D in plan), there was a sudden hissing sound, and a bright crimson glare over the crater turned the whole scene red. As I looked I saw three or four distinct jets of flame—like a line of powerful fire-hoses spraying fire instead of water—shoot across my fire-trench (see dotted lines in plan). How long this lasted it is impossible to say—probably not more than a minute; but the effect was so stupefying that, for my own part, I was utterly unable for some moments to think — collectedly. I remember catching hold of a rifle with fixed sword of a man standing next to me

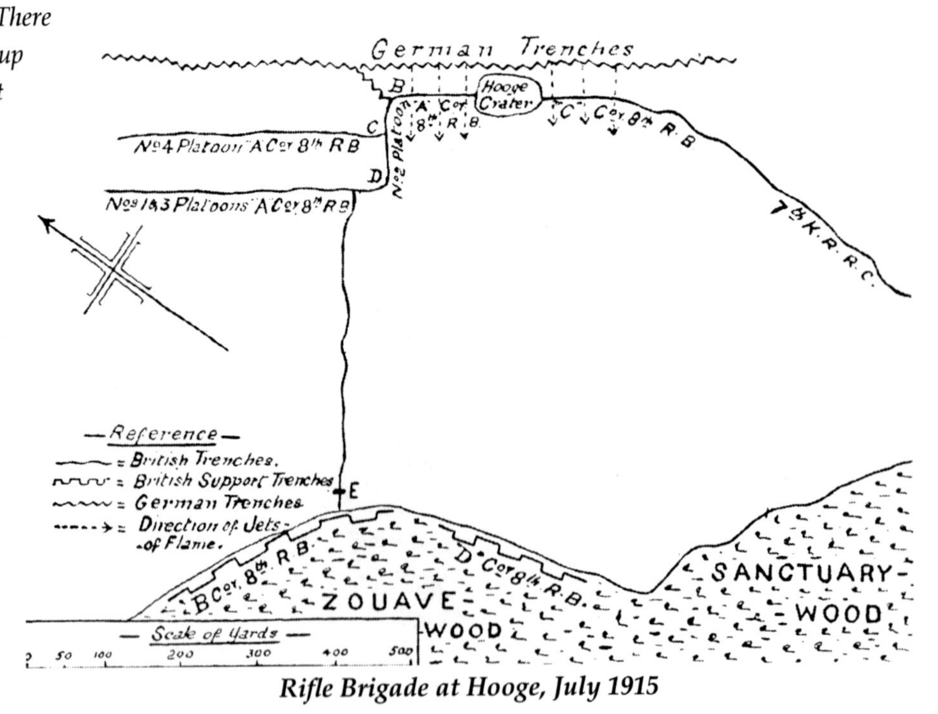

Rifle Brigade at Hooge, July 1915

and making for Point B, when there was a terrific explosion, and almost immediately afterwards one of my men, with blood running down his face, stumbled into me, coming from the direction of the crater. He was followed by one or two others, most of them wounded. The minenwerfer had started, and such men as had survived the liquid fire were, in accordance with orders, giving the crater a wide berth. Then broke out every noise under Heaven! 'Minnie' and bombs in our front trench, machine-guns from places unseen, shrapnel over the communication trenches and the open ground between us and the support line in Zouave Wood, and high-explosive on the wood and its vicinity. It was impossible to get up the trench towards the crater while men were coming down in driblets, so I got out of the trench to the right of Point C to try and get a better idea of the situation. I was immediately hit in the right shoulder by a shrapnel bullet, but I didn't have time to think much about it; still less did I realize that it was to prove my salvation. The first thing I saw was men jumping over the edge of the crater into 'C' Company's trench. It was still the grey light of dawn and for some moments I could not distinguish whether they were Boche or British; but, deciding soon that they must be Boche, I told the few survivors of my platoon, who by that time had joined me, to open fire on them, which they promptly did. At this point McAfee came up, followed by Michael Scrimgeour, and we had a hurried consultation. By this time the Boches were in my bit of trench as well, and we saw that my handful couldn't get back into it. It was a death-trap to stay where we were, under a shrapnel barrage; so Mac, after weighing the possibility of going for the Boche across the open with the bayonet, reluctantly gave the order for me to get the remnant of my platoon back to the support line, and said that he and Michael would follow with the rest of the company. About a dozen men of No. 2 Platoon were all that I could find—those who had faced the flame attack were never seen again—and we started back over the open. I doubt if we could have found the communication trench if we had wanted to, but for the moment there was open fighting to be done (we had no reason to suppose that the Germans were coming no farther than our front line). A retirement is a miserable business, but there can be nothing but praise for the conduct of the men in this one; there was nothing approaching a 'run,' and at every few yards they lay down and fired with the coolness of an Aldershot field day at any Bosches who could be seen coming over into our line. There was a matter of four hundred yards of open ground to be covered under a regular hail of machine-gun and shrapnel fire, and I have always marvelled how anyone got over it alive; as it was, most of my fellows were wounded during that half-hour's retirement, if not before, and one was shot dead within a yard of me while in the act of firing. Eventually, I (literally) fell into the main communication trench about twenty yards ahead of the support line (at Point E); it must have been then about 4.30 a.m. Here I was joined almost at once by Cavendish (O.C. 'B' Coy.), who, on learning that our front line was lost, suggested that we should there and then build a barricade in the communication trench—it was still expected that the Boche would come on. My small party set to, using sandbags from the side of the trench, and a supply of bombs came up while we were working. It was rather ticklish work when it came to the upper part of the barricade, as the Boche was using shrapnel very accurately, and there were a lot of rifle and machine-gun bullets flying about. But the men in the support trenches behind us were having a worse time, for Zouave Wood was being heavily bombarded and 'B' and D' Companies were 'suffering a lot of casualties. During this time, Mac, having got his survivors back to the supports, came up to see how I had fared. He was very cool, but terribly unhappy at our losses of men and ground; and especially at having been unable to get into touch with Woodroffe. I was thankful at finding him safe, and still more so to learn that Michael also was all right. He went off almost at once to reorganize the remainder of the company. We continued to stand by our barricade, and I borrowed a rifle and tried to do a bit of sniping; the Boche could be seen throwing up the earth in our front line, and it now looked as if he were going to stay there. About this time came our first bit of consolation. Our artillery had begun to retaliate, and we could see shells bursting in our old front line; but the effort was feeble as compared with the German bombardment. Some hour and a half later Mac came back with the grievous news that Michael Scrimgeour had been killed while reorganizing his men in the wood. He also began to fuss about my wound, and eventually gave me a direct order to go back to the dressing-station. I had to go, and that was the last I saw of poor McAfee, who was killed that afternoon leading his men in a counter-attack."

Of the officers mentioned in the narrative above, Captain Edward Prior died on Friday 15th September 1916 and is buried in Bernafay Wood British Cemetery, Montauban, 2nd Lieutenant Sidney Woodroffe won his Victoria Cross in this action and together with Lieutenant Michael Scrimengeour, 2nd Lieutenant Keith Rae and Lieutenant Lewis McAfee they died in the action and are commemorated on the Menin Gate.

Captain A C Sheepshanks wrote: *"He died splendidly leading his men over open ground up hill in the face of a tremendous fire from machine-guns. His Platoon Sergt. saw him pitch forward with a bullet in the head, and thinks he was hit again in the side as he fell. He must have been killed instantaneously as he was not seen to move afterwards. Both as his company commander and his friend I shall miss him enormously. His platoon all loved him, and he had somehow inspired them with a fighting spirit, and it was only a few days ago that I told the Col. that Bill's platoon was the best fighting platoon I had."*

On Saturday 31st July, Lieutenant Colonel Alexander Maclachlan*, Commander of the 8th Battalion, wrote to Lord Desborough: *"Billy was killed yesterday afternoon about 3.00pm when gallantly charging over the open at the head of his men. It is all too tragic and I dare not think what this double*

shock can mean to you." (* Lieutenant Colonel Maclachlan was killed and is buried in Savy British Cemetery.)
Billy had been killed less than a mile away from where his brother, Julian, had been fatally injured. Billy was one of the war poets.
At Taplow Court a sculpture of Apollo in his chariot of the sun, placed on a boulder, with an inscription that reads: *"In memory of the happy lives of Julian Henry Francis Grenfell Captain Royal Dragoons, died of wounds at Boulogne May 26th 1915 aged 27, and of Gerald William Grenfell, Second Lieutenant Rifle Brigade killed leading a charge near Hooge July 30th 1915, aged 25."*
The associated plaque has *'Into Battle'*, composed by Julian Grenfell, inscribed:

"The naked earth is warm with spring,
And with green grass and bursting trees
Leans to the sun's gaze glorying,
And quivers in the sunny breeze;
And Life is Colour and Warmth and Light,
And a striving evermore for these;
And he is dead who will not fight;
And who dies fighting has increase.

The fighting man shall from the sun
Take warmth, and life from the glowing earth;
Speed with the light-foot winds to run,
And with the trees to newer birth;
And find when fighting shall be done,
Great rest and fullness after death.

All the bright company of Heaven
Hold him in their high comradeship,
The Dog Star, and the Sisters Seven,
Orion's Belt and Sworded Hip.

The woodland trees that stand together,
They stand to him each one a friend,
They gently speak in the windy weather,
They guide to valley and ridges' end.

The kestrel hovering by day
And the little owls that call by night,
Bid him be swift and keen as they,
As keen of ear, as swift of sight.

The blackbird sings to him, 'Brother, brother,
If this be the last song you shall sing,
Sing well, for you may not sing another;
Brother, sing.'

In dreary, doubtful, wiling hours,
Before the brazen frenzy starts,
The horses show him nobler powers;
O! patient eyes, courageous hearts

And when the burning moment breaks,
And all things else are out of mind,
And only Joy of Battle takes
Him by the throat, and makes him blind

Through joy and blindness he shall know,
Not caring much to know, that still
Nor lead nor steel shall reach him, so
That it be not the Destined Will.

The thundering lines of battle stands,
And in the air Death moans and sings;
But Day shall clasp him with strong hands,
And Night shall fold him in soft wings."

In Eton College, Eton, a plaque was placed in the Cloisters with the inscription: *"In memory of the Hon Julian Henry Francis Grenfell, D.S.O., Captain 1st Royal Dragoons, died of wounds received in action at Ypres 13th May 1915. A.A. Somerville 1901-1906, The Hon Gerald William Grenfell Lieut. 8th Battalion Rifle Brigade, killed in action at Ypres 30th July 1915, sons of 1st Baron Desborough of Taplow Court Buckinghamshire. Francis Octavus Grenfell, V.C., Captain, 9th Lancers killed in action at Ypres 24th May 1915. Riversdale Nonus Grenfell, Captain, Bucks Hussars (Attached) 9th Lancers killed in action at the Aisne Friday 4th September 1914, also of Robert Septimus Grenfell, Lieut. 12th Lancers killed in action at Omdurman 2nd September 1898. Walter Durnford 1889-1893. Pascoe St Leger Grenfell, killed in the Matabele War March 1896. Reginald Du Pre Grenfell Lieut. 17th Lancers died of fever contracted on service in India March 1888, sons of Pascoe Du Pre Grenfell of Wilton Park, Bucks, W. Evans 1841-1846."*
Another memorial to the Grenfell Family and others, was erected at Mostyn House School, Parkgate, Cheshire:
Plaque 1: *"Captain Francis Octavius Grenfell, V.C., The 9th Lancers. Killed at Ypres, May 24th 1915. Saved the guns in retreat from Mons. Aged 34."*
Plaque 2: *"Lieut. Riversdale Nonus Grenfell, attached to 9th Lancers. Killed at Battle of the Aisne, Sept. 14th 1914. Aged 34."*
Plaque 3: *"Captain The Hon Julian H. F. Grenfell, D.S.O., The Royal Dragoons. Wounded at Ypres, May 13, & died at Boulogne, May 26th. 1915, aged 27. Author of 'Into Battle'."*
Plaque 4: *"2nd Lieut. The Hon G. W. Grenfell 8th Batt. The Rifle Brigade. Killed at Hooge, July 29th 1915, aged 25. Scholar of Eton & of Balliol Coll., Newcastle Scholar of Eton, Craven Scholar of Oxford."*
Billy is commemorated on the House of Lords War Memorial.
His brother, Captain Julian Grenfell, died on Wednesday 26th May 1915 and is buried in Boulogne Eastern Cemetery and his cousins Captain Francis Grenfell, VC, is buried in Vlamertinghe Cemetery and Captain Riversdale Grenfell died on Friday 4th September 1914

and is buried in Vendresse Churchyard.
'Julian Grenfell: his Life and the Times of his Death 1888-1915', was published by Weidenfeld & Nicolson, London 1976, also records considerable information about Billy. The comedienne and actress Joyce Grenfell was related to the family.

SECOND LIEUTENANT JOHN EDWARD GRESSON

3rd Battalion Cheshire Regiment
Died on Monday 24th May 1915, aged 23
Commemorated on Panel 19.

John Gresson

John was born at Woodville, Birr, King's County, on Friday 3rd June 1881, seventh and youngest son of Major W H Greeson and Mrs Greeson, of Fernleigh, Cheltenham. He was educated at Cheltenham College from 1896 to 1897 as a Day Boy followed by Rossall School until 1899. John was employed by Jardine, Matheson & Co in China. He was an excellent horseman, enjoying polo, steeplechasing, and coursing. He served with the Shanghai Light Horse and the Hong Kong Light Horse.
At the outbreak of war John was in England on leave, he volunteered and was gazetted in September 1914. Initially he served in Birkenhead and then on coastal defence in Scotland. He went out to France in March 1915. At dawn on Monday 24th May 1915 the Germans launched a gas attack. John and his men were getting ready to eat lunch when they were called to the line before they had the chance to eat it! At 5.00pm they commenced the attack; it was poorly executed mainly due to the fact the men were too exhausted and hungry, but they got within two hundred yards of the German lines, near Hooge Wood. John was killed and was buried in the field.
The Official History stated: "*... in the evening of the 24th May the German Fourth Army issued orders that operations should be stopped. The German Battalions were quite worn out and had suffered nearly as many casualties as the British.*"

CAPTAIN RUPERT HAROLD GRETTON

8th Battalion Bedfordshire Regiment
Died on Friday 17th December 1915, aged 30
Commemorated on Panel 31.

Rupert was born on Monday 8th November 1886, younger son of John Gretton, DL, and Mary Louisa Gretton. His brother, Colonel John Gretton, PC, CBE, VD, MP, JP, was Chairman of the brewers, Bass, Ratcliff and Gretton Limited. Rupert was educated at Marlborough College from January 1900 as a member of Preshute.

Rupert Gretton

Rupert volunteered at the outbreak of war and left for France in early September 1915. He was sent to Merville for further training before being sent to Vermelles to assist in the Battle of Loos on Sunday 26th. On Monday 4th October the Battalion was inspected by Major General John Capper before leaving for the Salient. They arrived at Vlamertinghe at noon on Monday 5th in the pouring rain. The Battalion undertook a series of duties including guard duty at Abeele and tours of duty into the line. On Wednesday 15th December Rupert took his men from camp to *'Forward Cottage'* where they relieved the King's Royal Rifle Corps. Throughout Friday 17th their trenches came under heavy shell fire and during one such attack Rupert was killed.

1675 PRIVATE HARRY GRICE

1st/5th Battalion King's Own (Royal Lancaster Regiment)
Died on Tuesday 27th April 1915, aged 16
Commemorated on Panel 12.

Harry was born at Scotforth, Lancashire, son of Alfred and Jane Grice, of 7 Ripley Street, Lancaster.
He enlisted in Lancaster and was sent for training. The Battalion embarked for Le Havre, arriving on Monday 15th February 1915. They entrained for northern France to continue training before taking the line for the first time. Harry was in the line which was under continuous pressure following the first gas attack that took place on Thursday 22nd April when he was killed in action.

SECOND LIEUTENANT JOHN HENRY CLIFFORD GRIERSON

3rd Battalion Gordon Highlanders
Died on Tuesday 31st July 1917
Commemorated on Panel 38.

John was the son of Mr and Mrs Grierson. He was educated at Christ's Hospital, Horsham, from 1906 to 1912.
John took part in the Battle of Arras before being sent to the Ypres Salient. In July 1917 he went into training for the Battle of Passchendaele. John took his men into the assembly positions on Monday 30th July 1917 ready for the attack that would commence at 3.50am. Their objective was the Frezenberg Ridge some distance ahead of them. John led his men forward and became involved in fierce

hand-to-hand fighting and John was seen despatching a German with a bayonet close to *'Wilde Wood'*. At 4.25am the first objective was taken and he moved towards the second which was taken a few minutes before 6.00am. There was a slight lull in the advance as the artillery had to be brought up into range. As they continued their advance later in the day, John was killed.

15613 Private John Griffin

8th Battalion King's Own (Royal Lancaster Regiment)

Died on Thursday 2nd March 1916, aged 25
Commemorated on Panel 12.

John was born at Gateshead on Sunday 13th April 1890, eldest son of Mrs Mary Eagles (formerly Griffin), of 28 Westbourne Street, Everton, Liverpool, and the late William Griffin. He was educated at St Francis Xavier's Roman Catholic School, Liverpool, and then was employed as a tobacco presser.

John enlisted in November 1914 and was sent for training. He left for France in August 1915. John was killed in action at *'The Bluff'*, close to the Ypres to Comines Canal.

Major West wrote: *"I remember him well when I was commanding 'A' Company, and always found him so willing and capable. It is indeed a great sorrow to us all. … In your sorrow it may be some little comfort to you to know that the action was a most brilliant one, and all behaved most splendidly, upholding well the traditions of the old regiment."*

His Chaplain, The Reverend Leonard, wrote: *"I know what a heavy blow this will be to you, and my heart goes out in sympathy; but nothing can take from you the pride you will always have that he gave his life in such a good cause. His is the death of a true man and a brave soldier, for he gave his life for England's honour and to protect our homes from German oppression."*

Captain Lord Hugh William Grosvenor

'C' Squadron 1st Life Guards

Died on Friday 30th October 1914, aged 30
Commemorated on Panel 3.

Hugh Grosvenor's family coat of arms

Hugh was born on Sunday 6th April 1884, eldest son of Hugh, 1st Duke of Westminster and his second wife, Katharine Caroline, Duchess of Westminster (daughter of William, 2nd Lord Chesham), of Combermere Abbey, Whitchurch, Salop and 2 South Street, Park Lane, London W. On Saturday 21st April 1906 Hugh married Lady Mabel Grosvenor (daughter of William, 3rd Earl of Enniskillen, who became Lady Mabel Hamilton Stubber), of 9 Southwick Crescent, London. They two sons Gerald Hugh, born in 1907 who became the 4th Duke of Westminster, and Robert in 1910 who succeeded his brother as 5th Duke of Westminster.

His Grace Hugh Richard Arthur, 2nd Duke of Westminster, GCVO, brother of Hugh. The Duke organised transport and support from the outset of war.

Hugh entrained at Ludgershall for Southampton, embarking on *SS Huanchaco* which left for Zeebrugge on Wednesday 7th October 1914, arriving in the early hours the next morning. The situation was confused, the *raison d'être* for being sent directly to Belgium had gone. The defence of Antwerp was abandoned as the city was already being evacuated. It was not until 3.30pm that they were ordered from the quay to ride south to Blankenberge. On Friday 9th they were ordered south to Jabbeke where they went into billets around Loppem. The next day they continued south to Beernem via Oostcamp.

On Tuesday 13th they arrived in Ypres and were marched out to Gheluwe, east of Gheluvelt as intelligence reported that Menin, just a few miles east, was occupied by the enemy, so they were ordered to Winkel St Eloi via Dadizeele. The next day Hugh was sent Ypres town where at 10.00am a Taube aeroplane flew low over the town square which was successfully shot down by Maxims. On Friday 16th he took his men from Vierstraat to Poelkapelle, via Ypres; that night they were billeted in Passchendaele. At 9.00am on Sunday 18th he took the men out along the Roeselare to Menin road where they came under attack and were able to see the explosions as Roeselare was being shelled. The Regiment was forced to retire to Moorslede and then Zonnebeke. He took the men back into the line where on Tuesday 20th he organised them to dig furiously and establish a line. The German artillery found their position and dropped shells onto them; the French on their flank retired which forced the line to be straightened — Hugh and the Regiment had no alternative but to retire also. On Thursday 22nd Hugh was sent to Hooge in reserve and billeted in Klein Zillebeke before being sent to support the line near Gheluvelt.

Four days later a fellow officer wrote: *"The Blues were ordered to make a mounted demonstration towards Kruiseecke. The Squadrons were rallied as quickly as possible, and we went off at a gallop towards the ridge, C Squadron leading. By this time it was getting dusk, and just as well for us that it was. We rode on to the crest between two trenches held by Hugh Grosvenor's Squadron, and here the Germans spotted us, and we came in for a hail of shrapnel and bullets. My horse was hit in the shoulder, and I got into a trench in which were Hugh Grosvenor and Gerry Ward. They seemed surprised at our selecting this spot for a point-to-point, as they can't put their heads out of the trenches without being shot at; I got out and shot my horse with a revolver. On reaching the crest we rode a left-handed course for a short distance. Alastair's horse was shot, and eventually Dick Molyneux rallied the Squadron and took them out of action, D Squadron being blocked by a very high fence and wire. D and B dismounted and opened a covering fire. The result of our little manœuvre seems to have been that the Germans thought the whole Cavalry Corps was behind us, ready to gallop their trenches, and turned every available gun on to the valley behind us. This was exactly what was wanted, as it relieved the pressure on the Twentieth Brigade. By now it was quite dark, the firing stopped, and all rode back to our billets via Pig Farm. Otto and his one gun are still in the trenches. There are only three machine-guns left in the Brigade. Thirty horses were killed in our little demonstration, but the human casualties, considering the fire we drew were small. Newcombe having been hit in the eye two days ago, Harradine becomes R.C.M."*

Hugh was on the Zandvoorde Ridge commanding 'C' Squadron when he was killed in action. The War Diary for the day records the following: *"6 a.m. Heavy bombardment of position opened. At 7.30 a.m. position was attacked by large force of infantry. This attack proved successful owing to greatly superior numbers. Regiment retired in good order about 10 a.m. except 'C' Squadron on left flank from which only about ten men got back. Remainder of Squadron missing. Also one machine-gun put out of action.*

Regiment retired behind 6th Brigade, which turned out to support. 2nd Dragoons and 2nd and 4th Hussars also came to support, but did not come into action. Having gained Zandvoorde ridge, enemy did not press the attack very vigorously, and second position occupied by 6th Brigade was not attacked. At dusk this position was taken over by 4th Guard's Brigade."

An officer wrote: *"One of the machine-guns of the First Life Guards had jammed and was useless, and Worsley, after seven days of ceaseless strain in the trenches, was asked by the Brigade Major to remain on for a further short spell of duty. 'All in the day's work' was the smiling reply of a young officer from whose lips a smile scarcely ever seemed to fade. Hugh Grosvenor and Gerald Ward, who perished side by side, were brothers-in-law as well as brother officers."*

Corporal of Horse Lloyd wrote: *"When the order to retire was given it did not reach the main body of 'C' Squadron owing to its position being slightly detached from, and in front on the left of, the rest of the Regiment. Lord Hugh Grosvenor, 'C' Squadron Leader, was not the man who would retire without orders, so they fought it out and died where they stood. No trace of Lord Hugh and his hundred-odd men was ever found."*

Hugh's brother-in-law, The Honourable Gerald Ward, died with him and is commemorated on the Menin Gate, his cousin, Captain Richard Grosvenor died on Wednesday 13th October 1915 and buried in Vermelles British Cemetery.

Hugh is commemorated on the House of Lords War Memorial. A bronze panel showing him in relief was erected in his memory in the Grosvenor Chapel, St Mary's Eccleston.

The Household Cavalry Memorial was erected on the slopes at Zandvoorde.

SECOND LIEUTENANT LAWRENCE ERNEST PELHAM GRUBB

2nd Battalion King's Own Yorkshire Light Infantry

Died on Sunday 15th November 1914
(recorded as Wednesday 18th by CWGC)
Commemorated on Panel 47.

Lawrence Grubb

Lawrence was born at Wembley, Middlesex, in 1892, the only son of Ernest Pelham and Emily Mary Grubb. He was educated at Rugby School from 1906 as a member of Town and went up to Brasenose College, Oxford, with an Exhibition in 1911, graduating with honours in 1914.

At the outbreak of war Lawrence gave up an opportunity of working abroad and with his experience in the OTC became a despatch rider. He received a field commission in October 1914.

In early November Lawrence was in billets at Neuve Eglise when Lieutenant Colonel Withycombe arrived from Singapore to take over the Battalion. He arrived to find that after the two and a half months the Battalion had been in the line, 2nd Lieutenant Slingsby was the only officer that went to France at the outbreak of war, and no sergeants or corporals had survived.

On Saturday 7th November Lawrence and the Battalion were sent to support the attack on Spanbroekmolen by the French. They did not get very far nor did they engage with the enemy to any great extent. During the night of Wednesday 11th and the early hours of Thursday 12th they went into the line south of Douve; the weather was foul and the French colonel showed Lieutenant Colonel Withycombe around the area and whilst doing so fell into a river up to his neck! The next night they

Algernon Smyth

were relieved and sent to the Menin Road and the area around Hooge Wood. The stables of Harenthage Château were in German hands; Captain Algernon Smyth, 2nd Lieutenants Boardman and Lawrence Grubb with fifty men were given the honour of carrying out the order to retake the stables. As they advanced the expectant Germans opened up with all they had — it was totally impossible to reach the stables. During the attack Lawrence was killed as was Captain Smyth (commemorated on the Menin Gate see below), and Boardman was wounded. As a result the Château was temporarily abandoned and over-run by the enemy until 2nd Lieutenant Corballis and 'D' Company retook it later in the day.

Lieutenant C R T Thorp, the Brigade Signalling Officer, wrote: *"The 2nd Battalion K.O.Y.L.I. were brought up into our line on the 14th; they did well as usual, but three officers, including A. B. Smyth, were missing when I went round near Harenthage at dawn yesterday (15th Nov.). Probably all killed. ... I am fit but it is snowing and raining, trenches half-full of water ..."*

The *'Oxford Magazine'* published: *"The death of L.E.P. Grubb has robbed both Brasenose and the world of a very vivid and effective personality. During his three years at Oxford he developed as few men do, and became a striking force in the life around him. His special love was the river, and it is difficult to say how much B.N.C. Rowing has owed to his enthusiasm. One likes to remember that last summer he enjoyed Henley as a member of a B.N.C. Four. His host at Henley writes of him, 'He struck both myself and my wife as the most lovable boy we had ever met'. Nothing but the best ever contented him, either him himself or in others."*

Lawrence is commemorated on the Hove Library War Memorial, Sussex.

51170 Private Charles Grundy

Princess Patricia's Canadian Light Infantry (Eastern Ontario Regiment)

Died on Saturday 17th April 1915, aged 36

Commemorated on Panel 10.

Charles was born at home on Sunday 2nd February 1879, son of Mary Grundy, of Oak Lodge, Prestwich, Manchester, and the late Albert Walker Grundy. He was educated at Shrewsbury School from 1894 to 1897 where he was Head of House, and went up to New College, Oxford, where he was a member of the OTC, graduating with an MA. He went out to Kootenay, British Columbia, Canada, and practised as a solicitor.

Charles volunteered in Victoria on Monday 9th November 1914. He was described as 5ft 7¾in tall, with a 38in waist, a fair complexion, grey eyes and dark hair. Charles joined the Battalion in the field on Thursday 11th March 1915. The Germans exploded mines at St Eloi and captured *'The Mound'* on Sunday 14th March 1915. Charles was ordered to 'stand to' then sent to assist in a counter-attack which was planned for the next day. It did not take place as the terrain was impossible to move across and deploy the men correctly. They were withdrawn at daybreak and ordered to dig support lines. After three days they undertook a two day tour of duty at St Eloi during which their Colonel, Francis Farquhar, DSO, was killed (he is buried in Voormezeele Enclosure No 3). On Wednesday 24th the Middlesex Regiment relieved The Pats who were sent to Poperinghe in reserve. On Tuesday 30th General Sir Herbert Plumer visited them followed by General Sir Horace Smith-Dorrien the next day — Charles would have delighted in all the cleaning and preparation for an inspection, two days running! Charles' first visit to Ypres took place on Monday 5th April when he marched through Vlamertinghe to the famous, now damaged, town where they were billeted overnight. On Wednesday 7th he was sent in front of Bellewaarde Lake for two days before moving to Polygon Wood for a further two days. They were relieved by the Rifle Brigade and marched back to Vlamertinghe. Their camp was bombed by a Zeppelin the next day, Monday 12th thankfully there were no casualties from the bombing raid. They rested and prepared for another visit by General Sir Herbert Plumer the next morning. On Wednesday 14th they returned to their trenches at Polygon Wood and relieved the Rifle Brigade. Shortly before the end of the tour of duty Charles was killed by a sniper.

Lieutenant Francis James Gunter

11th (Prince Albert's Own) Hussars

Died on Monday 24th May 1915, aged 21

Commemorated on Panel 5.

Francis Gunter

Francis was born at Eastcote House, Ruislip on Saturday 5th August 1893, the elder son of Mrs James Gunter, of Aldwark Manor, Alne, York, and the late Major General James Gunter. He was educated at Eton College as a member of Mr Matthew Davenport Hill's House, and was in the Shooting VIII. He went up to Brasenose College, Oxford, in 1912.

At the outbreak of war Francis volunteered and was gazetted in August to the 11th Hussars, and attached to the 12th Reserve Cavalry Regiment for training, promoted Lieutenant in September and went to the front on Wednesday 9th December 1914.

On Thursday 13th May 1915 he was involved in heavy action, recorded by one of the officers: *"At about four a.m. a terrific bombardment began against our front line trenches. The first was most intense, and heavier even than at Messines. At 7.30 a.m. Brigade Headquarters received a message from the 5th D. G.'s, saying that a great deal of their trenches had been blown in, and that their position was critical. The troops of C Squadron, 11th Hussars, under Norrie, were ordered up to support them. There was no communication trench to the front line, but by clever use of the ground they reached the 5th D. G.'s with very few casualties. There bombardment still increased. The Bays were holding on as well, but asked for more communication. A party from Renton's troop succeeded in getting some up, but had several killed in doing so. About 12 o'clock a regiment of the 3rd Cavalry Division, on the right of the Bays, came out of their trenches, and the Germans succeeded in getting a footing in them. General Briggs ordered a counter-attack, which was launched at 2.30 p.m. Renton, who had been twice up to the front line to get information for the Brigadier, volunteered to lead the 10th Hussars up to the Bays' right, where they were to commence their attack. The whole affair was carried out like an Aldershot parade movement. The men screamed at the top of their voices, the officers making hunting noises, as they charged across the open. It was a glorious sight. The Germans ran as if the devil himself was after them. The trenches were retaken, but in the excitement the attackers rushed on another half a mile.*

The Germans then turned on all their artillery, killing their own men as well as ours. Confusion followed, and the attacking line, being broken up, withdrew about half a mile. It was a pity they ever went beyond their original line, as the casualties were heavy.

To return to our own section of the line. The 5th D. G.'s reported that they had put Norrie's troop into their front line, keeping another troop in a support trench. Their casualties had been heavy, and the situation extremely critical. During the afternoon information came in that the whole of the 5th D. G.'s had been shelled out of their trenches, and were retiring. Shortly after this Lance-Corporal Watts came back from the front line with a message from Norrie, explaining the situation. He had held on with his troop when the 5th D. G.'s retired, and besides his own men had a troop of the 5th and one of their machine-guns, and was covering the left flank of the Bays — a grand piece of work. The line had to be held at all cost, so the 11th Hussars were ordered to advance and retake the lost trenches. Lawson's Squadron was sent in advance, with instructions to work up behind the Bays, and push in on the their left. Later, another message came in to say that a squadron of the 19th Hussars, under Tremayne, had pushed up to Norrie and had been put on his left; however, there still existed a considerable gap of unoccupied trench. Divine Providence must have come to our aid, as the shelling practically stopped as the regiment advanced. Soon after 6 p.m. Brigade Headquarters heard that Lawson had successfully got his squadron up to the front line. B Squadron, Stewart Richardson, followed on, and by dusk the line was re-established."

Francis was killed in action near Hooge on Whit Monday.

The *'Oxford Magazine'* wrote: *"F. J. Gunter came up to Brasenose from Eton in October 1912. Quiet, reserved, and self-contained, he made in those two years a place of his own in the College life, and the news of his death comes as a great sorrow to those who knew him more intimately. Under stoical mask of reserve lay hid a deep sense of loyalty and duty; though young, he faced the position which lay before him with a sober sense of the responsibilities it involved; to fear God and to honour the King he owned, in one of his rare moments of confession, as his ideal for himself and for those among whom he hoped to pass his life; a mysterious Providence has only allowed him to leave to them his example. A brilliant horseman, with no knowledge of what fear meant, he rode, as he lived, his own line quiet and straight. Faithful friend and gallant gentleman, he had died a soldier's death and has left his College and all who knew him yet another example of duty."*

In St Stephen's Church, Aldwick, North Yorkshire, a bronze plaque was placed in his memory that contains his 'Penny Plaque', with the inscription: *"In loving memory of Francis James Gunter Lieutenant 11th Hussars. Born 5th August 1893, fell in action in the Second Battle of Ypres 24th May 1915. Greater love hath no man."*

Second Lieutenant Reginald Augustine Jeremy 'Roy' Gwyn

2nd Battalion Lincolnshire Regiment

Died on Friday 3rd March 1916, aged 18

Commemorated on Panel 21.

Roy Gwyn

Roy was the son of Major Reginald P Jeremy Gwyn (7th Battalion Royal Fusiliers), and Isabel Jeremy Gwyn, of 72 Lexham Gardens, Kensington, London and Stanfield Hall, Wymondham. He was educated at Clongowes Wood College, followed by Stoneyhurst College as a member of Rudiments, from September 1910 to 1914 where he gained his nickname *'Roy'*.

At the outbreak of war Roy enlisted in the Empire Battalion of the Royal Fusiliers and rose to the rank of Serjeant. He passed into RMC Sandhurst and gazetted to the Lincolnshires, on Wednesday 12th May 1915. On Thursday 25th November 1915 he left for France and in mid-February 1916 was attached to the 7th Battalion when they were in camp at Reninghelst. For the last week of the month he moved the short distance to a camp in Ouderdom. The Battalion practised for the attack on *'The*

An idealised view of an officers billet

Bluff' with a full scale model which had been made for them to use. During the evening of Wednesday 1st March Reginald went into the line ready for the attack which commenced at 4.30am the next morning. The attack was successful and the front line trenches were taken.

During the night of Thursday 2nd to Friday 3rd March they were under heavy shell-fire, Captain Metcalfe (later Brigadier-General) wrote: *"I have always regarded the concentrated gun fire put down on us by the Germans during and after our recapture of the Bluff as the heaviest bombardment I ever experienced."* In the action at *'The Bluff'* Reginald and thirty-three men were killed and men of the Battalion won four Military Crosses and eight Distinguished Conduct Medals.

His death is described by the Medical Officer of the 1st Gordons: *"During the bombardment of March 3rd, 1916, Lieut. Gwyn was struck by a small piece of shrapnel. The fragment penetrated deeply into the neck, and I am very much afraid that the spinal cord was struck. I dressed him a few minutes after he was wounded. He was quite conscious and suffered no pain, but his lower limbs were completely paralysed. He was wrapped in blankets and removed to the 52nd Field Ambulance a few hours later. I very much fear that he may have died either there on the way to the Clearing Station."*

He was buried by a party of Royal Fusiliers in a wood near the Verbranden Molen on Wednesday 8th March.

The Major wrote: *"He was wounded in the attack on Ypres Bluff. The regiment was divided, as we were supporting four different battalions. Your son behaved very gallantly. He went over with his men in the attack in immediate support of the 1st Gordons, and as their front line was wiped out he and his men reached the enemy's trenches along with their second line. Up to this time he was unhurt. Later on, in the consolidation of the position we had won, he was arranging for a supply of bombs to be sent up to our front line, and was hit outside the bomb store by a shell.*

He was first of all taken to the dressing station of the 1st Gordons, and was dressed there, being sent on later to one of the other ambulances on a stretcher.

Your son was only with us a few days, but during that time he proved himself a gallant and capable officer.

All the casualties had to be carried through an exceptionally severe curtain of shell fire set up by the German artillery. This curtain stretch all along the immediate rear of the fighting, and was about 200 yards in depth — a belt of intensive fire, in fact. That there were cases of bearers, stretchers, and casualties being destroyed I know, and I must not disguise from you that here we have another case."

One of his Masters from Stoneyhurst wrote: *"I had always the highest opinion of his character — rugged and fiery at times, but always absolutely straight. He told me when he was in Rudiments that he had made up his mind to be a soldier, but was anxious then about his health.*

He was very keen on soldiering, and used to read of Wellington and his wars with great delight. I am not sure that he did not take a prize essay on that subject. He certainly won the Lower Line Prize Essay in 1912. He also won the Religious Doctrine Prize in 1911, and the B.C.A. Prize in 1911 and 1912. I hardly ever met a boy who was less influenced by human respect. What he considered right and honourable that he did, without apparently giving a thought to what other might think of him. He was indeed 'one of the very best'."

from

Habershon to Hyslop

Second Lieutenant Philip Henry Habershon

9th Battalion King's Royal Rifle Corps

Died on Saturday 25th September 1915, aged 23

Commemorated on Panel 51.

Philip was born on Thursday 16th March 1893 the third and youngest son of Mr and Mrs Edward Neston Williams Habershon, of Brook Lodge, Holmwood, Surrey and Bath. Philip was educated at Winchester College from 1907 to 1911 and went up to Clare College, Cambridge, in 1912.

Philip volunteered and was commissioned and was sent for training in Petworth and Aldershot until the Spring of 1915. He arrived in Boulogne on Sunday 20th May from where he entrained to northern France. He marched into Belgium and was trained for front line duties. His first major action was at Hooge on Friday 30th July when the Germans attacked in force using *'Flammenwerfer'* (flame throwers or 'liquid fire') for the first time. They were pushed back and commenced a series of counter-attacks that managed to recapture a short section of trenches; on Saturday 31st he was relieved from the line. On Friday 24th September Philip was again at Hooge ready to support an attack on Bellewaarde. The real battle was to take place at Loos: the attack on the Salient was to distract the Germans High Command. At 4.19am a mine was blown only fifty yards ahead of him. A fierce battle ensued, attack followed counter-attack. It was the most severe battle the Battalion had yet fought and during the day Philip was killed.

Philip was recorded in Debretts Obituary — War Roll of Honour published in the 1921 edition.

His brother, 2nd Lieutenant Sidney Habershon, died between Monday 8th and Saturday 13th April 1918 and is commemorated on the Ploegsteert Memorial.

Second Lieutenant Vernon Haddon

11th Battalion Royal Fusiliers

Died on Friday 10th August 1917, aged 19

Commemorated on Panel 8.

Vernon Haddon

Vernon was born on Wednesday 8th December 1897, son of Mr B P and Mrs Fanny Haddon, of 3 Marine Crescent, Bexhill-on-Sea, Sussex. He was educated at Dulwich College from 1911 to 1912 after which he went to Europe to complete his education. At the outbreak of war Vernon joined the Public School Battalion and went out to France in November 1915. He served through the Battle of the Somme and then returned to England in October 1916. He passed through the Cadet Battalion at Trinity College, Cambridge, being gazetted in March 1917.

Vernon went out to the front joining the Battalion in the Arras sector. In May he was opposite Cherisy, south of the Arras-Cambrai road firstly helping to mop up followed by providing support to the 54th Brigade. In the summer he moved to the Ypres Salient. On Friday 10th August 1917 after dawn the Fusiliers moved forward until the German machine-gunners directed fire on them from *'Inverness Copse'*. A gap opened up which left them in peril of being surrounded. The Germans mounted a counter-attack, but Vernon and the men bombed their way down *'Jargon'* and *'Jap'* trenches and were able to hang on. Vernon was killed in *'Glencorse Wood'* during the action. Losses were heavy, seventeen officers and three hundred and twenty-eight men became casualties in the twenty-four hours of the action.

102 Lance Corporal William Stephen Haig

4th Battalion Gordon Highlanders

Died on Saturday 25th September 1915, aged 23

Commemorated on Panel 38.

William was born in Lonmay on Sunday 6th November 1892, son of William Haig, of Ellen Cottage, Maud, Aberdeenshire. He was educated at Gordon's College, Aberdeen, where he was a member of the OTC, as part of the 4th Gordon Highlanders. He went up to Aberdeen University where he continued to serve in the OTC in 'U' Company. In 1914 he graduated with an MA.

William Haig

At the outbreak of war he was

mobilized and went into training at Bedford before leaving for Southampton where he embarked on *SS Archimedes* to Le Havre on Friday 19th February 1915. William was sent to camp at La Clytte, Belgium, arriving on Wednesday 27th. For the next two weeks the Battalion trained and went on short visits to the line to accustom the men to the front.

The Germans launched a gas attack at Hooge on Monday 24th May 1915 and William was sent into reserve at Zillebeke. He was ordered to attack Bellewaarde which was successful and a series of trenches were taken. Tours of duty continued without being involved in any particular action until the attack at Hooge on Saturday 25th September. At 4.10am the attack began and William charge towards the German lines. The preliminary artillery barrage had not done its job properly as the German wire remained uncut. Together with many of his friends and comrades William was killed, stuck on the German wire.

Lieutenant and Adjutant Charles Roderick Haigh

2nd Battalion The Queen's (Royal West Surrey Regiment)

Died on Saturday 7th November 1914, aged 26

Commemorated on Panel 11.

Roderick Haigh as a young boy at the Dragon School

Roderick was born on Wednesday 25th September 1889 the elder son of Arthur Elam Haigh, MA, a Fellow and Tutor of Corpus Christi College, Oxford. He was educated at the Dragon School from 1897 to 1902 as a Day Boy followed by Winchester College from 1902 to 1907 where he was an exhibitioner, appointed a School Prefect, a member of the Shooting VIII and the Rowing IV. Roderick went up to Corpus Christi College, Oxford, he rowed for the College and graduated with a BA in 1910.

On Wednesday 20th April 1910 Roderick was gazetted, promoted Lieutenant on Thursday 18th April 1912.

Roderick served in Bermuda followed by South Africa and was mobilized at the outbreak of war, returning to Southampton via St Helena. He was sent to Lyndhurst Camp for training and a period of rest before returning to Southampton where he embarked for Zeebrugge on Sunday 4th October as Adjutant. They were sent to help with the defence of Antwerp but arrived too late to make much difference, so instead they were sent to Ghent. After disembarkation they were sent to camp at Oostcamp, south of Brugge. Like so many who arrived at this time, they spent some time marching round in circles before going by train to Ghent, arriving on Sunday 11th. They were hardly in the line twenty-four hours before they were ordered to retire and march off. They arrived on the Salient via Thielt and Roeselare having to stop on many occasions due to the driving rain. On Thursday 16th they spent the day in Ypres, still intact and the splendid medieval town gave some respite to the footsore men of The Queen's. The next day their first experience of the Salient was provided as they took the line along the Zonnebeke to Langemarck road. Roderick wrote to his sister on Thursday 1st October: "*We are all inspired with the justice of our cause, and by the fact that we are fighting for the cause of honour and liberty throughout the world. The question at stake is whether liberty and justice or military despotism and tyranny are to prevail. I look forward to seeing you all again one day in England. But if I do not return, remember that it is the highest honour to which a man can attain (an honour which is open to officers and men alike), a higher honour than all the honour that can be showered on those who survive—to die for one's country.*"

Roderick Haigh

... leading the men forward in a counter-attack

On Wednesday 21st October Roderick was wounded but remained at the front. On Monday 2nd November they were sent for rest in Ypres — billeted in the Hôtel de Ville. The Germans opened a huge artillery barrage so their rest was cut short and were sent out in the direction of Dickebusch. At Klein Zillebeke a request was made for assistance by the 4th Guards Brigade. In the misty morning the Queen's advanced into the heavy machine-guns of the German infantry. Despite the heavy fire the Queen's pressed the attack and drove the Germans from their trenches. The Germans held good positions in the ruins of the houses and enfiladed them with machine-gun fire. During this action, Roderick was killed.

One of his men wrote: *"We had the order to attack some trenches at dawn. I saw our Adjutant cheering the men. We had only advanced a few yards when the enemy saw us and fired rapid fire at us, and then we charged through a terrible hail of bullets, and got the first line of trenches. Then Mr. Haigh gave the order to advance, which we did, quick; and we took another trench, and then were told to get ready again, and we took the last trench; but when we got into it we found it was a running stream. The Adjutant with myself and 14 others got into this ditch only to find that the Germans were only 10 to 15 yards away, strongly entrenched. We were firing point-blank range at each other, and all the time the Adjutant was standing up in the trench, head and shoulders showing. I actually stopped firing to look at him and admire him. He was using his revolver with great effect, and kept saying to encourage us, 'That's another one I hit'. Oh, he was a cool man. The Lance-Corporal went back for reinforcements, but couldn't return. We kept on firing for half-an-hour afterwards; then the brave Adjutant was shot through the temple. He died a noble death. I found myself alone, the only one of the fifteen alive, and I made a dash for it, and never got hit, though I had three bullets in my pack close to my neck. I got back safe and reported that the Adjutant had been killed."*

The Pelican wrote of Roderick: *"I can truly say that, during forty-five years of College life, I have met with very few who have given me such an impression of absolute truth and straightness, of unswerving loyalty to duty, of unfailing rightness, not only of action, but of thought and feeling. His devotion to the memory of his Father and Mother, his solicitude for his sisters and brother, his affection and admiration for his friends, were unbounded. What he had in himself he found in others. His brother officers, his College chums, were always 'simply splendid'. And some of us, who are sadly conscious of being only quite ordinary people, might have been surprised if we could have seen how his enthusiasm transformed us, and would have been moved, I hope, to try and become a little less unlike what he fancied us. Nor would it be right to omit, though it is a thing to be mentioned with reverent reserve, the deep and genuine religion which was the basis of his whole character. When the war broke out, he was recalled with his battalion from South Africa, and ordered to the front. I know that he went, fully realizing the possibility that lay before him, but counting it the highest honour which can befall a soldier, to be allowed to give his life for his country and his King. For him, therefore, we must not grieve. Almost ever since I heard of his death, Shakespeare's glorious words have been beating in my brain:*

Your son, my lord, has paid a soldier's debt.
Had he his hurts before ? Ay, on the front.
Why then, God's soldier be he!
Had I as many sons as I have hairs, I would not wish them to a fairer death !

May his memory and example long continue to inspire those who knew him."

Roderick left £500 in his Will to the Dragon School with instructions that the Headmaster should decide on how the money be spent. £200 went on improving the Rifle Range and for a silver cup for the 25 and 50 yard range, and part of the money was used as a bursary to educate the son of a brother officer who had been killed during the war.

... a dressing station in Zillebeke

14458 Serjeant Philip Haith, DCM

8th Battalion King's Own
(Royal Lancaster Regiment)

Died on Monday 3rd April 1916, aged 22
Commemorated on Panel 12.

Citation for the Distinguished Conduct Medal, London Gazette, Thursday 30th March 1916:
"For conspicuously gallantry and determination during operations. He held a grenadier post for twenty-four hours, and repulsed all enemy attacks."

Philip was born in Hulme, Manchester, brother of Mrs M Bailey, of 48/50 Ridgeway Street, Butler Street, Manchester. He was educated locally.

Philip landed in France on Monday 27th September 1915 as the Battle of Loos was raging. He entrained to northern France where he undertook additional training prior to taking the line. Philip was killed in action.

1539 Company Sergeant Major Frederick William Hall, VC

8th Battalion Canadian Infantry (Manitoba Regiment)

Died on Sunday 25th April 1915, aged 30
Commemorated on Panel 24.

Citation for the Victoria Cross, London Gazette No 29202, dated Wednesday 23rd June 1915:

"On 24th April, 1915, in the neighbourhood of Ypres, when a wounded man who was lying some 15 yards from the trench called for help, Company Serjeant-Major Hall endeavoured to reach him in the face of a very heavy enfilade fire which was being poured in by the enemy. The first attempt failed, and a non-commissioned officer and private soldier who were attempting to give assistance were both wounded. Company Serjeant-Major Hall then made a second most gallant attempt, and was in the act of lifting up the wounded man to bring him in when he fell mortally wounded in the head."

Frederick Hall

Frederick was born in Kilkenny, Ireland, on Saturday 21st February 1885 son of Mrs Mary Hall, of 43 Union Road, Leytonstone, London, and the late Bombardier F Hall. Frederick served twelve years with the 1st Cameronians. He then emigrated to Winnipeg, Manitoba, and became a clerk.
On Sunday 27th September 1914 he enlisted at Valcartier, his attestation papers describe him as 5ft 8in tall, a 36 in chest, ruddy complexion, brown eyes, auburn hair, and a tattoo of a scorpion on his right arm.
Frederick left with the first Canadian Contingent and

went to *'West Down South'* Camp on arrival in October before moving to *'Lark Hill'* Camp on Wednesday 16th December.
The Battalion received the traditional Royal Review prior to departure for France on Thursday 4th February 1915. The Battalion left camp on 2.30am on Wednesday 10th for Amesbury and entrained for Avonmouth to embark on *SS Archimedes*. The boat sailed at 11.00pm for St Nazaire, the Battalion disembarking at 4.00pm on Saturday 13th. They entrained for Strazeele and arrived at 3.00am on Tuesday 16th and finally were provided with billets in the early afternoon. From Thursday 18th the Battalion began to send groups into the front line for practical training and experience with battle-hardened troops. On Sunday 21st the Battalion was moved to Port de Nieppe and the next day they took the line and served in the Fleurbaix sector until Friday 26th March when, being relieved by the 7th Middlesex, they were sent to Estaires. Some rest was provided as well as training which continued until Monday 5th April. After a tiring march Frederick reached Steenvoorde where they were billeted and continued to train until Sunday 14th, when a fleet of motor buses arrived to collect the Battalion. A rough and bumpy ride took them to Vlamertinghe. Frederick formed the Battalion into marching order and they set off toward the sound of booming artillery. Passing Ypres they continued to the trenches at Gravenstafel. After a tour of two days Frederick was sent to billets in northern Ypres, close to the canal where they remained until Monday 19th. After being under shell-fire all day in Ypres the Battalion returned to the line, completing the relief at 10.30pm. After a couple of relatively quiet days in the line, the bombardment on their lines increased. At 5.00pm on Thursday 22nd the Germans launched the first gas attack to the left of their line and kept a constant bombardment on their lines. On Saturday 24th their line came under sustained attack and gas was also used. Reinforcements were required during the afternoon as the Germans pressed home further attacks that continued throughout the night.
On Sunday 25th a number of his men were lying wounded, exposed in *'No Mans Land'*. Together with Corporal Payne and Private Rogerson, they crawled out to rescue them in broad daylight and under heavy fire from high-explosive and gas shells. Both Payne and Rogerson were wounded in the attempt but made it back to the lines. Frederick went out again, alone, to rescue another man and in the attempt both were killed.
The street in which he lived in Winnipeg was renamed 'Valour Road' as three of its residents won the Victoria Cross, the other two being Leo Clark and Robert Shankland. A bronze plaque was erected in the street to record his bravery.

Second Lieutenant Harold Hall

'D' Company, 7th Battalion Lincolnshire Regiment

Died on Tuesday 15th February 1916, aged 20
Commemorated on Panel 21.

Harold was the son of Albert Frank and Clara Hall, of Keith House, King's Road, Westcliff-on-Sea, Essex. He went up to Magdalene College, Cambridge, in 1913, as a Scholar.
From Saturday 25th September 1915 Harold served on the Ypres Salient. In November they were in the line near *'Maple Copse'*, the trenches were in poor condition, continuously flooded, and many men were invalided with trench foot. In December Lieutenant Colonel Forrest wrote: *"The night of the 20th was on the whole the*

worst we have had. I cannot speak too highly of the behaviour of all ranks during a somewhat trying period of duty during which any sleep or rest were quite impossible ... the courage and devotion of the runners and orderlies were remarkable. Wires were cut practically throughout the forty-eight hours, and nearly all messages had to be sent by hand."

In January 1916 the Battalion was taken out of the line for rest and training at Hellebrouck, St Omer, not returning until Monday 7th February. Harold and his men went in to the line at *'The Bluff'* where the British were underground digging tunnels for mines. On Friday 11th a German officer broke through into one of the galleries and popped his head through — he received a bullet in the head for his efforts but had a enough time to blow his own gallery.

On Monday 14th February three mines were exploded and some initial German successes were made after fierce hand-to-hand fighting. Counter-attacks were launched and Harold was killed.

SECOND LIEUTENANT JOHN RAMSAY FITZGIBBON HALL

2nd Battalion Royal Dublin Fusiliers

Died on Monday 24th May 1915, aged 21

Commemorated on Panel 44.

John was the son of Mr and Mrs I FitzGibbon Hall, of The National Bank House, Cork.

John took a draft of one hundred men to the front in mid-November, joining the Battalion near Armentières. He moved to Nieppe where they were billeted and in early December they lined the streets when HM King George V visited the front. They remained in the area until Saturday 20th March when were they were sent to the Messines area between the River Douve and the Wulverghem to Messines road. It was a difficult tour as his trenches were below those of the Germans who could see quite clearly all movements. On Monday 12th April they were relieved to Bailleul and were inspected by General William Pulteney. At 7.30pm on Friday 23rd they were moved via Westoutre, Ouderdom, Vlamertinghe and Ypres, where the men discarded their packs, to St Jan, arriving at midnight on Saturday 24th. They went into the line at 4.00am, from where they made an advance at 6.30am on St Julien where the Canadians were still holding part of the village despite the appalling gas attack. Progress was difficult, no artillery cover could be provided as they were advancing into a 'friendly' village and the wire remained uncut. German machine-gun and rifle fire was heavy and the Fusiliers took very heavy casualties. By the end of the day John and the men had dug themselves in ¼ mile from the village. They remained there under heavy shell fire until Friday 30th. On Sunday 2nd May the Germans launched a gas attack along the line, however their advance made little headway. During the evening of Monday 3rd John was relieved and went into bivouac at La Brique, arriving at 2.00am, only to have two bombs dropped on them from a German aeroplane causing two casualties, both wounded. One of John's fellow officers wrote: *"One of the many instances of unrecorded gallantry and determination to put 'the Regiment' first at all costs came to my notice in this action. Lieutenant J. R. F. Hall, a bright, energetic and fearless young lad, who had survived the tedious though strenuous winter existence in the trenches, was sent back from the front line with a party to bring up rations from near St. Jean, just outside Ypres. When he reached the dump it was easy to see that he was greatly in need of even only a few hours' rest, and I got leave for him to remain for the night at the advanced Brigade Headquarters, and for somebody else to take the party back to the line. But I had done this without consulting Hall, who was furious when he heard of my action, and although almost exhausted from want of sleep and general overwork, pulled himself together and begged permission to be allowed to return with his party, using every possible argument, and finally gaining his point by saying — 'Now, what's the use of being in a good regiment if you can't stick it out?' He accordingly returned that to the line in command of his men, and was killed during a gas attack in a later stage of the same action."*

From the evening of the Wednesday 5th until 1.30pm on Saturday 8th, John was relieved to Château des Trois Tours from where he was sent to the woods by Potijze Château. The Battalion took part in the attack on Frezenberg which it was repulsed and by the end of the next day they were out close to *'Shell Trap Farm'*. On Wednesday 12th he was relieved to the grounds of Vlamertinghe Château, which today remains much as it was during the war. At 2.45am on Monday 24th May the Germans sent over gas that drifted slowly towards the line occupied by John and his men. It was more than three miles wide and forty feet in depth — the Germans then laid down an artillery barrage. Thankfully orders had been issued to all the men to prepare their respirators in anticipation of the attack. The Germans took *'Shell Trap Farm'* and orders were given to counter-attack and retake it. The heavy shell fire cut off effective communication: messengers were either killed or wounded taking messages to and from Headquarters. Orders got through to the artillery to shell the Farm with extreme accuracy, because the trenches surrounding it were still held by the British. Their work was effective and the shrapnel shells rained down on the Farm. The German shell fire and gas assaults forced some men to retire. During the close fire fight, John was killed.

4434 Private
Joseph Harrison Halliday

1st/4th Battalion East Yorkshire Regiment
Died on Saturday 29th January 1916, aged 23
Commemorated on Panel 21.

Joseph was born on Friday 30th June 1893, only son of Agnes Wilkinson Halliday, of 45 Corporation Road, West Marsh, Grimsby, and the late Joseph Halliday. He was educated at St James' College, Grimsby. Joseph undertook an apprenticeship and then went to work in the family drapers business. He joined the Territorials on Tuesday 10th January 1911.

At the outbreak of war Joseph volunteered and went into training, leaving for France on Wednesday 1st September 1915. He was given a month's leave in December, returning to the front on Wednesday 19th January 1916 and was killed ten days later whilst on sentry duty at Zillebeke.

His Captain wrote: *"He was on duty as a grenadier and had to patrol an empty trench. At the time of his death he was in a section of trench, resting and talking to three others, when a small shell, known as a 'whizz bang' breached the parapet, and was instantly followed by several others. All four men were badly hit, and only one has recovered. I was within a few yards of him at the time; within a very few minutes the stretcher bearers were there to render first-aid, but unfortunately nothing could be done. He was a man who always tried to do his duty, and one who will be greatly missed in the company."*

1530 Sergeant James Ham, DCM

34th Battalion Australian Infantry, AIF
Died on Monday 1st October 1917, aged 30
Commemorated on Panel 23.

Citation for the Distinguished Conduct Medal, London Gazette, Friday 16th August 1917:

"For conspicuous gallantry and devotion to duty. During a hostile raid he handled his Lewis gun with great courage and ability. He, with one other man, succeeded in accounting for five of the enemy, who were the only party who gained a footing in our trench."

James was born in Hall's Creek, New South Wales, son of John and Sarah Ann Ham, of Giant's Creek, New South Wales. He was educated locally.

On Saturday 12th February 1916 he volunteered and left for Plymouth from Sydney on Tuesday 2nd May on board *HMAT Horoata*, arriving at the end of June. For the next five months he continued his training at *'Lark Hill Camp'* before leaving for France from Southampton on Tuesday 21st November, arriving two days later. The Battalion entrained for Bailleul and marched to Outtersteene where they were billeted. From Monday 27th he undertook tours of duty at l'Épinette. He continued to undertake tours of duty for a month when he was sent to hospital in Bailleul with mumps. Following his recovery James rejoined the Battalion in the field at Houplines. He served in the line on tours of duty until Tuesday 10th April. The Battalion undertook training and provided fatigue parties until Saturday 5th May. Working parties were sent into the line at Le Bizet and they served in the sector until 10.00pm on Wednesday 6th June. James arrived in the assembly line at Messines to be greeted with German gas shells pouring down on the line and a number of the men became casualties *en route* to the trenches. At 3.00am on Thursday 7th four mines were blown in front of him, only seven seconds prior to Zero Hour. James charged forward under a heavy German barrage. The attack was successful and a considerable portion of ground was taken. After three days of constant fighting the Battalion was relieved at 2.00am on Sunday 10th, returning to *'Bunhill Row'* and *'Prowse Trench'*, and served in Ploegsteert Wood for a three day tour of duty. At 8.00am on Thursday 14th the Battalion was moved to Neuf Berquin for rest and training, and General Sir Alexander Godley inspected them the next day. From Saturday 23rd James was billeted in Neuve Eglise where baths were provided and sports competitions were organised. German aircraft were busy overhead and a number of balloons were brought down and the rear area was bombed. At 9.00pm on Wednesday 27th James marched to Messines and relieved the 36th Battalion at *'Middle Farm'*. He was back in the line where one month previously a battle had been raging, on Saturday 7th July it was a relatively quiet day. The German aeroplanes were again active, with one formation of more than thirty being spotted on Wednesday 11th. The tours of duty continued until the end of the month when, following relief, the Battalion

General Godley

was sent to *'Hillside Camp'* for two days' rest in the pouring rain before going to billets at Bleue followed by *'Aldershot Camp'*.
At 6.30am on Wednesday 15th August the Battalion entrained for Wizernes, arriving at noon and they marched to Vaudringhem where serious training commenced for the forthcoming offensive in which they would participate. At 6.00am on Wednesday 26th September James paraded with his men and marched twenty-one miles to Coubronne, via St Pierre, Lumbres, Blendecques and Heuringhem. At 4.00am the next morning the march continued to Godewaersvelde via Wardrecques, Ebblinghem, Staple, St Marie Cappel, and Eecke, a total of twenty-two miles. On Friday 28th a further eight miles took them to Winnezeele via Steenvoorde. Ypres was reached a lunchtime on Saturday 29th after they had been taken as far as Vlamertinghe from Abeele by motor bus and they marched through the Menin Gate out to *'Railway Wood'* to serve at Zonnebeke. The German barrage of high velocity shells fell from 7.00am until 9.30am and James was killed together with fifty-two of his friends and comrades.
He was promoted Lance Corporal on Saturday 3rd March 1917, Corporal on Monday 25th June and Sergeant on Monday 30th July.

CAPTAIN
THE LORD ARTHUR JOHN HAMILTON

1st Battalion Irish Guards

Died on Friday 6th November 1914, aged 30

Commemorated on Panel 11.

Arthur Hamilton and his family coat of arms

Arthur was born on Monday 20th August 1883 in Devon, the fifth son of James, late 2nd Duke of Abercorn, KG, PC, CB, and Mary Anna, Dowager Duchess of Abercorn, of 115 Park Street, London, and was grandson of Richard, 1st Earl Howe. The Hamilton family seat being Baron's Court, Newtonstewart, County Tyrone. He was educated at Wellington College from 1898 to 1900 where he learnt to speak both French and German fluently. Arthur was a member of the Royal Household serving as Deputy Master of the Household from 1913 to 1914.
Arthur was gazetted on Friday 4th December 1901, promoted Lieutenant in August 1904 and Captain on Thursday 2nd December 1909. He retired on Wednesday 5th March 1913 and joined the Special Reserve.
Arthur rejoined the regiment at Wellington Barracks when war broke out. On Tuesday 11th August 1914 Field Marshal Lord Roberts and Lady Eileen visited the Battalion to wish them well for their forthcoming duty. It was the last time the Battalion would see their Honorary Colonel who died in St Omer on Saturday 14th November 1914 (he is buried in St Paul's Cathedral). The next day they entrained for Southampton and boarded *SS Novora*, leaving at 7.00pm. They reached Le Havre at 6.00am and marched to Sanvic and *'No 2 Camp'*. The next morning they marched back into the town, being cheered on their way, and entrained at 11.00am for Wassigny — a seventeen hour journey. Over the next few days the Battalion rested and inoculations were given to the men against enteric fever. They marched across the border into Belgium and were positioned near Harveng at Mons; however they only witnessed the action. At 2.00am on Monday 24th their long march south commenced. On Tuesday 1st September they engaged the Germans at Villers-Cotterêts before continuing south. On Sunday 6th they turned eastward to engage the Germans; they found them later in the day at Villeneuve where four from the Guards were killed and eleven wounded in the short sharp action. The next day they came under fire from Boitron but the Germans were shelled from their position and the Battalion crossed the Marne at Charly on Wednesday 9th. On Monday 14th September they advanced on Soupir, with the support of the 2nd Battalion of the Grenadiers and the 3rd Battalion of the Coldstream. The village was cleared and later that day a large group of Germans were found in a field waving white flags. As British officers advanced to accept the surrender German machine-guns opened up on them. A fierce fight commenced and a large number of casualties were sustained.

Lord Roberts

Arthur remained on the Aisne until 13th October. The Battalion entrained at Fismes on Wednesday 14th for Hazebrouck — a very long and winding route via Paris, Amiens, Calais and St Omer! On Sunday 18th they were taken from Boeschepe, where they had billeted overnight, to Ypres. The town was still a medieval gem and relatively untouched by the horrors of war. The town was filled with refugees streaming through with a mixture of British soldiers, horses and limbers clogging the main square and the streets. They were provided with a hot meal in the northern outskirts before proceeding to St Jan. The situation on the Salient was fluid, and they were ordered to Zonnebeke where they were forced to retire. Their movement around the Salient continued. At

Irish Guards - from Mons to the Aisne

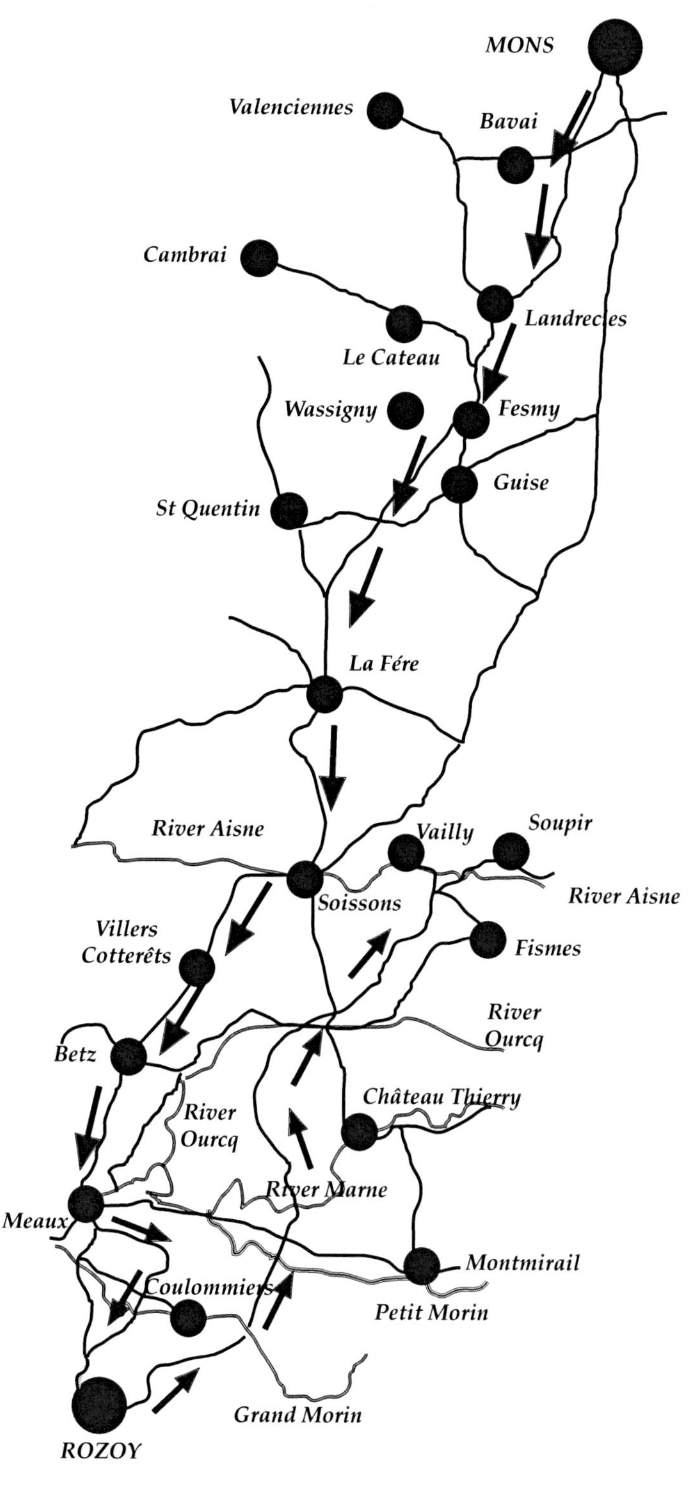

Route taken by the Irish Guards

9.00pm on Friday 23rd they were ordered to Zillebeke where they arrived at 2.00am the next morning. They had hardly settled down before being ordered to attack Reutel. They marched along the Menin Road to beyond Polygon Wood. On Sunday 25th they attacked the hamlet at dawn but were only successful in taking a couple of out-lying farmhouses. The next morning they attacked again and took significant casualties, being enfiladed from all sides. Arthur and the Battalion were billeted in *'Racecourse Wood'* from where they left on Friday 30th for Klein Zillebeke to support the 7th Division. An officer wrote: *"At the cross-roads near Klein Zillebeke we halted, lying down on each side of the road as shells were coming over. In the centre of the road lay a dead trooper of some British Cavalry Regiment, his horse also half dead across him. A woman passed by … She had all her household treasures strapped on her back and held the hands two very small children. She took no notice of any one, but I saw the two little children shy away from the dead man."* They came under intensive fire and remained in the line for thirty-six hours without supplies of food and water but eventually they were relieved and given sustenance, returning to the line immediately thereafter. On Sunday 1st the pressure was increased and every available man who could stand was utilised to repel the German attack. The battle for Ypres continued with the Germans throwing all they had into the attack. On Friday 6th an attack on the French lines next to the Irish Guards broke their line; the Battalion was now under attack from the flank too. The Household Cavalry galloped up the Menin road and dismounted. The 1st and 2nd Life Guards supported their line but Arthur was killed. He was initially listed as missing until sometime later a German officer confirmed his death.

Arthur is commemorated on the House of Lords War Memorial.

Irish Guards in action in the early engagements of 1914

Major The Honourable Leslie D'Henin Hamilton, MVO

1st Battalion Coldstream Guards

Died on Thursday 29th October 1914, aged 30

Commemorated on Panel 11.

Leslie Hamilton and his family coat of arms

Leslie was born on Friday 19th December 1873, third son of John Glencairn Carter, 1st Baron Hamilton of Dalzell, KT, CVO, JP, DL, (Lord in Waiting to HM Queen Victoria) and Lady Emily Eleanor (youngest daughter of David, 8th Earl of Leven and 7th Earl of Melville) and heir-presumptive to his brother Major Gavin, 2nd Baron Hamilton, KT, CVO, MC, who served throughout the war. He was educated at Eton College as a member of Sir Walter Durnford's House leaving in 1891. On Saturday 9th September 1905 Leslie married The Hon Mrs Amy Cecile Hamilton (née Riccardo), of 4 South Eaton Place, London, and they had a son, John born on Monday 1st May 1911. Leslie was a member of Guards' and Brooks' Clubs.

Leslie was gazetted in 1893, promoted Lieutenant in 1897, Captain 1901 and Major in 1910. He fought in the South African War receiving the Queen's Medal with four clasps.

Leslie went out to France Thursday 13th August 1914 as Second in Command of the 1st Battalion under Lieutenant Colonel John Ponsonby, leaving Blenheim Barracks, Aldershot, for Southampton. He embarked on *SS Dunvegan Castle*, arriving the next morning in Le Havre. He went out to camp five miles outside the town for less than twenty-four hours before he marched with his men back to Le Havre and entrained to go out to meet the enemy at Mons. The Battalion was not engaged in the Battle of Mons, but provided rearguard as the retirement began. On Thursday 27th Leslie organised his men at Oisy where they defended the bridge across the Sambre Canal and the Landrecies to Etreux road. Leslie and the Battalion marched southeastwards to Soissons and beyond; during the The Retreat they covered more than two hundred miles. On Saturday 5th September The Retreat ended and the next day turned to engage the enemy during the afternoon of Sunday 6th. Field Marshal Sir John French issued a Special Order that day: *"After a most trying series of operation, mostly in retirement, which have been rendered necessary by the general strategic plan of the Allied Armies, the British forces stand to-day formed in line with their French comrades, ready to attack the enemy. Foiled in their attempt to invest Paris, the Germans have been driven to move in an easterly and south-easterly direction, with the apparent intention of falling in strength on the Fifth French Army. In this operation they are exposing their right flank and their lines of communications to an attack from the combined Sixth French Army and the British forces. I call upon the British Army in France to now show the enemy its power, and to push on vigorously to the attack beside the Sixth French Army. I am sure I shall not call upon them in vain, but that, on the contrary, by another manifestation of the magnificent spirit which they have shown in the past fortnight, they will fall upon the enemy's flank with all their strength and in unison with their Allies drive them back."*

They marched onto the Marne and came under shell fire as they reached the slopes of the valley. They advanced onto the Aisne and fought on the Chemin des Dames.

Field Marshal Sir John French wrote: *"The Aisne valley runs generally from east to west and consists of a flat-bottomed depression of width varying from half a mile to two miles down which the river follows a winding course to the west, at some points near the southern slopes and the others near the northern. The high ground on each side is approximately four hundred feet above the valley itself, which are broken into numerous rounded spurs and re-entrants. The most prominent of the former are the Cheivre spur on the right bank, and the Sermoise spur on the left. Near the latter place the general plateau on the south is divided by a subsidiary valley of much the same character, down which the small river Vesle flows to the main stream near Dermoise. The slopes of the plateau overlooking the Aisne on the north and south are of varying steepness, and are covered with numerous patches of wood, which also stretch upwards and backwards over the edge on to the top of the high ground. There are several villages and small towns dotted about in the valley itself and along its sides, the chief of which is the town of Soissons. The Aisne is a sluggish stream of some hundred and seventy feet in breadth, but being fifteen feet deep in the centre, it is unfordable. Between Soissons on the west and Villers on the east there are eleven road bridges across it. On the north bank a narrow-gauge railway runs from Soissons to Vailly, where it crosses the river and continues eastward along the south bank. From Soissons to Sermoise a double line of railway runs along the south bank, turning at the latter place up the Vesle valley towards Bazaches. The position held by the enemy is a very strong one, either for a delaying action or for a defensive battle. One of its chief military characteristics is that from the high ground on neither side can the top of the plateau on the other side be seen except for small stretches. This is chiefly due to the woods on the edges of the slopes. Another important point is that all the bridges are under either direct or high-angle artillery fire. The tract of the country above described, which lies north of the Aisne, is well adapted to concealment, and was so skilfully turned to account by the enemy as to render it impossible to judge the real nature of his opposition to our passage of the river, or to accurately gauge his strength."*

During the Battle of the Aisne, Lieutenant Colonel Ponsonby was wounded on the Chemin des Dames, and Leslie took command of the Battalion. He remained on the Aisne until Friday 16th October when the 15th French Regiment relieved them. They marched to billets in Blanzy overnight and the next morning marched the two miles to Fismes where they entrained for Hazebrouck, arriving on Sunday 18th.

After a short period of rest in northern France Leslie took his Battalion into Belgium where at 5.15am on Wednesday 21st October he led the men along the refugee-strewn roads via Elverdinghe to their position at Pilkem. Despite coming under heavy fire on Thursday 22nd he was able to move forward. Attacks and counter-attacks continued with heavy shell fire falling down on them continuously until they were relieved late on Saturday 24th. Leslie was ordered to take the Battalion to Zillebeke which was reached by 10.00am on Sunday 25th. The Battalion was moved along the Menin Road to support the position around Gheluvelt. By Wednesday 28th Leslie only had three hundred and fifty men under his command, the Battalion having taken severe losses. A company of the Black Watch was allocated to their flank and a platoon of Gloucesters assisted in keeping the line properly connected. Further difficulties arose with ammunition, only nine rounds per man were available, made worse when their rifles and machine-guns either could not be supplied with the right ammunition or they jammed and stopped working. At 5.30am on Thursday 29th the 6th Bavarian Reserve Division advanced in the fog on their lines. The German attackers were able to move to within fifty yards of the Coldstream and Black Watch before they opened with accurate rapid fire. The Germans were in such superior numbers Leslie and his men were overwhelmed, the majority were killed or died of their wounds.

Those killed were: Major The Hon Leslie Hamilton, Captain Gordon Brown, Lieutenant Geoffrey Campbell, Lieutenant Granville Smith, Lieutenant The Hon Alan Douglas-Pennant, 2nd Lieutenant Vere Boscawen — all of whom are recorded on the Menin Gate, and 2nd Lieutenant Charles Williams-Wynn, the only one to have a grave, he being buried in Perth Cemetery (China Wall). Lieutenant F W Gore-Langton was wounded and Lieutenant Wavell-Paxton was taken prisoner when recovered from the field wounded, and Captain Gibbs and 2nd Lieutenant Alison who were taken prisoner. In addition, one hundred and eighty other ranks were either killed, wounded or captured.

Leslie is commemorated on the House of Lords War Memorial.

In the Guards Chapel a plaque reads: *"Major The Hon Leslie d'Henin Hamilton, MVO, Coldstream Guards. Killed at the First Battle of Ypres-Gheluvelt, 29th October, 1914."*

Lieutenant John Raphael Hamilton-Dalrymple

'D' Company, 2nd Battalion
King's Own Scottish Borderers
Friday 23rd April 1915, aged 25
Commemorated on Panel 22.

John Hamilton-Dalrymple and his family coat of arms

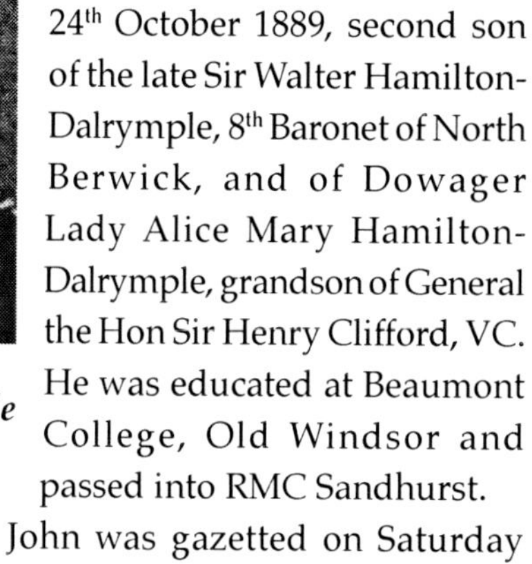

John was born at The Lodge, North Berwick, on Thursday 24th October 1889, second son of the late Sir Walter Hamilton-Dalrymple, 8th Baronet of North Berwick, and of Dowager Lady Alice Mary Hamilton-Dalrymple, grandson of General the Hon Sir Henry Clifford, VC. He was educated at Beaumont College, Old Windsor and passed into RMC Sandhurst.

John was gazetted on Saturday 18th September 1909 and promoted to Lieutenant on Thursday 8th May 1913.

He was ADC to the Governor and Commander in Chief of the Gold Coast from Wednesday 11th December 1912 to Wednesday 8th April 1914.

John went out with the BEF on Friday 14th August 1914 in charge of 'D' Company on board *SS Gloucestershire*, landing at Le Havre. He spent the night in camp about five miles outside the town before returning the next day where he entrained to Landrecies. He served at Mons where he mounted a counter-attack under heavy fire. He served through the Retreat, Le Cateau, the Battles of the Marne and Aisne. On Monday 14th September he was in action and wrote: *"Most awful day of my life: an eternity! 52 men in my company were casualties".*

In October he was wounded (together with ten other casualties) near Béthune and invalided home, returning to the front in December. He was on the Pilkem Ridge when he was killed, when the Germans used poison gas in the sector.

A brother officer wrote: *"He had always behaved magnificently, always fearless and calm, with keenest sense of duty. He was one of my greatest friends, and beloved by all who knew him. There is no man that I had a greater respect for. I hope it may be some comfort to you all in your anxiety to know that every officer and man who ever knew him would do anything to get him back again."*

John was Mentioned in Despatches on Monday 19th October 1914.

A plaque was placed in his memory in Buckfast Abbey, Leigh, Devon, that reads: *"Pray for the souls of Major General The Hon Sir Henry Hugh Clifford V.C., K.C.M.G.,*

C.B., late of the Rifle Brigade third son of the 7th Lord Clifford of Chudleigh and of his second son Brigadier General Henry Frederick Hugh Clifford, D.S.O., Suffolk Regt. who was killed in action near Devil's Wood, on the Somme 11th Sept. 1916 aged 49 years. And of his grandsons Theodore Hugh Galton, Worcestershire Regiment, killed in action at Illies 21st October 1914, aged 26 years Adjutant Captain Thomas Joseph Fitzherbert-Brockholes of the Rifle Brigade who fell at Neuve-Chapelle on the 12th March and died on the 14th March 1915, aged 27 years. Lieutenant John Raphael Hamilton Dalrymple, of the King's Own Scottish Borderers, who was killed at Pilkim in Flanders 23rd April 1915 aged 25 years Lieutenant Hugh Gilbert Francis Clifford, Lincolnshire Regiment killed near Albert on the Somme 1st July 1916 aged 19 years. Lieutenant Francis William Joseph Galton, Devon Regiment killed at La Coulotte on the Vimy Ridge, St George's Day 23rd April 1917 aged 21, Lieutenant Roger Hubert Fitzherbert-Brockholes R.N. killed in north Russia 2nd July 1919 aged 28 years Henry Clifford, Thomas Fitzherbert Brockholes, John Hamilton Dalrymple, and Hugh Clifford, had all been previously wounded at earlier periods of the war. R.I.P."

Brigadier General Frederick Clifford is buried in Albert Communal Cemetery Extension; 2nd Lieutenant Theodore Galton is commemorated on Le Touret Memorial; Lieutenant Francis Galton is commemorated on the Arras Memorial; Captain Thomas Fitzherbert-Brockholes is buried in Estaires Communal Cemetery; and Lieutenant Roger Fitzherbert-Brockholes is commemorated on Portsmouth Naval Memorial.

Lieutenant Lord Ian Basil Gawen Temple Hamilton-Temple-Blackwood

No 3 Company, 2nd Battalion Grenadier Guards

Died on Wednesday 4th July 1917, aged 47

Commemorated on Panel 9.

Basil was born at home on Friday 4th November 1870, third son of Frederick, 1st Marquess of Dufferin and Ava, PC, GCB, GCSI, GCMG, GCIE, FRS, DCL, LLD, JP, (late Governor General of Canada, Viceroy of India, Ambassador to Russia, Turkey, Italy and France) and Lady Hariot Georgina, VA, CI, of Clandeboye, County Down. He was educated at Harrow School, as a member of The Grove from 1885 to 1896, before going up to Balliol College, Oxford, in 1891. It was intended that he should be called to the Bar in 1896, but he was not inclined to a career in the law. He was a good friend of John Buchan. Basil was an accomplished artist and produced the illustrations for Hilaire Belloc's *'The Bad Child's Book of Beasts'*, *'More Beasts (for Worse Children)'* and *'The Modern Traveller'* using the signature *'BTB'*.

John Buchan

Ian Hamilton-Temple-Blackwood and his family coat of arms

Basil was a war correspondent during the South African War then a Judge Advocate on Lord Milner's staff in South Africa from 1901 to 1903, before being appointed Assistant Colonial Secretary at Bloemfontein until 1907. He went to Barbados as Colonial Secretary for two years, returning to England where he was Assistant Secretary to the Land Development Commission from 1910 to 1914.

Basil went out with the BEF on Thursday 6th August 1914 with the 9th Lancers and the Intelligence Corps. At the Battle of Mons he acted as Galloper to Colonel David Campbell, 9th Lancers. He saw service at numerous actions until he was severely wounded at Messines during the First Battle of Ypres and invalided to England where he became Secretary to the Lord Lieutenant of Ireland, Viscount Wimborne. In 1916 he was commissioned to the 2nd Battalion Grenadier Guards, No 3 Company, and returned to the Western Front at the end of September when his battalion left Morlancourt in French buses to Aumont for six weeks training.

On Monday 2nd July 1917 whilst in the Boesinghe sector he went out to reconnoitre the German lines with five men from No 10 Platoon. They had to cross the Yser Canal and he led his men toward the Germans. They did not find the trenches as expected but only a mass of wire and shell holes — his orderly was wounded and the Germans continued to throw bombs at them. Basil was last seen crawling forward and he died shortly afterwards.

One of Basil's brother officers wrote: *"His record is the finest imaginable and ought to be handed down and taught in every school as that of the ideal Englishman. With all his capabilities, age, influence, and record, to join as a Second Lieutenant is in itself a deed of which the country should be proud."*

Basil is commemorated on the House of Lords War Memorial.

Basil was recorded in Debretts Obituary — War Roll of Honour published in the 1921 edition.

Second Lieutenant Douglas William Hammond

2nd Battalion The Buffs (East Kent Regiment)

Died on Monday 24th May 1915, aged 18

Commemorated on Panel 14.

Douglas Hammond

Douglas was born on Wednesday 9th December 1896, the only son of Egerton and Ina Hammond, of St Alban's Court, Nonington, Dover, Kent. On the death of his parents the family estate was sold in the late 1930s.

He was educated at Castle Park School, Dalkey, County Dublin followed by Marlborough College from September 1910 until 1914 and passed into RMC Sandhurst.

... St Alban's Court

Douglas joined the Battalion in Winchester when it returned from India at the end of December 1914. Prior to their departure to France HM King George V and Field Marshal Lord Kitchener inspected the Battalion on Tuesday 12th January 1915. On Saturday 16th Douglas marched with his platoon to Southampton where they boarded heir transport ship and sailed for Le Havre. After a few days in camp they entrained for Hazebrouck, a journey was unpleasant for all ranks particularly the lack of toilet facilities. From the train station they marched to their billets in Rouge Croix. Additional kit was issued to the men that included gum boots, a fur coat and additional empty sandbags. On Thursday 28th Field Marshal Sir John French, accompanied by HRH The Prince of Wales inspected them and wished them well as they were about to take the line.

The Battalion was sent to the southern sector of the Ypres Salient near the Ypres to Comines Canal and they soon saw action. Late on Sunday 14th February Douglas was relieved and sent to *'Bedford House'* for rest that did not last long as the Germans were mounting an attack and they Battalion was required back in the front line. During the action he was wounded and invalided home, rejoining his Battalion in early May in the Salient itself. The Battalion had seen considerable service during the Second Battle of Ypres and on Saturday 20th May Field Marshal Sir John French addressed the men: *"I came over to say a few words to you and to tell you how much I, as Commander-in-Chief of this Army, appreciate the splendid work that you have all done during the recent fighting. You have fought the Second Battle of Ypres, which will rank amongst the most desperate and hardest fights of the war. You may have thought because you were not attacking the enemy that you were not helping to shorten the war. On the contrary, by your splendid endurance and bravery, you have done a great deal to shorten it. In this, the Second Battle of Ypres, the Germans tried by every means in their power to get possession of that unfortunate town. They concentrated large forces of troops and artillery, and further than that they had recourse to that mean and dastardly practice, hitherto unheard of in civilized warfare, namely, the use of asphyxiating gases. You have performed the most difficult, arduous and terrific task of withstanding a stupendous bombardment by heavy artillery, probably the fiercest artillery fire ever directed against troops, and warded off the enemy's attacks with magnificent bravery. By your steadiness and devotion, both the German plans were frustrated. He was unable to get possession of Ypres — if he had done this he would probably have succeeded in preventing neutral Powers from intervening—and he was also unable to distract us from delivering our attack in conjunction with the French in the Arras-Armentières district. Had you tiled to repulse his attacks, and made it necessary for more troops to be sent to your assistance, our operations in the south might not have been able to take place, and would certainly not have been so successful as they have been. Your Colours have many famous names emblazoned on them, but none rill be more famous or more well-deserved than that of the Second Battle of Ypres. I want you one and all to understand how thoroughly I realize and appreciate what you have done. I wish to thank you, each officer, non-commissioned officer and man, for lie services you have rendered by doing your duty so magnificently, and I am sure that your Country will thank you too."*

On Monday 24th the German mounted an attack at Hooge and the Battalion was sent forward to reinforce the 3rd Battalion Royal Fusiliers who had been driven from their line. As the counter-attack was being mounted and Douglas was leading his men forward when he was shot dead.

In St Mary's Church, Nonington, Kent, a marble tablet was placed in Douglas' memory with the inscription: *"Pro Rege Et Patria. In loving memory of Douglas William Hammond. 2nd Lieut. in the 2nd Battn. of 'The Buffs'. Only son of Egerton and Ina Hammond of Old Court House, in this parish. He fell in action near Hooge in Flanders on May 24th 1915. Aged 18½ years. 'He asked life of Thee and Thou gavest him a long life even for ever and ever'. Psa. XXI. IV. 'Thou hast chosen our inheritance for us'. Psa. XLVII. IV."*

Douglas is also commemorated on Nonington War Memorial.

Captain
Percival Campbell Hampe-Vincent

129th Duke of Connaught's Own Baluchis

Died on Monday 26th October 1914, aged 32

Commemorated on Panel 1.

Percival was born at Hyderabad on Saturday 27th August 1881, son of the late Robert W E Vincent, CIE, (late Indian Police), and Mrs Vincent. He was educated at Bedales and Northwood Park School. Percival was married to Blanche Hannington Vincent (née Robinson).
Pericval was gazetted in May 1901 and joined the Indian Army on Thursday 6th November 1902, promoted Lieutenant Saturday 8th August 1903, and Captain on Sunday 8th May 1910.
Percival served in the Somaliland Field Force and took part in the Expedition, receiving the Medal with clasp. On Monday 18th September 1905 he joined the King's African Rifles and served in East Africa until Friday 27th September 1912 before returning to India.
Percival accompanied the Indian contingent to Belgium. He was killed during an attack on Gappard leading his men against the Prussian Guard.

Indian troops during an attack on the German lines

199 Lance Corporal
John Latham Hampton

1st/5th Battalion London Regiment
(London Rifle Brigade)

Died on Monday 3rd May 1915, aged 38

Commemorated on Panel 52.

John was born in 1877, son of Mr C A Hampton of Ewell, Surrey and brother of Mr G C Hampton, of Firs, College Road, Epsom, Surrey. He was educated at the Whtgift School, Croydon, from 1889 to 1896, where he was a good all-round athlete, won the Fives Tournament, and was a member of VIII that won the Ashburton Shield at Bisley. He was employed by Le Blanc Smith & Co becoming a partner in 1904 and a member of the Stock Exchange in 1901. In 1912 he became a partner of Durham Stokes & Co. John was a member of The All England Lawn Tennis and Croquet Club (Wimbledon).
John served in the South African Campaign with the City Imperial Volunteers but was invalided home with enteric fever.
John volunteered at the outbreak of war but was initially rejected due to this age. However he enlisted in October 1914 and left for France on Wednesday 4th November on board *SS Cyhebassa*. During the evening on Friday 6th he entrained from Le Havre for St Omer and after a long and winding route they arrived twenty-four hours later. They were billeted overnight in the filthy cavalry barracks and were pleased to leave the next day for Wisques. Here they were billeted in the Benedictine Convent where the Chapel was converted into a rifle range. Field Marshal Sir John French arrived at the Convent to visit the troops, but John and the men were out training! On Friday 20th November Brigadier General Aylmer Hunter Weston addressed the Battalion at Bailleul before they went on their first tour of duty two days later at Ploegsteert. He was in the line during the Christmas Truce and fraternised with the Saxons. Whilst in billets in Ploegsteert he was promoted Lance Corporal on Thursday 7th January 1915. John remained in the southern sector until April. On Friday 23rd he left for Poperinghe in preparation to being sent to Wieltje, going into the trenches three days later. On Sunday 2nd May the Germans attacked their line although it was repulsed. In the early hours of Monday 3rd he was killed whilst on sentry duty when he was shot by a sniper.
His Company Commander wrote: *"There is no one whom we shall miss more than your son. The men have been*

An idealised view of a front line dug out

absolutely magnificent all through, and it is to your son and B— that I have put down the credit of most of it. They have always been so cheery and full of confidence, that they have infected the younger and less experienced men round them with something of their own spirit."

7689 Corporal James Handy, DCM

1st Battalion Connaught Rangers

Died on Monday 26th April 1915, aged 28

Commemorated on Panel 42.

Citation for the Distinguished Conduct Medal, London Gazette, Thursday 3rd June 1915:

"For conspicuous gallantry, marked ability, and initiative, from 14th to 22nd March 1915, near Rue du Bois, in reconnoitring the enemy's position at close quarters and obtaining very exact information under circumstances of great risk."

James was born at home the son of the late James and Norah Handy. He was educated locally. James was married to Margaret Jane Handy (subsequently remarried to Mr Carter), of 35 Dallfield Walk, Dundee.

At the outbreak of war the 1st Battalion was based in Ferozepore, India, and was ordered home. They embarked on *SS Edavana* at Karachi on Friday 28th August 1914 and sailed to Suez. Following four days in Cairo at Abassiyeh Barracks he entrained for Alexandria. James re-embarked on the *Edavana* bound for Marseilles, arriving at 6.00am on Saturday 26th September 1914. The Battalion entrained for northern France and were taken by London motor buses to Wulverghem, arriving at 3.30am on Thursday 22nd October where they remained for eight days when they were sent to Estaires. He sent into the line and immediately became engaged in heavy fighting. At 3.00am on Wednesday 16th December he marched to Givenchy to assist with an attack, however, the Battalion was not required so were sent to Béthune at 3.00pm. On Thursday 17th he returned to the La Bassée Canal, at Givenchy, for six days before being sent to billets in La Beuvrière where he spent Christmas out of the line.

James trained and rested until Friday 29th January 1915 when he moved into reserve first in Calonne and then in La Couture. He returned to the front line at Rue de l'Épinette on Tuesday 9th February. He continued on tours of duty in the Richebourg sector where in mid-March, whilst under heavy German shellfire, James was awarded his Distinguished Conduct Medal for reconnoitring. Following that particularly difficult tour of duty he was sent to rest billets in Paradis until Wednesday 31st March. James returned to the line at

General Keary

Croix Rouge where he spent eleven days in the line. He had two weeks rest and training in Paradis, where General Henry Keary inspected them on Monday 19th April. James expected to return to the line at Neuve-Chapelle, however, the German gas attack was launched, Father Peal recorded: *"Ominous cannonading warned us, early on Thursday, the 22nd April, that rough work was ahead. No one was therefore surprised, when, on Friday night, word was passed round that a sudden start was expected, and 'Belgium' whispered as our probable goad."* At 1.00pm on Saturday 24th he left on a forced march for Ouderdom where they bivouacked. Father Peal wrote: *"Leaving Merville and continuing our march to Vieux Berquin the country changes; the low flat land gradually disappears. We were going up a gentle slope, each step widening our view, and presently we had a huge map at our feet. Away to the right, Bailleul was clearly visible and Hazebrouck to our left recalled our first night on Belgian soil, when The Connaught Rangers were rushed up to the front at midnight in London motor-buses. A gentle rain settle the dust, and as the sun disappeared the lengthening twilight gave the country a touch of fairyland. It was beautiful, but for the incessant booming at Ypres becoming every minute more distinct. We crossed the railway near Strazeele and then Flêtre, on the main road from Cassel to Bailleul. As it became dark, we were skirting Mt. des Cats, on which stands a Trappist monastery, visible for miles around. We had done close on 15 miles now, we were hungry and wet, but as troops had been hurried up from all sides, billets were scarce and we had to wait by the roadside. ... It was now 9.30, dark and wet and cold. Presently there was a stir. One by one we slowly moved on, and found ourselves in Godeswaersvelde, a large frontier village. It was too dark and too wet to look around. Five of us secured a room. Some hot tea and bread, while steadily, ceaselessly, the guns thundered at Ypres."*

He continued: *"When a bit refreshed we looked about. The tower of the Cloth Hall at Ypres stood out gaunt against the dark sky, puffs of smoke showed how relentlessly shell was following shell. Every now and again a huge volume of black smoke burst into their air, followed by a heavy tremor marking the advent of an extra large high explosive."*

On Monday 26th marched into the front line, as described by Father Peal: *"At 3 a.m. on Monday the 26th we were astir. For this once I was allowed to follow the regiment going into action. As the companies passed me I raised my hand, the men understood the signal. Heads were bared and I have a general absolution. Many passed then never returned.*

A heavy mist favoured us as we moved on silently towards Vlamertinghe. Crossing the railway line we enter the town. At the Hôtel de Ville we turn sharply to the right, and our way leads straight to Ypres. The road runs parallel to the railway but crosses the line about midway. As the shelling

was heavy and were on the salient exposed to shell from three sides, the regiment left the main road near an estaminet and turned to the left along the beautiful grounds surrounding a château. This took us to the N.W. of the town. Crossing the canal, we were in full view of the church and Cloth Hall to our right. We kept to the outer streets, as far from the heart of the town as possible. Dead horses and dogs met us at every turn; shells screamed and hissed and crashed over and around us. Presently, as the Doctor and I walked behind the regiment, we noticed the Staff-Captain with his bleeding arm in a sling, helped along by an orderly. He told us that shell had struck the head of the regiment. We hurried up and there lay two of my boys on the pavement. Kneeling down by their side I gave absolution, but I fear too late, death was instantaneous. It seems this shell, besides killed these two, wounded our Colonel, the Adjutant, the Staff-Captain and five others. The Colonel's groom had a very narrow escape, the horse was killed by his side and he himself was covered with blood."

James took the line by 11.00am and prepared for the attack that should have commenced at 1.20pm. Whilst he waited to advance German machines patrolled the skies directing their artillery on them at La Brique. A distance of five hundred yards was covered as they reached the crest of the ridge ahead of them where the German artillery pounded shells onto them. During the afternoon a gas attack was launched against the advancing troops, in particular the Moroccan and Indian troops. James continued to fight on despite the constant counter-attack and shelling until he was killed.

Second Lieutenant John Henry Hanna

19th Battalion London Regiment (St Pancras Battalion)

Died on Thursday 20th September 1917

Commemorated on Panels 52.

John Hanna

John was the son of Mr and Mrs Hanna. He was educated at St Bees School from 1895 to 1901 with a Foundation Scholarship, and went up to Corpus Christi College, Cambridge, in 1901 with an Open Exhibition for Classics. He was elected to a Foundation Scholarship and won the Silver Cup, in his second year he won another Silver Cup for Latin Declamation. John was appointed Classics Master at Watford Grammar School. John was a polyglot, speaking Russian, German, French, Spanish, Italian, Portuguese and Dutch.

At the outbreak of war John volunteered and enlisted. He served for three years in the ranks, becoming an NCO before he was commissioned in June 1917.

John landed in Le Havre on Wednesday 10th March 1915 and was sent to northern France for further training. He took the line and participated in the Battle of Aubers Ridge in May followed by action at Festubert. Tours of duty and training continued before taking part in the Battle of Loos in September.

In 1916 John moved south and saw action at Vimy in May until taking part in the Battle of the Somme. He served through the Battle of Flers and fierce fights along the Transloy Ridges. His final participation on the Somme was at the Butte de Warlencourt from where he moved north to Flanders.

John trained for the Battle of Messines that was followed by tours of duty until the Third Battle of Ypres. He took his men into battle as an officer for the first time during the Battle of Pilkem Ridge from Tuesday 31st July 1917. John continued on tours of duty where he took part in a series of attacks and counter-attacks until he was killed in action in he front line.

Lieutenant Robert Hannah, DCM

13th Battery Australian Light Trench Mortar Battery
formerly 49th Battalion Australian Infantry, AIF

Died on Friday 12th October 1917

Commemorated on Panel 31.

Citation for the Distinguished Conduct Medal, Thursday 19th April 1917:

"For conspicuous gallantry in action. He led a party of men to assist the left flank of the battalion with great courage and initiative. Later, under very heavy fire, he maintained an adequate supply of bombs and ammunition to the front line."

Robert was born at 45 Well Street, Paisley, Scotland, son of Robert Hannah. He was educated locally until the age of 14 when he emigrated to Australia with his parents in 1906.

On Thursday 24th December 1914 he volunteered for foreign service. On Saturday 13th February 1915 he left from Brisbane, embarking on *HMAT Seang Bee* as a Corporal with the 9th Battalion.

On Sunday 27th February 1916 he joined the 49th Battalion, receiving a Field Commission on Saturday 16th September 1916.

On Friday 31st March 1916 the Battalion was based in Egypt and commenced a series of route marches that crossed the desert and Suez Canal. They covered more than forty miles in three days through high temperatures and deep sand. They arrived in Serapeum where they remained training for five days before moving the short distance to *'Railhead Camp'* to continue the training.

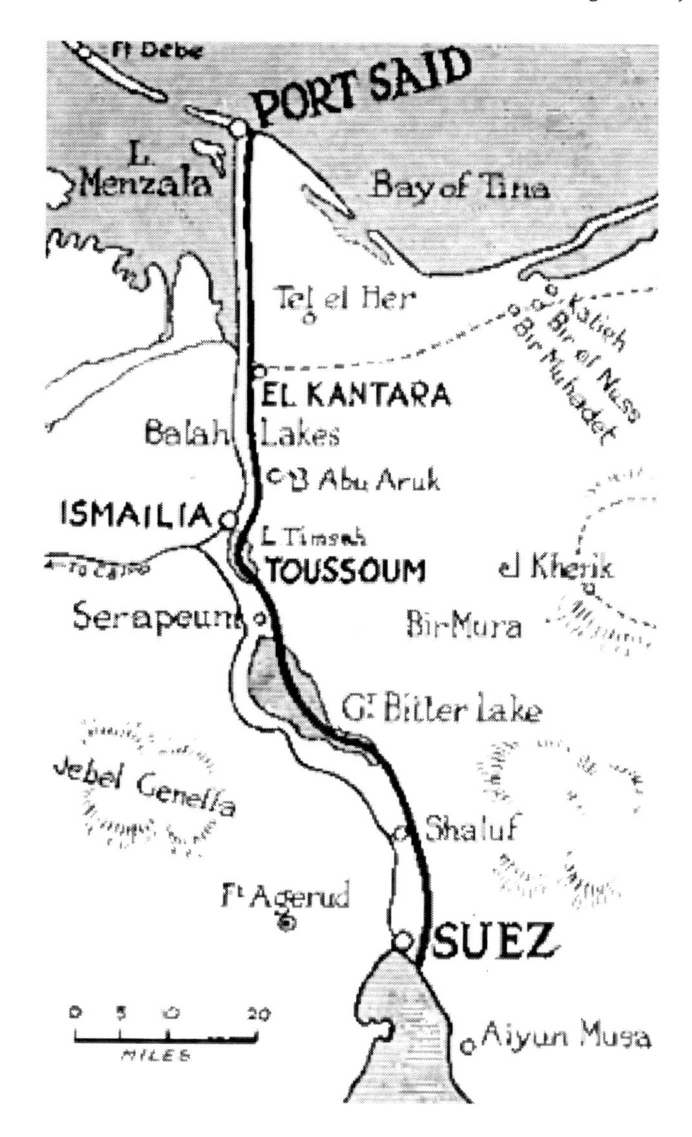

On Sunday 16th April Robert marched in the heat of 119° to *'Post 60'* and manned the front line defences. He continued to serve in the front line and spent time in *'Railhead Camp'* until Sunday 4th June. It was a relief to board the train in Serapeum and get away from the appalling dust storm that had blown up in the morning. They entrained for Alexandria and embarked on the *SS Arcadian* bound for Marseilles.

They disembarked at 10.00am on Monday 12th and were marched to a camp overlooking the town. Together with his friends and colleagues they were given the day to explore and enjoy Marseilles. At 10.30am the next morning he returned to the station and entrained for Strazeele. It was a long and tiring trip, with the train held up in Orange and Dijon amongst others, although it was recorded that most men enjoyed the green verdant scenery *en route*. They marched to billets that could not be accommodated and many had to sleep out in the open. The next morning a hearty breakfast of bacon, bread, jam and hot tea was followed by the Paymaster issuing money, much of it being spent on bottles of champagne that was being sold for three or four francs a bottle! On Monday 19th the Battalion set off via Estaires to the *'Cul de Sac'* and two days later took the line.

He continued to serve in northern France until the end of July when the move to the Somme began, arriving in Albert on Sunday 6th August. They marched out and took the line at *'Tara Hill'* before moving forward to Pozières and served on the Somme until Friday 8th September. The Battalion then returned to northern France, entraining to Godeswaersvelde and marching to billets in Steenvoorde.

Robert remained training in France until Thursday 21st when the Battalion crossed the border to continue their training at *'Quebec Camp'* at Reninghelst. From Saturday 7th October he took the line for the first time as an officer in the trenches at St Eloi.

After six weeks he left Flanders to return to the Somme, entraining from Hopoutre Sidings on Thursday 26th October. After a period of training the Battalion took the line at Flers on Monday 13th November where he was slightly wounded on Tuesday 21st November 1916 but remained in the line. He served on tours of duty on the Somme including at Delville Wood, spending Christmas out of the line in training at Buire. He returned to the line in January 1917 as well as spending considerable time training at Buire until Tuesday 15th May when the Battalion entrained at Albert for Caëstre.

Robert marched with his platoon to billets in Bleu where training continued until being sent to Neuve Eglise across the border in Belgium on Thursday 31st.

They were soon in action and successfully attacked the German line on Thursday 7th June 1917 as part of the Battle of Messines. On Tuesday 12th the Battalion was relieved to *'Canteen Corner'* where the next morning they cleaned their equipment and kit ready for an inspection by Lieutenant General Sir Alexander Godley. The Battalion moved to serve at Vieux-Berquin on Friday 21st September 1917 and Robert transferred to the 13th Battery Light Trench Mortar Battery. He was promoted Lieutenant on Monday 8th October 1917 and killed in action four days later.

General Alexander Godley

A desert ambulance

Captain Allen Humphrey Harden

2nd Battalion Oxford and Bucks Light Infantry

Died on Wednesday 21st October 1914, aged 23

Commemorated on Panel 37.

Allen Harden

Allen was born at Ealing, Middlesex, on Wednesday 23rd March 1881, son of Lieutenant Colonel John Edward Harden and Mrs Alice Mary Harden, grandson of Judge Harden and General Edwin Henry Atkinson. He was educated at Dulwich College in 1895. On Monday 3rd July 1905 Allen married Daisy (née Scott, cousin of the Rt Hon Lord Muskerry) and they had two children, Robert Allan George born on Friday 11th September 1908 and Daphne on Saturday 20th August 1910.

Allen was gazetted from the Militia on Saturday 5th January 1901, promoted to Lieutenant in September 1903 and Captain in January 1910. From 1908 to 1912 he was Adjutant.

He served in the South African War receiving the Queen's Medal with two clasps and the King's Medal with two clasps.

Allen went out with the BEF at the outbreak of war and saw action from Mons, through the Battles of the Marne and Aisne. Whilst fighting during the First Battle of Ypres, near Langemarck, he was with his Colonel, taking orders, when he was shot through the head. He was initially taken to a nearby farm building that was subsequently hit by German shell fire and totally destroyed.

Lieutenant Colonel Davies wrote: *"Your husband's death is a great loss to the regiment. He was one of the best company commanders we had ... I liked him so much personally. His death was quite instantaneous. I was talking to him at the moment that he was shot, and I feel sure that he felt nothing. We have lost a very good soldier, and all of us feel much for you in your sorrow."*

Captain Blewitt wrote: *"He was never downhearted in the depressing days of that retreat from Mons, and was so brave and capable in all the jobs we were given to do. I shall always be proud to have served under him, and had absolute confidence in his judgements and arrangements."*

Allen was Mentioned in Despatches gazetted on Thursday 14th January 1915.

... a German front line

646110 Private Alan Wilfred Harding

24th Battalion Canadian Infantry (Quebec Regiment)

Died on Tuesday 6th November 1917, aged 21

Commemorated on Panel 26.

Alan Harding

Alan was born in Buxton, Derbyshire, on Monday 11th November 1895, son of Mr L G and Mrs Hettie Kenny Harding, of 1121 Pender Street West, Vancouver. He was educated at Buxton College before emigrating to Canada and joined The Canadian Bank of Commerce, Vancouver, on Saturday 30th November 1912.

Alan enlisted on Friday 10th March 1916 in Vancouver where he was described as 5ft 9¾in tall, with a 37½in chest, fair complexion, blue eyes and medium brown hair.

Following a period of training Alan left for England and then onward to join the Battalion in the field in the Angres sector. On Wednesday 17th January 1917 the Battalion left Fosse 10 and was sent for training at Bruay and were billeted in the town. For the next two days the Battalion reorganised itself and absorbed the draft of one hundred and fifty-three men. On Sunday 11th February Alan paraded at 9.00am and marched twelve miles to Bois des Alleux from where he took the line in the La Folie sector. He served on tours of duty and in training before moving to Maisnil Bouche on Friday 23rd March. *En route* they came under heavy shelling as they passed through Villers-au-Bois and again when they arrived at Mont St Eloi. Alan was sent on working parties, continued his training and practised for the attack that would take place at Vimy Ridge at 5.30am on Monday 9th April — he had moved into the line two day previously. The attack went well, however, the Battalion was held up at *'Zwicshen Stellung Trench'* for a short period of time, and from 7.30am he helped consolidate the position.

In May the Battalion was moved slightly north, serving at Camblain-l'Abbé, Lens and Bully Grenay. From Thursday 23rd August they were sent to Gouy Servins for training from where working parties were organised. On Thursday 1st November Alan was taken by motor bus to *'Ten Elms'* at Poperinghe where spent the day studying the large model of the battlefield the Battalion was to attack. Two days later he paraded and marched to Caëstre and entrained for Ypres at 6.45am. Alan marched through the skeletal remains of the town to Potijze where he camped in a funk hole. During the evening of Sunday 4th the Battalion relieved the 19th Battalion in the front line. Throughout Monday 5th they came under heavy shellfire that intensified dramatically at midnight when an artillery duel began. At 6.00am Alan was led forward into the attack and shot down by machine-gun fire.

Lieutenant
Robert Denis Stewart Harding

4th Battalion attached 1st Battalion
Bedfordshire Regiment
Died on Saturday 7th November 1914, aged 28
Commemorated on Panel 31.

Robert Harding

Robert was the only son of the late Stanley Greville Harding and Edith Harding, of 15 Lowndes Square, London. He was educated at Harrow School from 1889 to 1903 as a member of Rendall's, and went up to Christ Church. He was a Lloyds Underwriter and a member of the Bath Club.

Robert was gazetted in 1912, promoted Lieutenant in March 1913.

At the outbreak of war the 1st Battalion was sent to Le Havre, arriving on Sunday 16th August 1914. They entrained to Le Cateau and went into billets at Pommereuil before being marched to Mons. They saw action at Wasmes on Sunday 23rd before the order to retire was given. The Battalion took part in rearguard action at Le Cateau and marched before receiving the order to turn and attack the Germans. He crossed the Marne followed by the Aisne that was reached on Saturday 12th September. They saw action at Missy until Saturday 17th after which they were given six days rest. On Sunday 11th October they had moved north and were first sent into the line at Essars before taking over Givenchy village. Givenchy came under heavy shell fire and they repulsed an attack. The Germans successfully counter-attacked until the Battalion drove them out again when they were able to rescue a number of their wounded colleagues whom the Germans had abandoned. From Friday 23rd to Sunday 25th they occupied the line a mile east of Festubert where they remained on tours of duty, being billeted in Gorre, until Wednesday 4th November. At 7.00pm on Thursday 5th he was sent to Locon. At 7.00am the next morning they were taken by motor buses to Ypres where they rested until 5.00pm when they marched along the Menin Road to Hooge. Robert was killed the next day as the Germans mounted an attack that broke their line.

His Captain wrote: *"The enemy had broken through the line of trenches held by a battalion on our left, and its break caused a part of our trenches to be vacated also. Our company was in reserve, and we formed up, and brought off an entirely successful counter-attack, driving the enemy back, killing many, and capturing twenty-five prisoners. It was in this counter-attack that Harding fell, leading his men up a lightly wooded hill. I did not see him fall, but missed him when we got to the ridge, and on gong back found him quite dead. Death had evidently been instantaneous. I had formed a very high opinion of his gallantry and coolness. I could rely on him always, and he had gained the confidence of his men, though he had only been with his company about a month. He was always bright and cheery, and it was a real pleasure to have his company on the line of march or in the trenches."*

Robert is commemorated on the Lloyds War Memorial.

Captain Ronald Montagu Hardy

'D' Company, 7th Battalion Rifle Brigade
Died on Friday 23rd July 1915, aged 33
Commemorated on Panel 46.

Ronald was born at Danehurst, Sussex, on Tuesday 12th April 1892, the youngest son of Herbert and A Louisa C Hardy, of Chilworth Manor, Surrey. He was educated at Eton College, a member of Mr Edward Compton Austen Leigh's House, leaving in 1890.

At the outbreak of war Ronald volunteered and enlisted in the Territorials, Sussex Regiment. He was gazetted in October 1914 to the Rifle Brigade and promoted Temporary Captain in November.

After training, on Wednesday 19th May 1915 Ronald sailed from Folkestone to Boulogne with his Battalion on *SS Queen*. He was sent to northern France for further training. After a week placed with the Lincolnshires and

... fighting in northern France, early 1915

Leicestershires for front line experience, he was sent into the line at St Eloi on Monday 7th June. For the next month he undertook tours of duty without particular incident until Monday 5th July when his line was attacked following an artillery bombardment. A group of twenty German infantry managed to break into their line; however the North Staffordshires, who were next to them came to the rescue and bombed the attackers out of the trenches. Life returned to 'normal' tours of duty for the next two weeks. He was due to relieve the Gordon Highlanders on Thursday 22nd but during the day the British blew a mine at Hooge and therefore it was a further twenty-four hours before Ronald reached the line close to the newly created crater. He arrived under a heavy barrage and was organising his men in the line when he was killed.

Ronald is commemorated on Danehill War Memorial, Sussex.

In All Saints Church, Danehill, East Sussex, a white stone statue of a knight holding a sword was placed in the Lady Chapel with the inscription: *"In memory of Roland Montagu Hardy, Captain in The Rifle Brigade, killed in action at Hooge, Flanders, on July 23rd 1915."*

His cousin, Captain Alfred Garthorne-Hardy, is commemorated on Loos Memorial, and Lieutenant Alan Hardy is buried in Chilham (St Mary) Churchyard.

Captain Gordon Hargreaves-Brown

1st Battalion Coldstream Guards

Died on Thursday 29th October 1914, aged 34

Commemorated on Panel 11.

Gordon was born on Saturday 31st July 1880, the only son of the late Sir Alexander Hargreaves Brown, 1st Baronet (former Liberal Member of Parliament for Wenlock), and Lady Henrietta Agnes Terrell Hargreaves Brown (née Blandy). He was educated at Eton College as a member of Mr Philip Williams' House, leaving in 1898 and passed into RMC Sandhurst.

Gordon Hargreaves-Brown's family coat of arms

On Friday 18th November 1910, in the Guard's Chapel, Wellington Barracks, Gordon married Editha Ivy Brown (daughter of Vice Admiral William Harvey Pigott), of Broome Hall, Holmwood, Surrey. They had three children, Joan Terrell Hargreaves-Pigott-Brown born on Monday 18th December 1911, John Hargreaves-Pigott-Brown (who succeeded to the Baronetcy on the death of his grandfather and also rose to the rank of Captain) on Saturday 16th August 1913 and Patience Hargreaves-Pigott-Brown, on Monday 15th February 1915.

Gordon was gazetted to the 3rd Battalion Coldstream Guards in January 1900. He served in the South African Campaign with the 2nd Battalion from 1901 to 1902.

Gordon left Blenheim Barracks, Aldershot, in the early hours of Friday 14th August 1914 for Southampton, arriving by train and embarking on *SS Dunvegan Castle* for Le Havre, commanding No 1 Company. Once they disembarked, a five mile march in the hot sun was required, including climbing up a long and tiring hill! Gordon entrained for the French Belgian border but he did not see action at Mons. He marched more than two hundred miles during The Retreat until Sunday 6th September when he turned to engage the Germans. Later in the afternoon they located over one thousand Germans at Voinsles and turned their guns on them. After the short sharp engagement they continued to move onto the valley of the Somme where it was their turn to be on the receiving end of an artillery barrage. They moved onto the Chemin des Dames and the Battle of the Aisne where he fought in the trenches until Friday 16th October. The Battalion was relieved and sent into billets before entraining from Frismes to Hazebrouck, arriving on Sunday 18th.

Gordon marched with his Company from Poperinghe at 5.15am on Wednesday 21st October. The roads were over-run with Belgian refugees with their meagre possessions fleeing the ever-advancing German armies. Their route via Elverdinghe to Pilkem was therefore slow and distressing. For the next four days they came under attack and mounted-counter attacks, until being sent to Zillebeke on Sunday 25th from where they were sent along the Menin Road towards Gheluvelt. Gordon was fighting in the streets, the houses, the gardens and fields, trenches were dug, just slight indentations for use as temporary cover only. At 5.30am on Thursday 29th October, Gordon and his Company were in an exposed position as the Germans advanced under the cover of fog. The German infantry were only seen when they were within fifty yards of his line. They did their utmost to hold on against the assaults made against their line, but their situation was made worse as the ammunition did not fit the rifles; the rifles and machine-guns jammed with over-use and clogged with mud. Eventually the German attack succeeded with all eleven officers killed, wounded or listed as missing. Those killed were: Major The Hon Leslie Hamilton, Captain Gordon Brown, Lieutenant Geoffrey Campbell, Lieutenant Granville Smith, Lieutenant The Hon Alan Douglas-Pennant, 2nd Lieutenant Vere Boscawen — all of whom are recorded on the Menin Gate, and 2nd Lieutenant Charles Williams-Wynn, the only one to have a grave, he being buried in Perth Cemetery (China Wall). Lieutenant F W Gore-Langton was wounded and

Lieutenant Wavell-Paxton was taken prisoner when recovered from the field wounded; Captain Gibbs and 2nd Lieutenant Alison were taken prisoner. In addition, one hundred and eight other ranks were either killed, wounded or captured.

3327 LANCE CORPORAL ERNEST MERTON HARRAP

59th Battalion Australian Infantry, AIF

Died on Wednesday 26th September 1917

Commemorated on Panel 29.

Ernest was the son of Mr E Harrap of Victoria. He was educated locally and became a farmer.
His brother, Lance Corporal James Harrap was killed on the same day and is commemorated on the Menin Gate, see below.
On Monday 17th July 1915 Ernest volunteered and enlisted, leaving on Wednesday 11th October from Melbourne on board *HMAT Nestor*.

HMAT Nestor

They arrived in Egypt where they remained on service and training until Sunday 18th June 1916 when the Battalion arrived in Alexandria. They embarked on *HMT Kinsaums Castle* for Marseilles, stopping *en route* in Malta. Ernest and James disembarked on Thursday 29th and entrained the same day for Steenbecque where they arrived at 7.00am on Sunday 2nd July. They marched to their billets and the next day training commenced. A week later they were in the line near Fleurbaix. Tours of duty to the front line, fatigues and training were the order of the day until Sunday 15th October when they moved to Estaires in preparation for going to the Somme where they arrived eight days later. They were first accommodated at Montauban where training began and they undertook fatigues. The first took the line at *'Carlton Trench'* before leaving for Dernancourt. Their tours of duty included serving at *'Delville Wood'* and *'Trônes Wood'*. Whilst based in Fricourt they undertook fatigues and saw considerable action at *'Deslaux Farm'*. From the first week of June they were sent for training at Rubempré where they remained until Monday 16th

Plan of Rubempré

July when they marched for nearly six hours to continue training at *'Lytham Camp'*. On Monday 30th a march to Belle Eglise took them to the train that proceeded to Steenbecque. Billets were provided at Sercus and training continued until Wednesday 19th September when they moved to *'Devonshire Camp'* at Blaringhem. Final preparations, planning and careful, detailed practise took place for the forthcoming offensive.
At 3.00pm on Saturday 22nd September the Battalion paraded and marched to camp and onward to *'Château Segard'* where they arrived at 7.00pm. At 4.00pm on Monday 24th Ernest and James were moved forward to Zillebeke Lake. Orders were received to proceed to *'Yeomanry Dump'* between Hooge and *'Zouave Wood'* to relieve the 57th Battalion. On Tuesday 25th they took the line near *'Clapham Junction'* and prepared to attack the German positions in Polygon Wood across a front of eight hundred yards. Brigade headquarters were in the crater at Hooge which came under constant attack; in addition it was an ammunition and stores dump although most had been destroyed by shelling. Tapes had been laid out that led to *'Black Watch Corner'*. At 5.53am Ernest and James clambered out of their trenches and charged the fifteen hundred yards towards the German lines under a creeping barrage. They successfully took their first objective, *'Cameron House'*; however, the right flank was terribly exposed as the troops that were to have supported them did not materialise. In the process of the attack a large number of prisoners were taken and were streaming back to 'the cage'. Counter-attacks commenced and the Battalion was forced to fall back and a large number of casualties were suffered including Ernest and James. Their bodies were not recovered then lost during subsequent actions.

3345 Lance Corporal James Wilfred Harrap

59th Battalion Australian Infantry, AIF
Died on Wednesday 26th September 1917
Commemorated on Panel 29.

James was the son of Mr E Harrap of Victoria. He was educated locally and became a farmer.
On Monday 17th July 1915 James volunteered with his brother, Lance Corporal Ernest Harrap, and was killed on the same day and is commemorated on the Menin Gate, for their story see above.

8793 Serjeant Major Arthur George Harrington, DCM

1st Battalion King's Royal Rifle Corps attached London Regiment (London Rifle Brigade)
Died on Wednesday 28th April 1915, aged 46
Commemorated on Addenda Panel 57.

Arthur was the son of the late John William Harrington (Serjeant Major, 3rd Battalion King's Royal Rifles) and Ellen Harrington. He was educated locally. Arthur was married to Florence Margaret Harrington, of 16 Arnos Villas, Bowes Road, New Southgate, London. Arthur was one of six brothers who, like their father, served in the King's Royal Rifle Corps.
Arthur served throughout the South African campaign where he saw considerable action and won the Distinguished Conduct Medal.
On Wednesday 4th November 1914 Arthur left for France, arriving in Le Havre. He entrained for a twenty-one and a half hour journey to northern France and went into billets. His training continued and for a short period of time he was attached to troops in the front line to learn trench duties and have practical front line experience. On Friday 20th Brigadier General Hunter Weston inspected the Brigade and the next day they took the line at Ploegsteert — remaining in the sector until early April. One of his comrades wrote in 1915: *"We are back again in the wood, and really almost glad, though I expect you will hardly believe it. Our quota of work in the winter no doubt did a good deal towards the transformation, and spring is now helping matters. The couduroy no longer stops at the worst parts, where we used to hold our breath and make a dive for it, Hunter Avenue, and right beyond it to the end of the wood, is now quite a pleasant walk. Rations and carrying parties, though they have developed a rather peculiar gait, can progress at a reasonable pace, and have no need to wade so long as they keep to the boards. On either side, however, we still have a reminder of the nightmare that is past. The possibility of getting material up has a corresponding effect on the work in the trenches. The trench we were in on December 9th, which we could not conceive ever being anything but a drain, has now found its proper use. It has a new C.T. behind, and breastworks pushed out in front into the hedge, with little bridges across to each; so that altogether everything in the garden is as near lovely as can be."*
On Friday 23rd April 1915 Arthur was in camp at Busseboom near Poperinghe from where he was sent to Vlamertinghe at 6.45am the next morning, marching through heavy rain and wind. At 6.00pm Arthur paraded and marched to the Salient. They prepared to go into the line at Wieltje where they arrived at 1.45am on Monday 26th. He had been in the line for two days when he was killed.
Arthur was awarded the Long Service and Good Conduct Medal.

Captain Arthur Lea Harris

4th Battalion The Loyal North Lancashire Regiment
Died on Tuesday 31st July 1917, aged 31
Commemorated on Panel 41.

Arthur Lea

Arthur was born on Sunday 2nd May 1886, son of the Reverend S F Harris, of Walton-le-Dale, Lancashire. He was educated at Marlborough College from September 1899 until 1904. Arthur studied law and was admitted as a solicitor in June 1901, employed with Edward Gerrish, Harris & Co of Bristol.
At the outbreak of war Arthur volunteered; he was commissioned and sent for training that continued in Bedford until leaving for France. On Tuesday 4th May 1915, 2nd Lieutenant Arthur Harris and the Battalion sailed on *SS Onward* for Boulogne from where they marched to *'Ostrohove Rest Camp'* for the day. That evening they marched to the station and entrained for Berguette, upon arrival they marched through Lillers to Châlons where they were billeted along the Robecq road. It was expected that a further period of training would be provided but on Friday 14th they were sent to billets at Méteren as GHQ Reserve. They were moved to Locon where on Tuesday 25th they went into the line, described in the Divisional History: *"… in the case of the front taken over by the Division, the normal difficulties were accentuated by the fact that digging in was only possible to a depth of from two to three feet. Everywhere in the Flanders mud, below that level, water was encountered. It was therefore necessary to erect above ground double rows of traversed breastworks, between which the men must live and have their being. The difficulty of consolidation in this mud country requires to have been experienced to be fully appreciated."* On Tuesday 15th June

Arthur participated in an attack near Rue d'Ouvert that was initially successful but the troops on their flanks failed to keep up with them and by 11.00pm the Battalion was desperately hanging on. At midnight the Germans launched a counter-attack and the Battalion was forced to withdraw. When they were relieved to Le Touret only two hundred and forty-three officers and men were able to answer the roll call. After further difficult tours of duty until Tuesday 27th July, following relief, Arthur marched with his men to La Gorgue and they entrained for Corbie to serve on the Ancre.

On Friday 7th January 1916 left the sector and spent a Mont of training at Airaines then moved to the sector south of Arras. They were not involved in any particular action but took part in a number of small and large raids. A raid that took place in mid-June is recorded by on of the privates: *"Captain Gregson was there — I never saw him look better, he was always on of the smartest officers in the Battalion, but he seemed to have been got up for the show with greater care than usual. The smoke lifted like a curtain. We were in full view of the Boche trench. We went on till within fifty yards of it, and then he opened out with machine-guns, rifles and trench mortars. It was hell let loose and somewhat shouted 'On the Kellys' and on we went but were cut down like corn. They Jerrys were two deep in their trench and we realized we were done."* On Tuesday 25th July Arthur was sent south to participate in the Battle of the Somme, taking the line at Guillemont and continued to serve in the sector until Saturday 30th September when they were moved to Belgium, Arthur now promoted to Captain. They arrived in camp at Brandhoek and served on the Salient between Wieltje and *'Railway Wood'* until the end of the year. On Christmas Eve the Battalion was relieved to Ypres town and Christmas was spent out of the line but under constant shell fire.

Until June 1917 the Battalion was involved in the usual routine of front line duties, training and resting. The Battle of Messines took place on Thursday 7th June and the Battalion was involved in a feint to assist in the success of the attack to their south. Throughout July intensive training took place to prepare all ranks for the Third Battle of Ypres. The battle began on Tuesday 31st and is described by the War Diary: *"... at zero, plus four hours forty minutes the 164th Brigade moved off from the assembly trenches in Congreve Walk, the Battalion and the 2/5th Lancashire Fusiliers in front on the right and left respectively, with the 1/4th Royal Lancaster and 1/8th Liverpool Regiment in support. During the actual advance the casualties were few, by 2nd Lieutenant Ashcroft was killed. At 10.10 a.m. the Brigade formed up under the protective barrage some 200 yards on the German side of the Black Line, experiencing some annoyance by the enemy snipers lying out in shell-holes, and then moved forward to attack and consolidate the Green Line, the Battalion, as it advanced, establishing touch With the flank battalion of the 15th Division.*

During the advance the casualties became very heavy, especially among the commissioned ranks, these being caused by machine-guns and by shells from guns firing from the high ground beyond the Green Line and by other on the right. Several strong points — known as Keir Farm, Gallipoli and Somme Farm — had to be dealt with while moving forward and from these some sixty prisoners were taken. The Green Line was occupied by 11.40 and consolidation was put in hand; but the protective barrage now ceased, ammunition was beginning to run short, and about 2.35 p.m. the enemy counter-attacked in strength, obliging the Brigade to fall back to the Black Line." It was a successful day for the Battalion but when it was withdrawn shortly after midnight, Arthur remained somewhere on the battlefield, his body was never recovered.

In St Leonard's Church, Walton Le Dale, Lancashire, a brass plaque was placed in his memory with the inscription: *"To the glory of God in loving memory of Arthur Lea Harris, Captain 4th Battalion Loyal North Lancashire Regiment, killed in action near Ypres, July 31st 1917, Only son of Rev. Seymour F. Harris, Vicar of this Parish 1889-1908. Be thou faithful unto death."*

SECOND LIEUTENANT ARTHUR STANLEY HARRIS

6th Battalion The King's (Liverpool Regiment)

Died on Tuesday 31st July 1917

Commemorated on Panel 6.

Arthur was the son of Mr and Mrs W S Harris. He was educated at Wellington College from 1896 to 1900.

Arthur was commissioned in 1917. Following training he was sent to France and joined the Battalion in the field. At the end of June he was in the Wieltje sector where on Sunday 1st July they repulsed a raid on their lines. Whilst in action, close to *'Observatory Wood'* he was mortally wounded at *'Strula Farm'*.

"In spite of the fact that our barrage was on the Farm it was at once attacked and captured with three German machine-guns which it contained. The capture of this strong point before the advance from the Blue Line considerably assisted the subsequent advance of the 7th and 8th King's to the Black Line.

The battalion attacked in four waves with 1/5th South Lancashire (166th Infantry Brigade) on the left, 1/5th Battalion The King's on our right. The German front and support lines were carried with little trouble, some slight opposition being encountered in the reserve line. This, however, caused no delay, and platoons from 'B' and 'C' Companies pushed on to the Blue Line and immediately commenced to dig in, strong points being dug, one on the left flank and one in front of Jasper Farm, between Jasper Farm and the Blue Line ... 1.T 5.05 a.m. the 9th Battalion The King's passed through the Blue Line to attack the Sutzpunkt Line and Pommern Redoubt."

Second Lieutenant Leslie George Hamlyn Harris

2nd Battalion Sherwood Foresters (Notts and Derby Regiment)

Died on Monday 2nd November 1914, aged 19

Commemorated on Panel 41.

Leslie Harris

Leslie was born in 1895 the son of the late Major General Noel H Harris (RA), and of Mrs Noel Harris, of 13 Brechin Place, London SW7. He was educated at Summer Fields from 1905 followed by Wellington College from 1909 to 1912. In 1913 he passed into RMC Sandhurst.

Leslie was commissioned on Saturday 8th August 1914. On Monday 7th September the Battalion entrained for Southampton embarking on *SS Georgian* for St Nazaire, arriving on the night of Tuesday 11th. It was a ghastly journey and the general view of

... a tented camp

the majority that the boat was not fit to transport cattle. They were sent by train to assist on the Aisne where they saw action on the Chemin des Dames where the fighting was intense.

On Friday 9th October Leslie entrained for Abbeville and onto St Omer where they marched to their billets in Arques. The next day they were sent by motor bus to Vieux Berquin where they were held in reserve. On Thursday 15th they moved closer to the French-Belgian border at Steenwerck from where orders were received for them to move to Sailly on the River Lys. They took charge of the village and as they arrived the church was shelled and was in flames. After covering the bridge and crossings during the day they were relieved during the night taking over at Ennetières. The next morning the German artillery bombarded the village and in the afternoon German attacks were attempted that were countered, but large numbers of casualties occurred. Retirement was not countenanced and they held on until 5.00am on Wednesday 21st.

Brigadier General Walter Congreve wrote: *"The Battalion had done exceedingly well all day; it was just worn out and overwhelmed by superior numbers."* On Monday 26th reinforcements arrived to replace the considerable casualties the Battalion had taken. Tours of duty continued and whilst in the line, Leslie was killed.

Captain Percy Cuthbert Harris

1st Battalion Suffolk Regiment

Died on Tuesday 16th February 1915, aged 26

Commemorated on Panel 21.

Percy was the youngest son of Colonel J E Harris (late Commander, 2nd Suffolk Regiment, 1888 to 1892) and Mrs Harris, of The Shade, Sharnford, Hinckley, Leicestershire.

At the outbreak of war Percy was about to leave for Japan to study the language, however, it was cancelled! He joined the mobilisation at Lichfield when the Battalion returned from Sudan.

On Saturday 16th January 1915 he embarked on *SS Mount Temple* for Le Havre. On Wednesday 20th he arrived by train in Hazebrouck. During the night of Thursday 4th and Friday 5th February they moved into the front line between the Ypres to Comines Canal and Hill 60. The front line was in very poor condition with the men having to wade constantly through two feet of water. 'O' Trench had been captured by the Germans and a counter-attack was launched when Percy was killed.

Percy was recorded in Debretts Obituary — War Roll of Honour published in the 1921 edition.

In St Mary's Church, Crown Street, Bury St Edmunds, Suffolk, a prayer desk was presented in his memory with the inscription: *"In memory of Captain P. C. Harris killed in action at Ypres 16th Febry. 1915."*

25911 Sergeant John d'Auvergne A Harris-Arundell

14th Battalion Canadian Infantry (Quebec Regiment)

Died on Wednesday 21st April 1915, aged 25

Commemorated on Panel 24.

John Harris-Arundell

John was born at Fairmount, Minnesota, USA, on Tuesday 14th May 1889, second son of Robert and Elizabeth Blanche Harris-Arundell of Halifax, Nova Scotia, grandson of John d'Auvergne Dumaresque, CMG. At the age of five the family moved to Canada. He was educated at the Collegiate School, Windsor, Nova Scotia. John was employed by Royal Bank of Canada in the Halifax branch.

John volunteered at Valcartier on Friday 28th August 1914, being a member of the Militia, described as 5ft 10in tall, with a 37in chest, a fair complexion, grey eyes and fair hair. He arrived in Plymouth on Wednesday 14th October. After training at Salisbury, he left for the front on Friday 5th February 1915. During action at Langemarck he went out two hundred yards under heavy fire to assist Lieutenant Whitehead who had been wounded but he was shot in the heart and died instantaneously.

461343 Private James Frederick Harrison, DCM

2nd Battalion Canadian Infantry
(Eastern Ontario Regiment)
Died on Tuesday 6th November 1917, aged 25
Commemorated on Panel 18.

Citation for the Distinguished Conduct Medal, London Gazette, Thursday 26th July 1917:

"For conspicuous gallantry and devotion to duty. He was instrumental in capturing an enemy machine-gun and the officer in charge of it. Later, he entered an enemy dug-out and captured three more officers and four other ranks."

James was born in Cheshire, England, on Friday 9th September 1892, son of Mrs Mary Kemery, of Granite Falls, Washington, USA. He was educated locally then worked in Canada as a farmer.

On Thursday 6th January 1916 James volunteered in Winnipeg where he was described as 5ft 7in tall, with a 37in chest, a clear complexion, brown eyes and dark brown hair.

Following training James was sent to England where training continued for a short period of time before he was sent out to France, where he joined the Battalion in the field. He first served in the line on the Ypres Salient and his tours of duty continued until Wednesday 9th August when he was sent to La Panne on the coast for three weeks training. At the end of the month he entrained for the Somme and arrived in Albert on Thursday 31st. James remained on tour of duty until December when he was sent to Ourton for intensive training that last until Saturday 20th January 1917 after which he returned to the line near Souchez. During Wednesday 28th March he moved the short distance to Ecoivres and the *'Maison Blache'* sector.

James continued to serve in northern France before being sent for training at St Marie Cappel on Monday 22nd October to prepare for the forthcoming attack on the Ypres Salient. On Friday 2nd November James marched to Bavinchove Station where he entrained at 6.00am for Ypres arriving at 9.30am. He marched through Ypres and out to Wieltje, which he reached at 11.45am. In the cold and rain he helped put up shelters in which he remained for two nights at *'Camp C'*. Throughout Saturday 3rd he undertook fatigues and was issued with his kit for the attack. James marched to the front line and his Battalion Headquarters

German prisoners taken at Passchendaele

were established at *'Waterloo Farm'*. On Monday 5th final preparations were prepared for the attack and Headquarters were moved to *'Meetcheele Pillbox'*. By 3.20am on Tuesday 6th all was prepared with a German barrage opening on their lines at 3.50am. At 6.00am a barrage was launched on the German lines and the attack commenced. Within fifteen minutes the first objective was taken. As James moved forward to attack the second objective, he was killed.

Second Lieutenant Leonard John Harrison

2nd Battalion Lancashire Fusiliers
Died on Monday 24th May 1915, aged 19
Commemorated on Panel 33.

Leonard Harrison

Leonard was born at Burton Rectory, Pembrokeshire, on Thursday 21st November 1895, son of Ethel Harrison, of Elysium, Framingham Pigot, Norwich, and the late Reverend Arthur Leonard Harrison, Rector of Yelverton, Norfolk, grandson of Major General John William Younghusband, CSI. Leonard was a chorister of St George's Chapel, Windsor, for five years followed by Haileybury from 1910 to 1912 as a member of Thomason, he then passed into RMC Sandhurst. Leonard was a keen sportsman, good rider, played cricket for the Norfolk Club and Ground, and was a member of the Cavendish Club.

Leonard was gazetted to the Indian Army in July 1914 and at the outbreak of war he was attached to the Lancashire Fusiliers at Barrow-in-Furness. He left for France in January 1915 and joined the Battalion in the field. He undertook normal tours of duty until the Second Battle of Ypres began on Thursday 22nd April. He fought through savage battle until he was killed in action at *'Shell Trap Farm'*.

His Commanding Officer wrote: *"Your son lost his life in endeavouring to retake some trenches which were lost. He behaved most gallantly in leading his men forward in the face of heavy fire and also gas. Nobody could have possibly shown better example to the men. We all miss him very much, as he made himself most popular whilst he was with us, both with officers and men."*

1201 Lance Serjeant Robert Harrison

1st/5th Battalion Northumberland Fusiliers

Died on Sunday 23rd May 1915

Commemorated on Panel 12

Robert was born and enlisted in Wallesend-on-Tyne. He served in the Territorial Battalion prior to the war. Following mobilisation he was sent for training and were on home defence duty; arriving in France in mid-April 1915.

The Battalion was sent to northern France where training was to continue but due to the Germans launching their gas attack on Thursday 22nd April the Battalion was sent into the line to support the Salient. The Second Battle of Ypres was raging as he first took the line. As the Battle of St Julien ended the Germans turned their attention to the sector to the south around Bellewaarde. During a German bombardment and attack that heralded the beginning of the Battle of Bellewaarde Robert was killed after only serving in the front line for three weeks.

... a German attack is repulsed

Captain Arthur Charles Hart

'A' Company, 2nd Battalion Northumberland Fusiliers

Died on Friday 7th May 1915, aged 33

Commemorated on Panel 12.

Arthur Hart

Arthur was born on Friday 7th October 1881, son Sir Israel and Lady Hart, 34 Holland Park, London. He was educated at Cheltenham College from 1896 to 1899. He held memberships of Queen's, the United Services and the Ranleagh, Roehampton.

Arthur was gazetted from the Militia in January 1901, promoted Lieutenant in February 1902 and Captain in March 1911. He served in South Africa, Antigua and India.

Arthur went out to the Western Front in January 1915, arriving in the Ypres Salient and went immediately into the front line.

On Saturday 20th February Arthur led 'A' Company forward through the remnants of a wood, across a field (by then a quagmire), and then charged at the German defenders. Sufficient warning was given to the Germans that they were able to pour heavy fire down on the attackers, wiping out all the leading men but luckily Arthur survived. The next day he took his men into the Infantry Barracks in Ypres for some much needed rest for two days.

On Tuesday 13th April Arthur marched from the billets in St Jans Cappel to a camp at Vlamertinghe. After two days they marched to Broodseinde, east of Zonnebeke. For the first couple of days it was relatively quiet; however, a small party of Germans had established a foothold in a gap in the line. Arthur led a group of men forward in the hope of taking a prisoner — he only captured a German rifle and took a slight wound for his trouble! He was subsequently wounded again, a fairly severe wound to his hand. During the gas attack the Battalion sent reinforcements to assist the Canadians. Lieutenant Hardy wrote: *"The greater part of the officers and men are asphyxiated by gas. I understand that the enemy is on three sides of me. Unless I am reinforced fairly well, it will be impossible to do anything great."*

On Wednesday 5th May the German artillery commenced a barrage that continued until Friday 7th, slowly increasing in intensity. Arthur was in the line and was rallying his men near Zonnebeke when he was killed. It is recorded that he personally killed at least twenty Germans.

Arthur was Mentioned in Despatches gazetted on Monday 31st May 1915.

Arthur was recorded in Debretts Obituary — War Roll of Honour published in the 1921 edition.

S/2506 Serjeant David Hart, DCM

1st Battalion Gordon Highlanders

Died on Thursday 2nd March 1916, aged 22

Commemorated on Panel 38.

David was born in Glasgow the son of the late Robert Hynd Hart and Mary Hart. He was educated locally. David was married to Margaret Inglis Hart, of St Andrew Terrace, Clydesdale Road, Mossend, Lanarkshire.

In February 1916 General Sir Herbert Plumer prepared for an attack on *'The Bluff'* and David with the Battalion was sent for training and preparation. General Plumer instigated the idea of marking the communication trenches as *'up to the line'* and *'down from the line'* to make life easier and more efficient. Some of the men were issued with steel 'shrapnel' helmets and were sent to attack on the left, supporting the Suffolks who were able to take a substantial portion of *'The Bluff'*. The Battalion took the left flank during the attack. They reached the German parapet but the machine-gun nests held them up until 2nd Lieutenant Sanderson rushed forward and bombed them into submission; for that action he was immediately awarded the Distinguished Conduct Medal. The Germans retaliated with a heavy bombardment and David was killed by shell fire.

General Plumer

2380 Private George Hart

'C' Company, 1st/4th Battalion

South Lancashire Regiment

Died on Sunday 27th June 1915, aged 16

Commemorated on Panel 37.

George was born at home, the son of Mr and Mrs George W Hart, of 4 Eustace Street, Warrington, Cheshire.

He enlisted in Warrington and was sent for training. On Friday 12th February 1915 he embarked in Southampton for Le Havre. The Battalion sailed on *SS Queen Alexandra* and *SS Trafford Hall* and after disembarkation marched to No 2 Rest Camp for two days. He returned to the town and entrained for Bailleul. He marched the short distance to the *'Grapperies'* where he was billeted for five days and undertook training. On Sunday 21st he was went the short distance to the Belgian border and onward to a camp in La Clytte via Locre. After a further five days of training and preparation for the front line he was sent to Kemmel on Friday 26th for his first tour of duty. On Thursday 25th March he marched further north to billets in Dickebusch where after a night's rest he was sent into the line at St Eloi. The view from the trenches was nothing short of a carnal house, bodies of soldiers and civilians who had been killed over the past months lay rotting in front of him. After six days he was relieved by the 2nd Battalion — he returned on tours of duty over the next three weeks. On Saturday 1st May George relieved the 2nd Battalion in the line near Elzenwalle Château. On Sunday 2nd a gas attack took place on Hill 60, the wind blew the gas in their direction, and George and his comrades suffered irritation of their eyes as a result. Throughout the rest of the month he undertook tours of duty without participating in any significant action. On Saturday 5th June the Battalion relieved the 2nd Life Guards and 8th Hussars at *'Sanctuary Wood'*. On Wednesday 16th he charged forward in the attack on Bellewaarde Ridge where he lost many friends who were killed as they advanced into the path of the British barrage. It was a furious fight, where they were pushed back and counter-attacked throughout the day. After a hard and long tour of duty he was relieved from the line and sent to the relative safety of Ypres, being billeted in the dug-outs in the thick walls of the ramparts. After three days rest he went back into the line for the last time, returning to Hooge. George's short life ended in the front line three days later.

Captain Clement Jesse Harter

3rd Battalion attached 4th Battalion Royal Fusiliers

Died on Wednesday 16th June 1915, aged 26

Commemorated on Panel 8.

Clement Harter

Clement was born on Wednesday 4th December 1889, third son of Charles B Hatfield Harter and Violet Harter, of 5 Onslow Houses, South Kensington, London. He was educated at Beaumont College, Old Windsor. Clement was a member of the Bath Club.

He originally served in the Royal Navy but was gazetted to the Royal Fusiliers in August 1911, promoted to Lieutenant in April 1914.

Clement left for France in March 1915. On Wednesday 16th June 1915 Clement was in the line east of *'Cambridge Road'*. At 2.50am a barrage opened up and two hours later he went 'over the top' and was successful in taking the German first line. They advanced on Bellewaarde Lake and Clement was killed leading his platoon forward.

His brother, Captain John Harter, died on Monday 3rd April 1916 and is buried on Lijssenthoek Military Cemetery.

Lieutenant Frank Lennox Harvey

9th (Queen's Royal) Lancers
Died on Friday 30th October 1914, aged 23
Commemorated on Panel 5.

Frank was the son of Reverend Edward Douglas Lennox Harvey and Constance Annie Harvey, OBE, JP, DL, of Beedingwood, Horsham, Sussex. He was educated at Eton College as a member of Mr Lionel Stanley Rice Byrne's House, leaving in 1909 and went up to Trinity College, Cambridge.

On Friday 30th October 1914 Frank was in the line at Messines when the Germans launched a major attack on their line after several days of shelling. At dawn they saw the Germans advance whilst positioned in front of the town. The 9th were repulsing them but orders were received to retire. The town was now split between defender and attacker. Barricades were constructed that came under shell fire. It was a fierce fight with Frank and many of his friends and men becoming casualties.

Frank is commemorated on Colgate War Memorial, West Sussex.

In St Saviours Church, Colgate, West Sussex, a decorated brass plaque was placed in his memory with the inscription: *"To the glory of God and in loving memory of Frank Lennox Harvey Lt. 9th Queen's Royal Lancers killed in action near Messines Oct. 30 1914 and Douglas Lennox Harvey 2nd. Lt. 9th Queen's Royal Lancers killed in action near Messines Nov. 3. 1914. They are numbered among those who at the call of King and Country left all that was dear to them endured hardness, faced danger and finally passed out of the sight of men by the path of duty and self-sacrifice giving up their own lives that others might live in freedom."*

His brother, 2nd Lieutenant Douglas Harvey died three days later, on Monday 2nd November 1914, and is buried in Dranouter Churchyard.

6948 Private Albert Fred Hass

10th Battalion Australian Infantry, AIF
Died between Thursday 20th to
Friday 21st September 1917, aged 24
Commemorated on Panel 17.

Albert was born in Greenville, Wisconsin, USA, son of Peter Heinrich Hass, of Peterborough, South Australia, and the late Lisette Hass (née Lohmann). He was educated locally, served in the cadets and became a clerk.

On Tuesday 8th February 1916 he volunteered leaving from Adelaide on Saturday 16th December on board *HMAT Berrima.*

After training Albert was sent out with a draft, joining the Battalion on the Somme in the Bancourt sector. The majority of May and June 1917 were spent in training at Bapaume, Ribemont and Henencourt before taking the line at Mailly Maillet on Sunday 24th June where he served until Friday 6th July. On Saturday 7th he returned to Ribemont to continue training and the Battalion was inspected by HM King George V on Thursday 12th before marching to Bray the next day where training and rest continued. On Thursday 26th the Battalion marched to Albert and entrained to Steenbecque from where they were billeted at Staple for three days before being sent to Seninghem until Sunday 5th August. They then returned for three days at Seninghem and marched to Bleue where they remained until Wednesday 12th September. On Sunday 16th they arrived in Ouderdom where they spent two days relaxing before moving to *'Château Segard'* and going into action at Polygon Wood where he was killed.

His brother, Corporal Walter Hass, died on Friday 12th October 1917 and is commemorated on the Menin Gate, see below.

2517 Corporal Walter Theodor Hass

48th Battalion Australian Infantry, AIF
Died on Friday 12th October 1917, aged 21
Commemorated on Panel 27.

Walter was born in Greenville, Wisconsin, USA, son of Peter Heinrich Hass, of Peterborough, South Australia, and the late Lisette Hass (née Lohmann). He was educated locally, served in the cadets and worked as a cleaner on the railways.

On Friday 5th May 1916 Walter resigned his commission in the cadets to volunteer for overseas service. He left on Monday 28th August from Adelaide on board *HMAT Anchises*. Walter arrived in England and after a period of training was sent to join the Battalion with draft on the Somme to serve in the Flers sector. He continued to serve on the Somme until April 1917 when he entrained at Aveluy at 3.30am on Sunday 13th May for Bailleul. Walter arrived at 5.10pm and they were billeted until Saturday 19th. He marched to *'Dou Dou Farm'* and they prepared for the Battle of Messines.

On Monday 4th June he marched to 'Antrim Lines' where he remained until Thursday 7th and was moved forward to *'Midland Support South Trench'* at 8.40am. During the evening the Battalion was ordered to support the 45th and 47th Battalions. On Friday 8th *'Owl Trench'* was captured and consolidated and he remained in the line until Tuesday 12th when the Battalion was relieved and sent to rest billets at La Creche. Walter was provided with a hot bath on Thursday 14th, a welcome event after so long in the mud of the battlefield with an

inspection taking place the next day of both clothing and equipment. A fleet of motor buses arrived on Sunday 17th and took the Battalion to Doulieu for training before returning to the front at Ploegsteert on Friday 29th. His tours of duty continued at Kemmel, *'Cabin Hill'* at Wytschaete, with rest and training at Doulieu.
The first three weeks of September Walter trained in northern France before returning to camp at Reninghelst in preparation to taking the line in the Salient. On Monday 24th he went into the trenches at Hooge; on Sunday 30th he moved forward to Nonne Bosschen as the Battalion relieved the 16th Battalion at the *'Green Line'*. It was a difficult relief as they were under heavy artillery fire and he proceeded with a small group in single file, with fifty yards between each group, until reaching the trenches. Their line came under heavy shellfire throughout the tour, including the twenty-four hours spent on Westhoek Ridge prior to being relieved to *'Halifax Camp'* late on Monday 1st October. After two days of rest and cleaning up Walter was taken by motor bus across the border into France to Steenvoorde for training. The Battalion received orders to proceed to Westhoek Ridge (*'Kit and Cat'*) and they marched to Abeele Station to entrain for Ypres where they arrived at 3.20pm on Thursday 11th October. A slow march into the front line followed, with the relief completed at 8.30pm. At 12.10am on Friday 12th the Battalion was led by Lieutenant Colonel Leane, DSO, MC, and took their position at the jumping off tapes on the Passchendaele Ridge eight minutes prior to Zero Hour. Walter advanced under a creeping barrage towards *'Assyria House'* where they came under very heavy machine-gun fire. They came under an intense counter-attack and during the fierce battle Walter was killed.
His brother, Private Albert Hass, died between Thursday 20th and Friday 21st September 1917 and is commemorated on the Menin Gate, see above.

LIEUTENANT FREDERICK HASWELL

3rd Battalion East Yorkshire Regiment

Died on Friday 23rd April 1915, aged 19

Commemorated on Panel 21.

Frederick Haswell

Frederick was born on Friday 14th June 1895, second son of Robert and Jessie Haswell, of 27 Thornhill Gardens, Sunderland. He was educated at Bede Collegiate College where he was awarded his cricket colours. He went up to Manchester University in 1913 and was a member of the OTC. Frederick was employed by the National Provincial Bank in Manchester.

Frederick volunteered for service and was gazetted on Saturday 15th August 1914. His promotion was gazetted posthumously. He was sent for training and went out to France to join the Battalion in the field with a draft.
On Thursday 22nd April 1915 Frederick was with his men in the huts at *'Camp A'* and moved off late that night. The Battalion Diary records: *"6.30 p.m. 22/4/15, Ypres. Battalion ordered to 'stand to' at 6.30 p.m. in consequence of the Germans having broken through the line held by the French Army near St. Julien. Marched to Brielen and bivouacked in field during the night. … About midday, news was received that the East Yorkshires were on their way across to come under Colonel Geddes' command and were being ordered to Wieltje. Orders were sent back to them to remain for the present at St. Jean, Wieltje at the time being very heavily shelled, and there was little or no cover there."* They now had to hold a much longer front line than before the gas attack in the line that connected them with the Canadians. At 4.10pm Frederick led his men forward to attack the German line. *"All ranks showed the most absolute indifference to fire and casualties, advancing splendidly under their officers."* The Germans opened up with machine-gun and rifle fire that caused severe casualties; however, the advance reached within thirty yards of their objective. Frederick was leading his men forward near St Julien when he was killed. Further advance was impossible, and holding on to the position was untenable due to lack of numbers through casualties — retiring was the only option. A heavy toll for so little, nine officers wounded, four killed (including Frederick) one missing; forty-one men killed, two hundred and Fifty-six wounded and seventy-two missing.
His Major wrote: *"Lieutenant Haswell had only been with us a short time, but quite long enough to endear himself to all ranks, and he leaves a gap very difficult to fill. I was not near him when he fell, but he was gallantly leading his men when he was shot in the head, death being instantaneous, which is always a comforting thing to know. He died bravely, as a brave man should."*

LIEUTENANT WILLIAM LEONARD RINGROSE HATCH

2nd Battalion Royal Irish Fusiliers

Died on Monday 25th January 1915, aged 24

Commemorated on Panel 42.

William was born in Bombay, India, on 27th November 1890, the elder son of Lieutenant Colonel William Keith and Clare Catherine Hatch, of Earlham Road, Norwich. Like his father, he attended Shrewsbury School from 1904 to 1907 where he was member of the OTC. He passed into RMC Sandhurst.
He was gazetted on Thursday 23rd March 1911 and promoted to Lieutenant Sunday 13th April 1913.

At the outbreak of war William was based in Quetta, India, and was sent to the Western Front with his regiment. Whilst in a forward observation post at Vierstraat he was wounded in the shoulder and killed shortly afterward whilst lying in a dug-out.
A brother officer wrote: "… *The next burst put a shell right in the trench. Some of the men had got along near him to try and move him at great risk just before, but he ordered them back, and was alone with one other man, a Private, who must have tried to get to him, when the next rounds commenced. Both must have been killed instantaneously. Five other men were buried with the falling parapet, but afterwards safely rescued. The men ordered back realize he saved their lives, for the shell burst before they could have moved him.*"
'The Salopian' wrote: "*Those of us who recollect him as a member of the Army Class … will feel sure that he died, as he lived, a sportsman, a gentleman, and a loyal Old Salopian.*"

Second Lieutenant Frederick Charles Hatton

2nd Battalion Yorkshire Regiment

Died on Friday 30th October 1914, aged 36

Commemorated on Panel 33.

Frederick Hatton

Frederick was born at Parkhurst, Isle of Wight, on Tuesday 9th April 1878, son of the late Alfred Charles and Louisa Frances Minetta Hatton. His father was for some time the Editor of the *'Yokohama Press'* in Japan. He was related to Sir Westby Brook Percival, KCMG, Agent-General for New Zealand. Frederick was educated privately.
Frederick was married to Mrs Elsie A M Hatton (née Thewlis, and niece of Alderman Thewlis, Lord Mayor of London), of 4 West Terrace, Richmond, Yorkshire. They had a son Frederick, born in 1902. Frederick was Secretary of the Green Howards' Old Comrades' Association and contributed to the *'Green Howards' Gazette'* and Sergeant Major of the *'Old-time Firing and Hand Grenade Display'*.
Frederick enlisted in the army and held various appointments including Gymnastic Instructor, Depôt Drill Instructor, Pay Sergeant Regiment Quartermaster Sergeant and Regimental Sergeant Major.
He served in the South African War and was seriously wounded at the Battle of Driefontein. Frederick received the Queen's Medal with three clasps and was also awarded the Long Service and Good Conduct Medal.
Frederick left for Zeebrugge on Sunday 4th October 1914, embarking on *SS California* accompanying Colonel Charles King together with 'A' and 'B' Companies, and was sent to Brugge where they were billeted and awaited the arrival two days later of 'C' and 'D' Companies. On Saturday 10th the Battalion was ordered to move south via Beernem, Koolskamp and Roeselare to Ypres. Shortly after his arrival on the Salient on 14th Frederick received his commission and was appointed Acting Adjutant.
Frederick took his men into the line near Gheluvelt at Pozelhoek on Friday 16th with the HQ being established in an *estaminet* on the crossroads in the centre of the village. Some excitement was caused when Lieutenant Richard Phayre (who was killed on Friday 30th and is commemorated on the Menin Gate, see below) returned from patrol with 'A' Company with a group of German prisoners. They had come under fire from a farmhouse and attacked and the Germans had moved into a barn and refused to surrender. Lieutenant Phayre set fire to the barn and eventually they came out! Throughout Saturday 17th Frederick organised his men to dig in although they came under intermittent fire. The next morning they moved to Becelaere during the day before returning to their lines later in the evening.
An advance on Gheluwe was under way on Monday 19th and the Battalion prepared to leave in the early afternoon to participate in the attack. The Battalion Diary records: "*The morning passed very quietly until suddenly, about 1.30 p.m. we got orders to be ready to move at a moment's notice, and at 2 p.m. off we went, not to the attack of Gheluwe as we thought, but back to our own entrenchments we had left the day before. On the way we were told that the attack on Kezelberg, though successful, had had to be abandoned because it was suddenly discovered that two German Army Corps were moving down on to us from the direction of Roulers. … We got back to our entrenchments about 4.30 p.m., that is to say, with roughly an hour and a half's daylight left.*"
The Battalion's first experience of being under a high explosive artillery bombardment was during the early morning of Tuesday 20th and a number of casualties were taken. Throughout the next day the men continued to dig in and improve the defences. At 3.00pm on Thursday 22nd columns of German infantry were advancing towards them and commenced rapid fire when they within range causing a large number of casualties. One of the men wrote: "… *we could see quite clearly columns of Germans massing on our left flank; our artillery made excellent practice, but bow we prayed for more and heavier guns. On the evening of this day we heard that the enemy had broken through the line on the left. They were attacking in mass for all they were worth and fully determined to break through, but were stopped in a most gallant manner by 'A' Company and the machine guns under Lieutenant Ledgard and by a party of our men who volunteered to attack and clear a wood under Captain Jeffery.*" (Lieutenant Frank

Ledgard was killed and is buried in Harlebeke Military Cemetery and Captain Claud Jeffery was mortally wounded and is buried in Ypres Town Cemetery.
The whole sector came under a sustained artillery barrage day and night from Friday 23rd to Monday 26th. The German infantry also mounted one raid or attack after another and they were repulsed on each occasion. The toll on ammunition was high, each night 96,000 rounds of ammunition were hauled up the Menin Road to replenish the front line, and on occasion additional supplies had to be sent during the day.
After a short break in reserve, at 6.30am on Tuesday 27th Frederick and the men were ordered back into the line as the pressure was mounting. Throughout the relief the shells rained down on them. At 11.00am on Thursday 29th the German infantry broke through the line that was pushed back one thousand yards. Colonel Charles King reorganised the line and led a counter-attack that regained two hundred yards of ground. The next morning the German attack increased in strength and whilst Frederick was with his Colonel he was killed by a sniper. Colonel King was also killed and is commemorated on the Menin Gate, see below.

4726 Squadron Serjeant Major Charles Burtwell Hawgood, DCM

4th (Queen's Own) Hussars

Died on Monday 24th May 1915, aged 35

Commemorated on Panel 5.

Citation for the Distinguished Conduct Medal:

"For gallantry and marked ability consistently displayed in every action in which his regiment has been engaged."

Charles was born in Kensington and was married to Alice Hawgood, of 87 Old Heath Road, Colchester.
On Friday 14th August 1914 Charles and the Queen's Own left the Curragh for Dublin, arriving the next day. They immediately boarded the *SS Atlantian* under the command of Lieutenant Colonel Ian Hogg (who died of wounds on Wednesday 2nd September and is buried in Haramont Communal Cemetery). They arrived in France at 7.00am on Thursday 18th, leaving the next day for Maubeuge. They went up to Mons and saw action, from where they took part in The Retreat, the Battle of the Marne and Aisne, before moving to the Salient.
On Friday 23rd April 1915, as a result of the German gas attack, Charles was marched from Vieux Berquin to Poperinghe, via the Mont de Cats, going into bivouac at 10.30pm. At 4.00am the next morning they went to the south of Elverdinghe where they left their horses. On Monday 26th they were in the line near *'Hell Fire Corner'*, remaining there until 10.00pm on Thursday 29th when they were moved to Wieltje. On Sunday 2nd May they were subjected to a gas attack: *"It should be noted here that we had as yet no gas masks, and our only protection against gas was 4-inch by 2-inch of flannelette, which we were told to dampen and hold over the nose and mouth."* The infantry caught by the gas were in a terrible condition: *"They were a very dreadful sight, and those not yet helpless were nevertheless oblivious to everything except the gas cloud which was following and enveloping them."* At 1.00am on Monday 3rd May they were relieved at dawn they watched in the distance the German counter-attack and on Hill 60. They went for rest and training at La Rue du Bois until they were ordered up to the front just before midnight on Thursday 13th as a result of a heavy attack on the Salient. They went into the line at Verlorenhoek; on Monday 22nd May they were relieved and sent to Vlamertinghe. At 3.00am on Monday 24th streams of men came passed suffering from the effects of a gas attack and Charles was told to get the men ready to move off to the front. At 10.30am they moved across country to Ypres and Charles was in a railway cutting south of Ypres. Whilst in the cutting they were heavily shelled and Charles was killed, twelve were wounded.

Lieutenant Lionel Hope Hawkins

1st (King's) Dragoon Guards

attached 6th Dragoon Guards (Carabiniers)

Died on Saturday 31st October 1914, aged 28

Commemorated on Panel 3.

Lionel Hawkins

Lionel was born at Chichester on Wednesday 28th July 1886, son of Isaac Thomas and Mary Hope Hawkins, of 90 Drayton Gardens, London SW. He was educated at Winchester College from 1900 to 1903 where he was a good all-round athlete, particularly running, winning the steeplechase for his House. He also played football, cricket and Fives. Whilst at school he gained the nicknames *'Agag'* and *'Diabolo'*.
In India he had a reputation as a fine polo player and competed in regimental competitions and helped win the Patiala Cup amongst many others. Lionel was a member of the Junior Army and Navy and the Junior Naval and Military Clubs and of the Hurlingham and Ranelagh.
Lionel passed into RMC Sandhurst in 1905 and was gazetted on Saturday 2nd February 1907, promoted Lieutenant on Tuesday 18th February 1908, and had

passed for his Captaincy In October 1912.
He served in India where he was awarded the Delhi Durbar Medal. He was the Signalling Officer of the Ambala Cavalry Brigade for two years.
At the outbreak of war Lionel was on home leave so he was therefore attached to the 6th Dragoon Guards and went with them to France on Saturday 15th August, seeing action from Mons through to Ypres. He was killed in action between Messines and Wytschaete when the Germans broke through during an attack.
The Adjutant wrote: *"It appears that after the enemy had penetrated our line a party was observed by your son approaching the trench which he held with his troop. He ordered fire to be opened on them, but they shouted 'Don't fire! We are the Scottish!' and he ordered his men to cease fire, and himself bravely, but incautiously, got out of the trench and went towards them. He had gone about thirty yards when the Germans — for it was the Germans, and not the London Scottish — opened fire, and your son was seen to fall. Two men at once went out and brought him back to the trench. He was seen to be badly wounded in the right side, and he was carried back by our men and the London Scottish towards Kemmel. On reaching a place of comparative safety two of the men went off to try and find a stretcher, and two remained with your son, who died very shortly afterwards. He had been unconscious from a few minutes after he had been hit, and passed quietly away. The men were unable to bury him then, and were obliged to leave him covered with a blanket at the edge of a wood, where I have no doubt he has since been buried. But as, unfortunately, the Germans now hold that piece of ground it has not been possible to do what otherwise would have been done. You have lost a gallant son, and we a brave and well-loved comrade who showed military qualities of a high order."*
Major S W Webster wrote: *"The farm we held was rushed by the Germans about midnight on 31 Oct. I at once went to the trench in which your son was. We retired from there to some reserve trenches about 200 yards in the rear. I was there with him for about half an hour. I then left him to go and see a troop who were holding a trench on his right. After I had gone I believe he went forward a little to see if they really were Germans, as he seemed to think they were our own troops — it was pitch dark at the time. He was shot through the body, and some of my own men carried him back. He died when they had carried him about ¼ mile to the rear. My man, Private Willings, then left the body under a fence. It was impossible to recover the body or even the wounded, as we had to evacuate the position at dawn. I am perfectly certain from what the men told me, that your son died within half an hour of his wound. It must seem strange to you, that we could not recover the body, but we were fighting for our lives through the night, in the pitch dark, over a front of at least half a mile. Three of our own officers and many men were left behind, and we do not even know if they are dead or prisoners."*

Wounded awaiting transfer to hospital

Brigadier General the Hon Cecil Bingham wrote: *"I only met your son, Lionel, when he became attached to the 6th Dragoon Guards, but I got to know him pretty well, and my regard for him grew as we got to know each other. During the retirement, and subsequently, he had several difficult patrols to carry out, and he always did his part with conspicuous success. He was a very brave man, and was careful of the lives of his men. On the night of his death, he, in company with many others, performed acts to their everlasting credit, but you will understand that all cannot be rewarded, the number was limited to two per unit, and a selection made from the reports."*

Captain Cyril Francis Hawley

2nd Battalion King's Royal Rifle Corps

Died on Monday 2nd November 1914, aged 36

Commemorated on Panel 51.

Cyril Hawley and his family coat of arms

Cyril was born in Lumby Dean, Lincolnshire, on Monday 24th June 1878, second son of Sir Henry Michael Hawley, 5th Baronet, and Lady Frances Charlotte Hawley (née Wingfield-Stratford) of Addington Park, Kent (late of Leybourne Grange, Maidstone, Kent) and 23 Albany Villas, Hove, Sussex. His elder brother, Henry Cusack Wingfield Hawley, inherited the title on Wednesday 5th October 1898 and Cyril became heir presumptive.
Cyril was educated at Malvern College from 1892 to 1894 on the Army Side.
On Wednesday 10th July 1912 he married Ursula Mary Hawley (née St John), of 14 Stafford Place, Buckingham Gate, London SW, and Stallington Hall, Blyth Bridge, Staffordshire. They had two sons,

David Henry born on Tuesday 13th May 1913 (who became the 7th Baronet) and Anthony Charles St John on Monday 7th September 1914.

Cyril was gazetted from the Militia on Saturday 25th February 1899, promoted Lieutenant on Friday 23rd February 1900, and Captain on Thursday 23rd November 1905. On Wednesday 5th August 1914 he was appointed a General Staff Officer, 3rd Grade.

Cyril served in the South African War where he was Mentioned in Despatches on Tuesday 10th September 1901, received the Queen's Medal with six clasps and the King's Medal with two clasps.

He arrived in Belgium on Wednesday 21st October being sent into billets at Boesinghe. On Sunday 1st November 1914 he was sent into the line at *'Sanctuary Wood'* with a draft of two hundred men and they were ordered to counter-attack Harenthage Château. It was successful, however, Cyril was killed.

The war diary for Battalion records: "*1st Nov. 1914. Early next morning the Germans with fresh troops again attacked, and at one time it seemed as if they would succeed in breaking through. The shelling was terrific and the enemy were able to bring up a field gun to within 700 yards of our front trenches, which they blew to pieces. They did not, however, succeed in breaking the line and by evening all was fairly comfortable. At about midnight Captain Hawley arrived with a draft of about 200 men, and shortly afterwards the 3rd Brigade were relieved by the 6th Brigade, the Berkshire Regiment taking over our trenches, with our 1st Battalion on their left. The Battalion withdrew to the woods S.E. of Hooge, where they bivouacked for the night.*

2nd Nov. 1914. The early hours of November 2nd were spent by the Battalion in digging themselves in, in case of shell fire, but their rest was short lived, as about 12 noon an urgent message was received from the 1st Battalion asking for assistance. The 1st Battalion was at this time just south of the Ypres to Menin road, and had been holding the trenches to which we were driven back on the 31st October.

Captain Currie and two signallers were sent forward to find out the situation, but within ten minutes one of the signallers returned and reported that Capt. Currie and the other signaller had both been hit by a shell. Lt. Dimmer was then sent forward to find out what was going on. When he returned he stated that our line had been broken north of the Ypres to Menin road. Meanwhile the Battalion had fallen in and advanced in very open order across the ground intervening between their bivouac and the Herenthage Chateau grounds. There had been no time to tell off the draft to companies so they were sent in as one company under Captain Hawley. The draft and A and B Companies crossed the main road west of the Chateau and pushed through the woods in the direction of Veldhoek. They pushed the enemy back and unfortunately Captain Hawley was killed during this operation."

Cyril was recorded in Debretts Obituary — War Roll of Honour published in the 1921 edition.

Lieutenant Colonel Archibald Walter Hay

52nd Battalion Canadian Infantry
(Manitoba Regiment)

Died on Saturday 3rd June 1916, aged 42
Commemorated on Panel 30.

Walter Hay

Archibald was the son of the late James and Magdalene Hay. He married Jessie A Knowles Hay, of 28 Artillery Street, Quebec.

During January and February 1916 Archibald was training his men at *'Whitely Camp'* and Bramshott. On Thursday 20th February they sailed from Southampton to Le Havre, arriving in a snow storm. They marched to *'No 1 Rest Camp'* before entraining for Hazebrouck the next day where he received orders to continue to Poperinghe. The Battalion marched towards Eecke where billets were provided and where they remained training. New kit was issued prior to being sent to billets in Locre on Wednesday 1st March. It was a long and hard march that took them via Caëstre, Flêtre, Méteren and Bailleul. Over the next week parties of men were sent into the line at Kemmel as part of their induction to the front attached to the Princess Patricia's Canadian Light Infantry. From arrival at Kemmel for a week each day a number of men were hospitalised with either influenza or measles. During the night of Friday 10th Archibald took his men into the line to relieve the 24th Battalion for a six day tour of duty. After being in the line the Battalion marched to billets between Flêtre and Caëstre, with all ranks being particularly tired and it was recorded that as a result their marching was somewhat poor! General Alderson inspected the Battalion on Saturday 18th. Later in the day Privates Batey and Limes were injured when Private Bannerman's rifle accidentally discharged; as result Archibald ordered that further inspections of the rifles should take place each evening.

General Sir Douglas Haig and General Mercer took the salute as Archibald took his men to *'Camp E'* at Ouderdom on Thursday 23rd where training continued until Saturday 1st April. The Battalion moved via Kruisstraat to Ypres and marched through the Lille Gate to *'Shrapnel Corner'* from where they went into the line at *'Sanctuary Wood'*. Archibald moved his Headquarters to *'Railway Dugouts'* from where he sent working parties which continued until Thursday 13th when they were sent to *'Camp A'* for rest and training. After two weeks the Battalion left camp and marched to the station at Brandhoek to entrain for Ypres Asylum at 6.30am. They marched to Hooge and completed the relief at 2.35am the next morning with Archibald's headquarters at *'Halfway House'*. The Battalion remained on tours of

duty in the sector until the end of May when they were sent to *'Camp B'* on Thursday 1st June. On Friday 2nd June the Battalion was taken to Poperinghe for baths from 8.00am until 1.00pm. At 10.00am Archibald attended a Brigade Conference and from 3.00pm he put the Battalion on half-an-hours notice. At 6.00pm the Battalion moved to take the line with the whole of the Salient under heavy fire. The Germans had blown two mines and had captured some ground at 'Armagh Wood' and a counter-attack was planned from *'Gourock Road'* to *'China Wall'*. They moved forward under a very heavy artillery barrage. Early in the morning of Saturday 3rd Archibald visited various sections of the front line and was attempting to locate Colonel Griesbach. He was in constant danger as he moved about and became separated from his runner when a shell burst. At 4.30am he met Colonel Gascoyne and appeared to be suffering from shell-shock. He was not seen again, and it is considered that he was killed by a shell.
His Adjutant wrote: *"In his loss the Battalion has suffered a severe blow. As a leader he was fearless, resolute and faithful; a most conscientious, thoughtful, hard working commander, who had the unqualified devotion and confidence of all officers, non-commissioned officers and men."*

16775 Lance Corporal William Ferguson Hay

7th Battalion Canadian Infantry (British Columbia Regiment)

Died on Saturday 24th April 1915, aged 32

Commemorated on Panel 24.

William was at home on Thursday 13th April 1882, son of the late James and Janet Hay, of Binghill, Murtle, Aberdeen, and his mother lived in London when he enlisted. He was educated at Stonyhurst College from 1895 where he was popular and good at sports. He emigrated to Canada and Worked as a broker. He served three years as a Lieutenant in the Highland Light Infantry.
William volunteered at Valcartier on Saturday 5th September 1914. His attestation papers describe him as a Roman Catholic, 5ft 7½in tall, with a 38in chest, blue eyes, brown hair and a scar on his left knee.
William arrived in England with the First Canadian Contingent and was sent to Salisbury Plain where training continued until Wednesday 10th February 1915 when he entrained at Amesbury for Avonmouth. He sailed on *HMT Cardiganshire* for St Nazaire the next day, arriving on Monday 15th. He entrained for Hazebrouck and was sent to billets in Strazeele. William went into the line attached to seasoned troops for practical instruction. His training completed he marched from Ploegsteert to billets near Fleurbaix on Monday 1st March. The Battalion relieved the Bedfordshire Regiment on Tuesday 2nd at La Boutillerie and they remained on tours of duty in the sector until Friday 26th when they marched to Estaires. Training, fatigues and periods of rest were provided. On 7.03am on Monday 5th April William marched in the rain to billets in Steenvoorde, arriving at 3.00pm. Further training continued until Wednesday 14th when embussed to Vlamertinghe from where he marched through Ypres to the front line at Gravenstafel. He was in reserve at Fortuin when the gas attack was launched at 5.00pm on Thursday 22nd. The Battalion was ordered back to Gravenstafel from where they were sent to St Julien to help defend the line. A counter-attack was prepared and during the attack in the early hours of Saturday 24th William was mortally wounded and died as a prisoner of war.

Captain Charles Wetherell Hayes Newington

2nd Battalion Cheshire Regiment

Died on Saturday 8th May 1915, aged 21

Commemorated on Panel 19.

Charles Hayes Newington

Charles was born on Saturday 17th June 1893, eldest son of Major P and Mrs Hayes Newington, of Ticehurst, Sussex and 16 Merton Road, Southsea, Portsmouth. He was educated at Dover College from 1908 as a member of St Martin's then Crescent House and passed into RMC Sandhurst as a King's Cadet. Charles enjoyed sports and was a good cricketer playing for his regiment.
Charles was gazetted to his father's old regiment in September 1912, promoted Lieutenant in July 1914, and Captain in January 1915.
Charles was stationed in Jubbulpore, India, at the outbreak of war. They embarked on *SS Braemar Castle* and sailed for England, arriving on Christmas Eve in Devonport. They marched to Winchester and camp — they remained for eleven days in the cold and wet without the opportunity of getting dry. They were moved to billets in the Peter Symonds School and the County Girls' School where they could at least dry out. On Saturday 16th January 1915 they embarked from Southampton on board *SS City of Chester* for Le Havre and entrained for the front. As soon as they arrived on the Salient they went into the line, immediately taking heavy casualties. On Saturday 22nd April the Germans launched the first gas attack and Charles was in the reserve line supporting the Suffolks. They were under heavy fire but were pinned down and unable to reply. The next day they were ordered forward in support of the Canadians who were suffering badly from the

effects of gas. Charles was killed in action at Hooge on the first day of the Battle of Frezenberg where they were heavily shelled and gassed.
Charles was Mentioned in Despatches.
His brother, 2nd Lieutenant Harold Hayes Newington, died on Wednesday 10th March 1915 and is buried in Vieille-Chapelle New Military Cemetery, Lacouture.

Second Lieutenant
Rycharde Mead Haythornthwaite

'B' Company, 2nd Battalion
The Buffs (East Kent Regiment)
Died on Monday 24th May 1915, aged 21
Commemorated on Addenda Panel 57.

Rycharde Haythornthwaite

Rycharde was born in Agra, India, on Thursday 4th January 1894, elder son of the Reverend John Parker Haythornthwaite, MA (Principal of St John's College, Agra and Fellow of Allahabad University) and his wife Izset Haythornthwaite, LRCP, LRCS, of Agra Lodge, Northwood, Middlesex. He was educated at Haileybury College with a scholarship from 1906 to 1913 as a member of Melvill. He was Head of School from 1912 to 1913 and Colour Serjeant of the OTC; he excelled at athletics winning various competitions. Rycharde went up to Sidney Sussex College, Cambridge, in 1913 with a History Exhibition where he won his College Colours for athletics and football.
At the outbreak of war Rycharde volunteered and was gazetted on Saturday 15th August 1914, training at Dover from September until May 1915 where he also organized the regimental sports events and competitions. He sailed for France and entrained for northern France, joining the Battalion on the Salient. Rycharde was killed in action and he was initially buried in the garden of a ruined cottage on the right hand side of the Menin Road, one thousand yards from the Ypres to Roeselare Railway level crossing.
On the day Rycharde died he had written to his parents: *"At 12.30 a.m. this morning the Germans started a terrific bombardment using their vile gas. Our lads were splendid and stuck it. About 5.30 a.m. we got a message to reinforce the firing line, with my Company, 'B'. Unfortunately there was very bad communication, and our 1st Platoon did not reinforce. I went out to try and find out what was happening, and worked my way up to the front line, about 1,000 yards ahead, and found out what was happening, and then returned to our trenches. 'B' Company immediately pushed forward, as the line wanted reinforcing, but I stayed back to report to Headquarters. After doing that I started with one other fellow to work my way up. The shrapnel was terrific, but our luck was in, and we reached a ruined house just behind the firing line, and found there was a good many wounded, poor beggars. I got a stretcher party together and we pulled several in several badly wounded fellows in a field, but unfortunately they sniped at us, the brutes! Two of our poor chaps were hit. Since then we have done what we can do to make them comfortable, but it is awfully hard for them. We can do so little for them till dark, and even then it isn't safe. The shelling is something terrific, one burst on this house knocking bits over our wounded, and gave a few more nasty cuts. All we can do is to keep boiling water – it is not safe to drink otherwise – and give them sips of tea and Bovril, of which we have luckily got a certain amount. Unfortunately it is very hot, and their thirst must be terrific. I know mine is. It is just that fiendish gas. I have had nothing to eat since 7 p.m. last night, it is now 4 p.m. Only a few sips of different things, and this gas keeps up a horrible choking feeling, which prevents one working as hard as one wants to. What will happen to us I do not know. I think we are advancing now, and in that case all ought to be all right."*
Sergeant Major W Dunlop, of the Durham Light Infantry, wrote: *"I was with him on that memorable day. 'Whit Monday', for about 10½ hours, at about 500 yds. from the Germans, without a British soldier in front and about 1,000 yds. from the nearest troops behind, attending to the wounded. First, I set away with a stretcher, my companion was either shot or fainted, so I went across to the ruins of an old cottage. There were a dozen or so wounded, with a wounded Corporal trying to dress the other poor souls. I could get no assistance there, so had to go to our reserves behind for someone to help me to get the stretcher in. I returned with two brave chaps, and on my return met Lieut. Haythornthwaite. He asked particulars and said it was certain death to venture out. I said, 'I'm risking it'. His answer was, 'If you go, I'm coming also'. The four of us set out, but could not find man or stretcher, and it was only by the protection of God Himself that we returned, for nothing human could have protected us from the murderous fire the brutes sent towards us, but not one of us was hit, thanks to God. It was after that I found the qualities of your son. The dressings of the wounded were not as they should have been, bandaged by little experienced hands, so your son and myself set about to try to sop the bleeding of the wounded. … After a while we got all made as comfortable as we could under the circumstances … It was during the time the water was boiling I saw your son sitting and writing the letter you eventually got, but the contents he did not mention at the time. After a while, the counter-attack started. Our troops started to advance. What a sight! Men falling right and left, but still the advanced continued until they reached our cottage. Your son collected men on one side of the cottage, myself the other, and got them to dig themselves in so as to stop the brutes from advancing, and after a while we got a position formed which seemed strong enough to hold them in check. And then came more work, the poor souls who had been shot were either helped,*

or carried to us for 'First Aid', and on several occasions your son and myself went out and brought men in, and it was on one of these that he got hit, the bullet passing through his left shoulder. I was dressing a chap with a finger blown off when it happened, but two men – I don't know their names – carried him in, and set about dressing him. He called for me, and asked me to adjust his bandages, and said, 'If there are any men about doing nothing tell them to try and get a rifle as every man in needed.' ... He was hit somewhere about 5 p.m. and after he was wounded he was calm and cool as ever. He ordered a man – I don't know his name – to take everything from his pockets, spectacles included, with the instructions, 'See these things handed over to my people'. The man repeated the words as he gave me the things I forwarded on to you."

Captain George Reginald Charles Heale, MC

10th Battalion Duke of Wellington's (West Riding Regiment)

Died on Thursday 3rd May 1917, aged 35
Commemorated on Panel 20.

Citation for the Military Cross, London Gazette, Friday 14th April 1916:
"For conspicuous gallantry. During a continuous and very heavy bombardment by the enemy he personally attended to the wounds of 15 men, and inspired his men generally by his cool bravery."

George Heale

George was born at Addington, Kent, on Thursday 26th January 1882, son of the son of the Reverend James Newton Heale and Isabella Margaret Heale of St Margaret's on Thames, and was related to the Viscount Powerscourt. George was educated at The King's School, Canterbury, from 1891 to 1898 then studied at Wye College with an exhibition.

George served in the South African War as a drummer boy and rose to private in Paget's Horse, then commissioned on Saturday 8th February 1902. He resigned from the army in December 1902 and became a school teacher in South Africa and in Jamaica.

At the outbreak of war George returned to England and volunteered. After training he left Bramshott for Le Havre, arriving in late August 1915. The Battalion was sent to northern France where training continued until taking the line the Armentières sector. In February 1916 the Battalion transferred south and was sent to serve around Souchez. George was awarded his Military Cross for action near Ablain in March 1916. With the Battalion, he was sent for training for the Battle of the Somme. He survived the battle including serving at Bazentin, Pozières, Flers, Transloy and Le Sars. In December 1916 he resigned his commission on health grounds but rejoined in February 1917. George was mortally wounded in action during an attack.

George was Mentioned in Despatches twice.

George is commemorated on the Nettlestead War Memorial, Kent, the Wye College Memorial and a plaque was placed in his memory in All Soul's, Twickenham.

George was recorded in Debretts Obituary — War Roll of Honour published in the 1921 edition.

His brother, Lieutenant Colonel Ernest Heale, died on Monday 12th June 1916 and is buried in Le Tréport Military Cemetery.

29524 Corporal Gerald Coussmaker Heath

16th Battalion Canadian Infantry (Manitoba Regiment)

Died on Friday 23rd April 1915, aged 26
recorded by CWGC as Thursday 22nd April
Commemorated on Panel 26.

Gerald Heath

Gerald was born at Mount Abu, India, on Thursday 3rd May 1888, son of Susan Wilhelmina Heath, of Failand, Paignton, Devon, and the late Colonel Lewis Forbes Heath (Indian Army). He was educated at Wellington College from 1900 to 1904, leaving for Canada at the age of 17. He was employed by the Canadian Bank of Commerce followed by the North Crown Bank in 1912, and served in the 72nd Seaforths (Militia) for three years prior to the outbreak of war. He was a keen athlete and won the British Columbia Hurdling Championship in 1912 and in 1913 won the National Championship, in addition to a considerable haul of other medals.

At the outbreak of war he volunteered and enlisted at Valcartier on Wednesday 23rd September 1914. His attestation papers describe him as 5ft 11in tall, with a 39in chest, a medium complexion, hazel coloured eyes, brown hair, and a V-shaped scar below his left knee-cap. Gerald came over with the First Canadian Contingent, the convoy forming up on Saturday 3rd October arriving in Plymouth on Saturday 17th. He was sent for training on Salisbury Plain before leaving for St Nazaire on Friday 12th February 1915 from Avonmouth. He arrived on Monday 15th from where he entrained for Hazebrouck, via Rouen. After marching to Caëstre in the rain, billets were eventually found in a hayloft. Until the end of the month his training continued preparing him for the front line at Bois Grenier. He served in the Fleurbaix sector until Friday 26th March when he was sent into reserve at Estaires. On Wednesday 7th April he was marched to Cassel, remaining there until Thursday 15th when he marched to Steenvoorde. After a night in billets a fleet of motor buses took the Battalion to Vlamertinghe. After a brief stop and rest, at 2.30pm he marched the five miles along the pavé to Wieltje.

Gerald was sent into the line, relieving the French 79th Division for a three day tour of duty from where he was sent into reserve; the Battalion was billeted in northern Ypres and along the Canal. For thirty-six hours he was able to relax in the relative quiet, bathe in the canal and visit the cafés and shops in Ypres. At 5.00pm on Thursday 22nd the Germans launched a major offensive against the French colonial troops using poison gas for the first time. The French line broke. At 5.30pm the Battalion was 'stood to' and by 6.00pm they were along the line of the Canal ready to repulse any German attack. Whilst lining the Canal bank the first terrorised refugees and gassed Zouave started to rush passed them — all they could do was watch and wonder what had happened. At 7.40pm he was ordered to march to St Julien, via La Brique. It was impossible to pass through Wieltje due to congestion and whilst they halted the gas wafting in the air caused many of the men's eyes to stream and they suffered with sore dry throats. Finally they were able to march through the village and advanced towards St Julien where they prepared for a counter-attack. At 11.45pm Gerald advanced against *'Kitchener's Wood'* (Bois des Cuisiniers) that was heavily defended. Flares were put up that illuminated the night and he came under very heavy fire. As they advanced Gerald was mortally wounded and despite being taken to a Dressing Station, died shortly afterwards.

Major Rae wrote: *"His work in the hard fighting in which we were engaged on 22 April, and afterwards, was most excellent, and he had been noted for distinction for his gallant conduct."*

One of his immediate officers wrote: *"Major Rae and all of his comrades have nothing but praise for his work. Several times he volunteered and took out stretcher parties with wounded officers and men, always under fire. His efforts were evidently of the finest. He has been recommended for distinguished service recognition."*

Gerald was Mentioned in Despatches gazetted on Tuesday 22nd June 1915.

8514 Private Harry Hedges

2nd Battalion Wiltshire Regiment

Died on Saturday 24th October 1914, aged 23

Commemorated on Panel 53

Harry was born in Hannington Wick, Wiltshire, son of the late Isaac and Hester Hedges. He lived in Farringdon, Berkshire. He enlisted in Swindon. His brother, Private Thomas Hedges, died on the same day and is commemorated on the Menin Gate, see below.

Harry and Thomas were sent to *'Lyndhurst Camp'* before being sent to Southampton from where they sailed to Zeebrugge, arriving on Wednesday 7th October 1914. The intention was for the Battalion to be sent to assist with the defence of Antwerp. As they arrived in Belgium the city was being abandoned with the Belgian and French armies retreating towards the coast. They marched along the straight road to Brugge where they were billeted. Orders were received to march south to Ypres which took them through Beernem, Wingene, to Roeselare. They arrived in Ypres, described by Reverend E J Kennedy who wrote: *"The first view of Ypres was glorious. As we marched through the great square in front of the Cloth Hall, I was struck with the mediaeval aspect of the place. The gabled houses carried one's imagination into the long ago; whilst the glorious Cloth Hall of the eleventh century, back up by the equally fine cathedral of similar age, presented a picture not easily to be forgotten."*

Harry and Thomas moved along the Menin Road towards Gheluvelt and took the line between the village and Kruiseik. The Battle of Ypres began and during a German attack the brothers were killed in action and neither body was recovered.

8450 Private Thomas Hedges

2nd Battalion Wiltshire Regiment

Died on Saturday 24th October 1914, aged 28

Commemorated on Panel 53

Thomas was born in Edington, Wiltshire, son of the late Isaac and Hester Hedges. He lived in Farringdon, Berkshire.

He enlisted in Devizes, Wiltshire, and was killed in action with his brother, Private Harry Hedges, and is commemorated on the Menin Gate, for their story see above.

"The King was pleased but I wasn't'"

Y996 Rifleman Arthur Heesom

9th Battalion King's Royal Rifle Corps
Died on Saturday 25th September 1915
Commemorated on Panel 53.

Arthur was the son of Arthur and Ann Heesom, 128 Knutsford Road, Latchford, Warrington.
Arthur was sent for training at Grayshott, Bordon and Aldershot from where he left for France, arriving in Boulogne on Sunday 20th May 1915. He entrained to northern France and marched across the border into Belgium where he was provided with training for the front line and re-kitted. Arthur undertook a series of tours of duty in the front line, but until the end of July did not participate in any major action. At 3.15am on Friday 30th July the Germans attacked in force at Hooge where *'Flammenwerfer'* (flame throwers or 'liquid fire') was used for the first time. The 9th and 7th Battalion were fighting side by side and the strength of the attack forced the line to retire. A series of counter-attacks took place in which Arthur participated and the 9th were able to recapture part of their lost line. During the night of Saturday 31st he was relieved from the line. He continued to on tours of duty; on Friday 24th September Arthur was again in the line at Hooge in preparation for the attack on Bellewaarde. At 4.19am a mine was blown under the German line, only a short distance in front of Arthur, whistles were blown and he went over the top attacking the German line when he was shot and killed.
His brother, Rifleman William Heesom, died on Sunday 10th October 1915 and is buried in Warrington Cemetery, Lancashire. (The brothers are related to the author.)

King's Royal Rifle Corps monument outside Winchester Cathedral

... flooded shell holes

Lieutenant Alexis 'Lex' Hannum Helmer

1st Brigade Canadian Field Artillery
Died on Sunday 2nd May 1915, aged 22
Commemorated on Panel 10.

Lex Helmer

Lex was born at Hull, Province of Quebec, on Wednesday 29th June 1892, only child of Elizabeth I Helmer, of 122 Gilmour Street, Ottawa, and the late Brigadier General R A Helmer. He graduated at the Royal Military College, Canada, and went up to McGill University where he graduated with a BSc in 1914 and from 1912 the Captain of their OTC.
In 1910 Lex was gazetted to the Canadian Militia. At the outbreak of war he applied to join the Expeditionary Force at Valcartier, and was gazetted in September as a Lieutenant in the Canadian Field Artillery. His attestation papers describe him as a Methodist, 5ft 7½in tall, a 37½in waist, blue eyes, light coloured hair, and a scar on his left leg. Lex saw action at the Second Battle of Ypres and was present when the Germans first used gas, where he was successful in bringing both his guns and men out. He was reporting to his Commanding Officer when a large shell exploded close to him, killing him instantaneously together with another officer. Lex was buried in the field near the Yser. He was a close friend of Lieutenant Colonel John McCrae who wrote: *"In Flanders Field"* in his memory. (John McCrae died on Monday 28th January 1918 and is buried in Wimereux Communal Cemetery, Boulogne.)

John McCrae

Essex Farm Cemetery close to where Lex died

In Flanders fields the poppies blow

Between the crosses, row on row

That mark our place; and in the sky

The larks, still bravely singing, fly

Scarce heard amid the guns below.

We are the Dead. Short days ago

We lived, felt dawn, saw sunset glow,

Loved and were loved, and now we lie

In Flanders fields.

Take up our quarrel with the foe:

To you from failing hands we throw

The torch; be yours to hold it high.

If ye break faith with us who die

We shall not sleep, though poppies grow

In Flanders fields.

His Commanding Officer wrote: *"We have been through a very severe battle which started about 5 p.m. on April 22nd. Doubtless you have already heard through the Department of your loss, which is ours as well. During all the strenuous fighting from April 22nd to May 2nd, Lex was in the middle of it, doing his duty in a most gallant and conspicuous manner. It seems hard that on May 1st I had sent his name in for gallantry under fire on April 27th, and also for his conduct on April 24th, when he was acting as Forward Observing Officer for the battery, and he was driven back by the poisonous fumes of the Germans, but still stuck to his post until I ordered him in. He was badly poisoned by the fumes, but begged and begged not to be sent to hospital, and after a period of twenty-four hours was once more in full charge of his section. He was full of pluck and fought his guns time and again to a finish, at times when we all though we were cut off and would never get through. His men adored him, and his section simply went to pieces when they saw what had happened. On the night of May 1st-2nd we changed the position of Lex's section. One of my last recollections of him was on the afternoon of May 1st, when I saw him standing in the dug-out in the middle of his section doing his job with shells falling all around. I was passing about fifty yards away, and he waved his hand and smiled. He was always in the best of spirits and kept his men in a fine shape. If I may say so, the battery has suffered a loss which cannot be remedied. Captain Cosgrave, who was at the Royal Military College and McGill with Lex, was near at hand when the shell came in, and immediately took charge of everything. You may know that Lex and the right section had been with me up in the salient, and when the Germans broke through our guns were the extreme left guns of the British Army. On the afternoon of the 24th April, Lex's section was run into the open at right angles to our usual line of fire, and opened fire on the Germans at 1,800 yards. The Germans were advancing out of a wood at the time, and we drove them back, and later in the day our Infantry occupied the woods. I could tell you many instances of Les's devotion to duty and care of his men."*

Lieutenant Maurice Hemmant

5th Battalion attached 11th Battalion Rifle Brigade

Died on Tuesday 14th August 1917, aged 29

Commemorated on Panel 46.

Maurice was the eighth and youngest son of William Hemmant, JP, and Lucy Elizabeth Hemmant, of Bulimba, Sevenoaks Kent. He was educated at Tonbridge School from May 1898 to Easter 1906 where he was a House Præposter, and played for the First XV and XI. He and went up to Pembroke College, Cambridge, playing golf for Cambridge University and represented the College in the XV. Maurice graduated in Mathematics and in 1909 was a Junior Optime. Maurice went out to the Straits Settlements and became a Manager on a rubber plantation. He was a member of Sevenoaks Golf Club. At the outbreak of war he returned to England and volunteered. He was commissioned on Saturday 15th May 1915, leaving for France in November. He was invalided home and when he recovered he returned to the front as Bombing Officer. Maurice was promoted Temporary Captain on Tuesday 7th November 1916 whilst on the Somme. The conditions in the trenches in November 1916 were dreadful, one of the men died from exhaustion extracting himself from the mud, related by Captain Hollond: *"... stayed throughout the whole night of the relief endeavouring to extricate one of his men who had stuck in the mud of the a front-line trench. No words could be too strong to describe the difficulties of that sector. The only communication trench was so deep in sticky mud that to venture into it was to invite the loss of one's boots. The track that ran beside it up to the front line was so slippery that men constantly slid off it into the shell holes on either side. Even gum-boots were insufficient to protect the feet. The cold was intense: the wind and sleet blew bitterly; and the enemy had the range of the track accurately registered by his field guns."*

Maurice spent Christmas out of the line — the Battalion was in Corbie and some of the officers were allowed to go to Paris, it is not known if he was one of them. He continued on tours of duty on the Somme, participating in the attack on *'Dessart Wood'* on Friday 30th March 1917 and Metz-en-Couture. Maurice moved from the Somme to the Ypres Salient and trained for the Third Battle of Ypres near Canaples from Sunday 1st July. They all took part in a musketry course, a riding school for the officers, and specialist training from the use of a Lewis gun to stretcher-bearing; sports and recreation were also organised. Maurice was sent back to the Ypres Salient where on Tuesday 7th August they were holding the line between the Steenbeek and *'Iron Cross'* and came under attack, including mustard gas shells. After three days they were relieved to the canal bank where Maurice organised parties carrying supplies to the front line. On Monday 13th Maurice took his men up into the line ready for the attack that was to take place the next morning at 4.00am. The British barrage opened on *'Zero Hour'* as they moved forward. The German machine-gun fire was intense, the crossing of the Steenbeek was slow and difficult, and the German block house at *'Au Bon Gite'* caused further problems. He was killed whilst in temporary command of his Company. Maurice had crossed the Steenbeek at Langemarck, accompanied by a few of his men, when he was shot dead by a sniper.

His Commanding Officer wrote: *"He had been with us some time, as he was bombing officer, and was kept here rather longer than he liked, I am afraid. He was an excellent officer in every way, and absolutely first-rate at his particular business of bombing, and took endless pains, and spent all his time in seeing that men were thoroughly trained in this before going to the Front. He certainly obtained excellent results and no men were better trained that those he sent out. It was reported to me on one occasion that a bomb having been badly thrown rolled back into the trench, whereupon he ran to it and threw it out again an instant before it exploded."*

His Major wrote: *"I am so sad that dear old Maisie has been killed. A clever man, a good soldier, a thorough sportsman, the most genial and delightful of companions, he was a very good friend to me and I regret his death more almost than any one I know who has been killed in this war."*

Lieutenant Alexander Rennie Henderson

4th Battalion Gordon Highlanders

Died on Saturday 25th September 1915, aged 26

Commemorated on Panel 38.

Alexander Henderson

Alexander was born at home on Wednesday 8th November 1888, son of Alexander R Henderson, of 46 Beaconsfield Place, Aberdeen, and the late Elizabeth J Thomson Henderson. He was educated at Robert Gordon's College and went up to Aberdeen University graduating with an MA. He was employed as a teacher at Aboyne Higher Grade School, Aberdeenshire. He was a member of the OTC from 1907 until 1912, being appointed Colour Sergeant in 1910. Alexander was a keen sportsman particularly fond of football and cricket.

At the outbreak of war he volunteered and was commissioned in September 1914, leaving for Le Havre on board *SS Archimedes* on Friday 19th February 1915. After a long and winding train journey Alexander arrived in northern France from where he marched to La Clytte to a camp, arriving on Wednesday 27th. Over the ensuing two weeks he undertook short trips to the line and continued training. He undertook his first tours of duty in the line at Kemmel. In April he was in camp at Brandhoek from where he was sent along the Menin Road to Hooge. On Monday 24th May Alexander came up in support from Zillebeke as the Germans launched a gas attack.

Shortly before Alexander took his men to their assembly positions for the attack on Saturday 25th September, Field Marshal Lord Kitchener inspected the Battalion and told them: *"Scotland expects that their work would be thoroughly well done."* Their trenches were along the Menin Road at Hooge and the advance commenced at 4.10am. However they were badly held up at the German wire that remained uncut. The wire was so thick that wire cutters made no impression and Alexander was mortally wounded whilst leading his men forward.

Lord Kitchener

His Commanding Officer wrote: *"The courage and pluck shown by him and his men that day are beyond words of mine."*

2486 Lance Corporal Charles Livingstone Henderson

'A' Company, 1st Battalion Black Watch (Royal Highlanders)

Died on Tuesday 27th October 1914, aged 18

Commemorated on Panel 37.

Charles was the son of William L and Margaret Livingstone Henderson, of 125 Taylor Street, Aberhill, Methil, Fife. He was educated locally.

His brother, Corporal George Henderson, died on Monday 2nd November 1914 and is commemorated on the Menin Gate, see below for their story.

2158 Corporal George Henderson

'A' Company, 1st Battalion Black Watch (Royal Highlanders)

Died on Monday 2nd November 1914, aged 21

Commemorated on Panel 37.

George was the son of William L and Margaret Livingstone Henderson, of 125 Taylor Street, Aberhill, Methil, Fife. He was educated locally.

Charles and George were at Aldershot when the order came through for them to parade on Tuesday 11th August 1914 for HM King George V prior to their departure for France. On Thursday 13th they entrained at Farnborough and sailed to Le Havre on *SS Italian Prince*. They were sent to Harfleur into camp for three days until entraining for Le Nouvion. They were sent to Mons where they were in support and could see and hear the action but did not participate. In the early hours of Monday 24th orders were received for them to commence the retirement, one that would last for more than two weeks. It was a difficult march, they carried full packs and tramped over poor roads. At La Ferté Milon additional mules and wagons were provided that helped considerably in lightening their load. On Thursday 3rd September they crossed the Marne and were billeted at La Férte-sous-Jouarre and on Friday 11th they crossed the Aisne. Three days later, on the Chemin des Dames, they engaged the Germans during

which their Colonel, Adrian Grant-Duff was killed (he is buried in Moulins New Communal Cemetery). For the next four days Charles and George dug themselves in and held the line. They remained on the Aisne until Friday 16th October when they were sent north by train to Hazebrouck. On Tuesday 20th they marched to Poperinghe from where they were sent into the line the next day to help support the Coldstream Guards. During the night of Thursday 22nd the Germans marched in close formation towards their lines, singing as they advanced. Charles, George and their colleagues opened up with rapid fire and the German losses were considerable, many bullets finding more than one mark. On Sunday 25th they were relieved by the French and on Tuesday 27th were on the Zandvoorde to Gheluvelt road when they came under sustained artillery fire and Charles was killed. Only 25% of 'A' Company survived. George remained in the line and the German pressure increased and during Monday 2nd he, too, died.
His brother, Lance Corporal Charles Henderson, died on Tuesday 27th October and is commemorated on the Menin Gate, see above.

Lieutenant Norman William Arthur Henderson

1st Battalion Royal Scots Fusiliers

Died on Tuesday 10th November 1914, aged 23

Commemorated on Panel 33.

Norman Henderson

Norman was born at Rosary Gardens, South Kensington, on Friday 23rd October 1891, eldest son of Arthur and Gareth Henderson of Farmile Court, Chobham, Surrey. He was educated Bath College followed by Rugby School from 1906 to 1911 as a member of School House, then passed into RMC Sandhurst.
Norman was gazetted on Wednesday 14th February 1912, and promoted Lieutenant on Thursday 12th June 1913. In February 1914 he was posted to South Africa, returning to England only a month later.
Norman left Southampton for Le Havre on Thursday 13th August 1914. He entrained for Landrecies where after five days he marched across the Belgian border to take up position at Ghlin. He engaged the Germans on Sunday 23rd before orders were received to retire to Frameries where a fierce fire-fight ensued for four hours. At Le Cateau the Battalion formed the Brigade's rearguard as the long retreat began. On Saturday 5th September orders were received to turn and move towards the Germans, first engaging them at Orly the next day. On Monday 14th they crossed the Aisne at Vailly and took the line a few hundred yards in front of the German line.
He remained on Aisne until Friday 2nd October when he was moved north. Two weeks later he saw action at Aubers where he remained until Saturday 7th November, moving further north to the Ypres Salient. During the First Battle of Ypres he was killed leading his platoon against the Prussian Guard at Harenthage Château. Norman had seen heavy action and acted bravely during the battle — at the end of the First Battle of Ypres the 1st Battalion was virtually wiped out. He was buried in the château grounds together with nine other officers.

1000291 Private William Henderson

43rd Battalion Canadian Infantry (Manitoba Regiment)

Died on Monday 12th November 1917, aged 26

Commemorated on Panel 28.

William Henderson

William was born in Eccles, Lancashire, on Thursday 4th December 1890, son of Joshua Henderson, of 297 Oxford Road, Manchester. He was educated at Manchester Grammar School from 1904 to 1906. He was employed by The Commerce Bank of Canada from Thursday 16th May 1912 at the Portage la Prairie Branch. He had served for a year in the Militia.
On Saturday 18th December 1915 William volunteered and enlisted in the 226th Canadian Battalion and after transferring to the 42nd Battalion, was promoted Sergeant in February 1916. He attestation papers describe him as 5ft 7½in tall, with a 36in chest, a fair complexion, blue eyes and brown hair.
William reverted to the ranks to get to France where he arrived with a draft to join the Battalion at the *'Reserve Camp'* Bray where he was inspected together the other eighty-four men in the draft on Saturday 25th November 1916. His training continued, with the rest of the Battalion, before taking the line for the first time on Friday 1st December. He tours of duty continued, including spending Christmas in the line. On Wednesday 31st January 1917 the Battalion was informed of a outbreak of mumps in the area so all estaminets, cafés, churches and meeting places were put out of bounds! During March he was

sent for training and in April took part in the operations at Vimy as part of the Battle of Arras. William served and trained in the Vimy and northern sector of France until mid-October.
At 3.00am on Sunday 21st October William marched to Caëstre Station and entrained for Ypres Asylum where he marched to *'X Camp'* near St Jan. His first task was to erect tents and by 5.00pm the kitchens arrived and hot food was provided. At 7.00pm German aircraft bombed the camp and caused a number of minor injuries; in addition the German artillery targeted the camp. At 8.30am the next morning he moved forward towards the *'Pommern Redoubt'* where he immediately dug in. The attack they had planned for commenced at 5.40am on Friday 26th. William advanced from the Ravebeek and consolidated his position. On Sunday 28th he moved to the support area on *'Abraham Heights'* with the Battalion Headquarters at *'Otto Farm'*. The next day they moved

... Canadians on the Passchendaele Ridge

to the transport lines at St Jan where he was issued with trousers to replace his kilt and given a hot bath.
At 11.00am the Battalion moved off to Ypres Asylum and entrained to Abeele from where he marched to *'Clyde Camp'*. The Battalion reorganised itself, rested and undertook training. A concert party was organised at the Pavilion Theatre, Poperinghe, by the 16th Battalion Canadian Scottish Concert Party and the Royal Canadian Regiment Band during the afternoon of Tuesday 6th November. Training continued during the morning of Wednesday 7th with a visit by the Queen's Own Cameron Pipe and Brass Band in the afternoon prior to a visit by General Currie who congratulated them on their work on the Passchendaele Ridge. At 5.45am on Saturday 10th William paraded with the Battalion and was marched to a fleet of buses that took them to the Kruisstraat road, Ypres, from where they marched to *'Camp D'* at St Jan. The rest of the day was spent resting in their tents in the pouring rain. Final preparations for moving to the front were made during Sunday 11th and he arrived in the line late in the evening under heavy shellfire. William was in a captured German pillbox under heavy shell-fire when it was struck and he died from concussion.

S/4955 Rifleman George Edward Hendry

1st Battalion Rifle Brigade

Died on Monday 26th April 1915

Commemorated on Panel 48.

George was born in Farlington, Hampshire, and lived in Twickenham. He was a British landscape and portrait painter — an Exhibitor at the Bruton Gallery in 1905. He enlisted in London and after a period of training George was sent out to France with a draft. On Wednesday 14th October 1914 the Battalion moved to Flêtre and the next day they joined the East Lancashire Regiment and entered Bailleul where they were billeted for the night. On Friday 16th George was marched across the border into Belgium and took the line between Steenwerck and Neuve Eglise with the objective of taking the Erquinghem crossing. However, they received orders to return to billets at La Crèche. For the third time in a week confused orders were issued to the Battalion that were then contradicted as the Battalion Diary records: *"... at 5 p.m. we received orders to attack l'Epinette—La Prevôte in conjunction with the East Lancashires in order to fill a gap; but at 5.45 p.m. the gap having already been filled, orders were cancelled and we went into billets on the outskirts of Armentières."* They were moved into the line near Le Bizet and Le Touquet where they remained until Friday 20th November moving the short distance north to Ploegsteert Wood where he served until March 1915. On Saturday 19th December George was involved in an attack on Ploegsteert Wood, Colonel Seymour wrote: *"The two assaulting platoons would take up a 'jumping off' position by the edge of the wood, under covering fire on German House from a pack gun detailed for the purpose. At 2.30 p.m. they would advance astride the road leading east-north-east to German House, being replaced on the edge of the wood by the remaining two platoons of 'I' Company, from the front line trenches, in readiness to reinforce. The attacking platoons, accompanied by Sappers detailed from No. 7 Field Company R.E., would then capture successively German House, Second House and Third House, detaching parties of one N.C.O. and eight Riflemen, together with a few Sappers, to consolidate the ground gained and put the captured houses in a state of defence. Meanwhile two platoons of 'A' Company would move up from Hunter Avenue to reinforce the front line, being replaced in Hunter Avenue by two platoons from 'C' Company in reserve."* The advance was held up by heavy machine-gun fire and the Colonel wrote: *"Present information, our line hung up just E. of Second House. Unless strong offensive possible on our right would suggest demolishing houses and returning to original line."* The request was agreed to and the next morning they destroyed the houses although they kept hold of *'German House'* and fortified it. George witnessed the Christmas Truce and participated in it. From the sector George was sent into the Salient itself in late March 1915. After serving at St Yves he was relieved on Thursday 15th April to Steenwerck for training until the morning of Saturday 24th when they entrained for the Salient. As they marched around the south of Ypres passing *'Hell Fire Corner'* and *'Deadman's Corner'* the Battle was raging ahead of them and the roads were congested with the wounded being taken back. They arrived in St Jan where they remained for some time as a lead company had been hit by shell fire and the badly wounded needed to be treated and removed. He passed through Wieltje and onward to Hill 37 where they took over some old trenches constructed by the French troops some time before. The Battalion came under heavy shell fire from the moment they arrived. On Monday 26th he was working hard on repairing and strengthening the trenches under a continuous artillery barrage when he was mortally wounded. He was buried in the field.

3305 Private
Graham Thornton Henery

1st/10th Battalion The King's (Liverpool Regiment)

Died on Wednesday 16th June 1915, aged 27

Commemorated on Panel 6.

Graham Henery

Graham was the second surviving son of Percival Jeffery Thornton Henery and Maria Henery (née Bullock), of Spring Bank, Olive Grove, Wavertree, Liverpool. He was educated at Cothill House, Abingdon, followed by (like his father) Harrow School as a member of Church Hill from 1902 to 1905. Graham was in business with a timber brokers, Messrs Duncan, Ewing & Co, of Liverpool.

In August 1914 Graham volunteered and enlisted in Liverpool. On Sunday 1st November 1914 he sailed for France. He served in the front line continuously from Sunday 29th November until he was killed in action on the first day of the Battle of Hooge.

At 4.00pm on Tuesday 15th June 1915 Graham was ordered to parade then marched from Busseboom to assemble at *'Cambridge Road'* that was under heavy artillery fire. Heavy casualties started to be taken shortly after midnight. Graham advanced through *'Railway Wood'* from where they advanced on Bellewaarde Farm when Graham was killed.

His brother, Lieutenant Hewett Henery, died on Tuesday 19th April 1917 and is buried in Gaza War Cemetery, Palestine.

Second Lieutenant
Edward Henry Lovett Henn

9th Battalion Rifle Brigade

Died on Saturday 25th September 1915, aged 23

Commemorated on Panel 46.

Edward was the son of Edward Lovett-Henn and Margaret Agnes Vaughan Henn, of Campagne Sidi-Merzoug, El-Biar, Algiers. He was educated at Frieburg University, Baden, and Trinity College, Cambridge, graduating with a BA in 1913. He passed his Civil Service Examinations and qualified for entry into the Foreign Office (Second in Competition) in August 1914.

Edward volunteered in September 1914 and went to France in August 1915. On Friday 24th September 1915 Edward was in the line at *'Railway Wood'*; it was difficult for them to take position as the majority of trenches had been badly cut up or destroyed by German shelling, and the trees reduced to mere matchsticks. At 3.50am the next morning the British artillery commenced their preliminary barrage and at 4.21am Edward blew his whistle and led his men forward. The Germans put up a fierce resistance and counter-attacked with bombs. Due to the shortage of ammunition Edward and his men soon ran out of bombs with which to retaliate, the German machine-gun fire was intense. Edward and the men were holding the lip of a crater when they were attacked at 8.00am which they repulsed. Support for their position was given by the King's Royal Rifle Corps and together they were able to pour machine-gun fire down on the German position. During the fierce fight Edward was killed.

412475 Private
Harold Albert Henry

26th Battalion Canadian Infantry
(New Brunswick Regiment)

Died on Sunday 18th June 1916, aged 16

Commemorated on Panel 26.

Harold was born at home, son of William and Margaret Elizabeth Henry, of 143 London Street, Peterborough, Ontario. He was educated locally.

Harold volunteered at Peterborough on Tuesday 23rd February 1915. His attestation papers describe him as a Presbyterian, being 5ft 3in tall, a 35in chest, fair complexion, brown eyes and dark brown hair and he claimed to have been born on Saturday 7th November 1896.

Harold was sent for training prior to sailing to England on *HMT Caldedonia*, arriving in Devonport on Thursday 24th June 1915. He entrained for a camp in East Sandling. He continued to train until Wednesday 15th September when he marched to Folkestone docks and sailed to Boulogne. After a night in camp at Ostrohove he entrained to Wizernes where they bivouacked overnight before being sent to billets near Hazebrouck. Generals Alderson, Currie and Turner accompanied by HRH Prince Arthur of Connaught inspected the Battalion on

Generals Alderson, Currie and Turner
HRH Prince Arthur of Connaught

Sunday 19th. The move into Belgium began on Tuesday 21st when they initially moved to Bailleul before moving to *'Hyde Park Corner'* and finally to billets on the Scherpenberg. Harold's first tour of duty took place on Tuesday 28th near Kemmel. He continued on tours

A post-war postcard of Kemmel
with a view of the road to Locre

of duty and served in the front during Christmas. The Germans attempted to fraternize but all efforts were rejected, in Harold's line there was no repetition of the *'Christmas Truce'* of 1914, but it was a very quiet day in the trenches. *'Normal service'* returned on Boxing Day with shelling from both sides of the line.

He was relieved on New Year's Eve and on New Year's Day was taken to the baths at Westoutre — during the afternoon his officers enjoyed a lecture by Colonel Fotheringham on 'trench foot'. On Monday 3rd January 1917 Harold took part in a practice attack using the taped trenches along the Westoutre to Berthen road. He undertook gas helmet drill before being sent to relieve the 22nd Battalion on Wednesday 5th. He continued to serve in the sector for the next month and from February was based in the *'RE Farm'* sector where he undertook fatigues, trained and tours of duty in the line. Harold spent a week training in Reninghelst in April until taking the line at St Eloi from Wednesday 12th. For the next two months he continued the usual routine of front line duties and training until he was sent in to the Salient on Thursday 8th June when the Battalion was sent to *'Railway Dugouts'*, *'Blauwepoort Farm'* and *'Woodcote Farm'*. From there they relieved the 1st Canadian Battalion in support of Hill 60 and *'Square Wood'*. Harold's last period of rest commenced on Sunday 11th when he was sent to *'Dickebusch Huts'* for three days. He returned to the line around Hill 62 taking the line from *'Hedge Street'* to *'Vigo'*. From Thursday 15th the weather improved with the German artillery increasing daily the intensity of its bombardment. Harold was killed by shellfire on Sunday 18th.

MAJOR
HERBERT ARTHUR HERBERT-STEPNEY

1st Battalion Irish Guards

Died on Saturday 7th November 1914, aged 35

Commemorated on Panel 11.

Herbert Herbert-Stepney

Herbert was born on Friday 10th January 1879, eldest son of George Herbert-Stepney, of Alberta House, Templeogue, County Dublin. His grandfather Colonel Arthur Herbert-Stepney had commanded the 2nd Battalion Coldstream Guards. He was educated at Rugby School from 1893 to 1897 as a member of Michell and passed into RMC Sandhurst from where he passed out first. Herbert was an all round sportsman and particularly fond of country pursuits.

Herbert was gazetted to the Coldstream Guards in 1899, transferred to the Irish Guards later in the year just after their formation and was appointed Adjutant throughout 1902, promoted Captain in September 1904 and Major in 1912.

Herbert served in the South African War and was slightly injured at Belfast: he received the Queen's Medal with three clasps.

Field Marshal Lord Roberts, Honorary Colonel, accompanied by Lady Aileen, visited Wellington Barracks on Tuesday 11th August 1914 to wish the

Battalion every success in the overseas adventure that would commence the next day. Herbert led his men to the station entraining for Southampton as the Senior Company Commander. At 7.00pm he embarked on *SS Novora* for Le Havre, arriving at 6.00am the next morning. After spending a night in camp he entrained for Wassigny in northern France. Herbert arrived at Mons on Sunday 23rd taking up position at Harveng, although he was not involved in any engagement. At 2.00am the next morning the retirement began ending on Sunday 6th September at Rozoy. Herbert and the Battalion turned eastward towards the Germans whom they engaged later in the day at Villeneuve. He crossed the Marne on Wednesday 9th re-engaging the enemy on Monday 14th at Soupir.

Lord Roberts

The Battalion remained in the Soupir sector for a further month before being sent to the Ypres Salient. After two days in Hazebrouck he billeted overnight in Boeschepe where, after Church Parade on Sunday 18th October, he was taken by London motor bus to Ypres via Reninghelst and Vlamertinghe. It was a long a tiring journey. They arrived in the crowded medieval town filled with escaping refugees, marching, resting or billeted soldiers, and all the paraphernalia of war. The town was still 'living' with open shops, bars and cafés. After a hot meal Herbert took his Battalion to St Jan, marching along narrow cobbled roads passed still intact hamlets, farmhouses and villages, and cheered by the local population living in their homes.

Until the end of October they moved around the Salient all the time under fire, seeing action at Zonnebeke, Gheluvelt, and were involved in a costly attack at Reutel. On Sunday 1st November the German attack intensified and the line was severely threatened. Every available man was put into the line: if they could fire a gun, they were used. One of the men wrote after the war: *"'Twas like a football scrum. Every one was somebody, ye'll understand. If he dropped there was no one to take his place. Great days! An' we not so frightened as when it came to the fightin' by machinery on the Somme afterwards."*

The Earl of Cavan

Captain Orr-Ewing

Lord Cavan wrote to Captain Orr-Ewing (then commanding the Battalion) on Friday 20th November: *"I want you to convey to every man in your Battalion that I consider that the safety of the right flanks of the British section depended entirely upon their staunchness after the disastrous day, Nov. 1. Those of them that were left made history, and I can never thank them enough for the way in which they recovered themselves and showed the enemy that the Irish Guards must be reckoned with, however, hard hit."*

Monday 2nd was spent holding the line, collecting the dead and wounded from the field, always under fire. Tuesday 3rd Herbert was pleased to receive reinforcements of sixty men under the command of Captain Edward Stafford-King-Harman (commemorated on the Menin Gate see below) but sadly many of the men were killed within hours of arrival. On Wednesday 4th the Germans established an effective machine-gun post in a farm overlooking the Battalion and Herbert ordered a field gun up to silence the offending position. The Germans were not amused and targeted both farm and the field gun. They succeeded in destroying the farm but missed the field piece. Friday 6th brought further pressure and danger to the line; Herbert requested support as the German onslaught was about to overwhelm his lines. The Household Cavalry (1st and 2nd Life Guards) galloped along the Menin Road, dismounted and charged into the field to support the Irish Guards. The line held and the Germans retired. The next day Herbert's men took over from the Life Guards after a night of relative quiet. He ordered the trenches to be re-dug and deepened despite being under heavy fire. Herbert was killed during a bombardment and Captain Orr-Ewing took over the command of the Battalion.

Captain Stafford-King-Harman

Herbert was Mentioned in Despatches gazetted on Thursday 14th January 1915.

2294 Rifleman Francis Mackay Herford

1st/9th Battalion London Regiment
(Queen Victoria's Rifles)

Died on Saturday 24th April 1915, aged 19
Commemorated on Panel 54.

Francis born on Wednesday 3rd July 1895, elder son of Mr and Mrs Robert Crow Henderson. He was educated at Charterhouse from 1909 as a Daviesite. He lived in Golders Green.

Francis enlisted in London and was sent for training in Winchester. On Wednesday 4th November 1914 he marched through Southampton Docks to embark on board *SS Oxonian* departing for Le Havre where he arrived the next day. He was marched to camp overnight before returning to the town to entrain for St Omer, a long tiring journey of over twenty-six hours! On Thursday 19th Francis and the Battalion marched to Hazebrouck and rested over night before continuing on to Bailleul where they remained in billets until Friday 27th. The Battalion paraded and marched across the border into Belgium to be sent into billets at Neuve Eglise. From the little village he marched into the line at Wulverghem, a village totally ruined by artillery. Captain Sampson wrote of one of their first tours of duty: "*5th December, 1914. I am back from the trenches and am very well indeed. There was nothing like an action, but there was continued sniping, etc., and we lost one man killed and one wounded, neither of them in my company. The battalion has, I believe, given a very good first impression to everyone. You know that life in the trenches is not pleasant, so I write to you exactly what happens without reserve, as I think you would like me to do so, even if it may be unpleasant reading, but you must remember that it is much worse to read of than to go through, and that I was perfectly happy and content the whole time. We marched off at dusk through the village where we are billeted, and two miles further on reached the next village* [Wulverghem]. *This is in the zone of artillery fire and presented a most melancholy appearance. Every other house is in ruins and there is not a pane of glass in any window, and in the road great holes where shells have burst. It was of course dark and no artillery firing goes on much after dusk. The inhabitants have of course all gone and you can imagine how melancholy was the appearance of this silent, ruined and deserted place. From here we marched some two miles through fields ankle deep in mud, once well-kept farms, now a deserted No Man's Land, with here and there dead cattle and more shell holes. As we get near the trenches bullets buzz by overhead. It is, of course, dark and one cannot tell where they come from. At last we file silently into the trench, passing those whose places we are taking. Imagine a grass field, 120 yards across, with a range of farm buildings on the further side; under the hedge on one side are our trenches, on the other side, 100 to 150 yards off, the German trenches are clearly visible in the moonlight. Here two armies have collided and dug themselves in six weeks ago. Since then they have carried on a kind of poachers' warfare, stealing up to one anothers' trenches and firing into them. The crack of rifles is almost continuous all night and bullets seem to be all round one's head, but it is quite extraordinary how soon one gets accustomed to it. Personally I never felt the slightest wish to duck my head or lie down, but felt strangely calm. The shots are simply fired on the chance of hitting someone and the chances of your stopping one are very small indeed unless you do certain obviously stupid things, such as showing your head above the top of the trench. I found my trench ankle deep in mud and falling down in parts, and we worked all night trying to improve it, as it had been shelled two days before and more protection from artillery fire was needed. I was either digging or looking through a loophole all night. It was a beautiful night, a clear sky and a full moon, so that it was practically broad daylight and the snipers were very busy. They are brave men and good shots, but it is extremely rare for them to bit anyone, and one has only to be careful. They are difficult to deal with actively though, and one comes to neglect them unless one of them gives you a good chance, which is seldom. Things are quieter here than they were, and well in hand, and they do not keep the same people in the front trenches long, so as it is now much warmer I do not anticipate any very great hardship. They seem inclined to take us very gradually up to our fences, so to speak, so as to get us slowly used to things.*"

Francis remained in the sector until Monday 22nd March 1915 when he moved to Ypres and from Thursday 1st April he was sent into the line at Hill 60. Captain Sampson wrote of the early experiences on the Salient where they had been billeted in the Cavalry Barracks in Ypres and at camp in Ouderdom: "*We have just done five days in the trenches. It is not really longer than usual, as we decided to do it in one dose instead of two, as the going to and from the trenches is tiring and there are generally one or two casualties on the way. It would be too long in bad weather, but here the soil is sandy, so that the trenches are dry. The trench I was in was very quiet in the daytime as they could not shell it, the reason being that it was under a hill, at the top of which, from 70 to 100 yards away, was the German trench. The result is that they cannot lob shells on to our trench without lobbing some of them onto their own, which even a Hun resents. We were extremely lucky, having only one casualty in the fire trench and one going up to it. A third was hit on the way back, but the shot only struck his entrenching tool, and he got off with a bruise on the place provided by nature for bruises!*

We are on historic ground here. There has been extremely heavy fighting on the ground where the line of trenches now is. Every building is wiped out by shell-fire, only the foundations and a pile of brickbats where a house once was, and in the woods there is hardly a tree whose top has not been lopped off by the fire. It is as if the seven plagues of Egypt had swept down the zone for half a mile each side of the trenches leaving behind it dead trees, dead horses and dead men. We get accustomed to all these things and hardly notice them, but when one is out of the trenches again one begins to think some times what this country would be like if there were no war, and then one realises what a pity it all is. Here as I write all is peaceful enough except that a captive balloon hangs in the air close by observing for artillery and occasionally one hears the bang of a gun. At night, if it is still, the sound of rifle fire is like crackers being pulled at a party, with the occasional boom of a trench mortar, and we can see the flares when they go up from the fire trenches. Their long-range gun could shell us here [Ouderdom] *if they tried, but they won't, as the camp is too scattered and heavy shell too precious.*"

Mines had been blown on Saturday 17th April that destroyed Hill 60, removing the top of the hill and creating large, deep craters. Francis and the Battalion were in position ready to support the offensive. The German counter-attack was soon mounted early the next day and in the afternoon they launched gas against the British defenders holding onto the Hill. One of his comrades wrote: *"About 2 p.m. they started using their 'stink' gas. They put most of it on the Hill and on a place called 'The Dump', on which we had a host of dug-outs. We got the waftings of the gas. It makes the eyes water and irritates the throat. It's devilish stuff. To be in the gas region must have been hell. It's the only word that describes it."*

Corporal H E Asser wrote of Hill 60: *"We had a pretty thick time of it up at Hill 60. It was some fight, I can tell you. When I heard the word to reinforce the hill I followed the man in front of me along the support trench and round the corner up the communication trench, which there was only about four feet high, and open to machine-gun fire from either side, with shrapnel bursting about and 'whizz-bangs' flying over by the dozen. We screwed our way along the narrow trench, passing many wounded coming back. At the end of the trench we were at the bottom of the crater. We saw the top of the hill and began scrambling up. It was all loose, sandy soil, because that part had been recently blown up. Our part of the hill ran up at about sixty degrees and was some twenty-five feet high. We were soon amongst those at the top and our job was to keep up a rapid fire on their trenches. You fired like blazes until your rifle boiled and you fairly ached. Then the man behind stepped in and took your place until his rifle was the same then you had another go. All this time they were sending their little black hand-grenades, but they all burst outside our trench—they could not chuck far enough. We were flinging ours, which are a very different kind, right into their trench. What did the damage was their trench mortars—filthy things. All you know is a tremendous report, and the thing has burst, probably in the trench, and two or three men roll back in the crater and others are wounded, some badly, some not. The low groans above all the rifle and shell-fire are horrible to hear. I lost many pals, and it was an anxious time to see who were left when the relief came for us. We had had four hours, but some of our chaps had been up much longer."*

6th Dragoons at Compiègne

During the morning of Thursday 22nd April the Battalion was relieved to Ypres where General Sir Horace Smith-Dorrien met them *en route* and addressed them. They marched to Brielen for some rest; it was not to last. At 5.00pm the Germans launched the first gas attack to the north of their position. That night the Battalion was moved to bivouac in Vlamertinghe, leaving in the early morning of Friday 23rd via Elverdinghe and took position on the canal bank. On Saturday 24th they moved forward to the line at Wieltje where they came under heavy shell fire and during one of the bombardments Francis was killed.

Captain Geoffrey Wilmot Herringham

6th Dragoons (Inniskilling)

Died on Saturday 31st October 1914, aged 31

Commemorated on Panel 5.

Geoffrey was born in London on Tuesday 7th August 1883, son of Major General Sir Wilmot Parker Herringham, KCMG, CB, MD (Oxon), FRCP, AMS, and Lady Christina Jane Herringham, of 30 Wimpole Street, London W. His father was Consulting Physician of the Forces during the Great War. He was educated at Eton College as a member of College, leaving in 1899 and passed into RMA Woolwich.

Geoffrey was gazetted on Friday 21st December 1900, promoted to Lieutenant on Monday 21st December 1903, transferred to the 6th Dragoons on Wednesday 21st November 1906, and promoted Captain on Wednesday 9th March 1910.

At the outbreak of war he assisted with the mobilisation and was sent out to France. He went to serve on the Marne and Aisne where he took part in a fierce action at Compiègne. In early October he rode northward and took part in the actions in northern France prior to crossing the border. As the First Battle of Ypres raged on the troops from the north (who had arrived in October at Ostend and Zeebrugge) met to the north of Messines with the BEF arriving from the Aisne. The battle at Messines was fierce. The village was split in two, with each half being occupied by the opposing armies. The battle lines were very close to each other and fierce hand-to-hand fighting took place. During the action Geoffrey was killed.

Geoffrey was recorded in Debretts Obituary — War Roll of Honour published in the 1921 edition.

475891 Private Ira Harry Heuhn

Princess Patricia's Canadian Light Infantry (Eastern Ontario Regiment)

Died on Friday 2nd June 1916, aged 20

Commemorated on Panel 10.

Ira Heuhn

Harry was born in Toronto on Monday 10th June 1895, son of Mr and Mrs Henry E Heuhn. He was educated at the Gladstone Avenue Public School followed by the Parkdale Collegiate Institute. He joined the Commerce Bank on Tuesday 28th January 1913 serving in the Market Branch, Toronto and was a member of the Militia.

He volunteered on Friday 13th August 1915 in Toronto where he was described as 5ft 9in tall, with a 36in chest, a fair complexion, blue eyes, fair hair, a birthmark on his left breast and scar from an appendicectomy.

After training he sailed to England where the training continued before being sent out to join the Regiment in the field with a draft. He entrained to northern France and arrived in the Kemmel sector where he saw service in the front line for the first time. In early March he undertook training from where he was sent to Zillebeke on Tuesday 21st, to serve at *'Railway Dugouts'* and *'Maple Copse'* for three days before moving forward to *'Sanctuary Wood'*. The Regiment was relieved on Tuesday 28th, although it took some time to extricate themselves and they did not arrive at *'Camp B'* on the Poperinghe road until the next morning. The range of the camp was known to the German artillery who shelled it on Friday 7th April. On Wednesday 12th Harry marched back to Ypres and went into the trenches at Hooge for an eight day tour which was followed by being in reserve at *'Camp D'*. He undertook training and fatigues before returning to *'Railway Dugouts'* and *'Maple Copse'* on Saturday 29th where he remained on tours of duty until Wednesday 31st May.

... billets in Westoutre

Harry was marched from *'Belgian Château'* to positions around *'Warrington Avenue'* and *'Zouave Wood'*. Thursday 1st June was relatively quiet from noon. Shortly after 1.00pm on Friday 2nd the German artillery laid down an immense barrage on their lines — The Battle of Mount Sorrel — with large portions of the Regiment being wiped out in their trenches in a short space of time, including Harry.

Captain The Honourable Archibald Rodney Hewitt, DSO

2nd Battalion East Surrey Regiment

Died on Sunday 25th April 1915, aged 32

Commemorated on Panel 34.

Citation for the Distinguished Service Order, London Gazette, Monday 9th November 1914:

"For moving out of the trenches at Le Cateau, under heavy shell fire, and bringing back men who were dribbling to the rear."

Archibald Hewitt and his family coat of arms

Archibald was born in Torquay on Friday 25th May 1883, second son of Archibald Robert Hewitt, 6th Viscount Lifford and Helen Blanche, Viscountess Lifford, of Hill House, Lyndhurst, Hampshire. He was educated at Dulwich College from 1899 to 1901 and passed into RMC Sandhurst. Archibald enjoyed hunting, shooting, fishing, golf and football, and held membership of the Naval and Military Club.

Archibald was gazetted on Wednesday 22nd October 1902, promoted Lieutenant on Saturday 18th June 1904, Captain on Tuesday 17th May 1910, and from June 1911 to May 1914 was Adjutant.

Archibald went out with the BEF on Thursday 13th August. He was sent out with the 1st Battalion embarking on *HMT Botanist* sailing at 6.00pm from Dublin, arriving in Le Havre at noon on Saturday 15th. After two nights in camp he entrained at 11.30am on Monday 17th for Le Cateau where they arrived at 4.00am the next morning. After breakfast had been provided, the Battalion marched to Landrecies where the men billeted in the *'Biron Barracks'* and the officers with local townspeople. General Sir Charles Fergusson visited the Battalion on Thursday 20th and addressed them, wishing them well for the forthcoming battle. The next morning, at 6.25am, the Battalion marched through the Forest of Mormal, crossing the Belgian border at 9.00am on Saturday 22nd and took the line at Mons. The Germans attacked the line and the battle was undertaken at close quarters. Late on Sunday 23rd the Battalion was ordered to retire and then rested for two hours at Boussu. At 4.00am on Monday 24th they continued to retire through Dour and continued on to Le Cateau. The Battalion took a frontage of two hundred yards and formed five lines. Heavy shrapnel fire was crashing down amongst two of the Companies when

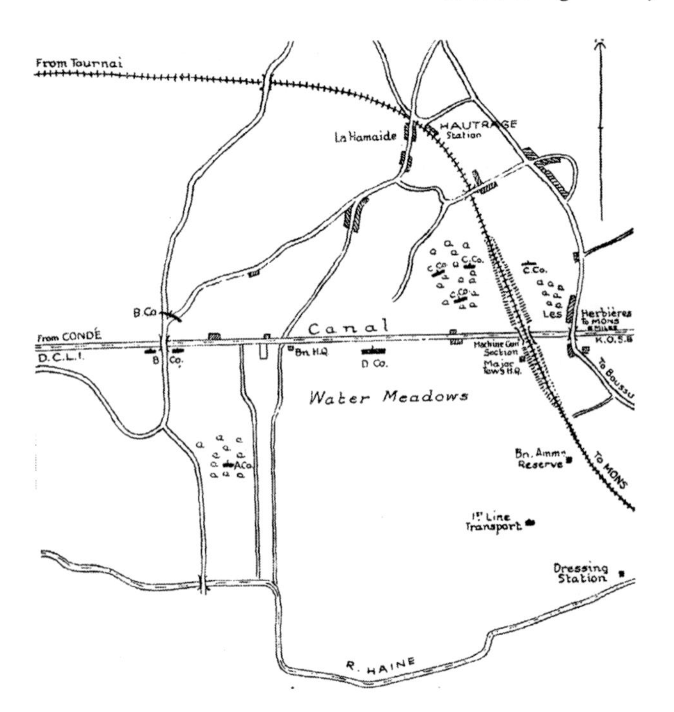

The East Surrey's at Mons

Archibald rallied the men, and they were able to hold onto their tenuous line. For this action Archibald was awarded the Distinguished Service Order.

Following the Battle of Le Cateau the Battalion continued to retire and arrived in St Quentin early on Thursday 27th. As the retirement turning into The Retreat, they passed throughout Noyon and shortly afterwards Field Marshal Sir John French was passing in his car when he halted and spoke to the men. He

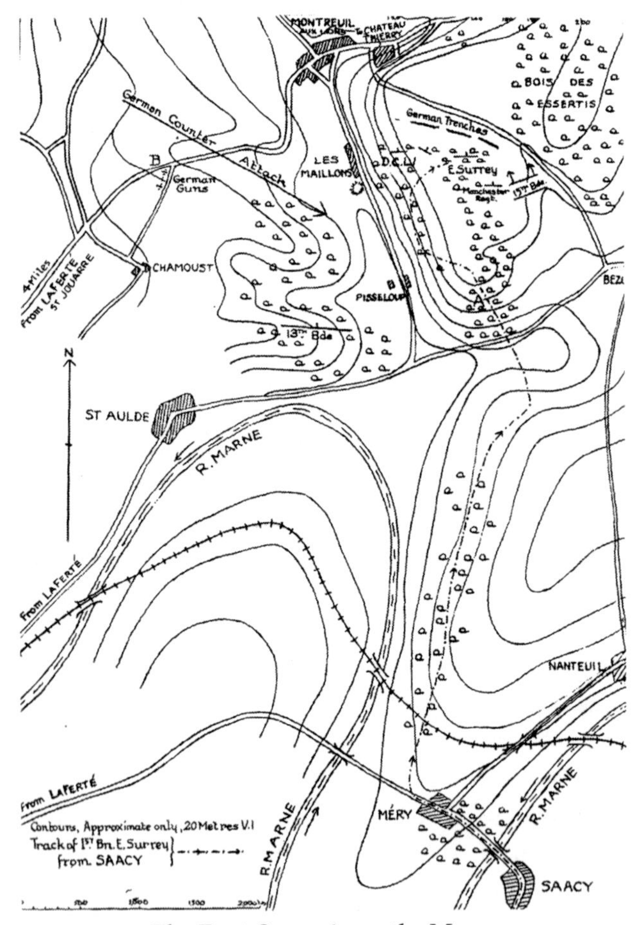

The East Surrey's on the Marne

congratulated them on their excellent work and its value. They crossed the Marne near Meaux and they finally arrived in Tournan — so ended The Retreat. On Sunday 6th September, with great delight, Archibald led his men towards the German armies, with their first night bivouac at Dammartin.

The Grand Morin was crossed at Coulommiers on Monday 7th where they whole village had been looted and broken wine bottles littered the streets. On Wednesday 9th September, Archibald was severely wounded whilst going forward with Lieutenant Colonel Longley during a reconnaissance in the woods near Bézu. He was taken to a cottage by the Medical Officer when they were cut off and surrounded by the Germans. Archibald feigned delirium and convinced them that he was dying so they left him behind — in short measure he rejoined the Battalion! From Tuesday 15th September Archibald took the line near Missy where he remained until the end of the month.

At the beginning of October Archibald moved to La Bassée. On Sunday 18th October he was Mentioned in Despatches, and on Thursday 29th Battalion Orders were published that included his award of the Distinguished Service Order. On Saturday 31st the Battalion continued is march north and after going in and out of the line at La Bassée finally arrived in Belgium on Monday 16th November. They immediately went to the front at Lindenhoek, close to Kemmel.

On Wednesday 2nd December the Battalion was paraded for an inspection by Field Marshal Sir John French, who addressed them: *"I am very glad to have the opportunity of addressing you to-day and thanking you for the work you have done. On the way here I asked your Corps Commander, Sir Horace, what special occasion I could mention in which you have distinguished yourselves. 'Whatever you mention, and whatever you say,' he said, 'it will be not be too much. They have been splendid throughout.' No regiment could wish for higher praise than this, and I thank you personally for what you have done and the way you have helped me. The 5th Division have had more than their share of the fighting in this campaign. On the terrible retirement after Mons and Le Cateau you had the brunt of the fighting, and immediately after, at the Battle of the Marne, you had to attack the most difficult section of the line, and the attack was brilliantly carried out. Not a week later you were engaged on the Aisne and held the extremely difficult position of Missy, into which an incessant rifle and shell fire was poured from the commanding German position above. Less than a month after this the Regiment was in the thick of the terribly severe fighting round La Bassée, where you were faced by three if not four times your numbers and experienced some of the fiercest fighting of the War. Lately in the trench fighting you have gallantly defended your lines against the most determined attacks and the most vigorous shelling. In fact,*

General Joffre and Field Marshal French at the front

you have crowded into the four months of this campaign enough fighting to fill the battle honours of an Army Corps, and by your conduct throughout you have not only upheld, but greatly added to the fame of a grand old Regiment. In conclusion, as Commander-in-Chief, I wish once more to thank you for your endurance and for the splendid work you have performed and to tell you how glad I am to have this opportunity of being able to tell you so." The next day Archibald paraded a company of the Battalion with those who had been awarded medals who were presented with them by HM King George V, including Archibald with the Distinguished Service Order.

For the rest of December Archibald remained in the line, including Christmas Day where the Christmas gifts from the King, Queen and Princess Mary were distributed. The New Year was ushered in by a bombardment of the German lines to which they replied in full measure.

In February 1915 the 2nd Battalion had arrived on the Salient and shortly afterwards he joined them. Archibald saw considerable action throughout the Salient, surviving several difficult actions. On Saturday 10th April Archibald took his men, with the Battalion, from Vlamertinghe through Ypres where they relieved the French 153rd Infantry northeast of Zonnebeke. They went through Ypres and as they passed the Cloth Hall they met the 1st Battalion and gave them a rousing cheer that was reciprocated — Archibald saw many of his old friends with whom he had fought over the past few months. The next evening Major Le Fleming was visiting each Company in the front line when he was sniped and Archibald took over command of the Battalion. On Wednesday 14th the Surrey's were badly shelled and so it was with relief they were taken from the line the next day: however, it was to support Zonnebeke as an attack was expected. On Thursday 22nd Archibald handed over the command to Lieutenant Colonel C C G Ashton (who had raised the 7th Battalion) and resumed his position as Second-in-Command. They were to be relieved but due to a heavy German artillery attack they remained in the line, also subjected to gas.

At 1.00pm on Sunday 25th the Germans attacked the whole of the Battalion's line under the cover of a gas attack and *'Trench 23'* gave way and was occupied by the Germans. *'Trench 25'* was also partially taken and counter-attacks were mounted against them. Archibald was leading one such attack when he was killed.

His Colonel wrote: *"He was one that could ill be spared; his influence was all for good, and his cheery and kindly disposition were invaluable on Service, as they were appreciated by all of us in peace time. His regiment has indeed suffered a severe loss. I know what they thought of him."*

His Major wrote: *"For your dear son I am not sorry; he lived like a man, the death we all hope for. He was the most gallant and faithful soul I ever knew."*

The Colonel of the 1st Battalion wrote: *"Your son joined under my command in Dublin, and has ever been one of our best friends in the regiment, and until the day before his death was commanding my battalion; the Major under whom he was early last monthly was loud in his praises of his zeal and dependability. I can honestly assure you the regiment's loss is very, very great. Ever bright and cheery, even under the most adverse circumstances, he was an asset of the greatest value when troops were called upon to do their best."*

A stained glass window in All Saints Church, Crondall, Hampshire was installed in his memory and a plaque with the East Surrey Regiment badge, with the inscription: *"The window is dedicated to the memory of The Hon Archibald Rodney Hewitt, D.S.O., Captain 2nd Battalion East Surrey Regiment younger son of the 6th Viscount Lifford. He was killed in The Second Battle of Ypres on the 25th April 1915 in his 32nd year."*

Archibald is commemorated on the House of Lords War Memorial and was recorded in Debretts Obituary — War Roll of Honour published in the 1921 edition.

His cousin, 2nd Lieutenant Denis Hewitt, VC, died on Tuesday 31st July 1917, and is commemorated on the Menin Gate, see below.

Punch cartoon:
"Tommy (finding a German prisoner who speaks English):
"Look what done to me, you blighters! 'Ere — 'ave you a cigarette?"

Second Lieutenant Denis George Wyldbore Hewitt, VC

2nd Battalion Hampshire Regiment

Died on Tuesday 31st July 1917, aged 19

Commemorated on Panel 35.

Citation for the Victoria Cross, London Gazette No 30284, dated Friday 14th September 1917:

"For most conspicuous bravery and devotion to duty when in command of a company in attack. When his first objective had been captured he reorganized the company and moved forward towards his objective. While waiting for the barrage to lift, he was hit by a piece of shell, which exploded the signal lights in his haversack and set fire to his equipment and clothes. Having extinguished the flames, in spite of his wound and the severe pain he was suffering, he led forward the remains of the company under very heavy machine-gun fire, and captured and consolidated his objective. He was subsequently killed by a sniper while inspecting the consolidation and encouraging his men. This gallant officer set a magnificent example of coolness and contempt of danger to the whole battalion, and it was due to his splendid leading that the final objective of his battalion was gained."

Denis Hewitt and his family coat of arms

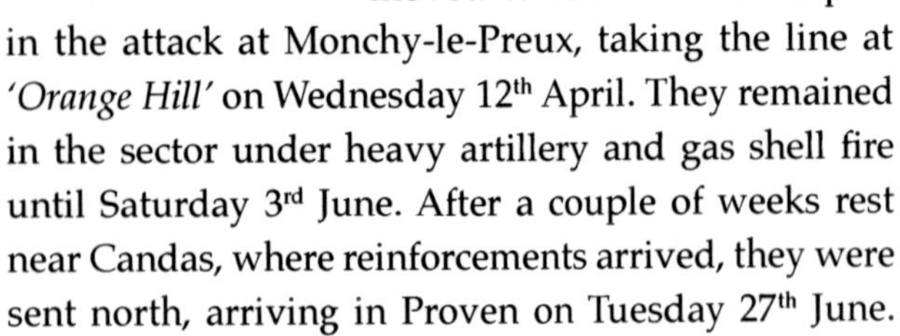

Denis was born in London on Saturday 18th December 1897, the elder son of the late Honourable George Hewitt, JP, and the Elizabeth Mary Hewitt (née Rampini), of Field House, Hursley, Winchester, grandson of James, 4th Viscount Lifford, DL. He was educated at Winchester College from 1911 to 1915 and passed into RMC Sandhurst.

Denis was gazetted on Friday 7th April 1916 and went out to France on Saturday 9th September joining the Battalion on the Somme. At Guedecourt on Monday 18th October an attack was launched at 3.40am. The Battalion consolidated their line and repulsed a series of counter-attacks. From the Somme Denis moved to Arras and took part in the attack at Monchy-le-Preux, taking the line at *'Orange Hill'* on Wednesday 12th April. They remained in the sector under heavy artillery and gas shell fire until Saturday 3rd June. After a couple of weeks rest near Candas, where reinforcements arrived, they were sent north, arriving in Proven on Tuesday 27th June. They were sent to assist in laying communication cables and undertook further training. From Monday 10th to Thursday 13th July they were allocated their first tour of duty in the Salient on the Ypres Canal. At 3.50am on Tuesday 31st July 1917, 'Zero Hour', the Hampshires advanced under the heaviest barrage so far of the war — or so it was then described. John advanced in conjunction with the 14th Royal Sussex on *'Kitchener's Wood'* (Bois des Cuisiniers) which was on the 'Black Line', the second objective. They were held up by the various German pill-boxes that were only taken when the Hampshires were able to work around them and take them from the rear. However, they took heavy casualties. In this action Denis won his Victoria Cross and was killed.

The War Diary records: *"Zero 3.50 a.m. Advanced from assembly positions, passed through 11th Royal Sussex Regiment on Blue Line, attacked, captured and consolidated Black and dotted Black Lines at FALKENHAYN REDOUBT. From there advanced onto Alberta and dotted Green Line on east of STEENBEEK which were captured. Here troops of 118th Infantry Brigade passed through to capture solid Green Line. Company on East of STEENBEEK retired with 118th Infantry Brigade on night of 31 July / 1st August. Captured two Field Guns and one 4.5 Howitzer, 17 Machine-guns (counted) and over 200 prisoners."*

His Colonel wrote: *"It may be a slight consolation to you to know that he died a glorious death. In the attack on 31 July he had a most difficult operation to carry out. During the earlier part of the attack he was hit on the back, on his haversack, by a piece of shell, which set on fire the rockets and flares he was carrying. By rolling in the mud he managed to get these extinguished. Then, although much shaken, he rallied his company, went forward, and drove back the Germans, attaining his object. It was while superintending his men digging in on their final objective that he was killed — hit by a bullet in the head. Death was instantaneous."*

In All Saints Church, Hursley, Hampshire a white marble plaque was erected in his memory with a moulded green marble frame, the Regimental crest of the Hampshire Regiment is in the top left corner and is in colour, in relief, additionally flower heads are in

The Battle of Passchendaele ... attacking a pill-box

the other corners. The inscription reads: *"In proud and loving memory of Denis George Wyldbore Hewitt, V.C., 2nd Lieut. The Hampshire Regiment, dearly loved elder son of The Hon George Wyldbore Hewitt and Elizabeth Mary his wife killed in action close to St Julien 31st July 1917 aged 19 years awarded the posthumous honour of The Victoria Cross 'For Most Conspicuous Bravery and Devotion To Duty' while leading his company against the enemy at The Third Battle of Ypres. Greater love hath no man than this, that a man lay down his life for his friends." St John 15.13.*

In addition his original battlefield cross is displayed with the inscription on the cross reading: *"Peace Perfect Peace 2nd Lt. D. C. W. Hewitt V.C. 14th Hants 31.7.17. Killed In Action."* A board below reads: *"Erected by the regiment and removed from the battlefield."*

His cousin, Captain The Hon Archibald Hewitt, DSO, died on Sunday 25th April 1915 and is commemorated on the Menin Gate, see above.

11460 Private George Hewitt

5th Battalion King's Shropshire Light Infantry

Died on Saturday 25th September 1915, aged 22

Commemorated on Panel 49.

George was the son of Emily Hewitt, of 26 Heywood Grove, Brooklands, Sale, Cheshire, and the late Thomas Hewitt. His brother, Private Thomas Hewitt, died on the same day and is also commemorated on the Memorial, see below.

The Battalion formed at Blackdown shortly after the outbreak of war. As the number of volunteers grew the Battalion took shape with training continuing at Aldershot until Thursday 20th May 1915 when Lieutenant Colonel H M Smith took his men by train to Folkestone where they sailed to Boulogne. After a rest at Ostrohove they entrained for Cassel that was followed by a tiring march to Erkelsbrugge and billets where they remained for a week. On Monday 24th General Stopford inspected the Battalion and immediately afterwards marched sixteen miles to new billets at Eecke. On Sunday 30th they moved to the Salient and camp at *'Canada Huts'*, Dickebusch. The next day General Sir Charles Ferguson addressed them and wished them well for their forthcoming work at the front.

Generals Stopford (above) Ferguson, (below)

The first experience under fire began on Tuesday 1st June when they were detailed to construct trenches near Zillebeke. Fatigues continued, including a week at Kemmel, and they prepared to assist in the attack on Bellewaarde. During the night of Tuesday 15th the Battalion was in dugouts in the walls of Ypres. At 10.00am the next morning they marched via *'Hellfire Corner'* to *'Gordon House'* where they came under from Hill 60, remaining in difficult circumstances for twenty-four hours. Following relief the Battalion was sent to rest in Vlamertinghe. The first tour of duty in their own right began when they relieved the Suffolks on Saturday 19th for a tour of five days near Hooge. Tours of duty to the front and fatigues continued throughout the summer in the sector.

On Wednesday 15th September the Battalion was relieved to the north of Poperinghe where they prepared for the attack that would take place on Saturday 25th as a feint for the Battle of Loos. General Plumer inspected the Battalion and addressed them. During the night of Thursday 23rd George and Thomas left by train from Poperinghe to the Asylum in Ypres from where they marched to their assembly positions at *'Railway Wood'*. At 3.50am on Friday 24th a British bombardment fell on the German lines for half an hour that started an artillery duel between the opposing artillery lasting throughout the day. At 3.50am on Saturday 25th the artillery began another heavy bombardment and at 4.20am the British attack on the German lines began. German defence was particularly fierce and the Battalion could not reach its objectives and they were forced back to their jumping off point by 8.15am. During the day seven officers were killed together with forty-one men, including George and Thomas.

General Plumer

9304 Private Thomas Hewitt

5th Battalion King's Shropshire Light Infantry

Died on Saturday 25th September 1915, aged 24

Commemorated on Panel 49.

Thomas was the son of Emily Hewitt, of 26 Heywood Grove, Brooklands, Sale, Cheshire, and the late Thomas Hewitt.

His brother, Private George Hewitt, died on the same day and is commemorated on the Memorial, for their story, see above.

... machine gunners in action at Hooge

617 Rifleman
Thomas Armitage Hewitt

1st/5th Battalion London Regiment
(London Rifle Brigade)

Died on Monday 3rd May 1915, aged 26
Commemorated on Panel 54.

Armitage was born on Thursday 27th December 1888, son of Thomas and Sarah Ann Hewitt, of Rostherne, Grove Street, Toowong, Brisbane, Queensland, Australia. He was educated at Mill Hill School from 1903 to 1905 as a member of School House where he was a Junior Scholar. He studied law and graduated with an LLB (London) then qualified as a solicitor, practising with Hewitt, Urquhart & Woollacott of 158 Leadenhall Street, London EC.

At the outbreak of war Armitage volunteered and enlisted in September 1914, turning down the opportunity of a commission. On Wednesday 4th November 1914 Armitage embarked on *SS Chyebassa* in Southampton and sailed for Le Havre, arriving the next day. He entrained for St Omer arriving on Saturday 7th and went into billets at the Benedictine Convent in Wisques and continued training. On Sunday 22nd he undertook his first tour of duty at Ploegsteert. He was in and out of the line with billets in Armentières. He took part in the Christmas Truce and until New Year's Eve no firing took place and he remained in the Ploegsteert sector until April 1915. On Friday 23rd they were sent to Poperinghe and on to Vlamertinghe the next day. At 6.15pm on Sunday 25th they marched in the pouring rain through St Jan to Wieltje and then moved into the line. On Thursday 29th they moved position and relieved the 4th East Yorkshires. On Sunday 2nd the Germans launched gas shells on their lines together with shrapnel and from 5.20pm to 6.30pm they pressed home an attack that was repulsed. Pressure was kept up on their line and retirement was about to be organised when he was killed.

2369 Corporal
Charles Leslie Tasman Hey

24th Battalion Australian Infantry, AIF

Died on Monday 8th October 1917, aged 24
Commemorated on Panel 26.

Charles was born in Tasmania son of George and Ann Hey, of Best Street, Devonport, Tasmania. He was educated locally and was employed as a cobbler.

On Saturday 10th July 1915 he volunteered and enlisted, leaving from Melbourne on Wednesday 29th September on board *RMS Osterley*.

After a period of training Charles was sent out with a draft joining the Battalion on the Somme. On Monday 15th January 1917 the Battalion was sent to Ribemont for training and *'Becourt Camp'*, returning to the line on Monday 5th February. After serving in the sector and a long period at Le Transloy, they left for training on Tuesday 24th July, spending the whole of August in Wardrecques and moving to Steenvoorde on Wednesday 12th September where they remained overnight before moving to *'Devonshire Camp'* in Ouderdom the next day. On Tuesday 18th Charles marched to *'Winnipeg Camp'*, arriving at 3.45pm from where parties were sent to the front acting as stretcher bearers between Westhoek Ridge and the culvert on the Menin Road and helping strengthen the trench system between Bellewaarde and Westhoek. On Sunday 23rd the Battalion was moved to *'Devonshire Camp'* where they remained at rest and training until the end of the month when they were sent to the Cavalry Barracks in Ypres. On Wednesday 3rd October they moved via *'Gordon Farm'* reaching the assembly positions early the next morning. From 4.00am on Thursday 4th the Companies moved forward into their jumping off trenches; the Germans had spotted the movement and laid down a barrage on their line from 5.30am. Zero Hour, 6.00pm, the British barrage opened and Charles was led forward into the attack. At 8.10am he moved forward towards the Broodseinde to Becelaere road where they came under machine-gun fire and sniper fire from the ridge. Charles was ordered to dig in and throughout the day their lines were continually sniped. At 7.00am and 8.00am on Friday 5th German planes flew low over their lines. At

11.00am Stokes Mortars were used, although in the afternoon the sector was relatively quiet. At 2.00pm on Sunday 7th Charles and the Battalion were moved to Zonnebeke via the Menin Road and took the Support Line by 7.30pm. Whilst in the line he was killed, one of ten killed that day.
His brother, Private Ernest Hey, died on Thursday 4th October 1917, and is commemorated on the Menin Gate, see below.

7016 Private Ernest Victor Hey

6th Battalion Australian Infantry, AIF

Died on Thursday 4th October 1917, aged 29

Commemorated on Panel 7.

Ernest was the son of George and Ann Hey, of Best Street, Devonport, Tasmania. He was educated locally and was employed as a mechanic.
Ernest volunteered and enlisted on Tuesday 19th September 1916, leaving for England on Thursday 23rd November 1916 from Melbourne on board *HMAT Hororata*. After more training in England he was sent out with a draft to join the Battalion in the field, on the Somme. He served at *'High Wood'*, Flers and Mametz until Tuesday 24th July 1917 when they commenced their move to Méaulte from where they moved north, arriving in Caëstre at 3.00pm on Friday 27th. They were sent to Cassel where they remained until Wednesday 8th August then going to the Le Verrier area to continue training.
On Thursday 13th September they moved to Berthen and were sent to camp near Mont de Cats overnight before moving across the border to Reninghelst where they bivouacked prior to being sent to *'Château Segard'* on Sunday 16th. They came under shell fire before relieving the 8th Battalion, London Regiment at Zillebeke Bund on Wednesday 19th. Here they prepared all day for an attack; at 2.30am the next morning an infantryman from the 15th Bavarian Regiment was captured when he wandered a little too close to their lines. At 4.00am the Germans laid down a barrage on their lines and at 5.40am the British barrage commenced and Ernest was led forward towards *'Glencorse Wood'*. Later in the night a blockhouse at *'Fitzclarence Farm'* was taken and the Farm was taken shortly afterwards and the position consolidated. The Germans shelled their new positions and mounted a counter-attack against the 7th Battalion, Australian Infantry next to them. British aeroplanes flew low over the German lines and let loose with their machine-guns for some time. The British artillery commenced a barrage to slow down any counter-attack; during the night of Friday 21st the Battalion was relieved to dug-outs at Zillebeke Bund. During the night of Saturday 22nd Ernest was marched to *'Cornwall Camp'* at Ouderdom where they rested until the next morning when they were sent for training near Steenvoorde until Monday 1st October. A fleet of buses arrived taking them to *'Dickebusch Huts'*, where they remained until 6.45pm the next evening. The Battalion marched to Westhoek Ridge where they bivouacked and during the night of Wednesday 3rd Ernest and his comrades were sent into their assembly positions. At 5.30am the Germans laid down a barrage on their lines killing the Adjutant. At 6.00am the whistles blew and Ernest went 'over the top' towards the crater on the Broodseinde Road. A series of concrete blockhouses slowed their progress and caused a large number of casualties including Ernest.
His brother, Corporal Charles Hey, died on Monday 8th October 1917 and is commemorated on the Menin Gate, see above.

Lieutenant Terence Hickman

2nd Battalion Leinster Regiment

Died on Monday 26th June 1916, aged 28

Commemorated on Panel 44.

Terence was the son of Mr W R J and Mrs Fanny Hickman, of Castle Grove House, Chobham, Surrey. He went up to King's College, Cambridge, in 1907.
At the outbreak of war Terence volunteered and enlisted in the Honourable Artillery Company on Tuesday 25th August 1914. One of his comrades wrote of his experiences at the front: *"Another problem is that of washing. When you get to the trenches or dug-outs, nobody ever thinks of such a thing. Water is generally very scarce, only to be obtained at considerable risk from snipers or shrapnel, generally from a farmhouse that has been destroyed, the pump perhaps surviving amid a mass of ruins. The water perhaps isn't as good as it might be, and orders are that it is not to be drunk unless boiled, but you are thirsty and have been inoculated against enteric, so you take a chance on it. Even when resting in billets a decent wash is hard to get. Probably there are a hundred or more of you on the farm, and only two buckets to be had, so if you get a lick and a promise it is all that can be hoped for as you struggle with a dull razor and cold water.*
And the mud! Never was there such mud since the Deluge dried up. You live in it, swim in it, splash in it all day long. Your boots are shapeless masses, and it is hopeless to keep them dry, let alone clean."
On Thursday 11th February 1915 he was commissioned to the Leinsters. On Monday 31st May 1915 he was sent to the Ypres Salient where he took part in the counter-attack at Hooge on Monday 9th August.
Terence remained on the Salient until Saturday 17th June 1916 when he was relieved to the area of Wormhoudt. On his first tour of duty in the Armentières sector Terence was killed.

3583 Private Samuel Denys Hillis

1st/10th Battalion The King's (Liverpool Regiment)

Died on Wednesday 16th June 1915

Commemorated on Panel 6.

Samuel Hillis

Samuel was the second son of Mr and Mrs Samuel Hillis of Birkenhead. He was educated from Birkenhead School from 1903 to 1910 and went up to Liverpool University. He graduated in 1913 with a BSc and continued to study for his MSc in metallurgy.

At the outbreak of war he volunteered and enlisted in September. After a short period of training he left for France, leaving camp in Tunbridge Wells, Kent, and sailed on *SS Maidan* on Sunday 1st November 1914. Samuel arrived in Le Havre and was sent to *'No 1 Rest Camp'* until Wednesday 4th when he entrained for St Omer. On Friday 20th Samuel marched via Bailleul to billets at Westoutre, a week later taking the line between Kemmel and Wytschaete. He remained in the sector until early March 1915 when he moved into the Salient itself, moving into the trenches at Zillebeke during the night of Wednesday 10th. Forty-eight hours later the Germans blew a series of mines close to the left of his position. Samuel served in the ghastly section of the line near St Eloi that came under intense attack on Wednesday 14th April that was successfully repulsed by the artillery and the good work of the Battalion. The Battalion Diary recorded: *"The Commanding Officer wishes to put on record the good work done by the men in the trenches during the night of 14th inst., when the mine exploded ... The thirty men, stretcher-bearers, first-aid men and signallers who were called on, responded magnificently, and their services will always be remembered in the history of the battalion."* Samuel was in the trenches at St Eloi when the gas attack began at 5.00pm on Thursday 22nd April, the Battalion Diary recorded: *"On the occasion of the enemy using poisonous gases on the 22nd inst. in the north, the fumes could be detected in our trenches and in Voormezeele. The men in the trenches complained of a smarting and watering of the eyes. Ypres was shelled for days on end with very heavy shells, and the noise of them was heard clearly by all ranks. The town must have been knocked into ruins and great fires were seen every now and then."* Samuel remained on tours of duty until Thursday 27th May when he was sent to Dickebusch. After a week he returned to the line at *'Armagh Wood'*. From midnight on Tuesday 15th a preliminary barrage began on the German lines at Bellewaarde. Samuel attacked in the second wave and passed quickly through the captured German front line. He was killed shortly afterwards in fierce hand-to-hand fighting.

Y/1109 Rifleman Arthur Robert Hilson (Served as Clarke)

4th Battalion King's Royal Rifle Corps

Died on Monday 10th May 1915, aged 16

Commemorated on Panel 53.

Arthur was born in St Barnabas, Birmingham, son of Arthur Hilson, of 184 Runcorn Road, Sparkbrook, Birmingham. He was educated locally.

He enlisted under the name of Clarke in Birmingham. After training he was sent out to France and onward to Belgium.

Conditions in the front line in the southern sector were dreadful: the trenches were totally water-logged; they could only be reached at night as no communication trenches existed. Many of his comrades suffered very badly from trench foot.

Arthur served at Polygon Wood in mid-April 1915 from where he was sent to Hill 60 where he was engaged in a furious attack and counter-attack. On Saturday 8th May the German artillery intensified. The next day it grew strong and their infantry attack was repulsed. The Battalion's front line trenches were totally obliterated. However they were able to hang on and repulsed each attack. On Monday 10th a further attack was made during which Arthur was killed.

Lieutenant Cyril De Villiers Hinde, MC

2nd Battalion Royal Berkshire Regiment

Died on Thursday 11th July 1917, aged 20

Commemorated on Panel 45.

Citation for the Military Cross:

"He led a patrol and inflicted heavy casualties on the enemy. Later, though wounded, he remained in command and successfully withdrew his men."

Cyril was the son of Lieutenant Colonel W H Hinde (late RE) and Mrs M Hinde, of Heathcote, Wellington College, Berkshire, where he was educated from 1910 to 1914.

After leaving School Cyril volunteered and was commissioned in 1915. After training Cyril was sent out to join the Battalion in the field. From Sunday 26th September to Sunday 21st November 1915 he served around Bois Grenier; he was then sent to Vieux Berquin near Sercus into reserve and training. Christmas was spent at Sercus with a good dinner provided from Battalion funds. On Sunday 9th January 1916 the Battalion was marched to Estaires where they relieved the King's Liverpool at Croix Maréchal. He remained in the sector until Tuesday 28th March when he marched with the men to Lestrem where he entrained for Longueau.

The Battalion moved into the line on the River Ancre, north of Albert. He undertook a series of duties, with the usual periods of rest and training, particularly in preparation for the Battle of the Somme. During the night of Friday 30th June Cyril organised his men and marched from *'Long Valley Camp'* to their assembly positions that came under shell fire throughout the night. At 6.35am on Saturday 1st July the British barrage commenced, with Cyril leading his men forward at 7.30am; the objective was Ovillers. The German machine-gunners halted the attack and heavy casualties were suffered. They withdrew to their old line later that evening before returning to camp. On Sunday 2nd the Battalion was sent out of the sector and moved north, arriving in Béthune on Friday 14th. After the Battalion was reorganised they served in the Vermelles sector until Tuesday 10th October when they returned to the Somme. On Sunday 22nd they were in the line ready to support an attack on *'Zenith Trench'* the next day. The attack commenced at 2.30pm, but the defences were strong and by 8.00pm they were forced to retire until mounting another attempt at 3.50am the next morning which also failed. He remained on the Somme until mid-May when the Battalion was moved round from one sector to another but not taking the line. At 1.00am on Thursday 11th July he led a raid; they moved forward from *'Kingsway'* and took the first objective quickly and within fourteen minutes the second was reached. Thirty were killed in hand-to-hand fighting, many dug-outs were bombed and a prisoner taken. Cyril was mortally wounded in the action and was awarded the Military Cross, posthumously, for his bravery.

SECOND LIEUTENANT HAROLD EDWIN HIPPISLEY

1st Battalion Gloucestershire Regiment

Died on Friday 23rd October 1914, aged 24

Commemorated on Panel 22.

Harold Hippisley

Harold was born at Wells on Wednesday 3rd September 1890, in Wells, Somerset, younger son of William John and Mary Hippisley of Northam House, Wells, Somerset. He was educated at King's School, Bruton, Somerset, where he was a good all round sportsman, Captain of both Cricket and Football. Harold passed the London University Matriculation Exam, and attended the Royal Agricultural College, Cirencester where he won the Gold Medal for East Management and Forestry. He was also their Captain of Cricket and Hockey and Captain in the OTC. He was a Fellow of the Institute of Surveyors. Harold played cricket for Somerset County Cricket Club from 1909 to 1913 and was capped for England. On Tuesday 4th August 1914 Harold married Ivy Gwendoline (née Hooper).

Harold sailed from Southampton to Le Havre, on board the *SS Gloucester Castle*, on Wednesday 12th August. He, with the Battalion, were sent to Rouen and from there to Le Nouvion, a long a tiring train journey. They marched to Mons, the Battalion Diary recording: *"The Gloucesters are pretty strong, but the whole position is very extended and not at all ideal for the defence (not half so good as the line we were on last evening)."*

The order to retire was given and after marching two hundred miles he arrived in Rozoy-en-Brie on Saturday 5th September when the order to advance on the enemy came through. The next day the march continued eastward passing the Marne and onto the Aisne which they reached on Monday 14th. Here Harold organised his platoon and dug in; they were to remain in the cold sodden trenches on the Chemin des Dames until Friday 16th October when the Battalion was withdrawn to move north.

Harold arrived in Poperinghe on Tuesday 20th and was given a period of rest. The next morning, at 1.45am, he marched via Elverdinghe to the Pilkem Ridge ready to attack Langemarck.

On Friday 23rd October, at 2.30am, under Captain Robert Rising (who died on Saturday 7th November and is buried in Zillebeke Churchyard) the Battalion went to Langemarck with Harold commanding No 3 platoon. At 9.00am the Germans started their advance under the cover of smoke from their artillery fire, reaching within one hundred yards of the British line. Every advance was repulsed but in the action Harold was killed, shot in the middle of the forehead at about 10.30am — all the officers and more than fifty per cent of the men were killed or wounded.

Captain Rising

"He was attended by his servant, Private Brown, who was under the impression that if he kept the brain from oozing out of the hole he would be alright. After a time he was convinced that the wound was fatal."

Harold was killed at the same time as Lieutenant William Yalland who is commemorated on the Menin Gate, see below.

Lieutenant Yalland

13711 Private Albert Hives

3rd Battalion Royal Fusiliers

Died on Monday 26th April 1915, aged 16

Commemorated on Panel 6.

Albert was born in Dalston, son of Mrs M A Southam, of 14 Alexandra Road, Heeley, Sheffield.

Albert enlisted in Stratford and was sent for training before leaving for the front, joining the Battalion with a draft. He was in the front line when the Germans launched the first gas attack on Thursday 22nd April 1915 and saw its horrific consequences. Terrible for anyone but one can only imagine what such a young, and relatively innocent, mind could conceive and comprehend. Another gas attack was launched on Saturday 24th whilst he was in the line at Gravenstafel which was followed by a major attack. The German shelling was fierce and they were able to advance around to the left rear of the Battalion and enfilade them. During the attack Albert was killed, one of three hundred and sixty three who were killed, wounded or listed as missing in the battle.

Second Lieutenant Herbert Edward Hobbs

2nd Battalion Northumberland Fusiliers

Died on Tuesday 25th May 1915, aged 21

Commemorated on Panel 12.

Herbert Hobbs

Herbert was born at Merton Park, Surrey, on Friday 9th November 1894, eldest son of Mr and Mrs Herbert Hobbs, of Riding Mill, Northumberland. He was educated at Malvern College from 1910 to 1913, and went up to Keble College, Oxford, where he was studying to enter Holy Orders. Herbert was a long-distance runner, winning the mile race for Keble.

Herbert volunteered at the outbreak of war and he was one of the first to receive a temporary commission, undertaking a month's training at Churn. He transferred to the Northumberlands and continued training, being promoted Lieutenant in November. He attended the Staff College at Camberley and was gazetted to the Regular Army and went out to Flanders on Sunday 2nd May 1915. After only three weeks he was killed in action at Hooge during an attack on Wittepoort Farm which was staunchly held by German machine-gunners. An attack was planned and executed successfully and the Farm was taken. From there they moved forward towards the *'Cambridge Road'* during which advance Herbert was killed.

Lieutenant Alwyne Chadwick Hobson

2nd Life Guards

Died on Thursday 13th May 1915

Commemorated on Panel 3.

Alwyne Hobson

Alwyne was the son of Mr and Mrs Hobson. He was educated at Eton College as a member of Mr Ernest Lee Churchill's House where he was a member of Upper Boats. He went up to Magdalen College, Oxford, in 1911 and rowed for their VIII in Ladies, 1912.

He was gazetted on 26th August 1914 and was sent for training. On Wednesday 7th October Alwyne embarked from Southampton landing the next day in Zeebrugge. Antwerp was in the process of being evacuated and General Joffre had wired Field Marshal Lord Kitchener: *"Important forces of German cavalry are at present moment in the neighbourhood of Ypres to Menin, in a somewhat difficult situation.*

Pray inform General Rawlinson that it would be highly advantageous if he could send light detachments to operate against their communications. Such action would have the result of clearing the district towards which the Belgian Army is to retreat."

Field Marshal Kitchener, Generals Joffre and Rawlinson and Field Marshal French

The Household Cavalry waited for instructions that finally arrived when Field Marshal Sir John French sent a message to General Sir Henry Rawlinson: *"… you should try and concentrate Belgians further west as soon as possible. I understand you will to-morrow hold a position on the Lys between Ghent and Courtrai. If you can retain this position without much trouble, do so as long as possible, but do not get involved in a big fight. If pressed, retire slowly on the line of Dunkirk and St. Omer. You will then be able to join me at St. Omer, where Third Army Corps will complete detraining on October 13th. If, however, you can hold your position on the Lys without incurring much risk or loss, the Second Army Corps or Cavalry will connect up with you at or near Courtrai by October 14th at latest. Let me hear at once what you can do."*

The Household Cavalry were sent to Brugge where the

next day, Saturday 10th, they were ordered to march south through Lichtervelde where they bivouacked and arrived on the Salient on Tuesday 13th. The next morning he was in Ypres town square when at 10.00am a Taube flew low and was shot down by rifle and Maxim fire —.the damaged machine was towed into the town together with the captured pilot and observer. One of his fellow officers expressed the frustration of many of his colleagues: *"So far, the war has not presented itself in all its grim reality. We have only heard the rumbling of the guns smashing at Antwerp, or smacking the Bosche on the Aisne. The first Uhlan captured and the first scouting cyclist scotched have been objects of curiosity, and perhaps the only thing realized is the importance of the map-reading, which in barracks seemed so boresome."* They were soon out along the Menin Road where on Monday 26th he took the line at Zandvoorde. On Friday 30th General Max von Fabeck directed two hundred and sixty heavy guns on their lines from 6.45am to 8.00am and this was followed by an attack where they were overwhelmed by superior numbers and forced to retire. Despite the odds against them they held the line and the attack subsided. At 3.00pm on Friday 6th November he was called forward as the French came under pressure and abandoned their line — a mile of front — and fell back from the Comines Canal to Zillebeke. He arrived at Zwarteleen and was deployed on the left of the line. The professionalism, enthusiasm and courage of the Household Cavalry rallied the demoralised French. They deployed all their men, including cooks and camp followers, and rushed forward to support the line. Major Hugh Dawnay led the 2nd Life Guards forward and as they moved forward Captain Arthur O'Neill was killed (he is commemorated on the Menin Gate, see below). The fire against them increased and Major Dawnay took them for cover in a shallow trench in a garden where he too was killed (he is buried in Harlebeke New British Cemetery). The line was held and late that night Alwyne was relieved to bivouac half a mile south of the village. After a further tour to the front he was relieved to the aptly named *'Mud Farm'*. He continued in and out of the line until January 1915 when he was sent for training and billets in Lynde. On Wednesday 27th January the Household Cavalry were inspected by the Commander-in-Chief, Field Marshal Sir John French. On Wednesday 3rd February Alwyne returned to the front line, relieving the French where they found the trenches in terribly poor condition. Captain Hon E H Wyndham wrote: *"A remarkable feature of the position due to the fact that the trenches were originally part of the German line, was an old communication trench, running from the centre of the line, straight into the German lines. At night small parties of the enemy were able to creep up this to within a few yards of our position and cut wire. It was only when pistols and flares were issued out, on Feb. 6th, that this trouble could be satisfactorily dealt with."*

General von Fabeck

Captain Dawnay

Captain O'Neill

Alwyne was relieved to Ypres on Friday 19th where they came under sustained artillery fire. He remained on tours of duty until being sent to northern France for the Battle of Neuve-Chapelle in March which was followed by further training near Merville before returning to the Salient.

Alwyne was in camp at Vlamertinghe from where he took a tour of duty before returning for his last period of rest back in the camp. At 8.30pm on Wednesday 12th May he marched through Ypres, now in ruins, through the Menin Gate, along the Menin Road to take the line between Verlorenhoek and Hooge. It was ominously quiet until 3.30am the next morning when the German artillery started to shell the line; at 4.00am a barrage was laid down on their line that lasted for three hours. At 7.00am the German infantry advanced in superior numbers on his line; at 8.30am the line was reorganised and straightened. The British artillery were not able to put up much of a show as they were very low on ammunition: one 'well directed' shell at a time was about as much support they provided. At 2.30pm Alwyne gave the order: *"Fix bayonets and dry your butts"* and Colonel Lord Tweedmouth ordered the advance. As they moved forward, Alwyne was killed.

The Household Cavalry Memorial was erected on the slopes over Zandvoorde.

LIEUTENANT JOHN COLLINSON HOBSON

1st/6th Company Machine Gun Corps (Infantry)
formerly 12th Battalion Royal Scots

Died on Tuesday 31st July 1917, aged 23
Commemorated on Panel 56.

John was the son of Thomas Frederick and Mary Innes Hobson, of Julianstow, Headington Hill, Oxford. He was educated at Westminster School as a member of Grants from 1907 to 1912. He went up to Christ Church, Oxford, as a scholar in 1912. John was a Liveryman of the Worshipful Company of Skinners and was a British poet: *'Poems'* (Blackwell, Oxford 1920).

At the outbreak of war John volunteered and was commissioned, leaving for France in May 1915 with the Royal Scots. He was sent for training before taking the line for the first time.

After seeing considerable service in both Flanders and France John joined the Machine Gun Corps. He trained with his men in July 1917 for the forthcoming offensive and was killed in action during the Battle of Pilkem on the opening day of The Third Battle of Ypres.
In St Peter's Church, Drayton, Oxfordshire, a stone tablet was placed in his memory with the inscription: *"In proud and loving memory of John Collinson Hobson, Scholar of Christ Church Oxford, Lieut. Machine Gun Corps, formerly Royal Scots killed in Battle near St. Julien, Belgium, on July 31st 1917, aged 23. Soldier by fate."*

Lieutenant
Andrew Buckland Hodge

3rd Battalion Leinster Regiment
Died on Tuesday 31st July 1917, aged 24
Commemorated on Panel 44.

Andrew was born on Wednesday 7th September 1892, son of Reverend John Mackey Hodge, MA, Vicar of St Luke's, Plymouth, and Jenny Hodge. He was educated at Plymouth College and went up to Exeter College, Oxford, in 1911, with the Dyke Exhibition, Dean Boyd Exhibition, and Cholmondeley Exhibition, graduating with Honours in Moderations.
Andrew was studying for 'Greats' and he wished to join the Indian Civil Service. He joined the OTC and was gazetted on Tuesday 26th January 1915, promoted Lieutenant in October. He was killed at *'Shrewsbury Forest'*, Zillebeke and buried where he fell.
His Colonel wrote: *"He was leading his company in front of our attack. He was a fine officer, and in common with a number of his comrades, he has died a fine death. The battalion has suffered severely, but the individual acts of so many gallant leaders have left an impression which never can die. Your brother fell in the hour of victory and died soon after he got his mortal wound."*

Second Lieutenant
Henry Burden Hodges

2nd Battalion King's Own Yorkshire Light Infantry
Died on Sunday 18th April 1915, aged 19
Commemorated on Panel 47.

Henry Hodges

Henry was born in Newtownreda, Belfast, on Wednesday 13th November 1895, the youngest son of John Frederick William Hodges, JP, and Mary Hodges, of Glenravel House, Glenravel, Ballymena, County Antrim. He was educated at Sherborne School from 1910 to 1914 where he was a member of the XV, a good golfer, swimmer (gaining his life saving certificate) and won the Public Schools Lightweight Boxing Championship. Henry's sporting interests including golf, football, and swimming winning several life-saving medals.
At the outbreak of war Henry enlisted in the King's Own Yorkshire Light Infantry and passed into RMC Sandhurst on Wednesday 23rd December 1914. In March 1915 he was gazetted and went to France on Saturday 6th. At 10.00am on Saturday 17th April Henry was sent from Reninghelst to assist in the attack on Hill 60. They formed up at *'Larch Wood'* and the order to attack was given. As they advanced up the Hill their route was not made any easier as every trench was filled with dead Germans and the badly wounded. The Germans were driven off the Hill. At dawn on Sunday 18th the Germans opened up a counter-barrage and several successful counter-attacks. During the attack to regain lost ground Henry was killed.
His Colonel wrote: *"... gallantly leading his men in a charge against the Germans."*

9419 Corporal
John William Hodges, DCM

2nd Battalion Oxford and Bucks Light Infantry
Died on Wednesday 21st October 1914, aged 21
Commemorated on Panel 39.

Citation for the Distinguished Conduct Medal, London Gazette, Thursday 17th December 1914:
"For gallant conduct and very good work during the attack on 21st October."

John was born in Southwell, Nottinghamshire, son of Frederick and Mary Annie Hodges, of 11 Livingstone Street, Red Hill, Worcester, where he was living when he volunteered in Birmingham.
John went out with the BEF at the outbreak of war and was sent to Mons. During the Battle of Mons he came under artillery fire prior to being ordered to retire that turned into The Retreat. Orders were received on Sunday 5th September 1914 to turn and attack the enemy. The Battalion recrossed the Marne and onward to the Aisne where they engaged the Germans on Saturday 12th and captured more than hundred prisoners. He continued to serve on Aisne until early October when he transferred to Flanders. The Battalion was sent into the line at Langemarck where they mounted an attack on Wednesday 21st October; the German lines were more than three hundred yards in front of them. All objectives were taken and very heavy casualties were sustained by the Germans. The 2nd Battalion lost over two hundred including John who was awarded the Distinguished Conduct Medal posthumously for his action that day.

27349 Private William Benjamin Hodges

15th Battalion Canadian Infantry
(Central Ontario Regiment)
Died on Saturday 24th April 1915, aged 20
Commemorated on Panel 24.

William was born at home on Monday 24th May 1894, son of Ephraim Alphæus and Myra Jane Hodges, of Hatley, Quebec. He was educated at the local Model School. William was a farmer and served for five years in the 26th Dragoons (Militia).
William volunteered at Valcartier on Thursday 20th August 1914; his attestation papers describe him as a Wesleyan, 5ft 5in tall, with a 37in chest, a light complexion, blue eyes and fair hair.
William went immediately into training then he sailed from Quebec on the *RMS Megantic* and arrived in Plymouth on Thursday 14th October 1914. He entrained for Patney from where they marched into camp on Salisbury Plain close to Stonehenge. They had a series of inspections, reviews and visits: on Saturday 27th Field Marshal Lord Roberts, VC, reviewed the Battalion; shortly afterwards by HM King George V and HM Queen Mary, accompanied by Field Marshals Lord Kitchener and Lord Roberts; and on Thursday 19th November Rudyard Kipling visited the Battalion. Over Christmas and New Year the Battalion was given a holiday and all men with relations in England received a free travel pass if they wanted it. In early February 1915 HM The King and Field Marshal Lord Kitchener visited them prior to their departure for St Nazaire. They entrained on a long winding route to Hazebrouck, from where they marched to Caëstre and undertook further training. They left on Tuesday 23rd February via Flêtre where, *en route*, General Alderson inspected them near the village and General Sir Horace Smith-Dorrien greeted them, then in the village General William Pulteney and General Turner, VC, met them! Their first tour of duty took place on Thursday 25th.

Generals Alderson, Smith-Dorrien, Pulteney and Turner

On Wednesday 3rd March they arrived in Sailly where they were billeted, going into the line at La Cardonnerie Farm, Fromelles on Saturday 6th. On Monday 8th he came under heavy shell fire with the German trenches only four hundred yards in front of them. The British and Canadian artillery laid down an immense barrage in preparation for the Battle of Neuve-Chapelle. William was sent forward and a report came through to Headquarters: *"They have carried the first line of trenches easily ... they are going after the second line of trenches right away."* At 10.30am the second line was taken and onward to the third line which was taken in the afternoon. That night William returned to his billets and the next day he went to Sailly for a hot bath and new clothes. After a further tour of duty they were sent to billets in Estaires. On Wednesday 7th April he was marched to Cassel where three days later he paraded for an inspection by General Sir Horace Smith-Dorrien. On 15th he marched to Beauvoorde on the French-Belgian border where he was billeted overnight before marching to Abeele from where a fleet of London buses took them to Poperinghe. William marched along the cobbled road to Ypres and was billeted in the town where he rested for four days. They heard the mines blown on Hill 60. During the evening of Tuesday 20th they took the line near St Julien. Early in the morning on Thursday 22nd the Germans launched gas against the French lines and the yellow-green mist was clear to see. Shortly afterwards dying Turcos passed them in agony. St Julien came under very heavy shell fire that intensified during the night. William was ordered to counter-attack at the point of the bayonet. The Germans launched a heavy artillery and gas attack on their lines, followed by intense machine-gun and rifle fire, during which William was killed and his brother, Ray, mortally wounded.
His brother, Private Ray Hodges, died on Tuesday 27th April 1915 and is buried in Bailleul Communal Cemetery Extension (Nord).

12604 Serjeant James Hartley Hodgkinson

2nd Battalion King's Own Yorkshire Light Infantry
Died on Friday 7th May 1915, aged 43
Commemorated on Panel 47.

James was born in Sheffield on Saturday 27th May 1871, son of James and Hannah Hodgkinson. He was educated locally and was then employed as a boiler founder. He was married to Ada Annie Hodgkinson (who remarried a Mr Walsh), of 27 Court, 5 House, Pond Street, Sheffield, and they had three children.
James volunteered at the outbreak of war and enlisted on Tuesday 18th August 1914. He went out to France and onward to Belgium. He was present at the capture of Hill 60 and for his leadership and bravery was promoted Serjeant. On Tuesday 4th May James was in Ouderdom and the Commander in Chief, Field Marshal Sir John French, inspected them and took the opportunity of addressing the men, thanking and congratulating all those responsible for the capture of

Hill 60. He had hardly finished the speech when the Germans launched a massive attack on Hill 60 using poison gas and recaptured it. On Thursday 7th May the counter-attack commenced at 2.30am under the command of Lieutenant Colonel Withycombe. The Germans defended their positions tenaciously and during the fierce fighting James was killed.
A friend wrote: *"He died a brave soldier. You have the consolation of knowing that your husband was a man who did his duty to the last, and was not afraid to meet death."*

Captain Michael Reginald Kirkman Hodgson

2nd Battalion attached 4th Battalion Royal Fusiliers
Died on Wednesday 17th March 1915, aged 35
Commemorated on Panel 8.

Michael Hodgson

Michael was born at 7 Charles Street, Berkeley Square, London, on Friday 26th September 1879, second son of Robert Kirkman Hodgson, JP, DL, and Lady Honora Janet Hodgson, of 13 Eaton Terrace, London SW1, grandson of Richard, 9th Earl of Cork and Orrery, KP, and Kirkman Daniel Hodgson, MP. Michael was educated at Eton College from 1893 to 1896 as a member of Sir Walter Durnford's House and passed into RMC Sandhurst.
Michael was gazetted in October 1899, promoted to Lieutenant in September 1900 and Captain in May 1907.
Michael served in the South African War, where he was Mentioned in Despatches on Tuesday 29th July 1902, and received the Queen's Medal with five clasps and the King's Medal with two clasps. He served in India, received the Indian Durbar Medal and was ADC to Lord Carmichael, Governor General of Bengal in 1912.
At the outbreak of war Michael went out with the BEF, transferring to the Yorkshire Light Infantry which he temporarily commanded in October 1914. He returned to his own regiment joining them in the field in the unpleasant southern sector of the Salient with their billets in Ouderdom, a muddy camp that was not much better than the front line. He served in the sector until Monday 8th March 1915 when he was relieved. The next tour of duty was at Rue des Berceaux where they arrived during the early hours of Saturday 13th. Shortly before the end of their tour of duty he was killed.
Michael was Mentioned in Despatches, gazetted on Monday 31st May 1915.
In All Saints Church, Barton Stacey, Hampshire, a bronze tablet was placed in his memory with the inscription: *"To the glory of God and in loving memory of their brothers, Michael and Maurice Hodgson. Killed in action March 1915. This panelling is dedicated by J.K.H., P.K.H., D.K.H., C.E.N. Nov. 1916."*
His brother, Captain Maurice Hodgson, died on Saturday 13th March 1915 and is buried in Estaires Communal Cemetery and Extension.

932 Corporal Albert George William Hogg

1st/12th Battalion London Regiment (The Rangers)
Died on Sunday 21st February 1915, aged 27
Commemorated on Panel 54.

Albert Hogg

Albert was born on Tuesday 3rd January 1888, only son of George and Julia Hogg of 11 Cornwall Gardens, Willesden Green, London. He was educated at Brondesbury College and the Polytechnic in Regent Street.
In 1909 Albert joined the Rangers and became secretary of the Polytechnic Company: he retired in 1913.
Albert embarked at Southampton on Christmas Eve 1914 for Le Havre from where the Rangers marched to camp for four days before entraining for St Omer. The Battalion was billeted in Blendecques and for the next month undertook training. On Monday 8th February Albert marched from Ouderdom to the Cavalry Barracks at Ypres. He went into the line where they remained for two weeks. Albert was killed shortly before they were withdrawn from the line and returned to Ouderdom; he was buried in a small cemetery near where he died.
Lieutenant G Rickett wrote: *"As an officer of the Polytechnic Company of the Rangers I am writing to you of some incidents that took place in the fighting of 20 and 21 Feb. We were ordered to go up to some very exposed trenches at dusk and remain until just before daybreak. We succeeded in taking up our position and remained all night under a fairly heavy fire, but managed all right and got away quite safely to our dug-outs in the rear just before dawn. We stayed in those dug-outs all day and again at dusk took up our position at the trench. We were relieved by another battn. during the night, and I regret to say our second attempt was not so successful as the first, for we had several casualties. Amongst those killed I grieve to say was your son and my friend. He was killed in action, doing his duty, and I am thankful to say his death was instantaneous."*

Second Lieutenant Gilbert Culcheth Holcroft

2nd Battalion Durham Light Infantry

Died on Monday 9th August 1915, aged 20

Commemorated on Addenda Panel 57.

Gilbert Holcroft's family coat of arms

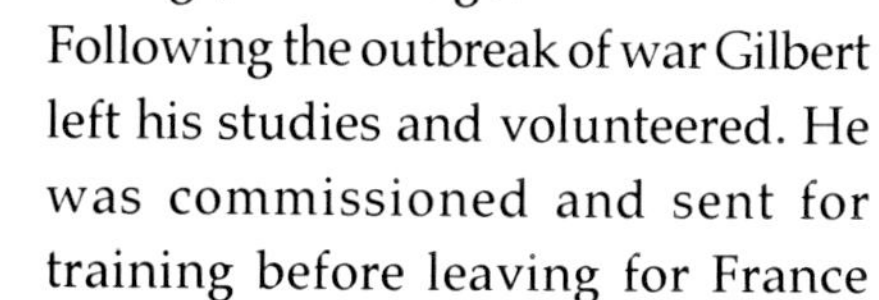

Gilbert was born on Tuesday 23rd October 1894, eldest son of Sir George Harry Holcroft, Baronet, MA, JP, Lord of the Manor of Berrington and Lady Anne Gertrude (née Coombs), of Easton Mascott, Berrington, Salop. He was educated at Radley College from 1909 to 1913 and went up to Queen's College, Cambridge.

Following the outbreak of war Gilbert left his studies and volunteered. He was commissioned and sent for training before leaving for France where he joined the Battalion in the field. The Battalion had arrived at Potijze from the battlefields around Armentières on Monday 24th May 1915. Gilbert undertook the usual series of tours of duty in the front line without being involved in any major action. On Friday 30th July the Germans launched a massive attack on Hooge using '*Flammenwerfer*' (flame throwers or 'liquid fire') inflicting heavy casualties and putting intense pressure on the line. A week later Gilbert led his men along the difficult route from Potijze to Hooge where they prepared to mount a major counter-attack. At 2.15am on Monday 9th Gilbert assembled his men; at 2.55am the preliminary barrage opened up and half an hour later he took his men over the top. With bayonets fixed they charged the German lines — at the end of battle more than five hundred Germans lay dead, most of them bayoneted. During the attack Gilbert was killed but his body was not recovered.

In All Saints Church, Berrington, Salop, his parents restored and rehung the bells in his memory. A bronze plaque commemorates the event with the inscription: *"To the glory of God and in loving memory of Gilbert Culcheth Holcroft, 2nd Lieutenant 2nd Batt. Durham Light Infantry, who fell in action at Hooge August 9th 1915. Eldest son of Sir Harry Holcroft, Bart., and Lady Holcroft of Eaton Mascott Hall in this parish by whom these bells were restored and rehung. The Dedication Service by The Lord Bishop of Hereford took place on Oct. 6th 1928."*

In St Mary's Church, Oldswinford, West Midlands, a bronze plaque was placed in his memory with the inscription: *"To the glory of God & in loving memory of Second Lieutenant Gilbert Culcheth Holcroft, Second Battalion Durham Light Infantry, killed in action whilst gallantly heading his men in the attack which succeeded in capturing the Hooge Ridge, Flanders on August 9th 1915. Born October 23rd 1894, eldest son of George Harry and Anne Gertrude Holcroft of The Grange in this parish. Be thou faithful unto death & I will give thee a crown of life. Pro Patria."*

51225 Private Frank Davenport Holland

Princess Patricia's Canadian Light Infantry (Eastern Ontario Regiment)

Died on Tuesday 4th May 1915, aged 19

Commemorated on Panel 10.

Frank Holland

Frank was born in Great Warford, Cheshire, on Friday 13th September 1895, son of Frank Bernard and Ada Holland, of 1284 Monterey Avenue, Oak, Bay, Victoria, British Columbia. He was educated locally and went out to Canada in October 1911 where he joined the Bank of British North America, in Prince Rupert, British Columbia. He was a member of Earl Grey's Own Rifles in November 1911 and was an excellent shot being in the winning team that won the Corporation Cup and the Northern British Columbia Championship in 1913.

At the outbreak of war Frank volunteered and enlisted. On Sunday 23rd August 1914 Field Marshal HRH The Duke of Connaught addressed the newly formed regiment: *"It gives me great pleasure to attend the first church parade that has been held by the regiment since its formation a week ago. I congratulate you upon its very creditable appearance, reflecting as it does the greatest credit on all ranks, and especially on the staff, upon whom so heavy a demand has been made. The attendance of the Duchess and myself to-day has given us an opportunity of accompanying our daughter on the occasion of the presentation by her to you of a camp colour which she has worked with her own hands. The Duchess and I are proud of having been asked by Major Hamilton Gault, to whose patriotism the inception of the regiment is due, to allow the regiment to be named after the Princess Patricia. I feel confident that you, the men of the regiment, representing every part of Canada as you do, many of whom are imbued with the great traditions of the army, in which you have formerly served, and who in every clime and in very part of the world have nobly done your duty toward your Sovereign and your country, will never forget the watchword of every true soldier — duty, discipline and mercy."*

Frank left for England with the First Canadian Contingent, on Sunday 27th September 1914

SS Royal George

embarking on *SS Royal George*. He arrived in Plymouth on Thursday 15th October. After training on Salisbury Plain and at Winchester, he was inspected by HM King George V and Field Marshal Lord Kitchener on Wednesday 16th December who wished them well for their overseas adventure. Four days later Frank marched to Southampton and embarked on *SS Cardiganshire* for Le Havre. After a night in camp the Battalion entrained for Arques and arrived in Blaringhem on Christmas Eve, his home for the next two weeks. One of the men wrote: *"It was getting on in December before we got our orders to go to the front. We gaily marched out of Winchester to Southampton. We managed that easily enough, although it was our first march with full ammunition pouches, every man receiving 120 rounds before starting. We crossed at night, and disembarked on the following afternoon. The French folk were wildly enthusiastic as we marched off to the cam seven miles off. On arrival we found there was no grub for us, and it was a sad and weary bunch that turned in for the night. Next day we marched down to the station and embarked in cattle cars — forty men in each car. If I had a grudge against a bunch of fellows, I think if I could put them, forty in a car, and haul them around for a few days and nights, with no stop longer than five minutes, and feed them twice daily on a couple of hard tack biscuits and a chunk of bully beef, I would feel my grudge was wiped out. At any rate, it was a most uncomfortable trip. Forty men cannot possibly lie down in one car. They can't even sit in comfort. We just squatted huddled up, and tried to forget cramp and such troubles. The second night we arrived at our jumping-off place, not far from —, and after some delay started off in the dark for our billets. We had about ten miles to go, and we were all about baked by the time we got there. Our billets were the large farmhouses of a fairly decent village, and there we made ourselves tolerably comfortable in the straw and hay in the various barns and stables."*

One of the Sergeants wrote of Christmas Day: *"At last we are where we wanted to be, and are contented with our little lot. We had a fairly good Christmas. Dinner consisted of bully beef and biscuits and whatever we could forage. My friend Sergeant — and myself did not do so bad, as we had one carrot, half a turnip, two leeks, one onion, two Oxo cubes, and 12ozs. of bully beef, with three hard biscuits, all mixed up and boiled in a bully beef tin. It sure made a tasty dinner. To-day we had our Christmas pudding, ½ lb. a man, 1-lb. tin of jam between four men, and a small bottle of wine also between four men. We are in good spirits, and within hearing distance of the big guns."* Their first main duty was to dig a series of trenches that took ten days of their time. On New Year's Day Field Marshal Sir John French visited them and wished them well for their first tour of duty in the line. On Tuesday 5th January 1915 Frank was marched to Méteren from where the next day he marched across the border to Dickebusch and immediately into the line to two days. Until late March Frank was on tours of duty around St Eloi, one of the worst places to be in the line. It was totally water-logged, the trenches regularly collapsed, as they were mainly held together by decomposing bodies. Communication trenches were often non-existent and movement could often only be made at night. A Corporal wrote on an incident: *"On the last day of February, just before dawn, our company was ordered to attempt to force one of the German trenches. As we climbed over the parapet the enemy, by means of their magnesium flares, spotted us, and immediately opened up on us a withering machine-gun fire.*

We lost men — some of my best friends and comrades — but on we kept plodding through a quagmire of mud, and when we jumped over the enemy's parapet into their trench we had to tramp over dead men. The rest of the Huns, afraid of the cold steel, fled screaming like children or went down on their knees and begged for mercy. This, in true British fashion, was granted them."

On Wednesday 24th March he was moved to Poperinghe and into reserve where Generals Sir Herbert Plumer and Sir Horace Smith-Dorrien inspected them on two consecutive days.

On Monday 5th April Frank paraded and started to march along the cobbled road connecting Poperinghe with Ypres. They passed through Vlamertinghe receiving a series of cheers from the troops in camps surrounding the village. He was billeted in Ypres before a two day tour of duty at Bellewaarde then moved for a further two days at Polygon Wood. On Saturday they marched to Vlamertinghe for rest that was disturbed the next day when a Zeppelin flew overhead and bombed the camp. General Sir Herbert Plumer visited them again on Tuesday 13th and was shown the damage caused by the Zeppelin. On Wednesday 14th Frank went back to Polygon Wood for three days, followed by three day in reserve at Ypres. On Tuesday 20th they returned to their line at Polygon Wood where he remained for eight days. After two days the Germans launched their gas attack to their left and all relief was postponed. Whilst the Germans were concentrating their fire on the St Julien sector, there was no let up at Polygon Wood. During the tour of duty The Pats suffered more than eighty casualties. At 3.00am on Tuesday 4th May Frank was sent to new, but incomplete, trenches on the Bellewaarde Ridge. They were subjected to a large barrage that was followed up by an attack. Frank was killed whilst helping a wounded comrade.

His comrades wrote: *"He was beloved by us all, and his behaviour when in action proved the he was both a son and a soldier to be proud of."*

A memorial was placed in his memory in St Andrew's Church, Prince Rupert.

2510 Company Serjeant Major Walter Frederick Hollis, DCM

1st/6th Battalion London Regiment
(City of London Rifles)
Died on Sunday 22nd October 1916, aged 21
Commemorated on Panel 54.

Citation for the Distinguished Conduct Medal, London Gazette, Tuesday 14th November 1916:

"For conspicuously gallantry in action. He assisted his officer in maintaining control of his men under very difficult circumstances, displaying a fine example to his men. Later he crossed the open under heavy fire to obtain connection with another unit, showing great courage."

Walter was the son of George Henry and Elizabeth Hollis, of 37 Campbell Road, Maidstone, Kent.
Walter enlisted in London. Mobilisation commenced and training of recruits continued until Wednesday 17th March 1915 when the Battalion entrained for Southampton. At 7.00pm they embarked on *SS Marguerite* and all the men sang *'Eternal Father, strong to save'* as the ship left the port. They arrived in Le Havre at dawn the next morning and marched to *'Camp No 6'* where they spent a bitter night out in tents without any bedding. Everyone was pleased to leave the camp and entrained for Berguette which took twenty hours and after a nine mile march they arrived in their billets at Raimbert. The Battalion settled in and were inspected the next day by Field Marshal Sir John French. On Wednesday 24th they marched along the cobbled roads to Béthune, a further nine miles, to billets in the orphanage. The officers' horses were stabled with those of the 2nd Battalion Staffordshires and 1st Battalion King's Royal Rifle Corps, one of the grooms wrote: *"Any one of them knew more about a quick and smart turn-out that all our Cockney amateur 'ostlers put together. Our accent amused them, and theirs amused us. In a few days they made old soldiers of us, taught us how to make wisps and pull and make swish tails for each of our horses; they cured the cracks and sore heels from which our horses had suffered from the heel-pegs at Le Havre. It was in this stable that Lieut. Neely saw the C.O.'s turn-out of the 1st K.R.R.C. He liked the effect of the Martingale, and before we moved on, Lloyd, the saddler, had plaited a very smart one for 'Nigger', a long-standing cause of amusement to the members of the transport."*
The Battalion was sent into the line attached to the South Staffordshires for practical training and experience at the front and from Thursday 1st April undertook tours of duty.
The Battalion participated at Festubert and whilst in the line, conditions were terrible and QMS Johnson could only deliver some of the rations to the front by wheelbarrow: *"Many wondered if it worse in the line than on the road to headquarters. Some of the 'Old Timers' in Béthune had said it was worse on the roads a mile behind the line than it was at the Breastworks. The Q. M. stores and the horse-lines were at Gorre, and one night, on the return journey, the rain just teemed down. Above the din and crashing of the 18-pounders, could be heard thunder, and the flashes of lightning seemed to light the whole of the convoy. Crash! A shell had burst about twenty yards away — horses were getting out of hand, and mules backed the limber into a ditch. What a night! And what a mix-up! Nobody could see anybody, and yet no damage was done. They were all shouting at the animals to get a move on.*
Batteries of artillery and transports were moving along the rain-sodden, cobbled roads; Canadians and Scottish regiments were straggling along in batches of platoons, or had halted by the roadside, most of them arranging their ground-sheets around their shoulders to resemble a cape. Roars of artillery began to succeed each other faster and faster. Thunder and lightning — what a combination! — the great bombardment becoming more and more intense. In the continuous chain of flashes, the limbers ahead could be seen. The horses were covered with white lather, through sheer fear of the terrible rendings all around. Everything becomes a jumble, and general confusion prevails. Limber-poles could be seen almost perpendicular; horses getting over the traces, and breetchings slipping over their hindquarters. The rear half of a limber in front had skewed into the ditch, waist-deep with mud, by the side of the road.
This was the night of hell prior to the great Battle of Festubert. On, on, ankle-deep in slime and mud, and, after another half-hour's trundling through this heavy going, the transport arrived, half-drowned, at battalion head quarters. Shrapnel was bursting overhead; machine-gun and rifle fire too near to be comfortable; the consistent ping, ping of stray bullets passing all around.
Many had volunteered to act as spare men with the rations and ammunition limbers that night. Some went forward from battalion headquarters to find a fatigue-party. After half an hour's wading through mud and slush, some of our 'boys' were found escorting prisoners through some breastworks.
A little way ahead the combined crashing of 'coalboxes' and the splitting tornado created by the overhead shrapnel, the mournful whizzing and whistling through the air as the fragments sought their final resting place. Ping, ping, ping, ping! Some of the Jerries were firing much too high. Pop-pop-pop-pop-pop-pop-pop! —sometimes a little quicker than others—tss-tss tss-tss, so the bullets would finally gasp, as they buried themselves in the earth around. Crash! A portion of the breastworks sagged! And so on. Through all this, men would duck and dodge, a muck-sweat creeping over everyone. The men in the companies didn't seem to mind much about things, but there was a persistent cry of 'stretcher-bearers'. At length a party from the foremost breastworks arrived and

unloaded the ammunition limbers.
Later, when back in the transport lines at Gorre, one could cast his mind over the events of the night, and determine that from that time on, the claims of the men in the line should always come first."
The Battalion continued to serve in the sector until it moved to Loos in June where they were involved in a number of engagements prior to training for the main battle that would take place in September.
On Friday 24th September the Battalion marched to Les Brebis prior to moving into the assembly position at 3.30am the next morning. Two hours later the British bombardment commenced and the gas was released from its cylinders. At 6.28am the gas was turned off and two minutes later the Battalion 'went over the top' wearing their gas masks. Despite a fierce defence of their position the Germans lost their first and second lines by 8.00am. One of the men wrote: *"The air was still thick with gas and smoke, and splinters, shrapnel, shells, and bullets were flying everywhere, and the hand-to-hand fighting in and above the German trenches provided a terrifying spectacle."* During the afternoon the rain fell with the battlefield becoming a mud-bath. Losses in the Battalion were heavy with many of their dead being buried in North Maroc. Rifleman Luce made a small wood cross and Rifleman Percy Garnsey painted the inscription to mark where many of the dead lay. The cross was taken after the war and installed in St James' Church, Croydon, and subsequently a granite stone replaced it with the inscription: *"In these Rows, H, J, K, and L, are buried without individual identification eighty-seven officers and men of the 6th Battalion London Regiment, who fell on the 25th September, 1915, in the capture of Loos, and whose names are commemorated on the headstone placed round the walls."* On Thursday 30th the Battalion was relieved by the French and they went to billets in Verquin the next day.
On Thursday 4th November the Battalion entrained for Lillers for re-fitting, rest and training for the rest of the month. The Battalion entrained for Nœux-les-Mines on Wednesday 15th December and after marching to Sailly Labourse they retook the line and spent the next six weeks in the sector. After a long period of training they moved to Vimy Ridge and were sent to the trenches near Souchez. Throughout May the Battalion was involved in considerable action; one of the mines blown at the end of April was named *'Mildren Crater'* after the Battalion's Colonel.

Colonel Mildren and the crater named after him

On Wednesday 26th July the Battalion was moved south to participate in the Battle of the Somme. On Tuesday 1st August they were billeted in Nœux and everyone had a coloured identification ribbon sewn onto their jackets: 'A' Company had blue, 'B' green, 'C' red and 'D' yellow. Further training continued at Millencourt until Sunday 20th August when they moved to Franvillers and finally to *'Black Wood'* near Albert. After a further three weeks training they were ordered to Bazentin-le-Grand at 3.20pm on Thursday 14th September. They eventually arrived at *'Worcester Trench'* at 6.30am just as the advance was commencing and as a result the Germans laid down a barrage on their line. Shortly afterwards a tank that had lumbered passed them became stuck in the mud. The tank then opened fire on them: *"A heated altercation between an infuriated company officer and the tank commander immediately followed, as a consequence of which the humiliated and gawky piece of mechanism refused to take any further part in the day's operations, and remained sullenly where it lay, an excellent target, no doubt for the German gunners. Nor was this the only machine that broke down; of the thirty-two employed along the whole of the battle-front, many developed mechanical defects or were 'ditched'."* The Battalion moved forward over a five hundred yard front, Walter being in the third wave, and they came under withering enfilade fire from the *'Cough Drop'*. The subsequent attack on the *'Cough Drop'* was

Butte de Warlencourt ... following its capture

successful with sixty prisoners taken, together with two machine-guns. They continued to attack *'High Wood'* and remained in the line before being sent to billets in Henecourt. For his bravery during the attack Walter was awarded the Distinguished Conduct Medal. After a period of rest the Battalion retook the line at Eaucourt overlooking the Butte de Warlencourt. They remained in the line and engaged the enemy but were not part of any of the main attacks that took place in early October. From the Butte the Battalion was sent to Flanders, arriving in Westoutre in mid-October where they remained for one night before moving to *'Victoria Camp'*. They were ordered to relieve the Australians near Voormezeele. Not long after they arrived two mines were blown close to their lines and during the ensuing action Walter was killed.

12008 Rifleman Harry Hollows

3rd Battalion King's Royal Rifle Corps

Died on Monday 10th May 1915, aged 16

Commemorated on Panel 53.

Harry was born at home, son of Edwin and Helen Hollows, of 486 Blackburn Road, Darwen, Lancashire. He enlisted in Blackburn and went into training before being sent out to France and onward to the Salient. At the end of March 1915 the Battalion was in reserve in billets at Poperinghe. Harry was sent to Polygon Wood in mid-April and undertook a series of tours of duty with billets provided in shell-damaged Ypres. In early May he was sent to Hill 60 where the Battalion came under heavy fire and considerable time was spent in reconstructing the trenches and consolidating their position. On Sunday 9th May the Germans commenced a significant counter-attack and after laying down a barrage they mounted an unsuccessful attack. The Germans attacked again the next day and whilst defending the line, Harry was killed.

Lieutenant Geoffrey Holman

2nd Battalion King's Shropshire Light Infantry

Died on Friday 9th April 1915, aged 22

Commemorated on Panel 47.

Geoffrey was born on Friday 9th December 1892, third son of Mr and Mrs Holman, Wynnstay, Putney Hill, London SW. He was educated at Rose Hill School, Banstead, then in Paris and Berlin, before passing into RMC Sandhurst.

Geoffrey was gazetted in September 1914 and was serving in India when war broke out. His battalion left Bombay on *SS Neuralia*, sailing via the Suez Canal,

Geoffrey Holman

Gibraltar, arriving in Plymouth in November, going to barracks in Winchester. On Sunday 20th December they marched down to Southampton, sailing on *SS Maidan* for Le Havre. They entrained to Aire on Wednesday 23rd and marched to Blaringhem where they remained for ten days spending most of their time digging trenches in pouring rain. On Tuesday 5th January 1915 they marched south to Strazeele and then the next day to Méteren where they were exposed to terrible weather conditions, made worse for the 2nd Battalion who had so recently returned from India. On Saturday 9th they went to Voormezeele. After three days in the line they were taken out to rest and given a hot bath, but many men were suffering with frost bite and other ailments which took them out of the line for some considerable time. Geoffrey spent February in the St Eloi area and was wounded in early March 1915 being invalided from the line. Geoffrey returned to the Battalion and on Monday 5th April left Reninghelst for Polygon Wood, and whilst in the line he was killed by a shell.

590311 Lance Corporal Stephen Robert Holman, DCM

1st/18th Battalion London Regiment (London Irish Rifles)

Died on Saturday 7th April 1917, aged 19

Commemorated on Panel 54.

Citation for the Distinguished Conduct Medal, London Gazette, Saturday 24th June 1916:

"For conspicuous gallantry during a bombing attack by the enemy. He remained the whole time exposed to the enemy's fire, and by his vigorous throwing succeeding in repulsing the enemy from his bombing post."

Stephen was born in Marylebone the son of Mr and Mrs S Holman, of 15 Cassidy Road, Fulham, London.

He enlisted in Chelsea and formerly was a member of the Royal Army Service Corps.

Stephen was serving at Vimy Ridge on Sunday 21st May 1916 when the Germans mounted an intense attack. He remained in France, serving on the Somme throughout 1916 including at Flers, Transloy and the Butte de Warlencourt. Stephen transferred to Flanders and was serving in the line during a tour of duty when he was killed.

Lieutenant
Carleton Colquhoun Holmes

7th Battalion Canadian Infantry
(British Columbia Regiment)

Died on Saturday 24th April 1915, aged 28
Commemorated on Panel 18.

Carleton Holmes

Carleton was born at Shipley, Yorkshire, on Friday 1st July 1887, only son of Adelaide Holmes, of 1502 Jubilee Avenue, Victoria, British Columbia, and the late Arthur Holmes. He was educated at Haileybury from 1900 to 1904 as a member of Hailey and was a member of the OTC.

Carleton joined the Honourable Artillery Company, serving with them for three years until he emigrated to Canada in 1906. In September 1912 he was commissioned Lieutenant to the Victoria Fusiliers and Acting Adjutant. He served with the Militia during the Nanaimo Coal Strike riots.

At the outbreak of war Carleton volunteered at Valcartier and commissioned on Wednesday 23rd September 1914. His attestation papers describe him as 5ft 10in tall, a 38½in chest, fair complexion and brown eyes.

Carleton sailed with the First Canadian Contingent to England, arriving in late September and was sent to *'West Down South Camp'* until Friday 4th December when they transferred to *'Lark Hill Camp'*. Following training he left with his platoon for Amesbury Station on Wednesday 10th February 1915 and entrained for Avonmouth. He embarked on *HMT Cardiganshire* the next day and arrived in St Nazaire on Monday 15th. The Battalion immediately marched to the waiting train that took them to Strazeele where training continued, including practical experience of the front line attached to seasoned troops at Ploegsteert.

Carleton first took the line at La Boutillerie in northern France on Tuesday 2nd March and continued on tours of duty until Friday 26th when he marched to Estaires. The next morning two bombs dropped on the Battalion's transport lines, however, little damage was caused. Training commenced which continued until leaving for billets in Steenvoorde on Monday 5th April. After further training the Battalion was taken by motor bus to Vlamertinghe at 8.00am on Wednesday 14th. After a short rest and a warm meal Carleton marched with his men along the cobbled road to Ypres, through the town, out to St Julien and to the line at Gravenstafel. They came under heavy shellfire during the relief that continued for more than forty-eight hours, with the Battalion losing four killed and ten wounded. The trenches were in poor condition and one of their first tasks was to improve and deepen the line. The 8th Battalion relieved them on Monday 19th and they were sent into reserve at Fortuin. At 5.00pm on Thursday 22nd the Germans launched the first gas attack: at 7.00pm the Battalion was ordered to 'stand to'. At 9.00pm they marched back to Gravenstafel where they remained until 3.00am on Friday 23rd when orders were received to move to St Julien. Their position, near Keerselaere, came under a heavy artillery barrage. From 3.30am on Saturday 24th an intense barrage was laid down along the line prior to the second gas attack at 4.00am. A further barrage was put down at 5.00am that was followed by a German advance at 6.00am which was repulsed. At 6.30am the Germans attacked again, this time with many of their troops dressed in British uniforms, however, the ruse was spotted and again the attack was repulsed. The German bombardment and infantry attacks continued and by 8.30am the right-hand flank was virtually surrounded and wiped out. In the fierce battle Carleton was killed.

Lieutenant
Francis Lermox Holmes

'B' Company, 1st Battalion
South Staffordshire Regiment

Died on Friday 23rd October 1914, aged 27
Commemorated on Panel 35.

Francis Holmes

Francis was born in Stoke, Devonport, on Tuesday 11th October 1887, younger son of Mrs Clara Bernal Harrison (formerly Holmes), of Evesham House, Cheltenham, and the late Major General Ponsonby Ross Holmes (RMLI); he came from a family of Army Officers. He was educated at Cheltenham College from 1901 to 1905 as a member of Southwood House and passed into RMC Sandhurst. Francis was a member of the Public Schools' Club.

Francis was gazetted on Saturday 19th September 1908, and promoted Lieutenant on Wednesday 14th July 1909. He served at Devonport, Gibraltar and in South Africa. At the outbreak of war Francis was ordered home from Pietermaritzburg, South Africa, landing in Southampton on Saturday 19th September 1914. After two weeks in camp in Lyndhurst he returned to Southampton and left for Zeebrugge as Signalling Officer. He arrived on Tuesday 6th October with orders to proceed to Antwerp and assist with its defence. Confusion reigned when they arrived as Antwerp was being evacuated and the Belgian and French armies were retreating towards the coast. They awaited fresh orders and were sent to Ypres,

arriving a week later. Francis was ordered down the Menin Road and took position around Westhoek.
He was killed in action; his Commanding Officer wrote: *"As his Commanding Officer I can truthfully say the Army has lost a fine and promising young officer, who as Signalling Officer and in other capacities, bought credit and honour to his regt. He was killed instantaneously, poor fellow, and had been exposing himself and working hard all through the operations. Capt. Dunlop told me he had been the greatest assistance to him in defending their position and he wished particularly to mention him."*
In the diary of the same officer, he had written: *"Lieut. Holmes was killed this day. He was in command of a half company of B Company and they had been doing excellent work the whole day. He had been looking after and superintending a machine-gun which did very good service. He also had done a lot of very dangerous work in scouting through the wood in front of his section of trenches, and had shown much pluck and coolness."*
Captain Evans wrote: *"On Tuesday and Wednesday, 20 and 21 Oct., the Germans attacked our position in point of the outskirts of Zonnebeke. Lennox was in charge of half a company, and was hit on the Wednesday afternoon by a ricochet."*
Corporal F Barrett wrote: *"On 22nd October 1914, I was working my machine-gun when Mr. Holmes came up and acted as my number two, also my observer, as the Germans were only five hundred yards from us, and he was quite excited, as I was moving them down in hundreds, and we got over that day all right. On the 23rd October he visited me again, and I shifted my position close to when Mr. Holmes was killed about three o'clock. He was in a trench just in front of some cottages — four of them I believe. He was at the back of his trench taking cover at the back of potatoes, bandaging up Private Millar, who had his three fingers blown off. After that he was taking aim at the Germans, and just going to pull the trigger when a bullet hit him straight between the two eyes. ... He never spoke at all: he died instantly. He was carried into some cottages at the back. ... I wish he had lived. I shall never forget him as long as I live."*

1690 Private Gilbert Holt

5th Battalion Australian Infantry, AIF

Died on Thursday 20th September 1917, aged 20
Commemorated on Panel 7.

Gilbert was born in Stratford, Victoria, Australia, son of Thomas Grosvenor Holt and Elizabeth E Holt (née Mitchell). He was educated locally and was employed as a butcher.
Gilbert volunteered on Saturday 29th January 1916 and embarked from Melbourne on *MHAT Ascanius* on Saturday 27th May 1916.
His brother, Private Thomas Holt, died on the same day and is commemorated on the Menin Gate, for their story see below.

HMAT Ascanius

6863 Private Thomas Mitchell Holt

5th Battalion Australian Infantry, AIF

Died on Thursday 20th September 1917, aged 22
Commemorated on Panel 7.

Thomas was born in Stratford, Victoria, Australia, son of Thomas Grosvenor Holt and Elizabeth E Holt (née Mitchell). He was educated locally and was employed as labourer.
Thomas volunteered in March 1916 and embarked for England on board *HMAT Ulysses* on Wednesday 25th October 1916. His brother, Private Gilbert Holt, died on the same day and is commemorated on the Menin Gate, see above.
Gilbert and Thomas sailed to England for training and were sent to France with drafts. Thomas joined Gilbert on the Somme serving at Thilloy. The continued to serve throughout the sector until the end of July. In July they were sent for training at Hondeghem for the first week and at Berquin for five weeks.
On Thursday 13th September they marched to billets in Berthen where they remained for two days before moving to camp at Reninghelst. After three days they moved to Château Segard prior to taking the line at Zillebeke Bund and *'Railway Dugouts'*. They marched in heavy rain to their assembly positions at *'Stirling Castle'*, arriving in the early hours of Thursday 20th. Thankfully the German shelling was relatively light and they arrived safely despite only being able to cover a mile and a quarter an hour. At 3.40am the preliminary barrage opened on the German lines that was the signal for them to move forward and as the barrage lifted they charged the German lines in the southeast corner of *'Glencorse Wood'*. Heavy machine-gun fire from *'Black Watch Corner'* opened on them as the consolidated the position and the front line took heavy casualties including Gilbert and Thomas.

Major Walter Gabriel Home

6th Dragoon Guards (Carabiniers)

Died on Saturday 31st October 1914, aged 41

Commemorated on Panel 5.

Walter was born on Friday 25th October 1872, son of the late Reverend Robert Home and Annie Home (née Swinton). He was married to Helen Gordon Home (née Davidson, she remarried to Mr Cole), of Avondale, Chesterfield Road, Eastbourne.

Walter was gazetted in October 1892 from the Militia, promoted Lieutenant in May 1897, Captain in July 1900, Brevet Major on Friday 22nd August 1902 and Major in November 1905.

Walter served in the South African War where he was an ADC to the Officer Commanding Cavalry Brigade, took part in the Relief of Kimberley, was Mentioned in Despatches on Tuesday 10th September 1901 and Tuesday 29th July 1902, received the Queen's Medal with six clasps and the King's Medal with two clasps.

Walter went out with the BEF at the outbreak of war and served in the Battle of the Aisne where he was Mentioned in Despatches gazetted on Thursday 8th October 1914. He moved to northern France in October and took part in the actions that led him across the border into Belgium. He was defending the southern sector at Messines when the Germans mounted a major offensive against the line and he was mortally wounded in action.

Second Lieutenant Geoffrey Phipps Hornby

3rd Battalion attached 1st Battalion Suffolk Regiment

Died on Saturday 8th May 1915, aged 24

Commemorated on Panel 21.

Geoffrey Hornby

Geoffrey was the son of The Venerable Phipps John Hornby (Archdeacon of Lancaster), and Agnes Eleanor Hornby, of St Michaels-on-Wyre, Garstang, Lancashire.

Admiral Hornby

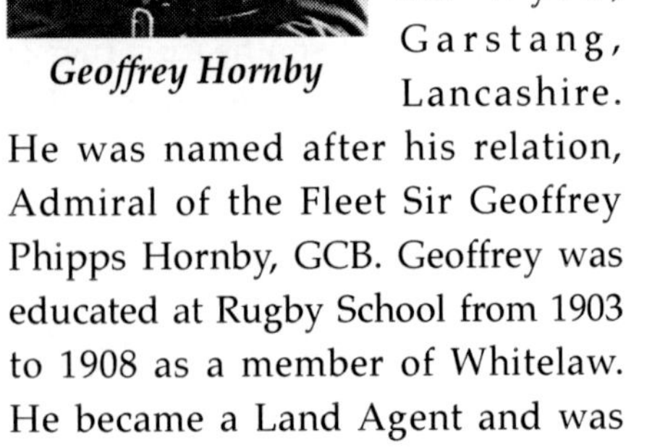

He was named after his relation, Admiral of the Fleet Sir Geoffrey Phipps Hornby, GCB. Geoffrey was educated at Rugby School from 1903 to 1908 as a member of Whitelaw. He became a Land Agent and was working for the War Office at the outbreak of war. Geoffrey volunteered and enlisted in the Suffolk Yeomanry before he was given a commission. In February 1915 he left for France and joined the Battalion in the field. On Monday 12th April 1915 Geoffrey marched from Dranouter to Poperinghe; whilst passing through Westouter they met the men of the 2nd Battalion and time was given for all to stop and meet old friends and family. All the officers were entertained in the Mess and a photograph was taken outside the church. Three days later they marched to camp in Vlamertinghe for two days before taking the line at Zonnebeke. The

... repulsing a German raid

German artillery were particularly active building up to the first gas attack that would take place on Thursday 22nd. During the night of Friday 23rd Geoffrey was sent into reserve between Frezenberg and Verlorenhoek. The next day he organised his men to hastily dig in whilst under heavy fire and in the open. They managed to create trenches four and a half feet in short order. On Wednesday 28th a German aeroplane flew low over their line that was successfully brought down by rifle fire. Finally, on Thursday 6th May, the German artillery slackened and their infantry quietened down. At dawn on Saturday 8th the German attack began again with increased intensity and at 10.00am their advance on the British line commenced. The Regimental History records: *"The din was terrific. The enemy were sending over projectiles of every calibre and description. High-explosive shell crashed in all directions, scattering bricks and timber like chaff before the wind. Huge guns and howitzers roared incessantly, shaking the earth; with the boom of mortars and bombs, make a noise that sounded like an army of riveters at work during some titanic thunderstorm. Amid the roar of battle vile yellow-green poison gas floated like a spectre through the British lines, and before it men reeled back, livid, chocking and blinded. Every engine of war, every invention of the devil, every device of wile of hell seemed to be in action against the Allies. All communication by wire was completely cut off for a distance of two miles behind the line, and getting into touch without anyone was almost an impossibility. The only road up to the Immortal Salient ran through the tow of Ypres itself, which was now in flames, presenting a wonderful spectacle."* The Battalion valiantly held on against the odds but by the end of the day the Battalion had lost over four hundred killed, wounded or missing.

A brother Officer wrote: *"Your son was last seen in the trench unwounded and doing all he possibly could, but I could get no further information."*

... a warm welcome in a billet!

Second Lieutenant Arthur Oscar Hornung

3rd Battalion attached 2nd Battalion Essex Regiment

Died on Tuesday 6th July 1915, aged 20

Commemorated on Panel 39.

Sir Arthur Conan Doyle

Arthur was born on Sunday 24th March 1895, son of Ernest William Hornung and his wife, Constance Amelia Monica (née Doyle). Arthur was Sir Arthur Conan Doyle's nephew and godson. He was educated at Eton College as a member of Mr de Haviland's House, leaving in 1914 and was to go up to King's College, Cambridge when the war broke out and he volunteered.

After training, Arthur was commissioned and sent out to France with a draft where he joined the Battalion in the field. Arthur continued on tours of duty, serving through the fierce battle of April and May 1915 at Ypres and was killed in the severe action of Tuesday 6th July.

Lieutenant Edwin Cecil Leigh Hoskyns

1st Battalion Royal Welch Fusiliers

Died on Tuesday 20th October 1914, aged 24

Commemorated on Panel 22.

Edwin Hoskyns and his family coat of arms

Edwin was born at Iffley, Oxfordshire, on Monday 22nd September 1890, only son of Sir Leigh Hoskyns, 11th Baronet, JP, and High Sherriff of Oxfordshire in 1907, and his wife, Lady Frances Hester Frederica Hoskyns (née Bowles), of Cotefield, Banbury. He was educated at Summer Fields from 1900 to 1903, followed by Eton College as a member of the Reverend Henry Thomas Bowlby's House, leaving in 1908 and passed into RMC Sandhurst. His interests included hunting and polo.

He was gazetted in September 1911, promoted in April 1913.

Edwin was stationed in Malta at the outbreak of war, returning to Southampton on Wednesday 16th September 1914, via Gibraltar, on *SS Ultonia*. They went into camp at Lyndhurst, three days later, they were joined by men from the 3rd Battalion. On Wednesday 7th October 1914 he left for the Ypres Salient. On Monday 19th October at 11.00am the Germans were seen advancing in columns. The only cover they had were shallow slit-trenches as the Germans came ever closer before the Fusiliers opened up with rapid fire. The Germans thought they were using machine-guns! Their artillery recommenced and at 4.00pm the Germans advanced again. *"Owing to dead ground, the enemy were able to get up to within a hundred yards of our trench, but we kept them from leaving the shelter of the wood to our front. Our chief danger lay in the enfilade fire, as our trench turned abruptly across the Broodseinde-Passchendaele road and our left was exposed.*

On our left were numerous cottages, which the Huns occupied and were thus able to fire down into the trench from the roofs and upper windows; to our front and within 120 yards was a thick wood in which the Germans were able to concentrate, especially as part of it was dead ground." That night Lieutenant Colonel Hal Cadogan and Captain Claude

Colonel Cadogan (left) and Captain Dooner (right)

Dooner (who would die at the end of the month and are buried side by side in Hooge Crater Cemetery) came to visit the front line at 7.00pm. Shortly afterwards Lieutenant Colonel Cadogan was in his headquarters in the sandpit when a shell burst and blew him off his feet: *"During the night there were several violent outbursts of fire, lasting some time, but nothing followed. The enemy were blowing bugles and whistles most of the night, but with what object I am unable to say."* The next morning a German aeroplane flew low over the Fusiliers trenches, looking for their artillery. At 10.00am, the Germans sent over coal-boxes, their position pin-pointed from the air, and continued bombarding them until 2.30pm. They remained under heavy shell fire and were continuously enfiladed and during the action Edwin was killed. *"For three days we remained in the trenches, firing and being fired at, without food or water. Lieut. Hoskyns, who commanded my platoon, was killed by a sniper, and about three hours later Capt. Kingston, D.S.O., was killed. He was a very fine officer, and would crack a joke in the trenches which would set us all laughing our sides out. It made us all made to avenge his death."* (Captain Miles Kington is commemorated on the Menin Gate, see below.)

Edwin was recorded in Debretts Obituary — War Roll of Honour published in the 1921 edition.

In St Blaise's Church, Milton, Oxfordshire, a black marble and brass plaque was placed in his memory with the inscription: *"To the glory of God and in memory of Alan John Bowles Captain Royal Berkshire Regiment killed in the trenches near Albert, France April 10th 1916, aged 20, Mentioned In Despatches for 'Gallant and Distinguished Conduct In The Field'. Only son of Capt. F.A.B. Bowles R.N. and Mrs. Bowles and great nephew of Colonel Sir Lonsdale Hale, R.E., Also in memory of Edwin Cecil Leigh Hoskyns Lieut., Royal Welch Fusiliers killed in action near Ypres Oct. 20th 1914, aged 24. Only son of Sir Leigh Hoskyns. Bt., and Lady Hoskyns and godson of Cecil Rhodes, grandsons of the late John Samuel Bowles, J.P., D.L., of Milton Hill."* (Captain Alan Bowles, died on Monday 19th April 1916 and is buried in Bécourt Military Cemetery, Becordel-Bécourt.)

Wounded arriving in London by train

475886 Private George Stuart Wright Hough

No 3 (University) Company
Princess Patricia's Canadian Light Infantry
(Eastern Ontario Regiment)
Died on Friday 2nd June 1916, aged 19
Commemorated on Panel 10.

George Hough

George was born in Picton, Edward County, Ontario, on Tuesday 1st December 1896, son of George L Hough, DD, and Edith W Hough, of 70A Melbourne Avenue, Toronto. He was educated at Picton Public School followed by the Harbord Collegiate Institute, Toronto. In September 1914 he joined the Bank of British North America in Toronto.

On Tuesday 27th July 1915 he volunteered and enlisted in Toronto where he was described as 5ft 10in tall, a 36in chest, dark complexion, grey brown eyes and dark hair. After initial training he was sent to England where it continued until he was sent to France.

The Battalion marched to Locre on Sunday 6th February 1915, going into the line at Kemmel the next day. George joined them on Wednesday 9th February where he remained on tours of duty until Monday 20th March. The Regiment was sent to Ouderdom for thirty-six hours rest before going into support at Zillebeke at *'Maple Copse'*. On Saturday 25th they took the line at *'Sanctuary Wood'* until Tuesday 28th. After being relieved, George undertook a slow, difficult march to *'Camp B'* on the Poperinghe road that was finally reached on the morning of Wednesday 29th. April and May was spent on tours of duty at Hooge, *'Railway Dugouts'* and *'Maple Copse'*. On Wednesday 31st May George relieved the 49th Canadian Infantry in *'Sanctuary Wood'*. On Friday 2nd June the Germans laid down a preliminary bombardment at 9.00am that lasted for four hours. They advanced and the Regiment took heavy casualties including George. In the three days the Regiment was involved in the Battle of Mount Sorrel they suffered four hundred and five casualties of all ranks.

Second Lieutenant John Howell

9th Battalion King's Royal Rifle Corps
Died on Saturday 25th September 1915, aged 20
Commemorated on Panel 51.

John was the son of Rex and Nona Howell, of Clive House, Esher, Surrey. He was educated at Sandroyd followed by Repton School from 1908 to 1914 where he was a member of Priory, becoming Head of House, and Head Prefect of the School. He played for both the First Cricket and Football teams taking over as Captain of Cricket from his brother, Miles. Mr F R d'O Monro wrote of him in *'Repton Cricket (1901-1951)'*: *"He played four times for Repton against Uppingham, and four times against Malvern. Of these eight matches, Repton won three, drew four, and lost one, namely the game with Malvern in 1914 and that only by the narrow margin of 25 runs. Against Uppingham and Malvern, during the four seasons he was in the XI, Howell went in fourteen times, and never once failed to reach double figures. His total runs in these engagements amounted to 690, which gives him the fine average of 49. Altogether Howell played 50 innings in foreign matches for Repton and made 1,892 runs. He was once not out, so that his average was 38.22. In 1913 he averaged 56, and in 1914, 52. None of those who played against him can doubt that had he lived, he would have been going in first for England very soon after he left School."*

Alfred Cochrane wrote of him: *"It is doubtful if we have ever had a better batsman at Repton than John Howell was during his last two seasons. Crawford and Francis Ford were more powerful and brilliant, but they were not more difficult to get out. Fry and Lionel Palairet were at their best some years after they had left school; and of that company of fine players who, a few seasons ago, won matches under Altham's captaincy there was not one who individually could compare with Howell as he was in 1913 and 1914. Long innings were characteristic of him. Many more boys can play a good innings than can play a long innings, indeed, the same may be said of many men. The success of getting runs is naturally exciting, and usually tempts a batsman, who has made his fifty or hundred, to more and more daring experiments with the bowling. Of such experiments, then when they succeed they constitute the great charm of cricket, there can be only one end. But Howell could go on hour after hour batting with the machine-like accuracy of a first-rate professional. Such proficiency requires certain qualities of concentration, as well as the power to recognise your own limitations. There may be something of a spectacular attractiveness wanting in the performance, but of its value to a side there can be no two opinions. In point of fact, the neatness of Howell's style made him always worth watching, while the variety of his strokes and his admirable onside play made him anything but a slow scorer. When he was in form it looked hopeless to bowl to him, and no player of his years gave his innings away less often."*

He was to have gone up to Oriel College, Oxford, but preferred to join the army.

At the outbreak of war John enlisted in the Artists Rifles in August 1914 with service number 2074, and was gazetted on Friday 11th December. He joined the Battalion at Petworth being sent to Aldershot in February 1915 from where he proceeded to France. He arrived in Boulogne on Sunday 20th May 1915 from where he entrained for northern France and onward to Belgium. Further training was provided for front line duties. His first major action was at Hooge on Friday 30th July when at 3.15am the Germans attacked in force using liquid gas for the first time. After a horrendous twenty-four hours of attack and counter-attack, John and what was left of the Battalion, was able to recapture a small section of their line. He continued on tours of duty without seeing any particular action until during the night of Friday 24th September he went back to Hooge in preparation for the attack the next day. At 4.19am a mine was blown under the German lines and John was led forward. During the attack John was killed.

Major Philip Llewellyn Howell-Price, DSO, MC

1st Battalion Australian Infantry, AIF

Died on Thursday 4th October 1917, aged 23

Commemorated on Panel 7.

Citation for the Distinguished Service Order, London Gazette, Thursday 27th July 1916:

"For conspicuous gallantry when leading a party, which he had previously trained, in a successful raid on the enemy trenches. In face of heavy opposition and uncut wire he carried through his attack with great coolness and resource and saw every officer and man back in our trenches before he returned."

Philip was born in Mount Wilson, New South Wales, on Tuesday 11th September 1894, son of Isabel Virginia Howell-Price and the late Reverend John Howell-Price. He was educated at Kogarah High School and was employed as a bank clerk.

Philip was an officer in the New South Wales Cadets before joining the 7th Australian Light Horse Regiment. On Thursday 3rd September 1914 he volunteered being commissioned to the 1st Battalion, leaving from Sydney on Sunday 18th October 1914 and embarking on *HMAT Afric*, sailing for Egypt. He served in Gallipoli, being Mentioned in Despatches for bravery at *'Lone Pine'* where he was wounded. After three months in hospital he returned to the front until the evacuation. After a period of time in Egypt he sailed from Alexandria to Marseilles.

He was sent to northern France to serve in the Armentières sector and there he was appointed Brigade Major of the 2nd Infantry Brigade (Victorians). Philip commanded a successful raid on *'Waterfort'* at Sailly at midnight on Wednesday 28th June, leading the men forward with the centre party. An initial barrage was laid down for five minutes and the raid moved forward. They successfully entered the German lines and after seven minutes Philip sounded the Claxton Horn for the men to withdraw. In the action Sergeant G R Downer was killed, and seventeen men wounded. Eleven Germans were killed, three were taken prisoner and considerable damage caused to the German trenches. Two telegrams were received:

From the 2nd Army Headquarters: *"Army Commander wishes to congratulate all the troops carrying out the successful raid last night."*

General Birdwood

From 1st ANZAC Headquarters of the 1st Australian Division: *"Glad to hear your raid again successful. Please convey my congratulations to 1st. Battalion. BIRDWOOD."*

Philip continued to serve in the line until Sunday 9th July when the move to the Somme began. He took the line at Contalmaison on Thursday 20th where preparations were made for an attack on Pozières that took place five days later. He continued to serve on the Somme until Friday 25th August when the Battalion was ordered to return to Flanders. They arrived at Hopoutre at 7.25am on Saturday 26th and marched to *'Eyrie Camp'* for training. Two days later the Battalion was sent to Poperinghe for baths and a complete clean-up. At 6.45pm on Friday 1st September he marched with his Company to Brandhoek Station where he entrained for Ypres Asylum, arriving at 8.10pm. They marched into the line around *'Railway Dugouts'* and Hill 60. Philip also served at *'The Bluff'* with rest and training at *'Devonshire Camp'* until Thursday 14th September when he returned to the Somme.

From the end of September he was in the line at *'Delville Wood'*. He continued to serve throughout the Somme sector until Thursday 26th July 1917 when the Battalion entrained for Flanders. They were sent to Wallon-Cappel for ten days training from where they moved to Sec Bois. Training continued until Tuesday 11th September when Philip was given leave to Paris for four days. He returned to join the Battalion at Ouderdom and the next day moved to *'Château Segard'* and took the front line. The tour of duty lasted until Sunday 23rd and he marched to *'Palace Camp'* over night. A fleet of buses took the Battalion to Steenvoorde and were sent for further training near Caëstre until Monday 1st October when they returned to the line. The Battalion took the line at Westhoek Ridge and took part in an attack on Thursday 4th. During an artillery barrage Philip was killed, he was first listed as missing before his death was confirmed.

The Australian War Museum holds a collection of his letters — reference 1DRL/0363.

Philip Mentioned in Despatches gazetted on Tuesday 2nd January 1917, and awarded the Military Cross later in the year.

His brother, 2nd Lieutenant Richmond Howell-Price, MC, died on Friday 4th May 1917 and is buried in Vraucourt Copse Cemetery, Vaulx-Vraucourt and Lieutenant Colonel Owen Howell-Price, DSO, MC, died on Saturday 4th November 1916 and is buried in Heilly Station Cemetery, Mericourt-l'Abbe.

Captain Adam Gordon Howitt, MC

12th Battalion East Surrey Regiment

Died on Sunday 5th August 1917, aged 33

Commemorated on Panel 34.

Citation for the Military Cross:

"The success of the raid was due to his good leadership and cool judgement."

Adam Howitt

Adam was born in Ellon on Wednesday 11th June 1884, son of Mr Howitt of Hazelhead and brother of Mrs A G Bulmer, of 81 Duthie Terrace, Aberdeen. He was educated at Robert Gordon's College and went up to Aberdeen University where he graduated with a BSc in agriculture in 1910.

Adam was employed by the Potash Syndicate in Germany, leaving for South Africa where he was Director of their office and a farmer.

At the outbreak of war Adam volunteered and enlisted in the Cape Town Highlanders, serving with General Botha in South West Africa, and was given a field commission. At the end of the campaign he returned to England and joined the East Surrey's in October 1915. He was sent to Ireland and served through the Easter Rising, leaving for France in May 1916 and entrained for Belgium. As the Battle of the Somme was beginning in France, on Saturday 1st July 1916, at 5.00am the 12th Battalion was relieved from *'Convent Trenches'* and returned to *'Soyer Farm'*. On Thursday 6th July they moved the short distance into billets at Grande Munque Farm, west of Ploegsteert Wood. They remained in the sector until Wednesday 23rd August when they entrained at Bailleul for Longpré, Amiens, where they went into camp and training. On Saturday 2nd September they were inspected by General Sidney Lawford and on Monday 11th by General Henry Horne at their camp near Albert before moving to the rear of the line at Fricourt. At 4.30pm on Thursday 14th they moved into the front line at a corner of Delville Wood; the next morning at 6.15am they advanced under artillery cover, supported by tanks, on

Generals Lawford and Horne

Flers. Men of the 12th Battalion were the first to enter the village under a heavy counter-barrage from the Germans, during which Adam was wounded. On Monday 18th the Battalion was relieved and went back to their camp near Albert, and Adam was invalided to England. On Friday 20th October the Battalion entrained for Godewaersvelde and went into training for nine days until they took over the line at St Eloi where they remained (in and out of the line) for the next four months. They were mainly billeted at Reninghelst in *'Ontario Camp'*.

Adam, under the command of Captain Hagen, together with 2nd Lieutenant H S Todd, were given the task of undertaking a raid. On Friday 1st June 1917 the British artillery, with their curtain bombardment, had practically destroyed all the German wire in front of the 12th Battalion. At 9.45pm they led sixty-eight men forward: it was a total success. They captured seven prisoners of the 44th Regiment, East Prussian Division, a machine-gun, a telephone and some rifles. For his gallantry and leadership, Adam was awarded the Military Cross.

On Thursday 7th June the Battle of Messines opened with the blowing of nineteen mines from 3.10am. At 5.10am Adam and his men moved forward to their assembly positions on the *'Dammestrasse'*. Their advance commenced at 6.50am moving forward fifty yards at a time and keeping close to the rolling barrage. They took *'Denys Wood'* and *'Pheasant Wood'* and in the process captured two hundred and sixty-eight prisoners during the day. For the rest of the month they remained in this sector of the Salient and during the month Adam was promoted Captain.

On Sunday 1st July the Battalion moved out of the line and to a new camp at Vierstraat for five days before marching south to Bailleul to a training camp until Monday 23rd. They marched to *'Wood Camp'* at Reninghelst and went into the line at Hollebeke the next day. At 5.30am on Tuesday 31st Adam and his men moved forward and attacked Hollebeke where Adam established the line in front of the village. Early on Sunday 5th the Germans advanced through a thick mist after a two hour preliminary barrage. Aerial signals could not be seen so the line was lost before reinforcements could be rushed up and during this action, Adam was killed.

His Colonel wrote: *"Although outnumbered, and under climatic conditions impossible to adequately describe, Captain Howitt and his men beat the enemy back in the fierce hand-to-hand fighting. I do not hesitate to say I have lost my best officer. 'Jock' Howitt died fighting to the last — one of the bravest of the brave. ... Had he survived he would have secured another well-earned decoration."*

Lieutenant
Geoffrey Morgan Hoyle

3rd Battalion attached 2nd Battalion
Sherwood Foresters (Notts and Derby Regiment)

Died on Monday 9th August 1915, aged 21

Commemorated on Panel 39.

Geoffrey Hoyle

Geoffrey was the youngest son of Edward Lascelles Hoyle, MA, JP, and Margaret Kupfer Hoyle, of Holme Hall, Bakewell, Derbyshire. He was educated at Rugby School from 1903 to 1913 as a member of Donkin. After leaving School he went out to Germany to study the language in Berlin followed by Weimar. Geoffrey returned to England only a couple of days before Germany declared war on Russia. He volunteered and was commissioned; his training continued until March 1915 when he joined the 2nd Battalion in northern France. At the end of April Geoffrey was sent to billets in Le Bizet and were sent into the line near Le Touquet on Tuesday 11th May. Shortly after their arrival in the line the Germans blew a series of mines causing considerable damage and casualties amongst the men.

On Saturday 15th Major Percy Dove was inspecting the line when he was shot and killed (he is buried Strand Military Cemetery) — Percy also had attended Rugby School. Geoffrey continued to serve in the sector until Friday 28th and on Monday 31st they marched via Bailleul, Poperinghe to hutments northwest of Ypres.

Percy Dove

En route the Battalion was inspected and addressed by Field Marshal Sir John French. Following the gas attacks mounted by the Germans over the previous five weeks, all ranks were issued with a primitive respirator that, in fact, provided no protection whatsoever. The Battalion was able to rest and train for five days before being sent into the line at Potijze. When they arrived they found a poor series of trenches as described in

the Battalion Diary: *"The relieved regiment don't appear to have done much work. No communication trenches even between the two companies in the front line, and 'C' Company has a post 150 yards in front of the main line which is absolutely isolated by day. … This Brigade seems to be the only one that takes the trouble to dig communication trenches. Whenever we move to a new piece of line we have to start digging them!"* After three weeks the Battalion was moved the short distance to St Jan and Wieltje. Throughout July the sector was described as quiet and Geoffrey was promoted to Lieutenant. The Germans mounted an attack on Friday 30th July and the Battalion ordered to 'stand to' but were not called upon to support the line. During the night of Monday 2nd August Geoffrey was relieved and marched to Poperinghe for three days rest. On Thursday 5th he marched with his platoon along the cobbled roads towards Ypres and came under carefully directed shell fire that killed one of the men and wounded twelve others, including Lieutenant Colonel Leverson-Gower. At 2.00am on Friday 6th they arrived at *'Maple Copse'* where they prepared for an attack. On Monday 9th from 2.45am a half an hour preliminary bombardment fell on the German lines before the whistles blew and the attack began. At 5.00am the German artillery began a retaliatory barrage that fell on the Battalion causing considerable damage, casualties and cut the telephone lines. Geoffrey was killed leading his men forward when he was killed. He had been recommended for promotion to Captain shortly before his death.
One of his men described the action: *"We, a party of four bombers, advancing up a communication trench, found ourselves held up by the fire of a machine-gun. Mr. Hoyle came up and deliberately risked his life to find out the position of this gun. Having found where it was, he took charge and led us to where we could bomb the gun in comparative safety. Owing to part of the trench being filled in we were compelled to get out on the top, a most dangerous position. Here Mr. Hoyle again took first chance. Waving us back, and telling us if he fell to push on at all costs, he stepped on to the top. He was no sooner there than he fell back, shot through the head."*
His Commanding Officer wrote: *"The death of your son was a great loss. He had been with us some time, was one of our most reliable Officers, and had proved himself a most gallant, brave gentleman. This War depends mostly on the Platoon Commanders, their work and their leading, and your son was one of the best Platoon Commanders I had."*
One of his men wrote: *"Whether barbed-wiring or reconnoitring he never followed, but led his men. It was not his way to give orders, but to ask us in a quiet way to do what was required, and he always set an example by working hard himself. We lost one of the best Officers we had out there, and he was a gentleman."*

L/12672 Private
Frederick George Hubbard

3rd Battalion Middlesex Regiment

Died on Monday 15th February 1915, aged 23

Commemorated on Panel 51.

Frederick was born in Earl's Court, London, on Tuesday 10th March 1891, eldest son of Alfred and Lucy Jane Hubbard, of 257 New King's Road, Fulham, London. He was educated at local schools and was a scholar at Fulham Congregational Sunday School until 1909.
Frederick enlisted in June 1909 and was stationed at Aldershot. He was part of the Special Guard at Buckingham Palace during the funeral of HM King Edward VII, and was part of the guard to the house used

… the funeral of King Edward VII

by HM King George V at Aldershot when he visited. He went out to India and was part of the King's Bodyguard during the Coronation Durbar.
At the outbreak of war Frederick returned to England and was sent for training before leaving for France on Monday 18th January 1915. He was sent by train to Hazebrouck and marched to Flêtre where he undertook intense training for the front line. At 6.00pm on Saturday 6th February he was sent into the line at St Eloi, for Frederick and his comrades it was their first experience in the front line and under fire. The conditions were terrible, the trenches were flooded, the trenches were collapsing (even without the assistance of German artillery) and the weather was freezing — many of the men suffered badly from frostbite. It must have been with great relief to Frederick when he was taken out of the line on Thursday 11th. The rest period was brief, twenty-four hours later he was sent back as the Germans had sapped up to the British lines in the whole sector. The Royal Engineers told Headquarters that the trenches were untenable and new ones should be constructed one hundred yards in the rear. Frederick and the men were set to that task immediately. The Battalion Diary records: *"… a small party to be left in the old trenches until the new ones were completed"*. The men worked night and day to complete the new trenches with Lieutenant Colonel Stephenson in the line with them supervising the work. On Sunday 14th the Middlesex, with the East Surreys, mounted a raid on 'O' Trench, at 4.00am on Monday morning it was successfully

retaken. During the day the troops moved into their new trenches but were under heavy fire from the Germans occupying the old British trenches. A number of casualties were taken, one being Frederick: later that evening his comrades were relieved from the line.

Second Lieutenant
Francis Stanley William Hubbert

2nd Battalion East Yorkshire Regiment

Died on Friday 23rd April 1915, aged 30

Commemorated on Panel 21.

Francis Hubbert

Francis was born at Grayling, Chichester, Sussex, on Sunday 4th October 1885, youngest son of Charles John and Mary Ann Hubbert, of 109 Walden Road, North End, Portsmouth. He was educated at Chichester Prebendary School and was a chorister at Chichester Cathedral.

Francis was married to Lilian May Hubbert, of 4 Dartmouth Road, Copnor, Portsmouth, and they had two sons, Stanley born in June 1911 and Charles in February 1913. Francis was an excellent billiard player, winning the Shorncliffe tournament twice and numerous other prizes.

Francis enlisted in the East Yorkshire Regiment serving in India and Burma, rising to the rank of Sergeant.

Francis returned from India to England in December 1914. On New Year's Day 1915 the Battalion was sent to billets in Winchester where on Tuesday 12th January they were inspected by HM King George V at Fawley Down. Three days later they marched to Southampton and embarked for Le Havre. At 9.00pm on Thursday 16th their train pulled out of the station, a long, winding and tiresome journey was completed at 5.30pm the next evening when they arrived at Hazebrouck. That night they were billeted in the hospital and the next morning they moved off to Bailleul where they remained in their billets — farm buildings and cottages — until the end of the month, during which time he received a field commission.

On Monday 1st February they marched the short distance to Méteren and were taken by motor bus to Vlamertinghe. Francis formed his men up and went into the line at St Eloi, remaining in the line for three weeks, and he continued on tours of duty until Saturday 3rd April when they moved to billets at Westoutre. They stayed there for six days before being sent to Zonnebeke, and the edge of Polygon Wood. The Brigade Diary records that on Friday 9th when Francis arrived: *"During the day the enemy threw a note into our trenches written in French asking the recipients to join with them against England, etc., thus showing they were not aware of the relief."* After a couple of tours of duty the Battalion was relieved to Vlamertinghe. On Thursday 22nd April Francis left *'Camp A'* at Vlamertinghe and marched to the front at St Julien. During Friday 23rd they were moved along the southern portion of the line three miles northwest of Broodseinde. At 4.10pm the Battalion 'went over the top' with the objective of taking a five hundred yard front. The Commanding Officer wrote: *"All ranks showed the most absolute indifference to fire and casualties, advancing splendidly under their officers."* The Germans opened up with artillery, machine-gun fire and intensive rifle fire which caused terrible casualties. Francis was leading his men into action against heavily defended German trenches when he was killed, getting to within 30 yards of them — he was buried in the field.

26202 Sergeant
Arthur John Hubble, DCM

12th Battalion Australian Infantry, AIF

Died on Tuesday 6th October 1917

Commemorated on Panel 17.

Citation for the Distinguished Conduct Medal, London Gazette, Monday 18th June 1917:

"For conspicuous gallantry and devotion to duty. He handled his machine-gun section with great skill, and although surrounded by the enemy succeeded in effecting his withdrawal. He was wounded.

Arthur was born at North Cottage, Cannonbury, Islington, London and was educated locally. He went out to Australia in 1913 aged 17 and was employed as a labourer.

On Friday 13th August 1915 he volunteered and enlisted, leaving on Wednesday 27th October from Melbourne embarking on *HMAT Ulysses*. He served on the Somme where he was awarded the Distinguished Conduct Medal on Sunday 15th April 1917 at Lagnicourt whilst in charge of a Lewis Gun. The Germans were forced back to Queant due to the artillery and the Lewis Gun fire taking heavy casualties. He continued to serve on the Somme until Friday 27th July when he entrained at Albert at 9.07am arriving in Steenbecque at 5.30pm, where he went into billets. Two days later he was sent to Nielle-les-Blequin for two weeks training, moving on Thursday 13th October to Thieushouck via Strazeele and Caëstre and onward to Wippenhoek then Ouderdom where they arrived on Saturday 15th. After three days in camp he marched through Dickebusch to bivouac near *'Château Belge'* prior to taking the line. The Battalion were in their assembly positions near *'Halfway House'* by

4.10am on Sunday 20th. Several casualties were taken as the German artillery opened up on their lines at 4.30am for over an hour before the Battalion moved forward in the attack on Polygon Wood, where they successfully took their objectives and consolidated their position. At 2.25am on Tuesday 22nd he was relieved and went to bivouac at Dickebusch Huts where they rested for a day before sent to Steenvoorde. On Wednesday 30th they were taken by motor bus at 11.00am to *'Château Segard'* into bivouac. The next evening they relieved the 48th Battalion, Australian Infantry, at Westhoek where they remained in the line for twenty-four hours under heavy artillery fire before returning to *'Château Segard'*. On Sunday 4th they returned to Westhoek for a further twenty-four hours before moving forward to Oosthoek. On Tuesday 6th they mounted a successful raid on *'Celtic Wood'* at 11.30pm where they captured ten prisoners and a machine-gun. In the action Arthur was mortally wounded, dying shortly afterwards.

17778 Private Albert Hughes

'A' Company, 2nd Battalion
Gloucestershire Regiment
Died on Monday 10th May 1915, aged 19
Commemorated on Panel 22.

Albert was the son of Mrs Annie Hughes, of The Wye, Charfield, Gloucestershire. He was educated locally. With his brother, Harry, they enlisted together and have consecutive enrolment numbers. His brother died on the same day and is commemorated on the Menin Gate, see below. They were sent for training before leaving for France with a draft.
They were killed in action near *'Sanctuary Wood'* during the Battle of Frezenberg Ridge. They had been taken to the second line, close to *'Hell Fire Corner'*, and were improving the line laying out wire when they were killed by shell fire.

17777 Private Harry Hughes

'A' Company, 2nd Battalion
Gloucestershire Regiment
Died on Monday 10th May 1915, aged 18
Commemorated on Panel 22.

Harry was the son of Mrs Annie Hughes, of The Wye, Charfield, Gloucestershire. He was educated locally. With his brother, Albert, they enlisted together and have consecutive enrolment numbers.
His brother, Private Albert Hughes, died on the same day and is commemorated on the Menin Gate, see above.

Captain and Adjutant Henry Kent Hughes

1st Battalion
King's Own Yorkshire Light Infantry
Died on Sunday 9th May 1915, aged 32
Commemorated on Panel 47.

Henry Hughes

Henry was born on Tuesday 6th February 1883 son of Frederick and Alice Hughes, of Wallfired Cottage, Reigate, Surrey. He was educated at Repton School from 1896 to 1900 as a member of Priory, and played for the cricket XI. His uncle, Reverend T E Hughes was Housemaster of Priory.
Henry was gazetted in May 1901, promoted Lieutenant in September 1903, and Captain in June 1909, Adjutant from April 1914. He saw service in Ireland, Gibraltar, South Africa, Hong Kong and Singapore.
Henry was stationed at Tanglin Barracks, Singapore, on Saturday 1st August 1914, *"where the rumour and expectation of war hung in the air like a peasouper"*. Minden Day was, however, celebrated. His Excellency The Hon Richard James Wilkinson, CMG, addressed the men with a 'stirring speech'! At 9.30am on Tuesday 4th, after the Declaration of War, mobilization commenced. On Sunday 9th the Battalion took their first enemy prisoners — thirty-three German Reservists tried to leave on a Dutch boat bound for the Fatherland. On Sunday 27th September Henry organised the embarkation on board *HMT Carnarvonshire* that included twenty-five wives and forty-four children. They sailed via Colombo, Ceylon, where they berthed for two days followed by Aden, arriving on Wednesday 14th October and remained there for three days. Ahead lay the Suez Canal; whilst off Ismailia they received the first real news — and casualty lists — of the war. Their spirits dimmed as they read of the horrendous losses suffered in France by their comrades, family and friends of the 2nd Battalion. On Monday 26th October they left Port Said and made for Malta, thence Gibraltar, arriving at Southampton on Monday 9th November at 11.00am. From the docks they left by train for Winchester and onward to *'Hursley Park Camp'* in terrible weather — not the best welcome for troops only accustomed to the tropics. Due to the poor weather they were moved, eventually, into billets in Winchester. On Tuesday 12th January 1915 the traditional Royal Inspection to place with HM King George V taking the salute and the next day they were inspected by General Sir Arthur Wynne as they prepared to leave for the front. They marched to Southampton on Friday 15th, embarking on *HMT City of Benares* for Le Havre.

After arriving in France they entrained for Hazebrouck, then marched to Outtersteene. Training for front line duty commenced immediately in dire weather. On Thursday 28th January the Battalion was inspected by Field Marshal Sir John French accompanied by HRH The Prince of Wales. The next day time was given for the men to meet up with the remnants of the 2nd Battalion near Bailleul where they learned first-hand of what to expect in the front line.

On Monday 1st February they were collected by motor bus and taken to Vlamertinghe from where they marched into the line south of Ypres, at Verbrandenmolen, relieving the French in trenches that straddled the Ypres to Comines Canal. Many of them going into the line for the first time were hoping for a reasonably comfortable and easy time, but for Henry and his men it was the opposite. *"It was an unpleasant experience for the newcomers, for the trenches were bad and isolated, many were waterlogged and filled with the bodies of dead Frenchmen, indeed some parapets appeared to be built of bodies."* After three days they were relieved from the line for rest, they remained on tours of duty in the sector for the rest of the month. For the first two weeks of March Henry served in the Wulverghem area.

On 7th April the Battalion was inspected by General Horace Smith-Dorrien whilst they were in camp. On Monday 12th they marched from their billets through battle-scarred but yet intact Ypres and out of the Menin Gate to Zonnebeke.

Henry was involved in heavy fighting at Frezenberg where their lines were heavily shelled. On Saturday 8th May 1915 the Battalion was forced out of their trenches and took new positions slightly to the rear, despite being under particularly heavy shell-fire and constant infantry attacks or raids. In the actions that took place Henry was killed by shell fire.

His brother, Captain Thomas Hughes, died on Thursday 15th October 1914 and is buried in Guards Cemetery, Windy Corner, Cuinchy.

A concert party in a mess behind the lines given by the Artists Rifles

5080 Serjeant William Osman Hughes, DCM

Machine Gun Corps (Infantry)

Died on Sunday 12th August 1917, aged 27

Commemorated on Panel 56.

Citation for the Distinguished Conduct Medal, London Gazette, Wednesday 18th July 1917:

"For conspicuous gallantry and devotion to duty. During lengthy operations he handled his guns with great skill, repelling counter-attacks, and displaying the utmost fearlessness in observing enemy movements, and passing on information to his guns."

William was born in Clapton-on-the-Hill, Gloucestershire, the son of William and Emily Hughes, of Clapton, Bourton-on-the-Water, Cheltenham.

He enlisted in Pontypridd and was formerly a member of the Gloucestershire Regiment.

Captain Frederick William Hunt

19th Lancers (Fane's Horse)

Died on Saturday 31st October 1914, aged 33

Commemorated on Panel 1.

Frederick was born on Wednesday 22nd December 1880, the second son of Mrs Hunt and the late Reverend William Cornish Hunt, of The Warrens, Ferring, Essex. He was educated at Marlborough College from May 1894 until December 1897.

He was commissioned to the Leicester Regiment from the Militia in April 1900, promoted to Lieutenant in June 1901, transferred to the Indian Army in July 1903, served with the King's African Rifles from April 1907 and promoted Captain in April 1909.

At the outbreak of war Frederick was in England on leave and joined the his Regiment in the field. Following action in northern France he moved across the border into Belgium and served near Hollebeke. As the Germans pressed home attack after attack Frederick went out with some of his men to destroy a couple of farms that threatened their line. On Friday 30th Frederick and his men were forced to retire. The Germans

... a shell burst

continued to press home their attack and when he went out to rescue Lieutenant Kenneth North of 4th (Queen's Own) Hussars, Frederick was killed by a shell. For this action he was Mentioned in Despatches.

Captain Bentley Moore Hunter

Royal Army Medical Corps attached
1st/1st Battalion Cambridgeshire Regiment
Died on Tuesday 31st July 1917, aged 29
Commemorated on Panel 56.

Bentley was born in Glenluce on Saturday 28th April 1888, the fifth child of Charles and Susan Bentley Moore Hunter. He was educated at Stranraer High School and went up to Glasgow University to study medicine, graduating with an MB on Tuesday 13th July 1909. He was a doctor in Consett, County Durham and then in Stevenston, Ayrshire. On Saturday 15th May 1915 Bentley was commissioned to the Royal Army Medical Corps and was sent to Lemnos to serve in the Gallipoli Campaign. Following the evacuation he was sent to Egypt. After a period of rest Bentley was sent to Alexandria where he sailed for Marseilles. He then served on the Western Front in France followed by

Bentley Hunter

... a motor ambulance

the Ypres Salient where he was killed in action at the opening of the Third Battle of Ypres.

The Battalion had been training hard for the forthcoming battle, having spent two weeks in Houlle before returning to camp in Brandhoek, prior to being sent into the line. At 9.30pm on Monday 30th July the Battalion marched out of their muddy camp to the sound of the pipes from the band of the Black Watch who cheered them on their way. They marched through the dark to their old trenches on the Ypres Canal bank, with headquarters nicknamed *'The Pike and Eel'*. Bentley had assisted in providing all ranks with ear-defenders that provided some respite from the booming of the guns and allowed some to catch a little sleep. At 3.50am the preliminary bombardment commenced, Brigadier General Riddell, CMG, recorded: *"A roar like thunder broke the stillness and thousands of flashes pierced the darkness. The air seemed filled with the hissing sound of shells passing overhead towards the enemy's lines. We shouted to one another, but the crash of the 18-pounders, standing almost wheel to wheel close by, made our voices inaudible. The flashes from our guns and their reflection in the sky lit up the surrounding scenery in a way I had not thought possible."*

General Riddell

At 4.45am breakfast was provided to all ranks prior to their advance to the front. After a mile the Battalion came under shell fire and Bentley's work began. The advance was going well and prisoners were being sent to the rear, a German officer was heading towards the rear, General Riddell recorded: *"I was speaking to an officer of another regiment when pointing to an approaching figure, he shouted:*

'Lor', blimy! Here comes Prince Rupprecht himself.'

The man walking towards us was a German officer immaculately dressed, wearing white kid gloves and carrying a black ebony cane with a silver knob. Addressing my companion, he said in excellent English:

'I am a German officer, and demand an officer escort to take to a place of safety.'

Field Marshal Crown Prince Rupprecht of Bavaria

'Hal a mo', cocky, you won't want these', casually remarked England's representative as he relieved the prisoner of his automatic pistol, field-glasses and cane, and dropped them into a sand-bag held open by an orderly. Then running his hands over the German's pockets he extracted a watch and note-case, adding 'Nor these'.

Here I intervened. The watch and money must be returned. 'Here you!' said my companion, addressing a diminutive Cheshire private who, with the aid of his rifle as a walking-stick, was limping back towards the place whence he had set out a dawn. 'Take this back with you, and see that he doesn't dirty his gloves'."

At 11.00am fog dropped across the battlefield as the Battalion consolidated their line. By 11.30am the fog started to lift. Bentley was working hard dealing with the wounded from both sides who were pouring into the gun-pit that he was using as a Dressing Station. General Riddell wrote: *"A wounded German boy, with a bayonet wound in the abdomen, had been slowly dying in the mud outside the gun-pit. We would not help him; Hunter, our doctor, was killed. Each one of us would have wished to put a bullet through the poor boy's head to end his agony, but no one had the courage or the right thing to do it. His pleasing eyes fascinated us until, his head falling back into the mud, they stared fixedly at the sky."*

His Commanding Officer wrote: *"Your son was killed trying to save the lives of others, as he had done so many times before. I, fortunately, had the satisfaction of telling him some few days before that I had recommended him for some sort of award."*

The Chaplain wrote: *"His staff say they will never have another like him. He was so generous-minded and willing to help others. I shall never forget the way he carried on down south when the other medical officer was killed. He was simply splendid."*

Lieutenant
Charles Gawain Raleigh Hunter

'A' Company, 2nd Battalion
King's Own Yorkshire Light Infantry
Died on Saturday 24th April 1915
Commemorated on Panel 47.

Charles Hunter

Charles was born at The Elms, Hunningham, third son of Captain William George and Kathleen Hayrer Hunter of Sunfield, Pirbright, Surrey. He was the sixth generation of his family to serve in the Army or Navy. Charles was educated at Christ College, Brecon, where he was a scholar and a member of the OTC. Charles was a good horseman, excellent shot and all-round sportsman.

In August 1911 Charles was gazetted and promoted Lieutenant in September 1914.

On Sunday 6th December 1914 Charles joined the Battalion in the field at St Jans Cappel. The Battalion spent December in the Dranouter sector, losing more men to trench foot and frost-bite than any other cause as they were spending as long as forty-eight hours up to their knees in freezing mud and water. On Christmas Day they were in their billets at St Jans Cappel where an inter-company football match was won by 'A' Company and they welcomed a new draft of men.

The new year brought them into reserve at Bailleul. On Friday 29th January 1915 the 2nd Battalion marched to meet the men of the 1st Battalion who were arriving at the front. They met together in a field and were given a couple of hours to socialise with old friends before marching back to their respective billets.

On Thursday 22nd April Charles witnessed the horrific results of the first gas attack. The Battalion was supporting the Canadians near Wieltje when he was killed advancing over open ground under heavy shell fire in command of 'A' Company. He was buried in the field at Wieltje.

In Hunningham Parish Church, Warwickshire, a brass plaque was placed in his memory with the inscription: *"In loving remembrance of Charles Gawain Raleigh Hunter, Lieutenant 2nd Battalion, The Kings Own Yorkshire, Lt. Infantry. Killed in action at Ypres in Belgium on the 24th of April 1915 aged 21 years. Beloved son of Capt. & Mrs. W. G. Hunter. And the spirit shall return unto God who gave it."*

CAPTAIN GEORGE EDWARD HUNTER

6th Battalion Northumberland Fusiliers

Died on Monday 26th April 1915, aged 28

Commemorated on Panel 12.

George Hunter

George was born at Newcastle-upon-Tyne on Sunday 27th March 1887, elder son of Edward and Anne Cunningham Hunter, of Wentworth, Gosforth, Northumberland. He was educated at Charterhouse from 1900 to 1903 as a Weekite. He studied architecture and was articled with Cackett and Burns Dick, obtaining his ARIBA in 1909. In 1913 George joined his father's firm, Hunter & Henderson, stockbrokers in Newcastle and became a partner in 1913.

In 1904 he joined the Militia and was promoted Captain in June 1908.

His brother, Captain Howard Hunter, was killed on the same day and is commemorated on the Menin Gate, see below. George and Howard went out to France in April 1915. He was sent to northern France. At 5.00pm on Thursday 22nd April the Germans launched their gas attack. George was in action at St Julien during the counter-offensive when he was killed by a shell splinter and Howard was mortally wounded, dying shortly afterwards. The brothers had been in the line for only a few days.

A brother officer wrote: *"He led his men with great courage and a total disregard for himself, and was right in front of the enemy's position when he was killed by a shell fired at short range."*

George and Edward are commemorated in St Nicholas Church, Gosforth, Tyne and Wear, where a stained glass window was dedicated to their memory. A plaque below was placed with the inscription: *"They were lovely and pleasant in their lives and in death they were not divided. To the glory of God and in proud and loving memory of Captain George Edward Hunter aged 28 years and Captain Howard Tomlin Hunter aged 26 years. Both of the 6th Northumberland Fusiliers (T) who were killed in action on 26th April 1915 near St. Julien at The Second Battle of Ypres.*

This window was erected by their father and mother Edward and Annie Cunningham Hunter of Wentworth, Gosforth."

CAPTAIN HOWARD TOMLIN HUNTER

6th Battalion Northumberland Fusiliers

Died on Monday 26th April 1915, aged 26

Commemorated on Panel 12.

Howard Hunter

Howard was born on Monday 1st October 1888 second son of Edward and Anne Cunningham Hunter, of Wentworth, Gosforth, Northumberland. Howard was educated at Charterhouse from 1901 to 1904 as a Weekite and went up to Durham University to study medicine, graduating with and MB and BSc in 1910. Howard continued his medical training at St Bartholomew's Hospital, London, then in Vienna. His brother, Captain George Hunter, was killed on the same day and is commemorated on the Menin Gate, see above.

In 1906 Howard was commissioned in the Militia being promoted Captain in 1912.

The Durham College Medicine Gazette wrote: *"We have all heard with pride and aching heart of his entry into action. The first torrent of bullet and shell only seemed to increase his absolute indifference to danger, and his example and courage infected the whole company. He led his men through a crossfire of machine-guns and shrapnel, trying to reach the German trenches by a series of rushes. When close to his objective he was struck on the leg but stuck to his job, gamely cheering on his men. We can imagine his bitter disappointment when he had to fall out so near the end of his task. While being helped to the rear he was struck again in the chest and almost immediately dropped dead."*

Lieutenant Norman Frederick Hunter

4th Battalion Royal Warwickshire Regiment attached 4th Battalion Royal Fusiliers

Died on Wednesday 16th June 1915, aged 36

Commemorated on Panel 8.

Norman was the son of the late Dr James Adam Hunter and Marion Hunter, of Edinburgh. He went up to Clare College, Cambridge, in 1897. He was married to Elizabeth Hunter, of Huntington, Ascot, Berkshire. Norman was a member of the Garrick Club.

On Saturday 24th May 1915 Norman was at Dickebusch as the Germans delivered a gas attack five miles away. However, the gas drifted in the wind, causing many in the Battalion to complain of sore eyes. By the end of May the Germans were in consolidating their captured positions at the Bellewaarde Lake. It was decided that the Bellewaarde Ridge would be stormed to enable the line to be straightened. On Wednesday 16th June Norman was in the line on the Menin Road, east of *'Cambridge Road'* when at 4.50am, after a two hour barrage, the whistles blew and he led his men 'over the top' towards Bellewaarde Lake. The attack was particularly successful and the first German line was taken without much difficulty. The German wire had been effectively cut or destroyed during the barrage and all around the laid the German wounded and dead. So shocked were they by the ferocity of the attack the defending German infantry were more than happy to surrender rather than face further attack. The British artillery had caused many casualties amongst their own men because they advanced their barrage slowly and the infantry advanced more quickly. The Germans mounted a counter-attack and the Battalion was forced to retire, making it back to their fire and communication trenches. During the action Norman was wounded and died of the wounds shortly afterwards.

Lieutenant George Hurry

15th Battalion Australian Infantry, AIF

Died on Thursday 18th October 1917, aged 32

Commemorated on Panel 17.

George Hurry

George was born at home on Saturday 6th December 1884, son of Henry and Mary Hurry, of Kyneton, Victoria. He was educated at Melbourne Grammar School from 1901 to 1902. On Tuesday 2nd June 1903 he joined the Bank of New South Wales in Kyneton and in 1907 George transferred to Melbourne; Sunshine in 1909; Fitzroy in 1910 before returning to Melbourne in 1911. He was a member of the Melbourne Cricket Club.

On Wednesday 17th February 1915 George volunteered and enlisted as a driver. He left from Melbourne on Monday 28th June 1915 on board *HMAT Berrima*, sailing for Egypt. After serving in Egypt he was sent to the Western Front.

In March 1917 George was commissioned whilst on the Somme near Bazentin. At 1.00am on Sunday 15th May he entrained at *'Edgehill Railway Sidings'* and left for Bailleul from where they marched fifteen miles to billets south of Doulieu where they trained for two weeks. They marched across the border arriving close to Neuve Eglise on Saturday 31st. After a week they moved to La Plus Douve Farm and served in *'Owl Trench'*. In early July the Battalion was serving in Ploegsteert Wood in *'Bunhill Row'*; the tunnels at *'Prowse Point'* and *'Ontario Avenue'*. At the end of the month the Battalion was sent for training at Outtersteene. General Godley visited them on Thursday 2nd August prior to their returning in the pouring rain to *'Hillside Camp'* at Neuve Eglise on Friday 3rd. On Sunday 26th they went into the Support Line at Messines Ridge. At the end of the month they were sent for further training where Generals Plumer and McLagan visited them, addressing the officers. On Sunday 23rd September they were sent to bivouac at

General Godley

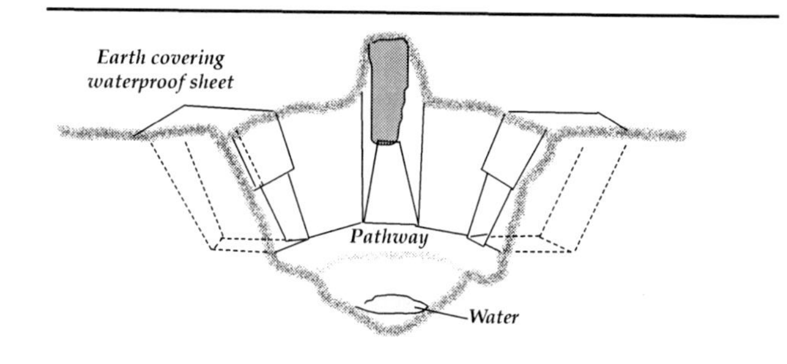

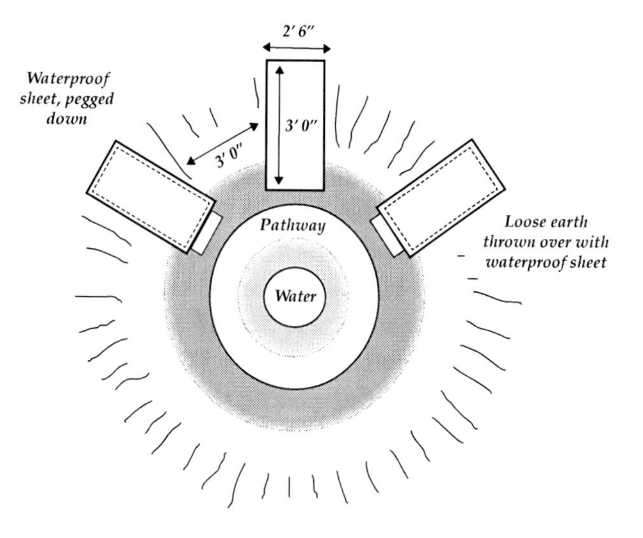

A consolidated shell hole

'Belgian Château' and then marched to Ypres Ramparts. On Tuesday 25th they marched via *'Gordon House'* out to the line for three days where they consolidated a captured position and where they came under attack by gas shells. After being relieved they were sent for training at Steenvoorde until Thursday 11th October when they marched to *'Halifax Camp'* at Vlamertinghe. The next morning the Battalion was sent to Ypres Ramparts before moving to the Westhoek Ridge on Saturday 13th, moving forward to Zonnebeke the next day. Throughout Wednesday 17th the Germans shelled their line heavily causing a large number of casualties. Whilst leading a party of men to cut the wire George was killed when a shell burst close to him and a splinter hit him in the heart. George was buried at the *'Soda Factory'* Zonnebeke.

A/36041 Private Henry Aloysius Hussey

4th Battalion Canadian Infantry
(Central Ontario Regiment)
Died on Tuesday 13th June 1916, aged 43
Commemorated on Panel 18.

Henry was born at home on Monday 27th July 1874, son of Thomas and Agnes Hussey, of 23 St Mary Abbotts Terrace, Kensington, London. He was educated at St Edmund's College, Old Hall, Ware, from 1886 to 1889. Henry served with the Civil Service Police in South Africa before he went out to Canada where he was employed as a builders clerk.

On Sunday 4th June 1915 Henry volunteered in Edmonton, where he was described as a Roman Catholic, 5ft 7½in tall, with a 36in chest, a dark complexion, brown eyes and black (turning grey) hair.

Following his initial training Henry was sent to England where training continued until he was sent out to France to join the Battalion in the field on the Salient.

Henry initially served in the Kemmel and Wulverghem sectors, in the front line and in reserve at *'Aircraft Farm'* until the end of March. On Saturday 1st April Henry marched to Poperinghe, via Reninghelst, where he was billeted in a convent. After two days of rest and training he marched to *'Dickebusch South Camp'* for a week of training that included route marches, practising rapid loading with and without smoke helmets, half an hour of saluting and the Medical Officer addressing them on sanitation. At 7.30pm on Saturday 8th a Zeppelin flew over the camp and dropped signal lights, however, they did not come under shellfire. During the night of Sunday 9th he marched to *'The Bluff'* where the next day they were attacked by a new form of German trench mortar (or torpedo) that effectively destroyed their parapets. Their lines were continuously sniped although it quietened down somewhat once the Battalion snipers got to work! In the early hours of Thursday 13th bombers went forward in *'Pollock Trench'* that brought an instant reply by the German artillery on the trench and *'Hedge Row'*. After six days in the line he was relieved and marched to Ypres Asylum to be taken by train to Poperinghe where he was billeted in the hop factory. Henry undertook fatigues and training until Easter Sunday (23rd) when he returned to the line near *'Blauwepoort Farm'*. In May he served at *'Dominion Lines'* and in reserve at Dickebusch until returning to *'The Bluff'* on Wednesday 26th.

Henry moved from *'Dickebusch Huts'* to the GHQ lines at *'Chateau Segard'* during the evening of Saturday 3rd June and he was set to work improving the trenches and making shelters. On Sunday 4th June 1916 the Germans launched an attack on Hooge using *'Flammenwerfer'* (flame throwers or 'liquid fire') under the cover of heavy artillery fire which was clearly witnessed by Henry and his comrades. The 16th Lancers relieved the Battalion on late on Thursday 8th June and he marched to *'Camp C'* for rest and training before returning to the line at *'Valley Cottages'*. At 1.30am on Monday 12th Henry was led in the attack supporting the 13th and 16th Battalions. General Henry Burstall commented: *"Now they can go over with their rifles slung if they want to"*. As they moved forward, at the point of the bayonet, heavy casualties were sustained. He moved forward and engaged the enemy. The fight was furious and late in the day Henry was killed.

Second Lieutenant Cecil Leigh Hutchinson

3rd Battalion East Lancashire Regiment
Died on Tuesday 31st July 1917, aged 21
Commemorated on Panel 34.

Cecil Hutchinson

Cecil was born in Manchester on Thursday 9th July 1896, elder son of Christopher Edward and Leonora Cecil Maud Hutchinson, of Moss Side, Lytham, Lancashire. He was educated at the King Edward VII's School in Lytham where he was captain of the football team.

On Monday 18th January 1915 Cecil volunteered and was sent for training and a commission. He left for France in March 1916 and joined the Battalion in the field.

Cecil was wounded and invalided to England in June, returning to the front in September in time to participate in the latter stages of the Battle of the Somme. The Battalion was moved north to the Ypres Salient in 1917. He was sent for training and visited the huge model of the battlefield of Passchendaele to study the plan of attack. In addition he took part in many mock attacks with his men on the life-sized 'taped' layouts before being sent into the line. Cecil was killed in action near Westhoek and buried in the field.

A brother officer wrote: *"We had reached our objective, and he was giving orders for consolidation of the position gained, when he was hit in the stomach by a sniper a few minutes after I had left him. He did splendidly, and led his men through with total disregard of danger."*

CAPTAIN AUSTIN HENRY HUTH

1st Battalion East Surrey Regiment

Died on Tuesday 20th April 1915, aged 33

Commemorated on Panel 34.

Austin Huth and his family coat of arms

Austin was born in Hertford Street, Mayfair, London, on Thursday 13th October 1881 younger son of Edward Huth, JP, DL, and Mrs Edith Wilhelmina Marshal Huth, of Avenue House, Bear Wood, Wokingham, Berkshire. He was educated at Eton College as a member of Mr Charles Lowry's House leaving in 1898 and passed into RMC Sandhurst.

Austin served in the South African War, receiving the Queen's Medal with clasp and the King's Medal with two clasps. At the end of the war he went up to Magdalen College, Oxford, graduating in 1903; he rowed in Torpids and was a member of the Oxford and Cambridge Club.

At the outbreak of war Austin joined the Pubic Schools' Battalion, Middlesex Regiment. He was commissioned Captain in October 1914. He went out to Flanders arriving at their camp in Flêtre with a draft of ninety men on Thursday 28th January 1915. The next day he had sight of his first German; an aeroplane flew low over the Camp, followed by his first experience of death in the war as two shells landed that killed one man and wounded nine others.

On Monday 1st February he went into the line in front of Messines, remaining in the line for three days, returning to billets in Neuve Eglise. On Wednesday the Battalion celebrated *Sobraon Day* and laid on special food, organised a football match against the Devons and put on a concert in the evening. The next the day the fun was over and he was back at Messines and they remained in and out of that line until the end of March. Austin spent the first four days of April at Kemmel that was particularly lively. The Battalion left the line and took billets in Locre before marching to Ypres the next day where they were billeted in the cavalry barracks. Ypres was not a safe place to be as it was under heavy shell fire and a good number of troops were wounded and some killed whilst billeted in the barracks. Whilst in Ypres the 2nd Battalion marched passed them *en route* to the front and both Battalions raised a great cheer when they saw each other. On Sunday 18th April they went into the line close to Hill 60, a fairly hot spot. Tuesday 20th was a very busy day for the Battalion being in action all day; the Germans were continuously counter-attacking, mounting raids, and pouring shells down on the new 'owners' of the Hill. Throughout the day many were killed by the shell fire — a considerable number buried alive. Both sides tried to bomb each other from their trenches and the snipers had rich pickings. By midday the barrages subsided and a little calm settled over the lines. In mid-afternoon further raids were made against the British lines culminating in a big push by the Germans to retake the Hill. Their artillery laid down a ferocious bombardment that made an even bigger mess of the defences. Everywhere the wounded lay untended, the dead unburied — it was difficult to move due to the piles of bodies. The battle went to and fro throughout the day and whilst holding onto his position Austin was killed.

His Brigadier-General wrote: *"I am fortunate enough to have in my brigade five splendid battalions, none of which I would change for any other in the Service, and amongst these battalion the East Surreys are second to none. In such a battalion it is necessary that the officers should set the highest possible example, and this was brilliantly the case in the work done by your son. I was wounded just a week before he was killed, and had a long talk to him in his trench that night. I was much impressed at the time with his zeal, keenness, and thoroughness and with the measure that he was taking to put his trench on a thoroughly sound footing ... His life was given, in the hour of victory for King and country, in the performance of a magnificent exploit in capturing and consolidating our hold on Hill 60, a point of extreme importance to the well-being of the Allied front."*

In St Mary Magdalene Church, Bolney, West Sussex, a plaque was placed in his memory with the inscription: *"Anno 1919. In loving memory of Captain Austin Henry Huth, East Surrey Regiment, of Wykehurst in this parish. Born 13th October 1881, killed 20th April 1915 at the capture of Hill 60 near Ypres in Flanders where he lies buried on the field where he fell, in an unknown grave."*

Lieutenant Frederick Robert Hughes Hutton

9th Battalion Argyll and Sutherland Highlanders

Died on Monday 10th May 1915, aged 33

Commemorated on Panel 42.

Frederick Hutton

Frederick was the youngest son of the late James Hutton, of Glasgow. He was educated at the Glasgow Academy and went up to Glasgow University graduating with an MA in 1905. Frederick qualified as a chartered accountant and was a partner in his father's firm, McFarlane, Hutton & Patrick.

In June 1913 he was gazetted in the Territorials and promoted to Lieutenant in September 1914. He was mobilized at the outbreak of war and sent for training with the Battalion. Frederick went to France on Tuesday 23rd February 1915 and entrained for northern France. He continued his training and gained front line experience attached to regular troops prior to being sent into the line. During the Second Battle of Ypres the Germans made a heavy attack at Hooge that resulted in a temporary retirement. Frederick and the Battalion was ordered to support and he was killed in action leading his men forward.

Second Lieutenant Richard Hutton

3rd Battalion Leicestershire Regiment attached 2nd Battalion Royal Warwickshire Regiment

Died on Saturday 7th November 1914, aged 23

Commemorated on Panel 33.

Richard born on Monday 20th April 1891, the youngest son of the late Reverend Joseph Henry Hutton and Mrs Hutton, of West Heslerton, Yorkshire. He was educated at Marlborough College from January 1905 and went up to Merton College, Oxford, with a scholarship in 1910.

At the outbreak of war Richard volunteered and was gazetted on Saturday 15th August 1914.

On Tuesday 6th October Richard arrived in Zeebrugge where he remained until Friday 9th when he entrained to Ghent. He marched four miles out of the city to support a battalion of French Marines, and they covered the retreat of the Belgian Army who were pouring back from Antwerp. Late on Sunday 11th the Battalion was ordered to leave the line and march southwest. They arrived in Ypres on Wednesday 14th via Thielt and Roeselare. Ypres was still occupied by civilians, the shops and cafés operating, selling souvenirs and drink, both in large quantities. Troops were coming and going, mingling with the refugees streaming into the town. During the morning a Taube had flown low over the town and had been brought down by rifle and Maxim fire. It remained a point of discussion, particularly when the wrecked machine was towed into the market square accompanied by its pilot and observer, now prisoners.

A German machine brought down, the contemporary illustration showing the 'chivalry' of the sky!

On Friday 16th Richard was sent to Zonnebeke where he remained before moving forward to Becelaere when on Monday 19th, he led his men to attack Menin. They went through Dadizeele and onto Kezelberg where they cleared the village. They were approaching Klijthoek when orders to retire were received as a large force of Germans had been spotted advancing on the Salient from the direction of Iseghem. As they returned to billets in Zonnebeke, a number of casualties were taken *en route* mainly from shell fire. The next morning he was sent into reserve at Harenthage Château before being called upon to rush up and help stem a German attack. On Wednesday 21st the Germans recommenced their attack on Zonnebeke where the Battalion defended the village from the cross-roads east of the village. Throughout Thursday 22nd Richard organised the men to re-dig the trenches, but they did not make use of them as the Battalion was ordered to Polygon Wood. The Germans had broken the line and a counter-attack was undertaken. Heavy losses mounted, many as a result of fire from a farm house that was eventually taken, together with the lost trenches. Finally a day of rest was provided on Sunday 25th after which they retook the line where they came under attack, and during the afternoon part of the line was lost. The Battalion was moved to billets in Zillebeke from where they took the line. During the morning of Saturday 31st the bombardment intensified; their trenches were blown in and again they were forced to retire. After nine consecutive days of constant service in the front line the Battalion was withdrawn on Wednesday 4th, but after only a short period of rest they were recalled. General Sidney Lawford led them forward on Saturday 7th to attack a German position which they successfully captured. However, during this action Richard was killed.

R/11830 Rifleman Alfred Henry Edgar Huxtable

7th Battalion King's Royal Rifle Corps

Died on Friday 6th August 1915, aged 15

Commemorated on Panel 53.

Alfred was born in Plumstead, son of Eliza Jane Huxtable, of 17 Alexandra Road, Erith, Kent, and the late Arthur Ernest Huxtable. He was educated locally. Alfred enlisted in Holborn and was sent for training. He arrived in Boulogne on Wednesday 19th May 1915 from where he entrained to northern France. His training continued in preparation for front line duties. In early June he crossed the border to a camp where he was trained for two weeks in trench digging and trench maintenance, before taking the line for the first time. Alfred marched through Ypres, no longer the beautiful medieval town of only a few weeks before, but a skeletal ruin; gone were the street cafés and shops, destroyed by shelling. It was not a place any more to wander around and relax. The cellars provided shelter but the town was a dangerous place, well pin-pointed by the German artillery. He undertook a series of duties without incident until the attack at Hooge on Friday 30th July. On Saturday 17th the British exploded a mine under the German lines at Hooge but were unable to exploit the action and push on further. Various attempts to attack and advance were made over the ensuing days but without success. A German counter-attack was anticipated from late July; the lip of the mine was held, but only just. No communication trenches ran to the rear and it was under constant sniper, shell and trench-mortar fire. During the afternoon of Thursday 29th Alfred marched to Ypres and during the night relieved the Rifle Brigade and their comrades in the 8th Battalion, King's Royal Rifle Corps. The relief went well and apparently unnoticed by the Germans who were, however, well aware that the relatively untried and inexperienced 7th Battalion was taking the line. The Germans had been tapping the British telephone wires and listened carefully to communications reporting all movements and reliefs to Headquarters. When Alfred arrived in the line he found himself very close to the German lines; in places they were only fifteen feet apart. Shortly before dawn Alfred was ordered to 'stand to', and not long afterwards an immense roar was heard as the Germans blew up the ruins of the stables of Hooge Château. At the same time they advanced on the British lines using *'Flammenwerfer'* (flame throwers or 'liquid fire'). Thick black smoke billowed everywhere and the sky turned crimson from the jets of flame, at the same time a heavy bombardment commenced, trench mortars rained down and the German front line opened rapid fire. Alfred's line was thus heavily attacked and he was ordered to rapid fire at the short distance that brought the *'Flammenwerfer'* to a halt in front of his line. At 11.30am reinforcements arrived and at 2.45pm he participated in the counter-attack that ended in failure. Alfred survived the horrific attack and was relieved from the line later that evening.

After a period of rest Alfred returned to the line and during a 'normal' tour of duty was killed — a young life lost that had experienced more than most of us today would wish to imagine.

The King's Royal Rifle Corps Memorial outside Winchester Cathedral

... a romantic view of resting behind the lines for the benefit of the British public

8479 Private Richard Hyslop, DCM

1st Battalion Gordon Highlanders
Died on Saturday 5th June 1915, aged 33
Commemorated on Panel 38.

Citation for the Distinguished Conduct Medal, London Gazette, Thursday 1st April 1915:

"For very gallant conduct on 14th December 1914, in undertaking the delivery of a most urgent message after six men had been killed in the attempt. He succeeded. Again, on the same day, he went forward at dusk to act as guide to an Officer's position, a place of danger situated only fifty yards from the enemy's main trench."

Richard was born in Govan, Lanarkshire, the son of Richard and Margaret Y Hyslop, of Kirkintilloch, Dumbartonshire. He was married to Margaret A Hyslop, of 29 Don Place, Woodside, Aberdeen.

He enlisted in Glasgow. At the end of October 1914 the Battalion left Fosse in northern France and went into the Ypres Salient. On Thursday 5th November Richard was sent into the line at Hooge, close to *'Shrewsbury Forest'*. At 9.00am on Wednesday 11th the Germans laid down a preliminary barrage prior to their attack along the line from Messines to Polygon Wood. The Pomeranians attacked the Gordons but they were successfully repulsed. Richard remained in the line until Friday 20th when he was relieved and sent south, a long hard march to Westoutre where they went into billets. On Monday 14th he was in the line on the Kemmel to Wytschaete road taking part in an attack on Messines. At 7.45am the whistles were blown and the advance began, however, the Germans put up a stiff resistance. Communication with Battalion headquarters was virtually impossible as the German artillery bombarded them and the German machine-guns continued relentlessly. By 4.00pm the Battalion had got to within fifty yards of the German line, Captain Arthur Boddam-Whetham managed to get into a German line but he and his men were killed (he is commemorated on the Menin Gate, see above). Richard's bravery on that day, acting as a messenger, won him the Distinguished Conduct Medal. Richard was in the line at Ploegsteert during Christmas and witnessed the Christmas Truce.

Captain Boddam-Whetham

When the Germans launched the first gas attack on Thursday 22nd April 1915 he was in the line at St Eloi, despite being a few miles to the south many of the men were complained of sore eyes. On Wednesday 12th May he was sent to Hill 60 and his first task was to clear the trenches of the dead who had been killed the week before. They also collected up weapons and ammunition that were then in short supply. On Thursday 20th he was relieved and sent to La Clytte for four days before being sent to Zillebeke at short notice when a gas attack was launched against Hooge. On Tuesday 1st June the Germans opened a huge barrage and four days later, whilst in the line Richard was killed.

Embarkation for France, One Day's Ration Per Man Consisted Of For The Men:

Meat	**1 ration (1lb nominal)**
Biscuit	**1lb**
Tea	**5/8oz**
Sugar	**3oz**
Salt	**½oz**
Pepper	**1/36th oz**
Mustard	**1/36th oz**
Cheese	**2oz**
Jam	**3oz**
Milk	**1oz**

For The Horses:

Bran	**3lbs (in lieu of 3lbs oats)**
Oats	**12lbs**
Hay	**12lbs**

from

I'Anson to Knox

Lieutenant Leonard Percy I'Anson

4th Battalion Yorkshire Regiment

Died on Sunday 25th April 1915, aged 27

Commemorated on Panel 33.

Leonard I'Anson and his family coat of arms

Leonard was born at home on Friday 19th April 1878, third and youngest son of William and Mary I'Anson, of Bardencroft, Saltburn-by-the-Sea, Yorkshire. He was educated at Bootham School, York, where he was Captain of the Football XI. Leonard studied law and was admitted as a solicitor in February 1901, practising in Middlesborough. He was an active and ardent Freemason.

In October 1913 Leonard was gazetted Lieutenant and at the outbreak of war was mobilized. He left for France on Saturday 17th April 1915 entraining at Newcastle for Folkestone where he sailed for Boulogne. After a short rest in camp — despite the benefit ruined by the exhausting march in both directions — the Battalion entrained for Cassel. From the hill-top town a view toward the battlefields of Flanders (both Belgian and French) could be gained and the sound of artillery was particularly clear. Leonard marched the few miles to the border village of Godeswaersvelde in the shadow of the Mont de Cats. From the top of the hill Leonard was able to look down upon the battlefield of Ypres and watch the flashes of the guns with the sound of battle echoing in his ears.

The Germans launched the first gas attack at 5.00pm on Thursday 22nd April to the north of Ypres against the French colonial troops. The effect was devastating: those who survived the initial attack fled in panic, many so badly affected by the gas that they died in agony shortly afterwards. Ypres was basically completely undefended in the northern section and the German troops could have simply marched into the town if they had not halted and consolidated their position.

The next morning the Battalion marched from the village to Poperinghe where they were taken to *'Camp C'* at Vlamertinghe. At 1.00am on Saturday 24th they marched to the Ypres Canal where they remained until noon when orders arrived for them to move forward to Potijze. Within twenty-four hours of arriving at the front Leonard would be killed. Leonard was ordered to lead his men to support the position at St Julien and they were able to reach Fortuin without taking too many casualties. From the hamlet they advanced across the open ground which was flooded as the water-table of the Hannebeek had been destroyed by constant shell-fire. Whilst crossing the thick mud Leonard was cut down at the head of his platoon.

The Divisional History records: *"On through Fortuin the two Battalions went, next encountering the enemy in force advancing south of St Julien.*

They forced the enemy to give ground and drove him back into the village. They then found themselves up against a muddy stream, known as the Hannebeek, on the southern exits of St Julien and, the crossings being swept by heavy rifle and machine-gun fire, the two Battalions were forced to take what cover presented itself.

Casualties during this affair were severe, but the counter-attack was completely successful and, besides preventing the Germans from making any further advance on the 24th reflected the greatest credit upon the two gallant Battalions."

Lieutenant John Eugene Impey

1st Battalion Lincolnshire Regiment

Died on Monday 27th March 1916, aged 19

Commemorated on Panel 21.

John was the second son of Edward and Katharine Impey, of Sheldon Manor, Chippenham. He was educated at Eton College, where his father was a Master. John was a member of Mr Philip Vere Broke's House, leaving in 1914.

Eton College

He was gazetted on Tuesday 10th November 1914. For the first six weeks of 1915 the Battalion was based in Kemmel before moving north to the Salient on Wednesday 17th February, taking the line by *'The Bluff'*. In mid-March they had moved to Hill 60 after the Germans blew a mine and their duties were to assist rebuild the shattered trenches. In early April he was sent to St Eloi for a tour of duty before being sent to the Ypres to Comines Canal. Here they experienced a strange odour on Thursday 22nd April as the gas used against the French Zouaves drifted down the canal. From Sunday 6th to Tuesday 15th June John was training ready for the attack on Bellewaarde. At 4.15pm on Tuesday 15th they moved from bivouac in Brandhoek, all men and officers were issued with a newly designed anti-gas hood before going into their assembly positions at *'Cambridge Road'*. At 2.30am the next morning the British artillery laid down a barrage, at 4.15am John led his men forward and captured the German front line trenches. At 4.30am they moved to the second line and captured them at the point of the bayonet. They fought through the day, countering attacks by the Germans, until 9.30pm when the Battalion was relieved. John remained in the sector

until Saturday 13th November when they moved south to the Houplines sector. John returned to the southern sector of the Salient and was killed at St Eloi.
John was recorded in Debretts Obituary — War Roll of Honour published in the 1921 edition.
At Eton College a green marble and stone tablet was placed in his memory with the inscription: *"To the dear memory of John Eugene Impey Lieutenant 1st Battalion The Lincolnshire Regiment. Second Son of Edward and Katherine Impey. Killed in action near St Eloi, Belgium, March 27 1916, aged 19. The lot has fallen unto me in a fair ground."*
St Mary's The Virgins Church, Steeple Ashton, Wiltshire, a stone tablet was placed in his memory with the inscription: *"To the dear memory of John Eugene Impey Lieut. First Batt. Lincolnshire Regiment. Second son of Edward and Katharine Impey, killed in action near St Eloi, Belgium, March 27 1916, aged 19."*

79940 Private William James Imrie

'B' Company 31st Battalion Canadian Infantry (Alberta Regiment)

Died on Monday 5th June 1916, aged 23

Commemorated on Panel 28.

William Imrie

William was born at home on Sunday 5th November 1893, son of Alexander and Emily Imrie, of Hayfield, Kinross, Scotland. He was educated locally and had intended studying law. He was serving an apprenticeship with a firm of solicitors when he decided to leave for Canada where he was employed by the Bank of Montreal in Medicine Hat.
On Wednesday 18th November 1914, in Medicine Hat, William volunteered and enlisted where he was described as 5ft 7in tall, a 35in chest, dark complexion, brown eyes, dark brown hair, and a small scar on the right of his forehead and the bridge of his nose. He went to England where he spent some time in training at Lydd and Otterpool, leaving for France at 6.15pm Saturday 18th September William embarked on *SS Duchess of Argyll* which sailed at 7.10pm for Boulogne, arriving at 9.30pm. He was sent to *'Ostrohove Rest Camp'* until the next morning. He marched to the station and at 10.30am left for Cassel, arriving at 3.00pm and went to billets in St Sylvestre. Final training was undertaken at *'Aldershot Huts'* before crossing the border to Kemmel on Saturday 25th.
William's first experience of the front line began on Thursday 30th September and he served in the Kemmel sector until the end of March 1916. He was sent for a reasonable period of rest, a minimum of five days, on Saturday 1st April, but it did not last long, as the next day the battalion was ordered to the Salient. He marched via Mont Noir and was sent to *'Camp A'* west of Dickebusch. William went into the line at the *'Spoilbank'* during the night of Monday 3rd. He served in the sector and around Voormezeele for nearly three weeks until being sent to *'Camp I'* for a week's rest and fatigues. William was then sent to Dickebusch
From Monday 1st May the Battalion went into reserve at *'Scottish Wood'* and Voormezeele when the village was bombarded and very badly damaged during the afternoon. Following a week under heavy shell-fire he was relieved to *'Camp E'* for rest and training until Monday 22nd. He again returned back to the line at Voormezeele where the Royal Flying Corps were particularly active, engaging the German machines above their lines. On Thursday 1st June he went to *'Quebec Camp'* for four days before leaving for *'Winnipeg Camp'* from where at 7.30pm, he was taken by motor transport towards the front line near *'Dormy House'*, Zillebeke. They came under heavy shrapnel fire as they marched into the line and passed many dead bodies which remained untended by the side of the road. William was killed, with two of his comrades, when a shell hit the dug-out where they were sleeping.

10065 Lance Serjeant James Inches, DCM

2nd Battalion Royal Scots Fusiliers

Died on Saturday 31st October 1914, aged 21

Commemorated on Panel 33.

Citation for the Distinguished Conduct Medal, London Gazette, Thursday 1st April 1915:
"Has been noted for conspicuous gallantry."

James was born at home, son of Mr and Mrs Andrew Inches, of 46 Reid Street, Dunfermline.
James enlisted in Dunfermline and in early October James was sent out to Belgium. Upon arrival in Zeebrugge the Battalion spent some time being sent hither and thither as Antwerp had fallen and they were now needed at Ypres. The Battalion arrived on Thursday 15th October where he took the line at Wieltje. James was moved to the line east of Gheluvelt between Poezelhoek and Reutel. The Battalion had difficulty holding their position as they were under constant attack by superior forces. During the night of Friday 23rd a party of forty Germans managed to break through a gap in their line but they were soon spotted and taken prisoner. Early in the morning a major advance on the line commenced with the 2nd Wiltshires on their left surrounded, and Polygon Wood under threat. The pressure was building;

General Capper

General Sir Thompson Capper, KCMG, CB, DSO, (who was killed on Monday 27th September 1915 and is buried in Lillers Communal Cemetery) sent the message: *"Hold on like hell: the Second Division is coming."* Hold on they did, but at great cost. During the night a burial party went out to collect bodies and were fired upon from a cottage, which they immediately attacked, taking a further twenty prisoners. Only during the afternoon of Sunday 25th was the pressure relieved as the 7th Cavalry Brigade made a spirited and successful counter-attack. After ten days continuous duty in the front line they were relieved and sent to Hooge for a rest. After only twelve hours they were sent back to support the line on Kruiseik Ridge. In the early hours of Thursday 29th the Germans attacked towards the Gheluvelt crossroads with HRH Duke of Würtemberg putting full force into the attack on Friday 30th. The 2nd Worcesters saved the day on Saturday 31st with their famous charge at Gheluvelt. James was one of the few men left to resist the German attacks and mount counter-attacks, but by the end of the day, he too had been killed and in effect the Battalion ceased to exist.

In March 1915 Brigadier General Herbert Watts addressed the men on their action at Ypres:

"Major Pollard, officers, non-commissioned, officers and men of the Royal Scots Fusiliers.

It is only within the last few days that I have learned the true history of the gallant doing of your battalion, on 31st October last, and in cases where troops are captured I think that the facts should be known.

On 30th of October, in order to cover the right flank of troops on our left, your battalion was ordered to take up a very bad and exposed position on a forward slope, and, sure enough, on the morning of the 31st you were exposed to a very heavy shell fire, followed by an infantry attack by vastly superior numbers. As far as your battalion was concerned all went well, until the troops on your left were driven back, and your left flank exposed.

The Germans came pouring through, and it soon became obvious that our position was untenable, and we were ordered to take up a position farther back. I tried to telephone to Colonel Baird Smith, but the wire had been cut by shrapnel. I then sent two orderlies with a message to withdraw, but the message was never received. Both orderlies must have been killed or wounded.

Colonel Baird Smith, gallant soldier that he was, decided — and rightly — to hold his ground, and the Royal Scots Fusiliers fought and fought until the Germans absolutely surrounded and swarmed into the trenches.

I think it was perfectly splendid. Mind you, it was not a case of 'Hands up' or any nonsense of that sort; it was a fight to a finish. What more do you want? Why, even a German general came to Colonel Baird Smith afterwards and congratulated him, and said he could not understand how his men had held out so long.

You may well be proud to belong to such a regiment, and I am proud to have you in my brigade. A regiment with a spirit like that cannot go far wrong, and I feel sure that when next called upon we need, none of us, feel nervous as to the results."

Lieutenant Gerald Sclater Ingram

'A' Company, 2nd Battalion The Queen's
(Royal West Surrey Regiment)

Died on Wednesday 21st October 1914, aged 24
Commemorated on Panel 11.

Gerald was born in South Kensington on Thursday 24th July 1890, only child of William R Ingram (sculptor) and Beatrice Eleanor Ingram (née Crofts) of 77 Eccleston Square, London, formerly of 25 Wilton Place, London. He was educated at Pemberton Lodge, Southbourne, Hampshire, followed by Winchester College from 1904 to 1907, and went up to Christ Church, Oxford, in 1909, graduating with a BA.

In 1912 he was gazetted as a University candidate to The Queen's.

At the outbreak of war Gerald returned from South Africa, via St Helena. After a short period in camp at Lyndhurst the Battalion sailed from Southampton to Zeebrugge. Gerald was posted to 'A' Company and promoted Lieutenant in September 1914. After some abortive efforts at helping to defend Ghent they were marched southeast to the Ypres Salient via Thielt and Roeselare. It was a particularly hard march, spending twenty-four out of twenty-six hours on the road. They took the line at Dadizeele and Gerald was sent with 'A' Company to the level crossing south of Ledeghem where he surprised a group of six Germans whom they killed or wounded. They were spotted and the German infantry enfiladed them forced them back towards Zonnebeke. On the morning of Wednesday 21st October the German artillery opened up on their lines, but 'A' Company were well dug in and held fast; during the engagement, Gerald was killed.

On Wednesday 4th November 1914 his obituary was published in *'The Times'*: *"LIEUTENANT GERALD SCLATER INGRAM, 2nd Queen's Regiment, who was killed near Ypres on October 21 was the only child of Mrs William Ingram of 77 Eccleston Square, SW. He was born in July, 1890, and was educated at Winchester and Christ Church, Oxford. He was gazetted to a Second Lieutenancy in his regiment in February last, and was promoted last month."*

Gerald is commemorated on the Chailey War Memorial, Sussex.

Second Lieutenant Walter Inkster

4th Battalion Gordon Highlanders

Died on Saturday 25th September 1915, aged 25

Commemorated on Panel 38.

Walter Inkster

Walter was born in Aberdeen, on Friday 21st February 1890, son of James Inkster. He was educated at Ashley Road School followed by Aberdeen Grammar School from 1903. In 1908 Walter went up to Aberdeen University where he graduated with an MA in 1911: he continued his studies, gaining a BSc in Agriculture in 1912. Whilst at College he played for a wide selection teams and in many sporting events. In 1912 Walter left to work in Berlin for the Potash Syndicate for two years before taking up a similar position in Australia.

After the outbreak of war Walter returned to Scotland and in March 1915 volunteered, enlisting with the 4th Battalion, being commissioned in April. In May he left for France, entrained for Belgium and joined the Battalion in the field. On Monday 24th May the Germans launched a gas attack on Hooge and he was sent to Zillebeke in reserve. He took part in an attack on Bellewaarde and captured a series of trenches. He remained on tours of duty until early September when he was given home leave. He had not been back in the line for a week before he was killed in action at Hooge when he took part in the feint for the Battle of Loos. At 4.10am on Saturday 25th September 1915 he blew his whistle and took his men forward against the German lines. They could not advance far as the German wire in front of them remained uncut and, whilst negotiating his way round it, Walter was killed.

Lieutenant Ambrose Constantine Ionides

15th Battalion attached 9th Battalion King's Royal Rifle Corps

Died on Saturday 16th October 1915, aged 37

Commemorated on Panel 51.

Ambrose Ionides

Ambrose was born at home on Tuesday 9th April 1878, second son of Alexander A and Isabella Ionides (née Sechiari), of 1 Holland Park, London, and The Homewood, Esher, Surrey, his father being the Consul-General for Greece. He was educated at Eton College from 1891 to 1895 as a member of Mr Francis Batten Cristall Tarver's House. Ambrose became a member of the Stock Exchange in 1900.

At the Greek Church in London on Saturday 29th July 1911, Ambrose married Euphrosyne (Effie) Ionides (née Spartali), of The Cottage, Carlisle Road, Eastbourne. They had two children, Denis who was born on Thursday 23rd May 1912 and Irene on Sunday 6th September 1914.

At the outbreak of war Ambrose joined the Inns of Court OTC, with service number D/1488 and rose to the rank of Corporal. He was gazetted on Tuesday 5th January 1915 and left for France on Thursday 5th August, joining the Battalion in the field in Flanders. Whilst in action near Hooge he volunteered to go with a party, in the thick mist, to mend and put up wire. Suddenly the mist lifted and his party was exposed, he ordered the men to get down and take cover, but there was not enough room for Ambrose: he was spotted by the Germans and shot.

His Colonel wrote: *"Although he had only been with us for a few months he was extremely popular, and had proved himself an excellent soldier. We all liked him and are proud to have had him as a brother officer."*

The sergeant of his platoon wrote: *"He was loved by his men for his kindness, his bravery and his many soldierly qualities. He set us a good example of coolness under fire, and his platoon was willing and ready to follow him anywhere."*

In St Martin's Church, East Horsley, Surrey, a stone tablet was placed in his memory with the inscription: *"To the memory of Ambrose Constantine Ionides of Rowbarns Grange in this parish, Lieut. King's Royal Rifles, who fell in action near Ypres on October 16 1915, aged 37."*

6890 Corporal Alfred Alexander Irish, DCM

'D' Company, 1st Battalion Hampshire Regiment

Died on Thursday 13th May 1915, aged 29

Commemorated on Panel 35.

Citation for the Distinguished Conduct Medal, London Gazette, Thursday 1st April 1915:

"For gallantry on 19th December 1914, in reconnoitring in daylight the ground over which an advance had to be made."

Alfred was born in Holborn, London, son of Alfred James and Georgina Emma Irish. He was married to Annie Marion Clutterbuck (formerly Irish), of 36 Chesterfield Gardens, Harringay, London.

Alfred enlisted in London. The Battalion sailed from Southampton to Le Havre on the *SS Braemar Castle* and the *SS Cestrian*, arriving on Saturday 22nd August 1914. After a short period in camp he entrained for Le Cateau at 4.00am on Tuesday 25th arriving as The

Retreat was beginning. He was marched to Solesmes and took part in the rearguard of the BEF as they passed through. On Wednesday they came under heavy fire from Cattenières with the German artillery causing a number of casualties. During the afternoon the Battalion was ordered to retire and reform at Ligny. As they retired the Germans moved forward with rapid fire halting them, and at 5.00pm orders were received to retire from Ligny. However, Major Hicks and three hundred men did not receive the order, remaining in position until 7.00pm. During the day the Battalion took more than two hundred casualties. By Thursday the Battalion had collected together and engaged the Germans at Nauroy. After the short skirmish The Retreat continued and another engagement took place on Tuesday 1st September at Vaucelles. Five days later the Battalion headed to the Marne followed by the Aisne where they dug in and fought on the Chemin des Dames until Sunday 4th October when the move to Flanders began. On Sunday 11th October the Battalion entrained via Amiens to Wizernes, arriving at 10.00pm, and went into billets. The next day they went close to Méteren and were in reserve but did not see action as the Germans were driven off the Mont de Cats and forced back to the Lys.

From Thursday 15th October the Battalion took position at Nieppe. On Wednesday 21st they crossed into Belgium to serve at Ploegsteert. For action on Saturday 19th December 1914 Alfred was awarded the Distinguished Conduct Medal whilst in the line at Le Gheer when he went out reconnoitring with Private Frank Glasspool (commemorated on the Menin Gate, see above). Until mid-April 1915 Alfred served in the Ploegsteert sector and was at rest at Noote Boom, Bailleul, when the Germans attacked with gas for the first time on Thursday 22nd April. At lunchtime on Saturday 24th Alfred was entrained in Bailleul and sent to Poperinghe. He marched to billets overnight before being sent into the line close to *'Berlin Wood'* to take part in a series of counter-attacks and halt the Germans from moving further forward. Each day the attacks were more intense and the Battalion took severe losses.

The Battalion was in front of *'Mouse Trap Farm'* on Thursday 13th May 1915 when the Germans opened a huge barrage: *"It was a shelling, at one time the whole line of trench disappeared in a yellow cloud of smoke and the earth was absolutely rocking."* Alfred was on the right flank and his Company took the heaviest of the shelling. Their trench took a terrible pounding and he was killed. Drummer Eldridge held on for some time until wounded — he and four others were the only ones out of the forty to retire from the trench (Drummer Eldridge was awarded the DCM and the French Croix de Guerre for his action).

Alfred was awarded the Russian Order of St George, 3rd Class.

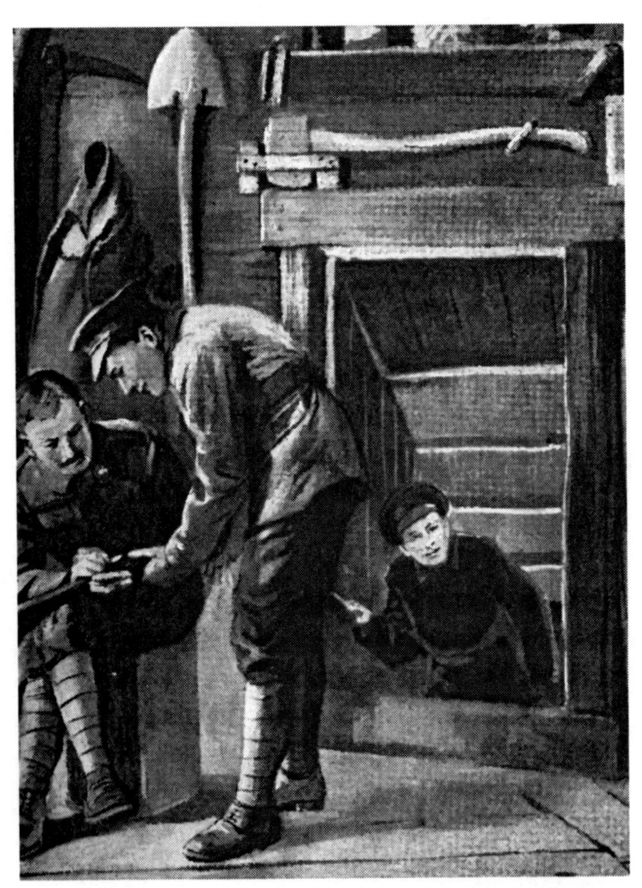

An idealised view of a front line dug-out, 1915

Honorary Captain De Witt Oscar Irwin

Canadian YMCA attached

10th Battalion Canadian Infantry (Alberta Regiment)

Died on Wednesday 28th April 1915, aged 29

Commemorated on Panel 32.

Oscar was born at home, son of Mary L Irwin, of Collingwood, Ontario, and the late John Irwin. He was educated locally and went up to Toronto University from 1908 to 1912, graduating with an MA. He studied for Holy Orders at Knox College, and was appointed to Victoria Church, West Toronto and Mount Albert Presbyterian Church.

At the outbreak of war Oscar volunteered and went out with the First Canadian Contingent being promoted Captain in Belgium.

The Battalion first saw service in Ploegsteert in the middle of February from where they were sent to the Armentières sector for a month. From Thursday 15th April they were in the line at Wieltje undertaking a difficult tour of duty in partly-dug trenches. Oscar encouraged the men in their digging and helped with the removal of the very many rotting corpses and supervised their burial — the dead being German, French and British. On Thursday 22nd he accompanied the Battalion and at 6.00pm they were sent into the line at St Julien ready to counter-attack after the German gas attack earlier in the afternoon. At 11.45pm their attack commenced and Oscar was fully employed in dealing with the scores of wounded taken from the moment of the advance. In addition, large numbers of German prisoners were taken, being herded back to the cages behind the lines. The German artillery retaliated with shrapnel shells followed by high-explosives, the Battalion was being badly cut up, retirement was the only salvation, and they withdrew to a line beyond their first objective. Nineteen officers and nearly six hundred other ranks were casualties. Oscar supported the men who were tired, hungry and thirsty; however, many were concerned that their ammunition had or was about to run out.

At 3.00am on Saturday 24th the Germans attacked again and gas shells rained down, their lethal contents pouring forth in huge waves towards them. Shortly afterwards the Battalion was ordered to take up position on the Gravenstafel Ridge, but just as they did so they were ordered to move again, to assist the 8th Battalion northeast of St Julien. Only one hundred and forty-six men under three officers took the line, and they were able to beat off several German attacks despite the gas and artillery pouring down on them. By noon the situation was hopeless and the Battalion had to retire. Later in evening, Tuesday 27th, orders were received to support the line which was again under immense pressure. During the day on Wednesday 28th the line broke for a short period and during the attack Oscar was killed. The next day only one hundred men of the Battalion were able to return to Vlamertinghe.

... relaxing in an estaminet when out of the line

Lieutenant Colonel Francis Edward Bradshaw Isherwood

2nd Battalion Commanding 1st Battalion
York and Lancaster Regiment
Died on Sunday 9th May 1915, aged 45
Commemorated on Addenda Panel 57.

Francis was born on Thursday 1st July 1869 son of John Henry Bradshaw Isherwood, JP, of Marple Hall, Cheshire. He was educated at Cheltenham College September 1882 to July 1885 as a member of Christowe, went up to Clare College, Cambridge in 1887 and passed into RMC Sandhurst. In 1903 he married Kathleen Machell, (daughter of Frederick Machell Smith), of 19 Pembroke Gardens, London, and they had a son, Christopher, born in 1904.

Francis was gazetted to the York and Lancaster Regiment in January, 1892, promoted Captain in 1901, Major in 1911, and Lieutenant Colonel on Thursday 18th February 1915.

Francis served in the South African War and was present at the Relief of Ladysmith and the actions of Vaal Kranz, Tugela Heights and Pieters Hill where he was Mentioned in Despatches twice, receiving the Queen's Medal with five clasps and King's Medal with two clasps.

Following the outbreak of war the Battalion was ordered to return to England from Jubbulpore, India, arriving on Wednesday 23rd December 1914. They were sent to Hursley Park for final training and re-kitting before leaving for France. From Southampton they sailed to Le Havre on Wednesday 17th January 1915 and entrained to northern France. The Battalion was sent across the border into Belgium to serve around St Eloi.

Following the beginning of the Second Battle of Ypres the Battalion was sent into the line in the Salient. Francis was killed in action.

'Kathleen and Frank' by Christopher Isherwood published in 1971 gives a particularly interesting insight into his parents somewhat 'different' lives.

The Band of the 1st Battalion played at the opening of the Menin Gate in 1927.

5099 Private Gilbert Ivall

1st Battalion Scots Guards
Died on Wednesday 11th November 1914
Commemorated on Panel 11.

Gilbert was born in Slough, Buckinghamshire. He was educated locally and became a member of the Royal Household serving as an Assistant in the Servants' Hall of the Lord Steward's Department.

He enlisted on Wednesday 5th August 1914 and following training Gilbert joined the Battalion in the field. On Sunday 18th October the 1st Battalion arrived in Hazebrouck and made their way up to Poperinghe. On Wednesday 21st Gilbert was ordered to march into the line in front of Langemarck on the Pilkem Ridge. From there he was moved into the line at Gheluvelt where he would remain until his death. At 6.30am on Wednesday 11th November the Germans launched another huge barrage on the trenches where Gilbert was serving which lasted for three hours. As the barrage lifted the Prussian Guard advanced in full strength. He was holding a position at a burnt-out farmhouse on the edge of Gheluvelt Wood and was subjected to heavy shell fire. The grey hordes descended on the line and it was impossible to hold on. Whether Gilbert was killed by shell fire or in the infantry attack is not known. By the end of the battle the 1st Battalion had been decimated when they finally marched out of the line on Sunday 22nd November to Westoutre — only Captain Stacey (lucky to be alive after being buried alive for an hour and half earlier in the month), the Quartermaster and seventy-three men were left.

Second Lieutenant David Ive

'D' Company, 2nd Battalion The Queen's (Royal West Surrey Regiment)
Died on Friday 23rd October 1914, aged 20
Commemorated on Panel 11.

David Ive

David was born at Kensington on Sunday 27th May 1894, son of Mr Ernest Ive, MICE, and Mrs St Claire Ive, of The Hermitage, Meadvale, Redhill, Surrey. He was educated at Reigate Grammar School and was a member of their OTC receiving his 'A' certificate in May 1912. David was subsequently educated privately in Eastbourne and London. He was a member of the 1st Reigate Troop, Scouts.

He was gazetted on Wednesday 1st October 1913.

David left South Africa when they were mobilized at the outbreak of war, arriving in Southampton. After a period of training in Lyndhurst he sailed to Zeebrugge on Sunday 4th October 1914 as a member of 'D' Company from where he was sent to help with the defence of Ghent. Their arrival in Ghent was too late for any meaningful assistance and almost immediately they were withdrawn and sent southwest to the Ypres Salient. On Sunday 18th The Queen's were in position around Dadizeele when 'D' Company were sent to support 'A' Company at Ledeghem in reinforcing the Royal Welch Fusiliers, and to bring in a large collection of bicycles that had been spotted in the village. They came under heavy fire from the German infantry and were forced to retire to Zonnebeke which they reached by 8.00pm. During the morning of Wednesday 21st the line was being heavily shelled. On Friday 23rd Major Crofts took two hundred and fifty men, under the command of Lieutenant Colonel Hal Cadogan (see Hooge Crater Cemetery), to take the trenches in Zonnebeke and help collect a large collection of abandoned equipment. During the work they came under fire and David was fatally wounded in the abdomen. He was buried where he fell.

Second Lieutenant Alan James Jackson

3rd Battalion Middlesex Regiment
Died on Tuesday 27th April 1915
Commemorated on Panel 49.

Alan was educated at Framlingham College from 1906 to 1913 and went up to Gonville and Caius College, Cambridge.

Alan left College and volunteered. He was commissioned and left for France on Monday 18th January 1915 and entrained to Flêtre where training for the front line continued. On Saturday 6th February he went into the line at St Eloi where he remained for the rest of the month; the majority of March was spent at Rossignol with the billets for the most part being at La Clytte. In early April he was sent into the line at St Jan. He witnessed the appalling effects of the German gas attack, seeing the French Turcos pouring back, in agony, after the dense yellow-green cloud of poison gas had flowed over their lines, although at the time the reason for their appalling condition was unknown.

Field Marshal Sir John French

Field Marshal Sir John French wrote: *"The effect of these poisonous gases was virulent as to render the whole of the line held by the French Divisions. ... The smoke and fumes hid everything from sight, and hundreds of men were thrown into a comatose or dying condition, and within an hour the whole position had to be abandoned, together with about 50 guns."* Alan and his men entrenched themselves straddling the crossroads at St Jan. Throughout Friday 23rd he was under heavy shell fire - one barrage lasting four hours - followed by a gas attack. Despite the desperate situation the Middlesex managed somehow to cling on. The next day they were forced to evacuate their trenches due to heavy artillery fire and move into a field close by and dig in. On Monday 26th Alan moved back to the GHQ lines in reserve to the Lahore Division and the following day Alan was killed.

Captain George Millais James

1st Battalion The Buffs (East Kent Regiment)
attached as Brigade Major,
22nd Infantry Brigade 7th Division
Died on Tuesday 3rd November 1914, aged 34
Commemorated on Addenda Panel 57.

George James

George was born in London on Monday 15th November 1880, elder son of the late Major William Christopher James (Scots Greys) and the late Effie Gray James (daughter of Sir John Millais, Baronet, the eminent painter). He was educated at Glenalmond from 1891 to 1894, followed by Cheltenham College until 1898 as a member of Hazelwell and was a member of the Shooting VIII. He passed into RMC Sandhurst. On Friday 16th October 1908, George married Hylda Madeleine (daughter of Sir James Heath, Baronet), of Oxendon Hall, Market Harborough, Leicestershire. They had two daughters, Eileen Alice born on Saturday 19th June 1909 and Daphne Millais on Friday 13th January 1911. His wife later remarried and became Mrs Bates.
George was gazetted on Wednesday 6th December 1899, promoted to Lieutenant on Saturday 17th February 1900, Captain on Monday 30th May 1904 and Brigade Major in 1912.
George served in the South African War where he was wounded during action at Venerskroon, Mentioned in Despatches on Tuesday 9th July and Tuesday 10th September 1901, received the Queen's Medal with three clasps and the King's Medal with two clasps. He then saw service in Mauritius and India.
George went out with the BEF as Brigade Major of the 22nd Infantry Brigade, 7th Division. He landed in Zeebrugge during the first week of October 1914. The Division was to have been sent to help support with the defence of Antwerp, but the German army had broken through and were beginning to advance towards Brugge and southeastward to Ypres. George was sent south to the Ypres Salient and assisted in organising the defence

German troops in Brugge, October 1914

of the town and Salient. The Division did not always get the best of billets; the Reverend E J Kennedy wrote: *"Then on and on after hour, halting ten minutes each hour for a needed breather and rest, until Ostend hove into sight. Visions of a comfortable billet rose before one's luxurious mind, but no luck; right through the city we marched, finding the station square crammed with terror-stricken and most wretched-looking refugees; until some four miles out, we lighted upon the most filthy and forsaken place to be found on the map of civilization — Steene. The houses were so vile and malodorous, that it was with great reluctance the O. C. allowed the men to enter. By this time it was very dark and very cold, and it was with purely animal instinct that we found the way to our mouths in the darkness, and tried to make believe that we enjoyed the biscuit and bully beef which formed our rations."* The Division was ordered back to Brugge where they were billeted before marching off to Beernem, followed by Wingene, Roeselare and onward towards Ypres. After marching through Zonnebeke they reached Ypres itself, the Reverend E J Kennedy wrote: *"The first view of Ypres was glorious. As we marched through the great square in front of the Cloth Hall, I was struck with the medieval aspect of the place. The gabled houses carried one's imagination into the long ago; whilst the glorious Cloth Hall of the eleventh century, backed up by the equally fine cathedral of similar age, presented a picture not easily to be forgotten. Alas! when I next saw it, the place was a heap of crumbling ruins.*
The Germans had passed through the city four days before we arrived; and according to their wont, had helped themselves very liberally to what they fancied. Many of the shopkeepers were loud in their complaints of the shameful manner in which they had been robbed."
George was initially established in Headquarters in Ypres before moving out with the Brigade Headquarters towards Gheluvelt. He was shot by a sniper, being killed instantaneously, and was buried in a small wood but the grave was subsequently lost.
George was recorded in Debretts Obituary — War Roll of Honour published in the 1921 edition.
His brother-in-law, Lieutenant Percy Heath, died on Friday 4th September 1914 and is buried in Baron Communal Cemetery.

G/7125 Private George Jarrold

4th Battalion Middlesex Regiment

Died on Wednesday 29th September 1915, aged 16

Commemorated on Panel 51.

George was born in Lambeth, son of Mrs Jarrold, of 27 Tower Street, Westminster, London.

George enlisted in London and was sent for training before being sent out to France.

From Monday 9th August to Monday 23rd 1915 George was in the line in *'Trenches 34'* to *'31'* and had a rough time of it. They were relieved and sent to Dickebusch for rest.

On Saturday 25th September 1915 an attack on Hooge commenced as a feint for the Battle at Loos taking places some miles to the south. The Brigade Diary records the difficulties that the British forces were under at the time: *"It was thought that the number of guns and the ammunition allotted to them was inadequate for the attack. ... Three trench mortar batteries are also to take part in the bombardment, but the ammunition for these is also very limited. ... The Brigade was ordered to hand over 90 pairs of wire cutters to 7th and 9th Brigades, as none were available in Ordnance Stores for them, it being thus seen that after 14 months of war even a sufficiency of wire cutters cannot be obtained before an action."* Not an auspicious start to the last battle George would see.

Following the usual preliminary barrage, four mines were blown, two at 4.19am, and within thirty seconds the second pair were blown. At 4.20am the whistles blew and George went 'over the top' and charged towards the German lines. At 6.30am the Battalion recorded that German prisoners and their wounded were being sent back. The Germans defended their positions well and put up a tremendous counter-barrage. Further gains, and consolidating those taken in the morning, were becoming increasingly difficult, partly due to lack of bombs. George and his comrades held on gallantly but by 2.20pm the supply of bombs was all but exhausted which meant counter-attacks could not be made. Much of the captured ground was lost. Throughout the night George worked on rebuilding the damaged or destroyed trenches. Late on Sunday 26th the opposing artillery commenced what became a mutual bombardment duel that lasted for nearly an hour. The next two days were, in relative terms, quiet and this allowed the men to rebuild the lines. At 4.30am on Wednesday 29th the Germans blew a mine to the left of the Middlesex lines which was followed by an immediate attack by the German infantry, including some dressed in the uniforms of the 2nd Royal Scots. Every man was wiped out on the left flank — they had stood their ground until the last, including George.

Lieutenant William Dummer Powell Jarvis

'C' Company, 3rd Battalion Canadian Infantry (Central Ontario Regiment)

Died on Saturday 24th April 1915, aged 23

Commemorated on Panel 18.

William Jarvis

William was born at home on Thursday 31st March 1892, eldest on of Æmilius and Augusta Jarvis, of 34 Prince Arthur Avenue, Toronto; he was grandson of Sir Æmilius Irving, KC. He was educated at Bishop Ridley College, St Catherine's, where he was Captain of the Cadet Force, and graduated with the Mason Medal for *'True Manliness'*. William won the lightweight boxing tournament at Toronto University in 1913. His family owned the bank Æmilius Jarvis & Co and he represented it on the stock exchange as a broker. William was a keen yachtsman, a member of the Royal Canadian Yacht Club, winning the George Cup in 1910 and successfully defended it in 1914 in his yachts *'Swamba'* and *'Nirwana'* respectively, and won the Prince of Wales' Cup twice. William was a quarter-back for the Argonaut Football Club. As a horseman he excelled at cross-country and in the show ring.

In 1911 William was commissioned as a Lieutenant in the Governor General's bodyguard.

On Tuesday 1st September 1914 William volunteered at Valcartier; his attestation papers describe him as 5ft 7½in tall, with a 38in chest, a medium complexion, brown eyes and hair, a small anchor tattoo on the left forearm, and the letter 'R' on the right leg.

He came over the England in October 1914 and trained throughout the winter at Salisbury Plain, leaving for France in February 1915. On Saturday 23rd April he was in the woods close to St Julien when the Germans first used gas, and he was sent forward to clear German snipers in ruined houses who were pinning down his section of the front. Thirty men set out and only four of them made it across the open ground to silence the snipers. William returned to report to his commander and was sent out again to help close the gap which was developing — this he did alone and was allocated more men from Lieutenant Colonel Loomis. The next day he was applying dressings to one of his wounded men when he was shot in the head, and within the hour the forty men who were left were totally surrounded and forced to surrender.

Colonel Loomis

Lieutenant Colonel Loomis wrote: *"I will never forget the officer's conduct. He seemed so competent and full of resource.*

He had absolute confidence in himself, and evidently did not know what fear was. It was a great relief to me at the time he reported, as I had previously been unable to find out what was taking place on our left. I had sent out several small patrols previous to young Jarvis's appearance, but they were never able to return and report, as most of them were killed."

Captain Streight wrote: *"Your son Bill was killed while defending his trench on the morning of 24 April. ... At noon on the 23rd I received orders to get in touch with St. Julien, which was some 800 yards to my right. Your son Bill volunteered at once to take on this dangerous task, and as he was the only Platoon Commander I had left, I gave him instructions to get his platoon out and form a connective file between our trench and the town, which he cleverly did with only two losses. Every inch of this ground was covered by all pulling themselves along on their stomachs, as the enemy were alert at all times trying to snipe them, and in a few cases they did. Before reaching the town he found himself short of men; he proceeded by himself alone into the town and found Col. Loomis in command there. Col. Loomis, after hearing his case, gave him twelve men to complete the chain, and a perfect line of communication was kept up all day. Bill returned to my trench when he had satisfied himself and reported the line to Col. Loomis connected up. Several times he went back and forward across this opening, and kept this line of communication in perfect order. No one could have operated this movement better or braver than Bill had done, and had he lived no doubt would have received some decoration for his services."*

10437 Private Frederick Arthur Jay

1st Battalion Royal Scots

Died on Tuesday 23rd March 1915, aged 26

Commemorated on Panel 11.

Frederick was born in Colchester, Essex, on Sunday 9th May 1889, eldest son of Ezekel and Ellen Jay, of 93 Harsnett Road, Colchester. He was educated locally.

On Tuesday 8th December 1908 Frederick enlisted initially serving in Scotland followed by four years in India.

Frederick was in India at the outbreak of war. The Battalion was ordered home, arriving in Devonport on Monday 16th November 1914 where he was sent to camp in Winchester. He sailed from Southampton to Le Havre on *SS City of Dunkirk*, arriving on Sunday 20th December 1914. The Battalion entrained for Aire taking billets in the barracks on Tuesday 22nd. On Wednesday 6th January 1915 he went to Dickebusch from where he undertook a series of tours of duty. Whilst they were not involved in any particular battle or action they did, however, come under constant fire from the German snipers, machine-gunners and artillery.

2nd Lieutenant Malcolm wrote of Frederick's death: *"It is with much regret that I writ to inform you of the death of your son, Private Jay. He was killed on the 23rd inst. by a shell which burst in the trench, and at the same time killed three and wounded two others. He was in my platoon, and had always proved himself a willing and capable soldier, and I deplore his loss greatly. The only consolation that I can offer is that he died doing his duty, and that his death was instantaneous. He was buried with his three comrades in the rear of the trench that same night."*

6378 Private William Arthur Jeffs

1st Battalion Gordon Highlanders

Died on Monday 14th December 1914, aged 16

Commemorated on Panel 38.

William was born in Highgate, Warwickshire, son of James William and Annie Florence Jeffs, of 100 Avon Street, Upper Stoke, Coventry. He was educated locally.

He enlisted in Aberdeen and after a short period of training he was sent out to France and joined the Battalion with a draft.

In early October the Battalion had moved from the Aisne and was taking part in the various battles in northern France around Armentières and La Bassée.

The ruins of La Bassée

On Thursday 5th November William was in the line at Hooge and the area of *'Shrewsbury Forest'*. On Wednesday 11th at 9.00am the Germans opened up a barrage along the line from Messines to Polygon Road. William and the Battalion came under attack from the Pomeranians who they repulsed. Over the next two days William came under sustained attack; during Thursday 12th a number of his friends and comrades were wounded by shell fire. The French infantry relieved the Battalion on Friday 20th and they marched to billets in Westoutre. When William took his first tour of duty near Kemmel he found the trenches half-filled with thick, cold, liquid mud. On Monday 14th December he took part in the attack on Messines, William was in front of Maedelstede Farm on the Kemmel to Wytschaete road. At 7.45am the whistles were blown and he advanced and came up against stiff resistance. In the attack William was killed.

Second Lieutenant Bernard Craig Keble Job

3rd Battalion Queen's Own (Royal West Kent Regiment)

Died on Sunday 18th April 1915, aged 27

Commemorated on Panel 45.

Bernard Job

Bernard was born in Liverpool on Thursday 9th June 1887, son of the Reverend Frederick William and Emily Frances Job, of Lower Gornal Vicarage, Dudley, Worcestershire, grandson of William Young Craig, Member of Parliament for North Staffordshire from 1880 to 1885. He was educated at Wolverhampton School from 1898 to 1901 followed by Radley College where he remained until 1904. Bernard was an all-round sportsman, being an expert fisherman, good shot, amateur boxer and a good athlete.

Bernard enlisted on Tuesday 4th August 1914 in the Liverpool Scottish and was gazetted in November 1914. He went out to the front in March 1915, joining the battalion in the field only three days before he was killed during a counter-attack on Hill 60.

The attack on Hill 60 took place on Saturday 17th April 1915: the mines were blown and the artillery barrage commenced. The top of Hill 60 simply went up in the air and it, together with the majority of the German defenders, their ammunition and materials, were scattered over a wide area. Late in the day Bernard and his men worked his way up the Hill and helped consolidate the position. They sat and awaited the expected counter-attack but it was some hours before it came. The Germans collected themselves together, commenced a counter-barrage and throughout the night attacked. During one of the morning attacks he was killed.

His Commanding Officer wrote: *"We have had altogether terrible losses in the last few days, but none will be felt in the 3rd Battalion more than this. He was a universal favourite. Had he lived he would have made a very fine officer. That his death was a glorious one I have no doubt. He was the soul of courage."*

Major Robinson wrote: *"He was shot by a bullet and died almost immediately on the morning of April 18 in the heavy fighting which followed our capture of a portion of the enemy's position called Hill 60, 2½ miles S.E. of Ypres. I understand that he died almost instantly, after being hit and that he could have felt no pain. It was not possible during the fighting to bury his body. I am, however, informed that all the dead have been buried, so your son no doubt lies at rest among the other officers and men who fought with him. Your son had only joined this Battn. a few days before his death, but from the little I saw of him, I formed the opinion that he was a gallant and valuable officer."*

In the church at Lower Gornal his parents donated the Lady Chapel Altar Screen in his memory which has the figure of St Alban in the form of their son.

Captain Bernard Digby Johns

10th Battalion Royal Welch Fusiliers

Died on Thursday 17th February 1916, aged 21

Commemorated on Panel 22.

Bernard was born in Bath, on Sunday 13th May 1894, only child of Honoria French (formerly Johns), of 3 Sion Hill, Clifton, Bristol, and the late Alexander Digby Johns of Carrickfergus, County Antrim. He was educated at Matfield Grange, Kent, followed by Repton School from 1908 to 1913 as a member of Mitre, where he was a House Prefect, Head of House and a School Prefect; he won the Crewe Exhibition and the English Literature Prize twice. Bernard won a History Exhibition at Hertford College and then a History Scholarship at Oriel College, Oxford, and decided to enter the latter College in October 1913.

At the outbreak of war Bernard volunteered and was gazetted in September 1914, promoted Lieutenant on Monday 23rd November and Captain in July 1915.

He left Dover for Boulogne on board *SS Onward* on Monday 27th September 1915. He entrained for northern France and went into training at Caëstre until Monday 5th October, when he marched with his men to Bailleul. Two days later the Battalion trained for the front line with the 2nd Battalion, Royal Scots, around Ploegsteert. On Friday 15th his first tour of duty was undertaken at Hooge. At the end of November the Battalion was moved to St Eloi, remaining in the sector until he returned home for a week's leave in February 1916. Almost as soon as he returned to the front he was shot by a sniper while supervising the strengthening of the trenches at Wytschaete, and buried close to where he fell.

His Colonel wrote: *"He was the life and soul of the officers' mess."*

In St Katherine's Church, Felton, Avon, a stained glass window was dedicated in his memory with the inscription: *"To the glory of God and in proud and loving memory of Bernard Digby Johns aged 21, Captn. Xth Batt. Royal Welsh Fusiliers, Scholar of Oriel College; grandson of The Revd. J. W. Hardman, LL.D., founder of this church, who gave his life for his King and country, falling in action near Ypres on Febry. 17th, 1916. This window was placed here by his mother and her brothers and sisters."*

426728 Private Frederick Slade Johnson

'A' Company, 28th Battalion Canadian Infantry (Saskatchewan Regiment)

Died on Tuesday 6th June 1916, aged 27

Commemorated on Panel 28.

Frederick was born at home on Sunday 26th August 1888, son of Kate Johnson of Bere Regis, Wareham, Dorset and the late John Josias Johnson. He was educated at Christ's Hospital, Horsham, from 1901 to 1904. He served for two years in the 4th Battalion, Devonshire Regiment, Territorials. He went out to Canada and became a farmer.

On Saturday 3rd April 1915 he volunteered at Regina where he was described as 5ft 11in tall, a 39in chest, fair complexion, brown eyes and light brown hair. Following training in Canada the Battalion left Winnipeg for Montreal where they embarked mid-May for Devonport. Upon arrival Frederick was sent to *'Shorncliffe Camp'* where training continued and various inspections took place by a wide range of senior officers including HM King George V and Field Marshal Lord Kitchener.

In the autumn of 1915 Frederick was sent to France from where he entrained for Belgium. After training they were sent into the line at Kemmel during the night of Saturday 25th September as the Battle of Loos raged and the feint on the Salient was in full swing. On Friday 8th October, during their second tour of duty, two mines were blown under their line and took a heavy toll on 'D' Company. The German infantry followed up but despite their relative inexperience in the front line, they were able to drive the assault back to their lines.

In January 1916 Frederick was involved in the Battalion's first major attack on German lines, in the area of the Spanbroekmolen. Their raid was carefully planned and successful, bringing back several prisoners. The first couple of months were spent in tours of duty, their billets being in Locre. On Monday 3rd April Frederick was in reserve at Dickebusch during the attack at St Eloi, the trenches being described: *"... our front line is no line at all. The men are unprotected and in mud and filth, and have to be relieved every twenty-four hours."* Three days later Frederick found himself in Voormezeele and under heavy shell fire. The ground was badly cut up and officers took parties out to reconnoitre the ground. Their Commander wrote: *"I told Captain Styles he was to come around north of the craters. He started off at 11.30 and left part of his men with Major Daly (31st Battalion). It was dark and raining hard, and we had never seen the ground before. The craters look just like the ordinary ground (a morass). Styles went up and found Lieut. Murphy at 4 o'clock, but had not time to fix up for an attack. The men were all in; they had only had three hours' sleep in forty-eight."* On Saturday 8th they were relieved after taking heavy casualties.

On Tuesday 6th June Frederick was in front of Hooge. The Germans blew a series of mines which killed Frederick and the majority of his comrades in 'A' Company.

Second Lieutenant George Arthur Moxey Tuker Johnson

19th Battalion London Regiment

Died on Monday 21st May 1917, aged 20

Commemorated on Panels 54.

George was the son of George Arthur Johnson, MRCS, LRCP (London), and Isabella Anderson Johnson, of 58 St Andrew's Street, Cambridge. He was educated at the Perse School and was to have gone up to Trinity College, Cambridge, in 1914 but the war intervened.

George was sent for training and received a commission. He was sent out to France where he served at the Battle of Loos in September 1915, at Vimy Ridge in May 1916 and through the Battle of the Somme. He was sent to Flanders in the spring of 1917 and during a tour of duty he was killed in action.

George is commemorated on the Cambridge St Andrew Great War Memorial.

Major Richard J Digby Johnson

3rd Battalion attached 2nd Battalion Royal Dublin Fusiliers

Died on Monday 24th May 1915, aged 38

Commemorated on Panel 44.

Richard Johnson

Richard was born on Friday 30th June 1876, younger son of the late Edward Mayson and Emma Jane Johnson, of 28 St Mary's, York. He was educated at St Peter's, York. On Wednesday 21st September 1904 in St Michael's Church, Camberley, Richard married Claudine Trower Johnson (née Hogg), of Camoys, Braintree, Essex and they had a son Richard Edward Digby born on Saturday 16th December 1911 and a daughter Claudine Blanche Mayson on Saturday 8th July 1905. Richard was a Freeman of the City of York. He worked for four years in the York City and County Bank before leaving on a world tour.

When the South African War broke out Richard was on his world tour in Cape Town. He immediately returned to England and volunteered where he was commissioned. Richard served throughout the war until he was invalided with enteric fever. He was awarded the Queen's Medal with four clasps. Richard was promoted Captain on Saturday 7th October 1905 and Major on Friday 18th December 1914.

In early December 1914 Richard went out to the front joining the Battalion in Nieppe where he remained until Saturday 20th March 1915. The Battalion crossed the border into Belgium and took the line at Messines, remaining in the sector until going into billets at Bailleul on Monday 12th April. At 7.30pm on Friday 23rd he marched his men to Westoutre where they billeted for the night before progressing to St Jan via Vlamertinghe and Ypres, arriving at 4.00am on Sunday 25th. At 6.30am their attack commenced over difficult ground where the barbed wire remained uncut — the Battalion had not had the opportunity of reconnoitring beforehand. As Richard led the men forward they came under heavy machine-gun and rifle fire; their tenacity during the advance successfully plugged the gap between St Julien and Fortuin. During the attack Richard was wounded and given one week home leave. He returned and went back into the line where he was killed during the fierce action at St Julien as they came under heavy shell and gas attack. Richard was buried with 2nd Lieutenant Christopher Considine (commemorated on the Menin Gate, see above) near *'Shell Trap Farm'*.

Richard was Mentioned in Despatches, gazetted on Tuesday 22nd June 1915.

113323 Private
William Hodson Johnson

4th Canadian Mounted Rifles
(Central Ontario Regiment)

Died on Friday 2nd June 1916, aged 16
Commemorated on Panel 32.

William was the son of William and Elizabeth Johnson, of Ottawa. He was educated locally.

William joined the Battalion whilst they were in training in Belgium on Saturday 29th January 1916. Two days later he was sent into the line near Messines and six weeks later they moved the line to Zillebeke in which sector they remained until mid-May. He went back into the line on Wednesday 31st May after being out of line for some considerable time at rest and training with some periods in reserve.

On Wednesday 31st May 1916 William paraded in the early evening in full kit with his gas mask and iron rations ready to go into the line. The Battalion was sent to Ypres by train then marched via *'Shrapnel Corner'*, *'Railway Dugouts'* to *'Transport Farm'* at Zillebeke. They moved slowly into the front line on Mount Sorrel where they found the trenches in good condition. Early on Friday 2nd the men were been made ready for a visit by Major General Malcolm Mercer (who died the next day and is buried in Lijssenthoek Military Cemetery) and at 6.00am Lieutenant Colonel Ussher made a preliminary inspection. The 'peaceful' sunny morning was shattered by an immense barrage that lasted for four and half hours. The well constructed trenches and dug-outs were destroyed or severely damaged. Ahead of them *'Sanctuary Wood'*, *'Armagh Wood'* and *'Maple Copse'* disappeared and when the smoke cleared only tree stumps were left. Shortly after 1.00pm, when the bombardment had finished, a huge mine was blown and the grey uniforms of the German infantry were seen moving swiftly towards them. Casualties were high, and during the barrage William was killed.

Lieutenant
Geoffrey Stewart Johnston

Essex Yeomanry

Died on Friday 14th May 1915
Commemorated on Panel 5.

Geoffrey was the son of Mr and Mrs Johnston. He went up to New College, Oxford, in 1908, where he served in the OTC and graduated with a BA.

Geoffrey was mobilized on Friday 7th August 1914, receiving a telegram from Lieutenant Colonel Ned Deacon and went to Ipswich to join the Yeomanry. He went into training, entraining at Woodbridge on Sunday 29th November for Southampton, sailing to Le Havre. He and the men went into camp which was little more than a muddy swamp. Geoffrey, together with his fellow officers, were invited by Colonel Harry Cooper, CMG, who was based in Le Havre, for a dinner. On Thursday 3rd December he entrained for St Omer and was billeted in Grand Sec Bois. On Monday 14th he was sent to Locre where he remained in the support line for an attack on Wytschaete. On Wednesday 27th January the Yeomanry were inspected by HRH The Prince of Wales and Field Marshal Sir John French.

Colonel Deacon

From early February he served at Zillebeke and on the Ypres Salient. On Wednesday 12th May he was in the line at Potijze prior to the main German attack the next morning. The German artillery was particularly effective and the German infantry were able to advance. At 2.15pm a counter-attack was organised: they charged the Germans at the point of the bayonet but at a huge cost. They were subsequently ordered to take up position around the Headquarters line, where Geoffrey was killed.

Captain Frank Charlton Jonas

'C' Company, 1st Battalion
Cambridgeshire Regiment

Died on Tuesday 31st July 1917, aged 36
Commemorated on Panel 50.

Frank was born on Thursday 21st July 1881 son of George and Jane Jonas, of Duxford, Cambridgeshire. He was educated at Westminster School from May 1895 to July 1898 as a member of Rigauds. Frank studied brewery in Copenhagen, Denmark, before being appointed a Manager of Miskin & Co (brewery) in India. In 1908 Frank married Maria Jonas (only daughter of John Swallow of Mosborough Hall, Derbyshire), of Grithow Field, Madingley Road, Cambridge.

At the outbreak of war Frank returned to England and volunteered. He trained with the Cambridge University OTC from September 1914 until he was commissioned the following month and promoted to Lieutenant in January 1915. From May 1915 he was appointed Temporary Captain and Adjutant with his captaincy confirmed on Friday 13th October 1916.

Frank left for France in November 1916 and joined the Battalion in Ypres, serving on the Ypres Canal and at Wieltje. As the winter set in the canal froze and provided an additional football pitch but the conditions in the front line were terrible. Even wearing additional items of clothing no-one could keep warm and blankets used during the night became frozen solid. A series of unofficial truces were arranged so that both sides when the thaw finally came that allowed balling out of trenches. The Battalion HQ was established behind the lines and given the name *'Pike and Eel'*, after the fish caught in the canal, and where a vegetable garden was established. Frank was given some fish hooks taken from a German prisoner that he put to good effect! Tours of duties continued with regular visits to Poperinghe where Frank visited *'Skindle's'* and was able to enjoy the relaxed atmosphere away from the front.

On Sunday 16th July 1917 Frank entrained with the Battalion at Poperinghe for Houlle where intensive training was provided for the forthcoming Third Battle of Ypres. They practised on a life-size model of the area they would be attacking, complete with trees, 'concrete' bunkers and trenches. Frank led his men forward in mock attacks to ensure that his officers and men would know the ground over which they would advance. The Battalion returned to a camp in Brandhoek and prepared for moving to their assembly positions in front of St Julien. Throughout Sunday 29th torrential rain fell that turned the camp into a muddy quagmire and it continued to fall incessantly until lunchtime on Monday 30th. After a period of rest the Battalion paraded at 9.30pm and to the sound of the bagpipes of the Black Watch they marched toward the Ypres Canal. They settled into their positions and took possession of the *'Pike and Eel'* the officers discussed the objectives for their sector: the Blue Line, *'Mousetrap Farm'*, the Black Line, *'Kitchener's Wood'* and the Green Line 1,000 yards northeast of St Julien. The preliminary bombardment began with Zero Hour at 3.50am and the night sky was filled with flashes of the deafening guns. At 4.45am breakfast were served to all ranks prior to setting off. As Frank looked ahead it was clear that the Blue Line had been taken. Frank was in the rear wave with 'C' Company and after marching for a mile they saw prisoners of war being taken to the rear and tanks moving slowly forward over the increasingly soft muddy ground. The Battalion halted briefly to issue rations and Frank visited the captured *'Mousetrap Farm'*. As the Battalion closed on *'Kitchener's Wood'* they were spotted by the Germans who began to shell them heavily and fired their machine guns that covered their advance. Frank's Company did not waver but continued to move forward without flinching. The desolate ruins of St Julien came into view and beyond it those of Fortuin. Frank was ordered to advance on *'Border House'* and hold it at all costs. They reached their objective and hang on. Despite the loss of their popular officer, Frank, his Company kept it in their possession for two days until the ammunition ran out. Sadly no-one was able to come to the rescue or relieve them and those left in the concrete bunkers were taken prisoner.

... a concrete blockhouse

Private Muffet related later: *"I received a message, by orderly, to retire, but as Captain Jonas, before he was killed, said we were not to retire without written orders from the C.O., I am holding Border House. There are only three of us left alive, and tow of those chaps is wounded. I am holding Border House until I get written orders to retire."*

He was Mentioned in Despatches.

Frank is commemorated on Duxford War Memorial and in St Peter's Parish Church, Duxford, a brass plaque was placed in his memory with the inscription: *"To the memory of Frank Charlton Jonas Captain 1st Battn. Cambridgeshire Regt. Killed in action near St. Julien, July 31st 1917, aged 36 years."* Frank is also commemorated in Ely Cathedral.

Lieutenant Adolphus William Percy Jones, DCM

15th Battalion Australian Infantry, AIF

Died on Wednesday 26th September 1917, aged 21

Recorded by CWGC as Monday 24th September 1917

Commemorated on Panel 17.

Citation for the Distinguished Conduct Medal, London Gazette, Monday 18th June 1917:

"For conspicuous gallantry and devotion to duty. He directed his machine-gun team through the enemy's wire under very heavy fire. He rendered invaluable service throughout the operations."

Adolphus was born at home, the son of Adolphus Percy and Theodasia Helena Jones (née Whitman), of Lutwyche Road, Brisbane, Queensland. He was educated locally and was employed as a bank clerk. Adolphus was a member of the Boy Scouts (becoming a Scout Master), served in the Cadets and in the Citizen Military Forces.

On Monday 7th February 1916 Adolphus enlisted once he was 19, his parents having refused permission before. He left from Brisbane, on Thursday 4th May 1916, embarking on *MHAT Sean Choon*. He served in Egypt followed by the Western Front. Adolphus won the Distinguished Conduct Medal whilst serving in the ranks as 5700 Lance Corporal Jones.

Adolphus was commissioned in the spring of 1917 whilst serving on the Somme.

On Sunday 15th May the Battalion moved north, arriving in Bailleul later that evening from where they marched to Doulieu where they were billeted. After two weeks of training they were sent to Neuve Eglise from Saturday 31st where he served for a week before moving the short distance to *'La Plus Douve Farm'*.

In July he served in Ploegsteert Wood before being sent for further training. On Saturday 22nd the Battalion was sent to bivouac by motor bus near *'Belgian Château'*, moving to Ypres Ramparts the next day where, throughout Monday 24th, the Battalion rested before being sent out to the line. At 7.30pm on Tuesday 25th Adolphus marched out via *'Gordon House'* where they stopped for food and a drink of tea. Just after midnight on Wednesday 26th they moved forward to Westhoek where at 5.50am he had formed up with his men and the creeping barrage opened as they moved forward. During the attack Adolphus was killed.

... a bivouac

Second Lieutenant Clifford Jones

15th Battalion Royal Welch Fusiliers

Died on Thursday 2nd August 1917, aged 25

Commemorated on Panel 22.

Clifford was the only son of Mrs E A Jones, of Bodlondeb, Whitland, Carmarthenshire, and the late Reverend Daniel Jones (the Baptist Minister of Whitland). He was an Hons Graduate of Wales, then went up to Jesus College, Oxford, in 1900, graduating with a BA.

In January 1916 he enlisted and was subsequently commissioned. He joined the Battalion in the field.

At the end of June 1917 he was marched to St Hilaire for training. Here Clifford, with his stop watch, led his men forward timing the practice advance to coincide with the imaginary creeping barrage. During the night of Thursday 19th / Friday 20th Clifford returned to the line which was filling with troops ready for an attack. He came under heavy artillery fire and mustard gas shells were intermittently sent over. The skies were filled with aeroplanes spotting activity on the ground: *"7.13 p.m., Albatross Scouts, flying high. 7.18 p.m., one D.F.W. Aviatik flying low over our lines. 7.40 p.m., three Aviatiks flying low over our lines and firing on same — they dropped a string of white lights over Lancashire Farm. 8 p.m., engagement between our A.E.5's and nine Albatross Scouts over the enemy lines — no result, but the Aviatiks retired. 8.30 p.m., three Aviatiks again fly over our lines. 8.45 p.m., four Aviatiks low over our lines —one drops a white light."* The attack was to take place on Wednesday 25th; however, it was postponed twice, the final date being Tuesday 31st. On Sunday 29th it was recorded: *"... early in the morning, four Germans were seen going towards Cæsar's Avenue, carrying what looked like packs. And at 8 a.m. a sniper in Harvey Trench reported that he had seen a party estimated at sixty strong, wearing full marching order, and visible from the waist upwards, enter dugouts about Kiel Cot and Caddie Trench. They entered from the right, and what appeared a relief moved out from the left. Rapid fire was opened on them."*

Royal Flying Corps over the front line

On Monday 30th July 1917, Major General Charles

Guinand Blackader sent the following message to the troops: *"To-morrow the 38th (Welsh) Division will have the honour of being in the front line of what will be the big battle of the war. On the deeds of each individual of the Division depends whether it shall be said that the 38th (Welsh) Division took Pilckem and Langemarck and upheld gloriously the honour of Wales and the British Empire. The honour can be obtained by hard fight and self-sacrifice on the part of each one of us. Gwel angau na chywilydd."* That night they assembled under a covering barrage of gas which the British artillery were firing into the German lines. Clifford was in reserve and once the attack on Pilkem Ridge commenced he was brought up and attacked *'Battery Copse'*, being ordered to consolidate *'Iron Cross Ridge'*. The fight was intense and during the ensuing actions Clifford was killed.

7755 Private Douglas Crosby Jones

2nd Battalion Canadian Infantry (Eastern Ontario Regiment)

Died on Thursday 22nd April 1915, aged 22
Commemorated on Panel 18.

Douglas was born at home on Saturday 20th August 1892, the son of Arthur Crosby Brett Jones and Amelia Margaret Jones, of 25 Luton Road, Chatham, Kent. He was educated at The King's School, Rochester, from 1901 to 1906. Douglas emigrated to Canada where he was employed as a clerk and joined the Militia.

On Wednesday 26th August 1914 Douglas volunteered at Valcartier; his attestation papers describe him as 5ft 6in tall, with a 34in chest, a fair complexion, blue eyes, brown hair and three vaccination marks on his left arm.

The Battalion sailed to Devonport on *SS Cassandra*, from where they were sent to *'Bustard Camp'*, Salisbury Plain, for training on Monday 26th October 1914. On Sunday 7th February 1915, following training they left from Amesbury and entrained for Avonmouth where they embarked on *SS Blackwell* for St Nazaire. They were sent for training in Merris before being sent into the line. Douglas had his first experience of the front line when he was attached to experienced troops in the line at Armentières.

The Battalion went into the line in their own right on Monday 1st March when they relieved the Royal Warwickshires at Bois Grenier. The rest of the month was spent in the line and training. On Tuesday 6th April Douglas marched to Winnezeele for twelve days when he marched across the border to Poperinghe. From Tuesday 20th he was in camp at Vlamertinghe and was ordered to 'stand to' shortly after the Germans launched the first gas attack at 5.00pm on Thursday 22nd April. He marched to the front and took part in the counter-attack which took place shortly before midnight. The plan was ill-conceived and badly executed with large numbers of troops being killed as they left their trenches, including Douglas.

2504 Private Harry Dukinfield Jones

1st Battalion Honourable Artillery Company

Died on Wednesday 16th June 1915, aged 22
Commemorated on Panel 9.

Harry was born in São Paulo, Brazil, on Tuesday 11th April 1893, youngest son of Edward Dukinfield and Bertha Jones. Harry was brought to England in 1905 and sent to Liverpool College Preparatory School followed by Lancing College. In 1912 he went to study piano in Vienna. He attended the Royal College of Music from January to July 1914 where he studied piano and singing. He was employed as a civil engineer and lived in Kensington where he was a member of the United Artist Rifles.

Harry volunteered and enlisted on Tuesday 13th October 1914, leaving for France on Boxing Day. He left his bivouac, on Tuesday 15th June 1915, south of Ypres and marched through the town, via the Lille Gate and the Menin Gate. They marched down the Menin Road passing *'Hell Fire Corner'* into the front line just before the battered remnants of Hooge. At 4.15am the two hour barrage finished and Harry went 'over the top' and assisted in taking the German front line. The Germans opened up with gas later in the day. During the heavy action, Harry was killed.

His obituary was published in *'The Times'* on Thursday 24th June 1915.

13368 Private Henry George Jones

1st Battalion Bedfordshire Regiment

Died on Tuesday 20th April 1915
Commemorated on Panel 33.

Henry was born in Battersea, London, and went to live in Millbank, London. He was educated locally then became a member of the Royal Household as a 'Hired Person' in the Lord Steward's Department.

Henry enlisted on Wednesday 2nd September 1914 in Westminster and was sent for training, before being sent out to France with a draft. At the beginning of March 1915 Henry was in billets in Bailleul and on Wednesday 3rd he was marched to Ouderdom Camp where they

... resting behind the lines

rested and trained until the next night, when he was marched into the line, relieving the Royal Scots Fusiliers on the canal bank, south of Ypres. *En route* three of his comrades were wounded by shell fire. They came under heavy fire and German snipers were particularly active. Over the next two weeks Henry spent his time in the line and in reserve. The tours of duty were particularly difficult as the German lines were very close and their snipers were on constant watch; they were pinned down all the time in the line, even the use of a trench periscope was useless as that was a target too; he also had to contend with bombing and shelling. At the end of the month they were relieved and whilst in reserve were visited by the Bishop of London who addressed the men — and by the time he arrived, very late, none of the men particularly impressed! On Monday 5th April Henry was in reserve until Sunday 11th when he was sent to take over *'Trenches 38 to 45'* in front of Hill 60. Over the next few days Henry was detailed to re-dig the trench line and prepare dugouts ready for the attack. The British blew their mines and the Royal West Kents advanced. The next day the Germans mounted a counter-attack and Henry was recalled from reserve and consolidated the front line under heavy artillery fire. On Tuesday 20th the Germans mounted a further counter-attack during which Henry was killed.

The battle at Hill 60 was intense. A Quarter Master Serjeant wrote of Tuesday 20th and the support from the 6th Battalion, The King's Liverpool: *"The approaches to our positions were swept by a storm of bullets and shells of all kinds and they had a large number of casualties, but they never flinched, and was largely owing to the manner in which they kept up the supply of hand-grenades and ammunition of all kinds that we were able to hang on and finally driven back the enemy's attacks."*

Lieutenant Henry Paul Mainwaring Jones

Machine Gun Corps (Infantry)

Died on Tuesday 31st July 1917, aged 21

Commemorated on Panel 56.

Henry Jones as a baby with his mother, as a student and in the army

Paul was born at 6 Cloudesdale Road, Balham, on Monday 18th May 1896, elder son of Harry and Emily Margaret Mainwaring Jones, of 29 Half Moon Lane, Herne Hill, London. His father was the Parliamentary Correspondent of the *'Daily Chronicle'*. He was educated at the Hoe Preparatory School followed by Dulwich College from September 1908 to March 1915. He was both a Junior and Senior Scholar. Paul was a member of the First XV from 1912 to 1915 (Captain in 1914 and 1915), Editor of the School magazine, a good athlete winning the mile, half-mile, steeplechase and the 'Victor Ludorum'. At school Paul was described: *"He absolutely reformed our School game, and was one of the best Captains we ever had. His influence at School was enormous."*

Paul was to have gone up to Balliol College, Oxford, in 1915 with the Brakenbury Scholarship in History and Modern Languages, and his Scholarship papers were described: *"... vivacity of expression, sound reading, strong mental grasp, excellent arrangement and method."* He joined the army rather than take up his Scholarship.

His father described him: *"... was a young man of herculean strength, tall, muscular, deep-chested and broad-shouldered. But he had one grave physical defect. He was extremely short-sighted, had worn spectacles habitually from his sixth year and was almost helpless without them. In fact, his vision was not one-twelfth of normal. Much to his chagrin, his myopia excluded him from the Infantry which he had tried to enter in the spring of 1915, and he had to put up with a Commission as a subaltern in the Army Service Corps."* Paul

was commissioned on Thursday 15th April 1915 and promoted Lieutenant on Thursday 18th May 1916.
Paul arrived at Waterloo Station on Tuesday 27th July 1915 to set off of France where he went to Headquarters and was appointed Requisitioning Officer to the 9th Cavalry Brigade, where he was described: *"... a most loyal subaltern and lovable companion; he was an idealist, but carried his theories into practice."* Paul was sent to serve on the Ypres Salient, he wrote home on Monday 23rd August: *"...A few days back I was in the city whose name practically sums up the character of British fighting — Ypres. Never have I seen such a picture of desolation. Not a house standing; only skeletons of buildings, shattered walls, and gaping window openings, from which all vestige of glass has long since disappeared. The Church and the Cloth Hall are simply piles of débris. To walk along the streets is like a kind of nightmare, even when the Boches are not indulging in a spell of hate against the place. Talk of Pompeii — why, this puts it quite among the 'also-rans'. What a pathetic spectacle to see a whole city in ruins! Stupefaction and sadness at the wholesale destruction is my impression of this melancholy ruin of an historic town."* In December he was given home leave spending six days at home and played a game of rugby for the Old Alleyians against the School XV. Paul was back on duty for Christmas; he wrote: *"We had a very jolly Christmas. The revellings have, in fact, only just begun to subside. Our Brigade Major spent his Christmas in the trenches along with his brother, a V.C. In that part of the line there was a truce for a quarter of an hour on Christmas Day, and a number of Englishmen and Germans jumped out and started talking together. A German gave one of our men a Christmas tree about two feet high as a souvenir. It is of the usual variety, covered with tinsel and adorned with glass ball."*
In early May 1916 Paul was again given home leave until Friday 12th when he left from Victoria Station and sailed to France via Folkestone before returning to the Salient. In June 1916 he transferred to the Divisional Supply Column; he was not pleased to leave the 9th Cavalry Brigade. He wrote on Monday 12th June: *"I am frankly and absolutely fed-up with this change! They tell me it is promotion. Well, as I told my colonel, promotion of that kind was not what I wanted. I loved my old job with its facilities for exercising my French, and its comparative variety. Now I am dignified with a job whose main element is seeing to the rations being loaded on to the motor lorries that feed the division."* In August Paul was given the command of an ammunition working-party on the Somme, on Monday 21st he wrote: *"I am delighted to tell you that I have been temporarily posted to a job of real interest and responsibility having been given the command of a working-party composed of infantry, artillery, and A.S.C. men, whose function it is to load and unload ammunition at an important railhead not far from the Front. We are about 150 in all, and a very happy family. We live in tents and work under the orders of the Railhead Ordnance authorities. There is a vast amount of work, and it goes on continuously, at present from 4 a.m. to 9 p.m. daily, and sometimes throughout the night as well. It is a revelation to see the immense quantities of explosives etc., that are sent up. ...*
Next door to us across the line there is a concentration camp of Boche prisoners. They work on the railway all day shovelling stones in and out of trucks and lorries. To the eternal credit of England the treatment the prisoners received, the food supplied to them, and the conditions under which they live are all of the very best. They have their being in tents within a barbed wire enclosure, not too crowded, and have excellent washing facilities (hot baths once a week), good food and conveniences for its preparation, including huge camp kettles for cooking — in short, every comfort possible. The work they do is hard, but no harder than many of our own fellows have to do in the normal course of events."
In October Paul was appointed Requisitioning Officer to the 2nd Cavalry Brigade and on Wednesday 22nd November he wrote of his ambitions: *"... To my mind there are only four really interesting branches in the Army; (1) Flying Corps; (2) Heavy Artillery; (3) Tanks, and (4) Intelligence."* On Thursday 7th December he undertook a medical and was passed fit for general service and the next day sent off his application form applying to join the infantry, the Machine Gun Corps and the artillery. On Thursday 11th January 1917 he was interviewed at headquarters of the Heavy Machine Gun Corps and was recommended for tanks and joined them on Tuesday 13th February. A week later he wrote of his joy on being a member of the Tank Corps: *"Am having a grand time — up to my eyes in oil, grease and mud from 8 a.m. to 5 p.m. I am finding my old hobby of engineering of the greatest value, and my enthusiasm for seeing 'the wheels go round' has returned in all its old force."* He continued to train before taking part in the Battle of Arras, writing home he said: *"... despite the horrors of war, it is at least a big thing;*

Troops leaving from Victoria Station

you are not living for your own self but have realised an ideal. I rejoice the war has come my way. ... There is nothing like the wild exhilaration just before a battle." He was killed by a bullet whilst advancing in action with his tank.

Major J C Haslam wrote: *"Your son went into action with his Tank, together with the remainder of the company, in the early morning of July 31st. He was killed by a bullet whilst advancing. From evidence of his crew I gather he was unconscious for a short time, then died peacefully. I knew your son before he joined the Tanks. We were both in the 2nd Cavalry Brigade together. I was delighted when he joined my company. No officer of mine was more popular. He was efficient, very keen, and a most gallant gentleman. His crew loved him and would follow him anywhere. Such men as he are few and far between. I am certain he didn't know what fear was. Please accept the sympathy of the whole company and myself in your great loss. We shall ever honour his memory."*

Corporal D C Jenkins wrote: *"I have been asked by your son's crew to write to you, as I was his N.C.O. in the Tank. Your son, Lieut. H. P. M. Jones, was shot by a sniper. The bullet passed through the port-hole and entered your son's brain. Death was almost instantaneous. I and Lance-Corporal Millward, his driver, did all we could for your son, but he was beyond all human help. His death is deeply felt not only by his own crew, but by the whole section. His crew miss him very much. It was a treat to have him on parade with us, as he was so jolly. We all loved him. Fate was against us to lose your son. He was the best officer in our company, and never will be replaced by one like him. I and the rest of the crew hope that you will accept our deepest sympathy in your sorrow."*

His Captain wrote: *"He was efficient, very keen and a most gallant gentleman. I am certain he did not know what fear was."*

His *'War Letters of a Public School Boy'* were published by Cassell & Co. The Paul Jones Memorial Prizes — one for an essay on History and one for English — were founded in his memory at Dulwich College.

Second Lieutenant Jesse Jones

2nd Battalion Oxford and Bucks Light Infantry

Died on Wednesday 11th November 1914, aged 31

Commemorated on Panel 37.

Jesse Jones

Jesse was born at Horton Cum Studly, Oxford, in July 1883, son of Mr Thomas Jones. He was married to Beatrice Lily Jones (née Johnson) and had four children, Ivy born in 1904, Evelyn in 1908, Ena in 1910 and Albert in 1911.

Jesse was a professional soldier and served in the South African War receiving the Queen's Medal with two clasps. He rose through ranks to become a senior NCO becoming a gymnastic instructor and was a noted shot.

Jesse went out to France with the BEF, arriving in Boulogne on Friday 14th August 1914 with the rank of Colour Sergeant. He took part in the Battle of Mons, and the Retreat which took them two hundred and twenty miles to the southwest, ending on Sunday 6th September when they turned to engage the enemy. The Battalion crossed the Marne and on to the Aisne, taking part in a major action on Saturday 12th and taking more than one hundred prisoners. Jesse moved north to Flanders where he took part in the Battle of Langemarck on Wednesday 21st October taking position along the Langemarck to Zonnebeke road. Following relief from the northern sector of Ypres they moved to the Zwarteleen where a successful counter-attack was launched against the advancing German troops. Jesse continue to serve at Zwarteleen until Monday 9th November when he was relieved by the London Scottish and took over the line at Verlorenhoek. Jesse was given a field commission by his Colonel but he did not live long to enjoy it.

During Tuesday 10th Jesse and his men were able to get some rest and General Charles Monro visited them to congratulate them on their efforts. At 10.00am on Wednesday 11th the Battalion was taken forward by Lieutenant Colonel Davies towards Westhoek. The Germans were in Nonne Bosschen and were entrenched on the southeastern corner of Polygon Wood. They charged the Prussian Guard and during the attack Jesse was killed, one of only five to die that day.

Lieutenant Ralph Egerton Norris Jones

'A' Company 27th Battalion Canadian Infantry (Manitoba Regiment)

Died on Thursday 6th April 1916, aged 38

Commemorated on Panel 26.

Ralph Jones

Ralph was born in St Mary's, Ontario, on Sunday 3rd June 1877, son of the late Charles S and Helen A McDougall Jones. He was educated at Upper Canada College. On Monday 22nd April 1895 he joined the Commerce Bank and the Manager of the Alexander Avenue Branch, Winnipeg. He served for three years in the Militia, two years in the ranks prior to his commission.

He volunteered on Tuesday 16th February 1915 in Winnipeg where he was described as 5ft 11in tall, with a 37½in chest, a dark complexion, blue eyes, dark brown hair, a birthmark on his right side and a tattoo on his left wrist.

Ralph sailed to England and was sent for training at Shorncliffe and Otterpool. At 8.30am on Friday 17th September 1915 the Battalion marched from Sir John Moore's Plain via Sandgate to Folkestone Docks. They sailed on the *SS Marguerite* for Boulogne arriving in the early hours of Saturday 18th and were sent to a rest camp. They entrained for St Sylvestre where they remained until Tuesday 21st when a march took them to *'Bulford Farm'* for four days where training continued. Ralph arrived in Locre on Saturday 25th where they prepared to take the line, from where he wrote on Tuesday 28th: *"We are still in comfortable billets marking time, But expect to be called to the trenches any day now. On the night I last wrote you I think we were off for the firing line; instead, we walked miles along cobblestone roads, through at least one shell-shattered village, to this Nuns' School for children, close to the local church and churchyard, with its many crosses of recent date, bearing some English Tommies' names, I see.*

General Alderson

After General Alderson's speech to us at our last billets, he called for the 'Maple Leaf', then 'God Save the King', which all sang lustily. Rain was falling, and the men were permitted to break off without reforming, after having surrounded the speaker in a great mass. Supper was soon served and kit got ready, and at 8.30 p.m. the regiment was drawn up on the muddy road opposite our huts. Major MacLeod brought out an acetylene gas lamp, and its bright light thrown on the long line of men, four deep, in dripping and shiny ground waterproof sheets, which they used as capes, made a picture never to be forgotten by some of us. Our Chaplain, Major Beatty, who was the 1st Division before, addressed us in manly tones, called for a well-known hymn, which all ranks sang heartily, and then offered up a prayer. Roll call had been checked over before, and a moment or two after the goodbye address, etc., the whole regiment moved off into the darkness in absolute silence but for the tramping of feet on the muddy road, not even smoking being allowed. As we marched along, it seemed we came fairly close to the firing line at different points, as we could see star shells being shot into the air now and again not very far away, and could hear intermittent firing as well. Star shells, are, as a rule, only used in the front line trenches, I understand. We passed much transport en route, of course, moor and horse-drawn vehicles, and a large gun drawn by six heavy draught horses made us move to one side until its whole equipment passed, creating no little interest, as few, I am sure, could help wondering where it would likely be lodged in our rear."

On Friday 1st October Ralph marched with his platoon via Dranouter to Lindenhoek where their headquarters were established in *'T Farm'*. He wrote on Tuesday 5th October: *"I am sitting in my own special little dugout, the walls of which are lined with sand bags. There are two small tables about two feet by two feet square, made of rough pieces of board and parts of boxes, and my door has even got an old fashioned handle and bolt, the latter on the outside and workable from the inside as well. The window is about two feet by eight inches wide and simply a hole. The roof is well covered with corrugated iron sheets, on top of which sand bags are piled, then dirt, and the whole supported by four stout timbers, none squared except the front one. The space I have inside is about four feet by seven feet and mostly taken up by a six feet by two feet bed. I am in charge of a 'Keep' for the support of the front line trenches and am well off indeed, the only danger being from shrapnel, 'Jack Johnsons' and stray bullets. They shell our immediate surroundings frequently, and while one bombardment was going on in response to an awakening our guns gave the Gerboys, I wrote a couple of letters indoors the while listening to the big fellows whistling and half wheezing and shrieking as they passed. It was most uncomfortable at times too, as one could not help wondering where, say, that one just this moment which is hovering hesitatingly, it would seem just overhead, would land. The very big ones come up something like steam engines and make an awful row when they crash to earth scattering steel, mud and twigs in every direction. The first day I spent in the front line I saw a tree cut as clean as one could wish by a small shrapnel shell. Most of the men seem to like trench life better than the huts of dugouts in rear, from which they have to come down here as fatigue parties often when they would sooner rest up.*

What amazes me now is how easily we get used to it all. My desire is to get out over a front line parapet and crawl along between the lines in search of annoying snipers. Others have done it and are doing it every night and meeting with success occasionally, when there is much rejoicing. It is a far safer operation too than you can imagine owing to the well known undulations of ground that are always likely to occur between lines 35 to 300 yards apart."

Ralph continued in the line and at *'Kemmel Shelters'*, on Friday 29th October he wrote from *'T Farm'*: *"Our first morning in the trenches this time was made interesting by the bringing down of an enemy aeroplane not long after breakfast. I was on duty and chatting with some of my men when the familiar buzz of a flying machine made me reach for glasses and look heavenwards in several directions. After searching about for a moment or two I suddenly discovered a plane of unfamiliar design (since learn an Albatross) heading towards the right of our battalion line directly in our rear. There was suddenly a bursting of anti-aircraft shells near it and one seemed so close under it that we expected to see the plane drop. On it came though, and then to our surprise we saw another plane swinging around behind and below it, and as they came closer there was the popping of a machine gun in place of the bursting of shells. It was not until we had decided in our own minds that a British machine was*

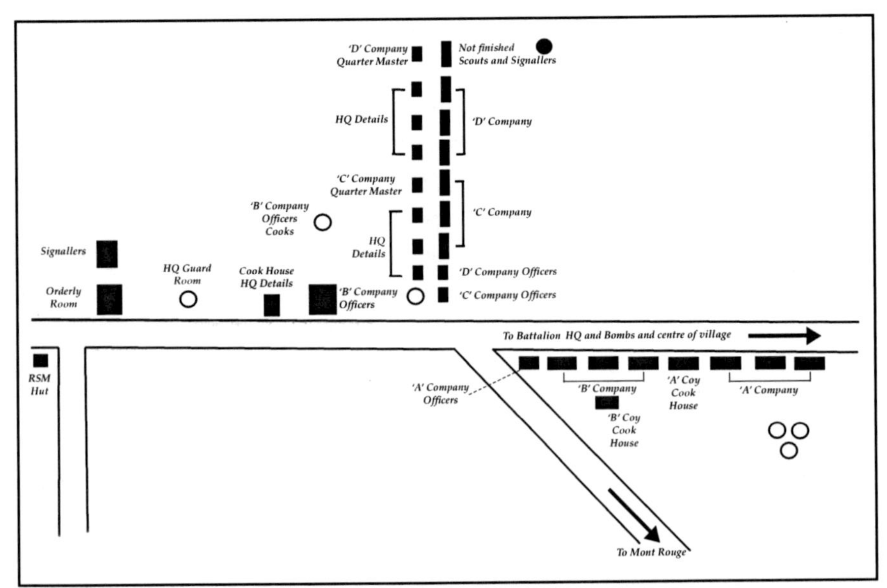

Layout of the billets provided in Locre for the 27th Battalion Canadian Infantry. (Where Ralph was billeted is now the village convenience store!)

catching up to it and firing at an enemy that I made out the Iron Cross on the lower wings of the leader which was not more than a mile from us and probably 2,000 feet up only. Machine gun fire is such a common sound and so difficult to locate along the front, in the daytime especially, one is usually little impressed by its occurrence, and so few enemy aeroplanes are seen over this section of the line, we seldom pay more attention to flyers than to identify them as a matter of principle. Hence our surprise and deep interest in the sudden battle which was on before our very eyes. The British plane steadily overhauled, keeping well below and popping away at short intervals, and to our delight the enemy began to show something was seriously wrong within and began to gradually descend, finally landing within the 3rd Battalion lines on our right. The pilot was killed and the observer, a lad of seventeen, escaped by a miracle, as in addition to having gone through our own fire, the plane on descending was fired upon by the enemy, with a view I suppose to destroying it completely. They are brutes without a doubt."

He continued on tours of duty until Wednesday 22nd December when the Battalion returned to Locre for rest. Ralph spent Christmas in billets with a lunch at 1.00pm that was followed by a Regimental Sports event at 3.00pm in the cement fields. At 6.30pm he attended the Regimental Dinner of roast turkey then plum pudding which was followed by a Concert Party. Their rest period ended on Monday 27th when they marched back to Lindenhoek and retook the line.

After two weeks of tours of duty Ralph returned to Locre where on Wednesday 19th January 1916 he wrote: *"Next day we threw over four trench mortar 60 lb. bombs from our own trench, and only two exploded because of damp fuses which were not properly attended to. We frequently landed them in their front line and on their front parapet, doing no end of damage. As a matter of fact we strafed Boche more this last time than on many previous occasions that I remember, and his 'come back' was remarkably weak. The regiment we relieved had four men buried by a German Minenwerfer (a thrown mine shaped like a large shell and called often a torpedo). All were fortunately dug out by willing and brave men who worked in full view of Boche not 65 yards away, and only one chap was injured, his collar bone being cracked, I believe. The breach in the parapet was soon closed, and when my men came in, we finished the job by strengthening with sandbags and making a perfectly good parapet. Towards noon one day as I was trying to disclose a loophole opposite to four bored men and a sniper, the report of a gun — a report I shall never forget since first hearing it — made me stop and instinctively look in the direction of the sound, even though I was just about to pull the trigger, and I knew what to expect. Up, up, crept a Minenwerfer, higher and higher, and coming our way. I called attention to it at once, of course, and we all watched, and wondered not a little as to its probable objective. It seemed about over our heads when it reached the apex of its flight, and I am sure there was not one of us who did not heave a sigh of relief when it became evident instantly that the torp. was going well over to our left a bit."*

Ralph continued to serve in the sector, including the Scherpenberg, St Eloi and *'Dead Dog Farm'*. He was sent to Méteren for twenty-fours on Saturday 1st April before moving back to *'Camp B'* at La Clytte on Sunday

2nd from where he took the line at St Eloi from the King's Own (Liverpool). From the moment they took over the line casualties were taken mainly due to shell fire. Ralph was with his men in *'P4'* Trench when a German deserter arrived and surrendered — he informed them of an imminent attack. Ralph ordered his men to open fire rounds of rapid fire on the German trenches. The German artillery continued to bear down on their line and Ralph was killed. By the end of the day sixty-three of his men were also killed or wounded.

2303 Serjeant
Jesse Frederick Jordan, DCM

1st Battalion Northumberland Fusiliers
Died on Wednesday 16th June 1915
Commemorated on Panel 12.

Citation for the Distinguished Conduct Medal, London Gazette, Thursday 5th August 1915:

"For conspicuous gallantry and devotion to duty at Hooge on 16th June, 1915, when he brought in a wounded man under shell and machine-gun fire. He then returned to rescue other men and was then himself wounded. Serjeant Jordan rendered excellent service in preparing trenches in front of Bellewaarde Farm."

Jesse was born in Croydon, Surrey, son of Mr and Mrs Jordan. He was educated in London.
He enlisted in London. For the first five months of 1915 Jesse served in the southern sector of Belgium initially around Kemmel. The Battalion moved slightly north to St Eloi where he was involved in some fierce actions, although for the most part it was 'normal duties' in the line.
On Tuesday 15th June 1915, at 4.45pm Jesse, with his men, paraded at their bivouac in readiness to march to the line a quarter of an hour later. They marched eight miles via Vlamertinghe, through the Menin Gate and via *'Hell Fire Corner'* moving carefully along the Menin Road to Hooge. He was crouched in very shallow assembly trenches that did not provide sufficient cover as the British artillery opened up and a good number were killed or injured by shrapnel (friendly fire). At 2.50am the next morning a huge barrage opened up on the German front line. Just after 4.10am the final barrage was complete, the whistles blew, and Jesse rushed forward with his men. The attack was well performed as was the defence. During the day Jesse was awarded the Distinguished Conduct Medal for bringing in a wounded man under fire. Sadly he lost his life shortly afterwards after attempting to rescue another.

Major Francis John Joslin

2nd Battalion attached 1st Battalion
Queen's Own (Royal West Kent Regiment)
Died on Sunday 18th April 1915, aged 30
Commemorated on Panel 45.

Francis Joslin

Francis was born at home on Wednesday 2nd September 1874, only surviving son of Mary A Joslin, of 7 Almorah Crescent, St Helier, Jersey, and the late John Joslin. He was educated at Victoria College, Jersey, from 1886 to 1892 playing for the First XV and XI and Captained the XV in 1892. Francis was also a military historian.
Francis was gazetted from the Militia on Saturday 7th December 1895, promoted to Lieutenant on Saturday 13th November 1897, Captain on Wednesday 7th January 1903, Adjutant from Wednesday 16th November 1904 to Friday 15th November 1907 and Major on Thursday 3rd September 1914.
Francis served in the South African War where he was Mentioned in Despatches, received the Queen's Medal with three clasps and King's Medal with two clasps. During the Coronation Durbar he served as Brigade Major to General Walter Braithwaite, CB, and was awarded the Durbar Medal.
On Saturday 24th October 1914 Francis left for the Western Front with the Indian Corps. He was appointed Commandant of Lines of Communication in Rouen but requested to rejoin his regiment and was appointed second in command in February 1915.
He served in the Zwarteleen sector until the end of March, spending the last three days of the month in camp at Vlamertinghe. He took the Battalion out to the line between Broodseinde and Zonnebeke where they relieved the French. The conditions of the trenches were very poor indeed, and they spent their tour of duty repairing and strengthening the line. General Edward Bulfin wrote: *"Their energetic and indefatigable work greatly improved and strengthened the line: their steadiness under trying circumstances gave a sense of security throughout the Division, and their boldness in small enterprises diminished to a great extent the aggressive attitude of the enemy."*

General Bulfin

Francis returned to Vlamertinghe to prepare the Battalion for the attack on Hill 60 and they spent a Few days rehearsing their part. Late on Friday 16th April he took the men into the line where they had to remain out of sight throughout the next day until 7.00pm when the mines were blown and the artillery barrage commenced. Francis then led the regiment forward on the attack on Hill 60 and held the hill all night despite major counter-attacks. He was being relieved from the line, handing over to Major Sladen of the King's Own Scottish Borderers, when he was killed, being the last man out — he was shot dead. *"On the evening of April 16th, 1915, the 1st Battalion Royal West Kent Regiment and the 2nd King's Own Scottish Borderers were ready to storm the Hill. All through the heat of the following day they waited in the narrow trenches until the preparations were completed. By 7 p.m. all was ready. Major Joslin, who was to lead the storming party stood with his whistle to his lips beside the Royal Engineer Officer who was to fire the first of the five mines … The five mines were exploded within a few seconds of one another; then Major Joslin sounded the charge on his whistle and the men were over the parapet and away. The Germans were taken completely by surprise, and by 7.20 p.m. the Hill was stormed. Early in the morning of April 18th, the Germans counter-attacked several times, and during on of these attacks Major Joslin was shot through the body as he was leaving a position after his men."*

In Victoria College a wooden seat was placed in his memory with a brass plaque with the inscription: *"To the memory of Major Francis John Joslin, The Queens Own Royal West Kent Regiment. Born in St Helier on 2nd September 1874, educated at Victoria College from 1886-1892. He was killed in action on 18th April 1915 following an assault under his leadership on Hill 60."*

Captain Ernest Nevill Jourdain

1st Battalion Suffolk Regiment

Died on Tuesday 16th February 1915, aged 35

Commemorated on Panel 21.

Ernest was born at home on Saturday 9th August 1879, son of Nevill and Rebecca Jourdain, of 51 Fellows Road, Hampstead, London. He was educated at Haileybury from 1893 to 1896 as a member of Bartle Frere. On Wednesday 30th June 1909 Ernest married Olive Jourdain (née Fernihough).

Ernest was commissioned in the Suffolk Regiment from the Militia in November 1899, being promoted Lieutenant in December 1900, Captain in September 1908, Adjutant from December 1807 to December 1910. In 1912 he was Acting Deputy Assistant Adjutant and Quarter Master General in Cairo and was Military Censor at Alexandria.

Ernest served in the South Africa War receiving the Queen's Medal with three clasps and the King's Medal with two clasps. He was certificated as an Army's Gymnastic Instructor and in musketry. He undertook a course in intelligence duties passing his examination in Malta. He reached the finals at the Naval and Military Tournament at Olympia in bayonet fighting for three years consecutively and one year he tied for first place. In all the competitions he entered in Malta and Egypt for bayonet fighting he was never beaten! Ernest was Captain of the battalion's cricket and hockey teams and played in the Association football team. He was a good rugby player and was a member of the Rosslyn Park Football Club, the Hampstead Wanderers and the Haileybury Wanderers.

Ernest was in Egypt when he commanded the Guard of Honour on New Year's Day 1914 when General Sir Ian Hamilton arrived in Cairo in his capacity as Inspector-General of Overseas Forces. He was then sent to Khartoum later in January.

At the outbreak of war Ernest was stationed in the Sudan, returning to Liverpool on Friday 23rd October 1914 on board *HMT Grantully Castle*. The Battalion embarked on Saturday 16th January on board *SS Mount Temple* sailing for Le Havre, with Ernest commanding 'B' Company. He arrived four days later after a long and winding trip in Hazebrouck. During the night of Thursday 4th and Friday 5th February the Suffolks moved into the front line between the Ypres to Comines Canal and Hill 60. The front line was in poor condition with the men having to wade constantly through two feet of water. 'C' Company were ordered to relieve the Buffs in 'O' Trench, and he took his men forward, bombing the Germans who had captured part of it. Ernest was wounded in the hand on Monday 15th February during an advance but remained with his men at the front. The next day the attack continued and despite their best efforts the Germans could not be moved. Ernest was hit by a bullet which killed him instantaneously.

Lieutenant Arthur Jowitt

1st Battalion Royal Warwickshire Regiment

Died on Sunday 25th April 1915, aged 37

Commemorated on Panel 8.

Arthur was born in Leeds, Yorkshire, on Thursday 17th January 1878, the son of the late Joseph and Margaret Jowitt of Tipping Street, Manchester. He was educated at local schools. Arthur was married to Ethel Sarah, daughter of William Harwood, and they had a son, William, born in December 1911.

In 1895 Arthur enlisted and served in the South African War receiving the Queen's Medal with five clasps.

He was gazetted in December 1914 and joined the Battalion in the field at St Yves. He served on tours of duty without any particular significance until the outbreak of the Second Battle of Ypres.

The Battalion was called up to Ypres as a result of the gas attack, taking the line at midnight on Saturday 24th April near St Julien. At 4.30am the counter-attack began and Arthur led his men forward. They proceeded slowly under very heavy machine-gun fire. He continued to fight on until he reached the German lines where he was killed.

His Company Commander wrote: *"We were to attack a wood: between us and the wood was a farm which we were told was unheld. I was told to extend the men close to the farm by the Commanding Officer, and did so. Whilst doing so the enemy opened on us from the supposed unheld farm. We ran to some dead ground within twenty yards of their trench, and were under cover. Your husband charged with his platoon, but they were all killed except one man. He fell with his arms on the parapet of their trench, and the men say that the Germans pulled him into their trench, but I did not see this myself. Am very much afraid there is no doubt your husband was killed, as he was so very close, and must have been hit more than once. A magnificent soldier, officers and men were all devoted to him."*

Arthur's medals and citation are displayed in the Royal Warwickshire Regimental Museum.

His brother, Private Clarence Jowitt, died on Wednesday 28th October 1914 and is commemorated on Le Touret Memorial.

1152 Private Alfred Allen Keates

Princess Patricia's Canadian Light Infantry
(Eastern Ontario Regiment)
Died on Saturday 8th May 1915, aged 37
Commemorated on Panel 10.

Alfred Keates

Alfred was born in Sotke-on-Trent, Staffordshire, on Tuesday 3rd December 1878, son of William Allen Keates, of 2 Victoria Road, Clapham Common, London. He was educated locally and then enlisted in the Royal Artillery, Mountain Battery, with whom he served for ten years. He was awarded the Tibet Medal for service between 1903 to 1904. After leaving the Army he was employed by the Bank of Montreal as a messenger in the Windsor Street Branch, Montreal.

On Thursday 20th August 1914 Alfred volunteered in Ottawa where he was described as 6ft tall, with a 41in chest, a fair complexion, brown hair and eyes.

Alfred went out with the First Canadian Contingent to England, sailing to Plymouth on board *SS Royal George* on Sunday 27th September 1914. He was sent for training at *'Bustard Camp'* Salisbury Plain before moving to *'Morn Hill Camp'* in Winchester. On Wednesday 16th December HM King George V and Field Marshal Lord Kitchener inspected them and wished them well prior to their departure for France. On Sunday 20th December he was marched from Winchester to Southampton where he embarked on *SS Cardiganshire* for Le Havre. He entrained to Arques and was sent to billets at Blaringhem, arriving on Christmas Eve. On New Year's Day Field Marshal Sir John French visited the Regiment to wish them well. A private wrote: *"After the first day or two we were taken out daily, with full equipment, and made to dig trenches. A continuous line of them was being constructed right across the country. Our division dug three miles a day, and our task was to complete thirty miles. We got very fed up with the job, especially toward the end. We had about eight miles to march each way. We were allowed to remove our picks and equipment, but had to pile everything, with bayonet fixed, on top, not more than two yards away. All over this country two feet strikes water, so trench digging was always sloppy work. Early on the morning of the 3rd we were overjoyed to hear that we were to go straight into the firing line. We marched steadily all day, and crossed the Belgian frontier with the rest of the division. The cobble-stones were very wearying for a march. Moreover, once again we had to make a full day's march without food. When we got within three miles of the trenches shells burst somewhere near every now and again.*

We were told we were to extend the British line and to relieve French troops in the trenches. The Patricia's were given the post of honour, that of holding the extreme British left, facing the German fortified position. Absolute silence was ordered and no smoking was allowed. It was most weird. Great shell holes were plentiful in the cobbled roads. By and by we left the shelter of the hedge and road and were out in the open. All around rifles were cracking and everyone was ducking to avoid bullets. We had to cross 400 yards of open ground to reach our trenches. The mud was so awful that we had laboriously to pull each leg out of with our hands at every step. Presently up went a flare from the enemy, turning the darkness into the brightness of day, and down we flopped and lay there until the light went out. Our chins were well under the slime and quite a lot got into our ears. Our rifles were so muddied that they resembled brooms, shovels — anything but rifles, just long chunks of mud. Our water-bottles and haversacks were indistinguishable from lumps of mud."

The Battalion took the line for the first time at Vierstraat on Wednesday 6th January 1915 for two days. Until Wednesday 24th March, Alfred undertook tours of duty at St Eloi from where he was sent to Poperinghe. His first experience of the Salient proper was on Wednesday 7th April at Bellewaarde where after two days he was moved to Polygon Wood and he was relieved on Sunday 11th April by the Rifle Brigade. After another tour of duty and rest Alfred was again in Polygon Wood where they came under heavy shell fire from Tuesday 20th. The tour of duty was extended after the gas attack on

Thursday 22nd. On Tuesday 4th May Alfred was moved to Bellewaarde Ridge at 3.00am where he occupied a new trench which was only partially constructed. The Germans attacked them at dawn but were repulsed and throughout the day they came under heavy shell fire. On Saturday 8th the Germans commenced a major attack on their line, heralded by an immense barrage. Their front line was taken but the Germans were then repulsed by rapid fire. During the opening of the Battle of Bellewaarde Ridge Alfred was shot and killed.

9217 Private Henry Kelleher

4th Battalion Canadian Infantry
(Central Ontario Regiment)
Died on Saturday 24th April 1915, aged 24
Commemorated on Panel 18.

Henry was born in Dalkey, County Dublin, in December 1890, son of Mrs M C Kelleher, of Main Street, Chippawa, Ontario, and the late James Kelleher, of Bengal. He went up to Christ's College, Cambridge, in 1910 then left for Canada to study law.

He volunteered at Valcartier on Wednesday 23rd September 1914, where he was described as a Roman Catholic, being 5ft 6in tall, with a 38in chest, a dark complexion, blue eyes, black hair, three vaccination marks on his left arm, a scar over his left eye and a mole on his left side. Henry arrived in Plymouth on Thursday 22nd October 1915 and was sent for training at *'Bustard Camp'*, Salisbury Plain. He continued his training until leaving for France, sailing from Avonmouth on Monday 11th February 1915, arriving in St Nazaire the next day. He was sent by train to Strazeele from where he was billeted at Outtersteene where training continued. At 8.30am on Wednesday 17th Henry was formed up and he marched to billets in Erquinghem where the Welsh Fusiliers and Middlesex Regiment assisted in providing instruction with the Cameronians and the Argyle and Sutherland Highlanders taking them into the line for practical experience. On Monday 22nd the Battalion marched to Armentières where a fleet of motor buses collected them and took them to billets in an unfinished hospital at Hazebrouck for two days before returning to Outtersteene. Training continued until 9.00am on Sunday 28th when they marched to Bac St Maur, remaining overnight before continuing to Rue Bataille. They marched through a terrible electrical storm and blizzard to take over the billets from the West Surrey's. On Tuesday 2nd March Henry assisted in cleaning up their billets and undertook drill. The next day drill continued and a bath party was arranged. Late on Friday 5th he marched into the front line where they came under constant sniper fire. The tour of duty lasted for three days then they were sent to Rue Delpierre for training before moving to the line at Bois Grenier. They served in the line until Thursday 25th when they marched twelve miles to Neuf Berquin for rest and training, and provided working parties to the front.

General Smith-Dorrien

At 7.00am on Tuesday 6th April the Battalion moved to Steenvoorde and en route General Sir Horace Smith-Dorrien reviewed them as they marched passed. Route marches, physical training, and training in describing targets were the order of the day until Sunday 18th when they marched the seven miles to Proven. The Medical Officer gave a lecture on sanitation to each Company. At 2.00pm on Tuesday 20th Henry marched a further nine miles to Vlamertinghe, arriving at 5.45pm. On Thursday 22nd they clearly heard the bombardment of Ypres and saw the French colonial troops retreating passed them in considerable distress. At 9.30pm Henry was ordered to 'stand to'. Shortly after midnight he marched towards the sound of battle, crossed the Yser at No 4 Pontoon Bridge and halted at a farm house near Pilkem at 4.30am. After an hour he moved forward under heavy machine-gun and artillery fire and entrenched four hundred yards in front of the German lines. Colonel Arthur Birchall joined them and took command of 'C' Company, in addition to his other duties, after their commander was killed. The Colonel was killed at 7.00pm, (commemorated on the Menin Gate, see above). Henry continued to serve in the line before moving to reserve trenches close to the old château near St Jan. They came under shell fire and Henry was killed.

Colonel Birchall

Canadian counter-attack on Friday 23rd April 1915

Chaplain 4th Class The Reverend John Kellie

Army Chaplains' Department
attached 6th Battalion Cameron Highlanders
Died on Wednesday 1st August 1917, aged 34
Commemorated on Panel 56.

John Kellie

John was born on Wednesday 4th February 1883 only son of Robert Luin Kellie, JP, and Janet Kellie. He was educated at Kilmarnock Academy where he was Dux. He went up to Edinburgh University, graduating with an MA in 1904 in mental philosophy and BD in 1907 after winning the Aitken Scholarship. He continued his studies, at Marburg, Heidelberg and Berlin, being awarded his PhD in 1909 after studying at the University of Erlangen. John was a good all-round sportsman whilst at the Academy and University, becoming a competent golfer and accomplished swimmer.

John served as an assistant in Cathcart Parish Church before he was ordained and appointed Minister of Kirkmichael, Ayrshire in 1910. He was awarded the Royal Humane Society Medal in 1910 for saving two lives during a village picnic.

A Chaplain in the front line

On Tuesday 12th August 1913 John married Margaret Orr Ramsay Kellie (née Ramsay), of 30 Park Circus, Ayr and they had a daughter Ada, born just after the outbreak of war.

John volunteered and was commissioned to the Army Chaplains' Department and was posted to the Cameron Highlanders. He arrived in Le Havre on Sunday 21st March 1915. He left for northern France where training continued prior to the Battalion taking the line. He was moved to the Somme, initially near Hamel. In 1916 the Battalion trained and took part in The Battle of the Somme. In 1917 he took part in the Battles of the Scarpe during the Battle of Arras and in the offensive again at the *'Hindenburg Line'*. The Battalion was sent north to Flanders and trained for the Battle of Passchendaele. John insisted on being with his men and went 'over the top' with them as they attacked during the opening of the Battle. He was killed moving forward.

John was Mentioned in Despatches and had been recommended for the Military Cross on three occasions.

Captain Edward Denis Festus Kelly

1st Life Guards
Died on Friday 30th October 1914, aged 23
Commemorated on Panel 3.

Edward Kelly's family coat of arms

Edward was born on Monday 3rd January 1881, son of Edward Festus and Constance Kelly, of Donnington Castle House, Newbury and 47 Prince's Gardens, London SW7. He was educated at Eton College as a member of Mr Thomas John Proctor Carter's House, leaving in 1899 and going up to Magdalen College, Oxford. He passed into RMC Sandhurst and was commissioned to the 7th Hussars, from where he joined the Life Guards.

Edward left from Ludgershall for Southampton where he embarked on *SS Huanchaco* for Zeebrugge on Wednesday 7th October 1914, arriving in the early hours the next morning. The defence of Antwerp was abandoned as the city was already being evacuated. It was not until 3.30pm that they were ordered from the quay to ride south to Blankenberge and billets. On Friday 9th they were ordered south to Jabbeke where they went into billets around Loppem. The next day they continued south to Beernem via Oostcamp. On Tuesday 13th Edward arrived in Ypres where he was given a good welcome and sent out to

Gheluwe, east of Gheluvelt. Intelligence reported that Menin was occupied by the enemy so they were ordered to Winkel St Eloi via Dadizeele. The next day he arrived in Ypres town where at 10.00am a Taube aeroplane flew low over the town square which was successfully shot down by Maxims. The 1st Life Guards were now part of *'Kavanagh's Fire Brigade'* as they moved from one sector to another assisting where required. Edward was sent from Vierstraat to Poelkapelle and that night they were billeted in Passchendaele. They were sent to Staden before being ordered to return and take the line along the Roeselare to Menin road. He was sent to St Julien then back to the line at Zonnebeke only to be sent to St Eloi. Movement was not particularly simple, the rain had turned the countryside into a quagmire as Corporal of Horse Lloyd recorded: *"... We became almost amphibious animals, wallowing in a sea of mud which normally reached our knees, and in shell-holes and trenches which threatened to swallow us up. Road developed into paved causeways, ten feet wide, with a river of mud on each side of the pavé. Two vehicles were unable to pass on the solid surface, and to leave it meant disaster. The state of the roads presented a serious problem to those concerned with the transport of wounded, rations, guns, and ammunition. Soon we ceased to worry about roads, and always travelled across country, wading to our destination on a bee-line through the mud."*

On Thursday 22nd Edward was sent to Hooge in reserve, being billeted in Klein Zillebeke before being sent to support the line near Gheluvelt. He was moved south to Zandvoorde where on Friday 30th the Germans put down an heavy barrage on their position from General Max von Fabeck's two hundred and sixty heavy guns. The Germans attacked in strength, so heavy that they were forced to retire. Severe losses were inflicted on the Regiment and during the action Edward was killed. The Household Cavalry Memorial was erected on the slopes overlooking Zandvoorde.

Ypres Town centre before the war ...

Lieutenant Colonel Patrick Butler recorded in his diary: *"14.10.14. 4.45 p.m. On Place at Ypres. Wonderful Town Hall. Coats of arms on roof. Aeroplane prisoners."*

He describes the town: *"Ypres is (or, alas, was) a very beautiful and quaint old town, containing wonderful buildings. The Place d'Armes is in the centre of the town, and along great portion of this is the historic building variously known as the Halles, the Linen Hall, the Markets, the Cloth Hall, and the Town Hall. This building struck my fancy in a way impossible to describe. In its vast ground-level vaulted chamber hundred of horses were stabled, while above in the great frescoed galleries soldiers were billeted. It was of grey stone, with a loft belfry that was in the process of restoration, and to which the scaffolding still clung. The roof was of enormous extent, sloping down over the wall from a great height, and on it, gleaming in the sun, were four painted escutcheons of the ancient Counts of Flanders. Behind the Town Hall was the Cathedral of St. Martin, a noble edifice. The houses round the square were all old, and had gables and overhanging eaves, and sun-blistered shutters opening flat against their walls. I marvelled greatly that I had scarcely even heard of Ypres; it was so beautiful.*

A hostile aeroplane had been brought down that morning by our Horse Artillery (of the 3rd Cavalry Division), and shortly after we entered Ypres it was brought in in triumph on a motor-lorry. I think there were two prisoners with it. They had been captured hiding in a wood."

... and after the bombardment.

Second Lieutenant Edward Rowley Kelly

3rd Battalion Border Regiment

Died on Wednesday 7th July 1915, aged 17

Commemorated on Panel 35.

Edward was the son of the late Lieutenant Edward Kelly, RN, and Mrs Ethel Kelly. He was educated at Hitchin Grammar School and was to have gone up to Merton College, Oxford, but the war intervened.

Edward volunteered on Wednesday 27th January 1915 and was sent for training. After receiving his commission Edward left for France joining the Battalion in the field, attached to the Lancashire Fusiliers. He was killed in action on the Pilkem Ridge, one of the youngest of his rank to be killed.

16274 Private Hugh Galfried Duplex Kemp

7th Battalion Canadian Infantry
(British Columbia Regiment)
Died on Saturday 24th April 1915, aged 28
Commemorated on Panel 24.

Field Marshal French

Hugh was a Canadian cousin of Field Marshal Earl French of Ypres.
Hugh was born in London, on Thursday 26th January 1877, son of Mr and Mrs Kemp. He emigrated to Canada where he was employed as a book keeper. He served for three years in the Trinidad Light Horse, a year in the Alberta Dragoons and seven years in the 6th District of Columbia's Own Rifles.

Hugh volunteered on Thursday 3rd September 1914 at Valcartier, where he was described as 5ft 10in tall, with a 42in chest, a fair complexion, blue eyes, red hair, a vaccination mark on his left arm, a scar on the left lower leg, and the initials *'H. G. D. K.'* tattooed on his left arm. He was sent for training before being sent to England where training continued.
The Battalion left *'Lark Hill Camp'* on Salisbury Plain for Amesbury Station to entrain for Avonmouth. He embarked on *HMT Cardinganshire* and sailed to St Nazaire where he disembarked at 6.30am on Monday 15th. He marched to the station to entrain for Strazeele. Training continued until he was sent to Ploegsteert for front line instruction and practical experience until Monday 1st March. Hugh first took the line at Fleurbaix on Friday 5th where he served for three weeks until being sent to Estaires. Training continued for a further three weeks when the Battalion marched to Steenvoorde.
At 8.00am on Wednesday 14th Hugh boarded a motor bus that took him to Vlamertinghe where he rested before marching to St Julien. He took the line on the Gravenstafel Ridge. He was in reserve at Wieltje when the Germans launched their gas attack on Thursday 22nd and the cloud of gas was clearly visible although its implications were not yet understood. Orders were given to stop any retreating Turcos and force them to join them in advancing against the Germans. They successfully persuaded about fifty Turcos to join them. They came under heavy shell fire and they passed large numbers of men and horses dead and dying. Hugh arrived at 11.00pm at St Julien under the command of Colonel Lipsett. He was immediately ordered to dig in and consolidate the position. At 4.00am on Saturday 24th the Germans launched a further gas attack, although only two of Hugh's comrades were killed. At 5.00am a huge bombardment fell on their line and they were forced to retire. At 6.00am the German infantry advanced on their lines, many of them dressed in British uniforms and when they were within fifty yards of their lines the order to rapid fire was given. The Germans dressed in the British uniforms turned and fled, but during the attack a machine-gun nest was established to their left flank which enfiladed them. Each attack was repulsed and the German artillery again pounded their line. During the fierce action Hugh was killed.

8498 Private Angus Kennedy

2nd Battalion Cameron Highlanders
Died on Tuesday 11th May 1915, aged 24
Commemorated on Panel 38.

Angus was born at home, the son of Mrs Jessie Kennedy, of 2 West End Terrace, Fort William, Inverness-shire. His brother, Private Neil Kennedy, died on 1st August 1917 and is commemorated on the Menin Gate, see below. Angus enlisted in Fort William.
The Battalion mobilized in England at Winchester and undertook training before leaving for Le Havre shortly before Christmas 1914. The Battalion was sent to northern France for final training before taking the line.
Angus served at St Eloi before being moved into the Salient during the Second Battle of Ypres where he was killed.

200179 Private Neil Kennedy

7th Battalion Cameron Highlanders
Died on Wednesday 1st August 1917, aged 24
Commemorated on Panel 38.

Neil was born at home the son of Mrs Jessie Kennedy, of 2 West End Terrace, Fort William, Inverness-shire. He enlisted in Fort William. On Sunday 29th April 1917 Neil and the Battalion left the Arras area and went to Bernville where they trained until Tuesday 8th May; they were moved to St George where training continued until Wednesday 20th June. The next day they started their move northwards eventually arriving in a camp two miles from Vlamertinghe. On Monday 2nd July they were sent into support trenches at Ypres and after a short tour of duty they were out of the line, training until Monday 23rd July. On the morning of Saturday 28th the Battalion undertook a significant raid on the German front line, a preliminary barrage was laid down at 7.00am as they went over the top and they followed the creeping barrage. The German front line was cut up by the artillery which helped in the success of the raid. The next day a further, and more substantial raid took place with the German advance trenches being captured. It was an unpleasant situation that Neil found himself in; the mud was particularly thick and glutenous, his men's rifles became jammed, filled with the mud. The Germans launched a counter-barrage and followed this up with an attack that was repulsed. Neil was relieved from the line from where they were sent to relieve the Gordons. On Wednesday 1st August he was moved forward to support then relieve the Seaforth Highlanders but yet again many of the rifles were put out of action as they were clogged by mud. At 3.00pm the Germans mounted a counter-attack against his line and as Neil and his comrades attempted to repulse the attackers, he was killed.

The History of the 7th Battalion records: *"The H.Q. at one time was in an old Boche strong point. Unfortunately, as it was the only place protected, some of the men in the trench round it would rush to it for shelter, whenever heavy shelling started. As many a possible squeezed inside, but it seldom contained all and as it was no doubt the enemy's target we had several casualties in the trench outside. It was little use telling the men not come, for each hoped to be fortunate enough to find room inside, and the desire for security over all else. The floor of the dugout was a foot deep in water, which kept slowly getting deeper as the water in the trench increased, and its smell was horrible, as it was partly mixed with the blood of the men killed outside."*

His brother, Private Angus Kennedy, died on 11th May 1915 and is commemorated on the Menin Gate, see above.

Lieutenant Nigel Kennedy

2nd Battalion Royal Scots Fusiliers

Died on Sunday 25th October 1914, aged 26

Commemorated on Panel 33.

Wellington College

Nigel was the younger son of Jessie Kennedy, of Daneswood, Ascot, Berkshire, and the late John Kennedy, JP, of Underwood, Ayrshire. He was educated at Wellington College from 1901 to 1906.

Lieutenant Colonel Baird Smith took the 2nd Battalion from Gibraltar, at the outbreak of war, to England when mobilization was ordered. In early October they sailed to Belgium with the intention of assisting in the defence of Antwerp, but when they arrived in Belgium it was clear it was too late to offer assistance, and they were sent from Brugge, via Roeselare, to the Ypres Salient. They were first sent to Wieltje from where they took the line at Gheluvelt and were under extreme pressure from continuous German attacks. The Germans had entered Polygon Wood and the situation became particularly difficult. General Capper sent a message: *"Hold on like hell: the Second Division is coming."* (General Capper was killed on Monday 25th September 1915 and is buried in Lillers Communal Cemetery.) The Battalion took very heavy losses but they held on and the German attack subsided despite their success in taking Polygon Wood. The morning of Sunday 25th October opened with heavy mist, the Germans made a counter-attack on the Fusiliers lines, and during the action Nigel was killed.

General Capper

Nigel was Mentioned in Despatches.

Lieutenant John Gibson Kenworthy

16th Battalion Canadian Infantry (Manitoba Regiment)

Died on Saturday 24th April 1915, aged 33

Commemorated on Panel 26.

John was born at Hurst, Lancashire, on Saturday 27th August 1881, son of John and Mary H Kenworthy, of Tenby, Pembrokeshire. He was educated at Rossall School from 1895 to 1899. John was married and lived in British Columbia where he was a stock rancher and a member of the Militia.

On Monday 7th September 1914 John volunteered in Valcartier where he was described as 6ft tall, with a 40in waist, a fresh complexion, blue eyes, brown hair, and a mark to the left of his navel.

John was sent for training. On Monday 28th September 1914 at 8.30am he paraded with his men and to the sound of bagpipes, marched to embark on *SS Andania*. The ship sailed two days later to join the convoy for England which formed up on Saturday 3rd October and two weeks later it arrived in Plymouth. He entrained for Salisbury Plain for training; the camp was described by a fellow officer: *"It is a camp of bell tents, beside a bluff on a big plain; and for miles around, these plains stretch far into the distance. Thousands of blankets were distributed on arrival. Some of them are lengths of rough tweed, others soft, fleecy, woollen blankets. It looks as if the country has been scoured for anything in the way of cover, regardless of cost."*

On Thursday 11th February 1915 the initial training ended and he entrained for Avonmouth to embark for St Nazaire, arriving on Monday 15th. After a winding tiring journey the train finally halted at Hazebrouck. Two days later from where they marched to Caëstre: *"It was raining, we sat down at the side of the street for over an hour, then marched out into the darkness over a muddy road to a farmhouse. We were kept waiting there for over half an hour and marched back to town. Again marched out to another farmhouse, but no room there, so back to the starting point, and into a hayloft some time this side of midnight."* Training for the front line commenced; during the night of Wednesday 24th he went with his fellow officers and NCOs on a tour of the line before taking the men on a tour of duty at Bois Grenier. Until Friday 26th March he was in the Fleurbaix sector from where he marched into reserve at Estaires. General Sir Horace Smith-Dorrien inspected the Battalion on Saturday 10th April at 8.45am. At 2.00pm on Thursday 15th he marched with his men to Steenvoorde where they were billeted overnight. At 9.00am the next morning a fleet of motor buses collected them, driving up to Vlamertinghe where they stopped, rested and had lunch before marching off at 2.30pm. They continued the five miles along the cobbled roads getting ever closer to the sound of battle arriving in Wieltje from where they were ordered into the line along the St Julien to Poelkapelle road, relieving the French 79th Division. They spent three days in the line strengthening the trenches and defences. They were in the line next to the Zouaves (French colonial troops) who often spent time fishing in the Steenbeek becoming very excited with every catch! They were relieved and sent into reserve in the northern part of Ypres and along the adjacent Canal bank. The men were able to take advantage of the warm weather and bathed in the Canal; time was given for visits into the town where they could still enjoy its amenities. Their pleasant time was shattered at 5.00pm on Thursday 22nd, one of his colleagues recorded: *"At five p.m. we sat down in our little mess to have tea. Everything was very quiet, when all of a sudden a bombardment broke out away off in the distance and the same minute we heard a huge shell coming in with the noise of an express train, such a one we hadn't ever heard before. When the terrific crash of the explosion took place I looked from under the buffet, and some of the others were under the table. I consider we all acted with one single thought and did excellent time. ... We sat down to resume our meal and all was quiet again, when suddenly we heard the warning roar in the air. Again, like streaks of lightning, we were in our corners. This time the crash was just outside our door. The glass blew in on the table and there was a crash of timber and falling brick-work. Then they started in earnest, shells, large and small, poured into the town. The cries of the people mingled with the crash of the houses falling to bits, the stampeding of frantic horses, and the shouts of the troops rushing to their quarters. There was the wildest confusion."*

The Battalion History recorded: *"Crowds of refugees, old men and women and children, were trying to push their way out of the town towards the west and south. Aged women were being wheeled in barrows by old men, babies being carried in the arms of mothers whose pale faces and staring eyes looked the picture of terror; and everyone in the procession, who had the strength, was carrying bundles of his or her belongings wrapped in handkerchiefs and sheets."* At 5.30pm orders were received to 'stand to' and by 6.00pm the Battalion was in position guarding the Canal against any potential German advance. As they stood guard the first casualties started to stream passed: artillery limbers rode by, the riders desperately holding each other up despite showing no signs of any form of injury; riderless horses galloped through the terrified refugees which caused a number of injuries amongst the civilians who were unable to get out of their way; the Zouaves were trotting back without any weapons, packs, hats or equipment in very obvious pain and complete distress. John, his fellow officers and men could only watch as the coughing, spluttering troops passed them: the only cry they heard was *"Asphyxié"*. Headquarters were aware that a large section of line had been abandoned and it had to be plugged. At 7.40pm the Battalion was Ordered to proceed to St Jan and await for further orders. The German shelling made their march all the more difficult, they were diverted via La Brique, continued to Wieltje where they were forced to halt. The village was crammed with troops and during their enforced stop the wind carried whiffs of gas across them which caused many of the men to suffer with streaming eyes and sore throats. As they started to move off the Battalion mules pulling their ammunition wagons

... getting the mules to move!

refused to budge; eventually they stirred and the march to the front could continue. Their orders were to move forward to St Julien where it had been decided that a counter-attack would be mounted against *'Kitchener's Wood'* (Bois des Cuisiniers). At 11.30am he synchronized his watch ready for the advance that commenced fifteen minutes later. The artillery support was poor — only one shell every five minutes being dropped into the wood. John ordered the men to fix bayonets and led them forward in close formation against the heavily defended German line. The Germans put up large numbers of flares that illuminated the sky as if it were day, helping them to pour forth their deadly rapid fire on the advancing troops. Despite the dogged resistance, John and his men rushed the line and took the wood; one of his colleagues, Lieutenant Victor Hastings, sat cross-legged on the parapet of the captured German line taking pot-shots at the retreating Germans! As the attack continued, John was killed.

His brother, Captain Donald Kenworthy, died on Monday 17th May 1915 and is buried in New Irish Farm Cemetery.

SECOND LIEUTENANT MILTON KERSHAW

'A' Company, 2nd Battalion Gloucestershire Regiment

Died on Saturday 7th November 1914

Commemorated on Panel 22.

Grave reference III. C. 19.

Milton was the son of Mr and Mrs Kershaw. He went up to Peterhouse, Cambridge, in 1905.

On Saturday 7th November 1914, at 6.00am, Milton was to the north of Zwarteleen where orders were received for an attack; however, due to the heavy fog it was cancelled. Later in the morning a telephone call was received to order them to move forward and occupy a section of the German trenches that had been captured earlier in the day by the 22nd Brigade. Captain Robert Rising and Major Ingram led the men forward and in doing so encountered fierce machine-gun fire from a collection of houses at the end of the village. The situation became confused due to the lack of orders and the men were totally exhausted. To make matters worse they found themselves stuck out in the open with slit trenches as their only cover. Milton, with 'A' Company, were on the right of the action and became totally cut off. Milton was killed and never seen again, Captain Rising was mortally wounded and died later in the day, being buried in Zillebeke Churchyard.

Captain Rising

SECOND LIEUTENANT EDWIN BLOW KERTLAND

3rd Battalion Royal Irish Fusiliers
attached 2nd Battalion Royal Irish Rifles

Died on Wednesday 16th June 1915, aged 19

Commemorated on Panel 42.

Edwin Kertland

Edwin was born on Wednesday 29th January 1896, son of Edwin Happer Kertland and Meta Blow Kertland, of Dunnimarle, Knockdene Park, Belfast. He was educated at Campbell College, Belfast, from September 1909 to July 1912 followed by the Royal Belfast Academical Institution. Edwin was employed as an apprentice manager in the linen trade.

Edwin volunteered at the outbreak of the war and was commissioned. He went out to the front where he was taken ill with pleurisy and invalided, rejoining the Battalion in the line in front of Wytschaete. On Thursday 3rd June 1915 he marched into a bivouac south of the Poperinghe to Vlamertinghe road. Whilst based at the camp he organised his platoon to take barbed wire up to the front until they returned to the line at Hooge on Wednesday 9th. On his second tour at Hooge he took part in the successful attack at Bellewaarde where they advanced the line two hundred and fifty yards over an eight hundred yard front, captured two hundred prisoners and three machine-guns. Throughout the day on Wednesday 16th June the Germans had been bombarding their line. At 3.35pm the preliminary barrage lifted which was the signal to advance; none of the men had slept for more than thirty-six hours, the last twelve under artillery fire. As he took his men forward Edwin was hit by machine-gun fire.

Rifleman Arthur McConville wrote: *"Lieut. Kertland was hit by machine-gun fire and fell - he must have been mortally wounded as I lay beside him for seven minutes and he did not move."*

Edwin was Mentioned in Despatches.

German machine-gunners in action

406863 Private William Christopher Kewley

25th Battalion Canadian Infantry (Nova Scotia Regiment)

Died on Wednesday 12th April 1916, aged 23

Commemorated on Panel 26.

William was born at Alpha Vicarage, on Tuesday 12th July 1892, only son of Margaret B Kewley, of 10 Vicarage Terrace, Kendal, Westmorland, and the late Reverend William Kewley.

He was educated at Kendal and Warrington Grammar Schools, then went up to Selwyn College, Cambridge, in 1910 where he was a member of the OTC. William went to Canada in March 1914 becoming a farmer at Cardale, Manitoba.

On Thursday 29th April 1915 William volunteered at Hamilton and came over to England in June 1915. His attestation papers give his next of kin as his sister, Frances Elizabeth Kewley, c/o London Hospital and describe him as 5ft 5in tall, with a 35¾in waist, a fresh complexion, hazel eyes, light brown hair, a scar on the fingers of his right hand and on his groin as a result of a hernia operation.

The Battalion trained at *'East Sandling Camp'* near Folkestone, arriving in Boulogne on Wednesday 15th September 1915. He entrained at the Pont de Briques for St Omer from where they undertook four days of route marches to Kemmel before taking the line.

During his second tour of duty the Germans blew a mine under 'B' Company which created a crater twenty-five feet deep, killing twelve and wounding twenty. The Germans charged the lines defended by William and his men but they were repulsed. He spent the winter months in the Kemmel area undertaking a series of trench raids in which the Battalion seemed to excel. William was close to St Eloi when he went out to rescue a wounded comrade and was shot in the head.

... a dug-out at Kemmel

His Commanding Officer wrote: *"It was a noble sacrifice; one of the other boys was badly wounded, and he volunteered to carry him out, and it was in doing this noble act that he was killed. He was a fine fellow, always willing to do more than his share of work, no matter how unpleasant it was, and he will be greatly missed by all who knew him."*

6193 Corporal Arthur King

1st Battalion Lincolnshire Regiment

Died on Sunday 1st November 1914

Commemorated on Panel 21.

On Thursday 13th August 1914, at 6.15am Arthur was paraded, marched from Victoria Barracks, Portsmouth, and entrained to Southampton where they embarked on *SS Norman*. That night they sailed for Le Havre, arriving at 2.30am the next day from where they were sent six miles out of the town to an orchard in the pouring rain and bivouacked. Arthur was sent by train to Landrecies before marching to Mons. The Battalion was ordered south, arriving in Frameries at 10.00pm on Monday 24th August where they participated in a four hour engagement. The Retreat continued for a total of two hundred and thirty-seven miles until Saturday 5th September when orders were received that the Battalion should turn and engage the enemy. The next day, at 6.00am, he marched back towards the Marne and onto the Aisne which was reached by Saturday 12th. From Monday 14th Arthur took position at Vailly on the Chemin des Dames where he served for seventeen continuous days in sodden trenches. When the Battalion was finally relieved they had to endure three days of forced marches before finally entraining for Abbeville. Their next action was in the La Bassée sector from Monday 12th October. He took part in the capture of Herlies before serving at Neuve-Chapelle. On Thursday 29th Arthur was sent to billets in Estaires for two days.

At 6.45am on Saturday 31st October Arthur was ordered to march twelve miles via Neuve Eglise, Lindenhoek to Kemmel. They had not arrived in the village for long before they were sent into the line. From midnight on Saturday 31st October a German barrage commenced along the whole line between Messines and Wytschaete. One hour later nine German battalions attacked Wytschaete village — an attack along the Messines Ridge was undertaken at the same time. The pressure on the British line was intense and they were outnumbered 12 to 1 — at 2.45am Wytschaete was taken. Arthur was sent with his comrades up to help rescue the situation. The Battalion Diary records: *"... at 1.30 a.m. a hurried order was received that the battalion was to march to Wytschaete and retake the trenches from which the cavalry had been drive."* When they arrived at a railway cutting close the village they were under attack *"by people whom we thought to be native troops, as they called out several Hindustani words"*. Arthur volunteered to go out to reconnoitre the position, he clambered up a bank when he heard someone calling out *"We are Indians, who are you?"*, Arthur replied *"We are Lincolns"*. He carefully advanced and was shot dead. One of his fellow NCOs subsequently went out and suffered the same fate.

Major Arthur Montague King

4th Battalion Rifle Brigade

Died on Monday 15th March 1915, aged 45
Commemorated on Panel 46.

Arthur was born on Thursday 21st October 1869, son of Captain Henry King, RN, of Chithurst, Sussex. He was educated at Haileybury from 1882 to 1888 as a member of Hailey and then went up to Trinity College, Cambridge. He married Mrs Dorothy Lee King (related to the Earl of Lovelace), of 18 Royal Avenue, Sloane Square, London, and they had a daughter, Diana Charlotte.

In October 1897 Arthur served in the Tochi Valley Expedition being awarded the Medal with clasps. He served in the South African War and was awarded the Queen's Medal with two clasps.

At the outbreak of war Arthur was based in Dagshai, India, when the Battalion was ordered home. He sailed to Devonport from where he was sent to *'Magdalen Camp'*, Winchester, arriving on Thursday 19th November 1914. The Battalion was re-kitted, mobilization completed and training for the front line undertaken. On Wednesday 16th December HM King George V inspected them prior to their departure for France. On Sunday 20th he marched with his men to Southampton and embarked for Le Havre. When they arrived the train was waiting at the docks to take them to St Omer from where they marched to billets in Blaringhem. Arthur organised the men into working details, strengthening the defences around St Omer.

Arthur's first tour of the line was at St Eloi on Wednesday 6th January 1915 where the Battalion relieved the French. Many of the men suffered badly in the cold winter conditions that differed somewhat from India. Throughout their time in the line they came under constant bombing from the German trenches which were very close to their own. The Battalion undertook a series of raids on the German lines. On Sunday 14th March Arthur was in camp at Reninghelst when the Germans blew a mine under *'The Mound'* near St Eloi at 5.00pm then followed it up with an attack that captured part of the village. The Battalion was ordered to 'stand to' and shortly afterwards marched to Voormezeele and halted outside the village on the St Eloi road where they fixed bayonets. Arthur was with 'B' Company in reserve at *'Bus House'* and was given orders that if no further orders were received he should return to camp at 5.00am. The rest of the Battalion advanced towards St Eloi where they became involved in a ferocious fight, but the counter-attack was beginning to falter. At 5.00am Arthur had not received any orders; he took the decision not to return to camp but await developments. The Battalion Adjutant arrived at 5.15am requesting that 'B' Company reinforce the line so they moved forward at the double led by Lieutenant Edwards, Major Harrington wrote: *"King, Moore-Gwyn, Edwards and I with the leading sections of the latter's platoon got through to where the Colonel was."*. They arrived to find total confusion; Colonel Thesiger* organised a counter-attack on *'The Mound'* with Arthur in charge. As he took the men forward he was instantly killed. (* Colonel, later Major General, George Thesiger was killed Saturday 26th September 1915 and is commemorated on the Loos Memorial.)

General Thesiger

Arthur was recorded in Debretts Obituary — War Roll of Honour published in the 1921 edition.

Colonel Charles Arthur Cecil King

2nd Battalion Yorkshire Regiment

Died on Friday 30th October 1914, aged 51
Commemorated on Panel 33.

Charles King

Charles was born in the Cape on Friday 6th February 1863, the third son of James and R Maria King. He passed into RMC Sandhurst. Charles was married to Adela Margaret King, of 33 Evelyn Gardens, South Kensington, London. Charles was a gifted linguist speaking fluent French, German, Hindustani and Persian. He was a good sportsman, particularly fond of riding, shooting and swimming.

Charles served in the Sudan during the Nile Expedition and for his action at the Battle of Ginnis he received the Frontier Field Force Medal and the Khedive's Bronze Star. He then went to India and onward to Burma in 1893 where he saw considerable action and received the Medal with clasp. He was promoted Captain in 1893 and Adjutant in November 1896. Charles served in the South African Campaign where he was twice Mentioned in Despatches, given the Brevet of Major and received the Queen's and King's Medals both with two clasps. In February 1905 he was promoted Major, Lieutenant Colonel in 1910 and Colonel in September 1914. He received the Coronation Medal of HM King George V.

Charles took the Battalion to Belgium on Sunday 4th October 1914. He sailed on *SS California* with 'A' and 'B' Companies, with 'C' and 'D' on *SS Victorian* which left in the early morning of Tuesday 6th. After arrival in Zeebrugge Charles was ordered to Brugge where they were billeted and awaited the rest of the Battalion to arrive. On Thursday 8th they marched to Klemskerke close to Ostend where they remained for twenty-four hours before returning to their billets in Brugge. The next day orders were received for the Battalion to proceed

Ostend in October 1914

to Ypres. As the advance guard, Charles led the men to Beernem where they established a post to guard the roads leading to the village. On Monday 12th the Battalion moved on via Koolskamp and Roeselare, arriving in Ypres at noon on Wednesday 14th. Major Pickard wrote: *"The Battalion marched with the Brigade up the Menin Road and after a time I received orders to proceed to Kruisstraat and billet the Battalion there. This village was about half a mile from the Ypres railway station on the road to Dickebusch. On arrival there 1 rode through the village in order to get an idea of the size of it and the type of houses it contained. I then came back to the Ypres side of the village and commenced to mark up the houses for the Battalion. Suddenly, a small boy appeared out of a by road, shouting 'Uhlan! Uhlan!' I had my regimental quartermaster-sergeant with me, and Sergeant Bell was actually at the door of the house. I seized Sergeant Bell's rifle and some ammunition off him and dashed off to the corner of the road. There about twenty yards away were two Uhlans. My Q.M.S. and I dropped on our knees and blazed off. The Uhlans who, in my opinion, should have charged us, turned round, crashed into each other, and dashed away, but not before we had got them both in the back. A naval party, who had an aeroplane on the Dickebusch Road, was in Ypres when we started firing, and thought their aeroplane was in trouble, so dashed out in a light lorry. I told them what had happened and asked them to get down the Dickebusch Road as fast as they could and try and capture those two Uhlans. Off they went as fast as possible and returned about ten minutes later with the two. One was an officer who was very badly wounded and died shortly after in Ypres, the second was a non-commissioned officer who was also seriously wounded in the back. … My Q.M.S. and I were the first to open fire in the 7th Division."*

...a German mounted soldier

Charles was ordered on Friday 16th to take the Battalion to the area of Pozelhoek and re-established his HQ in an *estaminet*. Shortly after arriving in the area Lieutenant Richard Phayre (commemorated on the Menin Gate, see below) went out with 'A' Company and captured a German patrol. On Sunday 18th they moved during the day to reserve at Becelaere before returning to their position near Pozelhoek. The Battalion was expected to take part in an attack on Gheluwe and on to Menin on Monday 19th. However, at 2.00pm orders were received to return to their line as large columns of German infantry had been seen advancing on the Salient. The German artillery opened on their lines from the early morning of Tuesday 20th which was followed by infantry attacks throughout the day; each time they were repulsed. *'The Green Howards' Gazette'* published an account of the events: *"That day was our first experience of shell fire and though we had only shrapnel against us it was not very pleasant. The enemy's snipers came into action too, and wonderfully good they are in utilizing ground for cover. … There was a certain amount of shooting on the left during the afternoon, and when dusk fell we were able to get out of our trenches and found out what had happened generally. We were told that among the casualties in 'D' Company, Walmesley had been killed."*

Lieutenant Phayre

After spending eight hours under constant shell fire

the Germans advanced on their lines yet again taking heavy casualties. One of the men wrote: "*... we could see quite clearly columns of Germans massing on our left flank; our artillery made excellent practice, but bow we prayed for more and heavier guns. On the evening of this day we heard that the enemy had broken through the line on the left. They were attacking in mass for all they were worth and fully determined to break through, but were stopped in a most gallant manner by 'A' Company and the machine guns under Lieutenant Ledgard and by a party of our men who volunteered to attack and clear a wood under Captain Jeffery.*" During the action Lieutenant Frank Legard was killed, who is buried in Harlebeke Military Cemetery, and Captain Claud Jeffery was mortally wounded, he is buried in Ypres Town Cemetery. For a further four days the Battalion remained in the line under non-stop shell fire and they repulsed many attacks, with the men using nearly 100,000 rounds each day.

'The Green Howards' Gazette' recorded the events that led to Charles' death: "*At daybreak on the 29th October, 'A' and 'C' Companies went up to support the Royal Scots Fusiliers; at about 11 a.m. the Germans in great strength broke through a regiment on our left and threatened our left rear, which forced those on the right to retire about 1000 yards. Colonel King reorganized the Regiment and, collecting anyone he could find from other units, led an attack which was successful in retaking our former position and gaining another 200 yards. This advance was terrible, as the enemy simply poured shrapnel into us and our casualties were heavy. Major Walker was killed whilst in charge of his Company, 'C,' by a shrapnel bullet; his death was very much felt as we lost a very fine soldier and a good friend. ...*

When dawn broke the Battalion took up a position which formed a salient, with 'D' Company on the left and the other companies in the order 'A,' 'C' and 'B.' We little knew what a terrible day it was going to be for us. We were fired at fairly heavily during the morning, but this caused no casualties; it was through the deadly accuracy of a few snipers who never seemed to miss, that the Battalion had a loss which those who get through this war will never forget — I refer to Colonel King; every officer and man felt his loss more than I can describe, Brown and Hatton were both killed by snipers." (Brown, or rather Captain Ernest Broun, and 2nd Lieutenant Frederick Hatton are both commemorated on the Menin Gate, see above.)

His Brigadier wrote: "*Colonel King, I am sorry to say, was killed yesterday; he was holding on to his trenches most gallantly, indeed he has done awfully well through out; nobody could have done better and I am most awfully sorry at losing him, and also many of the gallant fellows in his Regiment. He was splendid and I shall miss him greatly, he did such a lot of good work.*"

One of his officers wrote: "*I do wish the C.O. had lived to hear what the generals said about our Regiment and to read the splendid report they sent in. What is left of the Battalion has come through with flying colours. The Colonel could not have died a more gallant death. Right in the front trench he was, leading and cheering on the men. He was shot by a rifle bullet and death was absolutely instantaneous. He died like the true British officer he was, facing the enemy and doing his duty to the end.*"

Charles was twice Mentioned in Despatches, gazetted on Thursday 14th January and Monday 31st May 1915.

In St Mary's Church, Richmond, North Yorkshire a green marble plaque was placed in his memory with the inscription: "*In loving memory of Charles Arthur Cecil King, Colonel commanding 2nd Batt. Alexandra Princess of Wales's Own Yorkshire Regt. who was killed in action at Ypres on the 30th October 1914, aged 51 years. The path of the just is as the shining light that shineth more and more unto the perfect day.*"

B/2829 Rifleman Frank King

7th Battalion Rifle Brigade

Died on Friday 30th July 1915

Grave reference Panel 48.

Frank was born in Islington, London, and went to live in Holloway. He was educated locally.

On Wednesday 19th May 1915 Frank arrived in Folkestone where he embarked on *SS Queen* for Boulogne. The Battalion entrained for northern France from where he marched across the border into Belgium to continue his training in Dranouter prior to taking the line. He served on normal tours of duty in the trenches without being involved in any particular action until he took part in the counter-attack at Hooge. The Battalion had been relieved by their comrades in the 8th Battalion and had marched the long tiring route to Vlamertinghe where they looked forward to some rest, arriving just before midnight on Thursday 29th July. A sound sleep was enjoyed for only a short time when he was awakened; at 7.00am he paraded and was ordered back down the route he had only just taken a few hours earlier. The Germans had launched an attack on their comrades and the line at Hooge, where *'Flammenwerfer'* (flame throwers or 'liquid fire') was employed for the first time. At 1.30pm he arrived at the assembly position in *'Zouave Wood'*. As he was led forward 2nd Lieutenant Alan Godsal was hit in the face by a shell and Frank went to rescue him and was killed in the attempt. 2nd Lieutenant Alan Godsal is also commemorated on the Menin Gate, see above.

Lieutenant Godsal

LIEUTENANT LUCAS HENRY ST AUBYN KING

4th Battalion King's Royal Rifle Corps

Died on Saturday 8th May 1915, aged 20

Commemorated on Panel 51.

Lucas was born on Wednesday 8th August 1894 son of Sir Lucas White King, Kt, CSI, BA, LLB, LLD, FSA, JP, and Lady Geraldine, of 29 Abercorn Place, St John's Wood, London, and Roebuck Hall, County Dublin, and was a cousin of Lord Rothermere. He was educated at Winchester College from 1908 to 1912.

Lucas left for France shortly before Christmas 1914. After a period of training and undertaking short trips into the line he took his men to relieve the French on Wednesday 6th January 1915. The front line trenches were in terrible condition, water-logged as well as being difficult to defend. After a tour of three days they marched to Dickebusch where the next morning six officers and five hundred men reported sick, unable to walk after standing in the freezing water up to their knees. On Monday 1st March Lucas led his men in an attack at St Eloi where he was wounded. In early May he was in the front line at Hill 60; on Saturday 8th they came under heavy attack and during the day Lucas was killed. The Battalion managed to hold on: *"The stand of the 4th K.R.R.C., the Patricia's, the 1st King's Own Yorkshire Light Infantry, B Company 3rd Monmouthshire and 2nd Northumberland Fusiliers is indeed worthy to rank, with the counter-attack of the Rangers, among the historic episodes of the war."*

Lucas was recorded in Debretts Obituary — War Roll of Honour published in the 1921 edition.

CAPTAIN ROBERT NEAL KING

1st Battalion Lincolnshire Regiment

Died on Sunday 1st November 1914, aged 40

Commemorated on Panel 21.

Robert King

Robert was born on Friday 14th September 1874, only son of the late Robert King, FRCP, and his wife, Esther, of Moulton, Lincolnshire. He was educated at Rugby School as a member of Donkin from 1890. On Monday 19th December 1910, in St George's School, Hanover Square, London, Robert married Klara Alice Fanny King (née Kynoch Shand) and they had two sons, Robert McKerrel born on Friday 24th November 1911 (who died on Tuesday 3rd November 1914) and Philip Marshall born on Monday 23rd March 1914.

On Saturday 6th June 1896 he was commissioned, being promoted Lieutenant on Monday 31st July 1899 and Captain on Saturday 19th November 1904.

In 1898 he served in the Nile Expedition where he received the medal and the Egyptian medal with clasp. In 1902 he served in the South African War attached to the Mounted Infantry, and received the Queen's Medal with four clasps. On Wednesday 21st June 1911 he retired and joined the Reserve of Officers.

At the outbreak of war Robert was mobilized and left for France in September 1914 to join the Battalion in the field. In early October the Battalion moved from the Aisne northward towards Flanders. On Monday 12th October Robert took his men into the line near La Bassée. On Friday 16th the Battalion marched at 2.30am to relieve the 2nd Royal Irish Regiment near Croix Rouge.

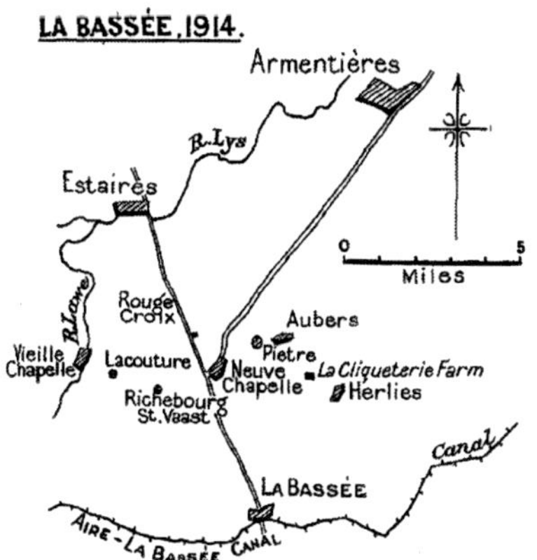

The Lincolns at La Bassée, 1914

At 7.00am Robert organised his men and dug in, holding the position until 3.00pm when they moved forward towards Pietre. At 7.00am the next morning the advance continued, at 1.30pm the order to attack Herlies was received. The Battalion Diary recorded: *"The village of Herlies, looking at it from the point of view of our attack, was situated at the foot of a long and gentle slope, perfectly open and at that time covered with beet. On our side the village was defended by strong entrenchments, further protected by barbed-wire entanglements. The enemy was in considerable force of infantry and was supported by machine-guns and a horse battery. The distance to be crossed was 1,450 yards. Battalion advanced in lines to within 1,000 yards of position, when we commenced to return the heavy fire poured into us. From thence we worked our way by short rushes to within five hundred yards of the forward trenches. At this point an urgent order was received that the village must be carried before dusk. Whereupon Colonel Smith gave the order to 'cease fire'. The battalion made three or four rushes, lying down between each. When near enough to the position Colonel Smith gave the order to 'charge'. At about three hundred yards from the position the enemy commenced to waver and many were seen to leave their trenches. Battalion pressed home and crossing the entanglements carried the trenches at the point of the bayonet, following the enemy through the burning village."*

That night they were relieved from the line overnight before relieving the Royal Scots Fusiliers on Monday 19th. From early the next morning the German artillery shelled along the line and at 10.00am they advanced;

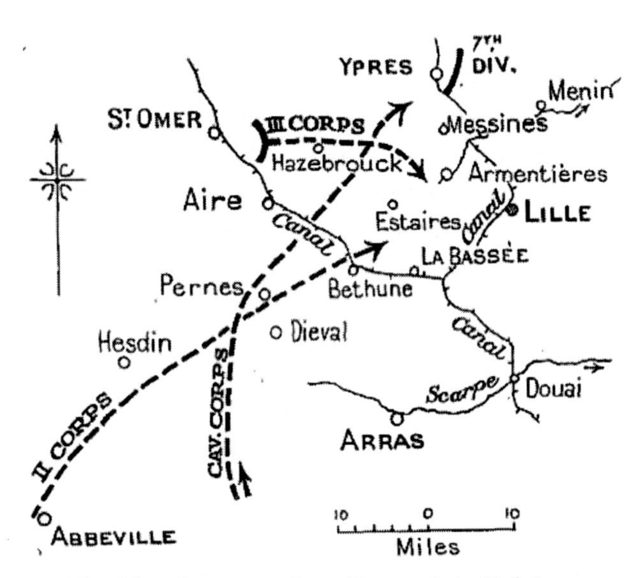

The Lincolns move from France into Belgium

however, the British artillery put paid to the attack until noon when they advanced again but were checked. At 1.15pm a third attempt was made which also failed. For the next two days they came under heavy pressure; on Friday 23rd the whole line withdrew with the Battalion acting as rear-guard. The Germans attacked their new line on Saturday 24th and Sunday 25th but they repulsed the attack and held on until 3.30am on Monday 26th when the Northumberland Fusiliers relieved them and Robert took his men to billets in Rouge Croix. After only twelve hours the Battalion was sent to support the hard pressed line at Neuve-Chapelle, deploying astride the Armentières to Neuve-Chapelle road. Despite being

Propaganda illustration of the Germans looting a château in Belgium, 1914

totally exhausted the Battalion defended their position and dug in from Tuesday 27th until late on Thursday 29th when they were relieved by the Indians. Billets were provided in Estaires in the farms on the far side of the town. At 6.45am on Saturday 31st Robert paraded with his company and marched north towards the Belgian border. They marched through Neuve Eglise and Lindenhoek to Kemmel. At 1.00am the Germans attacked in force at Wytschaete and the Battalion was sent to assist in a counter-attack. At dawn Robert took his men forward, charging the German lines that were very heavily defended. During the attack he was killed.

Lieutenant Charles George Dalegarth King-Mason

5th Battalion Canadian Infantry (Saskatchewan Regiment)

Died on Saturday 24th April 1915, aged 27

Commemorated on Panel 18.

Charles King-Mason

Charles was the son of Annie Gertrude King-Mason, of Vancouver, British Columbia, and the late Captain Charles T King-Mason who had been a master at St Bees from 1886 to 1887. His father served in the South African War and remained there at its conclusion.

Charles was educated at St Bees School from 1901 to 1902 when he left to join his father in South Africa before emigrating to Canada.

At the outbreak of war Charles volunteered and went to England for training at *'Lark Hill Camp'*, Salisbury Plain. From 9.00am to noon on Thursday 4th February 1915 Charles paraded with his men for the traditional Royal Review that heralded the imminent departure for France. On Monday 8th the Battalion marched to Amesbury and entrained for Avonmouth. They embarked on *HMT Lake Michigan* for St Nazaire and disembarked from 4.00am on Monday 15th and entrained for Strazeele. They marched to billets in Merris for training then moved to northern Armentières and were sent in small groups into the line for practical experience.

Charles first took his men into the line at the beginning of March near Fleurbaix where he served in the line for three weeks. At 6.30pm he marched to Estaires, arriving at 9.00pm, moving into dirty uncomfortable billets — there were no latrines or cooking facilities. A group of men broke into a wine cellar and somewhat over-imbibed — all were put under arrest!

On Monday 5th April the Battalion moved to Steenvoorde

where training continued until Wednesday 14th. A fleet of motor buses collected the Battalion and took them to Poperinghe where they remained in billets for a few hours. At 5.30pm Charles paraded his men and marched along the cobbled road to Ypres, through the town and out to Wieltje. They halted for two hours before marching into reserve in Fortuin and took over the billets from the French at 11.00pm — the billets were the worst yet experienced! At 8.00pm on Monday 19th he moved forward into the line at Gravenstafel, relieving the 10th Battalion at 10.00pm. Charles organised his men into strengthening the trenches and making them sanitary. From Tuesday 20th the line came under sustained shelling, both high explosive and shrapnel. Throughout the next day work had to be undertaken to rebuild the line that had been destroyed by the shelling. From 4.00am on Thursday 22nd the German aeroplanes constantly flew over their lines unchallenged and from 5.00am the German artillery bombarded them for an hour. From 2.00pm until 6.00pm Ypres became the target of the artillery and huge shells whizzed over their heads battering the town. Captain Clarke brought a group of Quartermasters, cooks, drivers and ancillary men who were sent into the line at 7.30pm to assist plug the gap created by the gas attack. At 11.00pm an attack took place to their right against the Surreys that lasted for two hours and was repulsed. Throughout Friday 23rd they came under sustained shell-fire with German aircraft patrolling constantly, directing their artillery. Early on Saturday 24th the German launched a further gas attack and the yellow-green cloud was seen drifting towards them from their left. Charles and all of his men suffered with sore eyes and choking coughs. The 8th Battalion were suffering badly and requested urgent assistance which 'C' Company provided. During the action Charles was killed by a shell whilst trying to save two men of his platoon.

Captain William Miles Kington, DSO

1st Battalion Royal Welch Fusiliers

Died on Tuesday 20th October 1914, aged 38

Commemorated on Panel 22.

William Kington

William was born in Cheltenham on Tuesday 25th April 1876, eldest son of Lieutenant Colonel William Myles Nairn Kington (4th Hussars) and Mrs Sophia Kington, of Charlton House, Wraxall, Somerset. He was educated at Winchester College from 1889 to 1890 followed by Glenalmond College until 1904 then passed into RMC Sandhurst in 1895. On Tuesday 11th August 1908, at St Giles Parish Church, Wrexham, Denbighshire, Wales, William married Edith Mary Agatha Kington (née Soames), of Bryn Estyn, Wrexham, Denbighshire, and they had a son, William Bereford Nairne, born on Friday 9th April 1909. William was a well-known cricketer, a member of the MCC; he also held memberships of the *I Zingari* and the Free Foresters. William was also a fine shot and said to be a musical genius.

William was gazetted in September 1896, promoted Lieutenant in January 1896, Captain in 1906, and appointed Adjutant in 1906.

William went out to Aden in September 1896 and served in the South African War seeing action at the Relief of Ladysmith. He was Mentioned in Despatches on Friday 8th February, Tuesday 9th July, Tuesday 10th September 1901 and Tuesday 29th July 1902. He received the Queen's

Medal with five clasps, the King's Medal with two clasps and gazetted for the Distinguished Service Order on Friday 31st October 1902: *"In recognition of services during the operations in South Africa"*. He then served with the South Africa Constabulary from April 1906 to 1910.

William left for Zeebrugge arriving on Wednesday 7th October 1915 at 9.00am from where he was sent to Brugge by train before marching to Oudenburg, south of Ostend. The Battalion entrained for Ghent to assist with its defence but they were not called upon to engage

The Germans passing through a Belgian village, 1914

the enemy. He was ordered to march via Roeselare and onward to Ypres where he was billeted in the army barracks. As they left Ghent Major Alston recorded: *"A battalion of Marine Fusiliers marched parallel to us through the broad boulevards of the town. We were impressed by their rapid and easy marching. We saw them several times during the march back to Ypres. Belgian cavalry were in the picture."*

In the early hours of Friday 16th he marched out to Zonnebeke arriving at 6.30am in time to witness an Uhlan patrol gallop out of the village. He was in the line near Zonnebeke on the day he died; the Germans started a bombardment at 10.00am that was particularly accurate after a spotter plane had identified their position. The bombardment continued for four and a half hours interspersed with heavy machine-gun fire. William was killed by a shell during the bombardment.

Lieutenant Hoskyns

"For three days we remained in the trenches, firing and being fired at, without food or water. Lieut. Hoskyns, who commanded my platoon, was killed by a sniper, and about three hours later Capt. Kington, D.S.O., was killed. He was a very fine officer, and would crack a joke in the trenches which would set us all laughing our sides out. It made us all want to avenge his death."* (* Lieutenant Edwin Hoskyns is commemorated on the Menin Gate, see above.)

William was recorded in Debretts Obituary — War Roll of Honour published in the 1921 edition.

Captain Rudolph Norman Clive Kirsch

'D' Company, 8th Battalion Australian Infantry, AIF

Died on Thursday 4th October 1917, aged 22

Commemorated on Panel 7.

Rudolph was born in Hawthorn, Victoria, on Thursday 17th August 1893, son of Simon and Julia Annie Kirsch, of 48 Auburn Grove, Auburn, Victoria. He was educated locally then employed as a clerk.

His brother, Private Vivian Kirsch, died on the same day and is commemorated on the Menin Gate, see below.

On Monday 17th August 1914, his 21st birthday, Rudolph joined the colours with the rank of Colour Sergeant, leaving Melbourne on Monday 19th October 1914 on the *Benalla*. He was commissioned and promoted Lieutenant on Wednesday 28th April 1915, and Captain on Sunday 12th March 1916.

Rudolph arrived in Alexandria on Tuesday 8th December 1914 and was sent to Mena for training until 3rd January 1915 when he was sent to Ismailia. He trained for the Dardanelles Campaign, and sailed for Mudros from Alexandria on Thursday 8th April from where he was sent to Gallipoli. He served through some of the most fierce battles in horrendous conditions until evacuated on Wednesday 15th December when he sailed for Mudros. On New Year's Day 1916 the Battalion received orders to move to Egypt. They sailed on *HMT Empress of Britain* on Monday 3rd January bound for Alexandria, arriving on Friday 7th from where they were sent to Tel-el-Kebir. After a month they moved to Serapeum where they remained until Saturday 25th March when they entrained for Alexandria. They embarked on *HMT Megantic* for Marseilles, arriving on Friday 31st.

The Battalion entrained and travelled through France, arriving at Godewaersvelde from where they marched eight miles to their billets near Steenwerck. They trained throughout April before taking the line near Fleurbaix on Monday 1st May where General William Birdwood visited them in the trenches the next day. After serving in northern France they crossed the border and were billeted at Neuve Eglise from Monday 19th June. They served at Messines until Saturday 8th July moving to *'Bulford Camp'* before moving south to the Somme. After a period of training they arrived in Albert on Thursday 20th and took the line at Pozières on Sunday 23rd. Rudolph served in the sector until Saturday 26th August when they entrained for Godeswaersvelde, marching to *'Ontario Camp'* where they rested before going into the line on the Salient until mid-October. Again they were sent to the Somme, serving at Mametz Wood. He served on the Somme until mid-April, moving to the *'Hindenburg Line'* until the end of May. The Battalion went into training at Bresle until the end of July, apart from a week's tour of duty at Mailly-Maillet. On Friday 27th July Rudolph entrained for Caëstre where he was sent to continue his training at Hondeghem until Wednesday 8th August, moving to Doulieu. On Thursday 13th September the Battalion was sent back to Belgium and from *'Chateau Segard'* went into the line near Zillebeke until Sunday 23rd from where they were billeted at Steenvoorde before returning on Sunday 30th. On Wednesday 3rd October 1917, Lieutenant Leonard Errey, DSO, MC, the Battalion Intelligence Officer, laid out the marker tapes for the men to follow the next day. At 5.30am on Thursday 4th, the German artillery opened up. Rudolph was killed together with Lieutenant Errey (buried in Menin Road South Cemetery) and Captain John Davidson (who is commemorated on the Menin Gate, see above).

General Birdwood

2347 Private Vivian Roy Kirsch

38th Battalion Australian Infantry, AIF

Died on Thursday 4th October 1917, aged 20

Commemorated on Panel 23.

Vivian was born in Hawthorn, Victoria, son of Simon and Julia Annie Kirsch, of 48 Auburn Grove, Auburn, Victoria. He was educated locally and employed as a bank clerk. His brother, Captain Rudolph Kirsch, died on the same day and is also commemorated on the Menin Gate, see above.

Vivian volunteered for foreign service on Friday 28th July 1916 from the Australian Army Service Corps, enlisting on Thursday 14th September. He left on *HMAT Port Lincoln* from Melbourne on Friday 20th October 1916. He sailed to England where he continued to train before being sent to join the Battalion in the field in northern France in the Armentières sector.

On Sunday 29th April 1917 Vivian crossed the border to take the line at Ploegsteert and serve in the sector, and at Messines.

Following a period of training Vivian was taken by motor bus to Vlamertinghe on Tuesday 2nd October from where he marched to a bivouac on the Ypres to Zonnebeke road. At 2.00am on Thursday 4th Vivian was in the assembly point. The Battalion followed the 33rd Battalion into action where they came under heavy machine-gun fire and Vivian was killed.

4320 Private Charles William Knox

29th Battalion Australian Infantry, AIF

Died on Thursday 27th September 1917, aged 23

Commemorated on Panel 23.

Charles was born in 1894 in Killesher, County Fermanagh, son of Marie Stuart Knox (née Adams), of 10 Proby Square, Blackrock, County Dublin, Ireland, and the late Reverend William Knox. He was educated at Christ's Hospital, Horsham, from 1903 to 1907, followed by Sydney Grammar School, and the North Shore Grammar School, Sydney. He worked on a sheep station as a manager, living in Parramatta, New South Wales.

On Tuesday 12th September 1916 he volunteered and enlisted, leaving from Sydney on 3rd November on board *HMAT Afric*.

After training in England Charles was sent to join the Battalion on the Somme where he served until Sunday 17th June when the Battalion was sent to Senlis for training. After a month the Battalion started to move north and trained at Blaringhem.

At 9.10am on Monday 17th September they moved to Steenvoorde and prepared to move into Belgium. On Monday 24th September 1917 he marched to *'Château Segard'* where he bivouacked and at 7.45pm the next day he was moved to *'Half Way House'* where he stopped for a short time. An attack on Polygon Wood was planned and he took the line at Hooge. On Wednesday 26th at 5.50am the covering barrage opened and Charles moved forward. By 7.30am the Battalion had reached their first objective where orders were received to halt. At noon they were ordered to advance again and came under fire from pill-boxes to the north of the Wood. They were silenced when bombs were thrown in and the occupiers, those still alive, surrendered. By 1.00pm the second objective was captured and the line consolidated. Later in the afternoon and during the next day the Germans launched counter-attacks which were repulsed. Before the Battalion was relieved later in the day on Thursday 27th Charles was killed in the front line.

Second Lieutenant George Knox

8th Battalion King's Own (Royal Lancaster Regiment)

Died on Sunday 9th April 1916, aged 34

Commemorated on Panel 12.

George Knox

George was born on Sunday 11th September 1881. He was educated at Dulwich College from 1893 to 1899 where he played for the Second XV. After leaving School he toured South America and when he returned to England he went to work in the City.

In December 1914 George volunteered, was commissioned, and went to train in Bournemouth, Winchester and Aldershot.

George left with the Battalion for France, arriving on Monday 27th September 1915. He was sent to the Salient where he served on tours of duty and he was killed in action at St Eloi.

... an attack at St Eloi

"AS PANTS THE HEART"
The recent order for the abolition of kilts on active service so preys on the spirits of one of gallant Highlanders that the mere spectacle of the hated 'trews' en gros is almost equal to shell-shock.

from

La Nauze to Lyon

Lieutenant William La Nauze

4th Battalion Royal Irish Rifles
attached Royal Irish Fusiliers
Died on Sunday 16th May 1915, aged 19
Commemorated on Panel 40.

William La Nauze

William was born at home on Tuesday 21st May 1895, fifth son of Thomas Storey La Nauze, of Manor, Highgate, County Fermanagh and Mrs E Scott Mansfield, of Ebnal Lodge, Shrewsbury. He was educated at the Abbey School, Tipperary, and went up to Trinity College Dublin in 1912.

At the outbreak of war William was studying for his degree but immediately volunteered being gazetted on Thursday 20th August 1914. He was initially stationed at Hollywood, Belfast, where he was promoted Lieutenant on Saturday 16th January 1915, leaving for France on Sunday 2nd May. He had not been in the trenches more than a few days when he was killed in action in the front line trenches, and only five days before his 20th birthday.

His brother, Lieutenant George La Nauze, died on Sunday 9th May 1915 and is commemorated on the Ploegsteert Memorial.

Captain Ronald Owen Lagden

6th Battalion King's Royal Rifle Corps
Died on Wednesday 3rd March 1915, aged 26
Commemorated on Panel 51.

Ronald Lagden

Ronald was born in Maseru, Basutoland, on Thursday 21st November 1889, son of Sir Godfrey Yeatman Lagden, KCMG, and Lady Frances Rebelah, of Selwyn, Oatlands Chase, Weybridge, Surrey. His father was the Commissioner for Native Affairs and a Member of the Legislative and Executive Councils of the Transvaal from 1901 to 1907.

He was educated at Mr Pellat's Durnford School, followed by Marlborough School from 1903 to 1908 where he played for their cricket, football, hockey, racquets and fives teams. He went up to Oriel College, Oxford, in 1908 where he played for their cricket, rugby, hockey and racquets teams, winning a Blue in all disciplines. He played cricket for a wide range of teams as a talented right hand batsman and bowler. He played as No 8 on the rugby field, and was capped for England whilst a member of the Richmond Club. In 1912 Ronald was appointed an Assistant Master at Harrow School.

In 1912 he joined the Army Reserve; at the outbreak of war Ronald was nominated by General Sir Edward Hutton and gazetted to the King's Royal Rifle Corps, joining them in Sheerness, Kent. He left to France just before Christmas 1914 and entrained for northern France, then marched into Belgium. After a short period of training the Battalion took the line in the grim water-logged trenches of the Messines to Kemmel sector. The conditions were so appalling that after a three day tour of duty six officers and more than five hundred men were invalided upon arrival at camp in Dickebusch, unable to stand up or walk. On Monday 1st an attack was mounted at St Eloi where two days later he was killed leading an assault. *"… Captain R. O. Lagden, a Harrow Master who had joined for the war, and was one of those of whom it might be said that it seemed to be impossible to find anything which he could not do, and do well."*

The '*Chronicle*', 1915 records: *"Proceeding to France at the end of February, 1915, he was posted to the 4th Battalion, and a few days later was called upon to lead his Company in an assault on the German trenches at St. Eloi. 'He behaved with the utmost gallantry', wrote his Colonel; 'the task was an impossible one, and D Company did all that was humanly possible to carry it out.' When last seen he was lying badly wounded on the parapet of the German trench, and although reported as 'wounded and missing', there is little hope of his survival. He died as he had lived, a hero among his fellows. Coming direct from Harrow, where as Assistant Masters their sympathies and interests were identical, the two friends, Charles Eyre* and Ronald Lagden, are essentially types of British manhood, which the Public School and University life of England has produced in such numbers to fight for the Empire in the hour of her peril. … Athletes of superlative excellence, scholars of high degree, conscious of their own physical strength and mental culture, both had been habituated from boyhood to lead, and to train the confidence of their fellows. … Such heroic spirits are of their very nature ideal officers and leaders of men."* (* Lieutenant Charles Eyre died on Saturday 25th September 1915 and is buried in Dud Corner Cemetery, Loos.)

Of the only two survivors who were taken prisoners in the attack, one, a Corporal, wrote from Germany: *"Captain Lagden, who was well away in front, was the first man to fall. I went and offered help, but he told me to go on with my men: then I saw him get up and struggle forward, but he was again wounded, and fell."*

Ronald was Mentioned in Despatches in 1915.

Ronald was recorded in Debretts Obituary — War Roll of Honour published in the 1921 edition.

A seat was placed in the Chapel of Harrow School in his memory with the inscription: *"To the fair memory of Ronald Owen Lagden Captn. 6th Battn. King's Royal Rifles Assistant Master 1912-1914. Killed in action at St Eloi Feb. 1915 aged 25 years. A man greatly beloved tender and true in friendship in bodily exercise supreme. Here I Am: Send Me."*
Ronald is commemorated on Langton Matravers, Durnford School War Memorial.

3087 Lance Corporal Rupert Laity, DCM

6th Battalion Australian Infantry, AIF
Died on Thursday 20th September 1917, aged 30
Commemorated on Panel 7.

Citation for the Distinguished Conduct Medal, Tuesday 21st August 1917:

"For conspicuous gallantry when on patrol. He crawled through the enemy wire to within a dozen yards of the enemy parapet and threw bombs into the trench. He has at all times set a splendid example of courage and devotion to duty."

Rupert was born in Oakliegh, Melbourne, son of William H and Elizabeth Laity, of West Reserve, Warmambool, Victoria, Australia. He was educated locally. Rupert was married to Isabella M Laity, of Mildura, Victoria.
On Monday 5th July 1915 he volunteered when he was described as 5ft 10½" tall. On Wednesday 29th September 1915 he left Melbourne embarking on *RMS Osterley* and sailed to Egypt. He was sent to join the Battalion at Gallipoli, via Lemnos, on Sunday 26th November. Rupert served at ANZAC and for the next few weeks until being evacuated to Egypt. He remained training and on guard duty near the Suez Canal until Sunday 26th March 1916 when he sailed from Alexandria to Marseilles and went by train to the Western Front.
On Thursday 6th July 1916 Rupert was sent into the line at Messines until 10.00pm on Saturday 8th when they were relieved by the 1st North Staffordshires. After bivouacking at Neuve Eglise they marched to Bailleul the next evening where they remained until 4.00am on Tuesday 11th, when they entrained for Doullens. The Battalion marched thirteen miles to Berteaucourt; the next day the march continued to Flesseles and after bivouacking overnight moved on to Cardonette.

Camp by the Suez Canal

The Battalion was sent to Albert, arriving on Saturday 22nd and was initially sent into the old British lines before moving forward to Pozières remaining in the line until Thursday 27th when they were sent for training.
On Monday 14th August Rupert was sent into the line on *'Tara Hill'* and remained in the Pozières sector until Tuesday 22nd.
On Saturday 26th August Rupert entrained for Godeswaersvelde from where the Battalion marched to Poperinghe, arriving in their billets on Tuesday 29th. At 10.00pm on Wednesday 30th he was sent by train to Ypres Asylum from where they were sent into reserve at *'Woodcote House'* and *'Bedford House'*.

Bedford House

He continued to serve on the Salient until Saturday 14th October when he was sent to *'Devonshire Camp'*, moved onward to Steenvoorde and then sent slowly down to the Somme, arriving in Dernancourt on Monday 23rd. He served at Guedecourt, Mametz, Flers, *'High Wood'* and Bullecourt until Tuesday 24th July 1917 when he was sent north, arriving in Caëstre at 3.00pm on Friday 27th.
After undertaking training until Thursday 13th September 1917, he crossed the border and bivouacked at Reninghelst. On Sunday 16th they moved to *'Château Segard'* from where they relieved the 8th Battalion, London Regiment at Zillebeke Bund on Wednesday 19th. The Battalion made preparations for the attack in which they would participate in the next day. At 4.00am on Thursday 20th the Germans put down a barrage, Zero Hour was fixed for 5.40am when Rupert advanced under a creeping barrage towards *'Glencorse Wood'*; some casualties were taken as the British artillery fell short. During the advance Rupert was killed.
His brother, Private Edward Laity, died on Thursday 4th October 1917 and is buried in Perth Cemetery (China Wall).

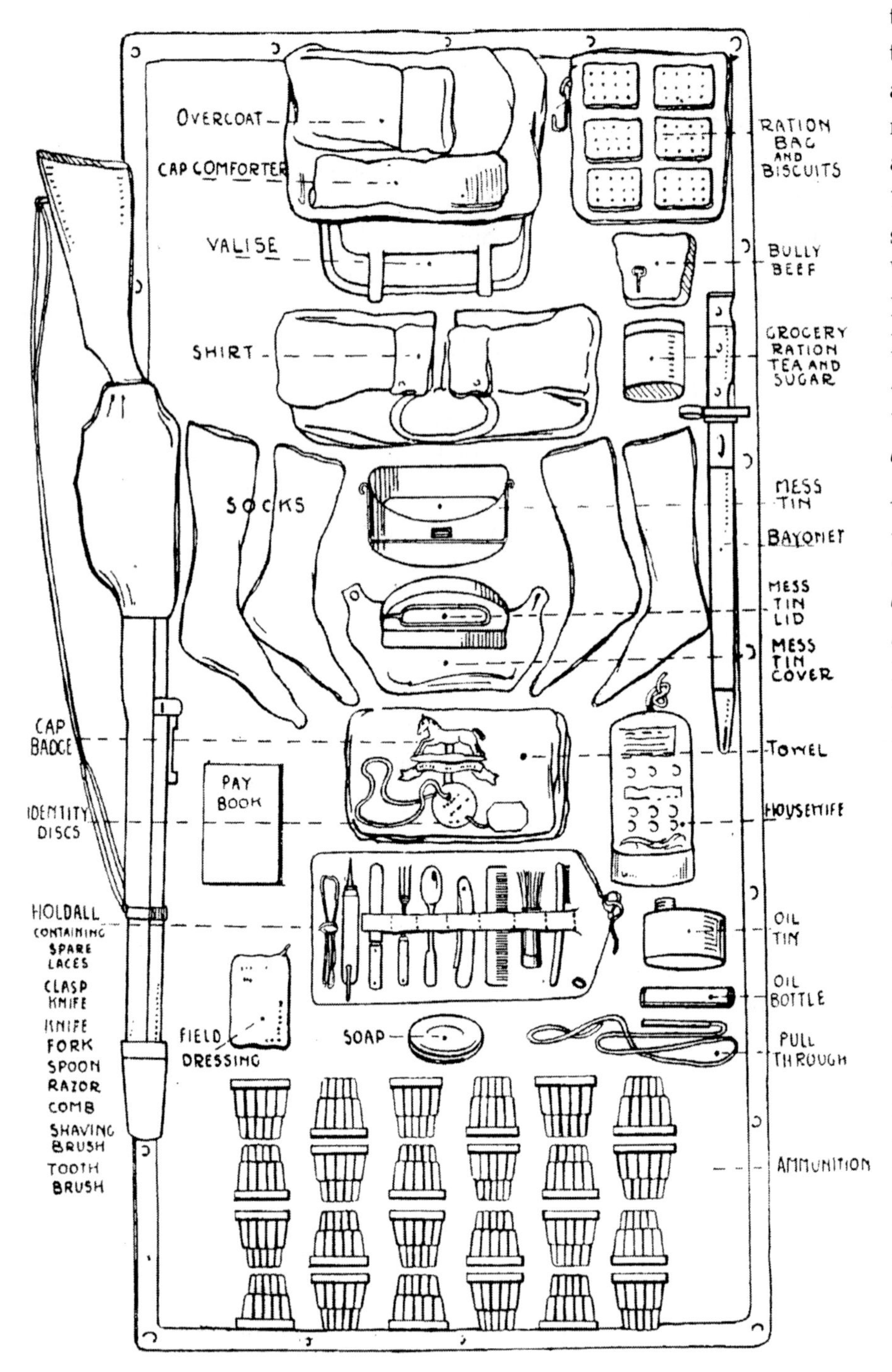

Layout for kit inspection

1065 Rifleman Harry Lamb

1st/5th Battalion London Regiment
(London Rifle Brigade)

Died on Monday 3rd May 1915, aged 22
Commemorated on Panel 54.

Harry was the younger son of Edward and Beatrice Lamb, of 7 Orchard Road, Bromley, Kent. He was educated at Tonbridge School from 1906 to 1908 as a Day Boy. He worked as a commercial banker with Messrs Dunn Fischer. Harry's hobby was sailing, in particular from Deal, an became an expert on the Goodwin Sands.

At the outbreak of war Harry volunteered and left for France on Wednesday 4th November 1914. He entrained to St Omer and spent three weeks training before going into the line at Ploegsteert on Sunday 22nd. He remained on tours of duty in the area until Monday 4th January 1915. In early January he was sent to *'Essex Trench'* on the River Warnave, near Lens, where on Friday 26th February Corporal T H Jenkin went across *'No Man's Land'* and captured a German flag that was reported in *'Punch'*: *"We are not surprised to hear that Cpl. Jenkin of the 1st Battalion London Rifle Brigade succeeded in capturing a German flag at the front. Cpl. Jenkin is an artist, and it was only natural that he should make for the colours."*

Harry returned to the Ploegsteert sector where the Battalion was visited by a series of senior officers and dignitaries. On Friday 23rd April he was sent to Poperinghe in preparation to being sent to Wieltje three days later. On Sunday 2nd May the Germans launched an attack on a ruined cottage in front of their line which was used as a forward listening post. This developed into a full scale attack at 5.20pm lasting for more than hours until it petered out. The Germans had used gas which had caused a number of walking wounded but for most of the men it was no more than a most unpleasant experience. At 8.25pm a report was sent to Brigade Headquarters: *"Situation quieter. Fear casualties very heavy, will report later. All supports now in trench. Improbable that we can hold length of trench without assistance. Men have had no sleep for seven nights. This, with the incessant shelling, had told on them. Germans are entrenching nearer to us, opposite to our centre. No. 3 Company, which is there, hopes that it did good execution on them. Can you send any Very lights?"*

The Germans continued to harass their line and during the action Harry had both legs blown off by shrapnel, as he was only one hundred yards from the German front line it was impossible to stretcher him to a Field Hospital or provide medical assistance, food or water. His comrades bandaged his wounds with their puttees and did the best they could for him but he succumbed to his injuries and was buried in the field.

LIEUTENANT CHARLES EDWARD KILCOURSIE LAMBART

'B' Company, 1st Canadian Mounted Rifles (Saskatchewan Regiment)

Died on Monday 5th June 1916, aged 38
Commemorated on Panel 30.

Charles was the son of the late Major and Mrs Frederick Lambart, one of three brothers who served in the Great War, and the family was related to the Earl of Cavan. He was educated at Wellington College from 1890 to 1895. Charles was married to Isabel Dora Lambart.

Earl Cavan

Charles served in the South African War including at the Siege of Mafeking.

At the outbreak of war Charles volunteered and was sent to England for further training at Shorncliffe. He marched with his Company from camp to Folkestone Harbour and embarked on *SS La Marguerite* for Boulogne on Wednesday 22nd September 1915. He entrained for Bailleul where he remained until Monday 27th and was sent to Ploegsteert where he was sent into the line for front line experience attached to seasoned troops. His first tours of duty were at the *'Brasserie Trenches'* followed by *'Westhof Farm'*. From November he moved to La Rossignol near Wytschaete.

In January 1916 Charles undertook training in Méteren until Monday 31st when the Battalion was sent to *'Red Lodge'* with their headquarters on the Rodeberg. The Regiment retook the line at *'McBride Mansions'* undertaking tours of duty and organising working parties until returning to Méteren on Sunday 20th February for further training. After a month the Battalion paraded and marched via Bailleul and Locre to *'Camp 'A'* where they rested overnight before being sent by train to Ypres Asylum from where they relieved the 1st Battalion North Staffordshire Regiment near Hooge. When they were relieved, the Battalion provided a series of working parties to the front line for a week before returning to the front line. From Saturday 1st April the Battalion spent four days on working parties before leaving for rest and training at *'Camp F'* until Thursday 13th. Charles returned to the line at *'Vigo Street'* for a tour of duty until early Thursday 22nd when he returned to *'Camp F'*. Each night working parties were provided, laying cables at Zillebeke Bund and cleaning and revetting the trenches around Hooge. Whilst with his men supervising the work Charles was killed, initially posted as missing. Charles was recorded in Debretts Obituary — War Roll of Honour published in the 1921 edition.

SECOND LIEUTENANT JACK FELLOWES LAMBERT

9th Battalion King's Royal Rifle Corps

Died on Friday 30th July 1915, aged 23
Commemorated on Panel 51.

Jack Lambert

Jack was born in Coombe, Malden, Surrey, on Wednesday 3rd September 1891, eldest son of Ernest and May Fellows, of 23 Terlingham Gardens, Folkestone, Kent. He was educated at Marlborough College from January 1906 as a member of Cotton and went up to Merton College, Oxford, in 1910 where he served in King Edward's Horse. Jack went out to the Malay States and was appointed manager of a cocoa estate.

At the outbreak of war Jack travelled back to England and volunteered, being commissioned on Tuesday 27th April 1915. He left with the Battalion for France arriving in Boulogne on Friday 21st May 1915. He entrained for northern France and then onward to the Ypres Salient where training continued for front line duties. He undertook a series of tours of duty until Thursday 22nd July when a huge mine was blown at Hooge. Jack and the Battalion were unable to make use of the crater as it was kept under constant fire. After a period of rest out of the line, during the late hours of Thursday 29th Jack took his men back into the line in front of Hooge. At 3.15am on Friday the Germans launched a significant attack on their line where liquid gas was used for the first time. The effect of this new weapon terrorised the defenders and terrible casualties were suffered, one of those being Jack. He remained on the 'missing' list until his death was confirmed in March 1916.

His Commanding Officer wrote: *"He was a splendid Platoon Commander and his men loved him."*

Liquid fire

61589 Private
Paul Adrien Lambert, DCM

Machine Gun Section

22nd Battalion Canadian Infantry (Quebec Regiment)

Died on Saturday 8th April 1916, aged 22

Commemorated on Panel 26.

Citation for the Distinguished Conduct Medal, London Gazette, Saturday 11th March 1916:

"For conspicuous gallantry and devotion to duty when, with another man, he carried a severely wounded comrade under heavy fire. Having no stretcher, they carried him on their shoulders and in doing so had to cross barbed wire and several trenches. Their bravery and physical energy was most marked."

Paul was born in Montreal on Monday 9th July 1894, son of the late Joseph Lambert and his wife, Eugenie Beauchamp. He was educated locally and was employed as a labourer. Before the war he served in the Militia.

On Boxing Day 1914 Paul volunteered when he was described as a Roman Catholic, 5ft 11in tall, with a 38in chest, a dark complexion, brown eyes, black hair and a tattoo on his right arm. He was sent for training at St John's until Friday 12th March 1915 when the Battalion was sent to Amherst, Nova Scotia, to continue their training. On Thursday 20th May Paul marched out of the camp being given a great cheer by the local population and the salute being taken by the Mayor. They arrived in Halifax and boarded *HMT Sconia* to sail to Plymouth where they disembarked during the morning of Saturday 29th. He entrained to Shorncliffe and was billeted at *'East Sandling Camp'* where training for the front was completed on Wednesday 15th September, when he marched to Folkestone harbour and embarked on the *SS Princess of Argyle* for Boulogne. The Battalion arrived at 11.30pm and were sent to camp until 4.00am when they boarded the train at Port de Briques for St Omer. Paul was bivouacked at Wallon-Cappel. The next day he marched to Méteren and was billeted at Rouge Croix for two days. He marched the relatively short distance across the border to the Sherpenberg to take the line where the Battalion took their first casualty; one man was wounded. Paul continued to serve at Vierstraat, the Sherpenberg and Kemmel until the end of the year.

Croix Rouge

Christmas was spent in billets at Locre, returning to the line on Wednesday 30th December.

New Year 1916 opened as 1915 had closed: tours of duty continued at Vierstraat, *'R E Farm'*, and Kemmel. Paul marched to rest billets in Berthen for two days before being sent to *'Camp C'* at Vlamertinghe which came under shell fire shortly after they arrived. At 4.00am on Thursday 6th he was ordered to 'stand to' and at 5.00am marched from the camp to Ouderdom where the Battalion waited in readiness to support the line, as a German attack was anticipated. At 7.15am on Friday 7th the Battalion was ordered back to camp in Vlamertinghe. Paul was killed during routine duties the next day.

Paul was awarded the Medaille Militaire (France).

Second Lieutenant The Honourable
Francis 'Pickles' Lambton

Royal Horse Guards

Died on Friday 30th October 1914, aged 43

Commemorated on Panel 3.

'Pickles' Lambton and his family coat of arms

Francis was born on Wednesday 18th January 1871, ninth son of George Frederick d'Arcy, 2nd Earl of Durham and Beatrix Frances, Countess of Durham brother of John, 3rd Earl of Durham, KG, GCVO, and Frederick William, 4th Earl (who were twins), and grandson of James, Duke of Abercorn, KG.

He was nicknamed *'Pickles'* and was educated at Eton College as a member of the Reverend Stuart Alexander Donaldson's House. Pickles was a member of the Turf Club and was a racehorse trainer at Newmarket.

At the outbreak of war Pickles volunteered and was gazetted in September 1914 joining the Guards during their mobilization. On Wednesday 7th October he embarked in Southampton and sailed for Zeebrugge, landing the next day. He was to have been sent to support Antwerp, but the city was being evacuated with the Belgian and French armies withdrawing westward. Instead he was sent to Brugge where orders were received to proceed towards Ypres. His route took him to the west, passing Lichtervelde, to Staden and Westrozebeke where he was billeted. A group of German Hussars were riding out searching for billets when they ran into a troop of Horse Guards, and Pickles was informed: *"… he was enjoying the luxury of a bath and*

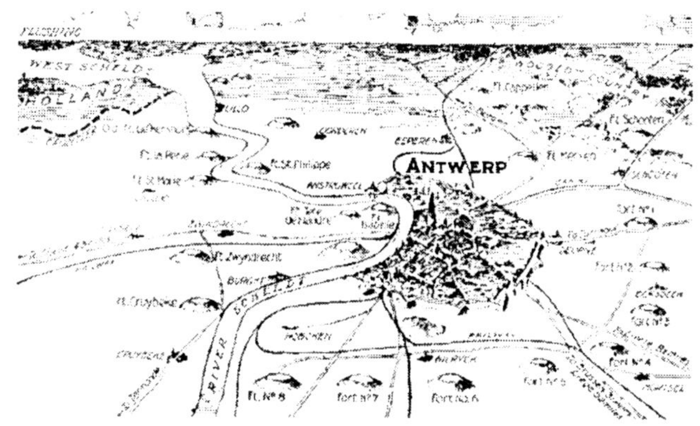

Plan of the forts around Antwerp

later paraded his troop wearing pink silk tights huddling on his clothes while giving his order."

On Sunday 18th a group of German cyclists were found, charged and 'put to the sword'. After taking their bicycles, they moved on until they came under fire from a farmhouse that they swiftly silenced. Pickles arrived on the Salient via Langemarck. On Monday 26th he rode out to Zandvoorde; one of his colleagues wrote of the action: *"The Blues were ordered to make a mounted demonstration towards Kruiseecke. The Squadrons were rallied as quickly as possible, and we went off at a gallop towards the ridge, C Squadron leading. By this time it was getting dusk, and just as well for us that it was. We rode on to the crest between two trenches held by Hugh Grosvenor's Squadron, and here the Germans spotted us, and we came in for a hail of shrapnel and bullets. My horse was hit in the shoulder, and I got into a trench in which were Hugh Grosvenor and Gerry Ward. They seemed surprised at our selecting this spot for a point-to-point, as they can't put their heads out of the trenches without being shot at; I got out and shot my horse with a revolver. On reaching the crest we rode a left-handed course for a short distance. Alastair's horse was shot, and eventually Dick Molyneux rallied the Squadron and took them out of action, D Squadron being blocked by a very high fence and wire. D and B dismounted and opened a covering fire. The result of our little manœuvre seems to have been that the Germans thought the whole Cavalry Corps was behind us, ready to gallop their trenches, and turned every available gun on to the valley behind us. This was exactly what was wanted, as it relieved the pressure on the Twentieth Brigade. By now it was quite dark, the firing stopped, and all rode back to our billets via Pig Farm. Otto and his one gun are still in the trenches. There are only three machine-guns left in the Brigade. Thirty horses were killed in our little demonstration, but the human casualties, considering the fire we drew were small. Newcombe having been hit in the eye two days ago, Harradine becomes R.C.M."*

General Max von Fabeck

On Friday 30th General Max von Fabeck turned two hundred and sixty heavy guns on their lines at 6.45am; at 8.00am the German 39th Division supported by three Jäger Battalions attacked, one of Pickles

... an Uhlan who escaped

fellow officers wrote: *"After an ominously quiet night, the enemy began at 7 a.m. to open a terrific fire against the ridge, and H.E. and big shrapnel burst round the support trenches and Echelon A. Willie Naper was limbered up and away before much harm was done. We retired slowly up the hill to Klein Zillebeke through the Sixth Brigade which occupied the reserve trenches. Pickles and five of his troops were buried in their trench. He was got out, but I am afraid killed afterwards. Otto and most of his M.G. section are missing, also Hugh Grosvenor's and Alex. Vandeleur's. Not one man has come in knows what happened to them."* Pickles was killed in action shortly after a shell burst in his trench, burying many of his men, he managed to get out from under the pile of earth only to be shot in the head. Corporal of Horse Meach and Corporal Hills returned to the trench to see if Pickles was alive and could be rescued, however, they were taken prisoner. Corporal Hills was deliberately shot in the head and killed, Corporal Meach was spared as the Germans thought he was an officer.

Pickles is commemorated on the House of Lords War Memorial and was recorded in Debretts Obituary — War Roll of Honour published in the 1921 edition.

In St Barnabas Church, Bournmoor, Durham, a stained glass window was dedicated in his memory, with the inscription: *"To the glory of God and in loving memory of Hon. Francis Lambton Lieut. Royal Horse Guards. Born Jan. 18 1871, killed in action near Zandvoorde Belgium Oct. 31 1914. Le Jour Viendra."*

His nephew, Lieutenant Geoffrey Lambton, died on Tuesday 1st September 1914 and is buried in Guards Grave, Villers-Cotterêts Forest.

Captain James Lancaster

3rd Battalion Monmouthshire Regiment

Died on Saturday 8th May 1915, aged 37

Commemorated on Panel 50.

James Lancaster

James was born at Wolston Heath, Rugby, on Tuesday 18th December 1877, younger son of the late Robert and Euphemia Lancaster of Allesley, Warwickshire, grandson of John Lancaster, MP, of Bilton Grange, Rugby. He was educated at Shrewsbury School from 1893 to 1896. After travelling around America he returned to England and became a member of the Institute of Mining Engineers. His interests included cricket and golf. James married Margaret Ormonde Lancaster (née Livingstone, of Vancouver Island), and they had three children, Robert born in January 1906, James in March 1910, and John in June 1914.

James was gazetted Lieutenant in February 1910 and promoted Captain on Friday 16th October 1914.

At the outbreak of war James assisted with the mobilisation and the Battalion was based at Northampton. In December they moved to Bury St Edmunds and in January 1915 to Cambridge prior to leaving for France on Sunday 14th February 1915. He entrained to northern France before moving across the border into Belgium to take the line for the first time. During the First Battle of Ypres James was killed in action.

Second Lieutenant Frank Ashton Lane

18th Battalion The King's (Liverpool Regiment)

Died on Tuesday 31st July 1917, aged 21

Commemorated on Panel 6.

Frank was born in Feltham, son of George and Alice Lane, of 53 Wroughton Road, Clapham Common, London. He was educated at the Emmanuel School, Wandsworth, and after school worked as a clerk.

Frank Lane

On Wednesday 9th September 1914 Frank enlisted in Royal Fusiliers. His attestation papers describe him as 5ft 8in tall, with a 34in chest, a pallid complexion, hazel eyes and brown hair. He left for France on Wednesday 17th November 1915 and served with the 5th Trench Mortar Battery.

On Saturday 16th December 1916 he was commissioned and trained at Peterhouse College Cambridge. Frank

returned to France on Friday 22nd June 1917 and joined the Battalion at Château Segard. On Monday 30th July Frank went with his men up to their assembly positions, arriving at 12.30am the next morning with Battalion Headquarters established at *'Crab Crawl Tunnel'*. The men were all given a tot of rum rather than hot tea at 3.50am, just before Zero Hour, due to the water supply being blown up by the German artillery! He led his platoon into *'No Mans Land'* and to the German front line.

"In the greater part of the front of the main attack the resistance of the German infantry was quickly overcome and rapid progress was made. The difficult country east of Ypres, where the Menin Road crosses the crest of the Wytschaete-Passchendaele Ridge, formed however, the key to the enemy's position, and here the most determined opposition was encountered. None the less, the attacking brigades, including a number of Lancashire battalions, regiments from all parts of England, and a few Scottish and Irish battalions (24th, 30th and 8th Divisions), fought their way steadily forward through Shrewsbury Forest and Sanctuary Wood, and captured Stirling Castle, Hooge and the Bellewaarde Ridge. After the capture of the German front-line system our troops on this part of our front (both sides of the Menin Road) had advanced in time with the divisions on their left against their second objective. Great opposition was at once encountered in front of two small woods known as Inverness Copse and Glencorse Wood, while further south a strong point in Shrewsbury Forest held out against our attacks till the morning of 1st of August."

The fighting was fierce and in the heat of battle the situation became confused and the troops mixed up, some going off course in their line of attack. During the attack Frank was killed.

His brother in law, Captain Albert Robson, died on Sunday 24th March 1918 and is commemorated on the Arras Memorial.

Lieutenant Hector Allan Lane

1st Battalion East Lancashire Regiment

Died on Thursday 13th May 1915, aged 25

Commemorated on Panel 34.

Hector Lane

Hector was born at Decorah, Iowa, America, on Sunday 2nd June 1889, only son of John Lane, of Cullisse, Parkstone, Dorset. He was educated at Newton College, Newton Abbott. He was a scholar of the Law Society, admitted as a solicitor in 1911, practising in Singapore with Sisson & Delay.

In March 1907 Hector was commissioned into the Dorsetshire Royal Garrison Artillery Volunteers and

served with them until 1911. Whilst in Singapore he was a member of the Singapore Volunteer Artillery.
At the outbreak of war Hector was in charge of one of the forts in Singapore. He wrote to the War Office and volunteered being gazetted in September 1914 and promoted Temporary Lieutenant in November, which was confirmed in December. He arrived in London in January 1915 leaving for the front in April 1915. He was killed in action on the Ypres Salient.
His Colonel described his death: *"I am very grieved to inform you that your son was killed on the 13th instant. On the evening of that day he led his platoon against a farm occupied by the Germans; he got in all right with his men, and was exchanging shots with them in the farm buildings when he was shot in the head and died at once. He was only with us a short time, but quite long enough to show what stuff he was made of. He was a valuable officer, and did his work very well, and I am very sorry to lose him. He made himself very popular with all ranks. He is buried at the farm he too, which is 1,200 yards north of Wieltje, a village north-west of Ypres."*
In St Mary's Church, Longfleet, Dorset, a stained glass window was dedicated to his memory with the inscription: *"To the glory of God in loving memory of Hector Alan Lane, Lieut. E. Lancs. Regt. killed in action near Ypres May 15th 1915, aged 25 years."*

Second Lieutenant
Henry Clarence Horsburgh Lane

'A' Company, 11th Battalion Border Regiment
Died on Tuesday 10th July 1917, aged 30
Commemorated on Panel 35.

Henry Lane

Henry was born at Sydenham on Thursday 16th December 1886, son of John Macdonald and Margaret Augusta Lane, of Devonia, Kew Road, Richmond, Surrey. He was educated at Dean Close School, Cheltenham, with an Exhibition. In 1906 he went up to St John's College, Cambridge, with a Choral Scholarship, graduating with a Second Class Honours degree in Classical Tripos and awarded his MA in 1912. Henry was appointed Assistant Master at Pocklington School from 1909 to 1910, at The King's School, Pontefract, from 1910 to 1912 and then left for the Malay States where he worked in the Education Department.
In 1916 Henry left his position in the Malay States and returned to England to volunteer. He trained with the OTC in Newmarket and was commissioned on Tuesday 19th December 1916.

British Navy pounding the Belgian coastline

Henry joined the Battalion in the field. He was in the line on the Belgian coast when at 10.00am on Tuesday 10th July 1917 the German started a preliminary barrage. However, due to strong winds the British ships off the coast were unable to reply. 2nd Lieutenant Cook-Gray, Assistant Adjutant, wrote: *"I have reached and examined the second line. On the right the trench is somewhat bashed about, but is not in really bad condition. There has been a continuous bombardment, particularly with heavy T.M.B.'s, since 6 this morning; 5 casualties are reported at present. Our 18-lb. shells are dropping short. I don't think there is any doubt of that fact this time.*
P.S. — 18-pounders have just smashed in a machine-gun dug-out in our second line."
The German barrage continued all day including the use of a new gas that caused violent sneezing, sickness and irritation of the eyes. At 3.30pm a report from 'C' Company was sent: *"Front line very badly smashed now, right half completely wiped out. Second line very badly knocked about. Communication trenches, many blown in and always shelled. Approximate casualties 40. The shelling is very heavy throughout and continuous on first, second and third lines and communication trenches."* Henry was leading his men forward to support another company when he was killed in heavy shell fire at Nieuwpoort.
His Captain wrote: *"Who can express the loss we have all sustained? How he was loved by everyone, and how he did his duty like the brave fellow that he was? Can I ever forget how cheerful he was when the orders came, and how he looked at me when he left me, saying 'Cheery O, sir', then led his*

men away. A better officer I have never had, a firmer friend I can never hope for, so I trust I may be allowed to share in the grief that this letter must bring you, and to offer on behalf of the officers and men of his company our deepest and most heartfelt sympathy in your distress."

The Chaplain wrote: *"I had known your son ever since he had joined our regiment, and am intensely sorry to think he has been taken away from us. I believe his men and all the officers had the greatest respect for him, and one of them was telling me yesterday how he was seen walking fearlessly round with his head up, encouraging his men in the thickest of the bombardment on that memorable day, 10 July. He will be a great loss to us."*

665 Private
Newton Frederick Seymour Lane

50th Battalion Australian Infantry, AIF

Died on Friday 8th June 1917, aged 39

Commemorated on Panel 29.

Newton was born in Shrewsbury son of Adela M Lane and the late Colonel Cecil Newton Lane, CMG, Resident in Cephalonia, and was related to the Earls of Abingdon. He was educated at Malvern College from 1893 to 1897. He was married to Mrs Vera A Lane, of High Street Cambelltown, Tasmania. He worked as a farmer.

His brother, Lieutenant Percy Lane, died on Monday 10th Mary 1915 and is commemorated on the Menin Gate, see below.

Newton served with the Imperial Yeomanry during the South African War.

Newton volunteered in October 1914, with the 3rd Light Horse Regiment, described as 5ft 11½in tall. He left for Egypt on *HMAT Thirty Six* on Monday 21st December

... rescuing the wounded under fire, Gallipoli

1914 from Newcastle, New South Wales.

Newton sailed to Egypt and undertook training prior to being sent to serve in the Gallipoli Campaign. He was wounded by a shell in the thigh on Friday 5th November 1915 but remained on duty. He was evacuated to Alexandria on Monday 20th December 1915 and then served in Egypt. He suffered with leg ulcers and was hospitalised to Port Said in June 1916 before being sent for treatment in London.

He left for France on Tuesday 12th December 1916 and rejoined the Battalion at Buire before undertaking further

The Somme, 1916

training at St Vaast. He spent Christmas undertaking a six mile route march and attending a Church Parade before, Christmas dinner was provided.

His first tour of duty on the Western Front was at Flers from Monday 8th January 1917. He continued to serve on tours of duty in the sector until he was invalided in the spring of 1917 with influenza to Rouen and Etaples.

Newton returned to the Battalion whilst they were training in Buire from where they marched to Albert on Tuesday 15th May and entrained for Flanders. They arrived in Caëstre at 1.30pm on Wednesday 16th and marched to Outtersteene. General Godley visited the camp and observed the Battalion at work.

General Godley

At 1.30pm on Thursday 31st May the Battalion formed up and marched to Neuve Eglise which took four hours, and they were sent out on fatigues. He continued on fatigues for the ensuing few days in the build-up to the beginning of the Battle of Messines. At 8.40am on Thursday 7th June the Battalion moved from Neuve Eglise and was sent into reserve in *'Midland North Support'* at *'Calgary Avenue'*. Prior to leaving for the front Newton was issued with: 170 rounds of SAA; 2 Mills grenades with detonators (one in each pocket) and an entrenching tool.

Their position came under shell fire and before the Battalion undertook their attack on Saturday 9th Newton was killed.

Newton was recorded in Debretts Obituary — War Roll of Honour published in the 1921 edition.

Lieutenant Percy Erwald Lane

Princess Patricia's Canadian Light Infantry (Eastern Ontario Regiment)

Died on Monday 10th May 1915, aged 34

Commemorated on Panel 10.

Percy was born in Boningale, Shropshire, on Saturday 15th January 1881, son of Adela M Lane, of Rycote House, Leamington Spa, Warwickshire, and the late Colonel Cecil Newton Lane, CMG, Resident in Cephalonia, and was related to the Earls of Abingdon. He was educated at Malvern College. He emigrated to Canada and became a rancher.

Percy served in the South African War receiving the Queen's Medal with clasp then served with the police for five years.

At the outbreak of war Percy volunteered and enlisted on Wednesday 9th September 1914 at Lewes Camp, where he was described as 5ft 8in tall, with a 37in chest, a medium complexion, grey eyes and brown hair.

Percy embarked on Sunday 27th September 1914 for Plymouth, sailing on *SS Royal George*, arriving on Thursday 15th October. After training he was sent to Le Havre on Sunday 20th December on board *SS Cardiganshire*. He entrained for Arques and was sent to Blaringhem for two weeks where he dug trenches at Mount Croquet.

On Wednesday 6th January 1915 he took his men into the line for the first time at Vierstraat. A private wrote: *"Our first job was to number off in threes, every third man standing guard and being relieved by the other two in rotation each hour. We had time to look around. Fourteen dark shapes were seen ahead. These were the dead bodies of Frenchmen, who had been mowed down as they left the trench for a charge. They were lying on their faces, still clutching their rifles. The German trenches were sixty yards away, and beyond them was a small wood on rising ground, every tree of which seemed to contain a machine-gun. The slush in the trenches was well above our knees, and the problem was how to get a footing and to keep our rifles out of the slime. A heavy, drizzling rain gave a finishing touch to our joys in the night. Next day there were lively exchanges of shots with the enemy, and in the afternoon the whole of German batteries in their rear were turned on our trenches. We were raked for about an hour by the most awful fusillade of shrapnel, 'Jack Johnsons', 'coal boxes', and every description of heavy artillery. We could only crouch back and hope that our trench would escape. Dozens of shells fell all around. One of them lifted three dead Frenchmen high in the air and threw mud and water all over us, but we had no casualty in our trench at all."*

For the next ten weeks Percy undertook tours of duty at St Eloi. He received a field commission on Sunday 7th February the same day that HRH The Prince of Wales visited them in camp. Three days later HRH Prince Arthur of Connaught, brother of HRH Princess Patricia, came to their camp and spoke to the officers and men. On Friday 12th he took his men into the line at St Eloi, for the first time as an officer, for a three day tour of duty. He continued on tours of duty until Monday 15th March when he was slightly wounded. On Wednesday 24th March they were sent to Poperinghe and after a period of rest marched to Ypres where they were billeted on Monday 5th April. For the next month Percy saw considerable action on the Salient, mainly at Polygon Wood. He was sent to Bellewaarde Ridge on 4th May where he occupied some new, partially constructed trenches. Almost immediately they came under attack and heavy shell fire. The Battle of Bellewaarde Ridge commenced on Saturday 8th with the German artillery demolishing their front line before advancing. Rapid fire eventually repulsed the German infantry. The attacks and counter-attacks continued — Percy was killed repulsing an attack.

HRH The Prince of Wales and HRH Prince Arthur of Connaught

Company Quartermaster Sergeant Allen wrote: *"The last seen of Lieut. Lane was in the firing trench leading his*

Princess Patricia's Canadian Light Infantry in action, 1915

men on like the true soldier he was, for he was a man who knew not the word fear, and he was beloved by all who came in contact with him."
Percy was recorded in Debretts Obituary — War Roll of Honour published in the 1921 edition.
His brother, Private Newton Lane, died on Friday 8th June 1917 and is commemorated on the Menin Gate, see above.

G/6735 Private Charles George Lang

8th Battalion Queen's Own (Royal West Kent Regiment)

Died on Tuesday 8th February 1916, aged 22
Commemorated on Panel 45.

Charles was born at home the son of Mr and Mrs Lang, of 171 Hanworth Road, Hounslow, Middlesex.
With his brother, Ernest, they enlisted on the same day in Hounslow and have consecutive service numbers.
From the end of November 1915 until January 1916 Charles, Ernest and the Battalion were in camp at Bonningues, St Omer. They undertook retraining, re-equipping and a draft of officers and men joined them which brought the Battalion up to full strength. They moved to the Ypres Salient and took position between Hooge and *'Sanctuary Wood'* and undertook a series of tours of duty. Whilst in the front line the brothers were killed.
His brother, Private Ernest Lange, died on the same day and is commemorated on the Menin Gate, see below.

... marching to the front

G/6736 Private Ernest Arthur Lang

8th Battalion Queen's Own (Royal West Kent Regiment)

Died on Tuesday 8th February 1916, aged 23
Commemorated on Panel 45.

Ernest was born at home the son of Mr and Mrs Lang, of 171 Hanworth Road, Hounslow, Middlesex.
With his brother, Charles, they enlisted on the same day in Hounslow and have consecutive service numbers.
His brother, Private Charles Lange, died on the same day and is commemorated on the Menin Gate, for their story see above.

Major Philip Martin Large

1st Battalion Middlesex Regiment

Died on Tuesday 27th April 1915
Commemorated on Panel 49.

Philip was a member of Kingston Rowing Club in their VIII and IV and rowed for the Thames Cup.
Philip sailed to Le Havre as part of the first Regiment of the BEF to arrive in France. Two companies disembarked on Tuesday 11th August 1914 and the second two the next day. Both were accorded a tremendous welcome as could be well imagined. They marched into camp outside the town where they remained for the next ten days.
On Sunday 23rd they arrived in Valenciennes and marched across the Belgian border to Mons taking position along the Mons to Condé Canal where they soon saw action. During the night the Germans launched an attack which was easily repulsed. From the Mons battlefield they were ordered to retire and arrived at Le Cateau at 10.00pm on Tuesday 25th, totally exhausted. They saw little action at Le Cateau although they came under heavy fire. *"After nearly six hours of incessant and overwhelming fire the right of the British line, which rested on Le Cateau, still stood firm. The German infantry was steadily increasing in numbers on their front and, despite all efforts, was drawing steadily nearer. Their right flank was open, they were searched with fire from right and left, and strong columns, betokening the advance of the German IIIrd Corps, were closing in upon the right flank. It mattered not: they had been ordered to stand."* A short engagement in conjunction with the Argyll and Sutherland Highlanders, the Royal Engineers and the Royal Scots Fusiliers resulted in forcing the Germans to retreat. This bought a little time and allowed the Battalion to retire as recorded in the Battalion Diary: *"About 4.00 p.m., on all remainder of force retiring, retirement was ordered by Lieut. Colonel Ward, Commanding Battalion. Retirement was successfully carried out in good order via Reumont, where hospital was established in Church, which was shelled. Battalion, after Reumont, now became somewhat broken up owing to congestion of road. Retirement proceeded S. of Estrées, where Battalion went into bivouac about 10 p.m."* The march south seemed endless

The Memorial erected by the Germans after the Battle of Mons to 'The Royal Middlesex Regiment' and the men they buried in St Symphorien Military Cemetery

particularly in the heat of the summer sun. On Monday 31st they marched into the Forest of Compiègne which provided some welcome shade.

On Tuesday 1st September they were involved in some fierce fighting at Néry including a dramatic bayonet charge that captured eight guns. Within the next few days they were heavily involved in the Battle of the Marne and the week thereafter, the Battle of the Aisne.

... crossing the Aisne under fire

They remained on the Aisne until Friday 9th October when they entrained via Amiens, Abbeville, Etaples, Boulogne to Watten, from where they marched into billets at St Omer.

On Friday 16th October they received orders to march to Vlamertinghe and go into reserve: *"Marched east 12.45 p.m. via Station-Ouderdom to Vlamertinghe, and went into billets at 8 p.m. — a long march, 17 miles."* Here they rested for two days before receiving orders to march twenty-seven miles back down the line to Laventie. They were billeted in Estaires ready for an attack on Fromelles and they remained in the sector until the completion of the Battles of La Bassée and Armentières on Monday 2nd November. The battles had been particularly hard as they were under continuously heavy shell fire which caused considerable casualties. The Battalion Diary records: *"Terrible in the extreme was the condition of officers and men as they stood in the trenches, often knee-deep in filthy mud and slush. For many days they had not taken off their clothes, which had become caked with mud, blood-stained and verminous; indeed it was with difficulty that many of them remembered there had been a time when they were clean and warm, when the concentrated misery of the trenches was unknown to them. But if their feet and hands were icy cold and numbed, if their clothes were soaked and clung like sodden rags about them, limbs racked with rheumatics, if they stood in three feet of water peering cautiously over the parapets across No Man's Land, dotted here and there with the rotting carcases of what had once been brave men and their 'pals', there still burned within them the old 'die-hard' spirit which made light of their troubles and their discomforts, for they were British soldiers."* They remained on the northern France-Belgian border sector until New Year.

On Sunday 3rd January 1915 the Battalion Diary records: *"Still in trenches, which are very bad, full of mud and water up to the men's knees in many places. Raining all day."* After a miserable couple of months the Diary records, in early March: *"The situation remains the same in our front; daily registration of our own and hostile artillery, but no organised bombardment on either side. Sniping by day active; by night little sniping except in front of our left. A great improvement in the weather makes the trenches drier, and there is more to show for work and material put into them. In addition to general strengthening of the front line, work in connection with supporting points and defence of the main second line is carried out by battalions in reserve."*

In April Philip was serving on the Salient and witnessed the first gas attack. He was in action at St Jan when they came under heavy shell and gas shell attack, and he was killed in action.

LIEUTENANT CHARLES KEITH LATTA

2nd Battalion Gordon Highlanders

Died on Thursday 29th October 1914, aged 24

Commemorated on Panel 38.

Charles Latta

Charles was born on Monday 2nd December 1889, third son of John Latta and Margaret Joppor Latta, of 17 Royal Circus, Edinburgh. He was educated at Edinburgh Academy from 1898 to 1908 and passed into RMC Sandhurst.

Charles was gazetted in November 1909 and promoted Lieutenant in August 1911.

Keith served in India and on Saturday 7th December 1912 he sailed from Bombay to Cairo, Egypt where he was stationed at Kaiser-i-Hind Barracks.

At the outbreak of war the Battalion was ordered home and Charles sailed to Southampton, arriving on Thursday 24th September 1914, from where the Battalion went to *'Lyndhurst Camp'*, only a short distance away. On

Sunday 4th October, at 11.00pm, the Battalion returned to Southampton, arriving three and half hours later. After some waiting about they embarked for Zeebrugge, arriving on Wednesday 7th. Charles entrained with his men to Brugge from where the next day they marched to Ostend to assist in covering the arrival of the 3rd Cavalry Division. They remained on the Brugge to Nieuwpoort Canal until ordered to entrain to Ghent during the evening of Friday 9th, arriving in the city at 1.00am on Saturday 10th. Whilst in Ghent they handed over their drums to the Mayor for safekeeping. The

French Marines marching into Ghent

city was lost shortly afterwards and it was not until 1933 that their Colonel, General Sir Ian Hamilton, visited Berlin and brought them home! After thirty-six hours in the rain and cold, without being able to cook or engage the enemy, orders were received to withdraw. Charles marched with his platoon via Somergem to Thielt. The march continued and they arrived in Roeselare at 10.00pm on Tuesday 13th. Ypres was finally reached on Wednesday 14th from where they were sent to Voormezeele. The march had been particularly hard on the men, many of them suffering with swollen feet from the pavé and their boots had shrunk in the rain.

General Hamilton

Charles led his men along the Menin Road and took the line near Amerika before being in position at Kruiseik. From Wednesday 21st October the Battalion was in the thick of the fighting defending Ypres and suffering numerous casualties. Throughout Sunday 25th they came under heavy shell fire and that night the Germans advanced on them from Kruiseik. The Scots Guards, under Major Fraser, mounted a successful counter-attack and he was killed, but two hundred prisoners were taken including officers. On Wednesday 28th they were in front of Gheluvelt when ordered to take the crossroads southeast of the village, and the Battalion went up accompanied by the Grenadier Guards, supported by the Scots Guards and the Border Regiment. They were stretched out across the fields as no trenches had been dug or prepared and as no German attack came they were withdrawn to Veldhoek. On Thursday 29th, the defending Gordons were enveloped in thick fog when the Germans commenced their advance; the grey-clad infantry were not seen and were able to take the British front line with hardly a shot being fired. The Grenadiers, under Captain Rasch, were forced back to the woods at their rear where he consolidated the position with the Gordon Highlanders. In the bitter fight Charles was killed.

His Colonel wrote: *"He gave his life for his country in a gallant fight, which was necessary for the safety, not only of his own regiment, but of a large force … He has always proved himself a fine example, and you may well be proud of him, as we are, and also all those of his own command. He is a great loss to us and the Army."*

His brother, Lieutenant Robert Latta, died on Monday 22nd October 1917 and is buried in Wimereux Communal Cemetery.

20789 Lance Corporal Arthur Edward Lawrence

10th Battalion Canadian Infantry (Alberta Regiment)

Died on Thursday 22nd April 1915, aged 34

Commemorated on Panel 24.

Arthur was born in Cheltenham, on Saturday 24th August 1878, son of Edwin and Fannie Lawrence, of 26 Victoria Mansions, Lethbridge, Alberta. He was employed as a clerk. He had served for three and half years in the Gloucestershire Regiment. His brother, Private Reginald Lawrence, died on the same day and is also commemorated on the Menin Gate, see below.

Arthur volunteered on Saturday 5th September 1914 at Valcartier, his attestation papers describe him as 5ft 7½in tall, with a 39in chest, a sallow complexion, grey eyes, grizzly hair, three vaccination marks and a mole on the inside of his right arm.

Arthur and his younger brother, Reginald, were sent to England and sent for training on Salisbury Plain. On Thursday 4th February 1915 HM King George V and Field Marshal Lord Kitchener reviewed the troops prior to their departure and three days later they sailed for France. On Wednesday 17th February 1915 they arrived in Hazebrouck at 7.00am after a long winding rail journey and after detraining the

… a troop ship sails

Battalion marched to Borre for two days rest.
Arthur and Reginald were paraded and marched across the border to billets in Romarin ready to take the line at Ploegsteert for a week. Their first experience of the line was a shock as Captain Holland related: *"Their trip into the line proved a revelation in more respects than one. The tenacious, icy-cold mud of the trenches, the evil odour of a much fought over battle ground, the necessity for keeping one's head down, and the constant unfightable menace of high explosive shells and trench mortar bombs of frightful killing power, effectively crushed old imaginations about the romance and glamour of war."* The majority of March was spent in the Armentières sector before going for training at Estaires until Wednesday 14th April when they boarded gaily advert-strewn London buses and were driven to Vlamertinghe. From the village they marched along the cobbled road through Ypres and onto Wieltje, arriving at 4.30am. Orders were given for them to immediately commence to dig and construct 'proper' trenches as the ones they were occupying were little more than slight ditches. Throughout their tour and digging the German artillery bombarded them.
Arthur and Reginald were in reserve when the Germans launched the first gas attack at 5.00pm on Thursday 22nd April. At 6.00pm they moved off towards St Julien and took a position ready to take part in a counter-attack. At 11.45pm they advanced against *'Kitchener's Wood'* (Bois des Cuisiniers) where the Germans were well placed and their position was heavily protected by machine-guns. In the first few minutes as they charged towards the German lines both brothers were cut down and killed.
Arthur is commemorated on the Cheltenham War Memorial.

20500 Lance Corporal Reginald Lawrence

10th Battalion Canadian Infantry (Alberta Regiment)
Died on Thursday 22nd April 1915, aged 32
Commemorated on Panel 24.

Reginald was born in Cheltenham, on Friday 9th May 1884, son of Edwin and Fannie Lawrence, of 26 Victoria Mansions, Lethbridge, Alberta. He was employed as a Clerk and served in the 103rd Calgary Rifles. His brother, Private Arthur Lawrence, died on the same day and is commemorated on the Menin Gate, for their story, see above.
Reginald volunteered on Saturday 5th September 1914 at Valcartier, his attestation papers describe him as 5ft 6½in tall, with a 36in chest, a light complexion, blue eyes, fair hair, with a scar under his right eye.
Reginald is commemorated on the Cheltenham War Memorial.

Major William Lyttleton Lawrence, DSO

1st Battalion South Wales Borderers
Died on Saturday 31st October 1914, aged 41
Commemorated on Panel 22.

Citation for the Distinguished Service Order, London Gazette, Wednesday 9th December 1914:
"For gallantry and ability in repelling the enemy on 28 Sept."

William Lawrence

William was born on Thursday 4th September 1873, youngest son of Dr Arthur Garnons Lawrence, of The Cedars, Chepstow, Monmouthshire. He wad educated at Epsom College from 1886 to 1891 where he was appointed a Prefect and played in the First XV and Hockey XI.
He was gazetted from RMC Sandhurst in July 1893, promoted to Lieutenant in 1896, Captain in September 1904, from September 1904 to September 1907 was Adjutant of the Battalion, December 1907 appointed ADC to the Divisional Commander in India.

... a despatch rider in action, 1914

William went out to France with the BEF, landing in Le Havre on Thursday 13th August 1914. He entrained to northern France to serve at the Battle of Mons, then took part in The Retreat and the Battles of the Marne and Aisne before being sent to support the action in Flanders.
As the First Battle of Ypres developed William was in line around Gheluvelt which was under threat of breaking. The 2nd Battalion, Worcestershire Regiment, supported by William and the South Wales Borderers charged forward and saved the day. During the fierce action he was killed.
He was Mentioned in Despatches on Thursday 8th October 1914.

Lieutenant
William Bernard Webster Lawson

1st Battalion Scots Guards

Died on Thursday 22nd October 1914, aged 21

Commemorated on Panel 11.

William Lawson and his family coat of arms

William was born in London on Tuesday 22nd August 1893, the younger son of The Hon Colonel William Arnold Lawson, DSO, DL, subsequently 3rd Baron Burnham, and his wife, Sybil Mary Lawson, of Barton Court, Kintbury, Berkshire, grandson of Edward, 1st Baron Burnham, KCVO (proprietor of the *Daily Telegraph*), and Lieutenant General Sir Frederick Marshal, KCMG. His parents divorced in 1912.

William was educated at Eton College from 1907 to 1911 as a member of Mr Edward Impey's House and passed into RMC Sandhurst. He was a good horseman riding to hounds and enjoyed polo. William was a member of the Royal Automobile Club.

William was gazetted in September 1912 and promoted Lieutenant on Wednesday 15th September 1915.

William embarked on *SS Dunvegan Castle* in Southampton on Thursday 13th August bound for Le Havre arriving at 1.00am the next day. After being sent to camp in Harfleur he entrained to northern France and was in reserve at the Battle of Mons, although they did not see any action. Orders were received for them to retire and so started The Retreat that continued for more than two hundred miles finally ending on Saturday 5th September when they were ordered to turn and face the enemy. The next day they commenced their march back towards the Marne. The Battalion crossed the Aisne and took the line on the Chemin des Dames where they remained until mid-October. The Battalion entrained at Fismes for Hazebrouck from where they marched to Poperinghe, arriving on Tuesday 20th October where they were billeted overnight.

At 5.30am on Wednesday 21st the Battalion marched into the line to assist in the defence of the sector at Bikschote on the Pilkem Ridge in front of Langemarck. Here they joined forces with a Brigade of French Territorials and various Cuirassiers. The Battalion took its first losses on the Salient, four killed and five wounded, whilst inflicting heavy losses on the German infantry who were brought down by rapid fire as they advanced in close formation. Whilst showing a French Officer the direction his men should follow William was shot and killed by a sniper.

A plaque in the cloisters of Eton College reads: *"To the memory of Captain Sir Edward Hamilton Westrow Hulse, 7th Bart, 2nd Battn. Scots Guards killed at the Battle of Neuve-Chapelle 12th March 1915. At Eton from 1903 to 1907, also his cousin William Bernard Webster Lawson, Lieutenant 1st Battn. Scots Guards, killed in action at Steenstraat Thursday 22nd October 1914, at Eton from 1907 to 1911."* (Sir Edward Hulse is buried in Rue-David Cemetery, France.)

In St Mary's Church, Beaconsfield, Buckinghamshire, a marble plaque was placed in his memory with the inscription: *"To the glory of God and in ever loving memory of William Bernard Webster Lawson Lieutenant 1st Battn. Scots Guards. Born 22nd August 1893, killed in action at Steenstraate 22nd October 1914 aged 21 years. All that life contains of torture, toil and treason shame dishonour death to him were but a name here a boy, he dwelt through all the singing season and ere the day of sorrow departed as he came."*

Lieutenant
Thomas Edward Lawson-Smith

13th Hussars

Died on Sunday 1st November 1914, aged 25

Commemorated on Panel 5.

Thomas Lawson-Smith

Thomas was born at home on Thursday 14th March 1889, son of Edward Maule Lawson-Smith, JP, of Colton Lodge, Tadcaster, Yorkshire, and the late Ethel Mary Lawson-Smith, grandson of General Sir William Davies. He was educated at Warren Hill, Eastbourne, followed by Harrow School from 1904 to 1908, as a member of Rendalls, and played for the first XI. Thomas passed into RMC Sandhurst and was gazetted in September 1909, promoted Lieutenant in December 1913.

At the outbreak of war the regiment was in India however he was *en route* to England on sick leave after enteric fever. As soon as he arrived he volunteered for active service, leaving for France with the 11th Hussars. During the First Battle of Ypres he was killed in action in the front line trenches near Messines together with several of his men when the trench received a direct hit from a shell. (The 13th Hussars did not leave India for four weeks after Thomas was killed.)

Colonel Pitman wrote: *"I hope it will be a comfort to you to know that your son had done most awfully well, and only a few days before I had written to Colonel Brooke to ask him to send me some more of the same sort. He knew no fear. Wherever he went his men followed him."*

Colonel A Symons wrote: *"He was just the kind of officer that we badly need — gallant, unselfish, and shrewd, always respected by the men and by his brother officers."*

Colonel Symons

A brother officer wrote: *"The fighting at Messines was desperate, and tremendous efforts were required of the troops to hold it. ... You cannot imagine what his loss means to the whole Regiment, which had every reason to be proud of him. 'Tommy' was the life and soul of everything; the whole of India knew Tommy and loved him; he was always the same — keen, cheery, and absolutely fearless."*

Thomas is commemorated on the Colton and Steeton War Memorial.

His brother, Lieutenant John Lawson-Smith, died on Tuesday 20th October 1914 and is commemorated on Le Touret Memorial.

Lieutenant
Louis James Penard Laycock

'A' Company, 7th Battalion
Northamptonshire Regiment

Died on Tuesday 31st July 1917, aged 25
Commemorated on Panel 43.

Louis was born on Wednesday 6th July 1892 son of the Reverend James Marshal Laycock, MA, of 74 Streathbourne Road, Tooting, London, and the late Louise Ellen Laycock. He was educated at Monkton Combe School, Bath, from 1907 to 1909, and graduated on Thursday 21st October 1915 with a BA in History from St John's College, Oxford.

After leaving College Louis volunteered and was commissioned, serving in France from 1916. In July 1917 Louis was sent to *'Dominion Camp'* from where the Battalion was sent to Redinghem by motor bus for ten days training. On Monday 22nd July they went into the line arriving the next day near *'Zouave Wood'*. On Monday 30th July at 9.00pm Louis took his men into the assembly trenches at *'Kingsway'* where a constant barrage from both sides was exploding above their heads.

The attack commenced, the men advancing one hundred yards every four minutes as the War Diary recorded: *"The barrage came down with a tremendous roar, and the battalion, lying on the parapets of Kingsway and Kingsway Support, advanced under its cover. Perfect order prevailed, the battalion keeping its formation as if on the practice trenches back at Bomy."* During the attack, and leading his men forward Louis was killed.

Captain
Frederick Neil Le Mesurier

2nd Battalion Royal Dublin Fusiliers

Died on Sunday 25th April 1915, aged 40
Commemorated on Panel 44.

Frederick Le Mesurier

Frederick was born in Brighton on Sunday 7th March 1875, youngest son of Colonel Frederick Augustus Le Mesurier, CB, LLB, and Mrs Louisa Le Mesurier (née Browne), of 31 St Margaret's Road, Oxford. He was educated at Marlborough College from 1886 to 1891 and passed into RMC Sandhurst from 1894 to 1895 where he won the two-mile race despite a sprained foot! In 1906 Frederick married Rachel Le Mesurier (née Gillham).

Frederick was gazetted in September 1895, promoted Lieutenant in October, and Captain in March 1900.

Frederick initially served in India and at the outbreak of the South African War the Battalion was sent out and he was taken prisoner during the action at Pretoria. He escaped in March 1900 and managed to reach Delagoa Bay where he rejoined the regiment but was invalided home with fever. When he recovered he returned to South Africa and was Mentioned in Despatches on Tuesday 10th September 1901, receiving the Queen's Medal with four clasps and the King's Medal with two clasps. In 1904 Frederick was seconded to the Sierra Leone Battalion, West African Frontier Force, serving in the action against the Kissis, assisting in their defeat, receiving the Frontier Medal with clasp. He was promoted to command the Battalion and remained in the area working with the local tribes. He worked hard to create a peace and established trade markets throughout the area. He retired from the Army in October 1910 when he was appointed Assistant Commissioner.

At the outbreak of war Frederick volunteered and rejoined the Army, serving in the trenches throughout the winter.

... Germans celebrating Christmas in 1914

During the Second Battle of Ypres he was ordered to help relieve the Canadians who were being attacked by gas at St Julien. In front of *'Shell Trap Farm'*, he, and his company, were at the wire when they were attacked by machine-gun fire: he ordered his men to lie low and started cutting through the wire. In the early morning Frederick made a second attempt to cut the wire but was killed in the process.
A brother officer wrote: *"The men spoke of him as their friend, worshipped him, and followed him anywhere."*

Lieutenant Clive Alfred Le Peton

8th Battalion Royal Inniskilling Fusiliers
Died on Wednesday 15th August 1917
Commemorated on Panel 22

Clive was the son of Alfred Edward and Rose Le Peton, of Earlfort House School, 3 and 4 Earlsfort Place, Dublin. Clive was gazetted on Wednesday 23rd September 1914. After training and serving in Ireland and England, he went out to France in February 1916.
On Monday 30th July 1917 Clive moved to Vlamertinghe ready for the attack the next day in the line between Langemarck and Gheluvelt. He died as a result of gas.
The War Diary records: *"The 4th Division relieved the Guards Division on the 25th, 26th and 27th July, the 1st Somersets taking over the front line trenches from the Scots Guards on the latter date. But the tour, which ended on the 31st, was uneventful and the battalion moved back into support on the Canal bank. At the close of the second tour, however, just as the battalion was being relieved by the 1st Rifle Brigade on the 8th August the enemy (about 10.30pm) made a violent gas attack, accompanied by heavy shelling. Dense clouds of the noxious fumes floated over the trenches and, although the Somerset men had only three casualties from shell fire, 12 officers and 161 other ranks became casualties from gas poisoning. Of these, six officers (2nd Lts. R. P. Thompson, V. F. De Ritter, R. C. Roseveare, D. E. Sully, H. J. Griffiths and D. A. Le Peton) and 27 other ranks died from the effects of gas. H Company, closest to the enemy lost most heavily - 5 officers and 72 other ranks. The gas, a mixture of chlorine, phosgene and prussic acid gas, was very insidious and clung to the ground and the men's clothes, so that if a man slept in his equipment he invariably developed gas poisoning and had to be evacuated to hospital."*

Desmond Le Paton's grave with Clive's commemoration

His brother, 2nd Lieutenant Desmond Le Peton, died on Wednesday 9th August 1916, and is buried in Lijssenthoek Military Cemetery, and Clive is commemorated on the headstone and they are commemorated on the War Memorial at St Matthias Church, Dublin.

Captain Ernest Geoffrey Carrington Le Sueur

1st Battalion Yorkshire Regiment
Died on Thursday 26th July 1917, aged 26
Commemorated on Panel 33.

Ernest Le Sueur

Ernest was born on Wednesday 21st January 1891 younger son of Arthur Le Sueur of Jersey. He was educated at Victoria College, Jersey from 1899 until 1910 when he passed into RMC Sandhurst. At School he was a Prefect, played for the First XV, XI and Shooting VIII, and was Colour Sergeant in the OTC. He then trained with the Sandhurst Company at RMA Woolwich and was then commissioned leaving to serve in India. On Saturday 5th May 1917 Ernest married Dorothy Le Sueur (daughter of Major Charles James Keene, CIE, VD, whose two sons had also attended Victoria College).
He was promoted to Lieutenant in September 1914 and Temporary Captain later in the year, confirmed on Monday 1st January 1917.
At the outbreak of war Ernest was with the Battalion in India and he was temporarily attached to the Mountain Battery at Bara Gali. On Sunday 29th November 1914 the Battalion was ordered to mobilise and move to Kohat. There were problems in Waziristan that runs along the Afghan frontier. He continued to serve in India until October 1916 when Ernest was invalided home with eye trouble, and when he recovered he was sent out to France to the 2nd Battalion. In July 1917 Ernest was resting and training with the Battalion at Zouafques until late in that month when the Battalion was moved to *'Dickebusch Huts'*. He had carefully prepared to lead a raid with his Company, 'C', on *'Jeffery Reserve Trench'*. A preliminary bombardment heralded their raid and they succeeded in getting into the trench and a German officer and ten men were captured. However, no artillery cover was provided for the return and the Germans were able to fire at will from *'Jackdaw Beek'* and Ernest was killed.

... taking prisoners

17297 Private
Frederick Charles Leach

5th Battalion Oxford and Bucks Light Infantry

Died on Saturday 15th January 1916, aged 19

Commemorated on Panel 39.

Frederick was born at home on Saturday 21st March 1896, youngest son of George and Mary Leach, of 17 Colley Street, West Bromwich. He was educated at the Beech Road Schools, West Bromwich.

Frederick volunteered and enlisted on Tuesday 5th January 1915 and was sent for training before leaving for France in September. He was killed in action.

Serjeant H W King wrote: *"We were proceeding to the trenches to relieve some more men, and on our way we had occasion to get out on the top owing to very deep water; as we did so one of the German snipers fired and, your son was hit. ... He has been in my platoon since he joined us last Sept. and I can honestly assure you he has always been a good lad, very willing and he died manfully doing his duty."*

... drawing lots for Christmas home leave

Lieutenant
Edward Hubert Leatham

12th (Prince of Wales's Royal) Lancers

Died on Saturday 31st October 1914, aged 28

Commemorated on Panel 5.

Edward was born at home on Tuesday 20th July 1886, the second and only surviving son of the late Mr Edward Ernest Leatham of Wenbridge House, Pontefract. He was educated at Eton College as a member of Mr

Edward Leatham and his family coat of arms

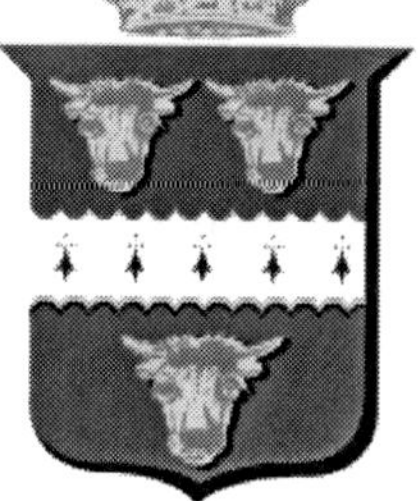

Charles Howard Allcock's House leaving in 1905 and passed into RMC Sandhurst. Edward was a successful polo player and with the regimental team won the Inter-regimental Cup and the Coronation Cup in 1914.

In October 1906 Edward was gazetted and promoted Lieutenant in August 1908.

On Sunday 16th August 1914 Edward entrained from Norwich to Southampton and embarked for Le Havre which he reached the next day. He entrained to Hautmont on Wednesday 19th from where he progressed across the border into Belgium when on Saturday 22nd a patrol encountered a German patrol. On Monday 24th Edward served in front of Harveng and Noyelles until Field Marshal Sir John French ordered the retirement. As the BEF retired the Brigade provided its rearguard. For five days they were in continuous action, including at 4.00pm on Friday 28th when the Colonel led 'C' Squadron in a full cavalry charge at the short-lived Battle of Moy.

The Retreat continued without incident until Sunday 6th September when they were ordered to ride out and engage the enemy. On Thursday 10th they attacked a large group of Germans at Chezy and Gandelu where they captured more than three hundred prisoners together with a large quantity of materials still on their wagons. The Aisne was reached on Saturday 12th which they crossed two days later at Vailly.

On Tuesday 15th the Regiment was relieved from the line to Couvrelles and they remained there in reserve until Wednesday 30th when they were ordered north towards Flanders. The infantry was sent by train, but the cavalry rode and marched — on Monday 12th they reached the Mont de Cats which was occupied by the Germans. They took part in the attack that cleared the hill and pushed forward taking Mont Noir, Mont Rouge, the Scherpenberg and Mont Kemmel.

On Wednesday 14th the Division linked up with the 3rd Cavalry Division that had landed in Ostend and Zeebrugge a week before and had been sent south. Edward was sent into the line opposite Wytschaete where they came under heavy attack. On Saturday 31st October whilst assisting an injured man back to a trench, he was killed by a shell.

Edward was recorded in Debretts Obituary — War Roll of Honour published in the 1921 edition.

Captain Edward Wilberforce Leather

3rd Battalion Yorkshire Regiment attached
2nd Battalion King's Own Yorkshire Light Infantry
Died on Sunday 18th April 1915, aged 35
Commemorated on Addenda Panel 57.

Edward Leather and his family coat of arms

Edward was born at The Friary, Trickhill, on Sunday 23rd November 1879, fifth son of Frederick John and Gertrude Elizabeth Sophia Leather, of Middleton Hall, Belford, Northumberland. He was educated at Wellington College from 1893 to 1896.

Edward was gazetted in 1899, promoted to Lieutenant on Thursday 13th December 1900, and retired in 1904.

Edward served in the South African War, receiving the Queen's Medal with two clasps and the King's Medal with two clasps.

At the outbreak of war Edward rejoined his regiment, leaving for France on Wednesday 11th November, joining his Battalion in the field on Sunday 1st December. He was promoted Captain on Monday 1st February 1915.

Edward immediately went into the line at Lindenhoek, Hill 75, a most unpleasant initial experience. Due to the very heavy rain that had fallen before they arrived the trenches were waist deep in water — on many occasions men had to be pulled from the trenches by rope as they were stuck in the glutenous mud. Twelve days later they were relieved and went into billets at Dranouter. Many of the men were invalided from the line suffering with the results of serving in freezing water up to their knees. Christmas was spent in billets in St Jans Cappel where various activities were organised including an inter-company football match, won by 'A' Company. Between Christmas and New Year they went into the line on the Douve before being billeted at Neuve Eglise — on Tuesday 5th January 1915 whilst in the village a German shell landed, killing fourteen officers and men, wounding twenty-five others. After an inspection by General Sir Charles Fergusson on Wednesday 7th at Wulverghem they continued to the front, serving in the sector until the end of the month. On Friday 29th they were billeted in Bailleul and were given the opportunity of meeting up with their friends of the 1st Battalion for a couple of hours during the afternoon.

From Sunday 11th to Saturday 17th April Edward was in rest billets at Reninghelst. On the Saturday morning he assembled with his men and marched to the front ready for an attack on Hill 60. At 7.00pm six mines were blown at ten-second intervals. Tons of explosives took the top off the Hill and, to make doubly sure of matters, the artillery laid down a curtain barrage that commenced from 7.00pm lasting fifteen minutes. At 7.15pm the infantry assault commenced. At dawn on Sunday 18th the Germans launched a large, and successful, counter-attack, retaking the summit. At 7.00am Edward and his men were moved by the railway embankment, immediately before the hill. At 12.30pm orders were received to move forward through *'Larch Wood'* and at 6.00pm they began the attack. As Edward attacked, the Germans launched a series of counter-attacks. He was badly wounded but continued to lead the assault despite his two serious head wounds. Shortly afterwards he collapsed and died of his wounds.

His brothers, Lieutenant Christopher Leather, died between Sunday 25th and Tuesday 27th October 1914 and is commemorated on the Le Touret Memorial, and Major Ernest Leather, died on Saturday 19th February 1916, and is buried in Rue-David Military Cemetery, Fleurbaix.

Lieutenant John Harvey Leckie

1st (Royal) Dragoons
Died on Sunday 13th June 1915
Commemorated on Panel 5.

John Leckie

John was the only son of Charles Stuart Leckie, of Little Cassiobury, Watford. He was educated at Rugby School from 1902 as a member of Donkin and went up to University College, Oxford, from 1907, where he was a member of the OTC and graduated with a BA in Law.

John joined the army in October 1911 and was with his Regiment in South Africa at the outbreak of war, returning to England for re-kitting and training. He left for Belgium, arriving on Thursday 8th October 1914. As Antwerp was being evacuated John was ordered to Ypres, arriving a week later. During the First Battle of Ypres he served at Langemarck, Gheluvelt and at Nonne Bosschen. John was slightly wounded on Monday 19th October 1914. He continued on tours of duty throughout the winter. He was killed in action during the Second Battle of Ypres near Hooge.

His Major wrote: *"Apart from his capabilities as a soldier, which were great, it was his sweet and loveable nature that made us all so fond of him. … He was a good soldier, good sportsman, and a great gentleman."*

His Colonel wrote: *"As for that boy Leckie, he was of the very best, everyone loved him."*

Captain Jack Lee, MC

6th Battalion Cheshire Regiment

Died on Tuesday 31st July 1917, aged 26

Commemorated on Panel 19.

Citation for the Military Cross:

"When commanding a raid his conduct throughout was of the highest order and a splendid example to his men; it was entirely due to his fine leadership that the enterprise was successfully carried out."

Jack was the son of Mrs I N Lee, of Woodside, Wilmslow, Manchester. He was married to Agnes Muriel Lee (she later remarried to Mr Tattersall), of Whitecroft Park Road, Timperley, Cheshire.

On the night of Wednesday 4th to the early morning of Thursday 5th July 1917 Jack commanded a raiding party of one hundred and thirty men and three other officers on an attack on *'Caliban Trench'*, north of Wieltje. After a short artillery barrage to help cut up the German wire, Jack led the men forward under a creeping barrage. The raid was successful and they returned with considerable reconnaissance information, only losing one officer and four men during the German counter-barrage.

On Tuesday 31st July Jack led his men passed the Hannebeek, through St Julien towards *'Tirpitz Farm'*. The weather was dreadful, constant heavy rainfall. To the Battalion's right flank the troops did not advance as quickly and a sizeable gap grew which the German infantry took advantage of. Some Germans had surrendered but when the attack on the right flank was spotted they took up their weapons to attack Jack and his men. The Germans supported their attack with a heavy barrage and by the end of afternoon the whole line had been forced back. During the afternoon Jack was killed together with a considerable number of his men.

Second Lieutenant John Mitchell 'Jack' Lee

7th Battalion Border Regiment

Died on Saturday 25th September 1915, aged 26

Commemorated on Panel 35.

Jack was born at Patterdale, Cumberland, on Thursday 4th July 1889, second son of Watson and Jane Marr Lee, of 38 Brunswick Square, Penrith, Cumberland. He was educated at Carlisle Grammar School and went up to Trinity Hall College, Cambridge, where he was a member of the OTC. Jack was awarded the Wiltshire Prize and graduated with a first class honours degree in chemistry. He worked for the British Cyanides Company in Birmingham.

At the outbreak of war Jack volunteered and was commissioned on Monday 16th November 1914, leaving for Boulogne in mid-July 1915. He entrained for northern France and was sent to camp in Reninghelst. An attack on Hooge was scheduled for Saturday 25th September. Jack and his colleague, 2nd Lieutenant White, were sent with a party of bombers to keep the enemy at bay; sadly they did not succeed and the Germans regained some of their lost ground. In this action he was mortally wounded.

His Commanding Officer wrote: *"It is with very great regret to tell you that your son, 2nd Lieut. J. M. Lee, of my battalion, has been wounded yesterday in an attack upon the German trenches. ... He showed the greatest courage and devotion to duty; his gallantry is a source of great pride to us all, and we feel his loss greatly."*

Lieutenant Howard Morgan wrote: *"In the early morning of 25 Sept. an attack was made on the German lines for half a mile north and south of H—. The Border Regt. was not making the assault, but later in the day, when our men were hard pressed, Mr. Lee volunteered to go out to the German trenches with three men and do some bombing. He went out to join up with the Royal Scots Fusiliers, who were on our left, but was unable to find any of their men in the German trench. Thus he probably held the Germans for two hours along, when he was severely wounded in the back. He was bandaged and placed in a German dug-out by his three men. Eventually the Germans turned their artillery on to their own trench which we had taken, and shelled us out. One of the bombers reported that a shell dropped on the dug-out in which Mr. Lee was lying. This is all we can gather of what happened. If we knew more there would probably be a tale of wonderful heroism. Jack as I always called him, was one of the bravest men I ever knew. He scoffed at bullets and shells. He undertook some of the most hazardous tasks, and was respected and loved by officers and men alike. On several occasions I know he was personally complimented by the Commanding Officer for his good work and great bravery."*

Bunkers at Hooge Château in 2002

Second Lieutenant Lionel Shaw Lee

5th Battalion Oxford and Bucks Light Infantry
Died on Saturday 25th September 1915
Commemorated on Panel 37.

Lionel the son of Mr and Mrs E H S Lee. He was educated at Wellington College from 1905 to 1910 and went up to Merton College, Oxford, where he graduated with an BA.
Lionel volunteered on Wednesday 26th August 1914 and was sent for training. The Battalion sailed to Boulogne on Friday 21st May 1915 and was sent to northern France before crossing the border into Belgium. He undertook a series of tours of duty on the Salient. During the feint for the Battle of Loos that took place at Hooge Lionel was killed in action. He was Mentioned in Despatches for bravery in France.
In St Peter's Church, Curdridge, Hampshire, a stained glass window was dedicated to his memory, is depicts King Alfred and St Alban, and has the inscription: *"To the glory of God in memory of those who fell in The War 1914-1918 & specially of Lionel Shaw Lee, B.A., aged 23. This window is offered by his parents."*

Captain Edmund Hastings Harcourt Lees

2nd Battalion Border Regiment
Died on Wednesday 28th October 1914, aged 38
Commemorated on Panel 35.

Edmund Lees and his family coat of arms

Edmund was born in Northampton on Tuesday 21st December 1875, son of Thomas Orde Hastings Lees, formerly the Chief Constable of Northamptonshire, and Grace Lees (née Bateman); grandson of the Reverend John and Lady Louisa Lees (daughter of Hans, 11th Earl of Huntingdon). He was educated at Marlborough College from January 1889, followed by the Royal Academy Gosport and RMC Sandhurst. Edmund was a member of the United Services Club and the Alpine Sports Club. He won many prizes for skiing and tobogganing and other winter sports.
Edmund was gazetted on Saturday 5th September 1896, promoted Lieutenant on Saturday 10th February 1900, and Captain on Sunday 24th June 1906, Adjutant from Tuesday 19th October 1909 to Tuesday 29th October 1912.
Edmund served in the South African War, was wounded, Mentioned in Despatches on Tuesday 10th September 1901 and received the Queens Medal with six clasps.
Edmund left Lyndhurst Camp for Southampton, the Battalion sailing for Zeebrugge on board *SS Turkoman* and *SS Minneapolis*, on Sunday 4th October 1914. They were sent to assist with the defence of Ghent from where they were relieved and ordered to march directly to Ypres where they arrived on Thursday 15th. The Battalion was in the line between Zandvoorde and Gheluvelt and Edmund was hit by shrapnel and killed near Kruiseik.
"Our men fought desperately from nine o'clock till six, when the Germans withdrew, and our little remnant was ordered to retire. We have only about 400 men left out of over 1,000 and hardly any N.C.O.'s".
One of his NCOs wrote: *"The regiment was holding an important position for eight days, during which time we were subject to the heaviest shell fire. Captain Lees was killed by a piece of shrapnel on 26th October, and was last seen by another man and myself in the open. We were then retiring with the enemy on top of us. The enemy gained about six hundred yards of ground, but were pushed back by the 21st Army Corps. Your brother was no doubt buried by the reinforcement that came up to our aid. Captain Lees was an officer, both brave and daring, who would always trust his men, and beloved and respected in return. Confidence in him was all that made us stick the shell fire as we did. No man can speak too highly of him."*

The Commander of the Artists Rifles wrote: *"His memory will always live in the hearts of the Artists' Rifles, and his old friends amongst us here desire me to convey to you both their sincerest sympathy."*
Edmund was recorded in Debretts Obituary — War Roll of Honour published in the 1921 edition.
In Guilsborough Cemetery, Northamptonshire, a cross was added to the family grave with the inscription: *"Capt. E. H. H. Lees 2nd Border Regt. 26 Oct. 1914 aged 38. Greatly beloved killed in action near Ypres."*

Captain Gerald Oscar Lees

13th Battalion Canadian Infantry (Quebec Regiment)
Died on Sunday 25th April 1915, aged 37
Commemorated on Panel 24.

Gerald was born at home on Wednesday 30th May 1877, the fourth and youngest son of William Lees, JP, and Rosa Lees, of Old Ivy House, Tettenhall, Wolverhampton. He was educated at Rugby School from 1892 until 1894 as a member of Whitelaw and left to work in Montreal, Canada. Gerald joined the Royal Highlanders of Canada (Militia) and remained with them until moving to Ottawa in 1910 where he worked as a broker. He was a keen golfer, in England and in

Gerald Lees

Canada, reaching the final of the Canadian Championships twice; he was asked to represent Canada against America but his business commitments prevented him joining the team.

Following the outbreak of war Gerald volunteered and rejoined the Battalion at Valcartier on Wednesday 23rd September 1914. He was described as being 5ft 11½in tall, with a 38in chest, a fresh complexion, brown eyes and hair, a scar on left hand and on his forehead.

Gerald left with the First Canadian Contingent, sailing on board *RMS Alaunia*, under Captain Rostron, RNR, who was the Captain of *RMS Carpathia* that rescued the survivors of *RMS Titanic*. They left at 3.00pm on Saturday 3rd October 1914 and arrived in Plymouth on Thursday 15th. Gerald continued to train at *'West Down South Camp'* until leaving on board the *SS Novian* on February 12th for St Nazaire. He entrained for Hazebrouck from where he marched the ten miles to billets in Flêtre and Caëstre where he remained for four days. Brigadier General Edward *'Inky Bill'* Ingouville-Williams (who died on Saturday 22nd July 1916 and is buried in Warloy Communal Cemetery) inspected the Battalion at Armentières from where they marched to take the line for the first time in northern France. On Tuesday 13th Gerald was sent to Abeele where they were billeted until they were collected by a fleet of motor buses and taken to Vlamertinghe. From the village they marched along the tree-lined cobbled road to Ypres that remained relatively intact, although within a few days would be reduced to a ruin. They passed through the town and through the Menin Gate to St Jan; after a short rest they moved into the line at St Julien with the French Colonial Troops to their left. At 5.00pm on Thursday 22nd the Germans launched the first gas attack that decimated the French troops to their left but the Germans failed to press home the advantage they had achieved. The Germans attacked their line and forced them to retire. They managed to hold their new line and assisted in the counter-attacks that were mounted later that night. Gerald fought hard with his men until he was killed by a shell.

'Inky Bill'

His Colonel wrote: *"We are all more grieved than we can say to hear of the loss of your son, and cherish with great pride and affection the memory of our association with so fine a soldier and gentleman."*

A brother officer wrote: *"He was a perfect hero, and by his cheerfulness helped to keep the men in good spirits, in spite of the terrible time we were having from German howitzers."*

Gerald is commemorated on St Michael & All Angels Church War Memorial Tettenhall, and on the Royal Ottawa Golf Club War Memorial.

... the artillery firing gas shells later in war

MAJOR THOMAS PRIOR LEES

'A' Company, 1st/9th Battalion London Regiment (Queen Victoria's Rifles)

Died on Wednesday 21st April 1915, aged 41

Commemorated on Panel 54.

Thomas Lees

Thomas was born at the Old Priory, Bedford, on Thursday 3rd September 1874, second son of Alfred and Rosa Matilda Lees, of The Pines, Bedford. He was educated at Bedford Modern School where he was Head of School and went up to Clare College, Cambridge, where he graduated with an MA and 8th Senior Optime.

Thomas was then employed by the Home Office.

Thomas was gazetted to the Territorials on Wednesday 22nd May 1889, promoted Captain in March 1905 and Major on Friday 15th August 1913.

During the South African War Thomas volunteered for service but was not sent out, and served in England. At the outbreak of war Thomas volunteered and arrived in Le Havre on Friday 5th November 1915. The Battalion entrained the next day for a twenty-six hour gruelling journey to St Omer from where they went into billets. On Thursday 17th the Battalion lined the streets for the funeral cortege of Field Marshal Lord Roberts, VC, and two days later they marched in the snow to Hazebrouck and twenty four hours later moved onto Bailleul. On Friday 27th General Sir Horace Smith-Dorrien inspected the Battalion as they marched across the border into billets in Neuve Eglise. On Sunday 29th Thomas took his men into the line at Wulverghem described by Captain George Culme-Seymour (commemorated on the Menin Gate, see above): *"The route for "A," old Lees, was quite easy and so I went with "B" and Stephen Shea. We were met by an officer in the village, which is not a village, but a mass of ruins, and he led us first to the Battalion Head-quarters, where the whole battalion will be in about six days' time. There were a few shells going over and a good many snipers at work, but beyond accustoming the men to the sound, etc., nothing happened. We had to walk through most awful mud, right up to our knees in places, and through a stream, though very small yet very wet. It was a bright night, moonlight, but with clouds every now and then, and we went along very slowly and quietly, the men doing very well and making no noise."*

Field Marshal Lord Roberts, VC

Captain Culme-Seymour

Thomas and the Battalion remained in the Wulverghem sector until Monday 22nd March 1915 when they moved to Ypres. On Thursday 1st April he took his men to Hill 60 where they would shortly see heavy action and Thomas would lose his life three weeks later. On Saturday 17th April, at 7.00pm, the British blew their mines on Hill 60 and the offensive commenced, Captain Sampson wrote: *"At the time of the great explosion the Q.V.R. were in rest billets five miles away listening to the distant gun-fire and watching the flashes. The Germans made three counter-attacks that night, losing very heavily, but their last attack retook a part of the new trench consisting of one of the craters formed by the explosions. On Monday evening this was retaken. On Sunday morning early we were called out of our rest billets at short notice and marched into Ypres, where we were billeted and our men employed to carry supplies of all sorts up to the fire trenches, an unpleasant job, in which we had a few, but not many casualties. Early on Monday morning we moved out of Ypres into reserve trenches and spent a quiet day there, having only a little carrying work to do. There was no fighting that day. However, on Tuesday morning the Germans opened a very heavy cannonade, shelling the fire trenches and our batteries, and also flinging huge shells from a 15-inch howitzer into the unfortunate town of Ypres. We were in a safe place about one and a half miles from the town, and these great monsters came roaring through the air and on their impact sending up a huge column of black smoke and debris, and causing a concussion which even at that distance struck one's ears almost with the force of a blow. In the afternoon I had the honour of a few minutes' talk with General Smith-Dorrien, who said he had watched the doings of our battalion and we had done 'splendidly.' He said he thought the Germans would attack again. All day the cannonade went on and about eight o'clock the Germans counter-attacked again and continued to do so all night, keeping up a tremendous artillery bombardment on Hill 60 and the ground in rear of it. We at once got orders to move up through this zone of fire to a place about 400 yards in the rear of the hill. Off we started, the C.O. and Seymour in front, then I and my company ('D') followed by Major Dickins and Capt. Cox with "B" Company, hoping for the best, but knowing we were in for it. We had some casualties on the way up, but the air seemed full of shells and it was wonderful we did not have more. Once a group of shells burst all round us in front, arid we were almost blinded by the gas escape, but uninjured. Finally we got to our rendezvous (Larch Wood) and after a long delay I was able to collect my company and get them into the dug-outs of sorts, where we were fairly well protected from the rush of shells. All this time hand-to-hand fighting was going on in the trenches. Soon 'A' Company (Major Lees) was ordered up into the fire trenches, and at about 1 a.m. I got an order to take my company up. The men fell in silently and as steadily as possible, and off we set along the railway cutting and from there up a communication trench. After I had gone a few yards up this I found it had been blown in and that it would take a long time to get the company over the various obstacles. So I went through a gap into the railway cutting to divert the rear half of the company along the cutting. Finding this feasible, I went back to the subaltern in front, who was in the communication trench, told him what I was going to do, and then returned along the cutting to do it. As I was going back, a shell burst very close to me, and a bit of it hit me on the side of the head. I was able to give Summerhays my orders and tell him what to do, and he took the company on. I hear that later on he was killed after doing very fine work. He had been as cool as a cucumber all night, and was a splendid little man whose loss I feel very much. A rifleman tied me up. I was quite able to walk back to H.Q. and later to the dressing station two miles in rear. I lost a good deal of blood in the first few minutes but it soon stopped, and I was in no pain and very thankful to find myself still alive."*

Lance Corporal H D Peabody wrote of Thomas' activities on Hill 60: *"We went up on fatigue, taking up ammunition, and as we came back Major Allason (Bedfords) asked for reinforcements for Hill 60 and refused to let us go. He told us that we could get rifles and swords on the hill if we had not got them. We then went up on hill, Major Lees taking over command. Major Lees decided that we should make a charge to the front of the crater where the Germans were supposed to be. The charge was made and only one German was found there. In the meantime the East Surreys went along the communication trench and occupied the right half of the hill. There they remained until morning, when their bombs had given out. Our own men had to retire when they were blown out with bombs, but they lined the rear of the crater and kept up a steady fire on the front to stop the Germans from occupying it. Just as dawn broke the Germans bombed and shelled us very heavily. Major Lees gave orders that where the bombs were falling very heavily then we could move left and right, but must be ready to line the crater again if the Germans came or in numbers. Shortly afterwards it was pointed out that the East Surreys were giving way on the right and Major Lees went across to stop them vacating the trench, and in doing so was shot."*

Thomas was shouting words of encouragement to the men and orders to hold on when he was shot in the head and heart; he fell backwards and was caught by a Sergeant of the Bedfordshires, but Thomas was dead.

Colonel Shipley

Lieutenant Colonel Shipley, CMG, wrote: *"He died like a hero, having retaken made good a position of primary importance which the enemy were on the point of re-occupying. His last gallant charge was, as he would have wished it, to the assistance of his county regt., the Bedfordshires. The last words I heard him speak as he led his company off into the trenches were: 'Now, remember, if anyone is wounded, the others must carry on. If I am hit, go on.' It was his initiative and courageous behaviour that has enable us to hold onto the position. I cannot even attempt to tell you what a stupendous loss he is to the regt. and myself, but we must console ourselves by remembering and tying to emulate your brother's unswerving devotion to duty and the unflinching gallantly shown by him in all times of stress; his life so earnestly devoted to others will live in our memories for all time."*

In Elstow Church a tablet was placed in his memory with the inscription: *"To the glory of God and in loving memory of Thomas Prior Lees, Major - Queen Victoria Rifles. Son of Alfred and Rosa Lees. Fell on Hill 60 near Ypres April 21st, 1915, aged 41. Immota Fides."*

Lieutenant Geoffrey Philip Legard

2nd Battalion Northumberland Fusiliers

Died on Saturday 8th May 1915, aged 22

Commemorated on Panel 12.

Geoffrey Legard's family coat of arms

Geoffrey was born on Friday 2nd June 1893, fourth son of Digby Charles and Eleanor Clementina Legard, of Heighington Hall, Lincoln, and related to the Baronets Legard of Ganton. He was educated at Charterhouse from 1906 to 1910 as a member of Gownboys.

On Saturday 20th February 1915 Geoffrey assisted in an attack on 'Y' and 'Z' Trenches north of the Comines Canal that was not successful and many casualties were sustained, Geoffrey was lucky only to be slightly wounded in the action.

At 5.30am on Saturday 8th May the German artillery commenced a huge barrage, the fourth day of bombardment that the men in the front line had to endure. At 8.30am the German attack commenced with hoards of grey uniformed soldiers climbing out of their trenches and streaming forward. Throughout the day the fight continued with counter-attack followed by counter-attack. In the fierce action the Battalion lost six of its officers including Geoffrey.

Geoffrey was recorded in Debretts Obituary — War Roll of Honour published in the 1921 edition.

In St John The Evangelist Church, Washingborough, Lincolnshire, a marble tablet was placed in his memory with the inscription: *"To the memory of Geoffrey Philip Legard, Lieutenant 2nd Battn. Northumberland Fusiliers, killed in action near Ypres, in defence of his King and Country on May 8th 1915 aged 22 years. Eternal God is thy refuge and underneath are the everlasting arms."*

His brother, Captain George Legard, died on Tuesday 27th October 1914 and is buried in Cabaret-Rouge British Cemetery, Souchez.

Ruins of the Cloth Hall

Lieutenant Hugo Molesworth Legge

3rd Battalion Royal Fusiliers

Died on Wednesday 5th May 1915, aged 23

Commemorated on Panel 8.

Hugh Legge

Hugo was born on Wednesday 29th July 1891, youngest son of the late Lieutenant Colonel the Hon Edward Legge, and Cordella Twysden Molesworth Legge, of Eversleigh House, Windsor, grandson of 4th Earl of Dartmouth. He was educated at Haileybury from 1905 to 1909 as a member of Lawrence and passed into RMC Sandhurst. His interests included cricket, polo and golf.

Hugo was gazetted in March 1911 and promoted Lieutenant in January 1913.

Hugo was in the line at Gravenstafel from Tuesday 20th April 1915 and witnessed the horrific first gas attack on Thursday 22nd. He was involved in the second attack three days later when they were under heavy attack and were forced to retire. Hugo was killed at Zonnebeke where he was shot through the head.

Hugo was recorded in Debretts Obituary — War Roll of Honour published in the 1921 edition.

Lieutenant Nigel Walter Henry Legge-Bourke

2nd Battalion Coldstream Guards

Died on Friday 30th October 1914, aged 24

Commemorated on Panel 11.

Nigel Legge-Bourke and his family coat of arms

Nigel was born at 45 Grosvenor Square, London, on Wednesday 13th November 1889, the only son of Colonel the Hon Sir Harry Charles Legge, GCVO, (Equerry to HM Queen Victoria, HM King Edward VII and HM King George V) and the Hon Lady Amy Gwendoline Legge (Maid of Honour to HM Queen Victoria, 1877 to 1884), grandson of William Walter, 5th Earl of Dartmouth, nephew of the William Heneage, 6th Earl. He was great-uncle to 'Tiggy' Legge-Bourke, nanny to TRH Princes William and Harry of Wales.

Nigel was educated at Eton College as a member of Reverend Henry Thomas Bowlby's House from 1902 to 1907 and passed into RMC Sandhurst, entering shortly after his 18th birthday in January 1908. In the Guards' Chapel, on Tuesday 3rd June 1913 he married Lady Victoria Carrington, youngest daughter of 1st Marquess of Lincolnshire, KG, PC, GCMG (now Lady Victoria Forester, of Furze Hill, Broadway, Worcestershire), they had a son, Edward Alexander Henry born on Sunday 16th May 1915. He was a member of White's.

Nigel was gazetted on Saturday 6th February 1909, and promoted Lieutenant in June 1910.

Nigel left Victoria Barracks, with No 1 Company, for Southampton on Wednesday 12th August 1914, sailing on *SS Olympia* and *SS Novara* bound for Le Havre. After going to camp some five miles outside the town the Battalion entrained the next day for the front but had to endure hours of waiting in the cold and rain on the station. Nigel served at Harveng during the Battle of Mons but did not engage the enemy. The Retreat commenced which ended after marching for more than two hundred miles to the town of Rozoy when on Sunday 6th September orders were received to turn and engage the German armies. The Marne was re-crossed on Wednesday 9th September and the Battalion engaged the Germans at Soupir on Monday 14th as they crossed the Aisne and took position on the Chemin des Dames.

German front line on the Aisne

During the Battle of the Aisne Nigel was Mentioned in Despatches on Sunday 4th October *"for his very excellent work and exceptionally good leading of his platoon on all occasions up to the battle of the Aisne"*.

The Battalion left the Aisne from Fismes by train for Calais, or rather that was the idea, but the train set off without warning leaving most of the officers and men watching it disappear into the distance! Luckily another train was found that took them to Hazebrouck and from there they marched through Steenvoorde to Boeschepe.

On Sunday 18th October, immediately after Church Parade, a fleet of London motor buses arrived to collect the Battalion and take them to Ypres via Reninghelst and Vlamertinghe. After a hot meal in the town Nigel marched with his platoon along the Menin Road towards Gheluvelt where he took the line. As each

day passed the German armies pressed hard on the British lines attempting to break through to the coast. Just before dawn on Friday 30th October the Germans mounted an attack that was repulsed. The Battalion was under heavy shell fire and was continuously sniped, one killing Nigel while he commanded No 1 Company in the advanced trenches at Reutel Wood.
Nigel was recorded in Debretts Obituary — War Roll of Honour published in the 1921 edition.
In St James Church, Fulmer, Buckinghamshire, a stone table was placed in his memory with the inscription: *"In loving memory of Nigel Walter Henry Legge-Bourke Lieut. Coldstream Guards. Only son of Colonel The Hon. Sir Harry and Lady Legge. Born November 13th 1899, killed in action near Ypres October 30th 1914. He died as he had lived, doing his duty."*

Captain Eoin Leitch

5th Battalion Argyll and Sutherland Highlanders
Died on Tuesday 31st July 1917, aged 25
Commemorated on Panel 42.

Eoin Leitch

Eoin was born at home on Wednesday 23rd September 1891, son of John and Jesse Leitch, of Greenock. He went up to Glasgow University in 1909 and graduated with a BSc on Friday 20th June 1913. He was member of the OTC at University and was commissioned to the Territorials in 1911. On Tuesday 7th December 1915 at Mid Parish Church, Greenock, he married Margaret Alexander Graham and they had a child.
Eoin was gazetted a Lieutenant at the outbreak of war and under took coastal defence duties. On Tuesday 1st June 1915 he sailed from Devonport to Egypt, arriving on Saturday 12th. Until the end of the month he was training, sailing on Thursday 1st July for Mudros, landing at Cape Helles on Saturday 3rd. He was wounded in action during action at Achi Baba on Monday 12th July and invalided home.

... action at Achi Baba

In 1917 he went out to France as a Captain and killed at Passchendaele. It was recorded of him: *"The support Company, under Capt. E. Leitch, realizing the 8th Division were not in line successfully formed a defensive flank. With this attempt, to touch personally with Battalion on right, Capt. Leitch was himself killed, a real loss to the Battalion."*

8073 Company Serjeant Major Frederick Lelliott, DCM

1st Battalion King's Own
(Royal Lancaster Regiment)
Died on Tuesday 24th May 1915
Commemorated on Panel 12.

Citation for the Distinguished Conduct Medal, London Gazette, Wednesday 30th June 1915:

"For gallant conduct and excellent work throughout the winter in the trenches. Company Serjeant-Major Lelliot's zeal, enterprise and example have had great effect on the men, and he has shown himself as always ready for any dangerous work; such a laying out wire entanglements, repairing parapets etc."

Frederick was born in Chichester. He was educated locally and enlisted in Winchester.
The Battalion was sent out with the BEF on Sunday 23rd August 1914 and took part in the Battle of the Marne and the Aisne. The Battalion entrained to northern France and onward into the Salient. He continued to serve on tours of duty throughout the winter. During the early stages of the Second Battle of Ypres the Battalion was sent to support the Canadians at St Julien following the gas attack on Thursday 22nd April. During the later stages he was killed in action at Bellewaarde.

5424 Corporal Harold William Lemme

6th Battalion Australian Infantry, AIF
Died on Wednesday 19th September 1917, aged 29
Commemorated on Panel 7.

Harold was born in Windsor, Victoria, son of Sweyn Harold and Catherine Lemme, of 341 Collins Street, Melbourne, Victoria. He was educated at Melbourne Grammar School from 1901 to 1903 and became a travelling agent. He served in the Cadets, was a member of St Kilda Cricket Club, Melbourne Cricket Club, Melbourne Rifle Club, and Harold played tennis for the State. In 1912 he had a serious motor cycle accident that cut short his sporting career and should have rendered him unfit for active service.
On Thursday 15th July 1915 he volunteered and enlisted, leaving from Melbourne on Tuesday 4th April 1916 on board *HMAT Euripides*, sailing for England. After training he was sent to France. On Tuesday 11th July 1916, after serving on the Salient and northern France, he was marched from Neuve Eglise to Bailleul. He entrained for the Somme where he served until Tuesday 22nd August when he was sent back up to the Ypres Salient until Monday 23rd October. He returned to the

Somme where he served at Guedecourt, Mametz, Flers, *'High Wood'* and Bullecourt until Tuesday 24th July 1917. Harold was again sent back to the Ypres Salient
After a period of training Harold arrived in Reninghelst on Thursday 13th September. Three days later he moved to *'Château Segard'* and moved forward to Zillebeke Bund on Wednesday 19th where he was preparing for an attack the next day. It was a relatively quiet day although there was spasmodic shelling and he was killed in the front line when a stray shell landed close to him.

Lieutenant
Alexander Henry Leslie

18th Battalion Australian Infantry, AIF

Died on Thursday 20th September 1917, aged 27
Commemorated on Panel 23.

Alexander was born in Aberdeen, Scotland, son of Samuel and Elizabeth Leslie, of Railway Terrace, Boat on Garten, Inverness-shire. He went to Australia where he lived at 60 Keppel Street, Bathurst, New South Wales, and was employed as a railway fireman.
On Tuesday 2nd March 1915 he volunteered and enlisted, leaving on Friday 25th June 1915 from Melbourne on *HMAT Ceramic*. In August he moved from Lemnos to sail to the Gallipoli Peninsular and took the line at *'Russell Top'*. He served at *'Courtney Post'* until arriving at Mudros on Monday 20th December. The Battalion spent both Christmas and New Year training and preparing to move to Egypt.
At noon on Tuesday 4th January 1916 the Battalion embarked on *HMT Simla* bound for Alexandria, arriving on Saturday 8th. They disembarked at 9.45am the next morning and entrained for Tel-el-Kebir where training continued until they were sent to the Dunkoon Plateau at the end of the month. On Saturday 5th February they moved to the trenches at Mount Kembla. After a month Alexander went with his comrades to Moasca from where they entrained for Alexandria on Saturday 18th March. They embarked on *HMT Ascania* and sailed at 2.00pm the next day via Malta to Marseilles. Alexander formed up with his men and marched through the town, entrained for Thiennes where they arrived at 9.00am on Wednesday 29th and were sent to billets. Training continued included instruction on gas, the use of the *'Tube Helmet'* and how to use Lachrymatory gas. After a month of training they took the line on Sunday 30th April. Whilst serving in the line billets were provided at Bois Grenier.
He continued on tours of duty until Friday 30th June when he was moved to *'Fort Rompu'* from where he was sent to the Somme. He took the line at Poziers on Wednesday 26th July and continued to serve in and out of the line until early on Tuesday 5th September when the move to the Salient began.
At 7.00pm on Tuesday 5th he detrained at Hopoutre Station and marched to Poperinghe and took billets in the Rue des Boeschepe. Alexander and his comrades were able to spend the next three days enjoying the town and relaxing — despite the sound of battle constantly booming in the distance. At 8.00pm the Battalion entrained for Ypres and marched out to Zillebeke Bund where they relieved the East Lancashires. They took position in *'Vancouver Street, 'Crab Crawl', 'Fort Street', 'Warrington Avenue'* with their Headquarters in *'Dormy House'*. He served in the sector until Tuesday 10th October when he was sent to Steenvoorde for training, followed by Nordausques and Bellancourt. They moved to Ribemont on Friday 27th and took the line at Montauban from Tuesday 7th November where the trenches were described as being in *"fearful condition"*. He served on the Somme at Delville Wood with hutments provided at Trônes Wood, followed by training at *'Adelaide Camp'*, Montauban. Whilst at *'Pioneer Camp'* on Friday 2nd February 1917 Alexander was promoted Lieutenant. He served at Bazentin, Contalmaison, Le Sars and Fricourt. From Friday 1st June the Battalion was sent to Contay for two weeks training before returning to Bapaume until the end of July.
Throughout August Alexander trained with his men until early September when they were sent to the Salient. They took the line at Westhoek Ridge before moving to the Bellewaarde Ridge at 6.30pm on Wednesday

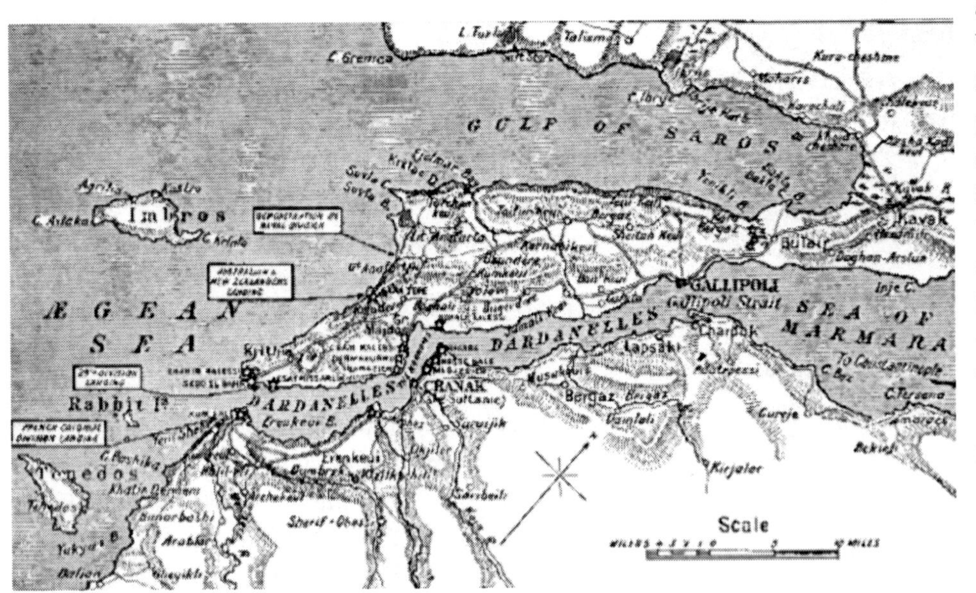

Map of the Dardanelles

19th September and took their assembly positions. At 1.40am they moved forward to the tapes at their jumping off point below the Westhoek Ridge. A preliminary barrage was laid down which began at 5.40am and they moved forward. Two hours later they had crossed the Hannebeek and consolidated their position. As they advanced Alexander was killed leading his men forward.

Second Lieutenant George Arthur Dunalley Lewis

4th Battalion South Staffordshire Regiment

Died on Thursday 8th July 1915, aged 20

Commemorated on Panel 35.

George Lewis

George was born in Hastings, Sussex, on Thursday 24th January 1895, elder son of Colonel Arthur W Drummond Lewis of 67 St John's Road, Jersey, grandson of the Hon Arthur James (Advocate-General of Bombay). He was educated at Victoria College, Jersey, from 1906 to 1912 where he was a member of the OTC. When George left School he joined the Capital and Counties Bank, Weymouth.

At the outbreak of war George volunteered and was commissioned. He undertook his training in Jersey, and then took a machine-gun course becoming the Machine Gun Instructor to his Battalion.

In May 1915 George went out to France and after a short period of training took the line on the Salient. He continued to serve on tours of duty until, whilst assisting to relieve the Lancashire Fusiliers George was killed and buried where he fell on the bank of the Yser Canal.

His Commanding Officer wrote: *"We all admired him; he had made himself very popular, and we all deplore his loss."*

Major Bernard Robert Liebert

Leicestershire Yeomanry

Died on Thursday 13th May 1915, aged 50

Commemorated on Panel 5.

Eton College

Bernard was the son of the late Edmund and Emily Liebert. Bernard was educated at Eton College as a member of Mr Henry William Mozley's House, leaving in 1882. He married Violet Mary Woods (formerly Liebert), of 3 Manchester Square, Marylebone, London.

He was killed on the Frezenberg Ridge in a fierce fight where the Germans also launched a gas attack prior to their attack for which Bernard and his men had virtually no protection.

Bernard was recorded in Debretts Obituary — War Roll of Honour published in the 1921 edition.

Germans attacking using gas and hand grenades

9620 Private William George Lilley

'A' Company, 1st Battalion

Royal Warwickshire Regiment

Died on Monday 24th May 1915, aged 16

Commemorated on Panel 8.

William was the son of William and Lucy Lilley, of 82 Conybere Street, Birmingham. He was educated locally. He enlisted in Birmingham and was sent for training before embarking for France to join the Battalion in the field. On Saturday 8th May 1915 William was sent into the line at Potijze Château where he remained for five days. He was relieved from the line and marched through the Menin Gate into the shattered town of Ypres. Very heavy shelling over the previous four weeks had taken a heavy toll on the town and William would have seen very little other than the movement of troops amongst the ruins. No longer were there open shops selling their wares or street cafés lining the streets and square. The

Ruins of Potijze Château during the war

town was also a dangerous place to be as the German artillery had the whole place pin-pointed. His march continued out along the Ypres to Poperinghe road, stopping in the relative safety of Vlamertinghe where he was able to rest for a few days. William was able to clean up, received clean clothes, had regular meals and was able to sleep. On Thursday 17th he paraded and marched back along the cobbled road to Ypres and out via Menin Gate, arriving at the front line in Wieltje. He had been trained and prepared for the attack on *'Shell Trap Farm'* which took placed on Monday 24th. William and the Battalion were in support some way behind the front line when the Germans used gas against the British lines. William, was not effected by it. His Company was in readiness to advance but the heavy machine-gun fire prevented their deployment. Despite not being in the heart of the battle William was killed: one of more than a hundred casualties.

Grave of an Unknown Soldier of the Warwickshire Regiment from the area where William was killed on the Salient

2199 Corporal Norman Frederick Lindhe, DCM

6th Battalion Australian Infantry, AIF

Died on Tuesday 30th October 1917, aged 21

Commemorated on Panel 7.

Citation for the Distinguished Conduct Medal, Tuesday 21st August 1917:

"For conspicuous gallantry and devotion to duty. With a few men he succeeded in driving off a strong party of the enemy. He set a fine example of courage and initiative throughout."

Norman was born in Hay, New South Wales, son of Mr J H B von Lindhe, of Swan Hill, Victoria.

Norman volunteered on Tuesday 13th April 1915, embarking from Melbourne, Victoria, on board *HMAT Wandilla* on Thursday 17th June 1915. He arrived in Egypt from where he left to serve in the Gallipoli Campaign until he was evacuated back to Egypt. He spent three months training whilst the Battalion was reorganised.

He was sent to the Western Front on Sunday 26th March 1916, sailing from Alexandria to Marseilles. Norman entrained to the Ypres Salient where he served until Tuesday 11th July when he was sent south to serve on the Somme until Saturday 26th August, after which he returned to the Salient. After a couple of months he was again sent to the Somme, arriving at Dernancourt on Monday 23rd. The Battalion saw action at Guedecourt, Mametz, Flers, *'High Wood'*, Thilloy and Bullecourt, amongst others, until Tuesday 24th July 1917. He was awarded his Distinguished Conduct Medal for bravery at Thilloy on Friday 2nd March 1917.

The Battalion marched to Méaulte from where they entrained to Caëstre arriving at 3.00pm on Friday 27th July. He was sent for training at Cassel and in the Le Verrier area before marching to Reninghelst and then into the line at *'Château Segard'* on Sunday 16th September. On Wednesday 19th Norman prepared with the Battalion for the attack that took place the next day against *'Fitzclarence Farm'* close to *'Glencorse Wood'*. The Battalion was relieved during the night of Saturday 22nd and sent for training until Monday 1st October when a fleet of buses collected them to take them to *'Dickebusch Huts'*. They remained there until 6.45pm the next evening. Norman marched into the line at Westhoek Ridge where he bivouacked before taking the line late on Wednesday 3rd. The following morning at 5.30am a German barrage fell on their lines and half an hour later Norman went 'over the top' and moved forward towards the crater on the Broodseinde Road. The tour of duty continued until Tuesday 9th when the Battalion was relieved to *'China Wall'* where they were collected by motor bus and taken to Reninghelst and *'Halifax Camp'* at Ouderdom. On Monday 22nd he marched to *'Belgian Château'* and onward to the Canal Dug-outs. The next morning he moved to Ypres, via the Lille Gate, along the Menin Road to *'Birr Crossroads'* and onto Westhoek where the Battalion was in reserve. At 5.30am on Friday 26th the British barrage commenced, the Battalion advanced and took *'Decline Copse'*. They continued to advance. The Germans put up a stiff resistance and Norman was killed in action shortly before the Battalion was relieved.

Second Lieutenant Richard Lintott

5th Battalion London Regiment (London Rifle Brigade)

Died on Monday 3rd May 1915, aged 19

Commemorated on Panel 52.

Richard Lintott

Richard was born at home on Monday 13th July 1896, eldest son of Bernard and Alice Lisle Lintott, of 11 the Carfax, Horsham, Sussex. Richard was educated at Hurstpierpoint School from 1907 to 1914 where he was a Prefect, was in the Cricket XI ('Best Bat' in 1914), won the Fives Cup and took the part of Octavius in *'Julius Caesar'* in 1914. He played for the School against the MCC: *"Lintott was very daring, for he hit three fours in the first over and settled down to enjoy himself."* Richard served in the OTC where he was promoted Sergeant and gained his 'A' Certificate.

At the outbreak of the war Richard was taking part in the School OTC Camp — he immediately volunteered. He was not accepted due to the fact he looked so young. However, was accepted by the Public Schools' Special Corps at *'Paddock Camp'*, in Epsom and after that he was able to enlist in the London Rifle Brigade. Richard went out to Le Havre on Wednesday 4th November on board *SS Chyebassa*. He went up to St Omer and spent three weeks training, mainly at the Benedictine Convent at Wisques. He undertook his first tour of duty on Sunday 22nd in Ploegsteert where he gained a reputation for catching rabbits and then producing an excellent stew. He was present during the Christmas Truce, what part he played is not known.

Christmas 1914
— an idealised view for the British public

In January 1915 he was sent to *'Essex Trench'* on the River Warnave, near Lens, before returning to Ploegsteert. On Thursday 29th April 1915 Richard was gazetted in the field.

Whilst in the line at Fortuin he was sleeping in a reserve trench that was accidentally hit by a British shell killing him instantaneously. Richard was buried in the field. Richard was related to Sub-Lieutenant William Lintott who is commemorated on the Helles Memorial.

20330 Private
William Alfred Lipsett

10th Battalion Canadian Infantry (Alberta Regiment)
Died on Friday 23rd April 1915, aged 29
Commemorated on Panel 24.

William Lipsett

William was born at home on Friday 29th January 1886, youngest son of the late Robert and Martha E Lipsett, of Ballyshannon, County Donegal, Ireland. He was educated at St Andrew's College, Dublin, and went up to Trinity College Dublin, graduating with a BA in 1908. William entered the Irish Bar and in the Spring of 1914 he left for Canada and practised there, becoming a member of the Militia.

On Saturday 5th September 1914 William volunteered and enlisted, refusing a commission. His attestation papers state his next of kin being Mr Lewis R Lipsett, of 56 Leeson Park, Dublin, and describe him as 5ft 8½in tall, with a 39in chest, a dark complexion, brown eyes and black hair.

William came back to England with the first contingent and after training he went to France in February 1915. At 7.00am on Wednesday 17th February he arrived in Hazebrouck from where he marched to Borre. After two days rest he was sent on his first tour of duty at Ploegsteert for a week. The Battalion was ordered to Fleurbaix, Armentières, where he remained for a month. He undertook training in Estaires until Wednesday 14th April when he boarded a London bus and was taken to Vlamertinghe. From there he marched to Wieltje, arriving at 4.30am the next morning. The trenches were merely ditches, so for the next twenty-four hours they dug at speed to create a line that gave them adequate cover. During the afternoon of Thursday 22nd the first gas attack was launched against the French Colonial troops which was spotted by Major Joseph McLaren (who died on the same day as William and is buried in Vlamertinghe Military Cemetery), Major Ormond and Captain Gledden as they were riding along the Elverdinghe road towards Brielen. Shells were bursting pouring forth a strange yellowish-green cloud that drifted gently along the line. The three officers galloped to Headquarters in Ypres and reported what they had seen, but their information was not understood. At 6.00pm the Battalion was paraded and William was sent to St Julien where he had to move up in a small party as the roads were clogged with gassed French troops streaming back in panic. At 11.45pm William was led forward in a counter-attack against a German strong point in *'Kitchener's Wood'* (Bois des Cuisiniers) that was strongly defended. As he charged forward, William was killed just short of the German lines.

Major Ormond wrote: *"I saw Lipsett the night that he was killed; we went into action charging the wood west of St. Julien at 11.50 p.m., April 22. The Grenadiers were grouped on our left flank and did exceptionally well, Lipsett being one of them. As soon as we had taken the trench, they continued along to the left until they were stopped. Lipsett like others was very cool and appeared to have no fear. They were subject to the most severe machine-gun fire I have known, but pressed on until all were killed and wounded. I regret to say that as he was killed within 10 or 15 yards from the German redoubt at the corner of the wood we were unable to recover his body. He was an excellent soldier."*

His relation, Major General Louis Lipsett, died on Monday 14th October 1918 and is buried in Queant Communal Cemetery British Extension.

Major General Louis Lipsett

and his funeral cortege

Second Lieutenant Andrew Little

9th Battalion Durham Light Infantry

Died on Sunday 25th April 1915, aged 28

Commemorated on Panel 36.

Andrew Little

Andrew was born in Hexham, on Tuesday 25th May 1886, son of Andrew and Sarah Little, of Oakfield, Hexham, Northumberland. He was educated at Bilton Grange, Harrogate. With his brother, John, he was joint owner of a flour mill in Hexham: Messrs A & G Little. His interests included playing hockey and tennis, both at county level, and he was a member of the Tyneside Athlete Association.

On Tuesday 3rd November 1914 Andrew was gazetted and sent for training. On Saturday 17th April 1915 he arrived with the Battalion in Boulogne, leaving for Flanders on Monday 19th April. They arrived at Cassel to continue their training which ended at 2.00pm on Friday 23rd when he paraded his men at Le Riveld, Cassel, and marched them to Steenvoorde. A fleet of buses arrived to convey them via Poperinghe to Vlamertinghe where they arrived at midnight. They had heard the guns booming away whilst in Cassel and now the night sky was illuminated by the full panoply of war. Andrew marched with his men up to Potijze where they were bivouacked before being sent to Verlorenhoek, and he was killed leading his men in action during his first day in the line.

Captain J E Raine wrote: *"He died at the head of his platoon, leading his men in an advance. We were being shelled and I had just walked up to him to say something, when a shell burst. Death was instantaneous, and we buried him later in a little churchyard near Voloerenhoek. Belgium, and marked the place with a cross. This was Sunday, about 6 p.m. Nothing could have been better than the magnificent way in which he behaved throughout the few days we were in this zone."*

Second Lieutenant Eustace Fernando Llarena

2nd Battalion Suffolk Regiment

Died on Saturday 18th June 1915, aged 23

Commemorated on Panel 21

Eustace Llarena

Eustace was born on Tuesday 19th April 1892, son of Mrs B S Llarena, of 39 Red Post Hill, Herne Hill, London, and the late Fernando Llarena. He was educated at Dulwich College from 1905 to 1910, where he was a Sergeant in the OTC, played for the Second XV and was a member of the gymnastic team. After leaving School he played for the Old Alleyian Football and Gymnastic Clubs. Eustace studied medicine at Guy's Hospital in 1910 where he played for their XV (being awarded his Blue), became Captain of the water-polo team and swam for the Hospital. He passed his First Professional and First Conjoint Examinations in 1912.

At the outbreak of war Eustace volunteered and enlisted in the Artists Rifles with service number 1416, leaving for France in October 1914. On Wednesday 27th January 1915 he was gazetted to the Suffolk Regiment.

For the last two weeks of April Eustace was in the

line at Vierstraat and during May served opposite the Wytschaete Ridge. On Monday 7th June he marched with his platoon from Brandhoek into the line at 'Moat Farm' near Hooge. On Wednesday 16th June an attack on the line of *'Railway Wood'*, Bellewaarde Farm and *'Y Farm'* commenced but despite initial success the attack did not achieve its objectives. *'Y Farm'* had been taken and Eustace and his men were ordered to dig a communication trench to help consolidate the position. During the work, and holding the position, Eustace was killed by a shell.

17552 Private David Isaiah Lloyd

5th Battalion King's Shropshire Light Infantry
Saturday 25th September 1915, aged 24
Commemorated on Panel 49

David was born at home, son of John and Sarah Lloyd, of The Village, Llangunllo, Radnorshire.
He enlisted in Knighton, Radnorshire and was sent for training at Aldershot. In March 1915 the Battalion was moved to Chiddingfold before returning to Aldershot from where they left for France. David arrived in Boulogne on Thursday 20th May 1915 and was sent to northern France before crossing the border to Belgium. He served on the Salient on tours of duty and during the night of Thursday 23rd September David was entrained to Ypres Asylum from where he was marched to *'Railway Wood'*. With his comrades he prepared for the attack that was a feint for the Battle of Loos. At 3.50am the British artillery commenced and after half an hour he leapt out of his trench to advance on the German lines where he was killed.
His brother, Corporal John Lloyd, died on the same day and is commemorated on the Loos Memorial.

Second Lieutenant Francis Oswald Lloyd

9th Battalion attached 6th Battalion
King's Shropshire Light Infantry
Died on Saturday 12th February 1916, aged 33
Commemorated on Panel 47.

Francis was born in Rangoon, Burma, on Thursday 26th April 1883, son of Major R O Lloyd, RE (India), of Treffgarve House. He was educated at Marlborough College from January 1895 until Easter 1900.
Francis served in the South African War before being employed by the Cape Police. He became employed as a civil engineer on the railroads in Canada.
Following the outbreak of war he volunteered at Valcartier on Saturday 5th September 1914 where he was described on 5ft 8in tall, with a 40in chest, a ruddy complexion, grey eyes, medium brown hair, two vaccination marks, a large scar on the left of his chest and on his back. Francis was appointed a Sergeant in the 10th Canadian Regiment and came over England with the First Canadian Contingent and was sent for training on Salisbury Plain. At 6.00am on Wednesday 10th February 1915 the Battalion marched from their camp to Amesbury Station and entrained for Avonmouth. At 2.55pm they embarked on *SS Kingstonian* to sail to St Nazaire. The ship was blown onto a sandbank off the port that delayed their arrival until Sunday 14th. Following a long and tiring rail journey the Battalion arrived in Hazebrouck from where they marched to billets in Borre on Wednesday 17th. After three days they moved to Strazeele where Field Marshal Sir John French inspected them. From Monday 22nd practical experience was provided for all ranks in the front line and undertook fatigues. On Monday 1st March the Battalion was sent to Bac St Maur, marching via Armentières, where General Edwin Alderson visited them and spoke to all ranks. Francis' first tour of duty took place near Fleurbaix and he remained in the line on high alert as the Battle of Neuve-Chapelle raged close to them. Francis moved from northern France to Belgium on Wednesday 14th April; a fleet of motor buses took the Battalion to Vlamertinghe from where they marched to Wieltje. They

Sir John French

... German in the front line, early 1915

were stretched out on the open ground and had to dig in at speed to provide cover and the next day 2,500 sandbags arrived to help create a parapet. Following the tour of duty Francis went into reserve and then were sent to camp at Vlamertinghe. Following the German gas attack at 5.00pm on Thursday 22nd April Francis was ordered to 'stand to' then was sent to support the line at St Julien where he participated in the counter-attacks that night and over the following days. After surviving the Second Battle of Ypres Francis was sent for officer training and commissioned, joining his Battalion in northern France. Francis was sent to serve in Belgium on Thursday 20th January 1916, taking the line near the canal below the Pilkem Ridge. The trenches were in very poor condition, they were flooded throughout and Francis and his men spent days standing up to their knees in cold muddy water. At 2.00am on Saturday 12th February the Germans began to bombard their line with 5.9 shells when a Nissen hunt on the canal bank was hit and collapsed. Francis was killed, together with 2nd Lieutenant Ivan Garnet, 2nd Lieutenant John Sidebotham (both now buried in White house Cemetery, St Jean-les-Ypres), and 2nd Lieutenant Barnes (buried in Etaples Military Cemetery). The Battalion lost twenty men in the same bombardment and a large number were rescued after hours of work digging them out from the mud and debris.

Ivan Garnett

17139 Private
Harry Edward Lloyd

7th Battalion Canadian Infantry
(British Columbia Regiment)
Died on Thursday 15th April 1915, aged 20
Commemorated on Panel 24.

Harry Lloyd

Harry was born at home on Saturday 24th November 1894, only son of Robert Henry and Beatrice Lloyd, of Spokane, Manor Road, Aldershot, Berkshire. He was educated locally, at Holmwood and Bexhill-on-Sea. Harry went to Canada to work on a ranch at Abbotsford, British Columbia. He served for a total of three years with the Territorials. Harry was travelling in Canada when the war broke out — he noticed troops on the move and he was invited to join them which he did! On Saturday 5th September 1914 he volunteered at Valcartier, his attestation papers describe him as 6ft 1in tall, with a 37in chest, a swarthy complexion, grey eyes, brown hair, with birth marks on his chest under the right arm and a vaccination mark on the left arm. Leaving everything behind him, Harry came with the first Canadian Contingent to England in October 1914. He was sent for training at *'West Down South'* before moving to *'Lark Hill'* on Friday 4th December.

HM King George V with senior officers undertake an inspection on Salisbury Plain

Harry paraded at 10.15pm on Tuesday 9th February 1915 and marched to Amesbury where he entrained for Avonmouth. He embarked on *HMT Cardinganshire* and sailed to St Nazaire where he disembarked at 6.30am on Monday 15th. He marched to the station to entrain for Strazeele. Training continued until he was sent to Ploegsteert for front line instruction and practical experience until Monday 1st March. The Battalion was sent south to billets at La Boutillerie from where they took the line at Fleurbaix from Friday 5th. Harry undertook a series of tours of duty until Saturday 27th when he was marched to Estaires. He went on a series of route marches and undertook training before marching to Steenvoorde at 7.03am arriving at 2.00pm in the rain. Inspections were carried out on Thursday 8th by General Edwin Alderson and General Sir Horace Smith-Dorrien on Sunday 11th. At 8.00am on Wednesday 14th Harry paraded and boarded a motor bus that took him to Vlamertinghe. At 4.00pm he marched along the cobbled roads, through Ypres, which remained basically intact and out to St Julien. The Battalion moved forward and relieved the 3rd Battalion at Gravenstafel which was completed

Generals Alderson and Smith-Dorrien

by 11.00pm. The German artillery laid down a heavy barrage from early the next morning and during the afternoon Harry was killed, one of four men from the Battalion to die that day.

Lieutenant Colonel Victor Odlam wrote: *"Lloyd was killed on afternoon of 15 April in the trenches in front of Gravenstafel Ridge, which is in the Ypres Salient. He was badly wounded in the abdomen and groin by shrapnel. I went down after he was wounded, and was with him when he died. He suffered a great deal, but the doctors were able to give him morphine tables, and he passed away in his sleep."*

Captain Leslie Haines wrote: *"He was in a section of the trench we are holding, in command of his section, when a shell from a German Howitzer Battery, which enfilades us, unfortunately exploded killing your boy. It will be some consolation to you to know that though his promotion had not appeared in orders, he had recently been placed in charge of his duty in that capacity, and during the very short period he lived after being struck, his thoughts were all for his section and the achievement of their object; the grit he showed was splendid."*

A German Howitzer being hauled into position

Lieutenant Lewis John Bucknall Lloyd

'B' Company, 9th Battalion, attached 1st Battalion
King's Shropshire Light Infantry
Died on Sunday 25th April 1915, aged 28
Commemorated on Panel 47.

Lewis was born in Toronto, Kansas, USA, on Sunday 19th September 1886, only son of John Bucknall Lloyd, JP, and Adela Maud Lloyd, of Dorrington Grove, Shrewsbury. He was educated at Charterhouse from 1900 to 1904 and passed into RMC Sandhurst.

Lewis Lloyd

He was gazetted on Wednesday 9th October 1907 and promoted on Wednesday 24th July 1912 and sent to serve in Secunderabad, India. At the outbreak of war Lewis was a member of the 9th Battalion that provided drafts for the overseas battalions, otherwise they remained on home duty. On Sunday 20th December 1914 he was sent out with the 1st Battalion and marched from Winchester to Southampton as a member of 'B' Company. He embarked on *SS Maidan* and sailed to Le Havre. After disembarkation he entrained to Aire and marched to Blarkinghem, spending ten days mainly digging trenches.

In March they were on tours of duty near St Eloi, and whilst Lewis was having breakfast in the front line he was annoyed by the constant bombing by the Germans which was disturbing his enjoyment of breakfast! In his annoyance he threw a half-used tin of marmalade into their trench that sent the Germans scattering thinking it was a real 'jam-pot bomb' — Lewis was then able to continue his breakfast uninterrupted! On Monday 5th April Lewis marched with his men into the front line at Polygon Wood and was slightly wounded during the tour. As the Battle of St Julien raged, Lewis brought up 'W' Company, some one hundred and forty, strong to assist capture a communication trench that had not yet been taken despite the best efforts earlier in the day (see Lieutenant Biddle-Cope above), this was to be supported by Lieutenant Voelcker with 'Y' Company, some ninety strong. They provided artillery support and at 2.40am whistles were blown when 'W' and 'Y' left their trenches and moved forward, getting to within thirty yards of the Germans line who then opened up on the attackers. The bright moonlight unfortunately gave the Germans perfect targets to aim at. Both main officers were killed and as a result the men were not provided with any direction and the attack failed. John and Lieutenant Voelcker were initially reported as missing, soon but it became clear that John had been killed. Later it was discovered that Voelcker had been taken prisoner; he had last been seen wounded and leaning against the German wire.

... German infantry attack

Captain Meyricke Entwisle Lloyd

1st Battalion Royal Welch Fusiliers

Died on Saturday 24th October 1914, aged 34

Commemorated on Panel 22.

Meyricke was born on Monday 31st May 1880, eldest son of the late Mr and Mrs Henry Lloyd, of Pitsford

Hall, Northampton. He was educated at Eton College as a member of Mr Edward Compton Austen Leigh's House and went up to Magdalene College, Cambridge, in 1898. He married Elizabeth Grace Lloyd (née Ramsey), of Rose Hill, Ruabon, Denbighshire. Meyricke was a keen horseman and huntsman.

In 1900 Meyricke was gazetted, promoted Lieutenant in September 1907, and Captain in April 1911.

On Saturday 19th September 1914 he left Wrexham with five other officers and three hundred and forty-two other ranks for Lyndhurst. Sunday 4th October he went out to Belgium as part of VIIth Division. He landed at Zeebrugge on Friday 9th at 9.00am with the intention of being sent to defend Antwerp. They entrained to Oostcamp, four miles south of Brugge and the next day they marched to Oudenburg along the refugee-clogged cobbled roads. Orders were received for the Battalion

General Joffre

to assist with the withdrawal of the Belgian and French forces, General Joffre wrote: *"... as things actually turned out, the troops which were landed at Zeebrugge and Ostend had no influence on the fate of the fortress, and what help they were in protecting the retreat of the Belgians and saving the Army from destruction might have been equally well rendered from a safer and more effective direction."*

On Saturday 10th he moved to Melle where they entrenched to cover the French and Belgian troops who had been in action near Ghent: *"French and Belgian troops were going to attack a small German force, and we were to co-operate by striking the German rear and left flank. The Germans, however, attacked first, and were surprised by the French and Belgians as they were coming over a railway embankment. The Germans left about 200 dead behind."*

The next day they commenced their retreat, arriving at Hansbeke at 7.00pm. The next day their march continued southwestward reaching Thielt during the night of Tuesday 13th from where they marched to Roeselare. Some of the men who were particularly fatigued or suffering badly from the march were sent by train to Ypres, the rest marched; the Battalion was billeted in the barracks.

On Friday 16th the Battalion marched down the Menin Road turning north to Zonnebeke where at 6.30am they saw an Uhlan patrol gallop out of the village. Two days later they were moved into reserve at Veldhoek from where he was sent to Becelaere into billets. At dawn they moved towards Dadizeele with orders to attack Klijthoek at 11.30am. They pressed the attack home, despite taking heavy casualties. Significant progress was made until orders to retire were received as the Germans were advancing in strength from Iseghem. They retired through Dadizeele, which was now under German artillery fire, to Broodseinde. At 11.00am on Tuesday 20th columns of German infantry were seen advancing and shortly thereafter the German artillery

trained their guns on them. The German infantry attacked in large numbers; their tight formation ensured that their losses were very high as Meyricke and his fellow officers ordered rapid fire. The Germans attacked again and were repulsed. Lieutenant Hindson recorded: *"Owing to dead ground, the enemy were able to get up to within a hundred yards of our trench, but we kept them from leaving the shelter of the wood to our front.*

Our chief danger lay in enfilade fire, as our trench turned abruptly across the Broodseinde—Passchendaele road and our left was exposed.

On our left were numerous cottages, which the Huns occupied and were thus able to fire down into the trench from the roofs and upper windows; to our front and within 120 yards was a thick wood in which the Germans were able to concentrate, especially as part of it was dead ground. This wood was occasionally 'searched' by machine-gun fire which covered some of the dead ground invisible from the trench, but with what result it is hard to say. One machine-gun was in the main trench on the extreme left, and had an all-round traverse, so as to be able to fire to our front or to our left flank and half-right; the other was in a well-concealed pit some thirty yards to our left front, in a cottage garden, and, in addition to lessening the amount of dead ground to our front, was able to bring enfilade and oblique fire on any party of the enemy attempting to rush the trench from the woods; it covered some 400-500 yards of the trench front, as far as I remember.

I had not good machine-gun targets, the best being a group of thirty to forty of the enemy, invisible from our trench, who were fully exposed behind some cottages about 150 yards away; only a few escaped, although some were only wounded. About 120 yards to our left front were three haystacks, which the enemy used as cover and so worked round to our flank. We had no wire in front of our trench. About 7 p.m. the Colonel and the Adjutant came up to the trenches from their headquarters in a small quarry north-west of the Broodseinde cross-roads. Shortly afterwards there was a sudden and evidently preconcerted outburst of shrapnel, machine-gun and rifle fire, which lasted for some time and then gradually died away. We carried on digging a communication trench back to the road; this was never finished."

At 10.00am on Wednesday 21st the Germans commenced an artillery bombardment lasting until 2.30pm which killed a large number of men and buried many alive. On Thursday 22nd they were defending the line at Polygon Wood under heavy shell fire. Two days later Meyricke was killed near Veldhoek whilst under heavy shell and machine-gun fire in shallow slit trenches and terribly exposed.

Meyricke was recorded in Debretts Obituary — War Roll of Honour published in the 1921 edition.

In Meifod Parish Church, Powys, a bronze plaque was placed in his memory with the inscription: *"In loving memory Meyricke Entwisle Lloyd Captain, 1st. Battalion, Royal Welch Fusiliers, died of wounds, October 23rd. 1914. Buried at Passchendaele, near Ypres, Belgium, aged 34 years. Elder son of the late Henry Lloyd of Pitsford Hall, Northamptonshire and of Dolobran Isaf and Coedcowrid Meifod, Montgomeryshire."*

Major John Frederick Loder-Symonds

Commanding 1st Battalion
South Staffordshire Regiment

Died on Sunday 1st November 1914, aged 40
Commemorated on Panel 35.

John Loder-Symonds and his family coat of arms

John was born at Dharwar, India on Tuesday 23rd December 1873, eldest son of Captain Frederick Cleave Loder-Symonds, JP, and Isabel Loder-Symonds, of Hinton Manor, Farringdon, Berkshire. He was educated at Eton College as a member of Dr Philip Herbert Carpenter's House, leaving in 1889. In 1907 John married Mary Josephine Loder-Symonds (daughter of Sir William Vavasour, Baronet) — they had no children.

John was gazetted from the Militia in June 1894, promoted Lieutenant in 1896, Captain in June 1901, Adjutant from August 1903 to August 1906, and Major in September 1911.

From July 1899 to August 1900 John served with the West African Frontier Force being seriously wounded in Nigeria. He was Mentioned in Despatches on Tuesday 16th April 1901.

At the outbreak of war John returned to England with his battalion from Natal and went to Belgium on Sunday 4th October 1914. After arrival he was forced to wait until General Sir Henry Rawlinson received orders and eventually the Battalion was ordered to march south to Ypres. They arrived in Ypres in mid-October and assisted with the defence of the Salient and halted the German march to Calais. During a fierce engagement John, together with several fellow officers, was killed instantaneously in action.

He was one of four brothers who died during the Great War: Captain William Loder-Symonds died on Thursday 30th May 1918 and is buried in Hinton Waldrist (St Margaret) Churchyard; Lieutenant Thomas Loder-Symonds died on Sunday 9th May 1915 and is buried in Rue-Petillon Military Cemetery, Fleurbaix; Captain Robert Loder-Symonds died on Wednesday 3rd March 1915 and is buried in St Sever Cemetery, Rouen.

John was recorded in Debretts Obituary — War Roll of Honour published in the 1921 edition.

Captain John Hastie Logan, MC

13th Battalion Royal Scots

Died on Wednesday 1st August 1917, aged 33
Commemorated on Panel 11.

John Logan

John was the son of the late Mr Thomas Logan, Berwickshire and brother of Mr James S Logan, of 189 Kemnare Street, Pollokshields, Glasgow. His parents died when he was a child and his aunt, Miss Stewart of 29 Leven Street, Pollokshields, brought the two boys up. He was educated at The High School of Glasgow. John was a Freeman of Berwick.

At the outbreak of war he volunteered and enlisted in the Glasgow Highlanders. He was commissioned during 1916 and joined his Battalion in the field.

On Saturday 7th April 1917 John was in Arras where he entered the Town Hall, descending into the underground city and network of tunnels, some of which dated back centuries. They moved forward underground occupying the newly dug and expanded tunnels with their exits in front of the German line. The 13th Battalion was allotted Blagny as their objective which was protected by two concrete pill-boxes. Mines were laid under them, but one remained intact making progress slow, difficult and dangerous. Sergeant McMilland bravely went forward and bombed the pill-box into submission. The defenders of Blagny did not give up easily so 'Stokes mortars' were brought up and this cleared the village by 10.00am. The weather was grim and anyone who found a thick German greatcoat kept it as a prized possession. At 5.45am on Friday 23rd John took part in an attack south of the Scarpe leaving their position at the crossroads at La Bergère on the Arras to Cambrai road. The Germans were well positioned in *'Dragoon Lane'* and poured fire on John and his men as they pressed the attack, until they ran out of ammunition. Their work was put to good effect and the Royal Scots Fusiliers followed up

Clearing the débris after an attack during the Battle of Arras

the attack that cleared *'Dragoon Lane'*. On Wednesday 25th John supported the 6th Camerons attacking *'Cavalry Farm'* remaining there until they were relieved on Sunday 29th. After being sent back to Arras for rest the Battalion went to the Ypres Salient. In June 1917 he was awarded the Military Cross and this was presented to him whilst on home leave.

John returned to the front rejoining the Battalion when they took the line along the Menin Road. On Tuesday 31st July he marched from camp to Ypres and through the Menin Gate moving along the Menin Road. As they approached *'White Château'* shell fire started that significantly intensified as they progressed to *'Cambridge Road'*. At 8.50am on Wednesday 1st the 6th Camerons commenced an attack with the 13th Battalion Royal Scots following them five hundred yards behind. *'Beck House'* was taken, German aeroplanes buzzed the skies directing their artillery on the British advance. John was shot through the head and killed instantaneously, whilst consolidating the ground that had been taken during the day.

John was Mentioned in Despatches in December 1916.

SECOND LIEUTENANT ROBERT 'BOBBIE' LONGBOTTOM

'D' Company, 7th Battalion King's Royal Rifle Corps

Died on Friday 30th July 1915, aged 19

Commemorated on Panel 51.

Bobbie was the son of William Henry L and Ethel Longbottom, of 83B Holland Park, Notting Hill, London; late of Wingfield, Bournemouth. He was educated at Wellington College from 1909 to 1914. He was a friend of 'Jack' Kipling, son of Rudyard Kipling, who was killed during the Battle of Loos on Monday 27th September 1915 and is buried in St Mary's ADS Cemetery, Haisnes, and commemorated on Loos Memorial.

Bobbie volunteered and was commissioned, being sent for training. He left his barracks in Aldershot and sailed for Boulogne, arriving on 19th May 1915. After entraining for northern France he marched across the border to Belgium where the Battalion undertook further training before taking the line. After a series of front line duties they saw their first major action at Hooge. During the night of Thursday 29th July Bobbie took his men back into the trenches beyond *'Sanctuary Wood'* in front of the huge crater at Hooge. At 3.15am the next morning the German infantry attacked with support from machine-guns, trench mortars and shrapnel. For the first time the Germans used *'Flammenwerfer'* (flame throwers or 'liquid fire') and during the attack on their lines Bobbie was killed.

His eldest brother, 2nd Lieutenant Henry Longbottom, died on Monday 9th August 1915 and is commemorated on the Helles Memorial.

SECOND LIEUTENANT ROBERT NELE LORING

5th Battalion Worcestershire Regiment

Died on Wednesday 16th June 1915, aged 27

Commemorated on Panel 34.

Robert was born in Hinstock, Shropshire, on Sunday 8th August 1897, second son of John and Annette J Loring, of Longstile, Connaught Road, Fleet, Hampshire. He was educated at Bradfield Junior School followed by Haileybury from 1901 to 1902 as a member of Melvill. Robert went to Canada where he worked in an estate agency in British Columbia.

At the outbreak of war he volunteered and following officer training was gazetted to the 5th Battalion on Thursday 3rd December 1914. He went out to France and joined the 3rd Battalion in the field in Belgium.

On Thursday 11th March 1915 the Battalion moved from their billets in Locre to take part in an attack on the Spanbroekmolen. A preliminary bombardment began but the results could not be seen as the mist and fog obscured the view. In the poorly dug, and flooded, assembly trenches provided little shelter as the German artillery answered the British guns. The attack ended in failure with the Battalion taking heavy losses and the survivors returned to their billets. The Battalion was reorganised itself before marching to St Eloi, opposite *'The Mound'*, to relieve the Gloucestershire Regiment; a sector they would come to know well over the ensuing weeks. They heard the blowing of the mines at Hill 60 and were anxious as the first gas attack took place to their north but had not been involved in either action. At the end of May the Battalion was to move round into the centre of the Salient, an officer wrote: *"Though we have put in a tremendous lot of work in this part of the line and though we are bound to have a thoroughly unpleasant time of it in the Salient, I am almost glad that we are going up there. Lately one has felt that one has been just out of the big fight, and, though we have had the fag ends of the bombardments and occasional whiffs of gas, we have been having a comparatively easy time, while the people on our left have been having a wretched time of it. We shall now be at the point of honour."*

The trenches of St Eloi were left behind them on Thursday 3rd June as they marched to a camp in Vlamertinghe for two days rest. On Saturday 5th they moved through Ypres and took the line in front at Hooge from the Menin Road towards *'Sanctuary Wood'*. Following a difficult tour of duty they marched in the pouring rain to bivouac at Busseboom, south of Poperinghe where they prepared for an attack on the Bellewaarde Ridge. Late on Tuesday 15th the return to the front began and reached their assembly positions at *'Witte Port Farm'* just before midnight. The preliminary bombardment commenced at 2.50am and the first wave of attack set off at 4.15am when the Battalion moved forward to *'Cambridge Road'*. At 3.15pm the orders for the Worcesters attack was given but their advance was slowed due to the confused and crowded conditions at the front line. The trenches were strewn with the wounded and these trenches had to be negotiated before they could move onto their objectives at Bellewaarde Lake. The German artillery accurately targeted the small area that contained thousands of British troops with an unacceptable number of casualties were taken. At 7.30pm the order to halt the attack was received at the front line and withdrawal began to the captured German front line. The Brigade Diary recorded: *"The result of these operations was the gain of 250 yards of ground on a front of 800 yards. Over 200 prisoners and 3 machine-guns were taken, and the enemy suffered severe losses."* Robert together with Captain Eric Buckler (who is commemorated on the Menin Gate, see above), Lieutenant Muir and thirty men were killed, eleven officers and two hundred and fifty-five men were wounded and twenty-four listed as missing presumed killed.

His uncles, Lieutenant Colonel Walter Loring, died on Friday 23rd October 1914 and is commemorated on the Menin Gate, see below; Captain William Loring died on Sunday 24th October 1915 and is commemorated on Helles Memorial; and Major Charles Loring died on Monday 21st December 1914 and is commemorated on Neuve Chapelle Memorial.

Charles Loring

... cutting the wire during an advance

Lieutenant Colonel Walter Latham Loring

Commanding 2nd Battalion
Royal Warwickshire Regiment

Died on Friday 23rd October 1914, aged 46
Commemorated on Panel 8.

Walter Loring

Walter was born at home on Friday 3rd April 1868, sixth son of the Reverend Edward Henry and Charlotte Loring, Vicar of Cobham and Rector of Gillingham, Suffolk. His mother and a sister were killed when their steamer foundered *en route* to Australia to visit his paternal uncle.

He was educated at Marlborough College from September 1882 where he gained a scholarship and went up to Trinity Hall, Cambridge, in 1886. Walter married Violet Loring (née Marshal) of 48 St John's Park, Blackheath and they had ten children, Constance and Grace (twins) born in 1899, Henry in 1900, Edward, 1901, Patience 1904, Madeline 1905, Faith 1910, Marion 1912, David and Joan (twins) in 1914. He

was a committed Christian and took a great interest in young boys particularly supporting the CEMS.
Walter was gazetted on Saturday 23rd March 1889, promoted to Lieutenant on Monday 1st December 1890, Captain on Tuesday 5th April 1898, Major on Wednesday 3rd February 1904, Adjutant from Wednesday 18th November 1908 to Sunday 17th November 1912 and Lieutenant Colonel in 1914.
He served in India, Malta and in the South African War where he received the Queen's Medal with four clasps. From 1908 to 1912 he was a Staff Officer at the Officers Training Corps for the Universities of Birmingham, Bristol, Manchester and the Royal Agricultural College, Cirencester.
At the outbreak of the war Walter was in Malta with the Regiment and they were ordered home, arriving on Saturday 19th September 1914. He took his men to camp for training, re-equipping and the completion of mobilization. Walter went out to Belgium landing at Zeebrugge on Tuesday 6th October. For three days they awaited orders as the intention of defending Antwerp was abandoned. On Friday 9th he entrained the Battalion to Ghent where they marched four miles out to support a battalion of French Marines until the night of Sunday 11th when he took the men from the line and marched towards Ypres.
After a hard march along the cobbled roads to Thielt and Roeselare they arrived at the Salient on Wednesday 14th. After two days the Battalion was ordered to take the

The onward march of the German infantry through Belgium, 1914

line at Zonnebeke where 7th Division was instructed to defend stretching south to Zandvoorde. Walter took the men forward to Becelaere on Sunday 18th from where General Sir Henry Rawlinson ordered an attack on Menin the next day. The advance went well and Dadizeele was passed without incident. As they approached Kezelberg they came under artillery fire although the village was easily cleared. As they prepared to attack Klijthoek orders were received to retire and return to billets in Zonnebeke as columns of Germans were advancing on Ypres Salient from the direction of Iseghem. Walter organised the retirement and disengagement; during their return a considerable number of casualties were suffered from shell fire. On Tuesday 20th the Battalion was in reserve and moved to Harenthage Château from where, during the afternoon, they were sent into the line at Zonnebeke as the Germans had launched an attack. Whilst organising the Battalion Walter was wounded by a stray bullet in the foot, remaining at his post with a bandage around his wound and puttee instead of a boot! At midnight the Coldstream Guards relieved them and they returned to their billets in Zonnebeke. The next day they returned to the line at the cross-roads east of the village, from where they moved to the ridge. Despite his wound Walter rode up and down the line encouraging the men and undertaking reconnaissance. Throughout Thursday 22nd the Battalion continued to dig in and improve the trench line. On Friday 23rd they were ordered to Polygon Wood which was under attack and its loss was threatened. Walter insisted on leading his men against the German lines on horseback: two of his chargers were killed under him. He was killed during an assault on the small farmhouse that was a German strong point.
Walter was Mentioned in Despatches gazetted on Thursday 14th January 1915.
An officer wrote: *"Again an attack on the line, and at 8 a.m. news that the line was broken. The Warwicks were sent up. They behaved splendidly: drove back the Germans, cleared a wood, and saved the situation. They lost one hundred and nine men and several officers, including the Colonel. Such a good sort, his death is a terrible loss to us."*
An NCO wrote: *"I am sorry to say our gallant Colonel was killed the same day, and my word! he was a brave man. He was always in front of his regiment. I have only written what I have seen with my own eyes, and it is enough to make anyone's heart bleed."*
In St Andrew's Church, Cobham, Surrey, a brass plaque was placed in his memory, with the inscription:
"To the glory of God and in honoured memory of his servants, three sons of the Rev. E. H. Loring once Vicar of this Parish, and of Charlotte Loring his wife. They fell facing the enemy in defence of freedom and right.
William Loring: Fellow of King's College Cambridge, Warden of Goldsmith's College, University of London. Captain 2nd Scottish Horse who died at sea of wounds received while leading an attack at Suvla, Gallipoli, October 24th 1915 aged 50 years.
Walter Latham Loring: Lieut. Colonel Commanding 2nd Battalion Royal Warwickshire Regiment who was killed heading an advance in the First Battle of Ypres. October 24th 1914 aged 46 years.
Charles Buxton Loring: Major 37th Lancers, Baluch Horse, Indian Army (attached Poona Horse) who was killed at Givenchy while leading an attack December 21st 1914 aged 43 years.
Who through faith subdued kingdoms. Heb. XI 33"

His brother, Major Charles Loring, died on Monday 21st December 1914 and is commemorated on Neuve-Chapelle Memorial, and Captain William Loring, died on Sunday 24th October 1915 and is commemorated on Helles Memorial. His uncle, Lieutenant Colonel Arthur Loveband, died on Tuesday 25th May 1915 and is commemorated on the Menin Gate, see below, and his nephew 2nd Lieutenant Robert Loring died on Wednesday 16th June 1915 and is commemorated on the Menin Gate, see above.

Lieutenant and Adjutant Bertie Charles Lousada

1st Battalion York and Lancaster Regiment

Died on Sunday 9th May 1915, aged 26

Commemorated on Panel 55.

Bertie was born on Monday 19th November 1888, son of Captain Charles Lousada (late Norfolk Regiment), of 3 Lansdowne Road, Cheltenham. He was educated at Cheltenham College from January 1903 to December 1907 as a member of Cheltondale then passed into RMC Sandhurst.

He was commissioned in 1909 and served in India.

At the outbreak of war Bertie was in Jubbulpore, India; the Regiment was ordered back to England, arriving on Wednesday 23rd December 1914 and was sent to camp for training and re-kitting. He was sent to France on Sunday 17th January 1915. After a short period of training he was sent into the line. As the intensity of the Second Battle of Ypres increased Bertie was killed in action.

Bertie is commemorated on his parents' grave in St Peter's Churchyard, Leckhampton.

His twin brother, Lieutenant Edward Lousada, died on Monday 2nd November 1914 and is commemorated on the Menin Gate, see below.

Lieutenant Edward Arthur Lousada

2nd Battalion Royal Sussex Regiment

Died on Monday 2nd November 1914

Commemorated on Panel 20.

Edward Lousada

Edward was born on Monday 19th November 1888, son of Captain Charles Lousada (late Norfolk Regiment), of 3 Lansdowne Road, Cheltenham. He was educated at Cheltenham College from January 1903 to December 1907 as a member of Cheltondale then passed into RMC Sandhurst.

On Wednesday 12th August 1914 Edward marched with his men to Woking Station and entrained for Southampton. The Battalion embarked for Le Havre on *SS Olympia* and *SS Agapenor* arriving at noon the next day. After a night in *'Bleville Camp'* he entrained for Wassigny. After further rest and training they marched towards Mons, arriving in the early hours of Sunday 23rd near Givry. They heard the sound of the artillery and saw the smoke and explosions, but the Battalion did not become involved in the Battle of Mons. When they were ordered to retire they provided rear-guard protection for the troops as they poured down the road passed them. The Retreat got into full swing and his march south continued until Sunday 6th September when orders were received to turn and face the Germans. On Monday 14th September they engaged the Germans at Vendresse for three days before moving to Paissy. Until Thursday 15th October he was in action in and around Troyon before moving to northern France, arriving at 3.00am on Monday 19th at Cassel.

With two overnight stops they marched to Ypres and were sent into reserve at Boesinghe on Wednesday 21st. He marched with his men to *'Chateau Wood'* where Battalion Headquarters were established on Tuesday 27th. At 8.00am the next morning orders were received to move to Polygon Wood and they arrived there under heavy shell fire. The Germans launched a major attack along the line from 5.30am on Thursday 29th until they were required again at *'Chateau Wood'*. During the morning of Friday 30th Lieutenant Colonel Hugh Crispin led the Battalion, on his horse, towards Gheluvelt across country, the most direct route. The Germans spotted the advance and sent over shrapnel shells and the Colonel was killed (he is commemorated on the Menin Gate, see above). The Battalion took the line and engaged the advancing Germans with rapid fire. The Germans broke into Gheluvelt and the Battalion was forced to alter its line before being ordered to counter-attack at the point of the bayonet. They were able to advance a reasonable distance before the German machine-gunners opened on them, the Battalion was enfiladed and forced to retire.

Colonel Crispin

At 1.00am on Sunday 1st orders were received to clear a small wood and Major Green blew his whistle, leading the men forward at the charge. Despite heavy fire from the Germans their objectives were secured. During the attack Edward was killed and buried in the field.

Edward is commemorated on his parents' grave in St Peter's Churchyard, Leckhampton.

His twin brother, Lieutenant Bertie Lousada, died on Sunday 9th May 1915 and is commemorated on the Menin Gate, see above.

3/6961 Private Robert Love

1st Battalion Gordon Highlanders

Died on Monday 14th December 1914, aged 28

Commemorated on Panel 38.

Robert was the youngest son of John and Mary Love, of Rockland, Rutherglen, Glasgow. He was educated at The High School of Glasgow, and then studied as a civil engineer and elected an Associate Member of the Institute of Civil Engineers from 1912. He was apprenticed to Messrs Warren & Stewart and worked with them for seven years until he was appointed Assistant Civil Engineer with Lanarkshire. In 1913 Robert went to work in Montreal followed by Quebec where he worked on water and sewer projects. Robert became an inspector in Smyrna before returning home. At the outbreak of war Robert was working for Rochdale Council when he volunteered and enlisted in September 1914 leaving for France in November, joining the Battalion in Locre. He was killed in his first main action at Messines on Monday 14th December 1914. As the Battalion advanced at 7.45am from the Kemmel to Wytschaete road towards Maedelstede Farm Robert was shot through the head.

Lieutenant Colonel Arthur Loveband, CMG

2nd Battalion Royal Dublin Fusiliers

Died on Tuesday 25th May 1915

Commemorated on Panel 44.

Arthur Loveband

At the outbreak of war Arthur was stationed at Aldershot. Initially Major Loveband and 'E' Company was sent to guard the station at Golders Green. The Battalion returned to barracks at Aldershot where, before they left for the front, they won several cups including the 'Obstacle Challenge Shield' which was presented by HRH Field Marshal the Duke of Connaught who then sent a telegram of congratulations: *"Duke of Connaught congratulates all ranks on having won his Obstacle Challenge Shield and is very glad it should have been won by his own Regiment."* Arthur was able to join the Battalion in the field on Sunday 25th October 1914 being given home leave in late November 1914.

HRH The Duke of Connaught

In April 1915 Arthur was in the front line at St Julien, where they were fighting amongst the ruined houses and attacking the wood occupied by the Germans.

A fellow officer wrote of him *"One unforgettable scene remains in the writer's memory; one company, which had lost all its officers and which had been ordered to retire, was doing so in disorder when the small untidy figure of Colonel Loveband, clad in an ancient 'British warm' and carrying a blackthorn stick, approached quietly across the open, making as he walked the lie-down signal with the stick. The effect was instantaneous, and for hundreds of yards along the front the men dropped and used their entrenching tools."* Later in the day, after this action, Arthur was wounded and Captain Bankes took over the command (he was killed, see above), after only a short period he returned to his command.

Arthur was in the area of *'Mouse Trap Farm'* (also known as *'Shell Trap Farm'*) and the gas attack was recorded by Captain Leahy: *"Colonel Loveband, Major Magan, second in command, Russell, R.A.M.C., and I, acting adjutant, had just finished dinner in our headquarter dug-out at 2.30a.m. Previous to this the Colonel and Magan had been round all the front line trenches and spent considerable time in Shell Trap Farm. Something suggested 'gas' to the Colonel during his round of the trenches as he personally warned all company officers to be prepared, and Russell had inspected all the Vermoral sprayers and warned each company about damping their respirators. These were ten sprayers in working order that night — one with each machine-gun and the remainder distributed along the trenches.*

At about 2.45p.m. the Colonel and I were standing outside our dug-out, some 400 yards behind the first line of trenches, looking in the direction of Shell Trap Farm, where we saw a red light thrown up in the German line to the north-west of the Farm, and immediately three lights (red) were seen directly over Shell Trap Farm and a few more lights (red) in the German lines from the direction of C.30 — south-east from where we were standing. A few seconds later a dull roar was heard — more like an explosion, certainly not a shell — and we saw the gas coming on either side of Shell Trap Farm. The Colonel shouted, 'Get your respirators, Boys, here comes the gas!' We had only just time to get our respirators on before the gas was over us — the doctor, Russell, who was seeing to other people got some gas before his own respirator was adjusted.

In the trenches the 'Stand-to' was just over and rum was being issued, so there could not have been any element of surprise other than the sudden appearance of gas; everyone was awake. There was a very gentle breeze, the gas was very dense and took considerable time to pass over — about three-quarters of an hour. From the nature of the ground — a gradual slope towards Battalion Headquarters from the first line of trenches — I do not think that the gas lasted as long over the trenches as it did over us at Headquarters, or the troops (two companies 9th Argylls) in the retrenchment. Colonel Loveband and I ran out to stop them, there were cover of the buildings out of his sight. The Colonel then sent a second message to the O.C. 9th Argylls:-

'Enemy are in Shell Trap Farm, please send up two companies at

once and counter-attack and reoccupy Farm. Germans are in the right side of farm. Inform 10th Infantry Brigade'. (5.55a.m.).
... The Colonel then sent the following message to the 10th Infantry Brigade: 'The Germans are in Shell Trap Farm and I can see a few in small building on right of farm. Get artillery to shell it. I believe my two platoons are still holding trench to left of farm. The Germans have occupied the right of Argylls in support line so far. Argylls in retrenchment have moved up, but I fear to my centre and right, and am not sure if any went up to the farm. Reinforcements are required. Situation not satisfactory.'
This message was untimed but I think it was sent about a quarter of an hour before Burt-Marshal arrived with us. The enemy were now using gas-shells which disturbed our eyes but did not seem to have any other effect. Meanwhile the Colonel, Russell and I were standing at the back of our dug-out, Major Magan was inside gassed and out of action since about 4a.m., and Russell was hit by a piece of shell, but remained at duty and did most gallant work throughout.
Colonel Poole then came up and Colonel Loveband explained the situation. As far as I can remember Colonel Poole had not gone very long before Burt-Marshal arrived, and he, the Colonel and I were standing at the back of the dug-out — the doctor was inside — when bullets came from behind and presently Colonel Loveband was hit through the heart; he died without a word though he tried to say something. Marshal was hit in the shoulder from a bullet coming from the same direction; he was most plucky, wouldn't wait, but raced off to stop the firing. Our guns were shelling Shell Trap Farm heavily by this time and our shrapnel appeared to be bursting well clear of our trenches.

... attacking under shell-fire

The enemy recommenced their shelling and 'heavies' were being dumped into our right trenches, while the rifle and machine-gun fire was very accurate from the 18th Royal Irish trenches which the Germans held in force. It was marvellous how quickly they converted the parapet and everything was done without confusion and with proper method."
His nephews, Captain Charles Loring, died on Monday 21st December 1914 and is commemorated on Neuve-Chapelle Memorial, and Captain William Loring, died on Sunday 24th October 1915 and is commemorated on Helles Memorial.
Arthur was Mentioned in Despatches gazetted on Wednesday 17th February 1915.

Second Lieutenant George Low

4th Battalion Gordon Highlanders

Died on Saturday 25th September 1915, aged 24
Commemorated on Panel 38.

George Low

George was born at home on Wednesday 20th January 1892, son of Jessie Low, of Dyce, Aberdeen, and the late William Low. He was educated at Robert Gordon's College and went up to Aberdeen University in 1910 where he was a member of the OTC rising to the rank of Sergeant. In 1914 he graduated with an MA, a First Class Honours in Classics and was awarded the Dr Black Prize in Latin.
At the outbreak of war George volunteered and was sent to Bedford as a musketry instructor. In March 1915 he left for France and was promoted Company Sergeant Major. He was sent to northern France from where he crossed the border and joined the Battalion at La Clytte. In April they were in camp at Brandhoek before being sent along the Menin Road and into the line at Hooge where he took part on an attack on Bellewaarde. In August he received a field commission and was given home leave. George returned to the front only to be killed shortly afterwards in the attack at Hooge when the Battalion advanced against the German lines. The Battalion took many casualties whilst attempting to find their way through the uncut wire.

24370 Private Robert Lowe

13th Battalion Canadian Infantry (Quebec Regiment)

Died on Saturday 24th April 1915, aged 22
Commemorated on Panel 24.

Robert Lowe

Robert was born in Edinburgh, on Thursday 15th June 1893, the second son of David Lowe, of 24 West Holmes Gardens, Musselburgh, and the late Annie Radcliffe Lowe. He was educated at George Heriot's School from 1905 to 1903 where he gained a reputation as a proficient golfer. He joined the Union Bank of Scotland and was a member of the 3rd Royal Scots Territorial Force. In 1913 he went out to Canada where he was employed by the Bank of Montreal and joined the Militia.
On Saturday 29th August 1914 he volunteered and enlisted at Valcartier where he was described as a Presbyterian, 5ft 11in tall, with a 36½in chest, a fair

complexion, grey eyes, and brown hair. He went to England with the First Canadian Contingent, sailing on board *RMS Alaunia*, under Captain Rostron, RNR, who was the Captain of *RMS Carpathia* that rescued the survivors of *RMS Titanic*. They left at 3.00pm on Saturday 3rd October 1914 in a convoy of thirty-three ships escorted by the British Navy under Rear-Admiral Wemyss.

Admiral Wemyss

Canadian troops leave for England

They arrived on Thursday 15th October in Plymouth and entrained for Patney, then marched ten miles to *'West Down South Camp'*. They did not enjoy their experience in the camp, one of his colleagues wrote: *"This is a God-forsaken hole and we are getting pretty sick of it. It is raining again to-day. Nothing but rain, mud and then more rain."* Robert sailed on the *SS Novian* on February 12th for St Nazaire from where they entrained to Hazebrouck, arriving on February 19th. It had been a long and tiring journey, and once they arrived a ten mile march was required to get them to billets in Flêtre and Caëstre. After four days of training they marched to Armentières where they were inspected by Brigadier General Edward 'Inky Bill' Ingouville-Williams (who died on Saturday 22nd July 1916 and is buried in Warloy Communal Cemetery) after which they undertook their first tour of duty. They remained in the sector until Tuesday 13th April when they crossed the border and were billeted at Abeele. An officer wrote: *"I have not been able to write for the last few days as we have been on the move, and are now about seventeen miles from our last billet. I learn today that next week we are to take up trenches some distance farther on. With these moves we are seeing a lot of the country and of the troops at the front. We are now amongst some hills, which is a welcome change after the flat country we have left. From the top of one of the hills we can see the blue water of the North Sea. I was sent ahead with the billeting party and found the work of billeting the regiment not altogether an easy job, as the farms are far apart."*

The Battalion was collected by a fleet of London motor buses and driven the short distance to Vlamertinghe. The officer wrote further: *"We are still moving about, and are now a long way behind the trenches. We are preparing for another move. It is lovely spring weather where we are, and there is a big bowl of wild flowers beside me which I picked this morning. The men are either resting or wandering about the fields, and everyone is contented. Sir H. Smith-Dorrien inspected us yesterday. It was a real inspection, and there was not a man who did not come under his eyes. Our regiment looked splendid in new kilt aprons. General Smith-Dorrien was very pleased with the men, and afterwards he gathered the officers and sergeants together, and spoke to us at some length. He said that he was glad to have us in his army, and considered that it was a great piece of luck for him. He went on to say that we had surpassed the best hopes he had of us. The Canadian artillery and engineers, he thought, were excellent, and he knew that we would do well in the coming weeks, during which we should have the hardest kind of trench warfare. He concluded by saying that he would be sorry for the Germans who encountered the Canadians. General Alderson also spoke, and said he was proud of us, and he praised us for our splendid work in the trenches and for the support we had given to him."*

They marched through the relatively intact town of Ypres, through the Menin Gate and out to St Jan. During the night of Wednesday 21st April they went into the line with the French Turcos on their left with Battalion Headquarters in St Julien and the German line only between fifty and seventy-five yards ahead of them. At 3.00pm on Thursday 22nd the German laid down a

An early gas warning with rather pathetic precautions

barrage for two hours then launched the first gas attack. The chlorine gas fell heavily on the Turcos to their left, and it drifted down onto their lines too, the reserve lines taking the worst of it. The Germans advanced and attacked their flank at 9.00pm, pushing them back. They continued to hold their line until they were withdrawn further back at dawn the next morning. The Germans came forward dressed in French uniforms but were caught out and the Battalion opened fire. On Saturday 24th the Germans launched a further gas attack at dawn and Robert was called forward. He was killed in action just as he arrived in the firing line.

Captain Sidney Henry Lowry, MC

Hertfordshire Regiment

Died on Tuesday 31st July 1917, aged 29

Commemorated on Panel 54.

Sidney was born Friday 8th June 1888, son of Henry and Alice Lowry, of Stevenage, Hertfordshire. He was educated at Charterhouse from 1902 and went up to Pembroke College, Cambridge, in 1907 and was a member of the OTC at both School and College. In 1913 he was appointed a partner in his father's firm, Lowry Brothers, and elected a member of the Stock Exchange in 1913.
At the outbreak of war Sidney joined the Inns of Court OTC with service number B/946 subsequently commissioned Captain on Wednesday 28th October 1914. He left for France in January 1915 and arrived at Cuinchy on Tuesday 2nd February. He remained in the sector until 1916 when he served on the Somme, leaving for the Salient on Tuesday 28th November 1916.
Sidney was sent to England where in early 1917 he undertook a course at Aldershot and was recommended for a post of Second in Command of a Battalion.
From April 1917 he served in Hooge sector and on the Ypres to Comines Canal before leaving for Wormhoudt on Thursday 29th May where the Battalion went into training. On Sunday 3rd June Sidney assisted in the arrangements for the King's birthday parade in the town. From Monday 11th they proceeded to undertake a series of route marches. On Thursday 28th Sidney attended a lecture by General Sir Ivor Maxse and the next day entrained to Poperinghe. On Saturday 30th he returned to the Canal bank, relieving the Sherwood Foresters. On Tuesday 17th July he was sent to Watten for further training in preparation for the Third Battle of Ypres. On Monday 30th July he took his men forward to the assembly positions. At 3.50am on Tuesday 31st he led his men forward from the Steenbeek towards Langemarck. A German strong point was stormed and taken; however, the advance became more difficult as the German wire remained intact and particularly thick. As they went forward toward their final objective Sidney was killed. His Commanding Officer wrote: *"Your son was killed in action, whilst gallantly leading his company against the final objective. I don't think a better officer or more gallant man is serving in the army. It is not only as a splendid officer but as a friend that we, who had the privilege of knowing him intimately, will always remember him."*
Sidney is commemorated on The Stock Exchange War Memorial and on a stone tablet in St Nicholas Church, Stevenage, Hertfordshire.

Lieutenant David Elmar Lucas

2nd Regiment (Infantry) South African Infantry

Died on Thursday 21st September 1917, aged 24

Commemorated on Panel 15.

David was the son of Frederick G C and Maggie Gordon Lucas, of Durban, Natal. He was educated locally.
His brother, Sergeant John Lucas, died on Wednesday 20th September 1917 and is commemorated on the Menin Gate, see below.
David and John served in Egypt until being sent to France. They arrived in Marseilles on Thursday 20th April 1916 and entrained for Steenwerck where two months of intense training in trench warfare began. They arrived at Ailly-sur-Somme on Wednesday 14th June. The served through the Battle of the Somme including at the infamous Delville Wood and at the Butte de Warlencourt. Following the Battle of Arras their Regiment was sent to Flanders to train near Brandhoek for the Third Battle of Ypres. On Sunday 17th September David and John were sent into the front line and prepared for the attack. From 10.00pm on Tuesday 19th the rain began to fall heavily making an already difficult battlefield even worse. Crossing the thick deep mud was treacherous — it was only safe to do so using duckboards. On Wednesday 20th they attacked *'Waterend Farm'* which was heavily defended, but it was successfully captured it although during the attack John was killed. Throughout Thursday 21st they came under very heavy shell-fire and David was killed.

6679 Sergeant John Gordon Lucas

2nd Regiment (Infantry) South African Infantry

Died on Wednesday 20th September 1917, aged 21

Commemorated on Panel 15.

John was the son of Frederick G C and Maggie Gordon Lucas, of Durban, Natal. He was educated locally.
His brother, Lieutenant David Lucas, died on Thursday 21st September 1917 and is commemorated on the Menin Gate, see above.

180267 Private John Richard Lumley

29th Battalion Canadian Infantry
(British Columbia Regiment)

Died on Tuesday 6th November 1917, aged 26
Commemorated on Panel 28.

John was born in South Salt Spring, British Columbia, on Saturday 31st October 1891, son of Mrs Mary Lumley. He was educated locally and was employed as a logger. His brother, Private Robert Lumley, died on the same day and is commemorated on the Menin Gate, see below.

On Friday 12th November 1915 he volunteered and enlisted in Victoria where he was described as a Roman Catholic, being 5ft 8in tall, with a 40in chest, ruddy complexion, brown eyes and black hair.

John and Robert were sent to England for training before joining the Battalion in the field in Ypres. On Tuesday 6th June 1916 the Germans blew four mines at Hooge, the Battalion was ordered to move from the southern sector to support the line near *'China Wall'*. They came under sustained shell-fire and continuous attack and counter-attack for eight days before being relieved to *'Dickebusch Huts'*. They found the camp in dreadful condition and following a bathing parade they spent their time cleaning up the Camp. Following a period of rest and training they returned to the line at St Eloi. They served in the sector until the end of August when the move south began that took the brothers to the Somme.

Canadians attack at St Eloi

On Monday 11th September they took position at Pozières beyond the *'Windmill'* on the ridge. As they took the line their Colonel, J S Tait, was buried by a 5.9 shell during a curtain barrage whilst *en route* to *'Copse Avenue'*.

... mules supply the front

After a month in the sector they moved north to Souchez and the *'Lorette Spur'* where they were in the line for Christmas. The first two weeks of February 1917 were spent training at Raimbert and they were then sent to Mont St Eloi where training continued. They went into support from the end of the month for two weeks. The Battalion was sent for training for an attack at Neuville St Vaast as part of the Battle of Arras. In June John and Robert were training at Maisnil les Ruitz from where they moved to the Lens sector around Maroc and Fosse. Another period of training was provided and they returned to Neuville St Vaast in September.

At the end of October they were at Hondeghem training from where they marched to Caëstre and entrained for Ypres. They arrived in their camp at 5.00pm on Saturday 3rd November where they rested over night. John and Robert marched to the front line at Passchendaele where they relieved the 21st Battalion. From 4.50am on Monday 5th the German artillery bombarded their line for an hour. One of their friends, Private McComber, shot down a German aeroplane that landed behind the German lines. The next day the Battalion came under sustained attack and all ranks were called into support, including the cooks, bandsmen, drivers *et al*. By the end of the day the brothers had been killed, two of twenty-one to die that day.

181014 Private Robert Charles Lumley

29th Battalion Canadian Infantry
(British Columbia Regiment)

Died on Tuesday 6th November 1917, aged 29
Commemorated on Panel 28.

Robert was born in South Salt Spring, British Columbia, on Friday 7th September 1888, son of Mrs Mary Lumley. He was educated locally and became an engineer.

On Tuesday 18th January 1916 he volunteered and enlisted in Victoria where he was described as 5ft 7½in tall, a 39in chest, with a dark complexion, brown eyes and black hair.

3/2086 Private Alexander Lumsden

'D' Company, 1st Battalion Black Watch (Royal Highlanders)

Died on Thursday 29th October 1914, aged 35

Commemorated on Panel 37.

Alexander was the son of Janet Lumsden, of 5 West Pans, Levenhall, Musselburgh, Midlothian, and the late Alexander Lumsden.

His brother, Private James Lumsden, died on Saturday 31st October 1914 and is commemorated on the Menin Gate, see below for their story.

Captain David Aitken Lumsden

4th Battalion The King's (Liverpool Regiment)

Died on Saturday 1st May 1915, aged 27

Commemorated on Panel 6.

David Lumsden

David was born at Broomknowe, Broughty Ferry, Forfarshire, on Thursday 29th December 1887 only son of David and Kate Lumsden, of Dalreoch, Dundee. He was educated at the Harris Academy and went up to St Andrew's University from 1909 to 1911 where he was a member of the Union. He was a member of the OTC and the first Colour Sergeant of 'B' Company, passing his 'B' certificate. David was described as tall, a fair physique, a commanding presence and bearing.

David was gazetted to the King's Liverpool Regiment, promoted Lieutenant in May 1914 and then spent a considerable amount of time training at Aldershot, Hythe and in Ireland.

David was mobilized at the outbreak of war and went out to France in September, promoted Captain in January 1915. He was wounded during the First Battle of Ypres and was invalided home but was able to rejoin the regiment in January at Liverpool.

On Saturday 6th March 1915 David left for Le Havre and entrained to St Omer from where he marched to billets in Lillers. He went into reserve with the Sirhind Brigade at the Battle of Neuve-Chapelle but did not see any action.

From Tuesday 27th April David was in action near St Jan and involved in daily attacks and raids supporting the Gurkha Rifles. Their last attack cost him his life, together with 43 men.

His Adjutant wrote: *"Captain Lumsden was killed in action on Saturday, 1st inst, in the fighting in which the battalion took part. He was shot through the head and killed instantly whilst gallantly leading his men, and his death is a great loss to the battalion, as in him we have lost a good officer and a very popular comrade. It will be a comfort to you to know that he had no suffering and that he did his duty nobly and behaved in a most gallant way throughout the fighting for the good of his country, and we shall one and all miss him in every way."*

His Commanding Officer wrote: *"I cannot tell you what a grief it was to me, and I feel that he lost his life in order to save mine. We were in a trench together, and I was on the point of rushing forward to lead some men who had stopped, under cover. Your son heard me say I was going, when he jumped over the parapet, saying, 'No, sir, I am going', and rushed forward. His loss to the battalion is very great. I miss him very much — both as a friend and as an officer. He was a fine fellow, an excellent soldier, and was much loved by both officers and men."*

9246 Private James Lumsden

'D' Company, 1st Battalion Black Watch (Royal Highlanders)

Died on Saturday 31st October 1914, aged 35

Commemorated on Panel 37.

James was the son of Janet Lumsden, of 5 West Pans, Levenhall, Musselburgh, Midlothian, and the late Alexander Lumsden. His brother, Private Alexander Lumsden, died on Thursday 29th October 1914 and is commemorated on the Menin Gate, see above.

James and his brother, Alexander, left Aldershot for Farnborough where they entrained and sailed on *SS Italian Prince* for Le Havre, arriving on Thursday 13th August. The Battalion was sent by train to Le Nouvion in northern France before being marched to Mons where they witnessed the action but did not participate. In the early hours of Monday 24th orders were received to retire which became The Retreat to the Marne — reached on Thursday 3rd September; then onto the Aisne where they arrived on Friday 11th. It was a long and hard march with full packs and in addition they had been involved in a couple of short, sharp rearguard engagements. They saw considerable action on the Chemin des Dames and the Aisne until they were sent north by train from Frismes to Hazebrouck at 6.00pm on Sunday 18th October.

On Tuesday 20th they were marched to Poperinghe and onward to the line at Pilkem. They supported the Coldstream Guards who were under great pressure and were ordered on Friday 23rd to take Cabaret. The attack success that released more than sixty Cameron Highlanders who had previously been captured by the

Germans. After being sent to *'Remi Farm'* they were attacked by the Germans who sang their way into battle and were mown down by rapid fire as they were in close formation. After a short relief from the line at 5.00am on Sunday 25th they were back at the front. In the early hours of Thursday 29th, in the fog and mist, the Germans attacked the Battalion along the Menin Road during which Alexander was killed. James fought on in the line until he too was killed two days later as the Germans broke through into Gheluvelt.

Second Lieutenant George John Lunnon

'B' Company, 2nd Battalion
Duke of Cornwall's Light Infantry
Died on Tuesday 27th April 1915, aged 27
Commemorated on Panel 20.

George was born at Great Marlow, on Wednesday 10th August 1887, son of William and Marie Elizabeth Lunnon, of 3 Portland Villas, Marlow, Buckinghamshire. He was educated locally and joined his father's building business. George was described a 'big lad' at 6ft 2in.
George was a bugler in the Buckinghamshire Rifle Volunteer Corps until he enlisted with the Duke of Cornwall's Light Infantry on Friday 10th November 1905. He served in Gibraltar and was promoted Lance Corporal, followed by Bermuda where he was raised Corporal, then South Africa where he was appointed Regimental Schoolmaster-Sergeant at Bloemfontein. He was a good athlete playing for the regimental football and cricket teams, and was in the Regimental Rifle Team that won the championship. He served in Hong Kong in 1913 returning to England at the outbreak of war. 
George was gazetted in December 1914, sailing to France on Saturday 19th December 1914 from Southampton for Le Havre. The Battalion entrained for St Omer and marched to Wardrecques and were billeted in two factories where they were able to keep clean: *"Hot baths arranged for the whole Battalion (factory engine heated the water which was run into a cistern holding twenty men at a time)."*
On Thursday 7th January 1915 George, and the Battalion, marched to Méteren in the pouring rain then crossed the border into Belgium arriving at their billets in Westoutre. After three days they moved north to Dickebusch before going into the line at St Eloi.
On Friday 23rd April George led his men forward from Wieltje being met with tremendous machine-gun and rifle fire. That evening 'B' Company reached *'Turco Farm'* where they surprised a German observer giving details of the attack; they killed him — he had kept reporting to the last with the receiver in his hand as he died. George organised the men to dig in south of the Farm. They only had entrenching tools to complete their task but were able to stay there overnight with some little cover.
The Battle of St Julien commenced on Saturday 24th April and on Monday 26th, at 3.00am, George was marched via St Jan to a wood close to Potijze Château. The Battalion was in support of the Sirhind Brigade, George was in command of 'B' Company when he was killed as they advanced on *'Hill Farm'*.
His Captain wrote: *"About poor Lunnon he was wounded twice during that awful attack whilst at the head of his company. He kept up wonderfully well, but his Sergeant-Major advised him to leave the lines, but at that moment Lunnon was shot in the forehead. For several days he was missing. One night after we were fighting over that same ground his body was discovered in a ditch, quite five hundred yards from where he was shot. He had evidently struggled back to the dressing station. I got some stretcher-bearers and buried his body by Lieutenants Morris and Stewart, of the Durham Light Infantry. We put up a little wooden cross and wrote the name on it. I had Lunnon's company afterwards, and I know how the men missed him."*
His Commanding Officer wrote: *"I only took over command of this battalion after the sad death of your son. I have asked the officers now left who were in the battalion at the time. Your son was in command of 'B' Company at the time of his death and during the attack made by the regiment near St Julien he was shot through the head. His company was one of the two leading companies of the battalion in the attack, and they came under a very heavy rifle and machine-gun fire. I did not know your son personally, but from what I have heard he was a most excellent officer and his death was much regretted by all ranks, and had he been spared we are all sure he would have done very well."*

Captain Ernest Hugh Lyddon

2nd Battalion Bedfordshire Regiment
Died on Saturday 31st October 1914, aged 27
Commemorated on Panel 31.

Ernest was born in Cheltenham on Saturday 14th May 1887, eldest son of Mr Frederick Stickland and Mrs J W Lyddon, of 5 Beaufort Road, Clifton, Bristol. He was educated at Weymouth College and passed into RMC Sandhurst.
Ernest was gazetted in October 1907, promoted Lieutenant in June 1909 and Captain in October 1913. He served in Gibraltar, Bermuda, and South Africa.
Ernest was sent to Lyndhurst Camp at mobilisation where he remained until Sunday 4th October 1914 when

he entrained to Southampton. The next morning he sailed on the *SS Winifredian* via Dover to Zeebrugge, arriving on Wednesday 7th. He was sent to Brugge and was billeted at St Croix. The Battalion received various orders that moved them around West Flanders before they eventually arrived in Ypres on Wednesday 14th. The next day he took his men along the Menin Road to take position close to Zillebeke and later that night orders were received to move forward to Gheluvelt village. As they moved from the village along the Menin Road they came under fire from a German advance and were withdrawn. On Wednesday 21st Ernest took his men to Zonnebeke to reinforce the line; however, within the hour they returned as the threat from the German attack had been repulsed, the Battalion suffering considerable casualties during the march that was subject to heavy shelling. At 5.00pm on Sunday 25th he led his men forward to attack Becelaere; as they were pressing the attack home orders were received to stop and retire to their trenches. On Tuesday 27th they were relieved from the front line and went into reserve, being bivouacked first at Veldhoek and secondly at Hooge. They had little rest before returning to the front line, relieving the Black Watch just an attack was anticipated — it was not delivered. Ernest was ordered to take his men to the Zandvoorde road where they reconstructed the trenches that were coming under fire, Captain Botfield and his machine-guns kept the Germans pinned down which provided some cover and additionally repulsed an attack on their line. On Friday 30th the Germans advanced and took Zandvoorde village from where they able to shell the Battalion's trenches until eventually the German guns were silenced. On Saturday 31st Ernest was close to *'Inverness Copse'* when the Germans opened a curtain barrage and advanced. Ernest was killed in a hail of shrapnel.
His brother, Lieutenant Frederick Lyddon, died on Monday 26th April 1915 and is buried in Vlamertinghe Military Cemetery.

130014 Private Alexander Muir Lyon

'C' Company, 72nd Battalion Canadian Infantry (British Columbia Regiment)

Died on Tuesday 30th October 1917, aged 28
Commemorated on Panel 18.

Alexander was born at home on Monday 26th August 1889, fourth son of Thomas and Margaret Lyon, of 49 South Hamilton Street, Kilmarnock, Ayr. He was educated locally and left for Canada in 1912. On Monday 25th November 1912 he joined the Royal Bank of Canada, East End Branch, Vancouver, employed as a clerk.

After three attempts to enlist, (having being rejected on medical grounds), in October 1915 he enlisted and sent for training. He went out to Le Havre on Sunday 13th August 1916. The Battalion was sent to northern France and into Belgium where they rested and trained prior to taking the line. Their first tour of duty was close to the Spanbroekmolen. Alexander continued on tours of duty near Kemmel until the end of September when he was sent to Houlle for training, prior to being sent to the Somme.
Alexander arrived in Albert on Thursday 12th October and was sent to bivouac at *'Tara Hill'* from where he was sent on working parties until taking the line at Le Sars on Thursday 26th. He served on the Somme through Christmas until early in the new year when he moved to Vimy Ridge. He continued to serve in the sector until mid-October when he was sent north to train at Wallon-Cappel. Here they were inspected by HRH Field Marshal the Duke of Connaught and General Sir Arthur Currie. The Duke and the General congratulated the Battalion on their turn out and wished them well for the forthcoming operations. On Tuesday 23rd October 1917 he was taken by motor bus to a camp at Brandhoek where his training continued.

HRH The Duke of Connaught and General Currie

On Sunday 28th October Alexander went by train from Brandhoek to the Asylum at Ypres. He marched to Potijze and at 4.45pm went into the line at *'Hillside Farm'* on the *'Abraham Heights'*. The next night they moved to the reverse slope of the hill in front of the line and dug themselves in ready for the attack the next morning. At 5.50am the whistles blew and they advanced. As they did so they were shocked to find a group of Germans in an old trench which was empty the night before. They took an officer and fifteen men prisoner, sending them to 'the cage' in the rear. They pressed forward passing *'Crest Farm'*, which they eventually surrounded, before breaking into Passchendaele village that was virtually deserted. *'Crest Farm'* had twelve machine-guns defending the position with another twelve in close formation spread over five hundred yards of the Farm. The Commander in Chief sent a despatch: *"... the unit which took Crest Farm had by this action accomplished a feat of arms which would go down in the annals of British history as one of the greatest achievements of a single unit."* The capture of *'Crest Farm'* cost the lives of a good number of men, including Alexander's.

His Commanding Officer wrote: *"Your son was in charge of a Lewis Gun Section in C Coy. I would like to take this opportunity of expressing to you my appreciation of his gallant conduct throughout his service with us in France. His example has always been an inspiration to all his comrades; he was the most popular man in the whole company, possessing qualities of an exceptional nature."*

One of his officers wrote: *"He was an excellent gunner, absolutely fearless, an ideal man to lead a Lewis Gun Section in the field; out of the line he was a good, steady soldier, bearing an excellent character; always of a bright and cheery disposition that made him one of the most popular men in the company."*

A fellow private wrote: *"Alexander was a great favourite among all the boys, and many a weary mile has been shortened by Sandy striking up a chorus or speak a word of cheer."*

Captain Charles James Lyon

1st Battalion Royal Scots Fusiliers

Died on Friday 13th November 1914, aged 24

Commemorated on Panel 33.

Charles Lyon

Charles was born in London on Friday 28th March 1890, fifth son of Walter Fitzgerald Knox Lyon and Isabella Romanes Lyon, of Tantallon Lodge, North Berwick. He was educated at Haileybury from 1905 to 1908 as a member of Trevelyan where he was a member of the Second XV. Charles passed first into RMC Sandhurst. He was a keen polo player and golfer and a member of the Junior Army and Navy Club.

He was gazetted in 1909 and promoted to Lieutenant in October 1911. He saw service in Harrismith, South Africa.

Charles went out to France with the BEF, sailing from Southampton for Le Havre on Thursday 13th August 1914. He entrained for Landrecies where he rested and undertook training with his Company for five days. He marched to the Ghlin where at 6.00am on Sunday 23rd an advance party of Germans rode to within five hundred yards of their position and one of the patrol was killed by machine-gun fire. After a short engagement at Mons the Battalion was ordered to retire to Frameries where they were involved in a four hour long skirmish. The retirement continued towards Le Cateau where they provided the rearguard for the Brigade. The march southwest lasted until Sunday 6th September when they turned to face the enemy finding them at Orly where a short engagement took place. On Wednesday 9th the Marne was crossed again, at Nanteuil and over the next few days they captured a considerable number of prisoners but did not engage the enemy. The Aisne was crossed on Monday 14th and they went into the line at Vailly coming under artillery fire. Charles served on the Chemin des Dames in the sodden trenches until Friday 2nd October when the Battalion started preparations to move to northern France.

From Friday 16th October until Saturday 7th November he fought at Aubers before transferring to the Ypres Salient. Charles was in reserve in *'Inverness Copse'* when ordered to take position close to Harenthage Château. The stables of the château were attacked and during the ensuing fight Charles was killed.

In St Baldred's Church, North Berwick, Lothian, a marble tablet was placed in his memory with the inscription: *"In memoriam. Walter Scott Stuart Lyon, Advocate, Lieut. 9th Batt. (Highlanders) Royal Scots. Born October 1st 1886 killed in action near Ypres May 8th 1915. Alexander Patrick Francis Lyon, born Aug. 5th 1888, killed in action at Bertry, Aug. 27th 1914. Charles James Lyon, Lieut. Royal Scots Fusiliers, born March 28th 1890, killed in action near Ypres Nov. 14th 1914. 'In Thee O Lord Have I Put My Trust'."*

His brothers, Lieutenant Alexander Lyon, died on Thursday 27th August 1914 is buried in Bertry Communal Cemetery, and Lieutenant Walter Lyon, died on Saturday 8th May 1915 is commemorated on the Menin Gate, see below.

Lieutenant Walter Scott Stuart Lyon

9th Battalion Royal Scots

Died on Saturday 8th May 1915, aged 28

Commemorated on Panel 11.

Walter Lyon

Walter was born on Friday 1st October 1886, son of Walter Fitzgerald Knox Lyon and Isabella Romanes Lyon, of Tantallon Lodge, North Berwick. He was one of five brothers, three of whom were killed during the war. He was educated at Haileybury College from 1899 to 1905 as a member of Trevelyan and went up to Balliol College, Oxford, in 1905 where he studied classics. In 1909 he enrolled at Edinburgh University where he took law, graduating in 1912, and was appointed a Sub-Warden. Walter embarked on a career as a Scottish Advocate. He was Scoutmaster of 25th Edinburgh Troop. In 1910 he was commissioned to the 9th Battalion Royal Scots and promoted Lieutenant in 1913.

Walter was mobilized at the outbreak of war and promoted Staff Captain to the Lothian Brigade. On Tuesday 23rd February 1915 he left Edinburgh by train for Southampton. The Battalion embarked on *SS Inventor* for Le Havre, arriving on Friday 26th staying overnight in a rest camp. The next day they entrained for northern France and marched across the border into Belgium. Their first tour of duty was in the line at St Eloi where on Sunday 14th March they repulsed an attack. Until the beginning of April Walter remained in the sector before being sent to billets in Ypres. At 8.00am on Wednesday 7th his billet was hit by a salvo of shells and more than fifty men became casualties. After a tour of duty he went to camp in Vlamertinghe where he could clearly witness the shelling and destruction of Ypres and on Thursday 22nd this was coupled with the first gas attack. Whilst in camp the first streams of refugees passed them, suffering from the effects of the gas attack, frightened out of their wits. At 7.00pm Walter led his men along the cobbled road towards Ypres; the noise of shell fire grew louder and its effects more apparent. After negotiating the town they marched to Potijze arriving at 3.00am the next morning. The Battalion was ordered at noon to move to support the Canadians where the Battalion consolidated at St Jan. On Saturday 24th they received their first food in forty-eight hours before making a series of minor counter-attacks to keep the Germans at bay. On Tuesday morning of the 27th they returned to Potijze en route to *'Sanctuary Wood'*. On Sunday 2nd they were marched to Potijze only to be sent straight back. Later in the day they were ordered to Frezenberg only to be sent back again. Each route was difficult and not without risk and the tired men were not impressed with the unnecessary and contradictory orders. Late on 4th May they took the line astride the Menin Road. On Saturday 8th the Germans laid a barrage on their line during which he was killed. Walter was buried in *'Sanctuary Wood'* next to Alastair Macfarlane, see below.

Alastair Macfarlane

Walter was one of the war poets, *'Easter at Ypres'* was published by Maclhose, Glasgow in 1916, in addition two of his poems are printed in *'A Deep Cry'*, an anthology of public school poetry, 1993.
Whilst in Ypres in April 1915 he wrote the poem below.

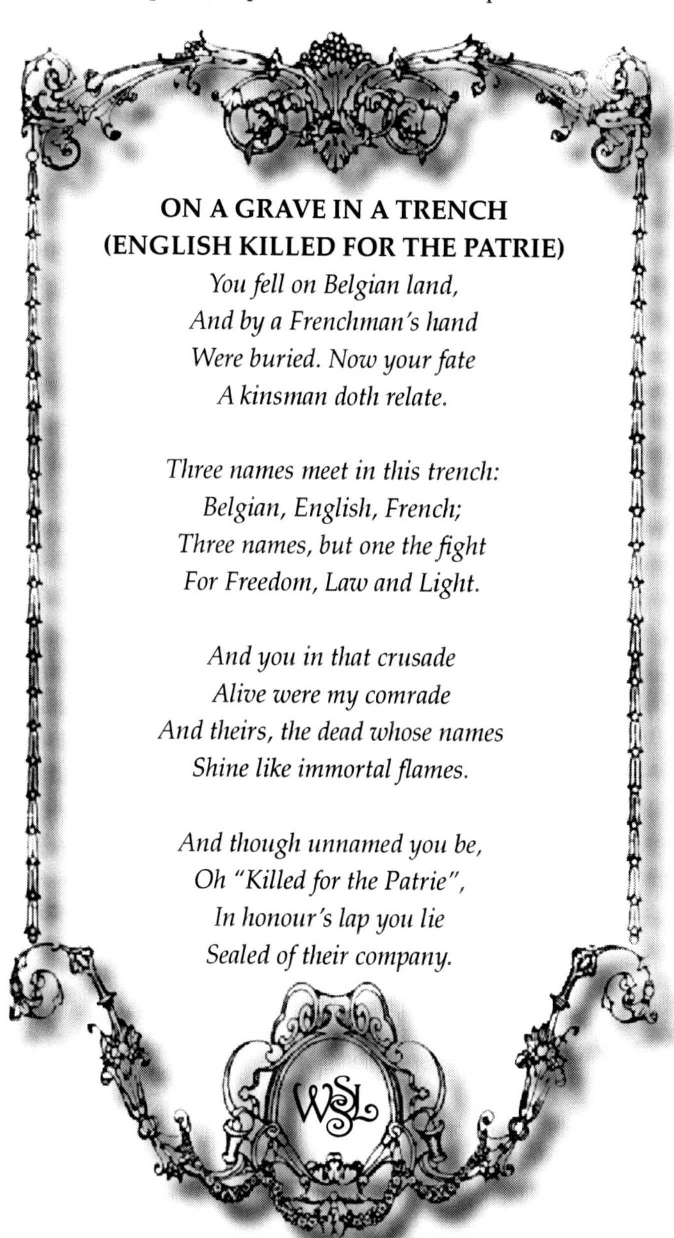

ON A GRAVE IN A TRENCH
(ENGLISH KILLED FOR THE PATRIE)

You fell on Belgian land,
And by a Frenchman's hand
Were buried. Now your fate
A kinsman doth relate.

Three names meet in this trench:
Belgian, English, French;
Three names, but one the fight
For Freedom, Law and Light.

And you in that crusade
Alive were my comrade
And theirs, the dead whose names
Shine like immortal flames.

And though unnamed you be,
Oh "Killed for the Patrie",
In honour's lap you lie
Sealed of their company.

... Germans surrendering

In St Baldred's Church, North Berwick, Lothian, a marble tablet was placed in his memory with the inscription: *"In Memoriam. Walter Scott Stuart Lyon, Advocate, Lieut. 9th Batt. (Highlanders) Royal Scots. Born October 1st 1886, killed in action near Ypres May 8th 1915. Alexander Patrick Francis Lyon, born Aug. 5th 1888, killed in action at Bertry Aug. 27th 1914. Charles James Lyon, Lieut. Royal Scots Fusiliers, born March 28th 1890, killed in action near Ypres Nov. 14th 1914. In Thee O Lord Have I Put My Trust."*
His brothers, Lieutenant Alexander Lyon, died on Thursday 27th August 1914 who is buried in Bertry Communal Cemetery and Captain Charles Lyon, died on Friday 13th November 1915, see above.

Another Figment From Flanders.
(By Major Wallace Bairnsbrother.)
September the First — Partridge-shooting beings to-day.

Lightning Source UK Ltd.
Milton Keynes UK
176133UK00003B/2/P

9 781908 345011